National

Life, Accident, and Health Insurance

License Exam Manual

At press time, this edition contains the most complete and accurate information currently available. Owing to the nature of license examinations, however, information may have been added recently to the actual test that does not appear in this edition. Please contact the publisher to verify that you have the most current edition.

This publication is designed to provide accurate and authoritative information in regard to the subject matter covered. It is sold with the understanding that the publisher is not engaged in rendering legal, accounting, or other professional services. If legal advice or other expert assistance is required, the services of a competent professional should be sought.

NATIONAL LIFE, ACCIDENT, AND HEALTH INSURANCE LICENSE EXAM MANUAL

If you find imperfections or incorrect information in this product, please visit www.kfeducation.com and submit an errata report.

Published in February 2009 by Kaplan Financial Education.

Printed in the United States of America.

ISBN: 1-4277-8589-9

PPN: 4103-5302

Contents

UNIT 4 Underwriting Basics 81

UNIT 5 Group Insurance 103

UNIT 6 Selling Life Insurance 115

UNIT 7 Policy Issuance and Delivery 135

UNIT 8 Types of Life Insurance Policies 151

UNIT 9 Policy Provisions 193

UNIT 10 Riders 223

UNIT 11 Policy Options 237

UNIT 12 Annuities 259

UNIT 13 Group Life Insurance 283

UNIT 14 Social Security and Tax Considerations 291

UNIT 15 Retirement Plans 309

UNIT 16 Health Insurance Basics 329

UNIT 17 Policy Underwriting, Issuance, and Delivery 365

UNIT 18 Policy Provisions 377

UNIT 19 Disability Income Insurance 411

UNIT 20 Medical Expense Insurance 437

UNIT 21 Special Types of Medical Expense Policies 463

UNIT 22 Group Health Insurance 481

UNIT 23 Social Health Insurance 497

UNIT 24 Long-Term Care 533

UNIT 25 Health Insurance and Taxation 551

Introduction

Important: Check for Updates

States sometimes revise their exam content outlines unexpectedly or on short notice. To see whether there is an update for this product because of an exam change, please go to **www.kfeducation.com** and check the Insurance Licensing Blog. If there is an update, it will be clearly noted in the blog entries.

We suggest that you check for updates when you first receive the course, again during your study period, upon completion of your studies, and one last time just before you take your insurance license exam.

HINTS FOR SUCCESSFUL EXAM PREPARATION

An examination must be taken and passed before an insurance producer's license is issued. This examination is designed to measure your basic knowledge of insurance coverages and practices to ensure that the public is served in a professionally responsible manner. The examination will also test your understanding of state laws and regulations pertaining to the insurance industry.

The Licensing Examination

All examination questions are four-part multiple-choice. The number of questions on the exam and the amount of time allowed to complete the exam varies depending on the state and the exam provider. Your exam may contain anywhere from 50–100 questions and have a time limit of 1–2.5 hours. Check with your state's license exam administrator for details.

Be sure to read each question carefully. While several of the possible answers may be partially correct, you must select the best answer to each question. Watch for words such as *all*, *never*, and *always*. They may help you eliminate some of the choices.

There is no penalty for guessing. If you can narrow the choice of four answers down to three or even two logical possibilities, you have a good chance of making an educated guess and picking the right answer.

Do not spend too much time on any one question. It is best to skip very difficult questions and return to them after you have completed all of the easier ones. Other questions on the exam may contain information that helps you answer more difficult questions.

Study Techniques

You may have a lot of experience taking training courses and their examinations or it may have been years since you've taken a course. Here are a couple tips we recommend to make your study most effective.

Read the Entire Course

Study the material in each unit until you understand it. A firm grasp of the material in the course is the best preparation for passing the exam.

Look for Question Areas as You Read Each Assignment

You can prepare for the exam by paying attention to the questions that appear throughout the course. They point to important areas that you should master. More importantly, study with the exam in mind. What questions would you put in the exam if you were creating it to test a student's knowledge of the material? This exercise will help you master the important material in the course and pass the exam.

UNIT

1

Introduction to Insurance

1. 1 INTRODUCTION

The future is notoriously unpredictable. Every day, each of us faces the possibility that something might happen that would result in a personal financial loss. Sickness, disability, premature death, and damage to property are all examples of things that might cause a financial loss. We know that these things will happen to some people and not to others, but we do not know which things will happen to any particular person. In the face of this uncertainty, the idea and business of insurance developed as a means for spreading the result of a financial loss among many persons so that the cost to any one person is small.

1. 2 LEARNING OBJECTIVES

After completing this lesson, you will be able to:

- define insurance;
- explain how the insurance business is regulated;
- describe how insurance law binds life and insurance policies;
- describe the underwriting process;
- explain group insurance;
- define the following key terms: *insurance*, *insurer*, *premium*, *insured*, *policy*, *claim*, *loss*, *risk*, *hazard*, *peril*, *indemnity*, and *law of large numbers*;
- list and describe two types of risk;
- list and describe four methods for managing risk;
- describe five characteristics of insurable risk;
- describe the following types of insurers: stock insurers, mutual insurers, nonprofit insurers, reciprocal insurers, fraternal insurers, Lloyd's of London, assessment insurers, reinsurers, excess insurers, and surplus lines insurers;
- describe the role of the federal government in providing insurance;
- list the two main insurance distribution systems and describe each; and
- list the five main types of insurance producers and describe each.

1. 3 WHAT IS INSURANCE?

Farmers in ancient China knew that some of the boats carrying crops to market would run into trouble and sink, but they had no way of knowing which boats. Instead of taking the chance that any one family in the community would lose its entire crop in an accident, the farmers began spreading their crop among several boats. That way, if one boat went down, only a small part of each crop would be lost. This spread the cost of the loss among several families, but each family's loss was manageable.

Insurance contracts originated in the 13th century with shipowners who wanted to make the possibility of loss manageable. Everyone knew that some ships would be lost at sea, but nobody knew which ones. A group of wealthy individuals agreed to take a definite amount of money from each shipowner in exchange for a promise that when a ship was lost, the wealthy individual would pay the costs of the loss. So, instead of a small possibility of losing everything, each shipowner paid a definite fee in exchange for the security that a catastrophic loss would not mean the end of future prospects for success.

As these examples illustrate, **insurance** is a social device for spreading the chance of financial loss among a large number of people. By purchasing insurance, a person shares the chance for loss with a group of others, reducing the individual potential for disastrous financial consequences.

The basic mechanism behind insurance is relatively simple. The insurance company or **insurer** receives relatively small amounts of money, referred to as a **premium**, from each person buying insurance. A large uncertain loss is exchanged for a specific small amount of premium.

The agreement between the insurer and the **insured**, the person who is covered by the insurance, is established in a legal document referred to as a contract of insurance or a **policy**. The insurer promises to pay the insured according to the terms of the policy if a loss occurs. **Loss** is defined as reduction in the value of an asset. To be paid for a loss, the insured must notify the insurer by making a **claim**. The **claim** is a demand for payment of the insurance benefit to the person named in the policy.

Insurance plays an important role in maintaining society. As a result of the sharing, or pooling, of a large number of similar risks, insurance coverage is available to most individuals for a reasonably affordable premium. When losses occur, insurance helps individuals to maintain their standard of living, which helps the whole economy. In the absence of insurance, a major disaster (such as fire or earthquake) could cripple the entire economy of local communities. If medical bills wiped out family savings and people did not have the funds to rebuild damaged homes, the uninsured losses could lead to a decline in all areas of consumer spending. Insurance is the device that allows individuals and society in general to recover from unexpected losses.

1. 4 RISK

To really understand insurance and how it works, you must first understand risk. **Risk** is the possibility that a loss might occur and is one of the reasons people purchase insurance. Notice that risk is not the loss itself but the uncertainty of loss. There are some losses that are certain to happen eventually, such as a rug that finally wears out after years of use or a car that runs out of gas if you stop refueling. Such losses are not risks because they represent a certainty, instead of uncertainty, of loss.

1. 4. 1 Types of Risks

There are two types of risks, only one of which can be covered by insurance.

Speculative risk is a risk that offers the opportunity for gain as well as the possibility of loss. Gambling is a common type of speculative risk. Insurance is not designed to protect against speculative risks. It is this type of risk that insurance and its underwriting practices are designed to avoid. Examples are found in new business ventures, stock market investments, and racetrack bets. There is a chance that the new business will not succeed, that the stock will not go up, or that the horse will not win, place, or show. However, there is a chance that in each of these instances, the speculator will make a profit.

Pure risk is the possibility of loss only and is the type of risk that insurers accept—for example, the possibility of financial loss resulting from an accident, sickness, or premature death. The purpose of insurance is to make the person whole again, to restore the insured to his original financial position. Insurance is not designed to provide a person with the opportunity of making a gain or profit.

1. 4. 2 Perils and Hazards

A **peril** is the cause of a potential loss. Accidents, fires, explosions, and floods are common perils that may be covered by insurance.

A **hazard** is a condition that increases the seriousness of a potential loss or increases the likelihood that a loss will occur. Slippery floors, unsanitary conditions, and improperly stored gasoline are hazards that might increase the severity or frequency of losses caused by perils. There are four types of hazards that may contribute to losses.

- **Physical hazards** arise from material, structural, or operational features of a risk situation. Slippery floors or unsanitary conditions are physical hazards.
- **Moral hazards** arise from people's habits and values. A moral hazard means that a person might create a loss situation on purpose just to collect from the insurance company. Filing a false claim is an example of a moral hazard.
- **Morale hazards** arise out of human carelessness or irresponsibility. This means that an individual, through recklessness or thoughtless action,

can increase the possibility of loss. Failing to wear a seat belt while driving is an example of a morale hazard.

- **Legal hazards** arise from court actions that increase the likelihood or size of a loss. Legal hazards are illustrated by the growing tendency of people to file lawsuits and of courts to award enormous sums for alleged damages or to require insurance payments that were not intended.

Once the risks and hazards are identified, they must be evaluated and analyzed and then steps to reduce the loss exposures must be examined and implemented. Finally, the results must be analyzed and techniques must be modified if appropriate.

1. 4. 3 Managing Risk

We spend our entire lives coping with risk: crossing a street, going swimming, and traveling by plane. These risks sometimes result in small losses, such as a stubbed toe or lost pocket comb, which we accept as a normal part of life, but risks may also result in serious financial losses, such as when a person is injured in a car accident or contracts a fatal disease.

There are four ways of managing risk. A risk may be avoided, reduced, transferred, or retained.

- The first method is to **Avoid risk**. For example, a person might avoid the risk of being in an automobile accident by never getting into a car.
- Risk may be **Reduced**, or controlled, by examining the perils and seeing which ones can be mitigated. For example, a person reduces the risk of health problems by living a healthier lifestyle.
- A risk is **Retained** when a person decides to assume financial responsibility for certain events. The deductible amount on a health insurance policy is one way the insured retains some portion of the risk. In addition, the premium may be reduced because the insured retains some of the risk.
- The final method of managing risk is to **Transfer** the risk to another party. This transfer may be done through any of a number of legal mechanisms, such as hold harmless agreements or lawsuits. However, for many risks, the best way for individuals to transfer them is through insurance.

1. 4. 4 Law of Large Numbers

When an individual purchases insurance, the risk is transferred from the individual to the insurer. To make a successful business of accepting the transfer of individual risk, the insurer needs to have some idea of how many losses will actually occur.

Insurance companies cannot predict the losses expected for a given individual. However, using the **law of large numbers**, insurers are able to predict how many losses will occur in a group. The basic principle of this law is that the larger the group, the more predictable the future losses in the group will be for a given period. The insurance company cannot reliably predict which people will die, but with a large enough population, statistics can accurately predict how many people in the group will suffer a loss.

Example

Experience might show that of a group of 100,000 people aged 40, about 325 will die each year.

For the law of large numbers to operate, it is essential that a large number of similar risks or exposure units be combined. An **exposure unit** is the item of property or the person insured. The exposure unit in life and health insurance is the economic value of the individual person's life. In property and casualty insurance, it is the number of cars, homes, and so forth.

The degree of error in predicting future losses decreases as the number of individual exposure units in a group increases. Thus, the larger the group, the more closely the predicted experience will approach the actual loss experience. Insurance companies deal only with averages, in the sense of establishing actuarial predictions of loss experience. By providing for the average risk, the extremes in loss experience cancel each other out.

1. 4. 5 Insurable Interest

In the early history of insurance, people profited by obtaining insurance on complete strangers. If the stranger died, the policyholder obtained the benefit of the policy with no appreciable emotional or financial loss. At best this was a form of gambling, and at worst it was an incentive to murder. For obvious reasons, this practice is now illegal in all states and provinces.

To avoid similar situations in the future, a basic rule governing insurance states that before an individual can benefit from insurance, that individual must have a legitimate interest in the preservation of the life or property insured. This requirement is called **insurable interest**.

A person is presumed to have an insurable interest in his own life. An individual is also considered to have an insurable interest in the life of a close blood relative or a spouse. In these cases, insurable interest is based on the love that individual would have for the family member and a real interest in protecting the life of that family member.

Insurable interest can also be based on a financial loss that will take place if an insured individual dies. Examples are two partners in a business, each of whom brings substantial expertise to that business. If one partner dies, the business could fail, resulting in a loss to the other partner.

For life insurance, insurable interest must exist at the time of the application for insurance, but it need not exist at the time of the insured's death. This prevents the insurer from needing to obtain proof of such emotional issues as existing love and affection in the emotional time following a death. In contrast, property and casualty insurance generally does require an insurable interest to exist at the time of loss. Loss of property is not generally as emotional as the loss of a life, and the existence of an insurable interest in property is more easily determined.

Insurable interest affects who may purchase a policy but not who may benefit from a policy. For example, an individual could purchase life insurance on her own life and name a charitable organization as the beneficiary. Because every person is presumed to have an insurable interest in his own life, the policy would be valid. As another example, a doctor who benefits from medical expense reimbursement payments may not have an insurable interest in the health of the insured, but the policyowner, usually the insured or the insured's employer, does have a personal or financial interest in keeping the insured healthy.

1. 4. 6 Insurable Risks

Not all risks are equally insurable. Insurable risks have certain characteristics that make the rate of loss fairly predictable, allowing insurers to adequately prepare for the losses that do occur. The more closely a risk aligns with the following characteristics, the more insurable it is.

1. 4. 6. 1 Large Numbers of Homogeneous Units

The expected loss experience of a group of exposure units cannot be predicted with any certainty unless there are a large number of exposure units in that group. Risks are not considered insurable unless the insurance company has a large enough number of similar (homogeneous) risks and knows enough about their previous loss experience to be able to reliably predict possible future losses.

1. 4. 6. 2 Loss Must Be Ascertainable

Because the purpose of insurance is to reduce or eliminate the uncertainty of economic loss, the insurer must be able to place a monetary value on the loss. In life insurance, monetary value is placed on the insured's human life value or ability to earn an income. In health insurance, economic loss is measured by lost wages or by actual medical expenses incurred. The potential loss must be measurable so that both parties can agree on the precise amount payable in the event the loss occurs. If the insured cannot determine the amount of his loss, the law affords no remedy.

1. 4. 6. 3 Loss Must Be Uncertain

Because the purpose of insurance is to reduce or eliminate uncertainty, it is obviously not in the public interest to permit the writing of insurance for intentional acts, such as a man jumping off a skyscraper two days after purchasing an insurance policy. Uncertainty arises out of not knowing what is going to happen or being unable to predict what is going to happen to the individual exposure unit. If insurance is provided for certain losses, the element of chance is not a factor, nor is there any element of uncertainty in losses occasioned by natural wear and tear or deterioration, depreciation, or defects in property covered under insurance. Losses are expected in these situations. Therefore, such losses would not be uncertain.

With life insurance, the uncertainty rests not with whether a certain individual will die but rather with when that individual will die and what financial obligations will be left behind when death occurs. With health insurance, the uncertainty rests less with whether a certain individual will have an accident or become ill sometime during his lifetime, but rather with how much expense will be incurred when an illness or accident occurs.

1. 4. 6. 4 *Economic Hardship*

The nature of the loss must be such that an economic hardship would occur should the loss occur. There would be little point in obtaining insurance to cover occurrences so minor that a loss would not produce economic hardship. For example, if a person loses two days' pay because of an injury, a loss occurs, but it is not significant enough to be covered by insurance.

The nature of the loss must be of such magnitude that it is worthwhile to incur the premium cost to cover potential loss. It must be economically feasible to insure. Thus, a comparison of the potential loss with the cost of premium is a major consideration to the insurance buyer.

1. 4. 6. 5 *Exclusion of Catastrophic Perils*

Although the ability to predict future losses with a reasonable degree of accuracy is critical to the insuring function, certain types of perils do not lend themselves to prediction. Such perils, when they cause losses, do not establish a pattern of predictability that can be relied upon for future predictions of anticipated loss. Accordingly, these perils are usually excluded from coverage. Examples of excluded catastrophic perils are war, nuclear risk, and floods.

1. 5 COVERAGE CONCEPTS

1. 5. 1 Indemnity

The concept of **indemnity** states that insurance should restore the insured, in whole or in part, to the condition he enjoyed before the loss. Restoration may take the form of payment for the loss or repair or replacement of the damaged or destroyed property.

In life and health insurance, the concept of indemnity has a slightly different meaning in that a person's economic value or human life value is the individual's present and future earning power. For example, a family is indemnified for the financial loss of the breadwinner by being provided with life insurance proceeds with which to replace present and future income, thus enabling the family to maintain its lifestyle. An individual is indemnified for the financial loss of a broken arm by being provided with health insurance proceeds to pay the medical bills and perhaps to cover wages lost as a result of the injury.

1. 5. 1. 1 Subrogation

Subrogation entitles one who has paid for another's loss to take over the other's right to recourse from the party responsible for the loss. A subrogation clause in an insurance policy gives the insurer the right to sue (for itself or on behalf of the insured) the responsible party. It prevents the insured from collecting from both the insurer and the liable party. Subrogation is never used in life insurance and seldom in health insurance.

1. 5. 2 Limit of Liability

Although the term *limit of liability* is not used in the life and health insurance field as commonly as it is in the property and casualty field, it means the maximum amount the insurer will pay for a specified insured contingency.

Life insurance policies usually use the term *face amount* to refer to the maximum liability of the insurer for a death claim. However, the face amount may not always be the maximum amount payable. In the case of a double indemnity provision, the limit of liability for an accidental death may be expressed as twice the face amount shown on the face of the policy.

Health and disability policies are more likely to specify a maximum benefit amount or period instead of a limit of liability. Basic medical insurance often has a maximum benefit amount (such as $10,000), and major medical insurance usually has a lifetime maximum benefit (such as $1 million). Disability income policies often limit benefits to a specified maximum benefit period (expressed in weeks or months). Within the maximum benefit limits found in health and disability policies, there may be various **sublimits**, such as daily dollar limits on covered room and board charges, scheduled maximum amounts for various surgical procedures, and weekly dollar limits for disability income benefits.

1. 5. 3 Deductibles

Deductibles are a common feature of medical insurance coverages (the term has no application in life insurance). A **deductible** is simply the initial amount of a covered loss (or losses) that the insured must absorb before the insurer begins to pay for additional loss amounts. For example, if a basic medical expense policy only pays losses above a $250 deductible and an insured incurs $1,000 of covered medical expenses, the insured would have to pay the first $250 and the insurer would then pay the additional $750 of expenses.

Although the term is not used in disability income policies, disability insurance usually has a time deductible. It is called the **elimination period** or a waiting period, but the concept is similar to a deductible. The **elimination period** is simply the number of days an insured must be disabled before disability income benefits become payable. For example, if a policy specifies an elimination period of 7 days and an insured is disabled for 30 days, the policy would pay benefits for only the 23 days following the elimination period.

The purpose of a deductible is to minimize small nuisance claims and to keep premiums down. It might cost an insurer much more just to process the paperwork on $10 and $25 claims than on the amount of the claims. Naturally, these costs would have to be reflected in insurance rates if such small claims were covered. Deductibles help eliminate this problem and keep rates down. Insurers usually offer a standard deductible but give applicants the option of purchasing higher deductibles that result in even lower premiums.

1. 5. 4 Coinsurance

Coinsurance is another concept commonly found in medical insurance policies. It means that within a specified coverage range, the insured and insurer will share the allowable expenses. It is usually expressed in percentages (e.g., 20–80%). For example, if a policy has a $500 deductible and a 20%/80% coinsurance provision for the next $10,000 of expenses, a $5,500 medical bill would be settled in the following manner: the insured would pay the first $500 (the deductible amount) and $1,000 of the additional expenses (the insured's 20% share); the insurer would pay the remaining $4,000 (the insurer's 80% share).

A coinsurance provision also is designed to keep insurance premiums down, but it does so primarily by discouraging unnecessary or excessive treatments. An insured who is faced with paying 20% of the bill is more likely to question the doctor about whether proposed treatments are necessary and whether there might be less costly alternatives.

1. 6 TYPES OF INSURANCE

Insurers market a variety of insurance products. The most common products offered are property, casualty, life, and health insurance and annuities.

Property insurance protects the insured against the financial consequences of the direct or consequential loss or damage to property of every kind. It includes a wide variety of insurance contracts for personal and business situations. Property insurance policies cover the risk of damage or loss to property. Property includes building, equipment, stock, or contents. Property insurance also includes many related and contingent property losses, such as business interruption.

Casualty insurance protects the insured against the financial consequences of legal liability, including that for death, injury, disability, or damage to real or personal property. It includes insurance policies covering losses resulting from a number of occurrences. Casualty insurance contracts include automobile policies, general liability policies, workers' compensation coverage, crime insurance and suretyship coverages, boiler and machinery coverages, and many others.

Almost every insured has a need for both property and casualty insurance coverage, whether personal or business (commercial). Some of the property and casualty coverages are sold together in special policies called **packages**.

Life insurance is insurance coverage on human lives, including benefits of endowment and annuities, and may include benefits in the event of death or dismemberment by accident and benefits for disability insurance. It is designed to protect against the risk of premature death—that is, dying too soon. Premature death exposes a family or a business to certain financial risks, such as burial expenses, paying off debts, loss of family income, and business profits.

An **annuity** is guaranteed income for the life of an annuitant. Annuities are designed to protect against the risk of living too long—that is, outliving one's financial resources and income during retirement.

Accident and health or sickness insurance protects the insured against financial loss caused by sickness, bodily injury, or accidental death and may include benefits for disability income. It may reimburse the insured for actual medical expenses incurred as a result of an accident or illness (hospitalization insurance), or it may provide protection for loss of income experienced by the insured during periods of disability resulting from accident or sickness (i.e., disability income insurance). Health insurance can be written on either an individual or group basis and may include medical expense, hospital indemnity, major medical, hospital, surgical, disability, cancer, accident, dental expenses, eyeglasses, prescription medication, and other health-related expenses.

Variable life and variable annuity products include insurance coverage provided under variable life insurance contracts and variable annuities. Variable products carry investment risk—that is, the insured may lose money because of a decrease in the price of the securities underlying the policy. For this reason, individuals selling such products are required to carry a securities license as well as an insurance license.

Credit is a limited line of insurance protecting the insured, who is usually a creditor, against the financial consequences should a debtor be unable to pay his debts as a result of illness or death.

Other types of insurance, such as title insurance or crop insurance, may be authorized in individual states. These limited lines of insurance are more narrowly focused than the types of insurance listed above, generally falling within the broad scope of one of the types of insurance listed above.

Insurance is provided to the public by three major sources: private commercial insurers (profit making), private noncommercial insurers (nonprofit service organizations), and the United States government (special nonprofit). Other types of private insurers include reciprocals, fraternals, Lloyd's, reinsurers, and self-insurers.

1. 7 TYPES OF INSURERS

Private life and health insurers are in the business to make a reasonable profit and are therefore called commercial insurers. Stock and mutual insurers are private insurers. Private noncommercial service organizations, such as Blue Cross and Blue Shield, operate on a nonprofit basis. A nonprofit status exists when profits are returned to subscribers in the form of reduced premiums or expanded benefits (similar to mutual insurers).

1. 7. 1 Stock Insurers

A **stock insurance company**, like other stock companies, consists of stockholders who own shares in the company. The individual stockholders provide capital for the insurer. In return, they share in any profits and losses. Management control rests with the board of directors, which is selected by the stockholders. The board of directors elects the officers who conduct the daily operations of the business. Capital stock companies control two-thirds of the premiums in the property and liability field and nearly one-half of the premiums in life insurance. If the board of directors declares a dividend, it will be paid to the stockholders. Often a stock company is referred to as a **nonparticipating** company because policyholders do not participate in dividends.

1. 7. 2 Mutual Insurers

In a **mutual company**, there are no stockholders. Formation funds must be contributed by someone or some group. Because of the difficulties involved today in obtaining the funds to organize a mutual company, many mutual companies start as stock companies and then mutualize.

In a mutual company, ownership rests with the policyholders. They vote for a board of directors, which in turn elects or appoints the officers to operate the company. Funds not paid out after paying claims and not used in paying for other costs of operation are returned to the policyowners in the form of policy dividends. As such, mutual companies are sometimes referred to as **participating** companies because the policyowners participate in dividends. Although in theory policyowners should share in losses as well as profits, these losses are actually felt only in the discontinuation of dividends. Mutual companies write nearly one-third of the property and liability business in the country and one-half of the life insurance business.

1. 7. 3 Reciprocal Insurers

Reciprocal insurers are unincorporated groups of people that provide insurance for one another through individual indemnity agreements. Each individual who is a member of the reciprocal is known as a **subscriber**. Each subscriber is allocated a separate account through which his premiums are paid and earned interest is tracked. If any subscriber should suffer a loss provided for by the reciprocal insurance, each subscriber account would be assessed an equal amount to pay the claim. Administration, underwriting, sales promotion, and claims handling for the reciprocal insurance are handled by an *attorney-in-fact*. The attorney-in-fact is often controlled and overseen by an advisory committee of subscribers.

1. 7. 4 Fraternal Insurers

Fraternal benefit societies are primarily life insurance carriers that exist as social organizations and usually engage in charitable and benevolent activities. Fraternals are distinguished by the fact that their membership is usually drawn from those who are also members of a lodge or fraternal organization. They operate under a special section of the state insurance code and receive some income tax advantages. One distinctive characteristic of fraternal life insurance is the open contract, which allows fraternals to assess their certificate holders in times of financial difficulty.

1. 7. 5 Lloyd's

Lloyd's of London is not an insurance company but may be compared to a stock exchange. Just as an exchange provides facilities for its members but does not buy or sell securities itself, Lloyd's provides a meeting place and clerical services to its members who actually transact the business of insurance. Members may be individuals or corporations.

Members are grouped into syndicates, but they remain individually liable and responsible for the contracts of insurance they enter into. Their individual fortunes and resources are pledged as the capital behind their assumption of risk. A syndicate is represented in a Lloyd's organization by an underwriter. Lloyd's of London assures full and adequate performance by its members through a governing committee and rules of eligibility. Such things as character, experience, business integrity, and amount of capital (funds held in trust at Lloyd's and personal wealth) are factors considered for any new member.

1. 7. 6 Reinsurers

Reinsurance is a form of insurance between insurers. It occurs when an insurer (the reinsurer) agrees to accept all or a portion of a risk covered by another insurer (the ceding company). In many cases, the original insured has no knowledge of the transaction. In the event of loss, the insured has no claim against the reinsurer. The ceding company is responsible for the coverage it has written, but it will have a legitimate claim against the reinsurer for any portion of its own loss that is reinsured.

Companies often use reinsurance to reduce the risk of a catastrophic loss. Insurance against loss by earthquakes, floods, and aviation accidents might not be available if a single carrier had to assume all of the risk. Large life insurance cases are also often reinsured. For example, a $1 million life insurance policy on an insured may be shared through reinsurance with one or more insurers. Reinsurance makes it possible for a carrier to issue a policy and then share the risk with another insurer or a group of insurers. Another reason for reinsurance is that it helps carriers avoid capacity problems. Insurers must keep unearned premium reserves and certain levels of surplus in relation to premiums written. A shortage of capacity occurs when the ratio of premiums to surplus and reserves gets out of balance. By reinsuring a risk, many insurers are able to avoid or minimize capacity shortages.

Specific, or **facultative**, reinsurance is negotiated on an individual risk basis. The reinsurer retains the faculty to accept or reject each risk offered by a ceding company, so there must be an offer and acceptance on each reinsurance contract. Some carriers form agreements under which they engage in **treaty** reinsurance, which involves an automatic sharing of risks assumed by the ceding company. Whether reinsurance is facultative or on a treaty basis, it may be written on an **excess of loss** basis. This means the reinsurer will pay only the portion of loss that exceeds a threshold **retained** by the ceding company, or on a **quota share** basis, meaning that the insurers will share loss on a pro rata or fixed percentage basis.

1. 7. 7 Excess and Surplus Lines

Occasionally, it may be difficult to place a risk in the normal marketplace. If the risk is very large or unusual in nature, typical carriers may be unwilling to assume it. For some special risks, the only market may be with specialty carriers. Excess and surplus lines is the name given to insurance for which there is no market through the original producer or that is not available through authorized carriers in the state where the risk arises or is located. Such business must be placed through a licensed excess or surplus lines broker, who will attempt to place it with an unauthorized carrier.

1. 7. 8 Risk Retention Groups

A *risk retention group* (RRG) is a mutual insurance company formed to insure people in the same business, occupation, or profession (for example, pharmacists, dentists, or engineers).

1. 7. 9 Self-Insurers

Self-insurance is a means of retaining risk. For a risk to be truly self-insured, two important characteristics will be present:

- A large number of homogeneous exposure units, so that the law of large numbers can be used to predict expected losses
- Sufficient liquid assets to pay claims and other costs of retaining risk

The advantages of self-insurance are that money can be saved if losses are less than those predicted, expenses may be reduced by the elimination of such things as administrative costs and commissions, and the self-insurer has use of the money that normally would be held by the insurance company. The main disadvantages of self-insurance are that actual losses may be more than predicted, and expenses could be higher than expected if additional personnel have to be hired to administer the program.

1. 7. 10 The United States Government as Insurer

The federal government provides life and health insurance through various sources. The federal government has offered a variety of military life insurance plans including United States Government Life Insurance (to veterans of World War I), National Service Life Insurance (in 1940), and Servicemen's Group Life Insurance. Additional occupations are eligible for federal government insurance provided through the Railroad Retirement Act, the Civil Service Retirement Act, and the Federal Employees' Compensation Act.

Because private insurance policies exclude catastrophic risks, the federal government has stepped in to provide war risk insurance, nuclear energy liability insurance, national flood insurance, federal crime insurance, federal crop insurance, and insurance on mortgage loans. At the state level, governments are involved in providing unemployment insurance, workers' compensation programs and second-injury funds, and state-run medical expense insurance plans.

Federal, state, and local governments provide **social insurance** to a segment of the population who would otherwise be without disability income, retirement income, or medical care.

Social Security provides survivor benefits in the event of death of a covered worker. These benefits include a lump-sum burial amount of $255 plus monthly income benefits to eligible survivors. Social Security also provides disability benefits in the event of the total disability of a covered worker. In addition, the program also provides retirement benefits to covered workers at age 65 or earlier if elected by the individual. The Medicare program is also part of Social Security and accordingly provides medical expense benefits for covered workers beginning at age 65. All of these programs will be discussed in more detail in later chapters.

Medicaid is primarily a state governmental program that provides health care benefits for the financially needy. Medicaid is financed by the states with some federal subsidies.

- Social insurance is distinguishable from private insurance in four significant areas.
- Participation is mandatory and automatic for all eligible citizens.
- Benefits are not provided under a contract or policy but are prescribed by law. Individuals do not elect changes to the benefit plan. Changes to the benefit structure and provisions are made by changes to the law.
- Social insurance seeks to be adequate, meeting the needs of the public, rather than equitable. As income is redistributed through the governmental system, insureds who put less into the system (the poor, the elderly, and those with many dependents) receive proportionally greater benefits.
- The government, as an insurance provider, has a clear and strong monopoly.

1. 8 DOMICILE AND AUTHORIZATION

1. 8. 1 Insurer's Domicile (Domestic, Foreign, and Alien Insurers)

An insurer is defined not only by its corporate status, but also by where it is located, or its domicile of incorporation. If an insurer is conducting business in the state where it is incorporated, that insurer is a **domestic insurer** in that state.

If an insurer conducts business in a state where it is not incorporated, the insurer is a **foreign insurer** in that state.

If an insurer is conducting business in a country where it is not incorporated, it is an **alien insurer** in that country.

Therefore, an insurer incorporated in California is a domestic insurer when it is conducting business in California. The same company is a foreign insurer when it is conducting business in New York and an alien insurer when it is conducting business in Canada.

1. 8. 2 Authorized Versus Unauthorized (Admitted Versus Nonadmitted)

Before an insurance company can conduct business, it must, by law, receive the authority to do so. Insurance statutes require a company to secure a license from the Department of Insurance to sell insurance in a particular state. Once the insurer receives the license, it is considered **admitted** into the state as a legal insurer and is **authorized** to transact the business of insurance. Insurers not licensed to transact insurance within the state are referred to as **unauthorized** or **nonadmitted**. This licensing power (sometimes companies are referred to as licensed and nonlicensed) is used to regulate company activities. Licenses may be issued to domestic companies, foreign companies, or alien companies. Stricter requirements are often imposed on alien and foreign companies because of their inaccessibility.

1. 9 TYPES OF DISTRIBUTION SYSTEMS

Insurance companies market their products generally in one of two ways: by using producers to sell their products or selling directly by mass marketing. The vast majority of policies are sold through producers.

1. 9. 1 Agency System

Companies that use producers to sell their products vary by whether the producers are employees or independent sales representatives.

Independent insurance producers sell the insurance products of several companies and work for themselves or other producers. They sell their clients the policy that fits their needs best among the many insurers they represent and are paid a commission for each sale. The independent producer owns the expirations of the policies he sells, meaning that the individual may place that business with another insurer upon renewal if it is in the best interest of the client.

Exclusive or captive producers represent only one company and have an agency relationship with that company. These producers are sometimes referred to as *career agents* working from *career agencies*. Most often, these captive or career producers are compensated by commissions. A career producer's compensation will normally consist of first-year commissions and renewal commissions in subsequent years. Usually, the first-year commissions may represent 50% or more of the first-year life insurance premium. Thereafter, the renewal commissions will usually be 10% or less each year.

However, frequently these producers also may be paid a training allowance that serves as a salary for a limited period during which the new producer is being trained. Generally, this allowance may be paid for several months or possibly a year or two. Most companies will require that the producer validate this training allowance by producing a certain amount of new business each month.

If a producer hires, trains, and supervises other producers within a specific geographical area, he is referred to as a **general agent** or **managing general agent (MGA)**. The MGA is compensated by commissions earned on business he sold as well as an overriding commission (overrides) on the business produced by the other producers managed by the general agent.

An MGA also may receive additional compensation for administrative and service functions performed for policyholders. This compensation is paid in accordance with a separate contractual agreement with the insurer. This supplemental agreement may be referred to as an expense allowance because it is designed to help cover some of the agency's overhead expenses.

Direct writing companies usually pay salaries to employees whose job function is to sell the company's insurance products. Technically, these salaried employees do not function as producers. Commissions are usually not paid, and the insurer owns all of the business produced.

1. 9. 2 Mass Marketing

Mass marketing has grown in general use over the past several years. The most common types of mass marketing systems are direct response, franchise, noninsurance sponsors, and vending machine sales.

1. 9. 2. 1 Direct Response

Direct-response marketing is conducted through the mail, by advertisements in newspapers and magazines, and on television and radio. Policies sold using this method have limited benefits and low premiums, such as disability only.

1. 9. 2. 2 Franchise Marketing

The franchise marketing system provides coverage to employees of small firms or to members of associations. Unlike group policies where benefits are standard for classes of individuals, persons insured under the franchise method receive individual policies that vary according to the individuals' needs.

Franchise plans are attractive to employers who do not, according to the laws of their state, meet the qualifications for a true group. It allows the employers to offer individual insurance to their employees at a lower premium than for insurance purchased on an individual basis. Premiums may be deducted from the individual's paycheck.

1. 9. 2. 3 Noninsurance Sponsors

Noninsurance sponsors are being used more and more. The most common are banks and companies that issue credit cards. This marketing system reaches a select group of individuals who have a history of periodic payments. Usually, the sponsor is responsible for the billing of premium, and it is added to the billing statement or deducted from checking accounts.

1. 9. 2. 4 Vending Machine Sales

Vending machine sales have traditionally been of travel accident policies sold from coin-operated machines at airports. A large amount of coverage is available at low premiums. The coverage is good only for the duration of a single trip.

1. 9. 2. 5 Internet Insurance Sales

Advertising and selling insurance through the Internet are relatively recent developments in insurance distribution. Insurance company Websites offer information about insurers, the various lines of insurance provided, and links to regulatory information, financial ratings, and quotation services, as well as locator services to put the consumer in touch with a local agent. Some companies are using the Internet to solicit leads, accept applications, and even issue insurance policies. Some insurance producers and agencies also have developed home pages advertising products and services over the Internet.

These practices raise some interesting questions about the regulation of Internet sales. Because the Internet essentially dissolves state geographic boundaries, at issue is whether the insurance company is licensed to do business in the state and whether the agent is properly licensed and appointed for the companies represented. Other challenges include how to track premium taxes, how to ensure the security of disclosed personal information, how to audit Internet transactions, whether Internet advertisements comply with state laws, and what the implications are for state guaranty associations. The NAIC has established an Internet Marketing Issues Working Group to further explore these issues.

1. 10 PRODUCERS

The term *producer* is becoming increasingly common for several reasons. Many states have replaced separate agent and broker licenses with a single **producer** license. In addition, a major law change in 1999 (discussed later in this course) removed prior legislative barriers between insurers, banks, and securities brokerages, allowing insurance to be sold by a wider range of professionals. Anyone who produces sales of insurance products is a producer.

1. 10. 1 Categories of Producers

Producers may function as agents, representing the insurance company, or as brokers, representing the potential insured. In some states, solicitors are still licensed and function as insurance producers.

Producers acting as agents are not only categorized by their function in the industry but also by the line of insurance they sell.

1. 10. 1. 1 Life and Health Agents

Generally, life and health insurance agents represent the insurer to the buyer with respect to the sale of life and health insurance products. The agents are appointed by the insurer, and usually the agent's authority to represent the insurer is specified in the agency agreement between them, which is a working agreement between the agent and the insurer. Life and health insurance agents generally do not have the authority to issue or modify insurance contracts. Customarily, life and health insurance agents are authorized to solicit, receive, and forward applications for the contracts written by their companies. The agent may receive the first premium due with the application, but usually not subsequent premiums, except in industrial life insurance. The insurance company approves and issues the contract after receiving the application and premium from the applicant through the agent. The agent cannot bind coverage. This means that an agent cannot commit to providing insurance coverage on behalf of the insurance company.

1. 10. 1. 2 Property and Casualty Agents

Agents appointed by property and liability insurance companies generally are granted more authority. These agents may **bind** or commit their companies by oral or written agreement. They sometimes inspect risks for the insurance company and collect premiums due. They may be authorized to issue many types of insurance contracts from their own offices.

1. 10. 1. 3 Brokers

In contrast to the agent-client relationship in which the agent represents the insurer to the purchaser, a broker represents the buyer to the insurer. A broker may do business with several different insurers. Brokers are independent sales representatives who select insurance coverages from these various companies for their clients.

Brokers must be licensed just like agents, and generally their routine activities and functions are similar to those of agents. Brokers solicit applications for insurance, may collect the initial premium, and deliver policies. Brokers do not have the authority to bind coverages.

1. 10. 1. 4 *Solicitors*

A **solicitor** is a salesperson who works for an agent or a broker. This working relationship is most common in the property and casualty insurance field. Most often the solicitor will be licensed as a solicitor. Depending on the state, the solicitor may obtain a producer's license. Solicitors normally have a working agreement with a producer. In accordance with this agreement, the solicitor's primary functions are to solicit insurance, collect initial premiums, and deliver policies. Solicitors cannot bind coverage.

1. 10. 1. 5 *Insurance Consultants*

A very small group of insurance professionals call themselves insurance consultants. Consultants are not paid by commission for the sales of insurance policies. Instead, they work strictly for the benefit of insureds and are paid a fee by the insureds they represent.

1. 11 SUMMARY

In this lesson, you learned about:

- key terms: *insurance*, *insurer*, *premium*, *insured*, *policy*, *claim*, *loss*, *risk*, *hazard*, *peril*, *indemnity*, and *law of large numbers*;
- two types of risk;
- four methods for managing risk;
- five characteristics of insurable risk;
- the types of insurers: stock insurers, mutual insurers, nonprofit insurers, reciprocal insurers, fraternal insurers, Lloyd's of London, reinsurers, excess insurers, and surplus lines insurers;
- the role of the federal government in providing insurance;
- the two main insurance distribution systems; and
- the five main types of insurance producers.

UNIT TEST

1. The term used to describe the individual who is covered by the insurance is
   A. insurer
   B. insured
   C. policyowner
   D. risk

2. Which of the following is a risk?
   A. A car may need to have new brakes installed after several years of regular driving.
   B. An individual may need medical attention after slipping on the ice and falling.

3. The application of the law of large numbers enables actuaries to
   A. estimate the future losses of a class or group of people
   B. predict the future losses of specific individuals

4. The estimation of future losses is more accurate when information is from a
   A. small select group
   B. large group

5. Which type of policy is designed to protect against the risk of living too long?
   A. Casualty
   B. Life
   C. Annuity
   D. Medical expense

6. Which of the following is a type of insurance company owned by its shareholders?
   A. Mutual
   B. Stock
   C. Lloyd's
   D. Reinsurer

7. The ZYX Insurance Company is incorporated in Alabama. While doing business in Texas, it is a(n)
   A. domestic insurer
   B. foreign insurer
   C. alien insurer
   D. export insurer

8. The ZYX Insurance Company is incorporated in Mexico. While doing business in Texas, it is a(n)
   A. domestic insurer
   B. foreign insurer
   C. alien insurer
   D. export insurer

9. Self-insurance is an example of which method of handling risk?
   A. Acceptance
   B. Transference
   C. Avoidance
   D. Reduction

10. Which of the following terms is used to denote insurance companies?
    A. Broker
    B. Exchange
    C. Corporation
    D. Insurer

11. A social device for spreading the chance of financial loss among a large number of people is the definition of
    A. hazard
    B. risk
    C. insurance
    D. peril

12. Which of the following risks is most likely to be insurable?
    A. George is concerned about the financial impact his premature death would have on his family.
    B. Talyn is concerned about the financial impact large betting losses at the horse track will have on his retirement savings.
    C. John is concerned about the financial impact on his savings when his car eventually becomes worn enough to need to be replaced.
    D. Jewel is concerned about the financial effect losing her hat would have on her weekly spending money.

13. Roger refuses to travel by airplane. Roger is managing the risk of being in a plane crash by
    A. reduction
    B. avoidance
    C. transference
    D. retention

14. Chianna becomes injured in a car accident caused when she took her eyes off the road to answer her cell phone. This is an example of a
    A. physical hazard
    B. moral hazard
    C. morale hazard
    D. legal hazard

15. Mathematicians who study and compile statistical data regarding exposure and risks for insurance companies are called
    A. solicitors
    B. insuraries
    C. underwriters
    D. actuaries

16. Which of the following is NOT an example of insurable interest?
    A. Jose wishes to take out a life insurance policy on his own life to provide for his family in the event of his death.
    B. Ana wishes to take out a life insurance policy on her mother to ensure that funeral costs will be covered when the time comes.
    C. Juan wishes to take out a life insurance policy on his neighbor because his neighbor is a careless driver—who Juan thinks is likely to die in a car accident.
    D. Carla wishes to take out a life insurance policy on her best salesperson to protect the business from lost sales in the event of the salesperson's death.

17. Kim is injured in a house fire. When the bills come, the insurance company pays 80% of the cost, and Kim pays the rest. This is an example of
    A. coinsurance
    B. a deductible
    C. extraneous insurance
    D. policy limits

18. Hoosier Insurance Company is owned by the policyholders. Hoosier Insurance is a
    A. stock insurer
    B. mutual insurer
    C. nonprofit insurer
    D. fraternal insurer

19. Which of the following people represents several insurance companies but owns the policy expirations?
    A. Independent agent
    B. Exclusive agent
    C. Direct writing agent
    D. General agent

20. Which of the following can bind an insurance company by oral or written agreement?
    A. Property and casualty producer
    B. Life producer
    C. Broker
    D. Solicitor

ANSWERS AND RATIONALES TO UNIT TEST

1. **B.** The term used to describe the individual who is covered by the insurance is insured.
2. **B.** A possibility that an individual may need medical attention after slipping on the ice and falling is a risk.
3. **A.**
4. **B.** The estimation of future losses is more accurate when information is from a large group.
5. **C.** An annuity is designed to protect against the risk of living too long.
6. **B.** A stock insurance company is owned by its shareholders.
7. **B.**
8. **C.** This insurance company is an alien insurer.
9. **A.** Self-insurance is an example of accepting the risk.
10. **D.** Insurer denotes an insurance company.
11. **C.**
12. **A.** George is most likely insurable.
13. **B.** Roger is avoiding the risk.
14. **C.** This is an example of a morale hazard.
15. **D.** Actuaries are mathematicians who study and compile statistical data regarding exposure and risks for insurance companies.
16. **C.** Juan's interest is not insurable.
17. **A.** This is an example of coinsurance.
18. **B.** Hoosier Insurance is a mutual insurer.
19. **A.** Independent agents represent several insurance companies but own the policy expirations.
20. **A.** A property and casualty producer can bind an insurance company by oral or written agreement.

UNIT

2

Insurance Regulation

2. 1 INTRODUCTION

Insurance is a public trust because it affects a large percentage of the general public and performs what can be construed as a public service by its very nature. The general public has an interest in making sure that insurance activity actually is provided as a service and not a disservice. Insurance is highly regulated to protect the public interest and to make sure coverage is available on an equitable basis.

Another reason the insurance business is regulated is the large amount of money involved in the industry. Insurance companies control vast sums of money. If used unscrupulously, especially in a concentrated effort, this money could disastrously affect the nation's economy.

2. 2 LEARNING OBJECTIVES

After completing this lesson, you will be able to:

- list the three major channels of regulation;
- explain the impact of federal regulations;
- explain the role of the Insurance Commissioner in insurance regulation;
- describe insurer solvency, annual statements, and investments imposed in most states;
- explain the functions and the purpose of the Mandatory Security Valuation Reserve;
- explain how life insurance companies are taxed by the states;
- describe the role of company ratings and how such information may be used with prospects;
- explain what market conduct exams are and how they differ from other state examinations;
- describe the role of state guarantee associations.
- describe how the Gramm-Leach Bliley Act affects producer regulation at the state level;
- list the qualifications the Producer Licensing Model Act suggests for receiving a producer license;
- list the standard exemptions from licensing requirements set out in the Producer Licensing Model Act;
- list the requirements suggested in the Producer Licensing Model Act for a nonresident producer license;

- explain the purpose of temporary producer licenses and list situations in which a temporary license might be granted;
- explain the requirements for maintaining a producer license;
- explain the procedure for reinstating a lapsed license;
- describe the function of producer appointments; and
- list possible causes for license denial, nonrenewal, or revocation as suggested in the Producer Licensing Model Act.

2. 3 REGULATION OF THE INSURANCE BUSINESS

Regulation of the insurance industry is divided among a number of authorities. The three major channels of regulation of the insurance industry are:

- federal regulation;
- state regulation; and
- self-regulation.

The National Association of Insurance Commissioners also plays an important role in insurance regulation, which will be explored later in this unit.

2. 3. 1 Federal Regulation of the Insurance Industry

Most insurance regulation takes place at the state level, but there are some important regulations at the federal level. Federal jurisdiction applies to individuals or companies whose activities affect interstate commerce, which includes most insurance activity. Federal regulation of insurance is primarily used as a means to oversee areas not covered by state regulation of the industry. The most important sources of federal regulation are outlined below and include both legislative and judicial aspects.

2. 3. 1. 1 Paul v. Virginia

In the case of *Paul v. Virginia*, an agent working for insurers in New York began to transact insurance in Virginia, where the New York insurers had failed to comply with state law. The case was brought before the Supreme Court to determine whether the individual states had the right to regulate the business of insurance. The Court's decision established, as law, that the transaction of insurance across state lines was not interstate commerce and therefore should be regulated by local law. This decision held in case after case for 75 years.

2. 3. 1. 2 *South-Eastern Underwriters Decision*

In 1944, the South-Eastern Underwriters Association was indicted for violating the Sherman Antitrust Act. The Association defended its action by stating the fact that federal regulation did not apply to the business of insurance. For the first time in 75 years, the issue of transacting insurance across state lines was looked at another way. The issue this time related to the effect of an act of Congress on insurance transactions conducted across state lines.

The Supreme Court overturned the previous decision by saying that insurance transacted across state lines was, in fact, interstate commerce. This decision had the capability of turning the insurance industry upside down because for the past 75 years, the states had been regulating the industry locally.

2. 3. 1. 3 *McCarran-Ferguson Act*

To waylay impending confusion, Congress enacted the McCarran-Ferguson Act in 1945. This act stated that the federal government had the right to regulate the business of insurance, but only to the extent that such business is not regulated by state law. The main intent of the law was to exempt the insurance industry from most of the provisions of the federal antitrust laws.

2. 3. 1. 4 *Privacy Act of 1974*

In the 1970s, the Privacy Protection Study Commission was established. The job of the Commission was to study (1) the collectors of personal information; (2) the users of personal information; and (3) the manner in which personal information is circulated. The study found insurers to be one of the major collectors and users of personal information. Because of the abundance of personal information and the numbers of agencies collecting and using personal information, it became vital that some controls be established to protect the public from inaccurate or misused information.

The Commission's findings were summarized in a report entitled **Personal Privacy in an Information Society**. A large portion of the report dealt with the insurance industry. The report outlined three goals:

- to minimize intrusiveness;
- to be fair and impartial in collecting, analyzing, and presenting information and reports; and
- to make it known to the public that they can expect personal information to be handled in confidence

2. 3. 1. 4. 1 Disclosure Authorization

Applicants for insurance must be given advance notice of the insurer's practices regarding the collection and use of personal information. Notice must be given promptly and in writing. Notice should be given in the following cases and in the following manner.

- If a third party is interviewed, the applicant must be given notice when the collection of information has begun.
- If only the applicant is interviewed, the applicant must be given notice when the policy is delivered.
- If a policy is being renewed, the insured must be given notice by the renewal date.
- If a policy is being reinstated, the applicant-insured must be given notice at the time the request is made.
- If an insured is requesting a change of benefits, the insured must receive notice at the time the request is made.

The notice must give the applicant or insured the following kinds of information:

- The people with access to personal information
- The kind of information to be collected
- The kind of information the insurer can receive without the applicant's prior approval
- The sources of information
- The persons to whom information may be disclosed without the applicant's prior authorization

Disclosure authorization forms are required by law to be prescribed and approved by the Commissioner. The disclosure form must be written in accordance with the plain language laws of the state and dated. Disclosure forms state the types of persons authorized to disclose private and personal information (e.g., neighbors, employers, and previous or other insurers) and the kind of information that may be disclosed (e.g., personal habits, work habits, health habits such as smoking and drinking). The form also must state the reason information is collected and how it will be used. For instance, the reason personal information is gathered is because the applicant requested a life insurance policy; the information will be used by the underwriting department for the purpose of determining the applicant's risk category.

The applicant's signature on the disclosure form authorizes the insurer to collect and disseminate information in the manner described in the notice. The authorization is good only for a certain period. For example, if authorization is given to an insurer to collect information with regard to a claim settlement, the authorization is good for 30 months. At the end of this period, another authorization must be obtained. The applicant or insured may request and receive a copy of the authorization form.

Personal information may be disclosed to persons other than the requesting parties under certain conditions. Among those to whom an insurer may disclose information are producers, other insurers, insurance organizations (such as the Medical Information Bureau), and insurance departments. This type of third-party disclosure may require authorization, but in some instances, authorization is not required as long as the applicant or insured has received proper notification of the insurer's information practices. In some cases, information is passed on to those conducting scientific research, audits, or marketing approaches.

2. 3. 1. 4. 2 Penalties

The Commissioner of Insurance has the authority to investigate any insurer or agency used by the insurer to collect information to determine whether the company is in compliance with the Insurance Act. If the Commissioner believes that a violation of the Privacy Act has taken place, he can conduct a hearing to determine the facts. If a violation is found, the Commissioner can issue a cease and desist order, but if the violator continues to violate the Privacy Act, the Commissioner can institute a fine of up to $10,000 for each violation. If the violation is one that happens with such frequency that it appears to be a general business practice, the fine for each violation can be up to $50,000.

The NAIC Model Privacy Act also provides for the enforcement of individual rights. The individual has the right to information concerning himself, the right to correct inaccurate information, the right to know the reasons for being turned down for insurance, or any other adverse underwriting decision. These rights are those found under the Fair Credit Reporting Act.

A fine of $10,000 or up to one year in jail is the penalty for any person who obtains information that he has no legitimate reason to receive.

2. 3. 1. 5 Fair Credit Reporting Act

When an application is submitted to a life or health insurance company, a consumer reporting agency may be hired to obtain personal information about the applicant to be used in the underwriting evaluation. To protect the consumer's right to privacy in this situation, the federal Fair Credit Reporting Act was passed in 1970. The act sets up procedures for consumer reporting agencies to follow in their dealings with businesses to ensure that records are confidential, accurate, relevant, and properly used.

2. 3. 1. 6 Consumer Reports

Consumer reports include written, oral, and other forms of communication that a consumer reporting agency has regarding a consumer's credit, character, reputation, or habits and are used or collected to determine whether a consumer is eligible for credit, insurance, employment, or other purposes authorized under the act. Consumer reports may be issued only to persons who have a legitimate business need for the information. Governmental agencies also may be provided with a consumer's name, present and former addresses, and present and past places of employment.

2. 3. 1. 7 *Investigative Consumer Reports*

An investigative consumer report includes information on a consumer's character, general reputation, personal habits, and mode of living that is obtained through investigation—that is, interviews with associates and friends and neighbors of the consumer. Such reports may not be made unless the consumer is clearly and accurately told about the report in writing within three days of the date on which the report was first requested. The consumer also must be notified that she is allowed to request additional information. If that person requests such information in writing, the person who caused the investigative report to be made must make a complete and accurate disclosure of the report to the consumer about whom it is written. The disclosure must be made within five days of receipt of the report or when the report was first requested, whichever date is later. If there is an investigative consumer report prepared subsequent to the first one, any adverse information must be verified or must have been received during the three months preceding the subsequent report.

2. 3. 1. 8 *Pretext Interviews*

A **pretext interview** is an interview whereby a person, in an attempt to obtain information about another person, pretends to be someone he is not, misrepresents the true purpose of the interview, or refuses to properly identify himself.

Generally, pretext interviews are prohibited. However, such an interview may be conducted when there is evidence of criminal activity, fraud, or misrepresentation.

2. 3. 1. 9 *Consumer Reporting Agencies*

Consumer reporting agencies collect information on individuals, prepare reports, and make the reports available to persons or organizations with a legitimate reason to receive such information. These agencies may operate for profit (e.g., Experian or Equifax) or agencies may be nonprofit (e.g., the Medical Information Bureau or a credit union).

A consumer may choose to have his name and address excluded from any list provided by a consumer reporting agency in connection with a credit or insurance transaction that is not initiated by the consumer. The consumer simply needs to notify the agency that he does not consent to any use of a consumer report relating to the consumer in connection with any credit or insurance transaction that is not initiated by the consumer.

Credit agencies are required to provide a notification system, including a toll-free telephone number, to allow consumers to request exclusion of their information. This notification is valid for two years. If notification is made in writing on a signed notice of election form issued by the agency, it is valid until the consumer revokes the request. The consumer may revoke the request at any time.

2. 3. 1. 9. 1 Prohibited Information

Consumer reporting agencies are specifically prevented from putting information in their reports about:

- bankruptcies over 10 years old;
- suits and judgments over 7 years old or in which the statute of limitations has expired, whichever period is longer;
- paid tax liens or accounts placed for collection or charged to profit that are over 7 years old;
- arrests, indictments, or conviction of crime reports; and
- any other adverse information that took place 7 years before the report.

These restrictions are not applicable when the consumer credit report is used in connection with a credit transaction of $150,000 or more, a life insurance policy of $150,000 or more, or when it concerns employment of an individual earning $75,000 or more.

2. 3. 1. 9. 2 Consumers' Rights

Consumers who feel that information in their files is inaccurate or incomplete may inform the consumer reporting agency of any information in dispute. The consumer reporting agency is then required to reinvestigate and record the current status of the disputed material (unless the agency has reasonable grounds to believe the dispute is frivolous or irrelevant) within a reasonable time.

If the agency's investigation finds that the information is no longer accurate or verifiable, it must be deleted promptly. If the dispute is not resolved after reinvestigation, the consumer may file a brief statement (not more than 100 words) concerning the problem. If this statement is filed, the consumer reporting agency must note it in future consumer reports that contain that information (unless it is determined to be frivolous or irrelevant). If credit or insurance is denied or charges are increased wholly or partially on the basis of information contained in a consumer report, the user of the information must notify the consumer of this fact and report the name and address of the consumer reporting agency that made the report. If credit or insurance is denied or charges are increased wholly or partially on the basis of information obtained from a person or organization other than a consumer reporting agency, the user of the information must disclose the nature of that information to the consumer if it has been requested within 60 days of the disclosure. It is the responsibility of the user of the information to inform the consumer of his right to request this information when the adverse action is communicated to him.

2. 3. 1. 9. 3 Penalties

Failure to comply with the provisions of the act makes the guilty party liable to the consumer for the sum of actual damages sustained as a result of the noncompliance, punitive damages deemed proper by a court, and the costs of an action that enforces liability, plus reasonable attorney's fees. When the noncompliance is a result of negligence, the guilty party must pay the consumer the sum of the consumer's actual damages and the costs of any successful action to enforce liability, plus reasonable attorney's fees.

Obtaining consumer information reports under false pretenses may result in a fine, imprisonment, or both. The same penalty is imposed on officers or employees of consumer reporting agencies who have knowingly and willfully provided consumer information to a person not authorized to receive it.

2. 3. 1. 10 Fraud and False Statements

Certain types of false or fraudulent statements have been specifically outlined in federal law as punishable by a fine, a prison sentence, or both. Federal law prohibits persons engaging in the business of insurance whose activities affect interstate commerce from knowingly and with the intent to deceive:

- making any false material statement or report that willfully and materially overvalues any land, property, or security in connection with any financial reports or documents presented to an insurance regulatory official or agency, or an agent or examiner acting for an insurance regulatory official for the purpose of influencing the actions of such individual;
- making any false entry of material fact in any book, report, or statement of such person engaged in the business of insurance with intent to deceive any person, including any officer, employee, or agent of such person engaged in the business of insurance regarding the financial condition or solvency of such business;
- willfully embezzling, abstracting, purloining, or misappropriating any of the moneys, funds, premiums, credits, or other property of any person engaged in the business of insurance; or
- corruptly influencing, obstructing, or impeding the due and proper administration of the law under which any proceeding is pending before any insurance regulatory official or agency or any producer or examiner appointed by such official or agency to examine the affairs of a person engaged in the business of insurance.

The punishment for any of the offenses described above may include fines, imprisonment, or both. If the statement, report, or activity was a significant cause of an insurer being placed in conservation, rehabilitation, or liquidation by a court, the fine and term of imprisonment may be significantly increased.

The attorney general may bring a civil action in the appropriate US district court against any person who engages in unfair and deceptive practices as defined in the law, and, upon proof of such conduct by a preponderance of the evidence, the person will be subject to a fine of not more than $50,000 for each violation or the amount of compensation the person received or offered for the prohibited conduct, whichever amount is greater. If the offense has contributed to the decision of a court to issue an order directing the conservation, rehabilitation, or liquidation of an insurer, the penalty will be remitted to the appropriate regulatory official for the benefit of the policyholders, claimants, and creditors of the insurer. The imposition of a fine under this section does not preclude any other criminal or civil statutory, common law, or administrative remedy available by law to the United States or any other person.

If the attorney general has reason to believe that a person is engaged in conduct constituting unfair and deceptive practices as defined in the law, the attorney general may petition an appropriate US district court for an order prohibiting that person from engaging in the conduct if the court finds that the conduct constitutes such an offense. The filing of a petition under this section does not preclude any other remedy available by law to the United States or any other person.

2. 3. 1. 11 Financial Services Modernization Act of 1999

Also known as the Gramm-Leach-Bliley Act (GLBA), this legislation was passed in 1999 primarily to remove Depression-era barriers between commercial banking, investment banking, and insurance. GLBA allows financial holding companies to engage in any activities that are financial in nature. Regulation of these holding companies is managed on a functional basis. This means that regulatory authority is based on what activity is occurring, rather than on what type of company is engaging in the activity. For example, the sale of insurance is regulated by state insurance regulators even if the company making the sale is a bank or securities brokerage.

Financial holding companies have the potential to capture unprecedented amounts of information about their customers. To address these concerns, GLBA also establishes a minimum federal standard for financial privacy. GLBA states that each financial institution has a responsibility "to respect the privacy of its customers and to protect the security and confidentiality of those customers' nonpublic personal information."

The law requires that all the functional federal regulatory agencies establish appropriate standards for each regulated institution with respect to technical, administrative, and physical safeguards:

- to ensure the security and confidentiality of customer records and information;
- to protect against any anticipated threats or hazards to the security or integrity of such records; and
- to protect against unauthorized access to or use of such records or information that could result in substantial harm or inconvenience to any customer.

Anyone about whom a company collects information is a **consumer**. A customer is a consumer who has an ongoing relationship with the financial institution. Different states define ongoing relationship using different guidelines, so be certain you understand what it means in your state.

GLBA protects the confidentiality of personal information. Business information is not covered under this statute. GLBA considers information to be **collected** when it is organized or can be retrieved by an individual's name or by an identifying number, such as a policy number. The source of the information is less important than how it is stored and organized.

Information that is publicly available, such as phone numbers listed in a telephone book, is not protected under GLBA. However, the fact that an individual has an insurance policy with a certain company is not public information, so publishing a list of policyholder names and listed phone numbers would not automatically be allowed.

In some cases, consumers and customers are given the opportunity to keep the company from sharing the information it has about them. This is known as the right to **opt out**. Health information, such as that acquired during a medical exam, is subject to a stricter **opt-in** standard, meaning that companies may not share some health information without receiving specific permission to do so from the customer or consumer.

The ability to prohibit information sharing would seriously limit a company's ability to manage a policy. For this reason, there are several exceptions to an individual's right to opt out of information sharing. For example, companies are always permitted to share information with their affiliates.

2. 3. 1. 11. 1 Requirements Under GLBA

GLBA requires that a company make two primary disclosures to customers: one at the time of the establishment of the customer relationship and the second before the company discloses protected information. The first disclosure is to be made at the time a consumer becomes a customer, usually by purchasing a policy. At this point, the company is required to give a clear and conspicuous disclosure to the new customer regarding its policies and procedures for customer privacy. The customer must, at least on an annual basis, receive an updated notice containing the same information.

The second disclosure required by GLBA explains the customer's right to opt out of information sharing. Each customer must be given the right to opt out and must be told explicitly how he may exercise that right. The notice must identify the products and services to which the opt-out right applies. The only other requirement is that the opt-out agreement must be in writing and may be electronic if the customer agrees. If the customer does not take advantage of this option within a reasonable time, the company may share the information with others.

A side issue of the opt-out right applies to joint accounts. A single notice of the opt-out right may be sent or given to joint customers, but either of the joint customers may individually opt out of disclosure. The financial institution has the discretion to apply the opt out by one person in a joint account to the entire account or to treat each individual separately regarding disclosure of information.

2. 3. 1. 12 *Other Regulating Agencies*

Some insurance products are regulated by both the federal and state governments. For example, the Securities and Exchange Commission (SEC) and the state Insurance Departments regulate variable contracts. Variable annuities and variable life insurance are insurance company products, but these products present a degree of investment risk to the buyer and, accordingly, have also been identified as securities in accordance with SEC regulations.

2. 3. 2 State Regulation of the Insurance Industry

Most insurance regulation takes place at the state level. The body of laws at the state level is called the **Insurance Code**. State regulation consists of statutes and rules and regulations. **Statutes** are the body of law developed by the legislative branch of government. They outline, in general terms, the duties of the Commissioner and the activities of the Department of Insurance. **Rules and regulations** are developed by the Department of Insurance, to expand upon statutory requirements and explicate legislative intent.

2. 3. 2. 1 *Commissioner's Scope and Duties*

The Insurance Code of each state authorizes the establishment of a department of insurance to administer and enforce the insurance laws. In each state, a public official will head the department—the title of the official will be the **Commissioner**, **Superintendent**, or **Director of Insurance**. The titles differ from state to state. A majority of the states use the title Commissioner. In all cases, the public official in charge of the department of insurance has broad powers to supervise and regulate the insurance affairs within the state. The insurance laws of the state usually confer upon the Commissioner all of the following powers and duties:

- To conduct investigations and examinations
- To make reasonable rules and regulations
- To hire employees and examiners and to delegate any power, duty, or function to such persons
- To examine the accounts, records, documents, and transactions of any insurer, agent, or broker
- To subpoena witnesses and administer oaths to further an examination, investigation, or hearing on insurance matters
- To issue orders and notices on decisions made or matters pending
- To issue insurance licenses and certificates of authority
- To impose penalties for violations of the Insurance Code, including but not limited to fines, suspensions, or revocations of licenses and certificates of authority, and to request that the attorney general prosecute a violator

- To approve insurance policy forms sold within the state
- To approve rates and rate increases for regulated lines of insurance

Notice that the Commissioner does not make the insurance laws. He is simply in charge of making certain all insurance operations within the state are in compliance with the laws made by the state legislature.

2. 3. 2. 2 *Regulating Insurance Companies*

The state Insurance Code prescribes the procedures that must be followed for an insurance company to be formed. It specifies the manner in which the company must be organized, the requirements for incorporation, such as the amounts for minimum capital and surplus requirements for a domestic stock insurer, and the minimum surplus requirements and securities deposit for a domestic mutual insurer. Although the bulk of the Code pertains only to domestic insurers, some of the laws regulate foreign and alien insurers' eligibility to transact insurance business as well as establish requirements for maintaining assets and liabilities.

Before individuals can form an insurance company, they must receive approval from the Department of Insurance to organize. They must meet the requirements for incorporation, certificates of intention, and bylaws just like any other corporation. They are required to draw up a charter that states the proposed name of the insurer, the location, the lines of insurance to be sold, and method of operation. The Department of Insurance will also conduct an investigation to ensure that the organizers are of good moral character.

The majority of individual life and health insurance is written by stock and mutual companies. A mutual company must have a minimum number of applications for insurance, the advanced premium payment for each application, and a surplus. A stock company must have a specified amount of capital, which is invested, and a surplus amount. In many states, domestic insurers must deposit securities that insurance regulations specify as relatively stable and safe, such as government bonds.

2. 3. 2. 3 *Insurer Solvency*

Insurance companies collect premiums before losses are paid. If the insurer later becomes insolvent, customers will have paid for protection the company is no longer in a position to provide. Protection against insurer insolvency is one of the principal concerns of the insurance industry. Insurance insolvency regulations govern such areas as the organization and ownership of a new company, capital and surplus requirements, reserves, accounting, investments, annual statements, and the rehabilitation and liquidation of impaired insurers. If an insurer gets into trouble, the Department of Insurance will attempt to rehabilitate the company or, if this fails, handle the liquidation. In addition, insurance departments in many states have adopted regulations for the establishment of guaranty associations in the event that an insurer does, in spite of regulations and precautions, become insolvent.

The Department of Insurance has the right to compute the reserve liabilities of a company, to value its assets, and to approve or disapprove its investments, dividends, and expenses and has the power to require it to deposit securities to cover its liabilities in the state.

Various state statutes impose capital and surplus requirements and require the preparation of annual financial statements and periodic examinations of insurers by the Department of Insurance. These laws establish initial financial requirements and help in the early detection of financial problems.

Each insurer's capacity to write new business is limited by the levels of capital and surplus it currently maintains. Most states discourage or prohibit the writing of net premiums in excess of some multiple of an insurer's existing surplus. Without such controls, a carrier might assume excessive amounts of risk, experience losses beyond the capacity to pay claims, and become insolvent.

Despite checks on policywriting capacity, there are a number of other factors that could undermine or improve the financial status of an insurer. Insurance always carries an element of uncertainty, and above-average underwriting profits or losses might cause a company's financial status to shift. Investment income or loss is another factor that can have a profound effect on an insurer's status. Producers and insureds therefore have an interest in having coverage placed with carriers who have a sound financial condition.

2. 3. 2. 3. 1 Annual Statement

Each insurance company must report its financial condition in an annual statement. The annual statement generally reports the following information:

- Summary of company assets (listed by type)
- Summary of company liabilities
- Summary of company surplus and other funds
- Summary of company operations
- Analysis of operations (listed by line of business)
- Analysis of reserve increases
- Statements regarding changes in financial condition

2. 3. 2. 3. 2 Investments

All states have regulations that are intended to ensure that insurers invest only in high-quality assets to prevent insolvencies. Life insurance companies may invest funds in concerns that are fairly stable in value. These safe investments include municipal bonds, corporate bonds, real estate mortgages, and even policy loans.

Regulations require that all investments and loans be approved by the company's board of directors and that no board members have a personal interest in the investment being made. Minutes must be recorded during committee meetings in which discussion of investment or loans has been undertaken. Such minutes will be open to inspection by the Commissioner.

Foreign companies seeking a license to transact business in a state must meet investment requirements similar to those required of a domestic insurer.

2. 3. 2. 3. 3 Company Financial Ratings

Producers have a responsibility to place coverage with financially sound carriers. Evaluating the financial health of an insurance company is a complex task. There are several organizations that rate the financial strength of insurance carriers on the basis of an analysis of a company's claims experience, investment performance, management, and other factors. These organizations include AM Best, Inc., Standard & Poor's Insurance Rating Services, Moody's Investors Service, Duff & Phelps Credit Rating Company, and Weiss Ratings. These ratings are one of the most widely used indicators of financial health (or the lack of it) in the insurance industry.

The firms do not all rate every company, and each firm has different criteria for which companies will be rated. Each firm also uses a different method for evaluating the financial strength of insurance companies. There are at least four different rating scales in use among the five firms.

Scaled in Use by Financial Rating Services

Firm	Scale, Highest to Lowest
A.M. Best Company	A++, A+, A, A–, B++, B+, B, B–, C++, C+, C, C–, D, E, F
Weiss Research	A+, A, A–, B+, B, B–, C+, C, C–, D+, D, D–, E+, E, E–, F+, F, F–
Standard & Poor's/ Duff & Phelps	AAA, AA+, AA, AA–, A+, A, A–, BBB+, BBB, BBB–, BB+, BB, BB–, B+, B, B–, CCC, CC, D
Moody's Investors Service	Aaa, Aa1, Aa2, Aa3, A1, A2, A3, Baa1, Baa2, Baa3, Ba1, Ba2, Ba3, B1, B2, B3, Caa1, Caa2, Caa3, Ca1, Ca2, Ca3, C1, C2, C3

Consumers might find a rating meaningless or even misleading if it is not presented in the context of the scale. For example, an A+ rating sounds like it belongs at the top of the scale, but only one rating service considers it the top possible rating. From other services, it may be the third or even the fifth highest rating.

2. 3. 2. 3. 4 Examination of Insurers

The state Department of Insurance must examine the financial affairs, transactions, and general business records of domestic insurers in accordance with specific state insurance laws. Generally, these laws will state that the Commissioner of Insurance may examine the insurer's records as often as necessary but at least once every three to five years.

The nonfinancial regulatory activities of an insurance department fall under the broad heading of market conduct. **Proper market conduct** means conducting insurance business fairly and responsibly. In a market conduct examination, state Department of Insurance investigators examine the business practices and operations of an insurer and its agents to determine their authority to conduct insurance business in the state. During a market conduct examination, state examiners investigate the records and practices of an insurance company and determine whether the company is in compliance with state laws regulating the sales and marketing, underwriting, and issuance of insurance products. Some states conduct market conduct exams in conjunction with their regular financial examinations of insurers; others conduct independent market conduct exams.

As part of these examinations, the insurer's records of commissions paid to agents will be reviewed to determine whether commissions were paid in accordance with state statutes. Most states require that commissions be paid or shared only with licensed producers. Generally, producers may share commissions with other producers provided they are both appointed with the same insurer and licensed in the same lines of insurance.

2. 3. 2. 3. 5 Rehabilitation and Liquidation

Despite regulatory controls, some insurers become insolvent or find themselves in financial difficulty. In this event, the Department has the authority to assume control over company funds and management. If an insurer becomes impaired (in financial difficulty), the Department will attempt to put the insurer back on a sound financial standing. If an insurer becomes insolvent (unable to meet financial obligations), the Department will attempt to make the insurer solvent again. Rehabilitation efforts are undertaken if the Department believes that an impaired insurer has a chance of restoring solvency. Liquidation proceedings are instituted when the insurer is insolvent and cannot be restored to solvency.

The 1977 NAIC Model Insurers Supervision, Rehabilitation, and Liquidation Act is divided into four sections designed to facilitate actions of insolvency. **General Provisions** establish the act's absolute authority for the rehabilitation or liquidation of insolvent insurers. **Supervision Proceedings** offer alternative plans for use before the need for the Department's full intervention. **Formal Proceedings** outline methods for transferring authority from the insurer to the Department. **Interstate Relations** provide for the transfer of an insurer's assets and records to the state of domicile.

Rehabilitation proceedings can occur for the following reasons.

- The company's continued operation would not serve the best interests of policyowners, creditors, or the general public.
- The company's officers and directors have violated the law by committing certain acts or omissions.
- The company's officers, directors, or owners have attempted to transfer a significant amount of assets or have attempted a merger without the Department's approval.

2. 3. 2. 4 Guaranty Associations

State **guaranty associations** are organized to protect claimants, policyholders, annuitants, and creditors of financially impaired or insolvent insurers by providing funds for the payment of claims and other related policy benefits. Associations are composed of insurers authorized to transact insurance business within the state. Association membership exceptions include fraternal organizations and nonprofit companies. Member insurers are assessed certain sums of money to cover the association's operating expenses. If insurer insolvency occurs, each member insurer will be assessed additional fees to cover the insolvency.

Guaranty associations are often compared to the Federal Deposit Insurance Corporation (FDIC), which protects bank depositors from bank failures. Like the FDIC, coverage by the guaranty association is subject to limitations, usually $300,000 for death benefits, $100,000 for life insurance cash surrender or withdrawal values, $100,000 for health benefits, and an overall cap for individuals.

Some characteristics of guaranty associations include the following.

- They establish accounts to collect funds for the administration and assessment of the association.
- They are supervised by the Commissioner and a board of directors (usually nine members).
- The duties of the board and the Commissioner are specified by law.
- An insurer's authorization to transact business in the state is contingent upon membership in the association.
- Member insurers are assessed on the percentage of premiums each insurer has individually earned in the state.

The NAIC has helped to establish the National Organization of Life and Health Insurance Guaranty Associations (NOLHGA), which helps facilitate cooperation and communication among the state guaranty associations.

2. 3. 2. 5 Marketing and Advertising Life and Health Insurance

States often regulate the marketing and advertising of life and health insurance policies to ensure truthful and full disclosure of pertinent information when selling these policies. As a rule, the insurer is held responsible for the content of advertisements of its policies. Advertisements cannot be misleading or obscure or use deceptive illustrations and must clearly outline all policy coverages as well as exclusions or limitations on coverage (such as preexisting condition limitations).

Most states require insurers to keep a permanent advertising file of all advertisements used in the state until the next regular examination of the insurer by the Department of Insurance or for a specified minimum number of years, usually two or three.

Also, many states require the delivery of a buyer's guide and policy summary or outline of coverage at the time of policy delivery. The buyer's guide is a document providing basic information about the insurance policies, and the policy summary (life insurance) or outline of coverage (health insurance) is a written statement describing the elements of the policy being sold. Generally, it must include the agent's name and address, the name and office address of the insurer, and the generic name of the policy and each rider.

2. 3. 2. 6 *Regulating Producers*

Producers may function as either agents or brokers. Agents represent their companies, and brokers represent their clients. Although agents and brokers seek to serve both their clients and companies by matching coverage with need, it is important to know the difference between the two roles. Regardless of their role, producers are governed by the Insurance Code with respect to licensing and unfair trade practices.

2. 3. 2. 6. 1 Licensing Regulation

GLBA, which was passed in 1999, contained a small but important section on the regulation of insurance producers, stating that 29 states must have uniform or reciprocal licensing regulations in place by November 12, 2002, or the federal government would begin licensing agents and brokers. Ideas about uniformity and reciprocity of state licenses had already been in the works for years, and the National Association of Commissioners had even drafted a Producer Licensing Model Act (PLMA) that satisfied GLBA. In addition, PLMA had the advantages of creating some standard statutory language, maintaining individual state authority over licensing and maintaining important consumer protections.

As of mid-2002, more than 40 states had passed PLMA and more than 45 states had met the GLBA minimum requirements. This text will discuss the general provisions of PLMA. However, no two states enacted PLMA exactly the same way. Refer to your *State Law Digest* for more information on licensing regulations in your state.

2. 3. 2. 6. 2 License Required

Under the statutes of most states, no person is permitted to act as an insurance producer unless he is currently licensed as a producer for the class or classes of insurance involved. Acting as a producer includes selling, soliciting, or negotiating insurance. In many states, adjusters, consultants, and service representatives also must be licensed.

PLMA streamlined the qualifications for insurance producers. Some states still require additional qualifications. According to the Model Act, insurance producers must:

- be at least age 18;
- have not committed an act that is a ground for denial, suspension, or revocation of an insurance license;
- where required by the Commissioner, complete a prelicensing course of study for the lines of authority for which they have applied;
- where required, pay the appropriate fees; and
- where required, successfully pass the examinations for the lines of authority for which they have applied.

A business entity acting as an insurance producer is required to obtain an insurance producer license. Before approving the application, the Commissioner must find that the business entity has:

- paid the appropriate fees; and
- designated a licensed producer responsible for the business entity's compliance with the insurance laws, rules, and regulations of the state.

The Commissioner may require any documents reasonably necessary to verify the information contained in an application.

2. 3. 2. 6. 3 Exceptions to License Requirements

PLMA also defines a standard set of exemptions from the licensing requirements. Generally speaking, people who are not paid commissions for selling insurance do not need a license. The list of exemptions according to PLMA includes:

- officers, directors, or employees of an insurer or a producer who do not receive commissions on policies written or sold in the state if the individual's activities are executive, administrative, managerial, clerical, or a combination of these and are only indirectly related to selling, soliciting, or negotiating insurance;
- officers, directors, or employees of an insurer or a producer who do not receive commissions on policies written or sold in the state if the individual's function relates to underwriting, loss control, inspection, or the processing, adjusting, investigating, or settling of a claim on a contract of insurance;
- officers, directors, or employees of an insurer or a producer who do not receive commissions on policies written or sold in the state if the individual is acting in the capacity of a special agent or agency supervisor assisting insurance producers where the person's activities are limited to providing technical advice and assistance to licensed insurance producers and do not include the sale, solicitation, or negotiation of insurance;
- a person who secures and furnishes information for the purpose of group life insurance, group property and casualty insurance, group annuities, group or blanket accident and health insurance or for the purpose of enrolling people under plans, issuing certificates under plans, or otherwise assisting in administering plans, or who performs administrative services related to mass-marketed property and casualty insurance, where no commission is paid for the service;
- an employer or association or its officers, directors, employees, or the trustees of an employee trust plan, to the extent that the individuals are involved in the administration or operation of a program of employee benefits for the employer's or association's own employees or the employees of its subsidiaries or affiliates, when the program involves

the use of insurance issued by an insurer, as long as the individuals are not compensated in any manner by the insurer issuing the contracts;

- employees of insurers or organizations employed by insurers who engage in the inspection, rating, or classification of risks or in the supervision of the training of insurance producers and who are not individually engaged in the sale, solicitation, or negotiation of insurance;
- a person whose activities are limited to advertising without the intent to solicit insurance through communications in printed publication or other forms of electronic mass media whose distribution is not limited to residents of the state, provided that the person does not sell, solicit, or negotiate insurance that would insure risks residing, located, or to be performed in this state;
- a person who is not a resident of a state who sells, solicits, or negotiates a contract of insurance for commercial property and casualty risks to an insured with risks located in more than one state insured under that contract, provided that the person is licensed as an insurance producer in the state where the insured maintains its principal place of business and the contract of insurance insures risks located in that state; and
- salaried full-time employees who counsel or advise their employers relative to the insurance interest of the employer or of the subsidiaries or business affiliates of the employer, provided that the employees do not sell or solicit insurance or receive a commission.

Other exemptions may be allowed in individual states. Check the *Law Digest* text for variations or additions applicable to your state.

2. 3. 2. 6. 4 Nonresident Producer Licensing

The majority of states allow for reciprocity in nonresident licensing as required in GLBA. Reciprocity means a mutual exchange of privileges. In the case of producer licensing, it means the recognition of two states of the validity of licenses or privileges granted by the other.

The NAIC has encouraged states to eliminate licensing and appointment retaliatory fees that might get in the way of reciprocity, suggesting that states avoid charging nonresident fees that are higher than resident fees and create a barrier to entry. Check your *State Law Supplement* to see what the rules are in your state.

PLMA suggests that an individual who wants to receive a nonresident producer license:

- is currently licensed as a resident and in good standing in his home state;
- has submitted the proper request for licensure and has paid the fees required by the state in which he wants to be licensed as a nonresident producer;
- has submitted or transmitted to the Commissioner the application for licensure that he submitted to his home state, or a completed uniform application; and

- is from a state that awards nonresident producer licenses to residents of this state on the same basis.

States generally will not require additional attachments to the uniform application or impose other conditions on applicants that exceed the information requested within the uniform application.

The Commissioner may verify the producer's licensing status through the producer database maintained by the National Association of Commissioners, its affiliates, or subsidiaries.

A nonresident producer who moves from one state to another state or a resident producer who moves to another state must file a change of address and provide certification from the new resident state within 30 days of the change of legal residence. No fee or license application is required.

2. 3. 2. 7 *Obtaining a License*

2. 3. 2. 7. 1 Application for Examination

A resident individual applying for an insurance producer license has to pass a written examination unless exempt as discussed above. The exam is developed by the Commissioner to test the knowledge of the individual concerning the lines of authority for which the application is made, the duties and responsibilities of an insurance producer, and the insurance laws and regulations of the state.

The Commissioner may, and generally does, make arrangements to contract with an outside testing service for administering examinations and collecting the nonrefundable fee as described by state law. Each individual applying for an examination must pay a nonrefundable fee. If the individual fails to appear for the exam as scheduled or fails to pass the exam, he must reapply for the exam and remit all the required fees and forms before being rescheduled for another examination. States may limit the frequency of application for examination.

2. 3. 2. 7. 2 Exemptions from Examination

A person licensed as an insurance producer in one state who moves to another state has 90 days after establishing legal residence to become a resident licensee. Prelicensing education is generally not required to obtain a line of authority previously held in another state. This exemption is available only if the person is currently licensed in another state or if the application is received within 90 days of the cancellation of the applicant's previous license. The Commissioner may require certification that, at the time of cancellation, the applicant was in good standing in that state or that the state's producer database records indicate that the producer is or was licensed in good standing for the line of authority requested.

2. 3. 2. 7. 3 Issuance of License

Licenses contain the licensee's name, address, personal identification number, date of issuance, lines of authority, expiration date, and any other information the Commissioner deems necessary.

2. 3. 2. 7. 4 Temporary Agent Licenses

In most states, temporary agent licenses may be issued for up to 180 days without requiring an examination if the Commissioner considers the temporary license necessary for maintaining an insurance business in the following cases:

- To the surviving spouse or court-appointed personal representative of a licensed producer who dies or becomes disabled to allow adequate time for the sale of the insurance business, or for the recovery or return of the producer to the business, or to provide for the training and licensing of new personnel to operate the producer's business
- To a member of a business entity licensed as an insurance producer, upon the death or disability of an individual designated in the business entity application or the license
- To the designee of a licensed insurance producer entering active service in the armed forces of the United States
- In any other circumstance where the Commissioner considers the temporary license necessary to ensure the public interest will be served

The authority of any temporary license can be limited in any way the Commissioner considers necessary to protect insureds and the public. The temporary licensee may be required to have a suitable sponsor who is a licensed producer or insurer and who assumes responsibility for all acts of the temporary licensee and may impose similar requirements designed to protect insureds and the public. Temporary licenses may be revoked if the interests of insureds or the public are endangered. A temporary license may not continue after the licensee disposes of the business.

2. 3. 2. 8 Maintaining a License

2. 3. 2. 8. 1 Change of Address

Every licensee must promptly give to the head of the Department of Insurance written notice of any change of business address. Most states require this notice be made within 30 days.

2. 3. 2. 8. 2 Assumed Names

An insurance producer doing business under any other than the producer's legal name is required to notify the Commissioner before using the assumed name.

2. 3. 2. 8. 3 Office and Records

Every resident producer must have and maintain in the state issuing the license a place of business accessible to the public. The designated place of business must be where the licensee principally conducts transactions under the license. The licenses of the licensee and solicitors appointed by the licensee must be conspicuously displayed in a part of the place of business that is customarily open to the public. The producer must keep at the place of business the usual and customary records pertaining to insurance transactions.

2. 3. 2. 8. 4 Continuation, Expiration, and Renewal of License

Producer licenses generally remain in effect unless they are revoked or suspended, as long as the appropriate fee is paid and the continuing education requirements are met by the due date.

An individual insurance producer who allows his license to lapse may, within 12 months from the due date of the renewal fee, reinstate the same license without passing a written examination. However, a penalty of double the unpaid renewal fee will be required for any renewal fee received after the due date.

An insurance producer who is not able to comply with the license renewal procedures because of military service or some other extenuating circumstance (for example, medical disability) may request a waiver of those procedures. The producer also may request a waiver of any examination requirement or any other fine or sanction imposed for failure to comply with renewal procedures.

2. 3. 2. 8. 5 Appointment

If a producer is going to function as an agent of an insurer, the producer generally needs to be appointed by that insurer. To appoint a producer as its agent, the appointing insurer needs to file a notice of appointment within 15 days from the date the agency contract is executed or the first insurance application is submitted. If an appointment fee is required, it will be paid by the appointing insurer. Any appointment renewal fees required in subsequent years are also paid by the appointing insurer.

In many states, the Commissioner verifies the eligibility of each producer appointed within the first 30 days after being notified of the appointment. If the producer is found to be ineligible, the insurer is notified within 5 days.

Like the insurance license, as long as the appropriate forms are filed and the appropriate fees are paid by the appointing insurer, appointments remain in effect until terminated or until the producer's license is revoked or terminated. If the filing of an appointment is late, additional fees may be charged.

Notice that producers are licensed by the state and appointed by an insurer. Loss of an appointment does not necessarily mean that the producer has lost his license. It simply means that the producer may no longer represent that particular company, although he is still licensed within the state.

2. 3. 2. 8. 6 Termination of Appointment

Subject to a producer's contract rights, if any, an insurer may terminate any of its appointed producers at any time. The insurer must give prompt written notice of the termination and the date to the Department of Insurance (and to the producer when reasonably possible) and must file a statement of facts related to the termination and reasons for it.

If the appointment was terminated because the producer was found to have done something that would be grounds for revocation, denial, or suspension of his license, the insurer is obligated to notify the Commissioner, generally within 30 days. If the insurer finds out after terminating the appointment that the producer did something while appointed that would have been grounds for revocation, denial, or suspension of an insurance license, the insurer has to notify the Commissioner when it makes the discovery. As long as this notification is made without malicious intent, whoever makes such notifications is immune from civil liability and no civil cause of action may be brought against such person.

2. 3. 2. 8. 7 License Denial, Nonrenewal, or Revocation

The Commissioner may place on probation, suspend, revoke, or refuse to issue an insurance producer's license or may levy a civil penalty for any combination of the following causes, listed in PLMA:

- Providing incorrect, misleading, incomplete, or materially untrue information in the license application
- Violating insurance laws or violating any regulation, subpoena, or order of the Commissioner or of another state's Commissioner
- Obtaining or attempting to obtain a license through misrepresentation or fraud
- Improperly withholding, misappropriating, or converting money or property received in the course of doing insurance business
- Intentionally misrepresenting the terms of an actual or proposed insurance contract or application for insurance
- Having been convicted of a felony
- Having admitted or been found to have committed insurance unfair trade practices or fraud
- Using fraudulent, coercive, or dishonest practices or demonstrating incompetence, untrustworthiness, or financial irresponsibility in the conduct of business in this state or elsewhere
- Having an insurance producer license or its equivalent denied, suspended, or revoked in any other state, province, district, or territory
- Forging another's name to an application for insurance or to any document related to an insurance transaction
- Improperly using notes or any other reference material to complete an examination for an insurance license
- Knowingly accepting insurance business from an individual who is not licensed
- Failing to comply with an administrative or court order imposing child support obligations
- Failing to pay state income tax or comply with an administrative or court order directing payment of state income tax

If the Commissioner nonrenews or denies an application for a license, the applicant or licensee must be notified and advised, in writing, of the reason for the denial or nonrenewal of the license. The applicant or licensee may make a written demand for a hearing within a reasonable time as specified in state law.

A business entity's license may be suspended if the Commissioner finds that an individual licensee's violations were known or should have been known by one or more of the partners, officers, or managers acting on behalf of the business entity and the violation was not reported nor was corrective action taken.

A civil fine may be imposed in addition to or instead of license denial, suspension, or revocation. Depending on the violation, fines can range from $100 to several thousand dollars. If a producer is in violation of civil law, the Commissioner can refer the matter to the state attorney general for criminal prosecution and possible imprisonment.

2. 3. 2. 9 Regulated Practices

2. 3. 2. 9. 1 License for Controlled Business Prohibited

Coverage written on a producer's own life or health and on the lives or health of such persons as the producer's relatives or business associates is called **controlled business**. Because of the effect that controlled business could have on the insurance industry if people became licensed solely to sell insurance to family and friends, the Commissioner limits such activities.

There is nothing wrong with a producer writing insurance for himself or on family members and close business associates such as partners. Generally, a licensee is not permitted to earn commission or compensation from controlled business in excess of a stated amount (35–50% of total compensation, depending on the state) during a stated period (usually a calendar year). If a greater proportion does come from controlled business, the practice is in violation of law and the license may be revoked or suspended.

2. 3. 2. 9. 2 Unfair Trade Practices

The Unfair Trade Practices Act is divided into two parts: unfair marketing practices and unfair claims practices. In each state, statutes define and prohibit certain trade and claims practices that are unfair, misleading, and deceptive.

2. 3. 2. 9. 2. 1 Misrepresentations

A **misrepresentation** is simply a lie. It is a violation of unfair marketing practices for any person to make, issue, or circulate any illustration, sales material, or statement that is false, misleading, or deceptive. Misrepresentations include (but are not limited to):

- misrepresenting the benefits, advantages, or terms of a policy;
- misrepresenting policy dividends by implying or stating that they are guaranteed;

- misrepresenting the financial condition of an insurer by means of an inaccurate or incomplete financial comparison; and
- misrepresenting an insurance policy by using a name or title that is untrue or misleading or by indicating that an insurance policy represents shares of stock.

In some cases, misrepresentation can occur unintentionally. To prevent this, the producer must know the products he is selling and accurately explain these products to a population largely ignorant about insurance. To assist in explaining the products being sold, many states require that life insurance buyer's guides be distributed by an insurance company to its prospects to explain basic insurance plans and identify the types of insurance available.

2. 3. 2. 9. 2. 2 False or Deceptive Advertising

It is illegal for any person to formulate or use an advertisement or make a statement that is untrue, deceptive, or misleading regarding any insurer or person associated with an insurer.

2. 3. 2. 9. 2. 3 Twisting

Twisting occurs when a producer convinces a policyowner to lapse or surrender a present policy in order to sell him another one, usually from a different company. This is not to say all policy replacements are wrong. If a producer proves to the policyowner that the protection he has is not the best available and the policyowner decides to replace the old policy with a better one, that policyowner has been well served. However, the producer must be careful that the arguments used on the policyowner can stand the scrutiny of the Commissioner. Any attempt by the producer to misrepresent another insurer by falsely making statements about the financial condition of the company or by giving an incomplete comparison of policies can create legal liability.

2. 3. 2. 9. 2. 4 Churning

Closely allied with twisting is **churning**, which is the practice of using misrepresentation to induce replacement of a policy issued by the insurer the producer is representing, rather than the policy of a competitor. The impetus behind churning is to allow the producer to collect a large first-year commission on a new policy. Churning is the result of a producer putting his interests above those of the client.

2. 3. 2. 9. 2. 5 False Financial Statements

It is a violation of unfair marketing practices for any person to deliberately make a false financial statement regarding the solvency of an insurer with the intent to deceive others.

2. 3. 2. 9. 2. 6 Defamation

It is illegal for any person or company to make oral or written statements or to circulate literature that is false, maliciously critical, or derogatory to the financial condition of any insurer or that is calculated to injure anyone engaged in the insurance business.

2. 3. 2. 9. 2. 7 Discrimination

It is illegal to permit discrimination between individuals of the same class or insurance risk in terms of rates, premiums, fees, and policy benefits because of their place of residence, race, creed, or national origin.

2. 3. 2. 9. 2. 8 Rebating

Splitting a commission with a prospect is prohibited in almost every state (California and Florida are exceptions). **Rebating** is any inducement in the sale of insurance that is not specified in the insurance contract. An offer to share commissions with the insurance applicant is an inducement in the sale of insurance that is not part of the insurance policy, and thus, constitutes rebating. Rebates include not only cash but also personal services and items of value.

2. 3. 2. 9. 2. 9 Illegal Premiums and Charges

It is unlawful for a person or insurer to collect premiums or make charges that are not specified in the insurance contract.

2. 3. 2. 9. 2. 10 Boycott, Coercion, and Intimidation

It is a violation of the act for a person or organization to commit or be involved in an act of boycott, coercion, or intimidation that is intended to create a monopoly or restrict fair trade in the transaction of insurance. For example, it is unlawful for a bank to force a person to purchase insurance from a particular company or agent as a condition for receiving a loan from the bank. The bank may require that adequate insurance be purchased or be in force to back such a loan, but the bank cannot force or intimidate a person into purchasing coverage from a specific insurer as a condition for the granting of a loan.

2. 3. 2. 10 Unfair Claims Practices

Claims settlement practices are regulated in the public interest for two main reasons.

It is for the purpose of settling claims that insurance companies have collected policyowners' money.

When insureds are denied claims or claim payments are delayed or altered, the consequences go beyond the policy benefits and can drastically affect other areas of the insured's financial situation. The unfair claims practices provisions of the Unfair Trade Practices Act are designed to protect insureds and claimants from any claims settlement practices that are unfair, deceptive, or misleading. The following are considered unfair claims practices:

- Misrepresenting pertinent facts or insurance policy provisions relating to coverage at issue
- Failing to acknowledge and act reasonably promptly upon communications with respect to claims arising under insurance policies
- Failing to adopt and implement reasonable standards for the prompt investigation of claims arising under insurance policies

- Refusing to pay claims without conducting a reasonable investigation based on all available information
- Failing to affirm or deny coverage of claims within a reasonable time after proof of loss statements have been completed
- Not attempting in good faith to effectuate prompt, fair, and equitable settlements of claims in which liability has become reasonably clear
- Compelling insureds to institute litigation to recover amounts due under an insurance policy by offering substantially less than the amounts ultimately recovered in actions brought by such insureds
- Attempting to settle a claim for less than the amount to which a reasonable person would have believed he was entitled by reference to written or principal advertising material accompanying or made part of an application
- Attempting to settle claims on the basis of an application that was altered without notice, knowledge, or consent of the insured
- Making claims payments to insureds or beneficiaries not accompanied by statements setting forth the coverage under which the payments are being made
- Making known to insureds or claimants a policy of appealing arbitration awards in favor of insureds or claimants for the purpose of compelling them to accept settlements or compromises less than the amount awarded in arbitration
- Delaying the investigation or payment of a claim by requiring an insured, claimant, or the physician of either to submit a preliminary claim report and then requiring the subsequent submission of formal proof of loss forms, both of which submissions contain substantially the same information
- Failing to promptly settle claims where liability has become reasonably clear under one portion of the insurance policy coverage to influence settlement under other portions of the insurance policy coverage
- Failing to promptly provide a reasonable explanation of the basis relied on in the insurance policy in relation to the facts or applicable law for denial of a claim or for the offer of a compromise settlement

Some states have added another provision that makes it an unfair claim practice to offer a settlement or payment in any manner prohibited by law.

2. 3. 2. 10. 1 Penalties

Following an investigation and a hearing, if the Department of Insurance finds that any person or insurer is engaged in any unfair trade or unfair claims practice, the Commissioner may issue a **cease and desist order** prohibiting the individual or company from continuing the practice. Failure to comply with the cease and desist order can result in a substantial fine (usually $10,000). In addition, fines and loss of license also may be imposed for a company or person guilty of violating the Unfair Trade Practices Act.

The Department of Insurance also may issue a **consent order**, which is a disciplinary action in which the party at fault (the insurance company or agent) agrees to discontinue a particular practice (usually an unfair trade or claims practice) through a written agreement with the Department of Insurance. Usually the individual denies the allegations but consents to the action taken by the Department of Insurance. Consent orders (also known as consent decrees) may or may not involve a fine.

2. 3. 3 Self-Regulation

The last channel of regulation of the business is self-regulation—that is, those restraints from within the industry either by individual company conscience or by group pressure of insurance associations. This was the first type of regulation of the business and is still the predominant type in the United Kingdom.

There are several intercompany organizations or associations that impose codes on their members. They include the National Association of Life Underwriters (producers) through its state and local associations, the International Association of Health Underwriters (producers), and the American Society of Chartered Life Underwriters (producers). In recent years, these industry associations have had a major impact on prelicensing and continuing education laws. For example, often the state Association of Life Underwriters will be the major force in obtaining passage of these laws through the state legislature. Continuing education laws are designed to protect the consumer by mandating certain continuing educational requirements if a producer is to maintain his license. These educational requirements usually focus on product knowledge, insurance regulations, and ethics. The majority of states have continuing education requirements.

2. 3. 3. 1 NAIC

The **National Association of Insurance Commissioners (NAIC)**, an association of state Commissioners, although without legal authority as a group, also imposes a strong influence in the area of the industry's self-regulation. The NAIC is the organization that has done the most to standardize law between the states. Although the wording and sometimes the provisions themselves differ from state to state, for the most part, the differences are only slight as each state attempts to follow the wording of the model laws established by the NAIC.

The model laws include the Individual Accident and Sickness Policy Provisions Law, Standard Nonforfeiture and Valuation Laws, Fair Trade Practices Act, Unauthorized Insurers Service of Process Act, Insurance Holding Company System Regulatory Act, Variable Contract Law, Group Life Definition and Standard Provisions Bill, and Credit Life and Credit Health Insurance Regulation Bill.

2. 4 SUMMARY

In this lesson, you learned about:

- the three major channels of regulation;
- the impact of federal regulations;
- the role of the Insurance Commissioner in insurance regulation;
- insurer solvency, annual statements, and investment requirements imposed in most states;
- the functions and purpose of the MSVR;
- how life insurance companies are taxed by the states;
- the role of company ratings and how such information may be used with prospects;
- market conduct exams and how they differ from other state examinations;
- the role of state guarantee associations;
- the effects of GLBA on producer regulation at the state level;
- the qualifications PLMA suggests for receiving a producer license;
- the standard exemptions from licensing requirements in PLMA;
- the requirements suggested in PLMA for a nonresident producer license;
- the purpose of temporary producer licenses and situations where a temporary license might be granted;
- the requirements for maintaining a producer license;
- the procedure for reinstating a lapsed license;
- the function of producer appointments; and
- possible causes for license denial, nonrenewal, or revocation suggested in PLMA.

UNIT TEST

1. Which of these cases first defined insurance as interstate commerce?
   A. South-Eastern Underwriters decision
   B. McCarran-Ferguson Act
   C. *Paul v. Virginia*

2. Pretext interviews are
   A. always illegal
   B. not permitted without a warrant sworn by a sitting judge
   C. generally accepted practice in the industry
   D. not permitted unless some evidence of criminal activity exists

3. A customer is
   A. anyone about whom a company collects information
   B. anyone with whom a company has an ongoing relationship
   C. anyone who prohibits the sharing of nonpublic personal information
   D. anyone who permits the sharing of nonpublic personal information

4. The federal government
   A. is the primary authority for regulating the business of insurance
   B. does not get involved in regulating the business of insurance
   C. has the right to regulate the business of insurance to the extent that such business is not regulated by state law

5. Insurance laws generally are written by
   A. the federal government
   B. the state legislature
   C. the state Department of Insurance
   D. the Commissioner

6. The head of the state Department of Insurance (usually called the Commissioner) is responsible for all of the following EXCEPT
   A. examining individual insurance policies before issuance
   B. administering and enforcing state insurance laws
   C. imposing penalties for violations of the Insurance Code
   D. issuing insurance licenses and certificates of authority

7. The nonfinancial regulatory activities of an insurance department fall under the broad heading of
   A. company conduct
   B. regulatory conduct
   C. market conduct
   D. producer conduct

8. To become licensed as an insurance producer, an individual must be at least age
   A. 16 years
   B. 18 years
   C. 21 years
   D. 25 years

9. Which of the following individuals would NOT be exempt from a producer licensing requirement?
   A. Alicia works in an insurance office conferring directly with or offering advice to prospective purchasers about the benefits, terms, and conditions of insurance policies and urges a person to apply for policies Alicia thinks would be a good match.
   B. Brenda works for an insurer acting in the capacity of a special agent or agency supervisor assisting insurance producers by providing technical advice and assistance to licensed insurance producers on nonsales-related areas.
   C. Cannie gathers information for the purpose of enrolling individuals under a group life insurance plan at her company. Cannie also issues certificates and assists in administering the plan.
   D. Del inspects, rates, and classifies risks. At times, Del also supervises the training of insurance producers.

10. An insurance producer who permits her license to lapse may reinstate the license within
    A. 3 months from the due date of the renewal fee
    B. 6 months from the due date of the renewal fee
    C. 9 months from the due date of the renewal fee
    D. 12 months from the due date of the renewal fee

11. Producers may act as
    A. agents representing the insurance company
    B. brokers representing the individual seeking insurance
    C. either agents representing the insurance company or brokers representing the individual seeking insurance
    D. neither agents representing the insurance company nor brokers representing the individual seeking insurance

12. Most insurance regulation takes place at the
    A. international level
    B. national level
    C. state level
    D. local level

13. Applicants for insurance must be given advance notice including all of the following types of information EXCEPT
    A. the persons who are collecting information
    B. the kind of information to be collected
    C. the sources of information
    D. the persons with access to personal information

14. Which of the following acts does NOT contain provisions protecting individual privacy?
    A. Gramm-Leach-Bliley Act
    B. Privacy Act of 1974
    C. McCarran-Ferguson Act
    D. Fair Credit Reporting Act

15. Consumer reporting agencies are prevented from putting information in their reports about all of the following EXCEPT
    A. bankruptcies less than 10 years old
    B. suits and judgments less than 7 years old if the statute of limitations has not expired
    C. arrests, indictments, or conviction of crime reports
    D. paid tax liens or accounts placed for collection more than 7 years ago

16. Under the Financial Modernization Act, an individual about whom a financial institution collects information is a
    A. customer
    B. consumer
    C. client
    D. patron

17. Under the Financial Modernization Act, an individual with whom a financial institution has an ongoing relationship is a
    A. customer
    B. consumer
    C. client
    D. patron

18. The Commissioner of Insurance has all of the following powers EXCEPT
    A. conducting investigations and examinations
    B. making reasonable rules and regulations
    C. promulgating insurance law
    D. approving insurance policy forms sold within the state

19. Nonfinancial regulatory activities of an insurance department fall under the broad heading of
    A. market regulation
    B. conduct regulation
    C. market conduct
    D. insurance conduct

20. Associations organized to protect claimants, policyholders, annuitants, and creditors of financially impaired insurers are known as
    A. insurance associations
    B. department associations
    C. liability associations
    D. guaranty associations

21. Which of the following is NOT a requirement for obtaining a producer's license in most states?
    A. Have not committed an act that is grounds for denial or suspension of an insurance license
    B. Be at least age 19 years
    C. Pay the required fees
    D. Complete any required prelicensing course

22. Which of the following people would be required in most states to obtain an insurance license?
    A. Rachel, a salaried employee of a large department store chain, who counsels her employer on insurance-related matters
    B. Ross, who works in an advertising agency, supervising the advertising business of a major insurer
    C. Phoebe, who works as an underwriter for a small insurer
    D. Chandler, who sells insurance to businesses only

23. A person licensed as an insurance producer in another state who moves to this state has how many days after establishing legal residence to become a resident licensee without taking prelicensing education or an examination?
    A. 30
    B. 60
    C. 90
    D. 120

24. Which of the following individuals is least likely to be granted a temporary license?
    A. Georgia, whose insurance producer-husband passed away unexpectedly, leaving her with a business to either learn or sell
    B. Kim, who wants to try selling insurance on a temporary basis before investing the time and money into being licensed
    C. Dave, an employee of a business entity, when the individual designated as the licensee in the business entity is disabled in an auto accident and unable to return to work for several months
    D. Lee, whose insurance producer-fiancée was recalled to active duty by the Navy and appointed Lee her designee

25. Business written on the producer's own life or interests is known as
    A. controlled business
    B. personal business
    C. conflicted business
    D. producer business

26. Which of the following is considered an unfair claims practice?
    A. Splitting a commission with a prospect
    B. Failing to affirm or deny coverage within a reasonable time after proof of loss
    C. Convincing a policyowner to lapse or surrender an existing policy to sell another policy
    D. Making any oral or written statement that is false, maliciously critical, or calculated to injure a competing producer

27. An organization that establishes model laws that are often adopted by states with only slight differences is the
    A. National Association of Insurance Companies
    B. National Association of Independent Commissioners
    C. National Association of Insurance Consultants
    D. National Association of Insurance Commissioners

ANSWERS AND RATIONALES TO UNIT TEST

1. **A.** The South-Eastern Underwriters decision first defined insurance as interstate commerce.
2. **D.** Pretext interviews are not permitted unless some evidence of criminal activity exists.
3. **B.** A customer is anyone with whom a company has an ongoing relationship.
4. **C.** The federal government has the right to regulate the business of insurance to the extent that such business is not regulated by state law.
5. **B.** Insurance laws generally are written by the state legislature.
6. **B.**
7. **C.** The nonfinancial regulatory activities of an insurance department fall under the broad heading of market conduct.
8. **B.** To become licensed as an insurance producer, an individual must be at least 18 years old.
9. **A.** Alicia would not be exempt from a producer licensing requirement.
10. **D.** An insurance producer who permits her license to lapse may reinstate the license within 12 months from the due date of the renewal fee.
11. **C.** Producers may act either as agents representing the insurance company or as brokers representing the individual seeking insurance.
12. **C.**
13. **A.** Applicants for insurance do not have to be given advance notice of the persons who will be collecting information.
14. **C.** The McCarran-Ferguson Act does not contain provisions protecting individual privacy.
15. **C.** Consumer reporting agencies can put information in their reports about arrests, indictments, or conviction of crimes.
16. **B.** Under the Financial Modernization Act, an individual about whom a financial institution collects information is a consumer.
17. **A.** Under the Financial Modernization Act, an individual with whom a financial institution has an ongoing relationship is a customer.
18. **C.** The Commissioner of Insurance does not have the power to promulgate insurance laws.
19. **C.** Nonfinancial regulatory activities of an insurance department fall under the broad heading of market conduct.
20. **D.** Associations organized to protect claimants, policyholders, annuitants, and creditors of financially impaired insurers are known as guaranty associations.
21. **B.** A person does not have to be at least age 19 years to obtain a producer's license in most states.
22. **D.** Chandler would be required to obtain an insurance license in most states.
23. **C.** A person licensed as an insurance producer in another state who moves to this state has 90 days after establishing legal residence to become a resident licensee without taking prelicensing education or an examination.
24. **B.** Kim is least likely to be granted a temporary license.
25. **A.** Business written on the producer's own life or interests is known as controlled business.
26. **B.** Failing to affirm or deny coverage within a reasonable time after proof of loss is considered an unfair claims practice.
27. **D.** The National Association of Insurance Commissioners establishes model laws that are often adopted by states with only slight differences.

UNIT

3

Insurance Law

3. 1 INTRODUCTION

Life and health insurance policies are legal contracts. As such, they are governed by many of the same legal principles that are applicable to the formation of any **contract**, plus specific principles that are pertinent to insurance only. A **contract** is an agreement enforceable by law. It is the means by which one or more parties bind themselves to certain promises. With a life insurance contract, for example, the insurer binds itself to pay a certain sum upon the death of the insured. In exchange, the policyowner pays premiums. Because contracts of insurance are binding and enforceable, certain legal concepts extend to those who bring together the contract parties—the applicant and the insurer. In most cases, bringing the parties together is done by an agent or a broker.

3. 2 LEARNING OBJECTIVES

After completing this lesson, you will be able to:

- explain the law of agency;
- list and define three types of authority granted in an agency relationship;
- define fiduciary and explain the role of an insurance producer as a fiduciary;
- explain the legal doctrines of waiver and estoppel;
- describe the responsibilities of an agent;
- describe the responsibilities an insurer has to its agents;
- explain what errors and omissions policies cover and their importance;
- define *contract* and list and describe the elements that form a valid contract;
- describe the four basic parts of life and health insurance contracts;
- list and describe the five areas reviewed when courts interpret contracts;
- list and explain the characteristics unique to insurance contracts;
- explain the difference between warranties and representations;
- explain the difference between misrepresentation, concealment, and fraud; and
- define *parol evidence* and describe how it impacts insurance contracts.

3. 3 AGENCY LAW

3. 3. 1 Agency Law Principles

An understanding of the law of agency is important because an insurance company, like other companies, must act through agents.

Agency is a relationship in which one person is authorized to represent and act for another person or for a corporation. Although a corporation is a legal person, it cannot act for itself, so it must act through agents. An agent is a person authorized to act on behalf of another person, who is called the **principal**. In the field of insurance, the principal is the insurance company and the sales representative or producer is the agent. When one is empowered to act as an agent for a principal, he is legally assumed to be the principal in matters covered by the grant of agency. Contracts made by the agent are the contracts of the principal. Payment to the agent, within the scope of his authority, is payment to the principal. The knowledge of the agent is assumed to be the knowledge of the principal.

3. 3. 2 Presumption of Agency

If a company supplies an individual with forms and other materials (signs and evidences of authority) that make it appear that he is an agent of the company, a court will likely hold that a presumption of agency exists. The company is then bound by the acts of this individual whether or not he has been given this authority.

3. 3. 3 Authority

The authority of an agent is of three types: express, implied, or apparent.

Express authority is an explicit, definite agreement. It is the authority the principal gives the agent as set forth in his contract. It is very important for an agent to know the limitations of the contract and to operate within its limits. To do otherwise could place him in a position of personal liability. His actions and knowledge are binding on the insurance company, so he must be alert to the consequences of his actions and words.

Implied authority is not expressly granted under an agency contract, but it is actual authority that the agent has to transact the principal's business in accordance with general business practices. For example, if an agent's contract does not give him the express authority of collecting and submitting monthly premiums, but the agent does so on a regular basis and the company accepts the premium, the agent is said to have implied authority. It is a general business practice to collect premium, and by accepting the premium from the agent, the company has implied that the agent has the authority to conduct this practice.

Lingering implied authority means that the agent carries signs or evidences of authority. By having these evidences of authority, an agent who is no longer under contract to an insurer could mislead applicants or insureds. When the agency relationship between agent and company has been terminated, the company will try, or should try, to get back all the materials it supplied to the former agent, including sales materials.

On the other hand, the public cannot assume that an individual is an agent merely because he says so. The agent must carry the credentials (for example, the agent's license and appointment) and company documents (such as applications and rate books) that represent him as being an agent for an insurance company.

Apparent authority is the authority the agent seems to have because of certain actions undertaken on his part. This action may mislead applicants or insureds, causing them to believe the agent has authority that he does not in fact have. The principal adds to this impression by acting in a manner that reinforces the impression of authority. For instance, an agent's contract usually does not grant him the authority to reinstate a lapsed policy by accepting past-due premiums. If, in the past, the company has allowed the agent to accept late premiums for that purpose, a court would probably hold that the policyowner had the right to assume that the agent's acceptance of premium was within the scope of his authority.

3. 3. 4 Collection of Premium

All premiums received by an agent are funds received and held in trust. The agent must account for and pay the correct amount to the insured, insurer, or other agent entitled to the money.

Any agent who takes funds held in trust for his own use is guilty of theft and will be punished as provided by law.

An agent may establish an account separate from a personal account to deposit the trust funds. All trust funds may be deposited into the single separate account. However, the agent's records must clearly distinguish the funds held for each individual.

3. 3. 5 Agent's Responsibility to Insured/Applicant

An agent has a **fiduciary** responsibility to the insured, the insurer, the applicant for insurance, current clients, and so forth. The agent has a fiduciary duty to just about any person or organization that he comes into contact with as part of the day-to-day business of transacting insurance. By definition, a **fiduciary** is a person in a position of financial trust. Thus, attorneys, accountants, trust officers, and insurance agents are all considered fiduciaries.

As a fiduciary, the agent has an obligation to act in the best interest of the insured. The agent must be knowledgeable about the features and provisions of various insurance policies as well as the use of these insurance contracts. The agent must be able to explain the important features of these policies to the insured. The agent must recognize the importance of dealing with the general public's financial needs and problems and offering solutions to these problems through the purchase of insurance products.

As a fiduciary, the agent must know and comply with the state's insurance laws. Many of these laws are for consumer protection. It is the agent's duty to comply with these laws and thus protect the interests of the insured at all times.

As a fiduciary, the agent must collect and account for premiums collected as part of the insurance transaction. It is the agent's duty to make certain that these premiums are submitted to the insurer promptly. Failing to submit premiums to the insurer or putting these funds to one's own personal use is a violation of the agent's fiduciary duties and possibly an act of embezzlement. The insured's premiums must be kept separate from the agent's personal funds. Failure to do this can result in **commingling**—mixing personal funds with the insured's, or insurer's funds.

3. 3. 6 Waiver and Estoppel

The legal doctrines of waiver and estoppel are directly related to the responsibilities of insurance agents. An insurer may, by waiver, lose the right to make certain defenses that it might otherwise have available. **Waiver** is defined as the intentional and voluntary surrender of a known right. An insurance company may waive its right to cancel a policy for nonpayment by accepting late payments.

Waiver and estoppel often occur together, but they are separate and distinct doctrines. **Estoppel** means that a party may be precluded by his acts of conduct from asserting a right that would act to the detriment of the other party when the other party has relied on the conduct of the first party and has acted upon it. An insurer may waive a right, and then, after the policyowner has relied on the waiver and acted upon it, the insurer will be estopped from asserting the right.

The agent must be alert in his words, actions, and advice to avoid mistakenly waiving the rights of the insurance company. As a representative of the company, the agent's knowledge and actions may be deemed to be knowledge and actions of the company.

3. 3. 7 Agent's Responsibilities to the Company

The agent's contract or agency agreement with the insurer will specify the agent's duties and responsibilities to the principal. As previously mentioned, the agent has a fiduciary duty to the insurer. In all insurance transactions, the agent's responsibility is to act in accordance with the agency contract and thus for the benefit of the insurer. If the agent is in violation of the agency agreement, he may be held personally liable to the insurer for breach of contract.

An agent has a duty to act with a degree of care that a reasonable person would exercise under similar circumstances. This prudent person rule protects the insurer and the insured from unreasonable insurance transactions on the part of the agent.

In accordance with the agent's fiduciary obligation to the insurer and his agency agreement, the agent has a responsibility of accounting for all property, including money that comes into his possession. The agent must not embezzle or commingle these funds.

As part of the agent's working relationship with the insurer, it is important that pertinent information be disclosed to the insurer, particularly with regard to underwriting and risk selection. If the agent knows of anything adverse concerning the risk to be insured, it is his responsibility to provide this information to the insurer. Withholding important underwriting information could adversely affect the insurer's risk selection process. In accordance with agency law, information given to the agent is the same as providing the information to the insurer.

It is the agent's responsibility to obtain necessary information from the insurance applicant and to accurately complete the application for insurance. A signed and witnessed copy of the application becomes part of the legal contract of insurance between the insured and the insurer; thus, it is critical that the application be accurate.

Finally, the agent has a responsibility to deliver the insurance policy to the insured and collect any premium that may be due at the time of delivery. The agent must be prepared to provide the insured with an explanation of some of the policy's principal benefits and provisions. If the policy is issued with changes or amendments, the agent also will be required to explain these changes and obtain the insured's signature acknowledging receipt of these amendments.

3. 3. 8 Company's Responsibility to the Agent

The company likewise has a responsibility to the agent. It is required to permit the agent to act in accordance with the terms of the agent's employment contract, and the company must recognize all of the provisions of that contract.

In addition, the company must pay the agent the compensation agreed upon in the contract, must reimburse the agent for proper expenditures made on behalf of the principal, and must indemnify the agent for losses or damages suffered without fault on the part of the agent but occurring on account of the agency relationship.

3. 3. 9 Potential Liabilities of Agent (Errors and Omissions Exposure)

Errors and omissions (E&O) insurance is needed by professionals who give advice to their clients. It covers negligence, error, or omission by the insurer or by the producer who is the insurer's representative. E&O policies protect producers from financial losses they may suffer if insureds sue to recover for a financial loss resulting from a producer giving them incorrect advice (error) or not informing them of an important issue (omission). A producer's office is very busy, so he must take special care to follow strict procedures (and train all employees to do the same) in regard to taking applications, explaining coverages, collecting premiums, submitting changes to policies upon an insured's request, and preparing claim forms. Any error or omission could result in losing a client and could also lead to a lawsuit. All E&O policies have certain basic characteristics in common.

- The policy covers only losses resulting from negligence, error, or omission. For example, a producer who fails to tell a client that his purchase of a new policy means that waiting periods have to be met again can be sued for this omission if the event that was previously covered occurs and the insured finds that he is not currently covered.

- The policy usually has a high deductible, such as $500 or $1,000. The high deductible provides an added incentive for a producer to reduce his errors.
- The coverage may be written with both a limit per claim and a limit for all claims during the policy period.
- Except for obvious exclusions, such as a producer committing unfair trade practices or intentional fraud, the policy has few other exclusions.

3. 4 FORMATION OF A LIFE OR HEALTH INSURANCE CONTRACT

The formation of a life or health insurance contract differs from the formation of other insurance contracts in that the life or health producer usually does not have the authority to bind the insurer.

The life or health insurance producer has no authority to put a policy into effect. The producer can solicit offers only from prospective insureds, securing their applications and initial premium payments. The application and premium must be sent to the insurance company underwriter, who determines whether the company wishes to accept the risk.

The restricted underwriting authority of the life insurance producer is related to the nature of life insurance contracts. Life insurance policies are generally noncancelable, long-term contracts. A life insurance policy is contestable for a one- or two-year period. Property and casualty insurance, however, involves a short-term contract often for one year or less, and the insurance company usually reserves the right to cancel the policy if the risk appears to be undesirable. In addition, life and health insurance underwriting decisions frequently rest on medical questions. The life or health insurer employs medical experts and has at its disposal various investigative reports that shed light on the desirability of a risk. The insurance company is in a much better position than the producer to evaluate the applicant's insurability.

3. 4. 1 Contract Elements

Insurance policies are legal contracts and are subject to the general law of contracts. This is a distinct body of law that is separate from criminal law (crimes against society) and tort law (legal liability issues usually involving damages for negligence). Contract law dictates the formation and enforcement of legal contract rights.

A contract is a legal agreement between two or more parties promising a certain performance in exchange for a valuable consideration. Under the law, the following elements are necessary for the formation of a valid contract:

- Agreement (offer and acceptance)
- Consideration

- Competent parties
- Legal purpose

3. 4. 1. 1 Agreement (Offer and Acceptance)

There can be no contract without the agreement or mutual assent of the parties. A common intention on all terms of the contract is essential to an agreement, and no essential terms of the contract may be left unsettled. Furthermore, the intention of the parties to a contract must be communicated to one another.

The parties to an insurance contract are the insurance company and the applicant, who may become the insured or may name another person to be insured. Unless otherwise indicated, it is assumed that the applicant is the prospective insured.

3. 4. 1. 2 Offer

An **offer** is a proposal that creates a contract if accepted by another party according to its terms. A contract arises only if the acceptance indicates clear assent to the exact terms and conditions of the offer. Generally, any words or actions by the person receiving the offer that imply agreement will be interpreted as acceptance of the offer.

The offer may come from the insurer (company) or the applicant. In either case, the offer must be definite and clear in its terms. If an applicant gives the insurer a completed application and pays the first premium, the application is an offer. If the policy is issued as applied for, the insurer accepts the offer.

There is no offer if the applicant sends the application to the insurance company without payment of the premium. Such an application is merely an invitation to the company to make an offer. The insurance company makes an offer by issuing the policy. The applicant accepts it by paying the first premium.

3. 4. 1. 3 Acceptance

An acceptance must be unconditional and unqualified. A qualified or conditional acceptance rejects the offer and may constitute a counter offer. If an insurance company, after receiving an application and premium payment, issues a policy with more restrictive coverage than that applied for, the company has made a counteroffer.

For example, a counteroffer occurs if an applicant applies for a standard health insurance policy, pays the premium, and receives a policy containing an exclusionary endorsement for specified physical conditions. The applicant must decide whether to accept the policy as modified. If he accepts the policy, there is a contract. If he rejects the modified policy, there is no contract and the applicant is entitled to a return of his premium.

3. 4. 1. 4 Consideration

Each party to the contract must give valuable consideration. In the insurance contract, the value given by the insurer consists of the promises contained in the policy contract. The consideration given by the insured consists of the statements made in the application and the payment of the initial premium.

- The consideration may consist of any of the following:
- A monetary payment
- An act
- A forbearance from action
- The creation, modification, or destruction of a legal right
- A return promise

In other words, each of the parties to the contract gives up something of value or forbears from exercising a right.

It is important to know that part of the applicant's consideration consists of the statements in the application. A great deal of importance is placed on the representations in the application because the insurance company's entire decision of whether to contract is based on its evaluation of the information in the application.

The application should be complete and accurate. The producer must take the time to ask each and every question and to record the answers fully and legibly. The producer must be careful to avoid haphazard or cursory completion of application forms on behalf of applicants because incomplete or inaccurate application information hurts both the insurance company and the applicant. Furthermore, the producer must not assist the applicant in deliberately deceiving the company regarding material facts in the application. Later discovery of false information in the application may be cause for denying coverage.

Failure to complete all required information on the application in a thorough, honest, and detailed manner could subject the producer to the embarrassment of having to explain to his client why the insurance policy is invalid. This failure also could lead to disciplinary action by his insurance company and by the state.

3. 4. 1. 5 Competent Parties

For a contract to be binding, both parties must have the legal capacity to make a contract.

To have the legal capacity to make insurance contracts, an insurance company must have authority under its charter to issue contracts and be authorized by the state to issue contracts. The company's representative also must be licensed by the state. The legal effect of a contract made by an unlicensed insurer depends on state law.

The insured or applicant must be of legal age and be mentally competent to make an insurance contract. Applications of minors usually must be signed by an adult parent or guardian to comply with the legal age requirement for making contracts.

3. 4. 1. 6 *Legal Purpose*

To be valid, a contract must be for a legal purpose and not contrary to public policy. Wagering or gambling contracts are contrary to public policy. An insurance contract, however, is not against public policy where an insurable interest exists.

3. 4. 2 Parts of the Insurance Contract

Although it is not a legal requirement that all contracts be in writing, insurance contracts always are in writing because of their complex nature. The number of pages that make up an insurance contract varies because of the types of insurance and the individual risks being insured, but all life and health insurance contracts contain four basic parts:

- Policy face (title page)
- Insuring clause
- Conditions
- Exclusions

3. 4. 2. 1 *Policy Face (Title Page)*

The **policy face** is usually the first page of the insurance policy. It includes the policy number, name of the insured, policy issue date, the amount of premium and dates the premium is due, and the limits of the policy. The policy face also includes the signatures of the secretary and president of the issuing insurance company. In addition, generally there are clauses required by law to give the insured information on his right to cancel and a warning to the insured to read the policy carefully.

3. 4. 2. 2 *Insuring Clause*

The **insuring clause** generally also appears on the policy face. It is a statement by the insurance company that sets out the essential element of insurance—the promise to pay for losses covered by the policy in exchange for the insured's premium and compliance with policy terms.

3. 4. 2. 3 *Conditions*

This section spells out in detail the rights and duties of both parties. **Conditions** are provisions that apply to the insured and insurer. For example, the conditions include the reinstatement provision, suicide clause, payment of claim provision, and similar standard policy provisions.

3. 4. 2. 4 Exclusions

In this section, the company states what it will not do. The **exclusions** are a basic part of the contract, and a complete knowledge of them is essential to a thorough understanding of the agreement. Certain risks must be excluded from insurance contracts because they are not insurable. Such risks would include war and acts of war, self-inflicted injuries, and certain exclusions for hazardous occupations or avocations, such as sky diving, scuba diving, and auto racing. In reality, it is likely that coverage for persons who engage in hazardous activities would be available for an additional premium. The war exclusion usually stems from the results of war or warlike acts, but it may also be based on the status of the insured as a member of the armed services.

3. 5 LEGAL REQUIREMENTS

3. 5. 1 Contract Construction

When the courts have a case involving contracts, they look at the **rules of construction** to interpret the contract. The **rules of construction** help to identify and establish the intent of the parties to the contract. There are five major areas that the courts review to interpret the contract, establish the intent of the parties, and hand down a ruling.

3. 5. 1. 1 Plain Language and Word Definitions

If the language of the contract is clear, the courts do not have to interpret the meaning of the contract. The courts give the words in the contract their ordinary meaning. In cases where ordinary words have been used in a technical capacity, the technical meaning of the word is accepted.

3. 5. 1. 2 Entire Contract

The courts look at the entire contract to determine the intent of the parties. They do not consider material added to the basic contract, nor do they take only parts of the contract to make a determination. Once the intent of the contract has been established, individual clauses that tend to contradict the general intent of the contract will not take precedence over the intent of the entire contract.

3. 5. 1. 3 Interpretation in Favor of Valid Contract

Because the courts assume that when people make a contract they intend for it to be valid, the courts will, if possible, render an interpretation of the contract that makes it valid rather than invalid. Even if a party to the contract did not have the intention of making a valid contract, the courts will, if possible, interpret the contract as being valid and the dishonest party then becomes involved with charges dealing with fraud.

3. 5. 1. 4 *Unclear Contract of Adhesion Interpreted Against the Insurer*

If a contract contains wording that is unclear, the courts will interpret the language used against the writer of the contract unless the wording used is required by law to be stated in a specific manner. Insurance contracts are contracts of adhesion, which means the insured had no part in determining the wording of the contract. Therefore, the courts will interpret the contract in favor of the policyholder, insured, or beneficiary.

3. 5. 1. 5 *Written Contracts*

If a contract contains unclear or inconsistent material between printed, typed, or handwritten material in the contract, the typed or handwritten material will determine intent. Where there is a discrepancy between typed material and handwritten material, the handwritten material will determine the intent. This procedure is used because printed material is standard and for general use, but typed or handwritten material is added to the existing printed material and is a better indication of the parties' intent.

More and more states are developing regulations dealing with these areas of contract construction. Regulations now govern areas of contract construction, which include the following:

- Commonly accepted definitions of words
- The use of plain language in the contract
- The kind of type or print used in contracts

3. 5. 2 Contract Characteristics

The insurance contract has certain characteristics not typically found in other types of contracts.

3. 5. 2. 1 *Utmost Good Faith*

The insurance contract requires utmost good faith between the parties. This means that each party is entitled to rely on the representations of the other, and each party should have a reasonable expectation that the other is acting in good faith without attempts to conceal or deceive. In a contract of utmost good faith, the parties have an affirmative duty to each other to disclose all material facts relating to the contract. That is not just a duty not to lie, but also a duty to speak up. Failure to do so usually gives the other party ground to void the contract.

3. 5. 2. 2 *Aleatory*

An insurance contract is said to be **aleatory**, or dependent on chance or uncertain outcome, because one party may receive much more in value than he gives in value under the contract. For example, an insured who has a loss may receive a greater payment from an insurer for the loss than he has paid in premiums. On the other hand, an insured may pay his premiums and have no loss, so the insurer pays nothing.

3. 5. 2. 3 Adhesion

In insurance, the insurer writes the contract and the insured adheres to it. Although the insured may request special provisions or coverages, it is the insurance company that ultimately draws up and issues the policy. This concept is important because when a contract of adhesion is ambiguous in its terms, the courts will interpret the contract against the party who prepared it. The courts usually will grant any reasonable expectation on the part of the policyowner or the beneficiaries from a contract that was drawn up by the insurance company.

3. 5. 2. 4 Unilateral

Contracts may be **bilateral** or **unilateral**. An exchange of a promise for a promise is **bilateral**, whereas an exchange of an act for a promise is **unilateral**. Generally, insurance contracts are unilateral. This means that after the insured has completed the act of paying the premium, only the insurer promises to do anything further. The insurer has promised performance and is legally responsible. The insured has made no legally enforceable promises and cannot be held for breach of contract. For example, the insured may stop paying premiums because he is not legally responsible to continue paying premiums.

3. 5. 2. 5 Conditional

Insurance contracts are also **conditional** contracts because when the loss occurs, certain conditions must be met to make the contract legally enforceable. For example, a policyholder might have to satisfy the test of having an insurable interest and satisfy the condition of submitting proof of loss.

A condition is a contract provision that limits the rights contained in the contract. A **condition precedent** means that an act must be performed or an event must take place before the right is met. For example, an insured must become injured to collect a medical benefit or the insured must die before his spouse can collect a death benefit. A **condition subsequent** exists when an act or event is of such nature as to cancel a right. For example, if the contract contains a provision that denies payment of the death benefit in the case of suicide within a two-year period of the policy effective date, the insured who commits suicide within one year cancels the existing right of payment of the death benefit.

3. 5. 2. 6 Personal Contract

Life insurance is not a *personal contract* or *personal agreement* between the insurer and the insured. The owner of the policy has no bearing on the risk the insurer has assumed. For this reason, people who buy life insurance policies are called policyowners rather than policyholders. These people actually own their policies and can give them away if they wish. Such a transfer of ownership is known as *assignment*.

To assign a policy, a policyowner simply notifies the insurer in writing. The company will then accept the validity of the transfer without question. The new owner is then granted all of the rights of policy ownership.

Most other insurance contracts are personal contracts. They constitute a personal agreement between the insured and the insurer, and they cannot be transferred to another person without the insurer's approval. Because of this personal nature of most insurance contracts, they cannot be freely assigned by the policyholder to other parties. To permit a fire insurance contract to be assignable without the insurer's approval, for example, would be unfair to the insurer. Only by knowing and investigating each applicant for insurance can an insurance company accurately appraise the risk it is accepting.

3. 5. 2. 7 Warranties and Representations

A **warranty** is something that becomes part of the contract itself and is a statement that is considered to be guaranteed to be true. Under a strict interpretation, a breach of warranty provides grounds for voiding the contract.

A **representation** is a statement believed to be true to the best of one's knowledge. An insurer seeking to void coverage on the basis of a misrepresentation usually has to prove that the misrepresentation is material to the risk.

Under most state laws, an applicant's statements or responses to questions on an application for insurance (in the absence of fraud) are considered to be representations and not warranties.

An example would be a question on the application asking for your sex or date of birth. You represent yourself to the insurance company as being male or female and a certain age. The accuracy of these items is very important to the insurance company issuing the policy. If they are incorrect, they may be considered misrepresentations and the policy may be voided as a result.

There is a difference between representation of a fact and an expression of opinion. A good example is a question on many applications: *Are you now to the best of your knowledge and belief in good health?* If the applicant answers *yes* while knowing in fact that he is not, there is a misrepresentation of actual fact. If, on the other hand, he has had no medical opinion and suffers from no symptoms recognizable to a layman, his answer is an opinion and thus not a misrepresentation.

3. 5. 2. 8 Impersonation

Impersonation means assuming the name and identity of another person for the purpose of committing a fraud. The offense is also known as **false pretenses**. In the case of life insurance, an uninsurable individual applying for insurance may ask another person to substitute for him to take the physical examination.

3. 5. 2. 9 *Misrepresentation and Concealment*

A **misrepresentation** is a written or oral statement that is false. Generally, for a misrepresentation to be grounds for voiding an insurance policy, it has to be material to the risk.

Concealment is the failure to disclose known facts. Generally, an insurer may be able to void the insurance if it can prove that the insured intentionally concealed a material fact.

Material information or a **material fact** is something that is crucial to acceptance of the risk. For example, if the correct information about something would have caused the insurance company to deny a risk or issue a policy on a different basis, the information is material.

3. 5. 2. 10 *Fraud*

Fraud is an intentional act designed to deceive and induce another party to part with something of value.

Fraud may involve misrepresentation, concealment, or both, but not all acts of misrepresentation or concealment are acts of fraud. If someone intentionally lies to obtain coverage or to collect on a false claim, it would be a matter of fraud. If someone misrepresents something on an application (perhaps a medical treatment the person is embarrassed to talk about) without intent to obtain something of value, no fraud has occurred.

3. 5. 2. 11 *Parol (Oral) Evidence Rule*

The parol evidence rule limits the impact of waiver and estoppel on contract terms by disallowing oral evidence based on statements made before the contract was created. It is assumed that oral agreements made before contract formation were incorporated into the written contract. Once formed, earlier oral evidence will not be admitted in court to change or contradict the contract. An oral statement may waive contract provisions only when the statement occurs after the contract exists.

3. 5. 2. 12 *Void and Voidable Contracts*

The terms *void* and *voidable* are often incorrectly used interchangeably. A *void contract* is simply an agreement without legal effect. In essence, it is not a contract at all, for it lacks one of the elements specified by law for a valid contract. A void contract cannot be enforced by either party. For example, a contract having an illegal purpose is void, and neither party to the contract can enforce it. A *voidable contract*, however, is an agreement which, for a reason satisfactory to the court, may be set aside by one of the parties to the contract. It is binding unless the party with the right to reject it wishes to do so. Say that a situation develops under which the policyholder has failed to comply with a condition of the contract: he ceased paying the premium. The contract is then voidable and the insurance company has the right to cancel the contract and revoke the coverage.

This raises another possibility under a voidable contract. In the situation previously described, the insurance company may choose not to exercise its right to cancel the contract after the policyholder fails to pay the premium. The same possibility does not exist under a void contract.

3. 6 SUMMARY

In this lesson, you learned about:

- the role of agency in insurance sales;
- the three types of authority granted in an agency relationship;
- fiduciaries and the role of an insurance producer as a fiduciary;
- the legal doctrines of waiver and estoppel;
- the responsibilities of an agent;
- the responsibilities an insurer has to its agents;
- errors and omissions policies and their importance;
- contracts and the elements that form a valid contract;
- the four basic parts of life and health insurance contracts;
- the five areas reviewed when courts interpret contracts;
- the characteristics unique to insurance contracts;
- the difference between warranties and representations;
- the difference between misrepresentation, concealment, and fraud; and
- parol evidence and its impact on insurance contracts.

UNIT TEST

1. Insurance agents are appointed by
   A. the federal government
   B. the state Department of Insurance
   C. the Insurance Commissioner
   D. insurance companies

2. Life and health insurance producers have the authority to bind an insurance company to a contract agreement.
   A. True
   B. False

3. Ralph is a producer for Hoosier Insurance Company. His contract states that he is allowed to put the company's logo on his business cards and the door to his office. This is an example of
   A. express authority
   B. implied authority
   C. lingering implied authority
   D. apparent authority

4. Tom has always made a practice of having his policyholders mail their premium checks directly to his home address and forwarding them on to the insurer so that he is aware of anyone missing a payment and can contact policyowners directly if that should happen. His contract does not allow this practice, but the insurer is aware of the actions and has not asked him to stop. This practice is an example of
   A. express authority
   B. implied authority
   C. lingering implied authority
   D. apparent authority

5. Gina accepts the initial premium when she sells an insurance policy and sends it to the company with the application. Nothing in her contract mentions handling of initial premiums. This is an example of
   A. express authority
   B. implied authority
   C. lingering implied authority
   D. apparent authority

6. Albert's life insurance premium is due on the 10th of the month. Because he gets paid at the end of the month, he has always sent the premium in late. The insurer has been accepting his premium this way for 3 years when a new CEO comes in and decides to crack down on late premiums, canceling Albert's policy for nonpayment of premium. Albert contests this decision legally and gets the policy reinstated. The decision to reinstate the policy is an example of
   A. estoppel
   B. waiver
   C. contract of adhesion
   D. express authority

7. When representing an insurer, a producer acting as an agent has a responsibility to act with the degree of care that
   A. a licensed insurance producer would apply under similar circumstances
   B. a reasonable person would apply under similar circumstances
   C. a lawyer would apply under similar circumstances
   D. any person would apply under similar circumstances

8. Which element is NOT necessary for the formation of a valid contract?
   A. Consideration
   B. Competent parties
   C. Written document
   D. Legal purpose

9. The initial premium payment sent with an application constitutes which part of the insurance contract?
   A. Consideration
   B. Acceptance
   C. Offer
   D. Legal purpose

10. Life insurance contracts contain all of the following EXCEPT
    A. a policy folder
    B. an insuring clause
    C. conditions
    D. exclusions

11. Ken has paid only 4 premiums on his health insurance policy when he is hit by a car. The insurance company pays out nearly half a million dollars to cover his treatment and a lengthy stay in intensive care. This is an example of
    A. contract of adhesion
    B. aleatory contract
    C. unilateral contract
    D. utmost good faith

12. Carol applies for a life insurance policy and pays the initial premium. Carol has
    A. accepted an offer from the insurer
    B. made an offer to the insurer
    C. accepted a counteroffer from the insurer
    D. made a counteroffer to the insurer

13. The insurer looks at Carol's application and decides to offer Carol a modified policy, including an exclusion Carol did not request. The insurer has
    A. accepted an offer from Carol
    B. made an offer to Carol
    C. accepted a counteroffer from Carol
    D. made a counteroffer to Carol

14. The failure to disclose known facts is
    A. misrepresentation
    B. concealment
    C. fraud
    D. impersonation

15. When one party may receive much more from the contract than she gives in exchange, this is known as
    A. utmost good faith
    B. concealment
    C. aleatory

16. Both parties to the contract have an affirmative duty to disclose all information relevant to the contract, whether or not it is requested. This is known as
    A. utmost good faith
    B. consideration
    C. aleatory

ANSWERS AND RATIONALES TO UNIT TEST

1. **D.** Insurance agents are appointed by insurance companies.
2. **B.** Life and health insurance producers do not have the authority to bind an insurance company to a contract agreement.
3. **A.**
4. **D.** This is an example of apparent authority.
5. **B.** This is an example of implied authority.
6. **A.** The decision to reinstate the policy is an example of estoppel.
7. **B.** When representing an insurer, a producer acting as an agent has a responsibility to act with the degree of care that a reasonable person would apply under similar circumstances.
8. **C.** A written document is not necessary for the formation of a valid contract.
9. **A.** The initial premium payment sent with an application constitutes consideration.
10. **A.** Life insurance contracts do not contain a policy folder.
11. **B.** This is an example of aleatory contract.
12. **B.** Carol has made an offer to the insurer.
13. **D.** The insurer has made a counteroffer to Carol.
14. **B.** The failure to disclose known facts is concealment.
15. **C.** An insurance contract is said to be aleatory, or dependent on chance or an uncertain outcome, because one party may receive much more in value than she gives in value under the contract.
16. **A.** Utmost good faith means both parties to the contract have an affirmative duty to disclose all information relevant to the contract, whether or not it is requested.

UNIT

4

Underwriting Basics

4. 1 INTRODUCTION

By definition, underwriting is the process of selection, classification, and rating of risks. Simply put, underwriting is a risk selection process. The selection process consists of evaluating information and resources to determine how an individual will be classified (standard or substandard). Once this part of the underwriting procedure is complete, the policy will be rated in terms of the premium the applicant will pay. The policy will then be issued and subsequently delivered by the producer.

4. 2 LEARNING OBJECTIVES

After completing this lesson, you will be able to:

- describe roles played by the applicant, policyowner, insured, and beneficiary;
- define third-party ownership and list situations where it might be appropriate;
- explain the importance of the underwriting process in regard to policy issuance;
- define adverse selection and explain why it is relevant to policy issuance;
- list five sources of underwriting information and briefly describe the type of information available from each;
- list the four parts of the typical life or health insurance application and describe the type of information requested on each;
- briefly describe the safeguards that must be used if a company wants to use a blood test for HIV before policy issue;
- list and define the three types of insurance risk;
- list and describe the factors used in determining life or health insurance rates;
- list the possible premium modes and explain the effect that varying premium modes have on the total cost of the policy;
- describe how loss and expense ratios work and what they indicate; and
- explain reserves as they are required in the insurance industry.

4. 3 AFTER THE PROSPECT AGREES TO BUY

Once the prospect has agreed to purchase the insurance contract, three important functions must take place.

- The underwriting process will begin.
- The application will be approved and the policy will be issued (or declined).
- The producer will deliver the policy to the policyowner.

Each of these activities is important, not only to provide the best possible service to the policyowners, but to comply with state laws regulating the writing of life insurance policies.

It is important to clearly understand all of the individuals who might be involved and the parts they play in the insurance process. They might include the **applicant**, the insured, the **policyowner**, and the beneficiary. Although they are four separate roles, they all may be played by one person or by two, three, or four or more persons. Let us define them individually.

An **applicant** is the individual who fills out the application and applies for the insurance.

A **policyowner** is the individual who pays the premium, accepts the policy when it is delivered by the agent, and has the special owner's rights, such as designating beneficiaries. The policyowner is usually, but not necessarily, also the applicant.

An **insured** is the individual whose life is covered by the policy.

A **beneficiary** is the individual or individuals who the policyowner has named to receive the benefits of the policy.

Most of the time, the applicant, policyowner, and the insured are the same person. For example, a person who applies for insurance on his own life will be the insured and most often will also be the policyowner.

The term **third-party ownership** refers to a situation where the policy is owned by someone other than the insured. For example, in a business situation, a corporation may apply for insurance on the life of a key employee. In this case, the corporation is the applicant and the policyowner, and the key employee is the insured. The corporation would also be the beneficiary.

4. 4 THE UNDERWRITING PROCESS

4. 4. 1 The Underwriter's Job

An underwriter's job is to use all the information gathered from many sources to determine whether to accept a particular applicant. Individuals applying for individually owned life and health insurance receive more underwriting scrutiny than do members of a group. The following concepts apply primarily to individual underwriting. Group underwriting considerations are discussed in the next unit. The underwriter must exercise judgment on the basis of his years of experience to read beyond the facts and get a true picture of the applicant's lifestyle. Are there any factors (occupation, hobbies, lifestyle) that make this individual likely to die before his natural life expectancy? Is there any reason to anticipate that this individual will be ill or involved in an accident that will cause high medical expenses? An underwriter cannot, and is not expected to, foresee all circumstances. However, the underwriter's purpose is to protect the insurance company insofar as he can against **adverse selection**—very poor risks and parties with fraudulent intent.

Adverse selection exists when the group of risks insured is more likely than the average group to experience loss. For instance, in a randomly selected group of 1,000 25-year-old individuals, only two might be expected to die in a given year. However, human nature is such that many healthy 25-year-olds do not see the need to buy life insurance and prefer to spend their money elsewhere. Only 25-year-olds who are ill or perhaps employed in dangerous occupations are likely to buy insurance. An underwriter must take care not to accept too many of these poorer-than-average risks, or the insurance company will lose money.

4. 4. 2 Sources of Underwriting Information

The underwriter has various sources of information to provide the necessary information for the risk selection process. These sources include:

- the application;
- medical exams and history;
- inspection reports;
- the Medical Information Bureau (MIB); and
- the agent.

4. 4. 3 The Application

The application is a vital document because it usually is attached to and made a part of the contract. The producer must take special care with the accuracy of the application in the interest of both the company and the insured.

Application forms vary as to the type and amount of information required to complete the form. Insurers may use different forms for different insurance coverages, or they may use a multipurpose form.

The application is divided into sections or parts. Each section is designed to obtain specific types of information. The form of the application may differ from one company to another. However, most applications provide the following information:

- Part I—General Information
- Part II—Medical Information
- The agent's statement or report
- Proper signatures of all parties to the contract

4. 4. 3. 1 Part I

Part I of the application asks for general or personal data regarding the insured. This would include such information as name and address, date of birth, business address and occupation, Social Security number, marital status, and other insurance owned. In addition, if the applicant and the insured are not the same person, the applicant's name and address will be included in Part I.

4. 4. 3. 2 Part II

Part II of the application is generally designed to provide information regarding the insured's medical history, current physical condition, and personal morals. If the insurance applied for qualifies as nonmedical, the producer and the insured will complete Part II of the information. In some cases, the proposed insured is required to take a medical examination and Part II of the application is completed as part of the physical exam.

Part II of the application provides information regarding the medical history of the insured by asking questions related to the types of illnesses and accidents experienced by the insured, periods of hospitalization, any surgery, and reasons for visits to a physician.

In addition, Part II requires information regarding the current health of the insured by asking for current medical treatment for any sickness or condition and types of medication taken. The name and address of the insured's physician are also required.

Usually Part II of the application also will include questions regarding alcohol and drug use by the insured. Avocations and high-risk hobbies are also usually reported in Part II. Generally, plans for a prolonged trip or stay in a foreign country also are reported in Part II. Naturally, questions regarding alcohol and drug use are designed to help determine the morale attitude of the insured.

4. 4. 3. 3 Attending Physician's Statement

Another source of medical information available to the underwriter is an **attending physician's statement (APS)**. After a review of the medical information contained on the application or the medical exam, the underwriter may request an APS from the proposed insured's doctor. Usually, the APS is designed to obtain more specific information about a particular medical problem.

4. 4. 3. 4 Medical Examinations and Testing

Medical examinations, when required by the insurance company, are conducted by physicians or paramedics at the company's expense. Usually such exams are not required with regard to health insurance, thus the importance of the agent in recording medical information on the application. The medical exam requirement is much more common with life insurance underwriting than with health insurance underwriting.

Simplified issue life insurance requires no medical exam and only asks very basic health-related questions on the application. Usually, this type of insurance is only available in low face amounts to reduce the risk of adverse selection against the company.

4. 4. 3. 5 AIDS Considerations

Beginning in the decade of the 1980s, a new concern for life and health insurers came to the forefront: the risk to life and health from acquired immuno deficiency syndrome (AIDS). Individual health insurance buyers and the providers of health coverages have been greatly impacted by the enormous threat of this problem for which no cure now exists.

State legislatures and the insurance industry began developing responses to AIDS as well as to two related conditions:

- AIDS-related complex (ARC), which is caused by the same virus as AIDS—HIV-III—but may have less severe symptoms
- Positive test results for antibodies of human T-cell lymphotropic virus type III (HTLV-III)

Together, AIDS, ARC, and HTLV-III are the subject of AIDS legislation covering a broad range of considerations, including testing, discrimination, reporting, jobs, and confidentiality. We are concerned here primarily with how these diseases and related laws affect health insurance.

That these are diseases, just like any other disease, is a key point of insurance legislation. Many states instruct insurers to treat AIDS, ARC, and HTLV-III infection exactly like other disease or illness in the following ways.

- Underwriting decisions must be applied in the same manner as for other diseases.
- Provisions regarding coverage limitations, deductibles, exclusions, coinsurance, and similar clauses must be applied in the same way as for other diseases.
- Claim settlement considerations (such as when an illness begins or when a new claim should be submitted, rather than being considered a continuation of an old claim) must be on the same basis as other diseases.

In general, it is accurate to say that legislation requires insurers to make no basic distinctions in the way insurers handle insureds or applicants with AIDS-related conditions and the way they handle insureds or applicants with other diseases.

State legislatures that have adopted specific AIDS insurance regulations often pointedly prevent insurers from attempting to identify in the applicant population those who appear likely to develop an AIDS-related condition. For example, insurers may be specifically prohibited from looking at certain characteristics of individuals to attempt to predict these health conditions, especially characteristics such as sexual orientation, marital status, and geographic area of residence. Instead, insurers are expected to develop sound statistical bases (just as they do for conditions such as heart disease or cancer) to draw upon in making decisions to do the following:

- Accept or reject an applicant
- Rate an applicant as a standard or substandard risk
- Renew, nonrenew, or cancel a policy

Basically, most state legislation concerning AIDS and AIDS-related conditions and insurance is designed to ensure that insurers do not discriminate when making underwriting decisions against persons who have certain characteristics.

Even as efforts are being made to ensure nondiscrimination in providing coverage for AIDS-related conditions, some interest groups are attempting to prevent insurers from using screening tests to detect AIDS antibodies. The argument generally addresses the issues of privacy, confidentiality, and unfair discrimination. Insurers, on the other hand, claim that prohibitions against using such tests set AIDS conditions apart from other diseases—exactly the opposite intent of insurance legislation—because insurers have routinely been able to order medical testing for other conditions such as diabetes, high cholesterol levels, or high blood pressure.

Although issues regarding privacy and underwriting may still be in a state of flux, one thing is certain: the costs for treating HIV and AIDS are going up. With the introduction of such powerful drugs as protease inhibitors, many of those infected with HIV or even those with full-blown AIDS are now able to lead normal or near-normal lives, living far longer than could have been expected just a few years ago. Unfortunately, these drugs can be very expensive—$24,000 per year or more. For those with health insurance, either group or individual, that covers prescription drugs, the cost of their treatment can have an effect on the overall cost of health insurance.

Currently, state laws vary widely in regard to using certain tests to detect AIDS antibodies and using the results to make underwriting decisions. Blood tests for HIV before policy issuance are a common underwriting requirement. Typically, the proposed insured must sign a consent form before the blood test is performed. AIDS testing is almost always required whenever a large amount of insurance is applied for. Each insurance company sets thresholds for the ages and amounts of insurance for when medical underwriting (including blood tests for HIV) will be required.

Test results are confidential, and certain procedures must be followed to inform the applicant of positive results. A signed release form is required whenever test results will be disclosed to a party who is not otherwise entitled to the information.

4. 4. 3. 6 Agent's Statement

The **agent's statement** is part of the application and requires that the agent provide certain information regarding the proposed insured. Generally, this includes information regarding the producer's relationship to the insured, data about the proposed insured's financial status, habits, general character, and any other information that may be pertinent to the risk being assumed by the insurer.

The application will also record information regarding the policyowner's/insured's choices with regard to the mode of premium (e.g., monthly or annually), the use of dividends, and the designation of a beneficiary. Finally, the signatures of the insured (and the policyowner if different from the insured) are required in the appropriate places on the application. Usually, the producer also signs the application as a witness to the applicant's signatures.

4. 4. 3. 7 *Inspection Reports*

To supplement the information on the application, the underwriter orders an inspection report on the applicant from an independent investigating firm or credit agency, which covers financial and moral information. This information is used to determine the insurability of the applicant. If the amount of insurance applied for is average, the inspector will write a general report in regard to the applicant's finances, health, character, work, hobbies, and other habits. The inspector will make a more detailed report when larger amounts of insurance are requested. This information is based on interviews with the applicant's associates at home (neighbors and friends), at work, and elsewhere.

4. 4. 3. 8 *Investigative Consumer Reports*

An **investigative consumer report** includes information on a consumer's character, general reputation, personal habits, and mode of living that is obtained through investigation (i.e., interviews with associates and friends and neighbors of the consumer). Such reports may not be made unless the consumer is clearly and accurately told about the report in writing.

This consumer report notification is usually part of the application. At the time the application is completed, the producer will separate the notification and give it to the applicant.

4. 4. 3. 9 *Medical Information Bureau (MIB)*

Another source of information that may aid the underwriter in determining whether to underwrite a risk is the MIB, based in Westwood, Massachusetts. This is a nonprofit trade association that maintains medical information on applicants for life and health insurance. The MIB has over 600 member companies that write 80% of the health insurance and 99% of the life insurance policies in the United States and Canada.

The MIB maintains a database of medical information and avocation risks on applicants for life and health insurance. For every 10 applicants, the MIB will have a file on one or two. MIB information is reported in code form to member companies to preserve the confidentiality of the contents. The database does not contain details about the risk. The codes simply alert companies to the fact that there was information obtained and reported by a member company on this particular impairment or avocation risk. The report does not indicate action taken by other insurers, nor the amount of life insurance requested.

Underwriters compare the MIB file with the information contained in the application. If the MIB file contains a code for a condition that should be listed on the application but is not, the underwriter would then inquire more specifically about that area. For example, an MIB file might contain a code indicating high cholesterol levels, but the application indicates that the applicant had no ongoing medical conditions. This would prompt the underwriter to investigate whether the applicant had misrepresented his health status or perhaps had been able to reverse the condition.

In addition to tracking medical and avocation information, the MIB also reports the number of times information has been requested about an individual in the previous two years. There are two reasons for this report, which is called the Insurance Activity Index (IAI). The first reason is to allow insurance companies to identify people who frequently replace their insurance policies. Most of the costs associated with issuing a policy occur in the first one or two years, so insurance companies are interested in identifying individuals who are likely to cancel their policies after only a year.

The IAI also may identify situations where an individual is loading up on insurance policies by applying for a series of smaller policies that might fall below the radar screen for other underwriting requirements. By purchasing several small to midsize policies, an individual may be trying to avoid drawing attention to the accumulation of an extremely generous death benefit. There have been situations where this has occurred as part of criminal murder for profit schemes.

An insurer may not refuse to accept a risk solely on the basis of the information contained in an MIB report. There must be other substantiating factors that lead an insurer to decide to deny coverage. The MIB must provide explanations to applicants who are denied coverage, allowing consumers to challenge possibly inaccurate information about their medical histories.

4. 4. 3. 10 National Do Not Call Registry

The National Do Not Call Registry is a list of phone numbers from consumers who have indicated their preference to limit the telemarketing calls they receive. The registry is managed and enforced by the Federal Trade Commission (FTC), as well as the Federal Communications Commission (FCC), and state officials.

The registry applies to any plan, program, or campaign to sell goods or services through interstate phone calls, including insurance. This includes telemarketers who solicit consumers on behalf of third parties. It also includes sellers who provide, offer to provide, or arrange to provide goods or services to consumers in exchange for payment.

Calls from or on behalf of political organizations, charities, and telephone surveyors are still permitted, as well as calls from companies that have the express written permission of the consumer. Calls are also permitted to consumers with whom the company has established a business relationship, as follows:

- A consumer can establish a business relationship with an insurer by requesting information from it or submitting an application to it. In this case the business can call for three months from the date of inquiry or application.
- A company with which a consumer has an established business relationship may call for up to 18 months after the consumer's last purchase or last delivery, or last payment, unless the consumer asks the company not to call again.

Telemarketers and sellers are required to search the registry at least once every 31 days and drop from their call lists the phone numbers of consumers who have registered.

A consumer who receives a telemarketing call despite being on the registry will be able to file a complaint with the FTC, either online or by calling a toll-free number. Violators could be fined up to $11,000 per incident.

4. 4. 3. 11 HIPAA Disclosures

The Health Insurance Portability and Accountability Act (HIPAA) imposes specific requirements on health care providers with respect to the disclosure of insureds' health and medical information, or protected health information. Health care providers must preserve patient confidentiality and protect this information. If this information is inadvertently disclosed, providers must mitigate the harm to patients. Insurers and producers are under similar requirements when dealing with the protected health information of applicants and insureds.

When examining an applicant for underwriting purposes, all medical information is to remain confidential and the insurer must protect the applicant's privacy. If the insurer wishes to share this information (such as in communications with medical professionals), including information related to HIV infection, the applicant must be given full notice of the insurer's practices with respect to the treatment of this information, his rights to maintain his privacy, and an opportunity to refuse the dissemination of the information.

4. 4. 4 Field Underwriting

A key element in the underwriting process is the role of the insurance producer. It can be argued that the producer is the most important part of the risk selection process. The producer is in a position to see and talk to the proposed insured, to ask the questions contained on the application, and to accurately and completely record the answers to those questions.

Thus, one of the most important functions of the producer is the completion of the application. Much of the information reported on the application becomes the basis upon which to accept or reject the proposed insured. In addition, a signed and witnessed copy of the application becomes part of the policy, the legal contract between the insured and the insurer.

As a field underwriter, the producer can help expedite the underwriting process by the prompt submission of the application, by scheduling the applicant for a physical exam (if necessary), and by assisting the home office underwriter with other requirements such as obtaining an APS.

The most important element of this process for the producer is the accuracy, thoroughness, and honesty displayed when completing the application. Answers to questions must be recorded accurately and completely by the producer. In addition, honest reporting is required. The producer may not omit pertinent information or report it inaccurately to get the policy issued. The ethical conduct of the producer with regard to the underwriting process must be above reproach.

Finally, if the proposed insured is rated or declined for the insurance, it is the producer's role as a field underwriter to explain the reasons for the underwriting action. Seldom is an individual declined for life insurance, but it does happen that an individual may be classified as substandard; thus, a rated or substandard policy may be issued in lieu of the one applied for. When this occurs, the producer must be prepared to not only explain the reasons for the substandard rating but also to explain the rated policy the company has issued. In addition, there are usually some underwriting forms (amendments or revisions) that must be signed by the applicant when the policy is delivered. It is the producer's responsibility to return these signed forms to the home office.

4. 4. 5 Required Signatures

Several signatures are required to complete a life or health insurance application. If any of the required signatures are not included, there will be a delay in issuing the policy. Required signatures include those of the applicant, the proposed insured (if different from the applicant), and the agent soliciting the insurance. In situations where a corporation is the policyowner, one or more of the partners or officers must sign the application.

If replacement of an existing life insurance policy is involved, the applicant must sign a completed replacement form stating that he realizes that a replacement is taking place. The agent must also sign the form.

When consumer reports are required or additional medical information is needed, forms authorizing these actions must also be signed by the applicant and the agent. Any form requesting information from the applicant's personal physician (such as an attending physician's statement), hospital, or any investigative agencies must also include appropriate signatures.

The agent's report must be completed and signed by the agent only. The Fair Credit Reporting Act Notice of Disclosure ("Notice to the Applicant") is also to be completed with the appropriate signatures.

4. 4. 6 Changes in the Application

Any changes made to an insurance application after it is completed must be initialed by the applicant. It is permissible to change information, but the insurer requires verification that the applicant is aware of any change: thus the requirement that the applicant initial the changes.

Some insurers require that the agent also initial application changes. The reason an insurer would require initialing is to protect itself in the event a dispute arises and the applicant and the agent do not recall the changes that were made.

4. 4. 7 Incomplete Applications

Since the application is the critical tool used by the company in the underwriting process, the agent has the responsibility to see that an applicant's answers to the questions are recorded accurately and completely. Any incomplete applications sent to the underwriting department will be returned to the agent for completion. This means that a delay in the underwriting process will ensue, requiring that the applicant wait to have the proper protection issued. It is advantageous for an agent to ensure that applications are filled out completely to avoid embarrassment and unnecessary inconveniences. In some cases, the applicant may simply withdraw the application for coverage if delays occur.

4. 4. 8 Selection Critera and Unfair Discrimination

While insurers must use actuarially sound principles to determine whether to insure a risk and at what premium, they cannot impose underwriting criteria that unfairly discriminate among members of the same or similar actuarial class.

4. 5 CLASSIFICATION OF RISKS

As was previously stated, underwriting is the process of selecting, classifying, and rating risks. Risk classification refers to the determination of whether a risk is standard or substandard on the basis of the underwriting or risk evaluation process. Basically, a standard risk is simply an average risk.

4. 5. 1 Standard Risks

Standard risks are those who bear the same health, habits, and occupational characteristics as the persons on whose lives the mortality table used was compiled. Most insurers offer special but higher rates to persons who are not acceptable at standard rates because of health, habits, or occupation. This is sometimes called extra risk insurance. Some companies have coined euphemistic names for it to avoid the rather insulting implication that persons offered this type of coverage are substandard. About 90% of individuals covered are standard risks. Fewer than 2% of individuals who apply are turned down for coverage completely.

4. 5. 2 Substandard Risk

A risk that does not measure up to underwriting standards is a substandard risk. It still may be written, but usually at a surcharged premium.

There are several methods of determining the extra rate for the substandard class of risk.

- **Rated-up age**—This plan assumes that the insured is older than his actual age, which is a way of saying that he will not live as long or remain as healthy as a standard risk. Thus, a 35-year-old impaired risk may be issued a policy he applied for but pay the rate of a 40-year-old risk. Although it is simple to handle, this method is no longer widely used.
- **Flat additional premium**—A constant (i.e., not varying with age) additional premium is added to the standard rate.
- **Tabular rating**—Applicants are classified on the basis of the extent to which mortality of risks with their impairment or degree of impairment exceeds that of the standard risk. Percentage tables are developed and used to calculate the amount of extra premium to be charged for any class of impaired risks. Extra percentage tables are usually designated as Table A, Table B, and so forth. Each usually reflects about a 25% increase above 100%, or standard. Insurers vary in the number of tables on which they will accept risks. One may not accept anything lower (or higher, depending on viewpoint) than Table C (175%). Another may write through Table F (250%). Companies can be found that will write up to 1,000%—or perhaps even higher. More and more high-risk cases are becoming acceptable (and, also, many conditions once considered high risk are now, on the basis of more experience, being accepted as standard). Today, it is a rare case when coverage cannot be found anywhere for almost any risk.
- **Graded death benefits**—The insured pays the standard premium for, say, $20,000 of insurance but receives a policy with a face amount of perhaps $15,000. After some time has elapsed, the company may increase the amount of insurance periodically, and when the company considers the substandard condition to no longer exist, the full $20,000 of coverage would be granted.

4. 5. 3 Preferred Risks

If a substandard risk presents an above-average risk of loss, a preferred risk presents a below-average risk of loss. In an effort to encourage the public to practice better health, the insurance industry has developed preferred risk policies with lower (or preferred) premium rates. Applicants who may be eligible for preferred risk classification are those who:

- work in low-risk occupations and do not participate in high-risk hobbies (e.g., scuba diving or sky diving);
- have a very favorable medical history;
- presently are in good physical condition without serious medical problems;
- do not smoke; and
- meet certain weight limitations.

4. 5. 4 Declined Risks

A declined risk is one that an insurer has decided not to insure. The insurer declines the application for insurance. Insurers rarely do this; rather, they seek to insure for a higher premium, by limiting or excluding certain losses, or by some combination of these.

4. 6 DETERMINING PREMIUMS OR RATING CONSIDERATIONS

The final step in the underwriting process is the rating of the risk or the determination of the premium. There are three factors used in determining insurance rates:

- Mortality (life insurance rates) or morbidity (health insurance rates)
- Interest
- Expenses

4. 6. 1 Mortality or Morbidity

If an underwriter could predict exactly how long each insured would live, he could charge a premium for each risk that was precisely correct for covering the policy face amount and expenses, while taking into account the interest to be earned on the premium paid. Of course, an underwriter cannot do this on an individual policy, but he can predict the probability of numbers of deaths for a large group of people. The larger the number of people and deaths recorded, the more reliably actuaries can predict how many will die at a specific age in the entire population of insureds of that age. If the records are kept for many millions of people over a long period, the predictability becomes very reliable. This is an example of the law of large numbers in action.

Insurance companies have kept the kind of records required to produce precise predictions, and the result is called a **mortality table**. The table is based on statistics kept by insurance companies over the years on mortality by age, sex, and other characteristics.

The **mortality rate**, which is defined as the number of deaths per 1,000 people, is taken from the mortality table and is converted into a dollar and cents rate. For instance, if the mortality rate for a particular age group is 3.00, it means that, on average, three people of every 1,000 can be expected to die at that age.

An insurance company would need to collect $3 from each of 1,000 policyowners to have sufficient premium to pay out $1,000 in benefits for those who die in that age group. To illustrate, 1,000 × $3 = $3,000, and 3 deaths × $1,000 = $3,000.

Health insurance policies use related but much more complex statistics to determine morbidity rates. **Morbidity** is the likelihood that a person will suffer an accident, contract a disease, or otherwise require medical care. For many years, insurance companies have kept records that document the outcome of insuring various types of risks. For instance, they know that older people are more likely to become ill than younger people, so health insurance premiums tend to be higher for older people. Similarly, insurers know that people employed in certain occupations are more likely to be injured than those in other occupations. These determinations are based on what has happened in the past and the company's and industry's experience.

To set rates for health insurance, however, insurers need to consider not only how often people will become ill or injured, but how much it will cost when they do. Insurers look at how frequently claims happen among a particular population, or the **claim frequency rate**, as well as the average dollar amount per claim. These two figures are multiplied to create the **aggregate claim** amount, which is a primary element in calculating health insurance rates.

4. 6. 2 Interest

Because premiums are paid in advance of claims, insurance companies have money to invest to earn interest. This interest helps to lower the premium rate.

As explained, the basic cost of life or health insurance is the cost of mortality or morbidity. However, in constructing a rate, interest enters in. It is assumed that all premiums are paid at the beginning of the year and all claims are paid at the end. Therefore, it becomes necessary to determine how much should be charged at the beginning of the year, assuming a given rate of interest, to have enough money at the end of the year to pay all claims.

4. 6. 3 Expenses

If the cost of mortality is calculated (discounting for interest), there is enough money to pay claims, but the insurance company has no money with which to pay operation expenses. The premium without expense loading is a **net premium**. (Do not confuse *net* as it is used here with the same term sometimes used to indicate a participating premium minus dividends paid.)

An expense loading is added to the net premium to:

- cover all expenses and contingencies;
- have funds for expenses when needed; and
- spread cost equitably among insureds.

Loading consists of four main items:

- **Acquisition costs**—All costs in connection with putting the policy on the books are charged as incurred in the insurance accounting. In most cases, these costs will be so proportionately high compared with those for ensuing years that they must be amortized over a period of years. One of the highest acquisition costs is the producer's first-year commission. This is the reason a policy that lapses during the first two or three years creates a loss for the insurer. It has not yet recovered acquisition costs.

- **General overhead loading**—Clerical salaries, furniture, fixtures, rent, management salaries, and so forth must be considered when determining expenses. The allocation of these costs is unaffected by the size of the premium and probably little affected by the face amount but is most likely affected by the number of policies.
- **Loading for contingency funds**—Once a level premium policy has been issued, the premium can never be increased. However, unforeseen contingencies could make the rate inadequate. Assessment companies reserve the right to charge additional premiums in such a case. Legal reserve companies establish contingency reserves to draw on in such cases.
- **Immediate payment of claims**—In rate making, it is assumed that all claims are paid at the end of the year. This is not literally true, of course. Relying on the law of large numbers, it is safe to assume that claims will be spread throughout the year. Therefore, theoretically, all claims will be paid six months before the end of the year. Allowance must be made for this loss in the expense loading.

The **gross annual premium**, or the amount the policyowner actually pays for the policy, equals the mortality risk discounted for interest, plus expenses. By definition, the **net premium** is the mortality risk discounted for interest, without any expense adjustment.

By formula: gross premium = mortality − interest + expenses; net premium = mortality − interest.

The risk factor increases with age. This is the reason that some life insurance policy premiums increase periodically. For example, the premium for a one-year renewable and convertible term insurance policy increases each year because each year the insured is one year older and thus the mortality risk is greater. This can result in very expensive premiums as the insured becomes older.

The **level premium** concept was devised to solve this problem of increasing premiums. Mathematically, the level premiums paid by the policyowner are equal to the increasing sum of the premiums caused by the increased risk of mortality. Accordingly, in the early years of the policy, the level premiums paid are actually more than the amount necessary to cover the cost of mortality. Conversely, in the later years of the policy, the premiums paid are less than the amount necessary to cover the increased cost of mortality. This shortage in the later years of the policy is accounted for by the overcharges (plus interest earned) in the early policy years.

Premium mode—Once the single premium amount has been determined, the company will break this amount into smaller amounts (annual, semiannual, quarterly, or monthly) that will be more convenient for the insured to pay. This frequency of payment is called the **premium mode**. This is important because the insurance company invests the premium amounts it receives and uses the income as part of the eventual settlement. The more payments the insured wishes to break his premium into, the higher the total premium. This is because of the interest lost by not receiving money for coverage in advance and because of increased administrative expenses.

4. 7 LOSS RATIOS

Loss and expense ratios are basic guidelines as to the quality of company underwriting. A **loss ratio** is determined by dividing losses by total premiums received. Loss ratios are often calculated by account, by line of insurance, by book of business (all accounts placed by each producer or agency), and for all business written by an insurer. Loss ratio information may be used to make decisions about whether to renew accounts, whether to continue agency contracts, and whether to tighten underwriting standards on a given line of insurance. An **expense ratio** is determined by dividing an insurer's operating expenses (including commissions paid) by total premiums. When the combined loss and expense ratio is 100%, the insurer breaks even. If the combined ratio exceeds 100%, an underwriting loss has occurred. If the combined ratio is less than 100%, an underwriting profit, or gain, has been realized.

For example, let's assume that the ABC Insurance Company realizes $3 million in underwriting losses for all term insurance policies. This same block of business also generates $10 million in premium. The loss ratio would be calculated as follows:

$$\text{Loss Ratio} = \frac{\text{Losses}}{\text{Premiums}}$$

$$\text{Loss Ratio} = \frac{\$3\text{ million}}{\$10\text{ million}} = 30\%$$

Furthermore, let's assume that the ABC Insurance Company has operating expenses totaling $2 million for this same block of term insurance. The expense ratio would be calculated as follows:

$$\text{Expense Ratio} = \frac{\text{Operating Expenses}}{\text{Premiums}}$$

$$\text{Expense Ratio} = \frac{\$2\text{ million}}{\$10\text{ million}} = 20\%$$

The combined loss and expense ratio equals 50%. Thus, the ABC Insurance Company has an underwriting gain or profit on this block of term insurance.

4. 8 RESERVES

Insurers are required to follow certain regulations and laws to be certain they will have the money needed to pay claims as they arise. Funds set aside to pay future, existing, and ongoing claims are known as **reserves**. Reserves are accounting measurements of an insurer's liabilities to its policyholders. Theoretically, the reserve is the amount together with interest to be earned and premiums to be paid that will exactly equal all of the company's contractual obligations.

Companies must also keep enough on hand to pay claims that might arise should some major catastrophe occur on a local, regional, or national basis. For instance, if a nationwide epidemic were to occur, causing widespread disability among insureds, insurance companies would need very large reserves to handle claims. Any reserves set aside to cover current or future claims are called unpaid claim reserves.

Because insurance premiums are paid in advance, an insurance company always has a certain amount of money that it has not yet earned by providing protection. This amount, too, is considered a reserve, called an **unpaid premium reserve**. When a policy is canceled before its term ends, unpaid premium is ordinarily returned to the former policyowner.

A life insurance reserve is a fixed liability of the insurer. This liability represents the insurer's promise to pay the face amount of the policy at some future time. By law, a portion of every premium must be set aside as a reserve against the future claim from the policy as well as other contractual obligations such as cash surrender and nonforfeiture values. Accordingly, the policy reserve is equal to the premiums paid plus the interest earned on those premiums and other policy obligations.

Insurance companies demonstrate their solvency to the state insurance departments by showing their assets as well as adequate funds to cover their reserve obligations. In addition to its assets, the insurer must show that it will continue to receive future premiums plus interest to cover its reserve obligation.

By law, the Insurance Commissioner requires that a specific reserve be maintained if a company is to be solvent. The reserve must be calculated using a mortality table and an interest specified by the Commissioner. Most states require that premiums be calculated using the Commissioner's Standard Ordinary table. In addition, the estimated investment return or interest rate paid on the premiums also will be determined by the Insurance Commissioner. Usually, a very conservative interest rate is specified.

4. 9 SUMMARY

In this lesson, you learned about:

- roles played by the applicant, policyowner, insured, and beneficiary;
- third-party ownership and situations where it might be appropriate;

- the importance of the underwriting process in regard to policy issue;
- adverse selection and its relevance to policy issue;
- the five sources of underwriting information and the type of information available from each;
- the four parts of the typical life or health insurance application and the type of information requested on each;
- the safeguards that must be used if a company wants to use a blood test for HIV before policy issue;
- the three types of insurance risk;
- the factors used in determining life or health insurance rates;
- the possible premium modes and the effect of varying premium modes on the total cost of the policy;
- how loss and expense ratios work and what they indicate; and
- reserves as they are required in the insurance industry.

UNIT TEST

1. The tendency for poor risks to seek and be covered by insurance more often than average risks is
   A. inappropriate selection
   B. adverse selection
   C. inappropriate risk
   D. adverse risk

2. John fills out an application for a life insurance policy to insure his own life, for which he plans to pay the premiums. John is playing all of the following roles EXCEPT
   A. applicant
   B. policyowner
   C. insured
   D. beneficiary

3. Life insurance that requires no medical exam and asks only basic medical questions is known as
   A. simplified policy
   B. simplified issue
   C. simplified risk
   D. preferred risk

4. In many jurisdictions, testing for the presence of HIV infection requires all of the following EXCEPT
   A. a signed consent form before the blood test is performed
   B. a signed release form whenever test results will be disclosed to a party who is not otherwise entitled to the information
   C. medical oversight of testing by a specialist in HIV research
   D. confidentiality of results in the absence of a signed release form

5. Which of the following pieces of information is NOT likely to be contained in an MIB report?
   A. Mr. Jones reported a heart condition on an insurance application 2 years ago.
   B. Mr. Smith was turned down for insurance by 2 companies in the past year.
   C. Mr. Green's information has been requested 14 times in the previous 2 years.
   D. Mr. Brown reported a hobby as a flight instructor a year ago.

6. If an applicant is rated or declined an insurance policy, the reasons for this decision will be explained to the applicant by
   A. the producer
   B. the underwriter
   C. the insurer
   D. the Insurance Commissioner

7. Robin is a 25-year-old man who drinks occasionally, does not smoke, and has no known health problems. He probably would be classified by an insurer as a
   A. standard risk
   B. substandard risk
   C. superstandard risk
   D. preferred risk

8. Which of the following factors does NOT have an effect on insurance premium rates?
   A. Mortality or morbidity
   B. Interest rates
   C. Producer certification
   D. Expenses

9. To be certain that insurers have the money available to pay claims as they arise, they are required to maintain
   A. a risk-based capital ratio
   B. reserves
   C. expense ratios
   D. reinsurance

ANSWERS AND RATIONALES TO UNIT TEST

1. **B.** The tendency for poor risks to seek and be covered by insurance more often than average risks is adverse selection.
2. **D.**
3. **B.** Life insurance that requires no medical exam and asks only basic medical questions is known as simplified issue.
4. **C.** Testing for the presence of HIV infection usually does not require medical oversight of testing by a specialist in HIV research.
5. **B.** The fact that Mr. Smith was turned down for insurance by 2 companies during the past year is not likely to be contained in an MIB report.
6. **A.** If an applicant is rated or declined an insurance policy, the reasons for this decision will be explained to the applicant by the producer.
7. **A.** Robin probably would be classified as a standard risk.
8. **C.** Producer certification does not have an effect on insurance premium rates.
9. **B.** Insurers maintain reserves to be certain they will have the money available to pay claims as they arise.

UNIT

5

Group Insurance

5. 1 INTRODUCTION

Group insurance provides coverage to many people under one policy. It gets its name from the requirements that several people must first be members of a group before they become eligible to purchase the insurance.

A person who is covered by group insurance does not receive a policy as proof of insurance. As the master policyowner, the group receives and holds the insurance policy. The insured group members receive a certificate of insurance that certifies the coverage, the benefits under the policy, the name of the covered individual or individuals, and the name of the beneficiary if applicable.

5. 2 LEARNING OBJECTIVES

After completing this lesson, you will be able to:

- explain certificates of insurance;
- list and describe five common types of groups that are eligible for insurance;
- list three characteristics of groups authorized for group insurance;
- explain the difference between contributory and noncontributory policies and list the minimum participation percentage for each;
- explain the difference between underwriting for group insurance policies and individual insurance policies respectively;
- define *adverse selection* and explain its importance to insurance underwriting;
- explain the probationary and eligibility periods;
- list and describe one statutory and seven optional underwriting requirements for group policies;
- list and describe three mechanisms for funding group insurance;
- list five types of groups eligible to purchase insurance and describe each; and
- explain the difference between contributory and noncontributory group insurance plans and how participation limits affect each type of plan.

5. 3 THIRD-PARTY OWNERSHIP

Third-party ownership exists when a party other than the insured is the owner of the policy. For example, third-party owners could include a wife who is the owner of a husband's policy, a parent who is the owner of a child's policy, or a corporation that is the owner of a director's or officer's policy.

5. 4 TYPES OF GROUPS

Employee or individual employer group—The first type of group would be the employees of an eligible employer. This is called an employee group or an individual employer group. The employer is the policyowner and establishes the eligible class of employees to be covered under the group policy.

Usually, this classification will include all full-time employees (including the employer). Furthermore, the classification can also specify full-time, salaried, nonunion employees. By classifying the employee group in this manner, the employer is legally able to exclude certain groups of employees (e.g., part time and union) from the eligible class of covered employees. The eligible class of employees also may include retired employees.

Multiple employer group—A second type of group could be composed of several employers forming a trust fund to combine their workers for life insurance eligibility. This is known as a multiple employer group. The trusts are called **multiple employer trusts (METs)**.

A policy may be issued to the trustees of a trust group if the fund has been established by:

- two or more employers in the same or related field; or
- one or more labor unions or associations (this is known as a Taft-Hartley trust).

The trustees are the policyholders of the plan that covers eligible employees. This type of plan must not be for the benefit of the employer, union, or association. The individuals who may be considered employees as defined by this section are the same as those previously listed under employee group.

Association or labor group—A third type of organization eligible for group insurance includes members of labor organizations, such as the United Auto Workers. An association or labor group must have the following characteristics to be considered an authorized group:

- Have a constitution and bylaws
- Be organized and maintained in good faith for purposes other than obtaining insurance
- Have insurance for the purpose of covering members, employees, or the employees of members for the benefit of persons other than the association or its officers or trustees

Credit insurance is written to provide payment of the insured's debt when he dies prematurely or is disabled as a result of accident or sickness.

The creditor is the policyowner and the debtor is the insured. Benefits under credit insurance are not permitted to exceed the amount of indebtedness.

5. 5 PREMIUMS

Group insurance policies are often able to provide coverage at a lower premium than individual policies can. One reason for this is that the administrative costs to cover a group of 50 people are much lower than those involved in writing 50 separate policies.

Group insurance premiums are based on the experience of the group as a whole. The premium may be paid entirely by the policyowner, or it may be paid jointly by the policyowner and the insured. If the insured contributes money toward the premium, the plan is considered **contributory**. In most states, at least 75% of eligible employees must participate under a contributory plan. If the premium is paid entirely by the policyowner, the plan is considered **noncontributory**. All of the eligible members must participate in noncontributory plans.

5. 6 GROUP UNDERWRITING CONSIDERATIONS

Group life insurance is usually written on a group basis as opposed to an individual basis. In other words, the underwriter focuses on the group as a whole, rather than individual members. Each group participant completes a very short application form that usually consists of the individual's name, address, Social Security number, dependent information, and beneficiary designation. There are no medical questions. Thus, no medical underwriting takes place. (However, evidence of insurability must be furnished by an employee who wants to join a contributory group after the period of eligibility has ended.)

It is therefore possible for individuals in poor health to receive group insurance benefits because there is no medical underwriting. All eligible participants obtain coverage. Underwriting, the risk selection process, does occur, however, to protect insurers from adverse selection.

5. 7 ADVERSE SELECTION

Adverse selection is the tendency for poor risks to seek and be covered for insurance more often than average risks. Thus, in a group situation, the underwriter must consider such things as the type of work done, the ages of the participants, and the probability of this particular group being an adverse risk to the company. For example, a group of coal miners presents a much different risk than a group of bank employees.

The larger the group to be insured, the more predictable will be the expected losses from the group. Thus, it is more difficult for the underwriter to anticipate expected losses from relatively small groups (10, 20, or 25 participants).

Once a group is written, the underwriter wants the business to stay on the books and thus is concerned about the financial stability of the company. If the company has a history of financial problems (i.e., bankruptcy, layoffs resulting from no work, or seasonal employment), the group may be declined for these financial reasons.

The group underwriter is concerned with the number of new group entrants. The insurer does not necessarily want a group in which there is no turnover. If the loss experience is to be favorable, employees must leave the group because of retirement or terminations and new (younger) employees must take their place. This turnover of employees helps bring some stability in terms of loss experience and possible adverse selection.

5. 7. 1 Adverse Underwriting Decisions

A risk will be rejected when the insurer believes the applicant cannot be profitable at a reasonable premium or with reasonable coverage modifications. If a risk is rejected on the basis of information in an investigative report, the applicant must be notified and given the name and address of the reporting company. In health insurance, when renewal is denied, the insured must be given a written explanation for nonrenewal or be notified that the explanation is available upon written request.

5. 8 PROBATIONARY PERIOD

Often, individuals coming into a covered group will be required to serve a probationary period before becoming eligible for group coverage. It costs the insurer money to enroll an individual in a group plan. Some groups experience high turnover among membership. It would be prohibitively expensive, for example, to cover all workers as of the first day of employment in businesses with high turnover.

To avoid this expense, the insurer usually requires that employees be on the job for a specified period before the insurance is put into force. This period is often 90 days, though it can be longer or shorter.

5. 9 ELIGIBILITY PERIOD

If the group plan is noncontributory, all individuals become covered immediately after the probationary period. If the plan is contributory, the employees first must fulfill the probationary period and then must enroll within the eligibility period to avoid medical underwriting. This is one way in which insurers protect against adverse selection.

The eligibility period typically runs for 30 or 31 days after the probationary period expires. If the group member does not apply during the eligibility period, he is generally required to take a medical exam before being eligible for coverage.

If an individual does not enroll during the eligibility period but wants to enroll later, he generally will be required to take a physical examination and will be selected on an individual basis, just as if the policy were an individual policy.

5. 10 STATUTORY REQUIREMENTS IN GROUP UNDERWRITING

The following factors and requirements represent the underwriting criteria for group health insurance.

5. 10. 1 Statutory Requirements

Nondiscriminatory Classifications

An eligible group must not discriminate in favor of individuals in a manner that increases the opportunity for adverse selection against the insurance company. For instance, if an employer has five typists in the same job classification (job title and salary range), the employer cannot single out one typist to receive benefits greater than the other four typists. Therefore, employees will be grouped under such classifications, as eligible full-time employees, clerical workers, hourly employees, salaried employees, executives, employees working one year or more, or employees earning between $10,000 and $15,000.

5. 10. 2 Optional Requirements

5. 10. 2. 1 Employer Control

The employer should be in charge of enrollment, premium payment, benefit selection, and all other areas of administration that are not an insurance company function. Because the contract is between the insurer and the policyowner, it is the employer's duty to see that plan administration is conducted in a confidential, legal, and objective manner that precludes the individual insured's active participation in the business end of the insurance administration.

5. 10. 2. 2 Group Size

Most insurers require a minimum number of employees or plan participants before a group health insurance plan may be written. This requirement may vary depending on state laws. Typically, the minimum group size for health insurance is 10, but it could be as few as 5 or some other number. The larger the group, the more predictable the loss experience will be.

Relatively small groups (25 employees or fewer) may require some form of individual underwriting for which each plan participant may be required to prove insurability. Generally, larger groups do not need to prove insurability.

5. 10. 2. 3 Predetermined Coverage Amount

The underwriter should determine that individual coverage is based on some plan other than individual selection. Individual members of the group cannot select the level of benefits for their own coverage. Coverage can be based on such things as the number of years with the company, occupation, or salary. Coverage must be uniform for plan participants.

5. 10. 2. 4 Enrollment Percentage

The underwriter should determine that individual participation meets his company's guidelines to prevent adverse selection. The insurance company requires that a majority of eligible individuals be members of the group of insureds. For example, under a plan of insurance where an employer pays the entire premium and the employee does not contribute to the premium payment (noncontributory plan), 100% of all eligible employees must be covered. Under a plan where both the employer and the employee contribute toward the premium payment (contributory plan), 75% of all eligible employees must be covered.

5. 10. 2. 5 Insurance Incidental to Group

The underwriter should determine that the group has not been formed only for the purpose of purchasing insurance. If individuals could form a group for the purpose of obtaining insurance, the chance of adverse selection would increase dramatically.

5. 10. 2. 6 Eligibility

The underwriter first should determine that the business is one that the insurer will cover. There was a time when certain occupations were of such a high risk or unstable nature that employees could not get insurance. Today, virtually all occupations can get insurance coverage. However, the higher the risk or instability of the occupation, the higher the premium.

Because death and illness rates differ in different parts of the country, underwriters may take geographic location into account. Also, certain parts of the country are more prone to catastrophic loss from natural disasters.

5. 10. 2. 7 Composition of Group

The underwriter should determine that the group is of such nature that there is a reasonably steady flow of new members into the group. Many states have regulations that specify the number of members who must join the group for the group to remain eligible. If a group were to keep the same individuals in the group, the chance of accident, illness, or death would increase as the group became older. Because of this increase in risk, rates also would increase.

The group underwriter also must be concerned about currently disabled employees or their dependents. A new insurer may decide to decline the entire group because of a large number of current claims unless the existing insurer agrees by contract to continue to honor these claims.

Also, a new insurer may establish a preexisting condition provision in the group contract that excludes coverage for any condition that exists before the effective date of coverage. This provision normally will exclude these conditions for a period of 6 or 12 months after the effective date of coverage.

Generally, there also will be a requirement that only employees currently working at least 25 hours per week are eligible for coverage. Employees not actively at work usually are eliminated from coverage.

Although there have been changes to underwriting standards because of the passing of unisex laws, there remain instances when a group composed largely of women in general, young women, or older employees pays higher premiums.

5. 10. 2. 8 Group Contract and Certificate of Coverage

The basic principle of *group insurance* is that it provides insurance coverage for a number of people under a single *master contract* or *master policy*. Because a group policy insures a group of people, it is the group—not each individual—that must meet the underwriting requirements of the insuring company.

Group insurance is most typically provided by an employer for its employees as a *benefit*. In these cases, the employer is the applicant and contract policyholder; the employees, as group members, are not parties to the contract. In fact, they are not even named in the contract. Instead, each employee who is eligible to participate in the plan fills out an enrollment card and is given a *certificate of insurance*, which summarizes the coverage terms and explains the employee's rights under the group contract. A list of individual employees covered under the contract is maintained by the insurer.

5. 11 FUNDING OF GROUP INSURANCE

Several mechanisms for funding group insurance have been developed. Alternative funding allows employers to absorb some of the risk and save premium dollars while increasing cash flow.

For example, a **shared funding arrangement** allows the employer to self-fund health care expenses up to a certain limit. The employer can select a deductible and pay covered expenses for any individual incurring claims up to that maximum, at which point the insurer assumes the risk.

Under a **retrospective premium** arrangement, the insurer agrees to collect a provisional premium but may collect additional premium or make a premium refund at the end of the year based on the actual incurred losses.

A **minimum premium** plan occurs when the employer agrees to fund expected claims and the insurer funds excess claims. The employer and insurer agree to a trigger beyond which the insurer is liable. The employer is responsible for a minimum premium consisting of administrative expenses, reserves, and a premium for stop-loss to fund claims over the trigger.

A large employer may elect to fully self-fund or may self-fund a plan but contract for administrative services only (ASO).

5. 12 SUMMARY

In this lesson, you learned about:

- certificates of insurance;
- the five common types of groups that are eligible for insurance;
- the three characteristics of groups authorized for group insurance;
- the difference between contributory and noncontributory policies and the minimum participation percentage for each;
- the difference between underwriting for group insurance policies and individual insurance policies;
- adverse selection and its importance to insurance underwriting;
- the probationary and eligibility periods;
- one statutory and seven optional underwriting requirements for group policies;
- the three mechanisms for funding group insurance;
- the five types of groups eligible to purchase insurance; and
- the difference between contributory and noncontributory group insurance plans and how participation limits affect each type of plan.

UNIT TEST

1. To be eligible to purchase insurance, an association group must
   A. have a constitution and bylaws
   B. be organized and maintained strictly for the purpose of obtaining insurance
   C. have insurance for the purpose of covering the association or its officers or trustees only

2. For group insurance policies, the covered individual receives proof of coverage in the form of a(n)
   A. insurance policy
   B. insurance contract
   C. certificate of coverage
   D. certificate of policy

3. If a group insurance policy is contributory, what percentage of employees must participate?
   A. No set percentage
   B. 50%
   C. 75%
   D. 100%

4. Albert works as a window washer at the top of skyscrapers. Bernie works as a window washer on the ground floor. The fact that Albert is more likely to seek insurance coverage than Bernie is an example of
   A. risk selection
   B. adverse underwriting
   C. adverse selection
   D. risk underwriting

5. Gianna starts work at a new job on March 1. She is not eligible for insurance coverage until July 1. The period between start date and her eligibility date is the
   A. probationary period
   B. eligibility period
   C. selection period
   D. waiting period

6. Gianna is eligible for coverage on July 1. She enrolls on July 15. She does not need to take a medical exam because she enrolled within the
   A. probationary period
   B. eligibility period
   C. selection period
   D. waiting period

7. Tom started work the same day Gianna did, at the same company. Tom does not try to enroll in the company insurance plan until August 15. What will Tom probably need to do?
   A. Pay an extra premium
   B. Fulfill the probationary period again before coverage is available
   C. Look for insurance somewhere else
   D. Submit to a medical exam and full individual underwriting

8. The baker's union and the butcher's union worked together to form a trust to provide insurance to their employees. This type of group is called a(n)
   A. employee group
   B. multiple employer trust
   C. Taft-Hartley trust
   D. labor group

9. Jimmy's Print Shop and Bryan's Boutique join together to form a trust to provide insurance to their employees. This type of group is called a(n)
   A. employee group
   B. multiple employer trust
   C. Taft-Hartley trust
   D. labor group

10. A candlestick maker offers insurance to its employees. This type of group is called a(an)
    A. employee group
    B. multiple employer trust
    C. Taft-Hartley trust
    D. labor group

11. The United Auto Workers union provides insurance to its employees. This type of group is called a(an)
    A. employee group
    B. multiple employer trust
    C. Taft-Hartley trust
    D. labor group

12. General Electricians offers insurance to its employees. About 80% of its eligible employees are currently covered under the plan. The plan is most likely
    A. contributory
    B. noncontributory
    C. inclusive
    D. noninclusive

13. Group insurance generally does NOT require
    A. stringent medical underwriting
    B. a short application form
    C. a minimum level of participation among eligible insureds
    D. a master policyowner to hold the policy

14. Sara is hired to work at a restaurant. She is not eligible to join the group insurance plan for 30 days. This is an example of a(n)
    A. introductory period
    B. weeding-out period
    C. probationary period
    D. eligibility period

15. Marie has worked at a restaurant for more than a year but never participated in its insurance program. She decides that it is now time to sign up. She is required to undergo a medical exam because she is signing up after the
    A. probationary period has expired
    B. weeding-out period has expired
    C. introductory period has expired
    D. eligibility period has expired

16. Which of the following group underwriting characteristics generally is required by law?
    A. Employer control
    B. Predetermined coverage amount
    C. Nondiscriminatory classifications
    D. Insurance incidental to group

17. Kelsey's Printing funds all the claims in a year, regardless of the amount of the claim. Kelsey's insurer just manages the paperwork for the claims. Which of the following option's is Kelsey's Printing using?
    A. Retrospective premium
    B. Minimum premium
    C. Variable premium
    D. Administrative services only

18. Al's Print Shop pays a provisional premium at the beginning of the year. At the end of the year, Al's insurer has the right to change that premium by charging more or issuing a refund. Al's policy is funded using which premium option?
    A. Retrospective premium
    B. Minimum premium
    C. Variable premium
    D. Administrative services only

19. PDQ Printing pays for all routine claims. PDQ's insurer pays for excess or unexpected claims beyond a specified trigger point. PDQ's policy is funded using which premium option?
    A. Retrospective premium
    B. Minimum premium
    C. Variable premium
    D. Administrative services only

ANSWERS AND RATIONALES TO UNIT TEST

1. **A.**
2. **C.** An individual covered by a group insurance policy receives proof of coverage in the form of a certificate of coverage.
3. **C.** To be a contributory group insurance policy, 75% of employees must participate.
4. **C.** The fact that Albert is more likely to seek insurance coverage than Bernie is an example of adverse underwriting.
5. **A.**
6. **B.** Gianna does not need to take a medical exam because she enrolled within the eligibility period.
7. **D.** Tom will need to submit to a medical exam and full individual underwriting.
8. **C.**
9. **B.** This type of group is called a multiple employer trust.
10. **A.** This type of group is called an employee group.
11. **D.** This type of group is called a labor group.
12. **A.** It is most likely that this plan requires employees to contribute toward the premiums.
13. **A.** Group insurance generally does not require stringent medical underwriting.
14. **C.** This is an example of a probationary period.
15. **D.** Marie is required to undergo a medical exam because she is signing up after the eligibility period has expired.
16. **C.** Nondiscriminatory classifications generally are required by law.
17. **D.** Kelsey's Printing is using administrative services only.
18. **A.** Al's policy is funded using the retrospective premium.
19. **B.** PDQ's policy is funded using the minimum premium.

UNIT

6

Selling Life Insurance

6. 1 LEARNING OBJECTIVES

After completing this lesson, you will be able to:

- list costs commonly associated with death;
- list two different approaches to needs analysis and describe each;
- list the three income periods a surviving spouse may encounter and describe the characteristics of each;
- explain the difference between the capital conservation and capital liquidation methods of determining the amount of life insurance required;
- list four living benefits of life insurance;
- explain the advantages of life insurance as property;
- describe the traditional net cost method and the interest-adjusted cost method of comparing insurance policy costs;
- explain the difference between accelerated benefits and viatical settlements and explain when each might be used; and
- list the types of organizations that might use insurance for business reasons and provide examples of how insurance might be used.

6. 2 MEETING CONSUMER NEEDS

6. 2. 1 The Importance of Insurance

The loss of human life is tragic in many ways. The financial results alone of such a loss can be devastating. If the principal breadwinner dies, the spouse might not be able to maintain the family on Social Security benefits. If there were two breadwinners in the family, the surviving spouse might not be able to maintain the family's lifestyle on his income alone. The death of a single parent might leave dependent children without an adequate source of support.

Life insurance products are designed to provide a number of unique and powerful features. The one benefit all life insurance products have in common is that they provide financial security—a measure of certainty in an area marked by risk and change. Although different clients may find different life insurance products appealing to them in their particular circumstances, the one reason they all buy life insurance is to obtain that measure of financial security.

Studies show that less than half of American adults own individual life insurance and the average American adult has just $45,000 of life insurance. Relying on the group life insurance provided at work can build a false sense of security because coverage is usually insufficient for family needs and generally ceases when employment terminates. Experts agree that few people protect their own full value with life insurance, leaving their families at risk.

6. 2. 2 Costs Associated with Death

When an individual dies, he typically leaves behind the unfinished business of a lifetime. This is particularly true of individuals who die earlier than normal life expectancy would predict. Costs associated with death include:

- doctor and hospital bills from a final illness or accident;
- funeral expenses;
- estate taxes; and
- paying off debts (credit cards and loans).

In addition, to individuals leaving behind a family or others who are financially dependent on them for support, the following financial needs will immediately become apparent:

- Mortgage payments
- Immediate income needs—to pay for groceries, utilities, car payments, and other day-to-day living expenses
- Longer-term needs—to pay for children's educations and retirement income for a spouse

The insurance producer is the person most qualified to help potential insureds select the contract of insurance that will best meet their needs.

This needs analysis can be accomplished by identifying the specific financial objectives of the individual by means of a fact-finding interview. This interview covers the following financial needs:

- Cash needs to cover the expenses of dying (e.g., funeral, taxes, and last illness)
- Cash needs for payment of debts (e.g., credit cards, loans, and bank notes)
- Home mortgage payments
- Family income needs during the dependency period and in later years
- Funds for children's college education
- Retirement income needs
- Health insurance needs such as hospitalization insurance and disability income coverage

After the needs analysis is complete, the producer should make recommendations as to the amount and type of insurance needed by the individual.

These recommendations should consider the following.

- Should the coverage be permanent insurance, term insurance, or a combination of the two?
- How much premium can the individual afford to pay?
- Should the premium be level, increasing, or decreasing?
- Is the individual insurable?

6. 2. 3 Human Life Value Approach

The human life value concept was developed in the 1920s by Dr. S.S. Huebner. His concept was based on the fact that when a working person dies, his ability to produce income or support a family is lost. By comparison, a piece of machinery can help its owner to generate income or help in the support and maintenance of the business until it breaks down. Although theoretically true, Dr. Huebner realized that value cannot be placed on a human life the way it is on a piece of machinery. So the value was placed not on the life itself, as the name of the concept implies, but on the earning potential of the insured, calculated and projected over a period of years (capitalized).

In formulating the items to determine need, Dr. Huebner looked at four general areas:

- The individual's net annual salary
- The individual's annual expenses
- The number of years the individual has left to work (the present to retirement age)
- The value of the individual's dollar as it depreciates over time (capitalized rate)

The human life value concept was a way of determining what a family would lose in income by the death of the principal wage earner. By this method, if the insured died, the family could be reimbursed for that loss.

6. 2. 4 Needs Approach

Looking at the needs of an individual and his dependents is considered the best method for determining the amount and kind of insurance a prospect should buy. Basically, the needs method looks at such things as:

- needs for last illness and burial expenses;
- maintenance income for the family for a period after the death of the principal wage earner;
- education for dependent children; and
- continuing income for the surviving spouse.

After determining needs, the agent must present a plan of insurance that will meet these needs. However, this is not always so simple. The agent also must determine how much the prospect can afford to pay in premium and make further adjustments based on the prospect's financial position, keeping in mind the various term policies and riders.

This is an example of the needs approach because it focuses on the financial needs that will arise as a result of Dwight's death.

6. 2. 5 Income Periods

A typical married couple with children will have fluctuating income needs based on the changes in their family. To properly determine how much life insurance protection they will need if an income earner dies, their needs should be divided into three different income periods:

- **Family dependency period**—The first period is called the *family dependency period* because the surviving spouse will have children to support during this time, which means the family's income needs will be greatest during this period.
- **Preretirement period**—When the children are no longer dependent on the surviving spouse, he enters the *preretirement period*. Because the surviving spouse only qualifies for Social Security survivor benefits when he has dependent children in his care or after reaching age 60, this period is also referred to as the blackout period. Usually, the surviving spouse's income needs lessen during this period.
- **Retirement period**—The final period is called the *retirement period*. During this period, the surviving spouse's working income ceases and his Social Security and outside retirement benefits begin. Because the surviving spouse's standard of living does not lessen, he will require an income comparable to the preretirement period during this time.

6. 2. 6 Capital Conservation and Capital Liquidation

There are two methods used to calculate the amount of life insurance needed to supply an individual or family with the desired amount of capital to generate income if an income earner should die prematurely. **Capital conservation** (sometimes called capital retention) and **capital liquidation** (sometimes called capital utilization) differ in how capital is used to generate income for the surviving family.

Under the capital conservation method, income is derived only from interest gained on the principal. Under the capital liquidation method, both interest and principal are used to generate income. Generally, this means that a smaller fund is needed when using the capital liquidation method because there is no concern for leaving the principal intact.

Some individuals find the required small fund an attractive feature of the capital liquidation method, but the capital conservation method has two significant advantages.

- It generates income indefinitely. No matter how long the survivor lives, the capital conservation fund remains intact and generates interest. Under capital liquidation, however, the fund generally gets smaller and eventually disappears. Survivors who live longer than expected will outlive their sources of income.

- It creates a legacy. Under capital conservation, when funds are no longer needed, they can be given away to loved ones or charity. Legacies are uncertain under capital liquidation because they depend on the survivor's premature death.

6. 2. 7 Estate Planning

Life insurance also can create an immediate estate for the insured and provide funds that will help preserve the greatest amount of value in the estate. The field of estate planning is very complicated. It requires expertise in the areas of wills, taxes, law, and life insurance. Some of the items to be considered when planning an estate are:

- the needs of the beneficiaries;
- the type and amount of property in the estate;
- how best to administer the estate to fulfill the wishes of the insured;
- the amount of insurance needed to cover expenses and costs;
- how to dispose of any business interest; and
- who will settle and administer the estate.

There are two methods of distributing the estate: inter vivos transfers or testamentary transfers.

Inter vivos transfers are made while the estate owner is still alive. Transfers can be made as:

- gifts;
- trusts; or
- policy ownership under rights of survivorship.

Testamentary transfers are made by will after the death of the estate owner. If the estate owner dies without leaving a will, which is called dying **intestate**, the property will be transferred as an intestate distribution under the laws of the state.

6. 2. 8 Other Sources of Funds

In determining the amount and kind of insurance an applicant needs, the agent must consider other sources of income or benefits the applicant currently has or for which he may be eligible under other insurance plans, government programs (such as Social Security), and retirement plans (e.g., pensions, IRAs, or Keoghs).

These other assets will help in determining the amount and kind of insurance necessary to meet the applicant's current and future needs. For example, Social Security benefits may not pay the retirement benefit a dependent spouse needs before age 65. It is important to remember that there is a period, often called the **blackout period**, after a surviving spouse no longer receives survivor's benefits (after her youngest child is no longer eligible) and before she is eligible for retirement benefits. Other sources of funds to be considered are:

- Medicare;
- Medicaid;
- group retirement plans;
- savings;
- investments;
- other income (e.g., income from property rental);
- annuities; and
- other insurance.

6. 2. 9 Living Benefits

The primary reason to own life insurance is the death benefit—the money the beneficiaries will receive when the insured dies. However, life insurance also can provide benefits for the policyowner while he is living. Let's call them living benefits of life insurance.

The living benefit of the most prevalent type of life insurance is the cash value it accumulates. Throughout the years of premium payments, part of these payments accumulates for the insured as a cash value. This cash accumulation may be used as collateral for policy loans or later as retirement income.

Another type of policy, which we'll study later in the course, provides for withdrawals from the policy's cash value, which can be used to meet emergencies or pay off debts, further meeting the policyowner's needs. Many policies also offer dividends, which we'll study later. For now, however, dividends may be defined as payments to policyowners when the insurance company makes a profit.

So, although not all types of life insurance policies accumulate cash values or make payments to policyowners, you should recognize these living benefits of life insurance:

- Loan values
- Retirement income
- Cash withdrawals
- Dividends

6. 2. 10 Advantages as Property

As we get further into the subject of life insurance, you're soon going to ask yourself why people aren't more eager to buy life insurance if it is such a rational purchase. One of the main reasons people don't come to an insurance producer as they do other types of salespeople is that they don't recognize life insurance for what it is—a type of property.

The problem is that although life insurance is a type of property, it doesn't look like property. To the average individual, it looks like just a piece of paper. In fact, many of the characteristics and advantages of property apply to life insurance.

A life insurance policy's cash value can be used as collateral for borrowing money. Suppose an insured goes to a bank to borrow money. The bank will want to determine the type and amount of property the individual can call on to pay off the loan should his income be suspended. Life insurance can act as collateral or backup property for the loan.

Another advantage of life insurance as property is one you have already learned—it creates an immediate estate.

Suppose a man invests in a piece of land. He may have to wait years and years for that land to appreciate. Its value may never quite reach what he had anticipated. If that man were to die the day after buying the land, whether or not he paid cash for it, his family might have difficulty getting back the money that was put in.

It is not so with life insurance. The instant a life insurance policy goes into effect, the insured policyowner has established a fund that will be paid to his beneficiary—even if only one premium payment has been made. There is no waiting for the property to appreciate in value and no worrying whether the value will actually rise as expected.

There are other advantages to life insurance as property.

- One is the convenience of paying for life insurance in installments. In the case of a $100,000 life insurance policy, the entire premium required to purchase the policy does not have to be paid up front. Rather, it may be paid in installments.
- Safety of principal is of considerable concern to anyone purchasing property. How safe is your money? Is it subject to market fluctuations, depreciation, or other loss? A $100,000 life insurance policy will pay that amount to the beneficiary at the death of the insured as long as premiums are met and there are no outstanding loans against the policy.
- As for return on investment, as we'll see later in the course, life insurance offers plans that can be very advantageous, especially with regard to taxation of cash values.
- Many kinds of property require physical maintenance or upkeep. Houses must be painted, car engines tuned, livestock fed, and so on. Apart from paying premiums, a policyowner has no other obligations with regard to life insurance.
- Finally, managerial care is a frequent concern of property owners. Stocks and bonds, real estate, and similar investments require constant attention with regard to market conditions, taxation, and so on. No managerial care is required of a policyholder toward a life insurance policy.

6. 3 COMPARING INSURANCE POLICIES

Life insurance cost comparison methods are used to compare the cost of one life insurance policy with that of another to guide prospective purchasers to policies that are competitively priced. Although the cost of life insurance depends on an individual's specific circumstances and cash flows experienced under the policy, attempts to estimate costs are useful so that a consumer may consider every factor when making a purchase decision. The comparative interest rate method and the interest-adjusted net cost method are just two of many cost comparison methods used in insurance.

6. 3. 1 Comparative Interest Rate Method

This analysis examines the rate of return that must be earned on a hypothetical side fund in a buy-term-invest-the-difference plan so that the value of the side fund will be exactly equal to the surrender value of the higher-premium policy at a designated point in time. The higher the comparative interest rate (CIR), the less expensive the higher-premium policy relative to the alternative plan. Outlays and death benefits are held equal. The CIR method requires a computer because the final interest rate is found through trial and error.

6. 3. 2 Interest-Adjusted Net Cost Method

This analysis is conducted over a set period and considers a policy's premiums, death benefits, cash values, and dividends, recognizing the accumulated interest over the set period. The NAIC Model Life Insurance Solicitation Regulation requires two interest-adjusted cost indexes for a policy—a surrender cost index and a net payment cost index.

To compare two different policies, it is not enough just to compare premiums. A lower premium does not automatically mean a low-cost policy. Cost indexes have been developed to help in the process of measuring the cost of a policy. These indexes use compound interest factors to produce interest-adjusted cost and payment figures.

Policy illustrations normally include a surrender cost index and a net payment cost index. These indexes show average annual costs and payments per $1,000 of insurance on a basis that recognizes that $1 payable today is worth more than $1 payable in the future. Both assume that the insured will live and pay premiums for a period of years. Most companies provide these index numbers on both a guaranteed and an illustrated basis.

6. 3. 2. 1 Traditional Net Cost Method

This method is also called the **surrender cost index**. There is a complicated formula used to calculate this index, but the basic process works like this. The policy's premiums and dividends are accumulated over a period of years (say 10 or 20) at some assumed annual rate of interest, often 4% or 5%. Then, the total accumulated dividends are added to the cash value at the end of the period (plus any terminal dividends), and this total is subtracted from the accumulated premium payments. In other words, the projected total cash value of the policy at some point in the future is subtracted from the total premium payments to that same point in the future to find out how much the policy costs. This net cost is averaged over the number of years in the period to arrive at the average cost per thousand for a policy that is surrendered for its cash value at the end of the period.

6. 3. 2. 2 Interest-Adjusted Cost Method

This method is also called the **net payment cost index**. This index is developed in the same way, but it does not assume the policy is surrendered at the end of the period. The same formula is used, but the cash value element is omitted. Instead, this index provides an estimate of the policyowner's average annual out-of-pocket net premium outlay, adjusted for time value of money.

Cost indexes can be of significant help to life insurance consumers. It's important, however, to understand that in using cost indexes, the consumer should compare index numbers only for similar kinds of plans and only for the kind of policy for the consumer's age and the amount she intends to buy. Policy features and company service could offset small differences in cost index comparisons. Cost indexes are just one of the many things to be considered when buying the best policy for the premium dollar.

6. 4 USES OF LIFE INSURANCE

6. 4. 1 Personal Uses of Life Insurance

Life insurance is the only financial services product that guarantees a specific sum of money will be available at exactly the time that it is needed. Bank savings accounts, mutual funds, stocks, bonds, and other investments cannot make such a guarantee. The death of the insured creates an instant estate for the benefit of the individual's family. From a personal perspective, life insurance may be used to provide:

- peace of mind and financial security for a family;
- cash for funeral costs and related expenses;
- cash to pay off a home mortgage;
- a college education for surviving children;
- income for a family and surviving spouse;
- cash for emergencies or to supplement retirement;
- a means of maintaining a family's lifestyle;
- funds to preserve an estate and avoid a forced liquidation of capital to pay estate taxes and debts;

- bequests to persons other than family members or to charitable or civic organizations; and
- advance payment of proceeds before death through accelerated benefits or viatical settlements.

If an insured has a terminal illness, a life insurance policy may be her last substantial source of money. The life insurance benefits may be made available for medical expenses and living expenses before death through accelerated benefit provisions or viatical settlement agreements. **Accelerated benefits** are living benefits paid by the insurance company that reduce the remaining death benefit. The government does not consider accelerated death payments to be taxable income, and the policyowner gets 50–95% of the policy's full benefit.

Under a **viatical settlement**, the policyholder sells all rights to the life insurance policy to a viatical settlement company, which advances a percentage (usually 60–80%) of the eventual death benefit. The viatical settlement company then receives the death benefit when the insured ultimately dies. Since 1997, proceeds from viatical settlements and accelerated benefits are not taxable as income. Although accelerated death benefits may require a life expectancy of one year or less, viatical settlements may be available for a person who has up to five years to live.

6. 4. 2 Business Uses of Life Insurance

There are generally three types of business organizations: the sole proprietorship, the partnership, and the corporation. Regardless of business type, a business has the same need as an individual—protection against premature death and the delivery of cash exactly when it is needed.

This cash need relates to the disposition of a business interest upon the death of the sole proprietor, a partner, or a corporate stockholder. Disposition of the deceased's business asset usually means the sale of the business, retention of the business within the family, or liquidation of the business. The difference between a sale and liquidation is that a sale will usually result in the family receiving fair market value for the business interest. Liquidation is a forced sale, which may only bring 10% of the true business value.

In some situations, liquidation of the business is necessary or mandated by law. However, liquidation is the least desirable method of disposing of the deceased's business interest. The sale or retention of the business requires:

- proper planning and implementation of business agreements;
- a willing and competent successor or buyer; and
- cash with which to implement the plan.

6. 4. 2. 1 Key Person Life Insurance

Key person life insurance protects the corporation from the financial loss sustained when a key employee (the owner, for example) dies. In addition to the corporate owner, a key person could be a sales manager, a vice president, or another individual. When a key person dies, the corporation could experience a loss of income, impaired credit standing, and loss of jobs and customers. To offset this financial consequence, the corporation may purchase a life insurance policy on the life of the key person. Some contracts include a **change of insured provision** that allows the employer to change the person insured when there is a change in personnel, without the need to cancel the existing policy and issue a new one.

The corporation would be the owner, premium payor, and beneficiary of the policy. The face amount of the policy would generally relate to the amount of lost corporate income plus the costs of hiring and training a replacement for the deceased key person.

6. 4. 2. 2 Buy-Sell Agreements

A partnership is a legal, nonincorporated business relationship involving two or more individuals who each contribute their unique skills, talents, and capital for the purpose of owning and operating a business enterprise. As a partnership, each partner has unlimited liability with regard to partnership functions. As such, business creditors may claim personal assets for payment of debts.

Generally, by law, when a partner dies, the surviving partner(s) must dissolve the business. The survivor becomes a liquidating trustee and in essence liquidates the business and his own job, as well as eliminates the family's principal source of income. Disposition of the deceased's business asset is required to settle the deceased's estate.

To a large degree, the problems created by the death of a partner can be resolved by means of a properly drawn buy-sell agreement. If there are only two or three partners, a **cross-purchase plan** may be advisable in which each partner is bound by the terms of the plan and agrees to purchase a share of the deceased partner's interest. If there are more than two or three partners, the **entity type plan** is usually recommended, in which the partnership agrees to purchase the interest of a deceased partner.

The key element for partnership planning is the funding of the agreements. Life insurance is the ideal choice that will guarantee that the required amount of money will be delivered exactly when it is needed. A cross-purchase plan covering two partners would require that each partner own, pay the premium, and be the beneficiary of a life insurance policy on the life of the other partner.

If the partnership consisted of six partners, each partner would be the owner of 5 policies for a total of 30 life insurance policies. This is the reason an entity agreement is usually recommended if there are more than two or three partners. Under an entity agreement involving six partners, the partnership would own 6 policies.

The principal advantages of the funded buy-sell agreement include the following.

- A fair market value is established, funded with life insurance, for the benefit of the surviving family.
- Buyers of the partnership interest are predetermined and legally bound by the agreement.

- The partnership and employee's jobs are secure.
- The necessary funding to implement the plan is readily available.

6. 4. 2. 3 *Executive Bonus Plans*

Deferred compensation is an executive benefit that enables a highly paid corporate employee to defer current receipt of income such as an executive bonus and have it paid as compensation at a later date (retirement, death, or disability) when presumably the employee will be in a lower tax bracket. Generally, the employee will enter into an agreement with the employer that specifies the amount of money to be paid, when it will be paid, and the conditions under which the deferred compensation may not be paid.

The agreement will specify that the amount deferred will be paid as a retirement benefit or in the event of the premature death or disability of the employee. It will further indicate that the individual will forfeit the right to this sum of money if he leaves the employer, except for retirement, death, or disability.

The advantage of this agreement for the employee is avoidance of current taxation because receipt of the money is deferred. This is allowed by IRS Section 457. However, there are some disadvantages. Usually, deferred compensation is a nonqualified plan, and as such, it may be funded or unfunded. An unfunded deferred compensation plan is nothing more than an unsecured promise to pay a future benefit. As a funded plan, the assets funding the plan are considered corporate assets and thus subject to the claims of corporate creditors or to other uses by the employer.

The principal advantage for the employer is that the services of the employee are usually secured for life because the employee will forfeit the right to the deferred compensation, except for retirement, death, or disability. In addition, deferred compensation can be viewed as a desirable executive benefit and thus enable the employer to attract and retain key personnel.

Funding for the deferred compensation may be life insurance contracts, disability income policies, annuities, mutual funds, and other sources.

6. 4. 2. 4 *Business Continuation Plan*

A **sole proprietorship** is an unincorporated form of business whereby an individual, using his own special talents and abilities, owns and manages a business. Even though a sole proprietorship may have several employees, it is the sole proprietor who is directly responsible for the success of the business.

The sole proprietor has **unlimited liability** with regard to the business operation. Creditors can claim both the sole proprietor's business assets as well as personal assets. When the sole proprietor dies, the business also dies. This business asset becomes part of the deceased's estate and is commingled with other personal assets subject to taxation, the payment of debts, and claims of creditors.

Generally, the business is the principal asset in the sole proprietor's estate. It is also normally the only source of income for the family. Upon the death of the sole proprietor, family income ceases and, unless adequate planning has occurred, the business may have to be liquidated for a fraction of its value to pay estate settlement costs.

Life insurance can be used to solve the problems created by the death of the sole proprietor. Life insurance may fund a **business continuation agreement** (also known as a **buy-sell agreement**) by providing necessary cash with which to keep the business doors open until possibly the business can be sold at its fair market value for the benefit of the family. Life insurance also can be used to provide funds for a competent employee or other qualified person to purchase the business from the surviving family members.

If the business is to survive the death of the sole proprietor and the family is to be able to maintain its standard of living, adequate planning and the implementation of certain business agreements (such as a business continuation agreement) are necessary. Finally, these plans and agreements must be funded with adequate amounts of life insurance to guarantee that the sole proprietor's financial plans will be realized.

6. 4. 2. 5 Corporate Owned Life Insurance

A corporation is an artificial person. It is a legal entity that is owned by its stockholders. One of the characteristics that distinguish a corporation from the other business forms is that its life is unlimited. When a working stockholder dies, the corporation continues. Another distinguishing characteristic is that stockholders have limited liability. A stockholder's risk is limited to his investment in the corporation. Personal assets are generally safe from the claims of creditors.

Generally, a corporation is a larger business concern than the sole proprietorship or the partnership.

Corporations may be classified as closely held or publicly held. A **close corporation** is typically one that is owned by a few stockholders, often members of the same family. A **publicly owned corporation** may be owned by several thousand stockholders, such as General Motors. This discussion of corporate insurance needs will be limited to the close corporation.

The death of a stockholder in a closely held corporation means the loss of services of this key person and quite possibly loss of business income. However, the most immediate effect will be the loss of income to the deceased's family. The choices available to the family are to sell the deceased's stock, attempt to live off of any dividends the corporation may pay, or assume a working position within the corporation.

Probably, the most desirable alternative is to sell the deceased's stock. Attempting to live on dividend income only will probably not enable the surviving family members to maintain their standard of living for very long. Assuming the surviving spouse has inherited the deceased stockholder's shares, he may not be knowledgeable or competent enough to assume the position of the deceased within the corporation. In addition, the surviving stockholders may not want a new, inexperienced stockholder working in the corporation. Thus, the purchase of the deceased's stock becomes a viable alternative, provided there has been adequate planning and there is cash available for the stock purchase.

Business planning to resolve the problems created by the death of a stockholder involves the implementation of a stock purchase or stock redemption plan. A **stock purchase plan** is similar to a cross-purchase partnership plan in which a price is determined and each stockholder agrees to purchase a proportionate share of the deceased shareholder's stock. The purchase price is naturally funded with life insurance, and each shareholder is the owner, premium payor, and beneficiary of a life policy on the lives of the other stockholders. This arrangement is feasible when there are only a few shareholders.

In situations with several shareholders, the **stock redemption plan** is better. Under a **stock redemption plan**, the corporation is the owner, beneficiary, and premium payor of the life insurance policies and the corporation agrees to purchase the deceased's stock.

The advantages of the life insurance-funded corporate buy-sell plan include:

- the establishment of a fair price for the stock;
- a binding agreement that identifies the buyers;
- security of corporate assets and jobs; and
- guaranteed delivery of the purchase price.

Example

Section 303 stock redemption is a special type of stock redemption that permits a corporation to partially redeem a shareholder's stock for purposes of providing cash to cover estate settlement costs. Tax laws generally require that stock redemptions be total to avoid taxing the proceeds payable to the family as a dividend. The Internal Revenue Service will permit a partial redemption by the corporation to pay funeral expenses, taxes, and related estate settlement costs.

6. 4. 2. 6 Split Dollar Plans

Split-Dollar plans are not actually types of life insurance policies but rather methods of purchasing life insurance. Under a split-dollar arrangement, a plan of permanent life insurance is jointly purchased by the employee and the employer. Permanent life insurance is used because it provides guaranteed cash values.

The employer's share of the premium is an amount equal to the annual increase in the policy's cash value. Accordingly, during the early years of the plan, the employee's cost will be higher than during the later years when the policy will contain higher amounts of cash value and the employer's share of the premium will be greater.

The death benefit is also shared between the employee and the employer in proportion to the amount of the premium each is paying. Usually, the employer is the policyowner and thus has control of the policy, including its cash value.

Split-dollar plans are an attractive benefit whereby a key employee is able to purchase life insurance at an attractive cost because of the joint premium payments.

6. 4. 3 Charitable Uses of Life Insurance

Another use of life insurance is for charitable purposes. In accordance with tax laws, a policyowner may purchase a life insurance contract on his life, pay the premiums, and designate a charitable organization as the beneficiary, such as a church, school, hospital, or similar organization. Generally, the premium paid by the insured donor is tax deductible.

6. 5 SUMMARY

In this lesson, you learned about:

- the costs commonly associated with death;
- two different approaches to needs analysis;
- three income periods a surviving spouse may encounter and the characteristics of each;
- the difference between the capital conservation and capital liquidation methods of determining the amount of life insurance required;
- four living benefits of life insurance;
- the advantages of life insurance as property;
- the traditional net cost method and the interest-adjusted cost method of comparing insurance policy costs;
- the difference between accelerated benefits and viatical settlements and when each might be used; and
- the types of organizations that might use insurance for business reasons and examples of how insurance might be used.

UNIT TEST

1. Which of the following costs are associated with death?
   A. Doctor or hospital bills from a final illness or accident
   B. Paying off debts such as credit cards and other loans
   C. Taxes
   D. All of the above

2. An insurance producer analyzed Bonita's life insurance needs, taking into account Bonita's net annual salary, her expenses, her current age, and depreciation of the dollar over time. This producer was using the
   A. analytical approach to needs analysis
   B. human life value approach to needs analysis
   C. needs approach to needs analysis
   D. planning approach to needs analysis

3. An insurance producer analyzed Dwight's life insurance needs, taking into account the amount of money Dwight anticipated needing for his funeral and the amount of income that would be required to maintain his family's standard of living in the event of his death, including projected college costs and the costs of supporting his spouse. This producer was using the
   A. analytical approach to needs analysis
   B. human life value approach to needs analysis
   C. needs approach to needs analysis
   D. planning approach to needs analysis

4. Wilma's husband died 3 years ago, leaving her with 2 grade school-aged children. Which income period is Wilma in?
   A. Family dependency period
   B. Preretirement period
   C. Retirement period
   D. Grieving period

5. Which of the following is an advantage of life insurance as property?
   A. Life insurance is generally paid for in one lump sum.
   B. Life insurance requires no physical upkeep.
   C. Life insurance requires careful managerial care on the part of the policyholder.
   D. Life insurance has little potential for a positive return on investment.

6. Life insurance proceeds are generally the only source of income for surviving dependents of a breadwinner.
   A. True
   B. False

7. Which of the following factors should NOT be taken into account when a producer makes recommendations as to the amount and type of insurance needed by an individual?
   A. How much premium can the individual afford to pay?
   B. Should the premium be level, increasing, or decreasing?
   C. How much commission does the product offer?
   D. Is the individual insurable?

8. Ana wishes to purchase enough insurance to support her husband for the rest of his life if she should die prematurely and then leave a sizeable inheritance for her children upon his death. Which method should be used to calculate the amount of insurance necessary?
   A. Capital conservation
   B. Capital liquidation
   C. Human life value
   D. Needs analysis

9. The type of estate transfer made while the estate owner is still alive is called a(n)
   A. inter venous transfer
   B. inter vivos transfer
   C. testamentary transfer
   D. trustee transfer

10. The type of estate transfer made after the estate owner dies is called a(n)
    A. inter venous transfer
    B. inter vivos transfer
    C. testamentary transfer
    D. trustee transfer

11. Suki dies without leaving a will. The distribution of her estate will be handled by a(n)
    A. intestate distribution
    B. inter vivos distribution
    C. testamentary distribution
    D. vivos testate distribution

12. Ken has terminal cancer and wants to access the death benefit of his life insurance policy to pay medical expenses. How might he be able to do this?
    A. He won't be able to access the policy funds until after his death.
    B. He may access the funds through accelerated benefits.
    C. He may access the funds through a viatical settlement.
    D. He may access the funds either through a viatical settlement or by use of the accelerated benefits provision.

13. Shane is a master carpenter in business for himself. His business is probably operated as a
    A. corporation
    B. sole proprietorship
    C. partnership
    D. limited liability company

14. Which of the following is NOT financed using life insurance?
    A. Buy-sell agreement
    B. Section 303 stock redemption
    C. Cross-purchase agreement
    D. Split-dollar plan

ANSWERS AND RATIONALES TO UNIT TEST

1. **D.** All of these costs are associated with death.
2. **B.**
3. **C.** This is an example of the needs approach because it focuses on the financial needs that will arise as a result of Dwight's death.
4. **A.** Wilma is in the family dependency period because she still has children to support.
5. **B.**
6. **B.** Surviving dependents are often entitled to benefits from retirement plans and government programs such as Social Security.
7. **C.**
8. **A.** The capital conservation method should be used to calculate the amount of insurance needed because of the concern to leave the principal intact for her children.
9. **B.** The type of estate transfer made while the estate owner is still alive is called an inter vivos transfer.
10. **C.** The type of estate transfer made after the estate owner dies is called a testamentary transfer.
11. **A.** Suki's estate will be handled by an intestate distribution.
12. **D.** Ken may access the funds either through a viatical settlement or by use of the accelerated benefits provision.
13. **B.** Shane probably operates his business as a sole proprietorship.
14. **D.** A split-dollar plan is not financed using life insurance.

UNIT

7

Policy Issuance and Delivery

7.1 LEARNING OBJECTIVES

After completing this lesson, you will be able to:

- list two important reasons for the potential insured to pay the premium at the time of initial application;
- list three types of receipt and explain the differences among them;
- describe the reasons for creating a temporary insurance agreement;
- explain what happens when a potential insured dies between the application and issuance of the policy and how that changes depending on the type of receipt issued;
- list three ways a life insurance policy may be issued;
- explain the importance of personally delivering life insurance policies when issued and what the producer should explain during the delivery;
- define replacement and explain when it is and is not appropriate;
- list duties commonly required of producers when replacing insurance;
- list duties commonly required of insurers when replacing insurance; and
- explain the importance of policy retention.

7.2 COLLECTION OF PREMIUM

The producer is encouraged to collect the initial premium with the application. Evidence shows that this procedure is most effective in having the insured accept the policy when it is issued. If the insured does not pay the initial premium at the time of application, chances increase that he will not accept the issued policy. Also a point that the producer can make to the applicant is that if the applicant waits to pay the premium, he may become uninsurable or may die before the policy takes effect. Remember, the policy is effective only after the initial premium has been paid.

When the initial premium is not paid with the application, no contract is in force. The applicant is not making an offer to the insurer. He is merely inviting the insurer to make an offer by issuing the policy. Because there is no insurance in force under these circumstances, when the producer delivers the policy and collects the initial premium, there may be additional underwriting requirements to be satisfied. Most commonly, the insurance company may require that the insured sign a health statement verifying that no change in health has occurred since the date of the application.

7. 3 RECEIPTS

Once the underwriting process is complete and the applicant has been approved, the life insurance policy will be issued by the insurance company. The coverage is not effective until the policy is delivered and the initial premium has been paid. Usually the applicant will pay the initial premium with the application. When this occurs, the producer will provide the applicant with a receipt for the initial premium and the effective date of coverage will depend on the type of receipt issued.

7. 3. 1 Conditional Receipt

Once the producer has completed the application, it is normal to collect the first full premium from the policyowner. The receipt for this premium is generally a **conditional receipt**. The receipt is conditional because the producer cannot guarantee that the policy will be issued. The conditional receipt explains to the proposed insured that the policy will be issued subject to the approval of the insurance company.

According to the conditional receipt, if the proposed insured should die before the policy is issued, one of the following will occur.

- The proceeds will be paid to the beneficiary named in the policy if the company would have issued the policy to the proposed insured if he had been living.
- The proceeds will not be paid to the policy's beneficiary if the company would not have issued the policy. Instead, the premium will be returned.

Example

An applicant has paid the initial premium and completed and signed the application. The producer provides the applicant with a conditional receipt, which basically states that the applicant is covered as of the date of the application (or receipt) provided he is insurable as a standard risk. Thus, if the applicant were to die before the policy was issued, the beneficiary would receive the face amount of the policy.

On the other hand, if the applicant was found to be a substandard risk, the conditional receipt would be null and void and no coverage would be effective until the substandard policy was delivered and additional premium was paid. If the policy is not issued as applied for (a substandard rating, for example), no coverage would be in force until the applicant accepted the substandard policy and paid the additional premium required by the rating.

This receipt makes the coverage effective on the date of the application if the applicant is found to be insurable under the company's general underwriting rules in effect at the time of application. However, some conditional receipts make coverage effective on the date of application or the date of the medical examination, whichever is later.

7. 3. 1. 1 Statement of Good Health

In many cases, the initial premium is not paid until the policy is delivered. In these instances, most insurers require that when the agent collects the premium, he must also obtain a statement signed by the insured attesting to the insured's continued good health before leaving the policy with the insured.

The agent submits the signed statement and the initial premium to the insurer. The purpose of this requirement is to make sure that the insured has remained in good health during the underwriting period.

7. 3. 2 Binding Receipt

A few companies use an **unconditional** or **binding receipt** that makes the company liable for the risk from the date of application. This coverage lasts for a specified time or until the insurer issues the policy or notifies the applicant that the policy is being refused. The specified time limit is usually 30 to 60 days.

With a binding receipt, regardless of the applicant's insurability, he is covered following completion of the application and the payment of the initial premium and remains covered for the length of the specified term or until notified of refusal. This type of receipt is rarely used for life insurance policies, though it is commonly used for auto or homeowners insurance.

7. 3. 3 Inspection Receipt

Occasionally, a situation will arise where the proposed insured wants to examine the policy carefully before actually purchasing it. In this situation, the policyowner does not pay the first full premium at the time the application is completed. The policyowner signs an inspection receipt for the policy, examines the policy, and then pays the first full premium.

7. 3. 4 Temporary Insurance Agreement

This type of receipt or agreement provides the applicant with immediate life insurance coverage while the underwriting process is taking place, whether or not the individual is insurable. In this instance, the insurance protection applied for becomes effective immediately, within the limitations stated in the temporary insurance agreement or receipt.

The insurer has the right to cancel this coverage if the applicant fails to meet the company's normal underwriting requirements. However, claims incurred during the underwriting period will be paid in line with the terms of the receipt, whether or not the application ultimately would have been approved.

Example

An applicant submits the initial premium and application and is provided with a temporary insurance agreement that states that coverage is effective immediately and will continue during the underwriting process. If the applicant should die during this period, the coverage is in force regardless of the individual's insurability or risk classification as a result of the underwriting process.

7. 3. 5 Amendments

The insurer may amend the policy's terms depending on the results of the underwriting process. The insurer may, for instance, amend the policy to exclude certain losses or conditions, or it may classify the applicant as a substandard risk for which it will charge a higher premium. The applicant is not obligated to accept the amended policy, however, and may withdraw his application.

7. 4 SUBMITTING THE APPLICATION AND INITIAL PREMIUM

It is important for the producer to submit the application, initial premium, and any questionnaires or other forms to the home office underwriter promptly. The producer should review all forms for completeness and be sure that they are properly signed. Not only does this make for good relationships with the home office underwriter, but it is extremely important to the applicant. Unnecessary delays in issuing the policy can cause the applicant undue anxiety and result in a loss of confidence in the producer.

Because producers are handling money belonging to their clients, it is extremely important that an accurate record of such transactions be kept. It is also wise for the producer to keep copies of applications and other information. This avoids unnecessary delay or other problems if the originals are lost.

7. 4. 1 Issuing the Policy

A life insurance policy may be issued as applied for, modified, or even amended if the applicant meets the underwriting standards of the insurance company. Although uncommon, an insurer may issue a waiver with the policy that states that death by a particular event will not be covered. This might be done if the insured had a particularly hazardous occupation or hobby. More commonly, an insurer might issue a more limited form of policy or at lower limits than that applied for.

7. 5 DELIVERING AND SERVICING THE POLICY

7. 5. 1 Personal Delivery

Delivery is necessary to complete the sale of a life insurance policy, so the best way to ensure delivery is to do it in person. If a conditional receipt has not been issued, the insurer may require the producer to obtain a statement of good health at the time of policy delivery.

In addition to knowing the policy has been delivered, this method also gives the producer an opportunity to:

- thoroughly explain all coverage provisions, exclusions, and riders to the applicant/policyowner (although most policies contain a provision barring a producer from changing the policy contract in any way, the company may be liable for errors made by the producer if the producer incorrectly represents the policy being sold; it is important for the producer to sit down with the insured at the time of policy delivery and explain all policy provisions, particularly the exclusions and any riders that may restrict the coverage given in the policy);
- review the purpose of the policy and how it fits into the policyowner's total life insurance plan;
- reinforce the relationship and good will established with the client;
- allow the producer to explain the possible need for additional coverage; and
- ask the insured for referrals under favorable circumstances.

7. 5. 2 Mailing the Policy

Legally, the policy is considered delivered when it is mailed or turned over to the policyowner or someone acting on his behalf. Some companies do mail policies directly to policyowners. However, many prefer to have the producer make a personal delivery.

In some cases, a **constructive delivery** is deemed to occur when the insurer mails a policy to its producer for actual delivery to the policyowner because the insurer has issued the policy and released it for delivery. However, a legal delivery has not yet occurred if the insurer requires personal delivery for verification of good health at the time of delivery or if the policy is being provided to the applicant merely to review and inspect at that time and not necessarily to buy.

7. 5. 3 Policy Review

Once the policy is delivered to the policyowner, the producer should thoroughly explain all coverage provisions, particularly the exclusions, and any riders that may restrict the coverage given in the policy. This also allows the producer the opportunity to review the purpose of the policy and how it fits into the policyowner's total life insurance plan.

7. 5. 4 Effective Date of Coverage

An important question that must be addressed in any life insurance sale is: When does the policy become effective? The effective date is important for two reasons: Not only does it identify when the coverage is effective, it establishes the date by which future annual premiums must be paid as well.

If a receipt (either conditional or binding) was issued in exchange for the payment of an initial premium deposit, the date of the receipt will generally be noted as the policy effective date in the contract.

If a premium deposit is not given with the application, the policy effective date is usually left to the discretion of the insurer. Often, it will be the date the policy is issued by the insurance company. However, the policy will not be truly effective until it is delivered to the applicant, the first premium is paid and a Statement of Continued Good Health is obtained.

7. 5. 5 Policy Summary

The policy summary addresses the specific product being presented for sale. It identifies the agent, the insurer, the policy, and each rider. It includes information about premiums, dividends, benefit amounts, cash surrender values, policy loan interest rates, and life insurance cost indexes of the specific policy being considered.

7. 5. 6 Buyer's Guide

An agent is required to deliver to the applicant a *Life Insurance Buyer's Guide* and a *Policy Summary*. These documents are usually delivered before the agent accepts the applicant's initial premium. Typically, the buyer's guide is a generic publication that explains life insurance in a way that average consumers can understand. It speaks of the concept in general, and does not address the specific product or policy being considered.

7. 6 HANDLING A CLAIM

A claim and its payment are the end result of the insurance process. With respect to life insurance, it means the insured has died and the beneficiary stands ready to collect from the insurer what is due. Unlike property or casualty insurance, claims made on a life insurance policy are rarely negotiated. They are either paid or denied. When proof of the death of the insured arrives at the insurer's claims department, the records are checked to make sure the policy was in force at the time of death and that the person to whom the policy proceeds are to be paid is indeed the rightful beneficiary.

7. 6. 1 Payment of Claims

When an insured dies, the life insurance company should be notified as soon as possible. In many cases, the family of the deceased is too grief stricken and shocked even to think about such matters as notifying the insurer. It is the producer's responsibility, in such a case, to make sure that the company is notified of the claim at the earliest possible moment.

Once a company has been given the proper forms, there is usually little or no delay in payment of the claim, especially when it is obvious that the claim is valid—the policy is in force, the beneficiary is available, there is no evidence of suicide within the limitations of the suicide clause, and so on. When an insurer is notified of a valid claim, the claim will be paid in very short order, usually within a few days.

Goodwill is one of the life insurance industry's most valuable selling tools. This is one of the many reasons most life insurance companies pay a valid death claim as soon as possible after they receive the proper notification and proof of death.

In most jurisdictions, life insurance companies are required to pay death claims within a specified period after proper notification of such claims is received. This period is usually two months (60 days).

If there is a delay in a death claim payment, the usual reason is that the company has not been properly notified of the insured's death. A formal proof of death form of some type is usually required by the company, in addition to a death certificate completed by the attending physician or the coroner. When an insured dies, the agent should complete any proof of death form the company requires, have it signed by the necessary parties, and forward it to the company as soon as possible along with a death certificate.

7. 6. 2 Payment Less than Face Amount

In property or casualty insurance, the amount of claims paid is often less than the face amount of the policy. In contrast, life insurance is generally paid for the full face amount of the policy. There are three exceptions.

The first exception is when there is an outstanding loan against the cash value of a policy. The amount of the loan, plus any interest outstanding, is deducted from the face amount of the policy before payment is made to the beneficiary.

The second exception is when a premium payment is due. With insurance premiums, as with many other types of bills, there is a grace period of somewhere between a week and a month after the due date but before the policy expires. If the insured dies within this grace period, the amount of premium due is deducted from the face amount of the policy before payment is made to the beneficiary.

The third exception happens when there is an error made in determining the age or gender of the insured when the policy was issued. If such an error is discovered at the time of death, the insurance company will compute the face amount that the premium would have purchased if the accurate information was used and pay that amount to the beneficiary.

Such errors are not an unusual occurrence in the life insurance business. Some are intentional, but most are simply mistakes. In either event, the discrepancy is not material enough to void the policy.

Each of these exceptions is explained in more detail later in this text. For now, just remember that unless one of these three exceptions applies, the full face amount of the policy is paid.

7. 6. 3 Producer Responsibilities Upon Insured's Death

When the producer is made aware of an insured's death, the first task is to notify the company immediately. On occasion, a beneficiary, the beneficiary's legal representative, or an heir of the deceased will notify the company directly of the insured's death. In these instances, the company will then contact the producer or will advise the beneficiary to do so.

Next, the producer should contact the person designated to receive proceeds of the policy or that person's legal representative. In other words, the producer should contact the beneficiary (or the beneficiary's legal representative).

As you've learned, the company will require a completed form of some type that serves as official proof of the insured's death. The producer should help the beneficiary complete a proof of death form and send it to the company along with a death certificate.

Most of the information on the proof of death form can be obtained without actually questioning the distraught family members of a deceased insured. The producer should personally complete the form and then take it to the beneficiary for signing.

When an insured dies, he often may have been insured by more than one company. Therefore, the producer may be meeting one or more producers from other companies when attempting to settle a death claim.

The important thing at this point is to render the best possible service to the beneficiary. So, when dealing with producers from other companies at the time of a death claim, the producer should cooperate fully with any other insurers' representatives.

As you know, life insurance policy proceeds can be taken in forms other than cash. The insured can indicate when buying the policy which settlement option should prevail upon death, or it may be left up to the beneficiary as to which option to select. Even if the insured had chosen an option, the right to change it to another one may have been given to the beneficiary.

If the insured chose a particular settlement option at the time the policy was bought, this option should be explained to the beneficiary. The logical person to explain this settlement option is the producer, who is on hand to answer questions and give a detailed explanation of the option.

The insured may have chosen a particular settlement option at the time the policy was purchased but, realizing how needs change over the years, may have given the beneficiary the right to change it. Alternatively, the insured may not have selected a settlement option at all. In this case, it is entirely up to the beneficiary. In either situation, the producer explains all of the available options to the beneficiary.

7. 7 REPLACEMENT

Replacement is the purchase of one life insurance policy to replace another. Because of the cash values that can build up in a policy and the favorable loan interest rates in older policies, replacement can be disadvantageous to consumers. However, there are good reasons to replace a policy, particularly if it does not meet the current needs of the consumer.

Commissions paid to producers for selling a new policy are particularly lucrative. For this reason, unscrupulous producers have persuaded consumers to give up old policies for new ones, even if it was not in the best interests of the policyholder.

When replacement of life insurance is involved, the producer must comply with all pertinent federal and state regulations. Each state has rules and regulations regarding replacement of life insurance products that are designed to protect the interests of the insuring public. Frequently, it is not in the best interests of the insured to replace existing life insurance with a new policy. There are many reasons for this.

- New insurance requires the applicant to prove insurability.
- Premiums may be higher for a new policy.
- New policy provisions will have to be complied with, such as a new incontestable period.
- The existing policy's provisions may be more liberal than a new policy's provisions.
- Generally, a new policy will not have current cash values.

The National Association of Insurance Commissioners (NAIC) has adopted a Model Life Insurance Replacement Regulation. The majority of states have replacement regulations based on this model.

7. 7. 1 Duties of Producers

Replacement means any transaction in which new life insurance or a new annuity is to be purchased, and it is known, or should reasonably be known, that as part of the transaction, existing life insurance or annuities will be:

- lapsed, forfeited, surrendered, or terminated;
- converted to reduced paid-up insurance, continued as extended term insurance, or reduced in value by the use of nonforfeiture benefits or other policy values;
- amended to produce a reduction in the benefits or in the term for which coverage would otherwise remain in force or for which benefits would be paid; or
- reissued with reduction in cash value.

Generally, the duties of the producer include obtaining, along with the application, a signed statement from the applicant as to whether insurance is to be replaced and submitting the statement to the insurer.

If replacement is involved, the producer is required to:

- list all existing life insurance policies to be replaced;
- give the applicant a completed Comparison Statement, signed by the producer, and a Notice to Applicants Regarding Replacement of Life Insurance (a copy of the forms should be left with the applicant); and

- give the insurer a copy of any proposals made and a copy of the Comparison Statement with the name of the insurer that is to be replaced.

The producer must take special care when replacing an existing policy with a new policy to make sure that the insured is not misled into purchasing a policy that is to the insured's disadvantage. The producer also needs to be aware of his own errors and omissions liability, particularly in the area of replacement.

7. 7. 2 Duties of the Insurer

The duties of the replacing insurer include the following:

- Making sure that all replacement actions are in compliance with state regulations
- Notifying each insurer whose insurance is being replaced and, upon request, furnishing a copy of any proposal and Comparison Statement
- Maintaining copies of proposals, receipts, and Comparison Statements

Each individual state has established time limits for the performance of duties. You should check your state's regulations to learn specific time limits, such as the following:

- The time within which a producer must supply the applicant with a Comparison Statement
- The time and manner within which the producer must notify the insurer of replacement activities
- The time within which the insurer must notify the insurer being replaced that such action is in operation
- The time within which the insurer being replaced must respond to the replacing insurer and the applicant

Also, individual state law specifically outlines the method in which records are to be maintained and the length of time the records are to be made available. A common wording for laws on recordkeeping is as follows: *These records shall be maintained for at least (three years) or until the next examination of the company by the Insurance Department.*

7. 8 POLICY RETENTION

Although much of the business of the producer is involved in attracting potential clients, retaining the account and servicing it through the years is very important as well.

The producer becomes involved with the client after original application and delivery at times of change. The client's needs change at such times as marriage, the birth of a child, and death. The producer acts as the representative of the company in changing beneficiaries when desired, adding amounts of insurance, and facilitating payment of claims. The effectiveness of the producer at these times will lead to retention of the account for the lifetime of the client and often over generations.

7. 9 PROFESSIONALISM AND ETHICS

All business transactions are based to a certain extent on trust. When it comes to life insurance, the trust factor is especially significant. When asked what factors matter most in a financial advisor, consumers choose ethical performance more than twice as often as financial performance. Ethics and professionalism are critical components of a successful career as an insurance producer.

Ethics means setting a standard of conduct or behavior based on established values. Insurance producers and other industry employees have long sought to distinguish themselves as professionals. A **professional** is defined as a person in an occupation requiring an advanced level of training, knowledge, or skill. Professionals enjoy privileges commensurate with their skills, but they also have higher responsibilities in caring for others because of the title of professional. Professionals relate to their clients in a way that reflects well on the entire industry. The highest standard of service is provided by preparing for a new client long before even meeting him.

7. 9. 1 Fiduciary Responsibility

Insurance producers have a **fiduciary** duty to just about any person or organization that they come into contact with as a part of the day-to-day business of transacting insurance. By definition, a **fiduciary** is a person in a position of financial trust. Attorneys, accountants, trust officers, and insurance producers are all considered fiduciaries.

As a fiduciary, the producer has an obligation to act in the best interest of the insured. The producer must be knowledgeable about the features and provisions of various insurance policies as well as know the use of these insurance contracts. The producer must be able to explain the important features of these policies of the insured. The producer must recognize the importance of dealing with the general public's financial needs and problems and offering solutions to these problems through the purchase of insurance products.

As a fiduciary, the producer must know and comply with the state's insurance laws. Many of these laws are for consumer protection. It is the producer's duty to comply with these laws and protect the interest of the insured at all times.

7. 9. 2 Summary of the Producer's Responsibilities

The insurance producer is a key person in the process of marketing, underwriting, and delivering of insurance policies. As a marketing representative of the insurer, it is the producer's responsibility to represent and market the insurer's products in an ethical and professional manner. This requires knowledge of various insurance products, awareness of a prospect's insurance needs and problems, and the ability to solve these needs with the proper insurance products.

The producer also has a responsibility to be aware of insurance laws that pertain to the marketing of insurance products, such as state-required standards for advertising and sales literature. Generally, all advertising, sales presentations, and illustrations must be truthful and may not misrepresent or omit material information.

As part of the underwriting process, the producer is the primary source of underwriting information. It is the producer's duty to accurately and thoroughly complete all applications for insurance, collect initial premiums, and promptly submit them to the company. In addition, the producer is responsible for providing the insurance applicant with privacy notices and information, such as the Notice of Insurance Information Practices, as well as necessary receipts for the initial premium collected.

Another objective of the producer as a field underwriter is to help protect the insurer from adverse risks. If an applicant is substandard, the producer is responsible for delivering the substandard policy and explaining its limitations and/or extra premium to the applicant.

7. 10 SUMMARY

In this lesson, you learned about:

- the importance for the potential insured to pay the premium at the time of initial application;
- three types of receipt and the differences among them;
- the reasons for creating a temporary insurance agreement;
- what happens when a potential insured dies between the application and issuance of the policy and how that changes depending on the type of receipt issued;
- three ways a life insurance policy may be issued;
- the importance of personally delivering life insurance policies when issued and what the producer should explain during the delivery;
- replacement and when it is and is not appropriate;
- the duties commonly required of producers when replacing insurance;
- the duties commonly required of insurers when replacing insurance; and
- the importance of policy retention.

UNIT TEST

1. Alice decides to buy a policy. She pays the first premium; the producer issues a receipt and tells her that she is covered immediately, until she is notified that the policy is either issued or declined. What kind of receipt has Alice received?
   A. Conditional receipt
   B. Binding receipt
   C. Inspection receipt
   D. Premium receipt

2. Brenda decides that she wants to buy a policy. She fills out the application but does not pay the initial premium. What kind of receipt will Brenda receive?
   A. Conditional receipt
   B. Binding receipt
   C. Inspection receipt
   D. Premium receipt

3. Camille decides to buy a policy. She pays the first premium, and the producer issues a receipt and tells her that she is covered immediately, unless the company decides she would have been a substandard risk. What kind of receipt did Camille receive?
   A. Conditional receipt
   B. Binding receipt
   C. Inspection receipt
   D. Premium receipt

4. Which kind of receipt is most commonly used in life insurance?
   A. Conditional receipt
   B. Binding receipt
   C. Inspection receipt
   D. Premium receipt

5. Insurers sometimes require personal delivery so that the
   A. producer has another opportunity to sell policies
   B. producer can verify the insured's good health at the time of delivery
   C. insurer can save mailing costs of delivering the policies
   D. first premium may be collected

6. If payment of a valid death claim is delayed, what is the usual reason?
   A. A dispute over the validity of the claim
   B. A dispute over the amount of the claim
   C. The insurer has not received proper notification of the death
   D. The insurer has not received proper notification of the policy

7. Lee applies for a policy, pays the initial premium, and receives a conditional receipt on March 14. On March 15, he passes the medical exam with flying colors. On March 16, an undiagnosed brain aneurysm bursts, killing Lee instantly. On March 17, the insurer receives the results of the medical exam, which includes no information about the aneurysm. On March 19, the insurer receives the notice of claim. The insurer will
   A. pay the claim
   B. return the premium
   C. pay the claim plus the amount of the first premium
   D. pay the claim minus a processing fee

8. Rich applies for a policy, pays the initial premium, and receives a binding receipt on Friday, September 1. On Monday, September 4, the underwriting department decides not to issue the policy and places the file in a pile for notification letters to be sent out at the end of the week. On Wednesday, September 6, Rich is killed in an auto accident. On Thursday, September 7, the insurer receives the notice of claim. The insurer will
   A. return the premium and not pay the claim because the underwriting decision had been made.
   B. return the premium and not pay the claim because death occurred before the policy was issued.
   C. pay the claim because a binding receipt ensures coverage until the potential insured is notified of a rejection.
   D. pay the claim because any receipt assures coverage until the potential insured is notified of a rejection.

9. Brit purchases a policy and tells the producer he wants immediate coverage, regardless of what the underwriting outcome is. To meet Brit's demand, the producer most likely will
   A. accept the premium and set up a temporary insurance agreement
   B. accept the premium and issue an inspection receipt
   C. accept the premium and issue a binding receipt
   D. accept the premium and issue a conditional receipt

10. A policy may be issued in all of the following ways EXCEPT
    A. as applied for
    B. as a modified or amended policy
    C. as an exchange policy, covering someone other than the original applicant
    D. with a waiver excluding death by a certain cause

11. Which of the following statements describes the best use of a producer's time when personally delivering the policy?
    A. Mr. Jones delivers a policy and makes a special point of finding out how the insured's son performed in the gymnastics competition.
    B. Ms. King delivers a policy and reiterates the same sales pitch she used to make the initial sale.
    C. Mrs. Ritley delivers a policy and restates the advantages of the policy and how it can be amended to meet future insurance needs.
    D. Mr. Bourne delivers a policy early in the morning, before the client is home, so that he can simply leave the policy in the mailbox.

12. Which of the following statements is NOT true?
    A. Replacement is illegal.
    B. Replacement is the purchase of one life insurance policy to replace another.
    C. Replacement laws are designed to protect the interests of life insurance purchasers.
    D. Replacement laws concern themselves with the use of false and misleading statements used in the sale of insurance.

ANSWERS AND RATIONALES TO UNIT TEST

1. **B.**
2. **C.** An inspection receipt is used when the applicant wants to inspect the policy before actually purchasing it.
3. **A.** This is a conditional receipt because Camille is covered conditionally. The receipt makes coverage effective on the date of the application if the insurer finds that Camille is insurable under the insurer's general underwriting rules.
4. **A.** Conditional receipts are the type most commonly used in life insurance transactions.
5. **B.** The insurer may require personal delivery so the producer can verify the insured's good health at the time of delivery, especially if a conditional receipt was issued.
6. **C.** Most insurance companies pay death claims as soon as possible after they receive proper notification and proof of death. If there is a delay, the usual reason is that the company has not received proper notification.
7. **A.**
8. **C.** The insurer will pay the claim because a binding receipt ensures coverage until the potential insured is notified of a rejection.
9. **A.** To meet Brit's demand, the producer most likely will accept the premium and set up a temporary insurance agreement.
10. **C.** A policy cannot be issued as an exchange policy, covering someone other than the original applicant.
11. **C.** When a producer delivers a policy personally, he should restate the advantages of the policy and tell the policyowner how the policy can be amended to meet future insurance needs.
12. **A.** Replacement is legal.

UNIT

8

Types of Life Insurance Policies

8. 1 LEARNING OBJECTIVES

After completing this lesson, you will be able to:

- describe the various types of insurance policies, including term insurance, whole life insurance, and various types of flexible policies;
- explain the death benefits for various types of insurance policies;
- describe industrial life insurance, home service life insurance, credit life insurance, and the various kinds of specialized policies; and
- describe viatical settlements and how they work.

8. 2 INTRODUCTION

All life insurance provides a death benefit. This benefit is easy to understand and universal. The living benefits, such as loan values, retirement income, and cash withdrawals, set certain life insurance policies apart from others. These additional benefits add to the enormous versatility life insurance has to meet a wide variety of needs.

Life insurance can be structured to provide:

- a guaranteed death benefit only, using term insurance;
- a guaranteed death benefit plus cash accumulation, using one of many types of permanent insurance;
- a guaranteed death benefit plus premium flexibility, using universal life;
- a guaranteed death benefit plus premium and investment flexibility, using variable or variable universal life; and
- liquidity for estates, using survivorship life.

8. 3 TERM INSURANCE

Term insurance is designed to provide life insurance protection for a limited time. It might be for 1 year or 10 years, but the face amount of the policy is payable only if the insured dies during the time specified in the policy. If the insured survives the limited term of the policy, the insurance company has fulfilled its part of the contract and no payment or refund is due.

Term insurance can be compared to a fire policy on a home. The fire policy is purchased to protect the homeowner from financial loss. However, if the home does not suffer a fire loss, the homeowner's premium is not returned. The homeowner had the peace of mind that comes with insurance protection but no cash value accumulation or refund.

8. 3. 1 Characteristics of Term Policies

The premiums for a term policy are usually level over the length, or term, of the policy. At the end of the policy, the policyowner must purchase another policy or allow the insurance protection to lapse. The new policy almost always requires a higher premium than the expired policy. This new, higher premium will then be in effect for the length of the new term, after which the process begins again.

Term policies are defined by the way the **face amount** of the policy changes throughout the life of the policy. The **face amount**, or **face value**, of the policy is the amount of money listed on the face page (first page) of the policy. This is the amount that will be paid in the event of the insured's death.

8. 3. 2 Types of Term Policies

8. 3. 2. 1 Renewable Term

A **renewable term policy** is one that may be renewed at the end of the specified period for another term period without evidence of insurability. Thus, a one-year renewable term policy expires after one year but is renewable for additional one-year periods. A five-year renewable term policy can be renewed for subsequent five-year periods. Renewability may be limited to a certain number of renewals or to a specified age.

The renewable feature must be written into the original policy at the time of purchase. Once it's there, the renewability feature guarantees that the policyowner will be able to purchase another policy just like the present one when the present policy expires.

When a renewable term policy is being renewed, however, the rates will be based on the age the insured has reached at the time of renewal. This is why premiums for renewable term coverage are often called step-rate premiums.

Step-Rate Premiums in Renewable Term

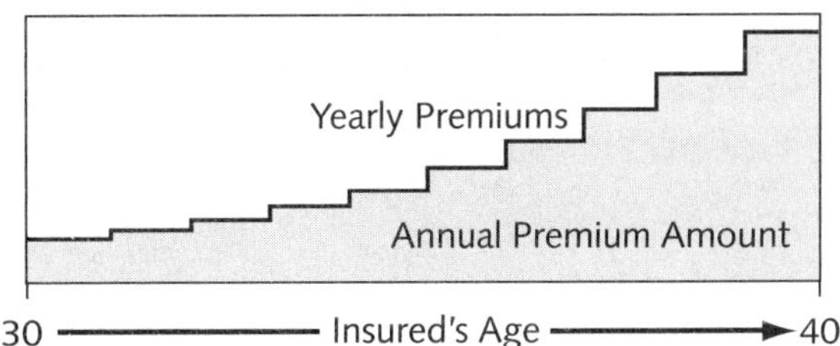

8. 3. 2. 2 Convertible Term

A **convertible term** policy allows the policyowner to convert or exchange the temporary protection for permanent protection without evidence of insurability. Usually, this conversion feature is used to convert term insurance to some form of whole life insurance. If the conversion privilege is exercised, it will be at attained age, meaning the premium paid for the new policy will be the insured's age at the time of conversion.

At the time conversion to permanent insurance is made, the insured generally has a choice of two ages:

- Present age, called attained age
- Age at the time the original term policy was purchased, called original age

Premium amounts depend to some extent on the age of the insured. If the insured converts to permanent insurance using original age, the premiums will be lower than if attained age is used.

When using original age, the policyowner must pay an additional sum, usually consisting of the difference between the lower term premiums over the years and the higher premiums she would have been paying if the permanent protection had been bought originally. The policyowner is also required to pay the interest that the insurance company could have earned on those higher premiums if it had invested them for those extra years.

By paying the difference in back premiums and interest, the policyowner is building an accumulated value in the policy much more quickly than if she simply began paying the higher premiums as for the attained age. The cash value will be well on its way to a meaningful amount.

Some life insurance companies place a time limit on the conversion privilege. This limit is usually based on the expiration date of the original term policy. The number of years excluded from the conversion privilege on a convertible term policy varies from company to company. For instance, some companies state that the policy must be converted as much as five years before expiration of the original policy, after which point the right to convert is lost.

8. 3. 2. 3 Reentry Term

A **reentry option** (also known as **reissue**) is also a common feature of term policies. This option gives the insured the opportunity to provide evidence of insurability at the end of the term to qualify to renew the policy at a lower premium rate than the guaranteed rate available without evidence of insurability. Essentially, the renewing insured is reviewed as a new applicant for term insurance.

8. 3. 2. 4 Level Term

Level term provides a level death benefit and level premium during the policy term. For example, if an individual purchases a 10-year term policy with a face amount of $100,000, both the premium and the face amount will remain constant for the entire 10-year period.

Assuming the level term policy is issued as renewable and convertible, every time the policy renews for a subsequent term period, the policy's premium will increase because of the increased age of the insured.

Example

An insured has purchased $50,000 of one-year renewable and convertible term insurance. Each year the policy is renewed at the same face amount by the payment of the new, higher premium. A new application is not required nor is a new policy issued. The only thing that changes is the age of the insured and subsequently the policy's premium.

8. 3. 2. 5 Decreasing Term

Decreasing term is also temporary protection for a specified period. The face amount decreases throughout the life of the policy to zero at the date of policy expiration. The annual premium for a decreasing term policy remains level during the term of the policy. A common use for decreasing term insurance is to cover a home mortgage. The policy amount decreases each year at the same rate as the balance on the mortgage.

Decreasing term is usually written as convertible but generally is not renewable at the end of the term period. The convertible feature allows the policyowner to convert to permanent insurance usually at any point during the decreasing term of the policy for the available amount of insurance at that point in time.

8. 3. 2. 6 Increasing Term

Increasing term is another type of term insurance that is not used as often as level or decreasing term. Increasing term is basically the opposite of decreasing term. The death benefit increases over the life of the policy, and the premium remains level.

8. 3. 2. 7 Interim Term

When a person wants immediate protection and is thinking of starting a permanent insurance policy in the near future, interim term may be used to cover the period before permanent protection is to begin. Many companies write interim term on an automatically convertible basis—that is, they provide the insured with temporary term protection that will covert automatically at some future date, usually no later than 11 months. The premium for the interim term is based on the age at application. The premium for the permanent coverage is also based on attained age when permanent protection begins.

8. 3. 3 Advantages and Uses of Term Insurance

Some of the advantages and uses of term insurance are as follows.

- Initially, the cost of term insurance is low, making it useful for individuals or businesses who may have a large need for insurance but limited financial resources to pay for it.
- As temporary protection, it often is used to help cover temporary needs. For example, decreasing term frequently is used to cover the decreasing financial obligation associated with debts.
- Term insurance can be flexible. It often is used to provide additional protection for an insured.

Example

A husband has a relatively small whole life policy and becomes a father of twins. His responsibilities have suddenly changed, and there is a need for large amounts of additional life insurance. Term insurance could provide the solution to this problem. Often, the additional insurance is added to the existing policy by means of a rider.

8. 3. 4 Disadvantages of Term Insurance

Some of the disadvantages associated with term insurance are as follows.

- Over a long period, renewable term insurance becomes very expensive. Although initially the level term premium is low, it increases with each renewal on the basis of the increased age of the insured and the increased risk of mortality for the insurance company. Thus, a relatively low premium at age 35 becomes an expensive and sometimes prohibitive premium at age 55 or 60.
- Even though the premium for decreasing term remains level for the life of the contract, this level premium pays for less and less insurance. In the later years of a decreasing term policy, the actual cost of the remaining insurance tends to be expensive.
- One of the disadvantages of term insurance is its very nature—it is temporary protection for a limited time. If the policy is not renewable or because of the increasing cost of the policy, the insured can be left without insurance at a time (older age) when he needs the protection the most. Some experts put it this way: term policies are actuarially designed to expire before you do.
- Term insurance is pure death protection only. It offers no living benefits such as guaranteed cash values.
- Even if the term policy is renewable, it generally is not renewable beyond a certain age, such as age 65 or 70. Again, there is the danger of losing or not being able to afford the protection at these ages.

8. 4 WHOLE LIFE INSURANCE

Whole life insurance, sometimes known as permanent insurance or ordinary insurance, is designed to provide protection for the whole life of the insured. Cash values accumulate within the policy as illustrated below.

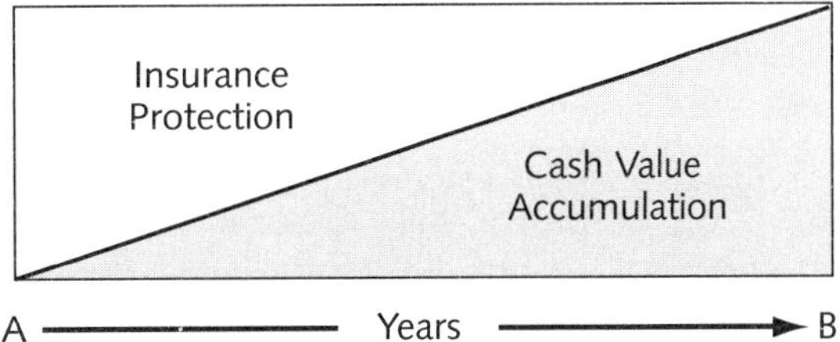

Assume the face value of the above policy is $100,000. The first day the policy is in force, the insured has $100,000 of protection. If the insured should die one week, one month, one year, 10 years, or 50 years later, his beneficiaries would be paid $100,000 at the time of his death. The face amount of the policy remains the same throughout the life of the policy (and the insured).

Because the face amount of the policy is payable upon the death of the insured, the element of risk to the insurance company is much different than it is for, say, an automobile policy. When an insurance company issues an auto policy, it hopes that the insured will be a safe driver and will never have an accident. When an insurance company issues a whole life policy, it knows it will someday be called upon to pay a claim because every human being dies. For the insurer, the only unknown is whether the claim will be made in one year or in 50.

8. 4. 1 Characteristics of All Whole Life Policies

8. 4. 1. 1 Level Premiums

Through mathematical science, the premiums for most permanent insurance policies are designed to remain level during the entire period the policy is in force. In the early years of the contract, the insured actually pays in more premium than is needed to provide the current year's insurance protection, whereas in later years less than is needed is paid in. The net result is that the premium remains the same for the entire period of the contract. In addition, the company has the opportunity to use the money—to invest it at a favorable return. This helps reduce the cost of insurance.

8. 4. 1. 2 Level Face Amount

Not only does the premium remain level for the life of the policy, but so does the face amount of the policy. Generally, the policy's basic face amount will not change for the life of the policy.

8. 4. 1. 3 *Guaranteed Cash Value*

As the policyowner continues to pay the premiums, the cash value in the policy accumulates year by year. The amount of pure insurance protection the insurance company must provide decreases as the amount of cash value increases.

Usually, in the first couple of years of the policy, the cash value is equal to zero, but over the life of the policy, there is a steady increase in the amount of the cash value until age 100, when the cash value is exactly equal to the policy's face amount. An increasing number of people do live past age 100, but they are so rare that they may be ignored statistically. Insurance company statistics generally assume that everyone has died by age 100.

The cash value built by whole life policies may be used by the policyowner in several ways, including withdrawing part or all of the cash value or taking a loan using the policy as collateral.

8. 4. 1. 4 *Nonforfeiture Value*

The cash value in the policy belongs to the policyowner. If he wishes, some or all of the cash value may be withdrawn from the policy. Any withdrawal of cash value will reduce both the face value of the policy and the amount of cash value available.

The policyowner is entitled to this living benefit at any time. If the policyowner decides to cease paying premiums, he may cash the policy in for the available cash value.

8. 4. 2 Types of Whole Life Policies

8. 4. 2. 1 *Continuous Premium Whole Life*

Continuous premium whole life is the most common type of whole life insurance sold. These policies stretch the premium payments over the whole life of the insured (to age 100). This type of policy is often referred to as straight life insurance.

8. 4. 2. 2 *Limited-Payment Whole Life*

Many insured policyowners want the lifetime insurance protection afforded by the whole life policy but do not like the thought of paying premiums for their entire lives. **Limited-payment whole life** policies allow the policyowner to pay for the entire policy in a shorter period. The premium for any whole life policy can be broken down into any desired number of installments.

Comparison of Whole Life and Limited Pay Life

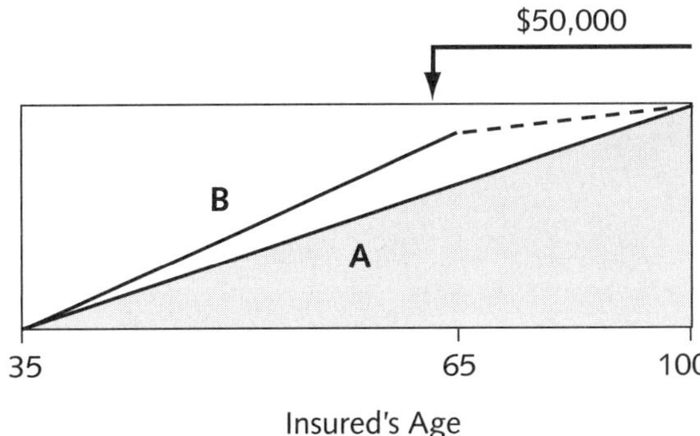

This figure shows a comparison of a whole life policy and a limited-pay policy. Line A is a whole life policy, whereas Line B (both solid and broken) represents a type of limited-pay policy. The dotted line continuing line B denotes insurance protection; however, the policyowner is not required to pay any more premiums.

Because the limited pay policy is paid up sooner than the whole life policy, all other factors being equal, the limited-pay policy would have a larger annual premium than the whole life policy. It's like buying a car on time. The payments on a $15,000 car paid over two years would be more per payment than if the car were purchased over the course of a four-year period.

Because the premiums are accelerated, the cash values of limited-pay policies build at a faster rate than that for whole life policies. This means that, for example, the loan value for a limited-pay policy after five years would be more than for a whole life policy owned for the same length of time.

Common forms of limited payment whole life are 20-payment life (meaning payments are spread over 20 years), 30-payment, and life paid up at age 65.

Example

20-pay life means premium payments for 20 years but lifetime (to age 100) protection. Life paid up at 65 means premium payments to age 65 but lifetime protection. A 20-pay life policy matures at age 100 or upon the death of the insured, whichever occurs first. The principal difference with limited-pay policies is simply the length of the premium paying period.

8. 4. 2. 3 Single Premium Whole Life

The most extreme version of a limited-pay policy is one that can be paid for with only one premium. For this reason, it is called a **single premium whole life policy**.

The premium for such a policy might be many thousands of dollars. The advantage offered by a single premium policy is that the policyowner will pay less for the policy than if the premiums were stretched over several years.

By the same token, the person insured by a single premium policy could die shortly after the single premium was paid, thus making the cost of insurance coverage much higher than it might have been had premiums been scheduled over a period of many years. Although this could be considered a disadvantage to the policyowner, such a circumstance would be favorable to the insurance company.

Single premium whole life policies fall into the category of modified endowment contracts. There are important tax consequences to be considered when purchasing a single premium policy or any kind of modified endowment contract. These consequences are discussed later in this unit.

How does a life insurance policy become an MEC? More importantly, how does a policy avoid being classified as an MEC? It must meet what is known as the "7-pay test."

This test states that if the total amount a policyowner pays into a life contract during its first years exceeds the sum of the net level premiums that would have been payable to provide paid-up future benefits in seven years, the policy is an MEC. Once a policy is classified as an MEC—which it can be at any time during the first seven years—it will remain so throughout its duration.

8. 4. 2. 4 *Current Assumption Whole Life*

Current assumption whole life policies (also known as **interest-sensitive whole life**) offer flexible premium payments that are tied into current interest rate fluctuations. The insurance company reserves the right to increase or decrease the premium within a certain range depending on interest rate fluctuations. During a period of relatively high interest rates, premiums could be reduced. During periods of low interest rates, premiums could be increased within certain limits. Usually, premium adjustments are made on an annual basis.

8. 4. 2. 5 *Economatic*

An **economatic** policy is a whole life-type policy with a term rider that uses dividends to purchase additional paid-up insurance. Let's assume that an individual wants $100,000 of whole life but can't quite afford it. Instead, he purchases $70,000 of whole life with $30,000 of term insurance. Thus, he has $100,000 of death protection at a lower cost.

As policy dividends are declared, they are used to purchase additional paid-up insurance. As the paid-up insurance is added, an equal amount of term insurance is removed from the policy, thus maintaining the full face amount of $100,000 at no additional cost. In reality, the cost of the insurance may decrease as the term amounts are eliminated if a level term rider were used. If a decreasing term rider were used, the reduction of the term insurance would become automatic but a level premium would be paid for the decreasing term.

When the paid-up additions equal $30,000, the insured now owns $100,000 of whole life but pays only an economical premium for $70,000.

8. 4. 2. 6 Interest-Sensitive Whole Life

Also known as *current-assumption whole life*, interest-sensitive whole life insurance is characterized by premiums that vary to reflect the insurer's changing assumptions with regard to its death, investment, and expense factors. Interest-sensitive products also provide that the cash values may be greater than the guaranteed levels, if the company's underlying death, investment, and expense assumptions are more favorable than expected. In this way, policyowners have two options: lower premiums or higher cash values.

If underlying assumptions turn out to be less favorable than anticipated, which otherwise would call for a higher premium than that at policy issue, the policyowner may either pay the higher premium or choose to reduce the policy's face amount and continue to pay the same premium.

8. 4. 3 Advantages and Uses of Whole Life

Some of the advantages and uses of whole life insurance are as follows.

- The principal advantage of whole life is that it is permanent insurance and can be used to satisfy permanent needs such as the cost of death, dying, and final burial expenses.
- The level premium allows the policyowner to know exactly what the cost of insurance will be and offers a form of forced savings.
- Whole life builds a living benefit through its guaranteed cash value, which enables the policyowner to use some of this cash for emergencies, as a supplemental source of retirement income, and for other living needs.

8. 4. 4 Disadvantages of Whole Life Insurance

Two of the disadvantages of whole life insurance are the following.

- The premium-paying period may last longer than the insured's income-producing years.
- It does not provide as much protection per premium dollar as term insurance does.

8. 5 FLEXIBLE POLICIES

Although traditional policies have served the needs of the public for many decades, more recently, several new types of life insurance products have been developed and marketed to meet the needs of the public. These new products include adjustable life, universal life, and variable life insurance. Each of these contemporary products has its own unique features and characteristics. However, one factor that each of these policies has in common is its flexibility. These newer life insurance products generally offer the policyowner flexibility in terms of premiums, face amounts, and investment objectives.

8. 5. 1 Characteristics of Flexible Policies

Ordinary whole life policies offer premiums, cash values, and face amounts that are determined at the time the policy is purchased and, unless the policyowner takes out a loan or partial withdrawal, generally do not change over the life of the policy.

Flexible policies, in contrast, offer the policyowner the opportunity to change one or more of these components in response to changing needs and circumstances. Each type of policy offers different types of flexibility.

8. 5. 2 Types of Flexible Policies

8. 5. 2. 1 Adjustable Life Insurance

Adjustable life is a policy that offers the policyowner the options to adjust the policy's face amount, premium, and length of protection without having to complete a new application or having another policy issued. Adjustable life introduces the flexibility to convert to any form of insurance (such as from term to whole life) without adding, dropping, or exchanging policies. Adjustable life is based on a money purchase concept.

The basic premise becomes not so much which type of policy a person buys but rather how much premium is to be spent. For example, if an applicant, age 25, states that he can afford to pay a $500 annual premium, it then becomes a matter of using this premium commitment to meet the individual's needs and to identify the type of insurance to be purchased.

To further illustrate, let's assume the 25-year-old applicant is married with three children and a large home mortgage and has no other life insurance. This person naturally needs a large amount of insurance. On the basis of the $500 premium, it might be recommended that all or most of that premium be used to purchase several hundred thousand dollars of term insurance.

In later years, this same individual may adjust the premium, the face amount, or the period of death protection to meet current needs.

Example

The insured is now 50 years old and planning for retirement. The same $500 premium now could be used for some form of permanent insurance protection with guaranteed cash values. The temporary protection would be changed to permanent coverage, and the death benefit (face amount) would be reduced because of the insured's age and premium commitment.

If the insured makes an adjustment in the policy that results in a higher death benefit, proof of insurability may be required for the additional coverage.

8. 5. 2. 2 Universal Life

Universal life was the insurance industry's answer to the extremely high interest rates we experienced in the decade of the 70s. Traditional whole life contracts have earned 3½–5% interest. In an effort to be more competitive, many insurers developed universal life products with relatively high interest rates (8–12%). Universal life is a flexible premium, adjustable benefit life insurance contract that accumulates cash value.

A prime feature of universal life is premium flexibility. Premiums paid into a universal life policy accumulate and, together with interest, make up the policy's cash value. Once sufficient cash value is accumulated, the policyowner has considerable flexibility with regard to subsequent premium payments.

An insured policyowner under a universal life insurance contract may increase the death benefit without buying another policy, although she may have to prove insurability. Also, the policyowner has the freedom to reduce the death benefit. Neither an increase nor a decrease in death benefit requires the issue of a new policy.

Most universal life policies are sold on the basis of the accumulation values and tax-deferred retirement income rather than on the proposed death benefit. However, policyholders often misunderstand that returns can and do fluctuate on the basis of investment performance and interest rates. The universal life policy was designed for people who need flexible coverage over the course of their lifetimes.

In earlier model universal life policies, a charge or **load** is deducted from each premium after the first-year premium to cover sales and administrative expenses. The remainder of the premium goes into a cash value account. The monthly amount needed to pay for the desired death benefit is deducted from this cash value account, usually on a monthly basis. When the policyowner pays more premium than is required to provide the desired death benefit plus other costs, the universal life policy will accumulate cash values.

As mentioned, a part of the premium goes to pay sales and administrative charges. A typical sales load is 7.5%. Thus, for a $1,000 premium payment, 7.5%, or $75, would be deducted and the $925 balance would go into the cash value account. Load charges range from about 7.5% to as high as 10%.

More recent universal life policies have adopted a back-end sales load. These back-end loads usually take the form of service charges for withdrawals from the policy, policy surrenders, and coverage changes. By postponing these sales loads until later, universal life policies could be illustrated showing more attractive returns than the earlier policies that subtracted the sales load at the front end.

Two adjustments are made to the cash value account of a universal life policy, usually on a monthly basis. The first adjustment is a charge against the account to pay the cost of the desired insurance coverage.

The second adjustment is a credit to the cash value account of interest at the current rate. The current rate consists of two parts:

- Guaranteed interest, guaranteed for the life of the policy, usually about 4%
- Excess interest earned by the insurer, which will vary greatly with the current level of interest rates

Current interest, then, is equal to guaranteed interest plus excess interest.

The cash value account isn't always fully credited with interest at the current rate. For some policies, there is an additional load that is generated by simply not paying excess interest on the first $1,000 in the cash value account. Thus, this load is the difference between the guaranteed interest rate and the current rate. For example, in a universal life policy with a guaranteed interest rate of 3.5% and a current interest rate of 8%, the annual load would be 4.5% and would amount to $45, which is 4.5% of the first $1,000 of cash value.

The current interest rate is commonly set once a year and guaranteed for the entire policy year. However, not all companies will guarantee their current rate for a full year and instead will choose periods as short as three months.

There are two options regarding the death benefit payable under a universal life policy. **Option A** (or **option 1**) provides a level death benefit equal to the policy's face amount. As the policy's cash value increases, the mortality risk decreases. Thus, the cost of the death protection actually decreases over the life of the policy and, accordingly, more of the premium can be placed in the cash account. This same concept applies to whole life.

However, because of the higher current interest rates credited to the account, if the cash value increases to an amount equal to or in excess of the policy's face amount, the death benefit will be increased automatically. Under current tax laws, if the universal life policy is to maintain its status as life insurance and thus provide a tax-free death benefit, there must be a degree of mortality risk until the insured's age 95. This is the reason for the automatic increase in the death benefit if the cash value equals or exceeds the policy's face amount. This buffer or corridor between the death benefit and the cash value must be maintained.

This corridor is shown at point B in the following illustration. At this point, further increases in cash value must be reflected by an increase in death benefit over the face amount. At point C, the cash value has increased even more and the death benefit reflects this increase, although the death benefit is still separated from the cash value by an amount at risk. This minimum separation is called the **risk corridor** and is determined by the Internal Revenue Code.

Option A—Universal Life Level Death Benefit

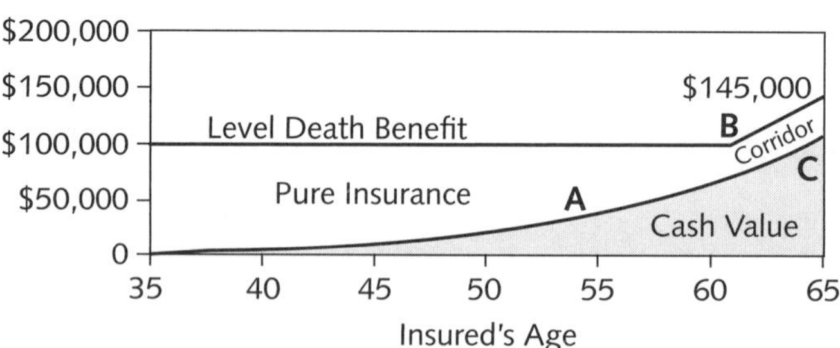

Option B (or **option 2**) provides for an increasing death benefit equal to the policy's face amount plus the cash account. Unlike option 1, the mortality risk remains at a level amount equal to the policy's face value. Thus, the policyowner will incur a higher expense for the cost of the death protection over the life of the policy and less of the premium will be deposited in the cash account.

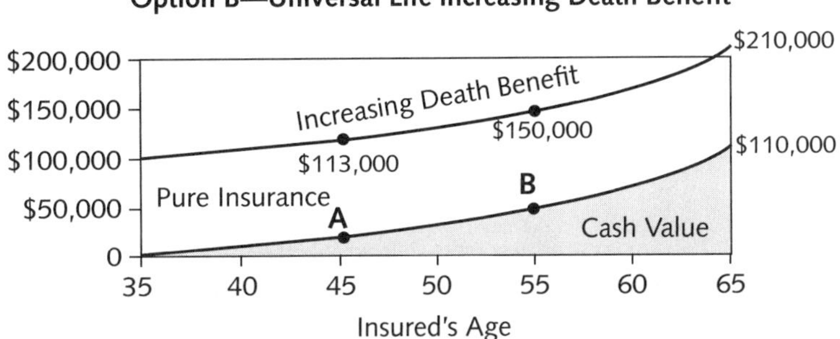

The contract illustrated above has a face amount and a death benefit of $100,000. In the beginning, this contract would have little or no cash value as shown, depending on the size of the initial premium payment. Later, at point A, cash value has increased to $13,000 and the death benefit would be $100,000 plus $13,000, or $113,000. Much later, at point B, cash value has increased to $50,000 and the death benefit is $150,000.

By comparing the diagrams for options A and B, you will see that at any specific age the policyowner is purchasing more pure insurance protection under option B than under option A. Thus, the policyowner will incur a greater cost for insurance under option B than under option A.

Universal life provides for cash value loans in the same manner that whole life or any permanent plan of insurance does. If a loan is taken, it is subject to interest, and if unpaid, both the interest and the loan amount will reduce the face amount of the policy.

Many universal life policies will also permit a partial withdrawal or surrender from the cash account. In such a case, the policyowner withdraws the desired cash directly from the cash value account and pays a small service charge for doing so. No interest of any kind is credited by the insurer or paid by the policyowner on the amount withdrawn.

Partial withdrawals may be repaid, although any money paid back will be treated as a premium payment and thus subject again to expense charges if it is a front-end load policy. With a current interest rate of 10% and a typical expense charge of 7.5%, the cost of a partial withdrawal that is repaid after one year is 17.5%, plus the amount of the service charge.

A universal life contract may be surrendered for its cash values whenever the policyowner wishes, although a surrender charge (or service charge) is usually applied.

Under a universal life insurance contract, the cost of insurance is deducted from the cash value account. When the cash value account reaches zero, coverage under the contract expires. However, there is a grace period, usually 30 to 60 days.

Although coverage under a universal life contract expires when the cash value account becomes zero, this does not mean that a policyowner must make regular and frequent payments. In fact, a featured benefit of the universal life contract is the flexibility of premium payments.

A policyowner might not make premium payments over, say, a one-year period. As long as there is sufficient cash value, the policy will continue in force even though no premiums have been paid recently. All the policyowner needs to do is make one large payment, or perhaps several smaller payments, and the cash value accumulation will continue the policy in force without further premium payments until the cash value is exhausted. At this point, to keep the policy in force, another premium must be paid. Otherwise, coverage expires.

8. 5. 2. 3 Variable Life

Variable life insurance is a securities-based whole life insurance product. Producers selling variable life must be registered with FINRA. This registration may be obtained by passing FINRA series 6 exam. In addition, an agent needs a valid life license, and in many states, a state-issued variable life or variable producer license.

Primarily, variable life insurance is a whole life policy designed to protect the policyowner and the beneficiaries from the erosion of their life insurance dollars as a result of inflation. Thus, it could be said that variable life is designed to be a hedge against inflation.

Historically, during periods of inflation, the stock market usually has kept pace with inflationary trends by increasing in value. In recognition of this fact, the insurers have established separate accounts, which consist primarily of a portfolio of common stock and other securities-based investments.

In contrast, the insurer's general account consists primarily of safe, conservative investments such as high-grade bonds, real estate, certificates of deposit, and so on. The premium from traditional life insurance contracts is placed in the company's general account, and the entire contract is fully guaranteed by the insurer.

In a variable life policy, a separate account holds the assets that are used as a basis for variable life policy benefits. These underlying assets may consist of equities, such as shares of common stock, or other securities such as bonds and money market securities. The values of these securities are subject to change, and the death benefit of the variable life policy also changes to reflect these changes in value. If the value of the separate account increases, the death benefit may increase. This is done to maintain a degree of mortality risk until the insured is 95 years old to maintain the policy's status as life insurance and provide favorable tax treatment. A drop in the investment results of the separate account will cause a decrease in the death benefit from the value in the previous year. However, the death benefit will never fall below the guaranteed minimum, which is the same as the face value of the policy.

Variable Life Insurance Death Benefit

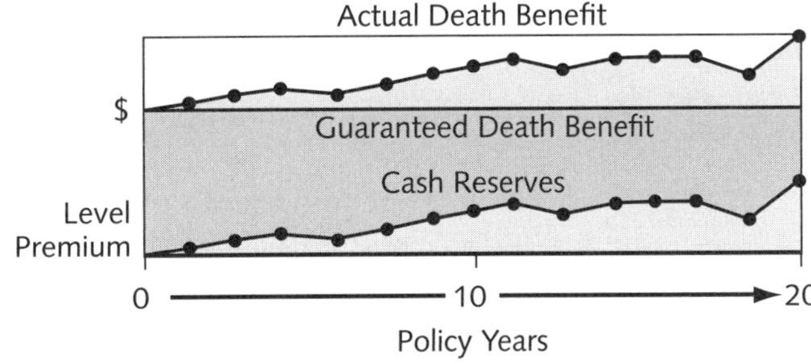

The previous illustration shows how the death benefit and the cash value may vary, reflecting the performance of the separate account in a variable life policy. This separate account performs on its own and is not an average of the entire company portfolio performance.

Technically, what happens in a variable life contract is that when the net investment return of the separate account exceeds the assumed rate of return, the excess is applied to increase the policy benefits.

Traditional variable life contracts provided for a fixed premium. Today, however, there are variable life benefit designs that provide for flexible or variable premiums, usually called variable universal life.

A variable life insurance (VLI) policy provides cash values. In fact, cash values in a VLI policy are determined on a daily basis according to the investment experience of the separate account, with no minimum amount guaranteed. So, although there is a guaranteed death benefit, there is no guaranteed cash value. The cash value at the end of any policy year is equal to the reserve for that policy.

The cash value may be withdrawn at any time on surrender of the policy. The exact amount payable will be the cash value calculated at the time the policy is surrendered.

Typically, up to 90% of the cash value of a VLI policy may be borrowed, subject to interest at a rate of 6%-8% compounded annually. The minimum that will be loaned is generally $100. Loans may be partly or fully repaid at any time as long as the insured is alive and the policy is in force.

If the policyowner defaults on a VLI premium payment, he has a 31-day grace period in which to pay the overdue premium. If the premium is not paid by the end of this period, the policy lapses.

Premiums paid for variable life insurance contracts are placed in a separate account consisting primarily of common stock; thus, there is considerable investment risk to the policyowner and few guarantees. Because of this element of investment risk, the federal government has declared that variable contracts are securities and are thus regulated by the Securities and Exchange Commission (SEC), FINRA, and other federal bodies.

The variable life product is regulated by the Securities Act of 1933, the Securities and Exchange Act of 1934, and the Investment Company Act of 1940. Following is a brief review of these acts as they apply to variable life insurance.

- The Act of 1933 requires that a prospectus be delivered at or before the point of sale of a variable life product.

- The Act of 1934 requires registration of the company and the company's sales representatives with the federal authorities.
- The Act of 1940 provides for the registration of separate accounts as an investment company.

Other requirements of the federal laws include a mandatory 45-day free-look provision from the date of policy application. Also, variable life policyowners have voting rights. Under the Act of 1940, the policyowner is allowed one vote for each $100 of cash value. The policyowner must be permitted to convert to traditional whole life insurance within 24 months of policy issuance.

Variable life insurance is often regulated by the state insurance department as an insurance product. This dually regulated product requires the following compliance.

- Producers selling variable life products must be registered with FINRA by passing the appropriate licensing exam (usually series 6 or series 7).
- The separate account backing the variable policies must be registered with the federal government in accordance with federal laws.
- Producers also must be licensed on a state level to sell life insurance.
- In some states, producers are required to have a separate state variable contracts license.
- All variable contracts must be filed and approved by the state insurance department

The 12% rule—At the time of solicitation, variable life illustrations may not be based on projected interest rates greater than 12%. This prevents both the producer and the policyholder from assuming excessive and unrealistic rates of return. A variety of policy performance illustrations at different rates would be the preferred method for clearly explaining variable life products. Producers should also stress that rates are not guaranteed and historical performance may not be duplicated in the future. Overreliance on the maximum permissible illustrated rates may mislead the buyer into thinking the rates are guaranteed.

There are two basic types of variable life insurance: scheduled premium variable life and flexible premium variable life.

Scheduled premium variable life requires a periodic level premium be paid to keep the policy in force. Because a specific premium will be paid, this type of variable life provides a guaranteed minimum death benefit equal to the initial face amount of the policy. Excess death benefit may be paid depending on the performance of the policy's separate account. If the portfolio of common stock in the separate account does well, the variable life policy will perform well. However, the policyowner is guaranteed a minimum death benefit regardless of the performance of the separate account.

The cash value of the scheduled premium variable life policy is not guaranteed. The values are solely dependent on the performance of the separate account. Because of this factor, any cash value loan is usually limited to 75% of the policy's available cash value.

In most other respects, the scheduled premium variable life contract is very similar to traditional whole life.

Flexible premium variable life is basically variable universal life. It provides the flexibility of universal life and the hedge against inflation of variable life. Although flexible premium variable life may provide a minimum guaranteed death benefit, most often there is no guarantee of death benefit or cash values. The performance of the policy is solely based on the performance of the separate account.

There is usually no guaranteed death benefit because of the flexible premium concept. It is very difficult to provide a guaranteed death benefit when the amount of premium to be paid is unknown. Thus, the principal difference between scheduled and flexible premium variable life is the method of paying the premium.

8. 5. 2. 4 *Variable Universal Life*

Variable universal life insurance is a combination of variable life insurance and universal life insurance. The benefits of such a plan are that it combines what are considered the outstanding features of both products.

The policy is variable in that the benefits vary according to the investments backing the contract, and many companies allow the insured to choose the type of investments she favors. The insurer will often permit the insured to switch from one investment to another at the insured's option. An insured will make her selection on the basis of the investment she believes will provide the greatest interest return. The investments the insured selects are not limited to the insurer's portfolio. Eligible investments may include any of the following: stocks, bonds, mutual funds, precious metals, diamonds, real estate in various forms, stamps, coins, and art objects.

Variable universal life does not require payment of specified premiums by given dates. Generally speaking and within certain limitations, the policyowner may pay premiums in any amount and at any frequency that's convenient. The life insurance benefit will be what the premium paid will purchase.

Premiums for variable universal life policies have deductions to cover sales and administrative expenses. These loads can be either front end, meaning they are deducted from each premium payment; back end, meaning they are deducted whenever the policyowner withdraws cash from the policy; or both.

Front-end loads are deducted from each premium as it is paid. For example, a company might deduct 9% of each premium payment to help offset sales expenses and 2.5% of each premium payment to pay premium taxes imposed by various states.

A flat fee representing a processing charge also may be deducted from premiums. Such a charge would be a specified dollar amount and would not vary with the size of the premium payment. For example, if a policy had total percentage deductions of 11.5% and a flat processing charge of $2, here's how to figure the amount going into the policy's separate account for a premium payment of $2,000.

Premium	$2,000
Less 11.5%	230
Less processing fee	2
Addition to separate account	$1,768

Once any front-end loads are deducted from the premiums, the remaining amount goes into the various cash value investment options according to the policyowner's instructions. Here's a diagram of the process for a front-load policy.

Separate Account Investment Options

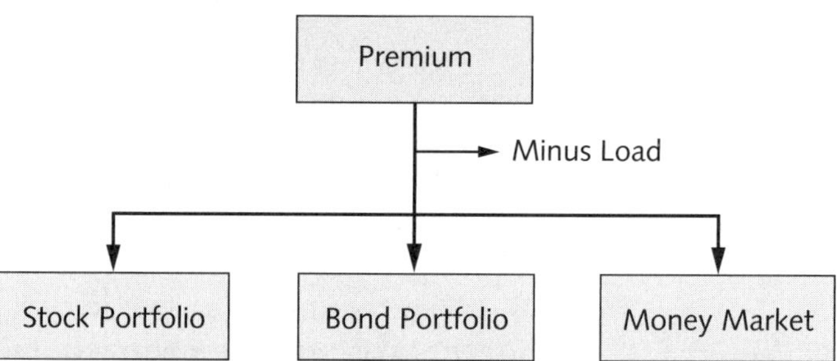

These options are separate accounts that will fluctuate in value according to their investment experiences. Policyowners can allocate premium payments among the available options with very few restrictions. They can make use of any number of the options and in any proportion they like, although most companies require a 10% minimum allocation. They can change the allocation with each payment as they choose, or their instructions will remain in force until they give notice to change them. Transfers of funds can be made among the various options, subject to minimum balance and minimum transfer requirements.

Monthly deductions are made from the funds in these separate accounts. These deductions principally pay for the insurance coverage provided by the policy. It's important to understand that without sufficient funds in a policy's account to pay for the insurance coverage, the policy will lapse.

Policyowners naturally hope that the cash value of their policies will grow, but with investments of any kind, there's always the possibility of a loss. If there should ever be a lack of funds in a policy's account to pay for insurance coverage, the policyowner is given a grace period to deposit enough money in the account to cover the minimum needed to keep the policy in force.

Variable universal life offers the policyowner access to the policy's cash value either through a policy loan or through a cash withdrawal. A policy loan not only will result in interest being charged, but also the amount of cash value representing collateral for the loan will be transferred out of the separate account and into the company's general account where it would likely earn a lower rate of interest than if it had remained in the separate account. The total cost of the loan, then, would be the interest rate plus the separate account earnings lost minus the interest credited from the general account.

If the policyowner wants cash without incurring interest consequences of a policy loan, money can be withdrawn from the policy. The death benefit is usually reduced by the amount of the withdrawal. There also may be a processing fee or back-end load charged per withdrawal.

With variable universal life, the policyowner may have the choice between two different death benefit options, just as you have already seen with universal life.

8. 5. 2. 5 Current Assumption Whole Life

Current assumption whole life goes by various other names, including interest-sensitive whole life and excess interest whole life. Although these types of policies are sometimes grouped along with universal life, they are different and need to be understood as separate products.

The premium and cash value amounts for a current assumption whole life policy may change on the basis of the insurer's experience. However, there is a minimum guaranteed cash value based on a minimum guaranteed rate of return.

The insurer guarantees a maximum annual premium on the policy but may charge less if the current return on the policy justifies it. The excess interest earned above the guaranteed rate may either lower the premium or increase the cash value accumulation.

Unlike universal life, current assumption whole life is a bundled policy. The pure insurance and investment elements are not broken out separately.

8. 5. 2. 6 Equity Indexed Life Insurance

Equity indexed life insurance is the life insurance equivalent of equity index annuities. The cash value of equity indexed life offers a guaranteed minimum rate of return with the opportunity for higher growth through participation in a stock market-related (equity) index, such as the Standard & Poor's 500 Index. The cash value cannot decrease because the market is flat or declining, but it may increase if the market is rising.

8. 5. 3 Advantages and Uses of Flexible Policies

Some of the advantages of flexible policies are as follows.

- Flexible policies provide the opportunity to customize the policy to the needs and wants of the insured.
- Flexible policies may include a securities component, which is considered an effective hedge against inflation.
- Premium flexibility allows policyowners to pay what they can, when they can. This provides the opportunity for much higher dollar amounts to be paid to increase cash value more rapidly when the policyowner has the resources to do so. It also provides the opportunity

for policyowners to skip payments when their financial circumstances dictate without losing insurance protection.

8. 5. 4 Disadvantages of Flexible Policies

Some of the disadvantages associated with flexible policies are as follows.

- Flexible policies that include a securities component may not have guaranteed returns. Returns may be low, or even negative, in policies based on separate securities accounts.
- Some policyowners need the forced discipline of a mandated premium schedule to ensure that they regularly contribute enough to ensure adequate cash value growth. Many flexible premium policies lack a required premium schedule.

Comparison of Life Products

Features	Term	Permanent Whole Life	Universal Life	Variable Life	Current Assumption Whole Life
Death Benefit	Fixed and level	Fixed and level	Adjustable level or increasing options	Varies with investment performance, guaranteed minimum	Fixed and level
Premiums	Fixed schedule, increasing amount	Fixed schedule, level amount	Flexible schedule, flexible amount	Fixed schedule, level amount	Fixed schedule, amount may rise to guaranteed maximum
Cash Values	None	Fixed and guaranteed	Current interest with guaranteed minimum rate	Varies with investment performance	Current interest with guaranteed minimum rate and cash value level
Mortality Rates	Fixed and guaranteed	Fixed and guaranteed	Current, guaranteed maximum	Fixed and guaranteed	Current, guaranteed maximum
Partial Surrenders	N/A	No	Yes	Some policies	Some policies
Regulated As	Insurance	Insurance	Insurance	Insurance and security	Insurance

8. 6 INDUSTRIAL LIFE INSURANCE

The industrial policy is written for a small face amount, usually $2,000 or less, and the premiums are payable as frequently as weekly and, occasionally, monthly. It derived its name from the fact that it was originally sold in England to the industrial class of factory workers. This form of insurance was originally sold in America to workers in industry.

The insured would determine how much he could pay each week and the face amount would be determined by the amount of premium the insured could pay. A company representative would call on the insured each week, usually at home, to collect the premium, which usually ranged from five cents to one dollar. The policy benefit primarily was used to pay for last illness and burial expenses.

This method of distribution is very expensive for two reasons. First, the mortality rates are higher for industrial policyowners because these insureds tend to have higher than average health risks and poorer than average living standards. Second, having the agent collect the premium each week at the customer's home increases the cost of this type of policy.

With the rising incomes of workers, increasing consumer awareness, and the growth of group life insurance, the need for industrial life has decreased considerably over the last several decades. Today, industrial life represents about 1% of life insurance in force. Federal Social Security benefits have also filled a need that was once met by industrial life insurance.

8. 6. 1 Characteristics of Industrial Life Insurance

The basic characteristics of industrial life insurance are as follows.

- Premium payments are made frequently.
- Benefits are usually less than $2,000.
- Premiums are collected, by the agent, at the insured's home or workplace.
- Sales are made in premium units rather than in insurance units. The rate book lists the amount of insurance that can be bought with a specified weekly or monthly premium. (This has been changing for larger amounts of insurance.)
- All family members are covered from birth to age 65 or 70.
- Usually a medical examination is not required.

8. 6. 2 Industrial Life Policy Provisions

Most of the provisions found in individual life insurance policies also are found in industrial life insurance. However, consideration should be given to these provisions and their unique application to industrial policies. Because the face amount of the policy is so small and the cost of this type of insurance is expensive, certain provisions do not have the same effect on industrial insureds as on individual insureds.

- A 31-day grace period (28 days for weekly premium policies) is provided.
- The application is not required to be part of the policy.
- Medical examinations are not required.
- Cash values do not accumulate sufficiently to provide loans.
- Settlement options do not apply because of limited cash value.

- Suicide provisions are not included in the policy because of the small benefit amount.
- Nonforfeiture provisions do not allow the cash option until premiums have been paid for five years (compared with three years for ordinary policies).
- Dividends are used to reduce the premium payment or to purchase paid-up additions.

8. 6. 2. 1 Home Service Life Insurance

Today we find a variation in the industrial life concept known as home service life insurance. The home service policy is written for a small face amount, usually $10,000 to $15,000 in face value, and is typically sold on a monthly payment plan, either by automatic bank payment or payment by mail. Often all family members are covered by this insurance, and a medical examination is usually not required. These insurance policies are subject to the same requirements for standard policy provisions as regular life insurance policies. The face amounts are so small that the primary use of this insurance is to pay for last illness and burial expenses.

8. 7 CREDIT LIFE INSURANCE

Billions of dollars of consumer credit are being used in this country today. Most of us make time payments on automobiles, bank loans, and similar obligations.

The unexpected death of an individual who has time payment obligations can create serious problems for his family. Credit life insurance provides that in the event of the death of an insured debtor, the outstanding balance is usually paid off in full.

Credit life insurance can be written on a group basis or in individual credit life policies. It is usually written as a decreasing term type of coverage so the amount of insurance decreases as the amount of the obligation decreases. Level term insurance that would remain level for the term of the loan also may be written. The benefits are payable to the policyowner (the creditor) and are used to reduce or extinguish the unpaid indebtedness. Most commonly, credit life insurance provides protection for 10 years or less.

Usually, the individual debtor pays the total premium. The premium is added to the finance contract amount so that, in effect, the insurance premium is being financed along with the item being purchased. The insurance company receives full premium up front. Life insurance companies write credit insurance through such lenders as banks, retailers, auto dealers, credit unions, and finance companies.

If a debtor prepays or refinances the loan, he is entitled to cancellation of the credit insurance and a refund of the unearned premium.

8. 7. 1 Credit Life Policy Provisions

Some of the major provisions found in credit life insurance policies are those that provide the following.

- Insureds must be given a certificate of coverage under the creditor's group policy, including their rights and obligations under the policy.
- The number of insureds under the policy must be maintained at a specified level (usually 100); if participation drops below that number, the insurer may not insure new debtors.
- The debtor's coverage will terminate when the debt is paid off, transferred to another creditor, or refinanced or becomes significantly overdue.
- Unlike standard group insurance policies, the policy does not have a conversion privilege.

8. 8 SPECIALIZED POLICY FORMS

There are a number of life insurance policies that have been designed to fit specialized situations. Some of the more frequently used forms will be discussed here. These forms are merely combinations or modifications of whole life or term life policies. Many of these special policy names vary by company, and many companies have produced variations of these basic combinations.

8. 8. 1 Endowments

The accelerated growth of the cash values of endowment policies resulted in legislation against them. According to the Tax Reform Act of 1984, any policy issued after January 1, 1985, that endows before age 95 will not qualify as life insurance. That would mean that the policy's cash value accumulation and its death benefit would be taxed. The endowment policy is included in this course because state insurance exams still cover it and because some clients may own existing endowment policies acquired before January 1, 1985. These contracts were not affected by the Tax Reform Act of 1984. Even though you are not likely to come across endowment policies issued after 1984, you still need to be familiar with them.

The endowment policy is another category of permanent insurance. As with other types of policies, the endowment pays a death benefit upon the death of the insured. Like the limited pay policy, the premiums are paid only for a specified period. If the insured is alive at the end of the premium-paying period, the policyowner would receive the face amount maturity benefit and the insurance coverage would terminate. Thus, the policy endows at the end of the premium-paying period.

The following represents a 10-year endowment policy. The policy's face amount is $10,000. The premiums will be paid up and the policy will endow when the policyowner is age 35. At that time, the policyowner will receive the $10,000 face amount of the policy.

10–Year Endowment Policy

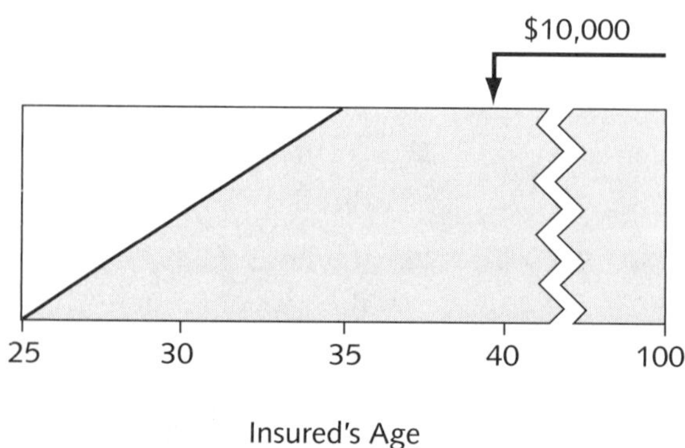

An endowment policy has all of the same elements as a whole life policy. The primary difference is that it matures earlier (at a specified age or date) so the cash value must build up more rapidly and the premium is higher per $1,000 of coverage.

If a person were to open a savings account in a local bank with the intention of accumulating $10,000 in a 20-year period but died one month later, his survivor would receive only what had been deposited (plus interest) in the savings account as of the date of death.

Conversely, if the same person had purchased a $10,000 20-year endowment policy and died one month later, the beneficiary would receive $10,000 (the amount the insured wanted to accumulate over 20 years). Thus, an endowment might be defined as a forced savings plan with a death benefit.

Specifically, an endowment provides for the payment of the policy's face amount if the insured dies during the endowment period or pays the face amount to the insured if the insured survives to the end of the endowment period. The endowment period is the length of time that the policyowner pays the premium. When the premium period ends, the endowment matures on the maturity date and pays the face amount to the insured (policyowner). Endowments are purchased for various periods—for example, 10 or 20 years or to age 65.

It should be noted that when the policy matures, insurance protection ends. The policy matures for the face amount as a living benefit. The overall concept of an endowment is very similar to that of whole life, except that the cash value accumulates more rapidly and the premiums are higher. It could be said that whole life matures at death or at age 100, whichever occurs first. It could be said that whole life is an endowment at age 100. By endowing after age 95, however, whole life maintains the tax advantages of life insurance that endowments lost in the mid 80s.

8. 8. 1. 1 Types of Endowments

Endowments generally are not sold today because the tax consequences have changed, eliminating many of the benefits that once made endowments attractive investment vehicles. Information on the most popular types of endowments sold is included here for historical context and to provide you with a better understanding of the needs these products were intended to fill when they were sold.

A **retirement endowment** was one of the most commonly sold endowment contracts. Typically, this type of policy was issued to mature at age 65 when the insured planned to retire. Like whole life insurance, the face value was payable as a death benefit if the insured died before the maturity date. However, at maturity, the full face amount became payable as a living benefit, usually in the form of monthly installment income.

Another version of the endowment concept was the **pure endowment**. This policy offered no life insurance protection. The pure endowment provided for the payment of the policy's face amount only if the insured lived to the maturity date. If the insured died before the endowment date, all benefits were forfeited. Because this was essentially a high-risk savings plan (all savings were lost upon early death), it was rarely sold.

Endowment life insurance was a combination of a pure endowment plus term insurance for a specified period. The pure endowment provided a living benefit at the end of the endowment period. The term insurance paid a death benefit to the insured's beneficiary if she died before the end of the endowment period.

Juvenile endowment policies were designed to mature at a specific age, such as age 18, so that the maturity value was available to help fund a college education.

8. 8. 1. 2 Family Income Policies

Family plans are uncommon but still included in most state exams. Combining whole life insurance with decreasing term coverage, the **family income policy** provides temporary protection and permanent coverage. The **family income policy** provides an income to be paid upon the death of the family breadwinner. The payout period, which is determined when the policy is purchased, is scheduled to last until the family's income needs diminish. Family policies are usually sold for periods of 10, 15, or 20 years. Coverage is provided by combining decreasing term insurance with a permanent policy. This may be accomplished by means of a special policy or by actually adding term insurance to a permanent policy—in effect, a rider. Family income coverage is generally referred to as a family income policy, so that's what we'll call it.

The family income portion of this type of coverage is supplied by a decreasing term policy. Income payments to the beneficiary begin when the insured dies and continue for the period specified in the policy, which is usually 10, 15, or 20 years from the date of policy issue, and not from the date of the insured's death. So the longer the insured lives, the less insurance will be needed to meet the income obligations of the policy. That's why decreasing term insurance is used for a family income policy.

For example, if Kim has a 15-year family income policy and dies two years after purchasing this policy, Kim's family can expect to receive income benefits for 13 years.

To prevent what might be a burden if the insured dies close to the end of the family income protection period, some companies permit an arrangement whereby the beneficiary would receive an income guaranteed for some specified period, say five years, if the insured dies within the family income protection period.

The amount of monthly income provided by the family income policy depends on the amount of insurance bought. A typical arrangement might be $10 of monthly income for each $1,000 of insurance. Some companies may offer more. If Kim purchases a $75,000 family income policy, Kim's family can expect to receive $750 per month during the family income protection period following Kim's death.

The death benefit from the permanent insurance protection of the family income is usually paid in a lump sum when the insured dies, even if that occurs after the family income protection period. However, some family policies stipulate that if the insured dies before the end of the family income protection period, the proceeds will be paid at the end of that period. The amount paid is the face value of the policy.

8. 8. 1. 3 *Family Maintenance Policies*

Family maintenance policies are similar to family income policies in that they both provide an income to be paid to the insured's beneficiary. The difference is that with a family maintenance policy, coverage is provided by combining level term insurance with a permanent policy. A family maintenance policy provides income for a stated number of years from the date of death of the insured , provided the insured dies before a predetermined time.

The family maintenance portion of the coverage comes from a level term policy. Here's how it works. Let's say Sandy, age 30, wants to provide funds for family maintenance for at least 15 years following her death, as long as death occurs before age 45. If Sandy were to die 10 years later at age 40 this family maintenance policy would pay monthly income to Sandy's beneficiary for 15 years from the date of Sandy's death.

The permanent insurance portion of the family maintenance policy pays a lump sum for the face value of the policy to the insured's beneficiary either when the insured dies or at the end of the family maintenance payout period, whichever is stipulated in the policy.

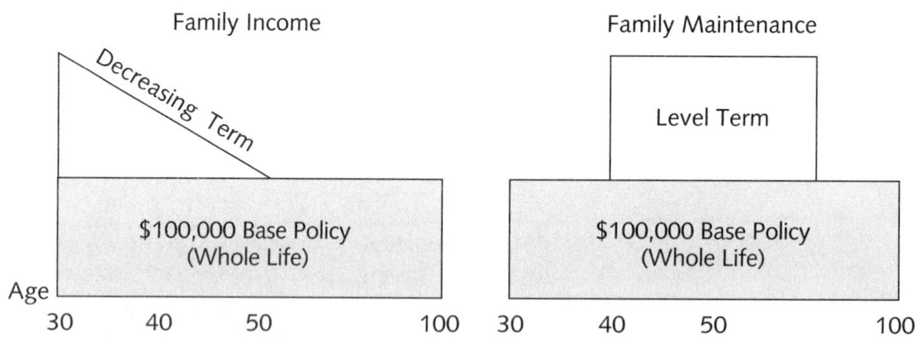

Family income and family maintenance plans are both designed to provide a period of monthly income following the death of the insured, if death occurs during the specified period.

8. 8. 1. 4 *The Family Policy (Family Protection Policy)*

Some companies offer contracts that provide coverage on each of the family members at the time the policy is issued. These combination policies or family plans customarily provide coverage on the principal breadwinner equal to four times the spouse's and five times the children's coverage amounts.

Example

Bob's policy might provide $100,000 on himself, $25,000 on his wife, and $20,000 on each child. In this example, the wife's and children's coverages would ordinarily be term insurance and Bob's would be a permanent policy. These additions to Bob's permanent coverage are sometimes referred to as riders, a concept we'll look at later in this unit. Spouse term rider and family rider are common names for these coverages.

Under a **family policy**, term insurance coverage is provided without additional premium for children born or adopted after the policy is issued. The term insurance expires on each child as he reaches a specified age—18, or perhaps 21, sometimes as late as 25. Coverage on the children is usually convertible to any permanent insurance without evidence of insurability.

8. 8. 1. 5 *Retirement Income*

A **retirement income policy** accumulates a sum of money for retirement while providing a death benefit. Upon retirement, the policy pays an income such as $10 per $1,000 of life insurance for the insured's lifetime or a specified period. These policies are expensive, and cash value accumulation is high to pay for the monthly income. Once the cash value in the policy approaches the face amount, the face amount must be increased to maintain the policy's status as life insurance.

8. 8. 1. 6 *Joint Life Policies*

Although most life insurance is written on the life of one person, policies are available to insure the lives of two or more people. A **joint life** policy may pay the face amount upon the first death among the persons covered by the policy or upon the last death among the persons covered by the policy. Under a **first-to-die** joint life policy, the contract ends at the first death and there is no further insurance protection for the other person or persons covered by the policy.

Suppose Esther, Sarah, and Rebecca are three sisters who have a $50,000 joint life policy covering all three of their lives. The proceeds are to be shared equally by the survivors upon the first sister's death. So, when Esther dies, Sarah and Rebecca each would receive $25,000.

Now, to continue with the example of the joint life policy for the three sisters, suppose Sarah dies soon after Esther. The last surviving sister will receive nothing more from the joint life policy because it terminated at the first sister's death.

Survivor life insurance, or **second-to-die insurance**, covers two lives and guarantees payment only when the second insured dies. Premiums are usually payable until the second death.

Second-to-die policies are very useful in estate planning. When a surviving spouse dies, the policy can provide money to pay taxes on assets that may have been sheltered at the first death by the marital deduction. They also can be used in certain business applications. Premiums on a survivorship policy can be significantly less than if the two lives were insured separately. Face amounts are usually more than $1 million.

8. 8. 1. 7 Juvenile Policies

Juvenile insurance can be any type of coverage—whole life, limited payment life, or term insurance, depending on the purpose of having the policy. The criterion for juvenile insurance is that it be written on the life of a person who is not yet considered an adult for life insurance purposes. In most places, this includes anyone who is under age 15 (16 in Canada).

A popular juvenile policy is called the **jumping juvenile** policy. It is normally purchased by a parent for a child. The face amount of this policy can be for as little as $1,000 initially. At the time the child turns age 21, however, the face amount automatically jumps by an amount usually five times greater than the original face amount, with no increase in premium and no evidence of insurability required.

The jumping juvenile has three advantages.

- A parent can provide insurance protection for children during their early years. Then, at age 21, an additional amount of insurance is automatically provided at a time when larger amounts may be needed.
- When a policy is purchased, the policyowner pays a premium based on the child's current age. At age 21, when the face amount has been increased fivefold, the premium is still based on the original age of the insured and the original face amount. At age 21, the insured takes over the policy and has insurance protection at a cost much less than would be required if the policy were purchased at the current age of 21.
- If the child becomes uninsurable before age 21, the face amount will still jump when increased life insurance protection is sorely needed.

8. 8. 1. 8 Minimum Deposit

Minimum deposit or **financed insurance** is technically a method of paying for insurance and not a type of policy. It is a high cash and loan value whole life policy. Such policies were devised in the late 1950s to take advantage of the fact that at the time, the Internal Revenue Service (IRS) allowed the interest paid on a policy loan to be deducted in full for income tax purposes. Thus, a prospect could buy such a policy and immediately borrow back the loan value so that, in effect, his initial premium outlay was very small. Since then, however, the IRS has placed restrictions on the interest deduction when the loan is to finance insurance so that its popularity has diminished.

As it is currently used, the cash value of a permanent policy is used to pay the premiums on that policy through the use of policy loans. To achieve sufficient cash value, the first two of these premium payments must be paid by the policyowner and then loans may be used—but only if during the first seven years of the policy at least four of the seven annual premiums are paid from funds other than policy loans. This is a rule imposed by the IRS.

One of the advantages of minimum deposit insurance is that under certain circumstances, interest paid on policy loans used to finance premium payments still may be deductible. Disadvantages include the fact that its administration is complex. Certain very specific criteria must be met to qualify for the deductions. Finally, interest payments in the later years of the policy can be high.

8. 8. 1. 9 Modified Premium Plan

A **modified premium plan** is an ordinary life policy in which the premium obligation is redistributed. Premiums are lower during the first three to five years of the policy, usually only a little more than would be paid for a level term policy for the same period. After this initial period, the premiums go up so that they're somewhat higher than would be paid for an ordinary whole life policy.

The advantage of the modified premium plan is that it allows the purchase of permanent insurance at a time when a person's income might otherwise not permit it and transfers much of the cost to a later period when the policyowner's income can be expected to be higher.

8. 8. 1. 10 Graded Premium Plan

A **graded premium plan** is similar to modified whole life in that initially the premium is very low. Unlike modified life, which has one increase to a higher, level premium for the life of the contract, graded premium policies provide for an increase in premium each year for the first 5 to 10 years of the policy. At the end of this step-rated premium period, the premium remains level for the life of the policy.

Graded premium policies, like modified life contracts, are designed to allow the policyowner to purchase a version of whole life without the initial cost of whole life. These contracts are aimed at the young individual just beginning a job or career and whose income will increase in future years.

It should be noted that graded premium (and modified life) policies build cash value but the amount of the cash value is usually less because of the smaller outlay of premium. Typically, a graded premium policy will have very little, if any, cash value during the graded premium period.

8. 8. 1. 11 Mortgage Redemption

The **mortgage redemption policy** or **rider** is simply decreasing term insurance. The benefit amount of the term element is intended to be sufficient to pay off the unpaid remainder of the mortgage loan if the insured dies before paying it off himself.

8. 8. 1. 12 Multiple Protection

Multiple protection policies are combinations of whole life and term in which the amount of protection is higher in the early years of the policy and less in the later years.

Example

The current death benefit may be described as equal to two times the benefit at age 65 (double protection). If the age 65 (and thereafter) benefit is $5,000, the insured has $10,000 of protection up to age 65. In essence, the additional death benefit before age 65 is term insurance.

8. 8. 1. 13 Index-Linked Policies

As a hedge against high inflationary periods, many companies offer policies with face amounts that increase by the amount of inflation. The policy amounts are generally linked to the Consumer Price Index. There are two ways of providing this additional coverage. Either the premium is increased every year to cover the increased insurance amount or the life insurance company makes assumptions about what it expects the increases to be at policy inception, and the insured pays the same (but higher than average) premium over the life of the policy.

8. 8. 1. 14 Deposit Term Insurance

Deposit term insurance is a level term insurance policy that has a much higher premium for the first year than for subsequent years. The initial premium is significantly higher than the average premium needed to cover the cost of mortality during the term period. The excess front-end premium (the deposit) is then set aside to earn interest, and these dollars (deposit plus interest) will be applied to reduce the premium payments required in the following years. The premium levels are set so that the entire deposit will be exhausted when the final annual premium is paid. In effect, this arrangement provides a method of paying a portion of the premium in advance.

Example

The annual premium for a 10-year level term policy for a particular insured may be $500 (total outlay of $5,000). The same type of policy may be purchased as a deposit term contract for an initial premium of $2,500 followed by annual premiums of $200 (total outlay of $4,300). The initial deposit and interest are used to make up the difference in premium. Mathematically, the insurance company actually receives an equal amount of premium for these two policies when the time factor and interest earnings are taken into account.

8. 8. 1. 15 Preneed Funeral Insurance

Funeral insurance or preneed burial insurance is a type of life insurance used to pay for an insured's funeral at a particular funeral home. Funeral insurance pays the face amount upon an insured's death. Really, it is just a contract to provide a preplanned funeral and cemetery services funded by a life insurance contract or annuity. Typically, the funeral home has the insured buy a life insurance policy on himself, naming the funeral home as the beneficiary. The funeral home usually is paid a commission on the policy sale as well. The policy will have an increasing face amount so that the funeral will be fully funded, even if burial costs increase.

Some states have begun regulating this type of insurance. In some cases, premiums must be deposited in trust funds to increase the likelihood that the funeral home will be able to meet the need when it arises. Other regulations address disclosure, requiring that advertisements disclose the relationships between the funeral home and the agent selling the policy, requiring the disclosure of geographical or other restrictions on the policy, and requiring disclosure of the fact that a sales commission or other compensation will be paid on the sale of the contract. Such disclosures must be made at the time of application.

Although the number of funeral insurance policies sold seems to be increasing, an alternative for most insureds would be a more standard form of life insurance, the proceeds of which could be used by the insured's family for the funeral or any other needs at the time of death.

8. 8. 2 Advantages and Uses of Specialized Policies

Some of the advantages and uses of specialized policies are as follows.

- Specific combinations of term and permanent insurance can be used to match the need exactly.
- The cost of the policy may be lower than ordinary whole life insurance.

8. 8. 3 Disadvantages of Specialized Policies

The following are two of the disadvantages of specialized policies.

- Policies set up to meet a specific need may become obsolete if the need changes over time.
- Certain policies, if not set up carefully, may incur negative tax consequences.

8. 9 VIATICAL SETTLEMENTS

If a chronically or terminally ill insured does not have an accelerated death benefits rider under his life insurance policy or wants another option, he may want to consider a viatical settlement. Under a viatical settlement contract, the insured, or viator, sells his insurance policy to a viatical settlement provider for a reduced percentage of the policy's face value. After the exchange, the viatical settlement provider becomes the owner of the policy and the beneficiary. While the viator lives, the provider must continue to pay premiums to keep the policy in force. When the insured dies, the viatical settlement provider receives the entire death benefit.

Because of the delicate nature of viatical settlements, some states require viatical settlement providers and brokers to be licensed before entering into viatical settlement contracts, and NAIC has drafted a Viatical Settlements Model Regulation for states to adopt. State requirements and the NAIC Model Regulation should be consulted before advising insureds about viatical settlements or soliciting them.

Although a few providers may enter into a viatical settlement contract with a policyowner based on old age, most will solicit contracts from only terminally or chronically ill insureds. A chronically ill person is either unable to perform at least two activities of daily living (eating, toileting, transferring, bathing, dressing, or continence) or needs substantial supervision because of cognitive impairment. A person is considered terminally ill if he is not expected to live more than 24 months because of a medical condition. Tax laws require viators to be chronically or terminally ill to receive payments from viatical settlements tax free.

Time plays a significant factor in viatical settlements because the viator probably needs funds quickly and may have a short amount of time to live. Most requirements dictate that settlements must be made within four to six weeks after the application is submitted unless circumstances require additional time. However, both sides of the settlement need to approach the process carefully to make sure their best interests are considered.

During the underwriting process, the viatical settlement provider will contact the insured's physician or clinic to verify records and determine his life expectancy. The issuing insurer of the life insurance policy also will be contacted to confirm policy terms and ascertain whether outstanding policy loans exist. Throughout this process, the insured's information may be shared only with the appropriate people involved in the settlement to protect the insured's privacy. If the issuing insurance company has a favorable rating and the settlement is in compliance with state laws, the provider will issue the viator an offer. NAIC's Viatical Settlement Model Regulation prescribes the following percentages of the policy's face value for viatical settlements on the basis of the insured's life expectancy. State requirements and company policies may differ.

NAIC's Viatical Settlement Model Regulation

Insured's Life Expectancy	Minimum Percentage of Face Value (not including any policy loans received by the viator)
Less than 6 months	80%
At least 6 but less than 12 months	70%
At least 12 but less than 18 months	65%
At least 18 but less than 24 months	60%
24 months or more	50%

8. 10 SUMMARY

In this lesson, you learned about:

- various types of insurance policies, including term insurance, whole life insurance, and various types of flexible policies;
- death benefits for various types of insurance policies;
- industrial life insurance, home service life insurance, credit life insurance, and the various kinds of specialized policies; and
- viatical settlements and how they work.

UNIT TEST

1. Term insurance provides
   A. cash values
   B. the ability to take a loan against the policy
   C. pure insurance protection
   D. lifelong protection

2. Carl's insurance policy is designed to cover the mortgage on his house if he should die before paying it off. The policy is
   A. convertible term
   B. renewable term
   C. increasing term
   D. decreasing term

3. The least common of the following types of insurance is
   A. convertible term
   B. renewable term
   C. increasing term
   D. decreasing term

4. Pam owns a 1-year term policy. At the end of the year, she may purchase another identical policy without showing proof of insurability. Pam's policy is
   A. convertible term
   B. renewable term
   C. increasing term
   D. decreasing term

5. Whole life insurance policies provide all of the following EXCEPT
   A. cash values
   B. the ability to take a loan against the policy
   C. pure insurance protection
   D. an opportunity for significant investment gains

6. Zelda agrees to pay premiums on her policy every year for 20 years. After that, she will no longer have to pay premiums, but her insurance protection will continue until she dies. Zelda has a(an)
   A. whole life policy
   B. limited-pay policy
   C. single premium policy
   D. economatic policy

7. Jerry has a policy that pays dividends, which are used to purchase additional paid-up insurance to increase the face value of the policy. Jerry has a(an)
   A. whole life policy
   B. limited-pay policy
   C. single premium policy
   D. economatic policy

8. Joan makes only one premium payment to acquire a paid-up policy that will probably be classified as a modified endowment contract. Joan has a(n)
   A. whole life policy
   B. limited pay policy
   C. single premium policy
   D. economatic policy

9. Cosmo has a policy that he must pay premiums on until he is 100 years old or until he dies. Cosmo has a(an)
   A. continuous premium whole life policy
   B. limited-pay policy
   C. single premium policy
   D. economatic policy

10. Which of the following is NOT flexible in a universal life policy?
    A. Premium amounts
    B. Premium schedule
    C. Guaranteed interest rate
    D. Death benefits

11. Adam purchases a universal life policy. In his second year, he decides to pay a $1,000 premium. What happens to the cash value of his policy at this point?
    A. Adam's cash value is increased by $1,000.
    B. The front-end load is deducted from the premium and the premium is added to the cash value.
    C. The front-end load is deducted from the premium, the premium is added to the cash value, and the cost of insurance is deducted from the cash value.
    D. The front-end load is deducted from the premium, the premium is added to the cash value, the cost of insurance is deducted from the cash value, and the current interest rate is credited to the cash value.

12. Martha has a universal life policy she purchased several years earlier. At that time, the death benefit in the policy was $100,000. Her cash value is now $20,000, and she has selected death benefit option A. How much is her current death benefit?
    A. $20,000
    B. $80,000
    C. $100,000
    D. $120,000

13. Karen has a universal life policy she purchased several years earlier. At that time, the death benefit in the policy was $100,000. Her cash value is now $20,000, and she has selected death benefit option B. How much is her current death benefit?
    A. $20,000
    B. $80,000
    C. $100,000
    D. $120,000

14. Assume that Martha and Karen are identical twins. Martha selects death benefit option A, and Karen selects death benefit option B. Who is probably paying more for her universal life policy?
    A. Martha
    B. Karen
    C. They are probably paying the exact same amount for their policies because they are twins
    D. None of the above

15. Which of the following is NOT required to be able to sell variable policies?
    A. A state insurance producer license
    B. Registration with FINRA
    C. Registration with the NAIC
    D. A passing score on the series 6 exam

16. Which of the following must be the case once a year for a variable policy to meet the federal definition of life insurance?
    A. The face amount must be higher than the cash value by a certain percentage.
    B. The cash value must be higher than the face amount by a certain percentage.
    C. The cash value and the face amount must be exactly equal.
    D. The cash value must equal zero.

17. Julia's variable policy deducts a certain percentage from the premiums as they are paid. What type of load does Julia's policy have?
    A. Back-end load
    B. Front-end load
    C. Premium load
    D. Face-value load

18. At the time of solicitation, variable life illustrations may not be based on projected interest greater than
    A. 8%
    B. 10%
    C. 12%
    D. 15%

19. A policy loan on a scheduled premium variable life policy is usually limited to
    A. 85% of the policy's available cash value
    B. 75% of the policy's available cash value
    C. a term of 5 years
    D. a term of 1 year

20. Laura collects insurance premiums every Friday at the home of several policyholders. Which type of policy do these policyholders probably have?
    A. Home service life insurance
    B. Credit life insurance
    C. Term life insurance
    D. Industrial life insurance

21. George has several policyowners at the factory set up on a plan that deducts the premium automatically from their bank accounts every month. Which type of policy do these policyowners probably have?
    A. Home service life insurance
    B. Credit life insurance
    C. Term life insurance
    D. Industrial life insurance

22. Which type of insurance policy is most common today?
    A. Home service life insurance
    B. Credit life insurance
    C. Industrial life insurance

23. Charlie has a policy to protect his family that will provide a monthly income for 10 years from the date of Charlie's death, provided that he dies within 10 years of establishing the policy. Which type of policy does Charlie have?
    A. Family security policy
    B. Family maintenance policy
    C. Family income policy
    D. Family plan policy

24. Sarah has a policy that will pay her family a monthly income until 2020 if she passes away before that time. Which type of policy does Sarah have?
    A. Family security policy
    B. Family maintenance policy
    C. Family income policy
    D. Family plan policy

25. Tracy has a policy that provides permanent life insurance on him, along with term insurance on his wife and children. Which type of policy does Tracy have?
    A. Family security policy
    B. Family maintenance policy
    C. Family income policy
    D. Family protection policy

26. Which type of policy would not provide a tax-free death benefit under current law?
    A. Joint life policy written on a survivorship basis
    B. Minimum deposit policy
    C. Endowment policy
    D. Mortgage redemption policy

27. Which of the following types of insurance is designed to provide life insurance protection for only a limited time?
    A. Whole life insurance
    B. Variable life insurance
    C. Term life insurance
    D. Universal life insurance

28. Which of the following types of insurance requires a level premium and provides lifelong protection?
    A. Whole life insurance
    B. Variable life insurance
    C. Term life insurance
    D. Universal life insurance

29. A flexible premium, adjustable benefit life insurance contract that accumulates cash values is called
    A. whole life insurance
    B. variable life insurance
    C. term life insurance
    D. universal life insurance

30. Securities-based whole life insurance is called
    A. whole life insurance
    B. variable life insurance
    C. term life insurance
    D. universal life insurance

31. Christy has a term policy that will allow her to switch over to a whole life policy at any time during the first half of the term without providing evidence of insurability. What type of policy is this?
    A. Level term insurance
    B. Renewable term insurance
    C. Convertible term insurance
    D. Reentry term insurance

32. Which of the following is an advantage of term insurance?
    A. The initial cost of the policy tends to be low.
    B. The policy becomes more expensive over time.
    C. It provides temporary protection for a limited time.
    D. Even if the policy is renewable, it is probably not renewable beyond a certain age such as 65.

33. Which of the following is NOT an advantage of whole life policies?
    A. Low initial cost
    B. Level face amount
    C. Guaranteed cash value
    D. Nonforfeiture values

34. Janice and Julie are identical twins who both work as teachers and live next door to each other. They each purchase a $75,000 whole life policy at the same time. Janice chooses continuous premium whole life, and Julie chooses a 20-pay whole life policy. Which sister is probably paying a higher premium?
    A. Janice is probably paying more.
    B. Julie is probably paying more.
    C. They are probably paying the same amount.
    D. It is not possible to determine from the information provided.

35. Sally purchases $100,000 of participating whole life and $50,000 of term insurance. Over time, she intends to use the dividends from the whole life policy to purchase paid-up additions to replace the term insurance. Sally owns a(n)
    A. adjustable life insurance policy
    B. economatic life insurance policy
    C. universal life insurance policy
    D. variable universal life insurance policy

36. Gerald has a state insurance license but no other training or licenses. Gerald can sell any of the following EXCEPT a(n)
    A. adjustable life insurance policy
    B. economatic life insurance policy
    C. whole life insurance policy
    D. variable universal life insurance policy

37. LaKita buys a policy that allows her to adjust the face amount, premium, and length of protection without having to complete a new application or have a new policy issued. LaKita has a(n)
    A. adjustable life insurance policy
    B. economatic life insurance policy
    C. whole life insurance policy
    D. variable universal life insurance policy

38. Which type of policy is least likely to be sold today?
    A. Term
    B. Whole life
    C. Endowment
    D. Variable universal life

39. Which type of policy combines whole life insurance with decreasing term coverage?
    A. Family stability policy
    B. Family maintenance policy
    C. Family income policy
    D. Family protection policy

40. Which type of policy combines whole life insurance with level term coverage?
    A. Family stability policy
    B. Family maintenance policy
    C. Family income policy
    D. Family protection policy

41. Which type of policy combines whole life insurance on one family member with term coverage on other family members?
    A. Family stability policy
    B. Family maintenance policy
    C. Family income policy
    D. Family protection policy

42. Dan and Dawn want to purchase a single policy that will provide a death benefit upon the death of either of them. The type of policy that might best fits this need is a
    A. juvenile policy
    B. minimum deposit policy
    C. joint life policy
    D. multiple protection policy

43. Devon wants to purchase a policy that will cover his nephew until the nephew turns 21, to help his nephew start out on the right foot in terms of insurance. The type of policy that best fits this need is a
    A. juvenile policy
    B. minimum deposit policy
    C. joint life policy
    D. multiple protection policy

44. Tim has a life insurance policy that will pay $100,000 if he dies before age 65 and $50,000 if he dies after age 65. Tim probably has a
    A. juvenile policy
    B. minimum deposit policy
    C. joint life policy
    D. multiple protection policy

45. Minimum deposit policies have become less popular as a result of tax regulations, but they still can be used as long as a certain number of the initial payments are made from sources other than cash value. How many payments must be made from other sources?
    A. 2 of 7
    B. 3 of 7
    C. 4 of 7
    D. 5 of 7

ANSWERS AND RATIONALES TO UNIT TEST

1. **C.**
2. **D.** This policy is decreasing term because it provides a decreasing death benefit as the balance on the mortgage declines.
3. **C.** Increasing term is not used as often as level term or decreasing term.
4. **B.** Renewable term may be renewed at the end of a specified period without proof of insurability.
5. **D.**
6. **B.** This is a limited-pay policy because Zelda is required to pay premiums for only a limited period.
7. **D.** An economatic policy is a whole life policy that uses dividends to purchase additional paid-up insurance.
8. **C.** Joan's policy requires only one premium to acquire a paid-up policy, so it is a single premium policy.
9. **A.** Cosmo's policy is a continuous premium whole life policy because he is required to pay premiums for his whole life or until he is 100.
10. **C.**
11. **D.** With a universal life policy, the front-end load is deducted from the premium, the premium is added to the cash value, the cost of insurance is deducted from the cash value, and the current interest rate is credited to the cash value.
12. **C.** Option A in a universal life policy provides a level death benefit equal to the policy's face amount.
13. **D.** Option B provides for an increasing death benefit equal to policy's face amount plus the cash value.
14. **B.** Option B is generally more expensive than option A for the same coverage because, unlike the case with option A, the mortality risk under option B does not decrease over the life of the policy.
15. **C.**
16. **A.** For a policy to meet the federal definition of life insurance, the face amount must be higher than the cash value by a certain percentage at least once a year.
17. **B.** The percentage is deducted from the premiums, so this is a front-end load.
18. **C.** This is known as the 12% rule.
19. **B.** Loans are usually limited to 75% of the available cash value because the cash value is not guaranteed and depends entirely on the performance of the separate account.
20. **D.**
21. **A.** These policyowners probably have home service life insurance because premiums are deducted automatically from the policyowners' bank accounts.
22. **B.** Credit life insurance is common because almost everybody uses credit.
23. **B.**
24. **C.** This is a family income policy because it provides an income for a stated number of years from the insured's death.
25. **D.** This is a family protection policy because it insures each member of the family at the time the policy is issued.
26. **C.** Under current tax law, endowments do not provide a tax-free death benefit.
27. **C.**
28. **A.** Whole life insurance requires a level premium and provides lifelong protection.
29. **D.** A flexible premium, adjustable benefit life insurance contract that accumulates cash values is called universal life insurance.
30. **B.** Securities-based whole life insurance is called variable life insurance.
31. **C.** A term policy that will allow the insured to switch over to a whole life policy at any time during the first half of the term without providing evidence of insurability is a convertible term insurance policy.
32. **A.** The initial cost of a term insurance policy tends to be low.
33. **A.** Low initial cost is not an advantage of whole life policies.
34. **B.** Julie is probably paying more than her sister is.
35. **B.** Sally owns an economatic life insurance policy.
36. **D.** Gerald cannot sell variable universal life insurance policies.
37. **A.** LaKita has an adjustable life insurance policy.

38. **C.** Endowments generally are not sold today because the tax consequences have changed, eliminating many of the benefits that once made endowments attractive investment vehicles.
39. **C.** A family income policy combines whole life insurance with decreasing term coverage.
40. **B.** A family maintenance policy combines whole life insurance with level term coverage.
41. **D.** A family protection policy combines whole life insurance on one family member with term coverage on other family members.
42. **C.** A joint life policy will provide a death benefit upon the death of either of them.
43. **A.** A juvenile policy will cover Devon's nephew until the nephew turns 21.
44. **D.** Tim probably has a multiple protection policy.
45. **C.** Four of seven payments must be made from sources other than cash value.

UNIT

9

Policy Provisions

9. 1 LEARNING OBJECTIVES

After completing this lesson, you will be able to:

- list the rights of policyowners;
- explain the provisions and clauses of various types of life insurance policies;
- describe the various types of beneficiaries and explain their rights; and
- explain the Uniform Simultaneous Death Act and Common Disaster Provision.

9. 2 INTRODUCTION

An insurance policy is a legal contract. The validity of life insurance policies as such has been established in the United States since 1815 (*Lord v. Ball*, 12 Mass. 115 [1815]). As does any contract, it contains provisions setting forth the rights and duties of parties to the contract. Although it is necessary to look beyond the actual wording of the policy contract and into the statutes and court decisions for a full interpretation of these provisions, they are, nevertheless, the basis of the agreement between the company and the policyholder (and the beneficiaries, heirs, and assignees of the policyholder).

There are no standard policies in life insurance in the sense that there are in the property and casualty insurance field. However, many states have provisions that are required in all life policies so that the following provisions have become more or less standard in such policies.

This chapter will summarize standard provisions, restrictions, and limitations in life insurance policies. It also will review beneficiary provisions and permitted exclusions and limitations on coverage.

9. 3 STANDARD PROVISIONS

9. 3. 1 Insuring Clause

The **insuring clause** contains the basic promise of the life insurance company to pay a specified sum of money in a lump sum or an equivalent income stream to the beneficiary upon the death of the insured. It sets forth the basic agreement between the company and the insured.

9. 3. 2 Entire Contract Clause

As you know, a contract is an agreement between two or more parties, and a life insurance policy is a contract between the insurer and the insured. Each party has obligations and rights that are spelled out in the contract. To make sure that there will be no misunderstanding of just what each insurance contract provides, one of the provisions contained in every policy states that the insurance policy itself and the application, when attached to the policy, make up the entire contract between the parties. No company rules, no oral understandings, and so forth have any bearing on the contract unless they are included in the policy or the attached application.

With regard to the obligations contained in the entire contract, the insured has a major responsibility in a life insurance contract—to pay for the coverage received.

The policy conditions also list the obligations of the insurance company. The insurer promises to pay the face amount of the policy if the insured dies or the cash surrender value to the insured, if so desired, while still living. The policy conditions, then, represent the obligations and promises of both the insurer and the insured.

Note that we're considering the insured to be the policyowner. As you know, this is not always the case.

Both the insured and the insurer have certain rights in a life insurance contract. The insurer can terminate the coverage if the insured fails to pay the premium (after the appropriate grace period), for example. The policyowner has certain rights in the policy—to name a beneficiary and to use cash value the policy accumulates, for instance.

In addition to the rights and obligations of the insurer and the insured, the policy conditions also designate restrictions, limitations, and exclusions of the policy. We'll discuss formal exclusions in detail later. For now, let's assume that John qualifies for life insurance coverage. However, his hobby is road racing. The insurer might issue a policy on his life with an exclusion—a provision that states, in this case, that no claim will be paid if John is killed while participating in a sports car race.

A life insurance policy is a legal contract, so restrictions, limitations, or exclusions in the coverage must be stated among the policy conditions as a written part of the life insurance policy.

The policy conditions must be a part of the policy itself to be effective. Most of these provisions are standard; the policyowner always pays premiums, the insurer always pays the face amount in the event of the insured's death (provided the policy is in force at that time), and so on.

Standard policy conditions—the rights and obligations of the insurer and the insured—are included when the company's standard contract is printed. If it's necessary to adjust the standard contract to satisfy the particular situation of a given policyowner, the alterations can be inserted (often typed) into the contract at the time the policy is issued. If a policy provision is typed into the contract, the company must make certain that the policyowner knows the provision has been inserted and that he accepts it.

On occasion, it's necessary to amend a life insurance policy after it has been issued. This occurs when a policyowner requests that the company add some coverage after the policy has been issued. In such instances, the company simply types or prints up the necessary addition to the policy—or stamps the data on the policy itself—to amend the policy contract. Such changes or additions are called riders, endorsements, or simply amendments.

Note that the policyowner must be aware of and accept the change, which must be reflected in the policyowner's copy of the contract.

For common additions to policies, most companies have printed forms that can be attached to the policy. In addition, some very short common amendments can be rubber stamped onto a policy. Whatever the method, when a printed, stamped, typed, or written change or addition is made to an in-force policy, we call it an amendment, an endorsement, or a rider.

To sum up, policy conditions are the provisions of the policy contract—printed, written, or typed in or added by rider, endorsement, or amendment. These conditions represent the rights and obligations of the insured and the insurer, plus any limitations, restrictions, or exclusions that apply.

A producer is never permitted to make a change in a policy, whether at the request of a policyowner or for some other reason. Only authorized company officers can make changes or amendments in life insurance policies, and such changes must have the policyowner's acceptance before they take effect. An authorized company officer can make a change in a policy, with the policyowner's acceptance, by issuing an endorsement, an amendment, or as it's more commonly called, a rider on the policy.

9. 3. 3 The Consideration Clause

The consideration clause is the second important clause found in every life insurance policy. As its name implies, the consideration clause deals largely with the consideration paid by the policyowner for life insurance protection—the premium.

Part of the insuring clause states that the company promises to pay the policy benefits in consideration of the premium payments. The consideration clause identifies the fact that the policyowner must pay something of value for the insurer's promise to pay benefits. This valuable consideration is the premium.

9. 3. 4 Payment of Premium

This provision specifies when, where, and how premiums are to be paid. Usually premiums are to be paid in advance either at the company's home office or to the agent. The various modes of paying the premium also are identified, such as monthly, quarterly, semiannually, and annually.

In addition, most insurers permit the premium to be paid by means of a monthly bank draft. This method is referred to as **monthly bank plan** or **automatic check plan**. The insurer simply sends a monthly premium notice to the policyowner's bank, and the bank sends the insurer a check for the monthly premium.

The least expensive way to pay the premium is annually or by a monthly bank plan. The other premium modes require the payment of a service charge added to the basic premium. For example, an annual policy premium may be $300. The monthly premium may be $25.50, which would total $306 of premium in a year.

9. 3. 5 Ownership Rights

In most instances, the owner of an insurance policy is also the applicant and the insured. However, for various reasons, it may be advantageous for the policy to be owned by a third party. The three parties would then be the insured, the insurer, and the policyowner.

Ownership of a policy by a third party usually means that the value of that policy will not be included in the estate of the insured. This can be of great benefit when the insured has a very large estate but is short on liquidity.

The policyowner (who may or may not be the insured) has certain rights regarding the policy he owns. The first is the right to name the person or persons to receive the policy's proceeds in the event of the death of the insured—that is, the policyowner can name the beneficiary.

The policyowner also has the right to decide how the proceeds of the policy are to be paid out. As we'll see, there are a number of options available regarding the way in which insurance benefits may be distributed, including leaving the decision to the beneficiary. Right now, we'll just say that the initial right to select how the policy proceeds are to be paid out belongs to the policyowner.

The policyowner also has the right to assign the policy. For example, the policyowner could borrow funds from a bank and assign the policy to the bank as collateral security for the loan. When the loan is fully repaid, the policy would be reassigned to the policyowner.

A policy also may be assigned permanently and irrevocably. This is called an **absolute assignment**. For example, the policyowner may wish to make a gift of a policy to his daughter. He would accomplish this by making an absolute assignment.

The policyowner might state that a creditor (such as the bank mentioned previously) has the right to take whatever amount is necessary from the policy's proceeds to pay a debt if the insured dies before the debt is repaid, or he might sign a contract that says a creditor can obtain a portion of the policy's cash value if he fails to pay the debt as agreed. In either event, the policyowner is using the right to assign the policy.

Another right the policyowner has is to use the policy's cash value. As we learned, permanent policies accumulate a cash value that may be borrowed, so the policyowner may use his policy to obtain a loan or cash.

As we'll learn when we study the various options that are available for an insurance policy, any cash value accumulated by a policy must be turned over to the policyowner in the event he can no longer pay the premiums and the policy lapses or in the event the policyowner surrenders the policy for whatever reason. When a policy lapses because of nonpayment of premiums or upon the surrender of a policy, the policyowner is entitled to the policy's cash surrender value.

The policyowner also has the right to decide his payment schedule for the coverage—annually, semiannually, quarterly, or monthly. Thus, the policyowner has the right to establish the policy's premium payment schedule.

Once the policyowner and the company have established the payment schedule, the policyowner might decide that it is inconvenient or disadvantageous. He can then exercise the right to change the schedule.

Finally, the policyowner has the right to decide how to use dividends paid by the company. There are a number of choices regarding dividends available to the policyowner. Right now, you just need to be aware of the policyowner's right to designate how dividends may be used.

With convertible term life insurance, the policyowner can change coverage to permanent protection—that is, he can convert the policy.

9. 3. 6 Applicant Control or Ownership Clause

When the proposed insured is a minor, the applicant can be the minor's parent or other relative or legal guardian. In such a situation, the applicant—let's say a parent who is applying for insurance on her son's life—will probably want to maintain control of the policy until the insured is of age. This can be accomplished by including a clause that designates the parent (the applicant) as the controller (or owner) of the policy. Because this clause designates the applicant as the person in control of the policy, it is called the **applicant control clause**, or the **ownership clause**.

The parent-child relationship is the most common one in which the ownership or applicant control clause occurs. Other common situations of this type are the guardian-child and grandparent-grandchild relationships. Whatever the relationship, by using the applicant control clause, the applicant for insurance on the life of a minor can retain control of the policy until the minor reaches a given age, at which time control of the policy passes to the insured.

9. 3. 7 Grace Period

When you owe money to someone—let's say you've borrowed money from the bank—you usually have regular payments that you are expected to make. If you don't make your payments on time, the bank will soon institute collection proceedings against you. They'll come after their money or repossess the product you bought.

However, they won't take action immediately. They'll give you the benefit of the doubt for at least a few days. In other words, they'll give you a few days' grace.

The same thing is true with life insurance premiums. If the policyowner fails to make the premium payment, the company won't immediately cancel the policy; it will allow a specified period in which to pay the overdue premium—again, a few days' grace. We call this period the **grace period**.

As you can imagine, this grace period is of tremendous advantage to the policyowner. For instance, suppose the premium payment has simply been forgotten, or suppose the policyowner intends to make the payment but is short of funds for a few days. Because of the grace period, life insurance protection is still available and the beneficiary still would receive the proceeds if the insured died within that period even without having paid the premium. The amount of premium owed, however, is deducted from the proceeds.

The grace period can vary, but for most ordinary life policies, it is one month (30 or 31 days).

9. 3. 7. 1 *Automatic Premium Loan Provision*

The ***automatic* premium loan provision**, when included, allows the company to use automatically whatever portion of the cash value is needed to pay premiums as they become due. This keeps the policy in force when it would otherwise lapse because of nonpayment of premiums.

Because the company is to use the cash value to pay any given premium as it becomes due, it's obvious that the automatic premium loan provision applies only to permanent policies.

Even with the automatic premium loan provision, the policy must have sufficient cash value to pay the premium due. This means that the automatic premium loan provision is meaningless if the policy has no cash value.

Money lent to the policyowner under the automatic premium loan provision is treated just like any other loan of the policy's cash value. This means that interest is charged on the loan and the cash value payable on surrender or death is reduced by the outstanding loan amount.

Example

The cash value on Susannah's policy has accumulated untouched to $5,000. When she misses her annual $500 premium for the first time, the automatic premium loan provision of her policy is activated and $500 is deducted from her policy's cash value to meet the premium obligation. To restore her policy's full cash value, Susannah must repay the $500 along with interest.

In addition, the company realizes that a policy is more likely to be kept in force if the policyowner has an equity—a cash value—in it. For this reason, a company often will limit the number of consecutive premium payments it will make under the automatic premium loan provision.

One final point: just because this provision has the word automatic in its title, don't get the idea that it's automatically included in every policy. In many instances, this provision must be requested and written into the policy. When selling situations arise in which you're trying to convince the policyowner that this is the policy to buy, never indicate that the automatic premium loan provision is included unless you're certain that it is.

9. 3. 8 Reinstatement

When a policy lapses because of nonpayment of a premium, it would be unfair to the policyowner if, shortly thereafter, he requested its reinstatement and the company refused (provided certain conditions are met—we'll discuss these shortly). On the other hand, it would be just as unfair to require the company to reinstate a lapsed policy—especially if no cash values have yet accrued—long after the last premium payment. Some jurisdictions permit insurers to refuse to reinstate a lapsed policy if the policyowner does not request reinstatement within three years.

Reinstatement can happen, however, provided three conditions are met. These conditions are spelled out in the reinstatement clause of the policy.

- The policyowner must pay all back premiums due plus interest on this amount.

- The insured must show proof of insurability.
- Less than three years must have elapsed.

Usually the reinstatement process includes the submission of a reinstatement request or application by the policyowner, evidence of continued insurability, and the payment of all back premiums plus interest. In addition, outstanding loans or other indebtedness against the policy will have to be paid.

The insurer has the right to decline the request for reinstatement if, for example, the insured is unable to provide satisfactory evidence of continued insurability. Statements made on the reinstatement application are subject to a new incontestable period (usually two years). Normally, the reinstatement request will be approved.

If the policy has not been in force for some time, the policyowner may think it is better to simply purchase a new policy rather than pay back premiums plus interest to reinstate the lapsed policy. However, there are several reasons for considering reinstatement.

- The lapsed policy may have more liberal policy provisions.
- The older policy may offer lower interest rates on policy loans.
- Suicide and incontestable clauses may no longer apply if the policy is two years old or older.
- The lapsed policy probably has a lower premium than a new policy.

This last point is especially relevant if the policyowner had purchased the lapsed policy 10 or 15 years earlier. Instead of paying attained age rates for a new policy, the policyowner could reinstate the lapsed policy at original issue age rates.

9. 3. 9 Policy Loan Provisions

Policy loan provisions are found in policies that include cash values. After a policy has been in force for a specified period (usually three years), it must contain some cash value, which may be borrowed by the policyowner.

A policyowner always has the right to surrender or cash in a policy in exchange for the full cash value. In many cases, however, a policyowner might want to make only a partial withdrawal of the available funds and not fully surrender the contract, so a policy loan is often a more appropriate solution.

Generally, a policyowner may borrow up to the amount of the current cash value *less any indebtedness against the policy* (previous loans and interest charges).

The insurance company will charge interest on cash value loans. The amount of interest is usually relatively nominal and regulated by state laws. Often, if the policyowner agrees to pay the interest in advance, the amount charged will be reduced. A slightly higher interest rate is charged if it is paid at the end of a loan year. Most states allow the insurer to use an adjustable rate of interest in lieu of a fixed loan rate.

If the loan amount and interest due are not paid, these amounts will be considered indebtedness against the policy and will result in a reduced death benefit if the insured dies while the indebtedness is outstanding. In most policies, after the policy has been in effect a certain number of years, failure to repay the loan or to pay interest on it will not void the policy unless or until the total amount of the loan and accrued interest equals or exceeds the cash value of the policy, and then only after 30 days' notice has been mailed to the last known address of the policyholder and his assignee, if any.

The insurer may defer a loan request for up to six months from the date of the loan application unless the reason for the loan is to pay premiums due.

9. 3. 9. 1 *Withdrawals and Partial Surrenders*

Partial cash value distributions may be classified as loans or withdrawals; which of the two is chosen depends on several factors.

A *loan* is just that—a loan against one's own money. It is withdrawn with either the presumption that it will be repaid (with accrued interest) or the understanding that by not repaying it the amount of future benefits—including the death benefit—will be reduced by the loaned amount (plus accrued interest).

A *withdrawal* has generally the same impact on policy benefits, but there is no presumption that it will be repaid. The withdrawn amount is treated as a permanent withdrawal, thus immediately reducing the death benefit and, of course, the cash value. The withdrawn amount does not accrue interest against future policy values, as it does with a loan. However, from an actuarial perspective, the impact on future policy values is identical with either approach.

Generally, only universal life and variable universal life policies, with their inherent policy flexibility, permit withdrawals. Traditional whole life and variable life do not lend themselves to this type of flexibility and, though there may be a few exceptions, they typically provide only for loans.

Because cash value withdrawals (versus loans) are recognized as taxable income to the extent they exceed the policyowner's cost basis in the contract, most sizeable withdrawals are technically regarded as "withdrawals" up to the owner's basis; withdrawn amounts above basis are regarded as "loans," which are not taxable. By recognizing withdrawn amounts that exceed basis merely as loans and not permanent withdrawals, this technique defers and possibly avoids income taxation of the full withdrawn amount.

9. 3. 10 Incontestability

The **incontestability clause** states that after the policy (term as well as permanent) has been in force a certain length of time, the company can no longer contest it or void it, except for nonpayment of premiums. The length of time varies, but it's usually one or two years.

If the company discovers some reason to void the policy during the contestable period—the first year or two the policy is in force—it can take such action. Once the policy has been in force for the specified period, even if fraud is discovered, the company cannot void the policy.

Thus, the policy becomes incontestable after the two-year period (in a few states, one year). This provision makes the insurance contract a little different from other types of contracts. Usually, contract law specifies that if a fraudulent contract has been enacted, it may be voided or canceled at any time. The incontestable period limits the period in which the insurer may contest the insurance contract for misrepresentation or fraud on the part of the applicant.

9. 3. 11 Suicide Clause

The **suicide clause** is designed to prevent people who are contemplating suicide from obtaining life insurance. To accomplish this, the clause states that if the insured commits suicide within a specified period, the policy will be voided. The length of time varies, but it's usually the same as the incontestable clause time limit: one or two years.

Once the period specified in the policy has elapsed, the company will pay the claim even if the insured commits suicide. If suicide occurs within the time limit, however, the company usually refunds any amount the policyowner has paid for the coverage. In other words, the company refunds the premiums paid.

When refunding premiums in the case of suicide occurring within the specified time limit of the suicide clause, the company usually doesn't pay interest the premium has earned because the interest earned is used to offset part of the costs the company incurred in setting up the policy.

Life insurance companies are allowed in many states to protect themselves from suicide through the suicide clause. Several jurisdictions don't specifically mention the clause in their laws, but by making no mention of it, they thereby permit its inclusion in policies. Check your state's law to see how the suicide clause is handled.

One final point: when included in a policy, the suicide clause applies whether the insured is sane or insane at the time he commits suicide.

9. 3. 12 Assignment

When a policyowner assigns a policy, she transfers rights in the policy—either all of them or a stipulated portion—to another party. The **assignment clause** in a policy states that any assignment the policyowner decides to make must be filed in writing with the company or it will not be valid when the claim is paid.

Suppose Henry decides to borrow money from the bank. He assigns enough of his policy proceeds to the bank to repay the loan if he dies before repaying it himself. Through an oversight, both Henry and the bank forget to notify the insurer of the assignment. If Henry dies before paying off the loan, the insurance company will pay the entire face amount (proceeds) to the beneficiary because the assignment wasn't filed with the company.

The policyowner can assign all of the rights or just a portion of them. The extent to which the policyowner's rights are assigned must be spelled out in the assignment agreement made with the assignee.

Keep in mind in this section that the type of beneficiary designation (which we'll discuss later in this unit) has a great deal to do with the policyowner's capability to assign policy rights. For example, if the beneficiary has been named irrevocably, he must agree in writing to the assignment.

9. 3. 12. 1 Collateral, Partial, Conditional Assignment

A policyowner, as you know, names the beneficiary of the policy. Under normal circumstances, the proceeds of the policy go directly to this named beneficiary upon the insured's death. However, the policyowner can, if so desired, direct that a certain amount of the money is to go to another party.

Suppose a man borrows $5,000. He uses the proceeds of his life insurance policy as part of the collateral for the loan. To do this, he signs an agreement that states that if he dies before repaying the entire $5,000, a portion of the proceeds of his policy is to be paid to the assignee—the person or party he's borrowing from—to pay off any outstanding loan balance.

Because the policyowner is using his policy as collateral for a loan, this is known as a **collateral assignment**.

Another way to look at it is this: only a portion of the proceeds is to be paid to the assignee and then only if the insured dies before having paid back his loan. Keep in mind, too, that if certain policy rights are restricted in the policy itself, the policyowner cannot make assignments involving those rights. Because just part of the proceeds are assigned, we sometimes call a collateral assignment a **partial assignment**.

In addition, the assignee is to receive a portion of the proceeds only under certain conditions, the main one being that a balance remains on the loan when the insured dies. Because this condition must exist, this collateral or partial assignment also is referred to as a **conditional assignment**.

Regardless of the exact title given to this kind of agreement, it occurs when the insured (policyowner) assigns all or part of the policy's proceeds as collateral for a loan.

Obviously, a lending institution or bank won't lend more than the face amount of the policy under a collateral assignment alone. In fact, most institutions probably won't lend an amount equal to the face amount but will limit the loan to something less than the face amount of the policy. Because this is the case, under a collateral, partial, or conditional assignment, the policyowner is usually assigning only part of the policyowner rights in the policy.

9. 3. 12. 2 Absolute, Voluntary, Complete Assignment

It sometimes happens that the policyowner decides to sell or make a gift of a life insurance policy by assigning all rights in the policy to the assignee. For instance, a man might want to give a policy on his life to his son. This type of assignment is made voluntarily, so it's sometimes called a **voluntary assignment**.

A voluntary assignment usually involves turning all rights—including the right to use the cash value—over to the assignee. For this reason, it can be called an **absolute** or **complete assignment**.

When a collateral assignment is made, the proceeds (or a portion of them) are assigned only for as long as there's a balance on the transaction involved. In other words, it's a temporary assignment.

When an absolute assignment is made, on the other hand, the original policyowner usually has no means of recovering surrendered rights. In effect, he has designated another policyowner to take over—a change in policy ownership is taking place. This type of assignment is usually permanent.

9. 3. 12. 3 Beneficiaries' Assignment Rights

In some cases, the policy's beneficiary can assign a portion of the proceeds (or all of them, technically, although this is unlikely) in about the same manner as the policyowner. However, unless the beneficiary has been named irrevocably, there is actually little to assign.

A revocable beneficiary has only an expectancy as far as the policy is concerned. He expects to receive the proceeds, unless the policyowner changes the designation to another person. This makes it unlikely that a lending institution will advance money on the strength of this expectancy.

An irrevocable beneficiary, on the other hand, has more than a mere expectancy in the policy; receiving the proceeds upon the insured's death is more likely because the policyowner cannot designate another person in his stead. An irrevocable beneficiary, then, is more likely to find a lending institution willing to lend money on the strength of the policy than is a revocable beneficiary.

One final point about assignments made by beneficiaries: if the beneficiary dies before the insured does, an assignment made by the beneficiary is no longer valid in most jurisdictions, unless the policyowner agrees in writing that the assignment remains valid if the beneficiary dies first. The proceeds of the policy are paid just as if the assignment had never existed, then, unless a written agreement to the contrary exists.

9. 3. 13 Misstatement of Age or Sex

If the insured's age or sex is misstated on the application, the insurer has the right to adjust the policy's benefits to reflect the amount that the premiums paid would have purchased on the basis of the correct age or sex of the insured.

The insured's age is a factor in computing the amount of premium to be paid. If a man said he was 30 at the time his policy was issued and it was discovered upon his death 20 years later that he was actually 32 when the policy was issued, this means that the insured has been paying a lower premium than he should have been for the entire 20 years.

Because the company computed the insured's premium rate at an age two years younger than his actual age, the premium paid over the years was lower than it should have been. In this case, because only two years' discrepancy exists, the difference probably wouldn't be a tremendous sum. Still, the company must meet its obligations to all of its policyowners.

The misstatement of age clause in an insurance policy provides that when a discrepancy in age exists, if the insured is alive, the company must adjust the amount of future premiums and request payment of the additional premium the policyowner should have paid. If the insured has died, the company must compute the amount of insurance that the actual premium paid would have purchased at the insured's correct age and pay the beneficiary that amount.

For example, suppose an insured purchases a policy with a face amount of $50,000. He states his age at the time of purchase as 30 when in fact he was 34. Let's assume that the premium he was paying would purchase only $47,000 of insurance at age 34. After he dies, the error in age is discovered. His beneficiary will receive $47,000 in proceeds rather than $50,000.

Misstatement of age is not an unusual occurrence in the life insurance business. Some of the misstatements are intentional, but most of them are simply mistakes. In either event, the difference in actual and stated ages is not material enough to void the policy. Most policies contain this misstatement of age clause to rectify this situation if it occurs. You should be aware that if an overstatement of age occurs, the company will reduce premium payments or adjust the face amount of the policy upwards if the insured dies before the error is discovered.

The same concept applies to misstatement of sex. Because of life expectancy (females have longer life expectancy), males pay more for life insurance than females. Therefore, if the insured's sex was misstated on the application, an adjustment to death benefit will be made, or if the mistake was found while the insured was alive, an adjustment to premium will be made. The premium adjustment will include a new, higher premium for the future and a request for additional premium to take care of the amount that should have been paid by the policyowner in the past.

This provision allows the insurer to make a change in the policy even though the error is discovered beyond the incontestability period.

9. 3. 14 Medical Examinations and Autopsy

Some states require life insurance policies to include a provision that gives the insurer the right and opportunity at its own expense to conduct a medical examination of the insured as often as reasonably required when a claim is pending and to make an autopsy in case of death where it is not forbidden by law.

9. 3. 15 Modifications

Modifications or changes in the policy, or any agreement in connection with the policy (such as changes in the beneficiaries, face amount, or additional coverage), must be endorsed on or attached to the policy in writing over the signature of a specified officer or officers of the company. No one else has authority to make changes or agreements, to waive provisions, or to extend the time for premium payment.

Some modification clauses also specifically state that no agent has the right to waive policy provisions, make alterations or agreements, or extend the time for payments of premiums.

9. 3. 16 Policy Change Provision (Conversion Option)

The policy may contain a provision that permits the insured to exchange a policy for another type of policy form permitted by the company. This exchange usually is made from one policy type to another policy form with the same face amount.

If the exchange is to a policy with a higher premium, the insured merely has to pay the higher premium and no proof of insurability would be required.

If the exchange is to a policy form with a lower premium, proof of insurability may be required as this could result in adverse selection against the insurer.

Example

If Charlie discovers that he has only six months to live, he might decide to exchange his higher-premium 20-pay life for one-year term insurance with the same face amount. The insurer's risk has increased while its premium income has decreased. Thus, Charlie will have to prove insurability.

9. 3. 17 Free Look

No policy of individual life insurance can be delivered legally or issued for delivery in most states unless it has printed on it or attached to it a notice stating in substance that during a period of 10 days (some companies allow 20 days) from the date the policy is delivered to the policyholder, it may be surrendered to the insurer together with a written request for cancellation of the policy and in such event, the policy will be void from the beginning and the insurer will refund any premium paid.

This provision allows the policyholder an opportunity to review the entire contract and reevaluate the purchase decision.

9. 3. 18 Beneficiaries

The beneficiary is the person or interest to whom payment of the life insurance proceeds will be made upon the death of the insured. The beneficiary provision allows the insured or the policyowner to direct the payment to any person she chooses.

A variety of different parties or interests may be designated as beneficiaries under the life insurance policy. The beneficiary can be a person or an institution, such as a foundation or charity. A specifically designated person, more than one person, or a class or classes of persons may be named as beneficiaries. The insured may name her estate, an institution, a corporation, a trust, or any other legal entity as a beneficiary.

As you should recall, to form an insurance contract, the policyowner must have an insurable interest in the insured at the time of application but not necessarily at the time of death. After a policy is in effect, the policy remains valid even if the insurable interest of the policyowner ceases to exist.

A beneficiary is not required to have an insurable interest but often does. In many cases, a spouse, parent, or child of the insured person is named as the beneficiary, so the beneficiary does happen to have a coincidental insurable interest in the life of the insured. Nonetheless, insurable interest on the part of the beneficiary is not required, and there is no need to change a beneficiary designation if the original family relationship changes.

Example

A couple is married, and each spouse is the owner and beneficiary of a life insurance policy covering the other spouse's life. Insurable interest exists at the inception of the insurance contract. Later, this married couple divorces. Legally, the policies remain valid, even though insurable interest has ceased and there is no obligation to change the beneficiary designations.

However, more than likely, there will be a change in ownership rights, the beneficiary designations, or both, or the policies will be surrendered when a marriage terminates. If there are children from the marriage, ownership rights might be transferred to the children or the children may be designated as new beneficiaries. If there are no children, the policies probably will be surrendered because people generally don't continue to pay life insurance premiums when financial and emotional interest in an insured has ceased.

9. 3. 18. 1 Revocable Versus Irrevocable

One of the rights of the life insurance policyowner is the right to designate a beneficiary and to change that beneficiary designation at will. Almost all life insurance beneficiary designations are **revocable** (changeable). Usually, the insured retains the right to change the beneficiary, unless he has specifically given up that right. Most policies have a revocable beneficiary.

It is possible, however, for the owner of the policy to give up the right to change the beneficiary designation at will. In such cases, there is an **irrevocable** beneficiary, and the designation cannot be changed without the consent of the beneficiary. An irrevocable designation might be used when a court orders a husband in a divorce settlement to continue payment on an insurance policy on his own life, with an irrevocable beneficiary designation on behalf of his wife (the primary beneficiary) and his children (the contingent beneficiaries). In the event that the irrevocable beneficiary dies before the insured, the right to select the beneficiary may revert to the policyowner on a reversionary basis.

When an irrevocable beneficiary is named, the policyowner gives up the usual ownership rights to the policy and cannot exercise them without the consent of the beneficiary. For example, the policyowner could not take out a policy loan without the consent of the irrevocable beneficiary.

Even when an irrevocable beneficiary designation has been made, the designation can be changed if the irrevocable beneficiary agrees to it.

Example

Suppose that Harry named his wife Sarah the irrevocable beneficiary of his life policy. Later, it turns out that Sarah has made a fortune in the stock market and if Harry dies prematurely, she won't need the proceeds of the policy at all. Harry and Sarah, therefore, decide to change the beneficiary designation from her name to that of their son. In this instance, because the irrevocable beneficiary agrees to the change, the son can be named beneficiary.

9. 3. 18. 2 Naming Beneficiaries

There are two methods for naming and changing beneficiaries: the filing method and the endorsement method.

9. 3. 18. 2. 1 Filing Method

This method of effecting a beneficiary change is also known as the **recording method**. Under this method, the request must be filed in writing to the insurer. The request is made effective by the insurance company recording the change in its records. Once recorded, the change takes effect as of the date the insured signed the request.

9. 3. 18. 2. 2 Endorsement Method

This method requires that the beneficiary change be typed or affixed directly to the policy. The insured must make a written request and mail the request along with the policy to the insurance company. The insurance company will then make sure that the beneficiary change is made to the policy.

9. 3. 18. 3 Succession of Beneficiaries

The beneficiary designation, however, may be one of several different choices. Perhaps the most common is the **primary** beneficiary.

The word **primary** means first or most important. Therefore, if Jane is named the primary beneficiary, she is the first person in line to receive the proceeds of the life insurance policy.

It's possible to name more than one primary beneficiary for the proceeds of an insurance policy. If Jane and her brother Bob are both named primary beneficiaries, they both will receive their shares of the proceeds before any others.

Because there's no guarantee that a beneficiary will outlive the insured, it may be wise to name a contingent beneficiary as well. Whether the contingent beneficiary receives anything depends on—or is contingent on—something happening to the primary beneficiary that keeps him from receiving the proceeds. Thus, a contingent beneficiary will receive the proceeds of the policy only if the primary beneficiary dies before the insured.

It is also possible to designate a tertiary beneficiary. A tertiary beneficiary occupies the third level in the succession of beneficiaries and is entitled to receive the life insurance proceeds following the death of the insured, provided that both the primary and contingent (secondary) beneficiaries have died before the insured.

After the death of the insured, the proceeds belong to the beneficiary. What is left after the beneficiary dies, of course, depends on the settlement option selected to go into effect at the death of the insured. If a lump-sum benefit is paid, the insurance company has no further obligation to the beneficiary. If an option other than a lump-sum payment is selected or an arrangement is made whereby benefits continue over a certain period, the beneficiary should name his own beneficiary.

If the primary beneficiary dies before the insured and there is no contingent or tertiary beneficiary, the insured's estate automatically becomes the beneficiary.

9. 3. 18. 4 Changing Beneficiaries

Careless wording of beneficiary designations can result in undesirable consequences. A tremendous amount of time is spent each year in courtroom litigation attempting to determine the beneficiaries and heirs. For this reason, the life insurance producer should insist that the applicant word his beneficiary designation carefully.

Example

If the insured designates his wife (not specifically named) as the beneficiary, a problem may arise. If the insured has married several times, it may be difficult to identify the true beneficiary. In such case, does wife mean the insured's present wife or does it mean his wife at the time the beneficiary was designated? Does it apply to a wife who is now caring for the insured's minor children? Who was the intended beneficiary in such a case? It is important that the beneficiary be designated by full name to avoid misunderstanding.

If children are designated as a class to receive the proceeds, and if it is apparently the intention of the insured that an adopted child be included, a disposition of the proceeds will be made to follow that intention.

The insurer will make every effort to make a disposition of the proceeds of the policy in compliance with the wishes of the insured, as long as the insured makes it clear what his intention is. When the intention is not clear, the insurer must distribute the funds according to the apparent intent of the insured or pay the funds into court and seek a judicial determination of the proper distribution.

9. 3. 18. 5 Designation Options

9. 3. 18. 5. 1 A Minor as Beneficiary

Naming a minor as the beneficiary of a life insurance policy presents problems. The most immediate of these problems is that a minor would not be competent legally to receive payment of and provide receipt for the policy proceeds if the insured dies before the minor came of age. If an insurance company paid the policy proceeds without a proper receipt from the beneficiary, it might be liable to pay the proceeds again when the beneficiary reached her majority.

To avoid this, insurance companies may hold on to the proceeds, paying interest on them until the beneficiary reaches legal age, or the company may insist that a trustee or guardian be appointed for the minor, someone who is legally entitled to receive and manage the policy proceeds.

If a minor becomes eligible to receive life insurance proceeds because of the death of both parents, any of their estate left to the minor would have to be administered by a general guardian whether or not it includes life insurance proceeds. Thus, the life insurance proceeds would be paid to that guardian. Also, some parents anticipate this problem by establishing a trust to administer the life insurance proceeds and all other property in the estate of the parents in the event that both parents die leaving minor children.

9. 3. 18. 5. 2 A Trust as Beneficiary

Up to this point, we've talked about beneficiaries of policies as if they were always one or more individuals—living human beings. However, this is not always the case. For example, if Jack wishes, he can name his estate as the beneficiary of his policy. The same is true of a company or a trust. All may be named as a beneficiary, as can the surviving stockholders of a closely held corporation.

A trust is formed when the owner of property (the grantor) gives legal title of that property to another (the trustee) to be used for the benefit of a third individual (the trust beneficiary). This fiduciary relationship allows the trustee to manage the property in the trust for the benefit of the trust beneficiary only. The trustee legally must not benefit from the trust.

When a trust is designated as the beneficiary of a life insurance policy, the policy proceeds provide funds for the trust. Upon the death of the insured, the trustee administers the funds in accordance with the instructions set forth in the trust provisions.

Although there are many benefits in naming a trust as beneficiary of an estate or a life insurance policy, particularly for minor children, there are drawbacks as well. A trustee will charge a fee for managing a trust. The way the trust property is managed is often left up to the trustee, leaving the trust beneficiary powerless to intervene if the trust is poorly managed. Also, the trustee may not provide resources for the trust beneficiary as he or even the grantor would have wanted. The trust beneficiary must request resources from the trustee; he cannot make free use of the property in the trust.

Life insurance trusts often are used to provide management of insurance proceeds on behalf of a beneficiary. Rather than allow the insurance company to administer the proceeds, a policyowner may wish that the proceeds be invested, managed, and paid out on a discretionary basis through the use of a trust.

An **inter vivos trust** is one that takes effect during the lifetime of the grantor. A **testamentary trust** is a trust created after the grantor's death, according to the provisions of the grantor's will.

9. 3. 18. 5. 3 The Insured's Estate as Beneficiary

The insured's estate can be named as beneficiary. The insured may direct that the policy proceeds be payable to his executors, administrators, or assignees. Such a designation might be made by an insured to provide funds to pay estate taxes, expenses of past illness, funeral expenses, and any other outstanding debts before the settlement of the estate. Designating the insured's estate as beneficiary aids in the settlement of the estate by avoiding the need to sell other assets of the estate to pay these last expenses.

Frequently, it is not desirable to name the estate as beneficiary. When money enters an estate and there is no will, the court handling the disposition of that estate is required to distribute the assets according to state law, which may or may not be the way the deceased would have wished.

In addition, estate costs usually are determined by the size of the probate estate. This means that adding life insurance policy proceeds to the probate estate increases the costs of settling the estate.

When policy proceeds go into an estate, they also could be tied up for a considerable time, especially if the estate is involved in a dispute.

Finally, when a policyowner leaves policy proceeds to a named beneficiary, there are ways to protect these funds from the beneficiary's creditors. (We'll discuss these methods later in the course.) When the proceeds go into the estate, however, the heirs receive the proceeds in the form of cash, which makes the money more vulnerable to creditors.

9. 3. 18. 6 Class Designations

Another way of designating beneficiaries of life insurance policies is by group or by class, rather than by individual name. An example of such a designation would be "all my children" or "my brothers and sisters still living."

This designation saves the policyowner the trouble of making changes if the membership of the group is altered because of births or deaths.

Let's use an example to see how beneficiaries may be designated by class. In 1995, Julio purchased a life insurance policy and listed as the beneficiaries "all my children." At the time he purchased the policy, Julio had three children—Maria, Jose, and Elizabeth. All three were, therefore, the beneficiaries of Julio's policy.

In 1997, Elizabeth dies, so the beneficiaries are Maria and Jose, Julio's surviving children.

In 1998, Julio's wife has twins, Raoul, and Margaret, at which point the beneficiaries to Julio's policy are Maria, Jose, Raoul and Margaret.

By designating his beneficiaries by class rather than individually by name, Julio saved himself the trouble of having to change the beneficiaries after Elizabeth's death and then again after Raoul and Margaret were born. More importantly, Julio made sure that the policy proceeds would be distributed according to his wishes (i.e., that all his children would share the proceeds). If Julio had designated his beneficiaries individually by name rather than by class, it could have led to confusion and, worse, the distribution of the policy proceeds in a manner not in accordance with Julio's wishes.

Example

Suppose Julio had named Maria, Jose, and Elizabeth as beneficiaries and then neglected to eliminate Elizabeth as a beneficiary after her death. If Julio had died, part of the policy proceeds might have been paid into Elizabeth's estate and distributed according to state law rather than to Julio's remaining children as he intended.

9. 3. 18. 7 *Per Capita and Per Stirpes*

Let's say two men have done a day's work, each sharing equally in the task. They receive $100 for the day, and they've agreed to divide the money on a per capita basis. **Per capita** is derived from Latin and literally means per head and, therefore, per person. Under the per capita distribution method, each of these men receives $50 for the day's work and thus shares equally in the day's earnings.

Now, apply what we've just said to a life insurance situation. Suppose when Zeke dies, he has a $150,000 life insurance policy that names his three sons, Abe, Ben, and Carlos, per capita primary beneficiaries. Each of the three sons would receive $50,000.

Under a per capita beneficiary designation, if one of the named beneficiaries is already dead when the policy matures, the remaining beneficiary or beneficiaries divide his share in addition to receiving their own. In the situation we've just described—three sons named per capita primary beneficiaries of a $150,000 policy—if Carlos dies before the father, when the father dies, Carlos's share is divided equally between the other two sons who would each receive $75,000.

Now, under a **per stirpes** designation, the proceeds belonging to the deceased brother would not go to the other beneficiaries. Per stirpes, again derived from Latin, means through the root, and in this case, the deceased brother is the root—if, that is, he has heirs of his own. To those heirs—usually his children—he is their root and the proceeds of the father's policy pass through the root to his children.

So, if we have three brothers named primary beneficiaries per stirpes of a $150,000 policy but Carlos has died, followed by the death of the father, each surviving brother would receive $50,000 and Carlos's $50,000 share would pass on to his heirs.

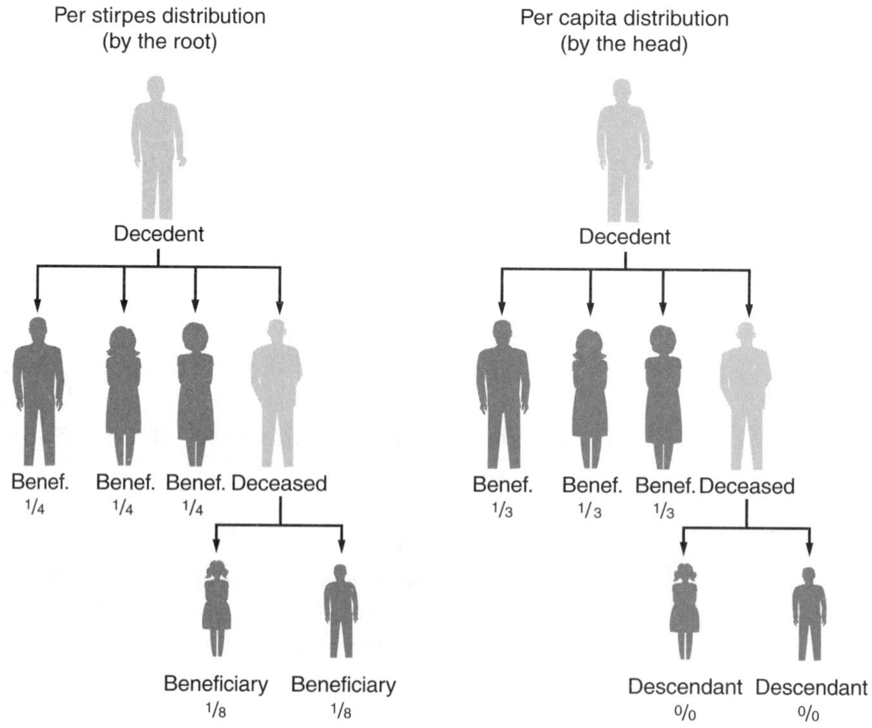

9. 3. 18. 8 *The Uniform Simultaneous Death Act*

Beneficiary designations may seem perfectly clear when read in a life insurance policy. Nevertheless, if an insured and the primary beneficiary are both killed at the same time, problems arise. How can it be determined who outlived whom?

Many states have adopted the Uniform Simultaneous Death Law. Under it, if there is no evidence as to who died first, the policy will be settled as though the insured survived the beneficiary.

Accordingly, the life insurance proceeds would be paid to the estate of the insured, not the estate of the beneficiary. Of course, if contingent beneficiaries are designated, the proceeds would be payable to them. If there is clear evidence that the beneficiary survived the insured, the proceeds are payable to the beneficiary's estate.

Let's say Melvin is the insured and his wife Melody is the primary beneficiary of the policy. Their children, Mike and Melissa, are the contingent beneficiaries. Melvin and Melody are killed in a plane crash.

If Melody, the primary beneficiary, lived longer than Melvin, she should get the proceeds and they should be paid into her estate. The proceeds would then go to people designated in her will or in accordance with state intestacy laws if she has no will.

If Melvin lived longer than Melody, the contingent beneficiaries, Mike and Melissa, should receive the proceeds. If there were no contingent beneficiaries, the proceeds would go to the insured's estate. The insured's will would then designate who should receive the money, or if he had no will, the intestacy laws would control the disposition.

As a practical matter, it is often impossible to determine whether one person outlived another in this type of situation. To deal with this type of problem, the Uniform Simultaneous Death Act has been adopted by most states.

The Uniform Simultaneous Death Act states that if the primary beneficiary and the insured die in the same accident and there's no proof that the beneficiary actually outlived the insured, the proceeds are paid as if the primary beneficiary had died first. This means that the proceeds of the policy are paid to any named contingent beneficiary(ies) or into the estate of the insured if contingent beneficiaries were not named. If there's any proof—such as a witness who says he saw the primary beneficiary move, thus showing signs of life, after an accident that kills both the beneficiary and the insured—then the primary beneficiary outlived the insured and the money must be paid to the primary beneficiary's estate.

9. 3. 18. 8. 1 Common Disaster Provision

There are times when it is most desirable to avoid this problem of the primary beneficiary living a short time longer than the insured and receiving the proceeds of the policy. It can be accomplished by using a common disaster provision.

A policyowner can make certain that the rights of the contingent beneficiary are protected by including a common disaster provision in the policy. This provision simply writes into a policy that the primary beneficiary must outlive the insured a specified length of time in cases of simultaneous (or nearly simultaneous) death or the proceeds are paid to the contingent beneficiary.

The common disaster provision paves the way, legally, for the policyowner to make certain that the contingent beneficiary receives the proceeds if both the insured and the primary beneficiary die within a short time of each other. The policyowner requests this provision in the policy. It states that the primary beneficiary must outlive the insured by a specified period, usually 10, 15, or 30 days, to receive the proceeds. This provision comes into play most frequently when the insured and the primary beneficiary are killed in (or die as a result of) a common disaster—an accident of some kind—which is the reason the provision covering the situation is called a common disaster provision.

Example

Suppose you buy a life insurance policy, naming your wife the primary beneficiary and your son the contingent beneficiary. You want to protect the rights of your son, in respect to the policy, in the event you and your wife die in a common disaster—and especially if you die first, because in that case, the proceeds might pass on to your wife and then into her taxable estate at her death a short time later. You can do this by adding a common disaster provision to your policy.

9. 3. 18. 9 Spendthrift Clause

One of the unique features of life insurance is that the life insurance proceeds are exempt from the claims of the insured's (deceased's) creditors as long as there is a named beneficiary other than the insured's estate. A similar provision with reference to the beneficiary is the spendthrift clause.

A person who spends money extravagantly is known as a **spendthrift**. The insured can protect the proceeds of an insurance policy from the actions of a spendthrift beneficiary through the use of a **spendthrift clause**. This clause in a life insurance policy provides the following features.

- The proceeds will be paid in some way other than a lump sum.
- The proceeds or payments to be made to the beneficiary are protected from the beneficiary's creditors while they are still held by the insurance company.

The spendthrift clause is designed to protect the proceeds of a life insurance policy from the beneficiary's spending habits and creditors.

The spendthrift clause also prevents the beneficiary from:

- transferring the proceeds—assigning payments to a creditor;
- commuting the proceeds—taking the present value of future payments in a lump sum; and
- encumbering the proceeds—borrowing money on the strength of the proceeds of the policy.

If the beneficiary fails to pay his creditors as agreed, one or more of them may be forced to take legal action to recover the money. If the beneficiary is receiving payments from a life policy that has a spendthrift clause, the creditors cannot attach those payments before they are made to the beneficiary. After the beneficiary has received the payments, however, the creditors can take steps to attach those payments.

The insured normally elects to have this provision as part of the policy at the time of the application for insurance. As long as the proceeds are paid on one of several settlement options whereby the insurer keeps the proceeds and sends a monthly payment to the beneficiary, the amounts are exempt from the claims of the beneficiary's creditors until they are actually received.

9. 3. 18. 10 Facility of Payment Provision

This provision allows the insurer to select a beneficiary if the named beneficiaries cannot be found. This provision is found most commonly in group life insurance contracts and industrial life policies.

When a named beneficiary cannot be found (after a reasonable time), to facilitate the payment of the death proceeds, the insurer may select a beneficiary if this provision is in the policy. Typically, this provision is found in policies with relatively small death benefits, such as industrial life. Normally, the insurer would select someone who is in the family's immediate blood line (e.g., a brother, sister, aunt, or uncle).

9. 3. 19 Exclusions and Limitations

For many years, life insurance policies were written with a number of exclusions. These exclusions spelled out the circumstances under which the policy proceeds would not be paid. Today, most life insurance policies no longer contain these exclusions. However, many policies containing exclusions of one kind or another are still in force, so you should know about the most common policy exclusions.

With the exception of the suicide clause, which we studied earlier and which can be considered a kind of exclusion, these exclusions are no longer found in policies being issued today. Companies may charge higher premiums for persons in situations such as those described below, but the policy proceeds will be guaranteed to the beneficiary.

9. 3. 19. 1 Aviation Exclusion

This exclusion restricts payment of benefits in case of death from aviation activities, except when the insured was a fare-paying passenger or commercial crew member. The following are among the types of aviation restrictions still found:

- Exclusion of all aviation caused or related deaths, except those of fare-paying passengers on **regularly scheduled airlines** (some policies do not include the phrase regularly scheduled airlines, thus covering non-scheduled flights also, but only for a fare-paying passenger)

- Exclusion of deaths in military aircraft only or death while on military maneuvers
- Exclusion of pilots, crew members, student pilots, and (sometimes) anyone with duties in flight or while descending from an aircraft (e.g., parachuting)

Companies using any or all of these restrictions will afford coverage of civil aviation deaths for an extra premium. The exclusions or restrictions apply only to those unwilling to pay the extra premium required and to military duties.

9. 3. 19. 2 War or Military Service Exclusion

In wartime, it has been common for companies to include restrictions that limit the death benefit paid to usually a refund of premium plus interest or possibly an amount equal to the policy's cash value. Often in the past, the policy's benefits were suspended during a war or an act of war. The term act of war has been used to describe the Korean and Vietnam conflicts.

Today, most insurers will provide some form of life insurance coverage for those on military duty. Traditionally, there are two types of restrictions or clauses that may be used. The **status clause** excludes the payment of the death benefit while the insured is serving in the military. The **results clause** excludes the payment of the death benefit if the insured is killed as a result of war.

Most insurers today do not use a war exclusion or clause. Instead, they may limit the amount of insurance that a person may apply for if military service is contemplated, or a higher premium may be charged to cover the slightly higher risk involved.

9. 3. 19. 3 Hazardous Occupation or Hobby Exclusion

By today's underwriting standards, few applicants are declined life insurance because of their occupations. For example, firefighters and police personnel can purchase life insurance at standard rates. Even commercial airline pilots can purchase life insurance (although possibly at higher than standard rates).

Much of the underwriting attention is focused on the applicant's avocations or hobbies. If an applicant participates in a hazardous hobby such as auto racing, sky diving, or scuba diving, the amount of insurance that may be purchased may be limited or an extra premium may be charged because of the additional risk. Depending on the hobby, the death benefit may be excluded if death was caused as a result of the hazardous avocation.

9. 3. 20 Prohibited Provisions

By law in most states, life insurance policies are not permitted to contain the following provisions:

- A provision that limits the time for bringing any lawsuit against the insurance company to less than one year after the reason for the lawsuit occurs
- A provision that allows a settlement at maturity of less than the face amount plus any dividend additions, less any indebtedness to the company and any premium deductible under the policy
- A provision that allows forfeiture of the policy because of the failure to repay any policy loan or interest on the loan if the total owed is less than the loan value of the policy
- A provision making the soliciting agent the agent of the person insured under the policy or making the acts or representations of the agent binding on the insured (agent must only be an agent of the company, not the insured)

The law of the state in which the policy is sold governs the contract. The policy may not contain a provision by which the laws of the home state of the insurer govern the policy provisions.

9. 4 SUMMARY

In this lesson, you learned about:

- the rights of policyowners;
- the provisions and clauses of various types of life insurance policies;
- various types of beneficiaries; and
- the Uniform Simultaneous Death Act and Common Disaster Provision.

UNIT TEST

1. Which clause contains the basic promise of the life insurance company to pay a specified sum of money to a beneficiary upon the death of the insured?
   A. Consideration clause
   B. Insuring clause
   C. Policy loan clause
   D. Payment clause

2. Which clause identifies the fact that the policyowner must pay something of value for the insurer's promise to pay benefits?
   A. Consideration clause
   B. Insuring clause
   C. Entire contract clause
   D. Payment clause

3. Which clause identifies the components of the contract?
   A. Consideration clause
   B. Insuring clause
   C. Entire contract clause
   D. Payment clause

4. Which of the following is NOT generally an ownership right in an insurance policy?
   A. Naming the beneficiary
   B. Deciding how the proceeds are to be paid out
   C. Assigning the policy when an irrevocable beneficiary has been named
   D. Using the cash value

5. How long is the typical grace period?
   A. 10 days
   B. 30 days
   C. 60 days
   D. 90 days

6. Which of the following is NOT usually a condition of policy reinstatement?
   A. The policyowner must pay all back dividends due plus interest on the amount.
   B. The policyowner must pay all back premiums due plus interest on the amount.
   C. The insured must show proof of insurability.
   D. Less than three years must have elapsed.

7. Which of the following statements about an automatic premium loan provision is TRUE?
   A. It applies only to term policies.
   B. It is included automatically in all policies.
   C. It keeps the policy in force when it would otherwise lapse because of nonpayment of premiums.
   D. Money used to pay premiums is treated as a partial withdrawal and is not subject to interest charges.

8. The incontestable clause is usually in effect after
   A. 2 years
   B. 4 years
   C. 5 years
   D. 6 years

9. Harry decides to borrow some money from a bank. What type of assignment will Harry probably use to secure the loan?
   A. Voluntary assignment
   B. Partial assignment
   C. Complete assignment
   D. Absolute assignment

10. Carol has a policy on her ex-husband that she wants to give to their daughter. Carol no longer wants any control over this policy. What type of assignment will Carol probably use to accomplish this?
    A. Collateral assignment
    B. Voluntary assignment
    C. Partial assignment
    D. Conditional assignment

11. Ginny is a revocable primary beneficiary on her mother's life insurance policy. Which of the following statements is TRUE?
    A. Ginny can probably assign her rights in the policy as collateral on a loan.
    B. Ginny will receive benefits only if another beneficiary has died before her mother dies.
    C. Ginny's mother may not change the beneficiary without Ginny's permission.
    D. Ginny will receive benefits before any other beneficiary upon her mother's death.

12. Carl purchased a life insurance policy when he was 44. The insurer accidentally recorded his age as 42. When the accident is discovered in a review of the files 5 years later
    A. the policy will be canceled because of misrepresentation
    B. the policy will not change because the incontestable period will have passed
    C. Carl will be charged the difference in premium between his actual age and his stated age, along with the interest on the back payments
    D. Carl will be credited the difference in premium between his actual age and his stated age, along with the interest on the back payments

13. How long is the free-look period in most states?
    A. 5 days
    B. 7 days
    C. 10 days
    D. 30 days

14. Steve is the beneficiary on his wife's life insurance policy. When they divorce, his wife cannot remove him as beneficiary on the policy without his written permission because
    A. most states require the beneficiary's written consent
    B. Steve is a revocable beneficiary
    C. Steve is an assigned beneficiary
    D. Steve is an irrevocable beneficiary

15. When Tom dies, Rosemary receives the death benefit. If Rosemary had died before Tom, George would have received the benefit. Which of the following statements is TRUE?
    A. Rosemary is the primary beneficiary, and George is the contingent beneficiary.
    B. Tom is the primary beneficiary, and Rosemary is the contingent beneficiary.
    C. Rosemary is the contingent beneficiary, and George is the primary beneficiary.
    D. George is the contingent beneficiary, and Rosemary is the tertiary beneficiary.

16. John leaves his $300,000 estate to his 3 children to split equally according to a per capita distribution. One of his children dies before John does. Upon John's death, which of the following statements is TRUE?
    A. The proceeds are split 3 ways between the remaining children and John's estate.
    B. The proceeds are split 2 ways between the remaining children only.
    C. The proceeds are split 3 ways between the remaining children and the beneficiary of the deceased child's estate.
    D. The proceeds are split 4 ways between the remaining children, John's estate, and the deceased child's estate.

17. John leaves his $300,000 estate to his 3 children to split equally according to a per stirpes distribution. One of his children dies before John does. Upon John's death, which of the following is TRUE?
    A. The proceeds are split 3 ways between the remaining children and John's estate.
    B. The proceeds are split 2 ways between the remaining children only.
    C. The proceeds are split 3 ways between the remaining children and the beneficiary of the deceased child's estate.
    D. The proceeds are split 4 ways between the remaining children, John's estate, and the deceased child's estate.

18. Alice and Ken are in a fatal car crash that kills them both. Alice is the primary beneficiary of a policy on Ken's life. What happens to the policy proceeds?
    A. The proceeds are retained by the insurance company.
    B. The proceeds are paid to Alice's estate.
    C. The proceeds are paid to any contingent beneficiaries or to Ken's estate.
    D. The proceeds are paid directly to Ken's estate.

19. Which of the following is allowed when policy proceeds are being paid through a spendthrift clause?
    A. The proceeds are paid directly to the beneficiary in monthly installments.
    B. The proceeds may be transferred directly to a creditor by the beneficiary.
    C. The proceeds may be commuted by the beneficiary to receive the present value of future payments in a lump sum.
    D. The beneficiary may borrow against the strength of the proceeds.

20. Under the facility of payment provision
    A. the insurer may select a beneficiary if the named beneficiaries cannot be found
    B. the insurer may retain the proceeds if the named beneficiaries cannot be found
    C. the state may select a beneficiary if the named beneficiaries cannot be found
    D. the state may retain the proceeds if the named beneficiaries cannot be found

ANSWERS AND RATIONALES TO UNIT TEST

1. **B.**
2. **A.** The consideration clause identifies the fact that the policyowner must pay something of value for the insurer's promise to pay benefits.
3. **C.** The entire contract clause stipulates that the documents, attachments, forms, etc. are to be considered parts of the insurance contract.
4. **C.** Assigning the policy when an irrevocable beneficiary has been named is not generally an ownership right in an insurance policy.
5. **B.** The typical grace period is 30 days.
6. **A.** Requiring the policyowner to pay all back dividends due plus interest on the amount is not usually a condition of policy reinstatement.
7. **C.** An automatic premium loan provision keeps the policy in force when it would otherwise lapse because of nonpayment of premiums.
8. **A.** The incontestable clause is usually in effect after 2 years.
9. **B.** Harry will probably use a partial assignment to secure the loan from a bank.
10. **B.** Carol will probably use a voluntary assignment to give the policy to her daughter.
11. **D.** Upon her mother's death, Ginny will receive benefits before any other beneficiary.
12. **C.** Carl will be charged the difference in premium between his actual age and his stated age, along with the interest on the back payments.
13. **C.** The free-look period in most states is 10 days.
14. **D.** When they divorce, his wife cannot remove him as beneficiary on the policy without his written permission because Steve is an irrevocable beneficiary.
15. **A.** Rosemary is the primary beneficiary, and George is the contingent beneficiary.
16. **B.** The proceeds are split 2 ways between the remaining children only.
17. **C.** The proceeds are split 3 ways between the remaining children and the beneficiary of the deceased child's estate.
18. **C.** The proceeds are paid to any contingent beneficiaries or to Ken's estate.
19. **A.** The proceeds are paid directly to the beneficiary in monthly installments.
20. **A.** Under the facility of payment provision, the insurer may select a beneficiary if the named beneficiaries cannot be found.

UNIT

10

Riders

10. 1 INTRODUCTION

Riders take their name from the concept that they have no independent existence. They have force and effect only when they are attached to a policy. Riders are special policy provisions that provide benefits that are not found in the original contract or that make adjustments to it. These special provisions are, in effect, attached to the policy, or ride it. A rider also can refer to a term policy that is attached to (or rides) a permanent policy to provide additional or specially needed coverage. Riders can be used to enhance or add benefits to the policy, or they can be used to take benefits away from the policy.

A **waiver** is a type of rider that is used to exclude benefits and for which no premium is charged. For example, for underwriting reasons, a waiver may be attached to a policy that excludes benefits for death by a specified cause such as a particularly hazardous hobby or occupation.

The other riders discussed in this section all require the payment of a relatively small additional premium for the benefits provided.

10. 2 LEARNING OBJECTIVES

After completing this lesson, you will be able to:

- define a policy rider;
- explain why riders are used in policies; and
- describe how various riders affect policies in enhancing, expanding, or reducing policy benefits.

10. 3 TYPES OF RIDERS

10. 3. 1 Accidental Death (Double Indemnity)

An accidental death benefit (ADB) rider may be added to an insurance policy to provide for an additional amount to be paid to the beneficiary if the insured dies as the result of an accident. This amount, usually referred to as the principal sum, is usually the same as the face value of the policy and is therefore often referred to as double indemnity. It could, however, be three or more times the face value.

Whatever the amount, the accidental death benefit may be paid only when the insured dies as the result of an accident.

Example

Rhonda has a $100,000 policy on her life that includes an accidental death benefit providing for double indemnity if Rhonda dies as the result of an accident. If Rhonda is hit by a bus and killed while crossing the street, the policy will pay $200,000 to Rhonda's beneficiary.

The accidental death benefit rider must be specifically requested and paid for. Because the inclusion of this rider naturally increases the company's risk, the extra premium adds nothing to the cash value of the policy. The extra premium is needed to cover the extra risk the company incurs.

Companies differ in their interpretations of what constitutes accidental death, so check your company's policies to see how the accidental death benefit rider is worded. In general, we can say this: accidental death benefits apply if the insured dies in an accident or within a specified period after and as the result of an accident. The period permitted between the accident and the insured's death also varies, but it's most often three months, or 90 days.

Not every type of accidental death is covered by an accidental death benefit rider. Certain causes of death are excluded. Three of these exclusions are common to many types of riders, namely:

- death as a result of self-inflicted injury;
- death while committing a crime; and
- death as a result of war.

In addition, the accidental death benefit rider usually excludes the same general cause of death as may be found in the aviation exclusion—that is, death of a passenger in other than a regularly scheduled commercial airline flight. However, if the insured is merely a passenger and has no duties on a private flight, the accidental death benefit still applies with many companies. Check your company's regulations on this point.

A fifth exclusion in an accidental death benefit rider is death as the result of riot or insurrection. These are situations in which people unlawfully gather to cause a disturbance and innocent bystanders are often hurt or killed. Riots are generally spontaneous; insurrections are usually planned rebellions or uprisings against authority involving more people than riots.

The insurer may elect to have a very liberal definition of accidental death or a very strict, limited definition. Regardless, if a death claim is submitted, it must comply with the policy's definition if the additional accidental death benefit is to be paid.

The inclusion of the accidental death benefit in a policy does not affect the handling of outstanding indebtedness—whether a policy or premium loan, or past-due premiums—on the policy. If a policy loan exists at the time of accidental death and the accidental death calls for double indemnity, the company will pay twice the face amount of the policy minus the loan balance and any interest due on it.

The accidental death benefit usually ceases either five years before or after an individual's normal retirement age—that is, age 60, 65, or 70 unless the accident occurs before that age. Note, however, that the rider itself can stipulate that the accidental death benefit is to apply for the entire lifetime of the insured or for the length of the contract. If a policyowner is paying an extra premium for the accidental death benefit and reaches the age at which this benefit no longer applies, the premium drops.

An accidental death benefit rider to a policy also may include additional benefits for dismemberment. If so, it is called an accidental death and dismemberment (AD&D) rider. The dismemberment portion of this rider provides for the payment of the **capital sum** (the face amount) in the event that, because of an accident, the insured loses two arms, two legs, or two hands or suffers the irrecoverable loss of vision in both eyes. Loss is generally defined as the actual severance or removal of the arm or leg as a result of the accident. Again, the loss usually must occur within 90 days of the accident.

Some companies will pay a reduced capital sum if the insured suffers the loss of only one arm, for example. The full capital sum would be paid for the loss of both arms.

Strictly speaking, dismemberment benefits are not life insurance, but because they sometimes are included in the accidental death benefit rider, you should be aware of them.

10. 3. 2 Waiver of Premium

The waiver of premium rider exempts a disabled policyowner from needing to pay premiums during the term of disability while keeping the policy in force. Although it is one of the most common riders attached to life insurance policies, it isn't attached to every policy automatically. It must be specifically requested and added, even though it's so commonly used that most companies include it in many of their standard policies, assuming that a fairly large percentage of their future policyowners will want it.

The waiver of premium rider subjects the company to greater risks than would be experienced if it were not included because it provides that the company will pay the premiums if an insured becomes disabled. Because this is true, most companies must charge a higher premium for polices that include the waiver of premium rider.

When additional premium is charged for waiver of premium benefits, the extra charge does not increase the policy's cash value but simply helps meet the costs of providing the waiver of premium benefit to policyowners requesting it.

For the waiver of premium to apply, the disability must be permanent and total. *Total*, as it is used here, can have two connotations.

- The insured is prevented (by disability) from engaging in his usual occupation.
- The insured is prevented from engaging in any work for gain or profit.

Technically, the first definition of *total* sometimes applies for a stated period, and then the second definition might take over as the criteria for deciding whether the disability is total. In other words, the company may state that for the first year, all that's necessary to qualify a disability as *total* is that the insured be prevented from engaging in his usual profession. After the year has elapsed, the company will then apply the broader definition of *total*—whether the insured can engage in any (not just his own) work for gain or profit. Check the exact wording of your company's waiver of premium rider to see how total disability is defined.

Understanding what constitutes permanent disability is somewhat more standardized. In most instances, whether the disability is considered permanent involves a waiting period after the onset of disability. If this waiting period elapses and the insured is still disabled in the judgment of a company-authorized physician, the disability is considered permanent.

The length of the waiting period involved varies by company, usually ranging from three to six months. The waiting period is necessary to provide the company with a yardstick it can use to determine whether the disability is permanent.

During this waiting period, the permanency and totality of the insured's disability have not yet been established, so the policyowner must continue making normal payments. Once the disability proves to be permanent and total, the company refunds the premiums paid during the waiting period because they were paid while the insured was, in fact, disabled.

Although premiums are being paid by a company under the waiver of premium rider, the policy remains in full force in every respect, just as if the policyowner personally were making the payments. This means that the cash value of a policy in this situation, and any dividends if it is a participating plan, continue to increase at the usual pace.

What happens when a disabled policyowner recovers from a disability? Suppose John, who is both the policyowner and the insured, was disabled for two years, during which time the company paid more than $1,000 in premiums for him under the waiver of premium rider. John has now recovered, so he simply begins paying his premiums again, starting with the next premium when it falls due.

The waiver of premium rider is usually not available when the policyowner reaches a specified age, commonly 60 and sometimes 65. When the waiver of premium rider expires because the insured reaches a certain age, the company lowers the premium to compensate for the loss of the benefits the rider provided—unless the company provides waiver of premium benefits free of charge.

If the insured becomes disabled after the period in which the waiver of premium is effective, for example, after age 60, the waiver of premium rider obviously does not apply and the insured can pay the premiums or allow the policy to lapse.

If the insured becomes disabled shortly before reaching age 60, she still would be eligible for the benefit under the waiver of premium rider of the policy. This is true even if the waiting period extends past the normal cutoff age of 60.

Once a waiver of premium rider is attached to a policy, the company cannot arbitrarily drop the rider. It must remain a part of the policy as long as the policyowner continues to pay premiums as agreed. However, if the policy should ever lapse and then be reinstated, the company can refuse to reinstate the waiver of premium rider.

Waiver of premium riders usually contain exclusions for suicide, military service, or injury received while committing a crime.

10. 3. 2. 1 Waiver of Premium for Universal Life Policies

Because premiums on a universal life policy may fluctuate considerably, most companies provide that a waiver of premium rider on a universal life policy will guarantee only the monthly cost of insurance, not the total premium the insured was paying. The policy's cash value will remain intact and continue to earn interest.

Some companies, however, will waive the guaranteed minimum annual premium, rather than just the monthly cost of insurance. In this case, the policy's cash value will grow not only with the interest credited, but also by the amount of the additional premium payments less the cost of insurance.

10. 3. 3 Disability Income Rider

In addition to making certain that life insurance premiums will be paid on schedule through the waiver of premium rider, the insured policyowner can guarantee a regular monthly income from the insurance company if he becomes totally and permanently disabled. Logically enough, this rider is called the **disability income rider**.

Under the disability income rider, the company guarantees the insured policyowner a regular monthly income for as long as he remains totally and permanently disabled. The amount of the income is usually based on the face amount of the policy—for instance, $X per month per $1,000 of coverage. In addition, most disability income riders include waiver of premium.

Example

If a policyowner has the disability income rider on a $100,000 policy and the company guarantees $10 per month on each $1,000 of coverage, the policyowner will receive $1,000 per month.

An income under the disability income rider continues for the length of the disability. However, a waiting period is required by most companies to ensure that the disability is, in fact, permanent (by the company's definition) and total (as determined by a company-approved physician). As in the case of the waiver of premium rider, this waiting period is usually three to six months.

Although the disability income rider usually includes the waiver of premium rider, it is possible to have one without the other. It's essential that you understand the difference between these two important riders.

- The waiver of premium rider states that the company will pay the premiums on the policy during the insured's total and permanent disability.
- The disability income rider stipulates that the company will pay the insured policyowner a monthly income during any period of total and permanent disability.

Remember, the amount paid under the waiver of premium rider depends on the amount of the policy's premium. The amount paid under the disability income rider is based on the face amount of the policy.

10. 3. 4 Payor Rider

With most juvenile insurance policies, a parent is the policyowner and pays for the coverage; the child, of course, is the insured. If the parent dies, premium payments will probably cease, so the policy would lapse. Policyowners can protect their (and their child's) interest in the policy through what's known as the **payor rider**.

The **payor rider** states that if the person who's paying the premiums—in most cases, the parent—dies or becomes disabled before the child has reached a specified age, the company will waive all further premiums until the child reaches that age. This means that if the payor dies or becomes disabled before the insured reaches the age specified in the policy, the policy remains in force. This waiver can apply to death only or to death and disability.

The payor rider makes it possible to guarantee that a juvenile policy will accomplish what its owner wants it to, whether or not he is around to see it happen. In simple terms, all the rider does is guarantee that the company will keep a juvenile policy in force, without premium payments from anyone, until the insured juvenile reaches a specified age—usually either 21 or 25—if the payor dies or becomes disabled and unable to pay the premiums.

Obviously, this rider exposes the company to a greater risk. For this reason, the company must charge higher premiums for policies that include payor riders than for those that don't.

In many jurisdictions, most life insurance companies consider a person who has reached age 15 (16 in Canada) an adult, as far as signing an application for coverage is concerned. However, the companies also realize that very few 15- or 16-year-olds will be financially able to pay for life insurance. Therefore, payor riders in juvenile policies usually stay in effect until the insured juvenile reaches either of two ages, 21 or 25. This gives the child an opportunity to earn enough money to pay the premiums on the insurance policy.

Finally, because the payor is, in effect, insured for the amount the premiums will cost the company in the event of the payor's disability or death, the payor must prove qualified for the benefit in many respects—morally, financially, and medically. In addition, before the company includes a payor rider in a juvenile policy, the payor probably has to prove insurability.

10. 3. 5 Guaranteed Insurability

There are times when an insured discovers that because of some circumstance, usually health reasons, she has become uninsurable. There may be some existing life insurance, but the insured wants more coverage and discovers he is no longer able to purchase it. There is a rider that will guarantee that the insured can purchase more permanent insurance at specified ages, without proof of insurability. This is the **guaranteed insurability rider (GIR)**, sometimes referred to as the **insurance protection rider (PIR)** or **future increase option.**

This rider guarantees that on specified dates in the future (or at specified ages or upon the event of specified occurrences such as marriage or birth of a child), the insured may purchase additional insurance without evidence of insurability. As the option age is reached, the insured normally has 90 days in which to exercise the option or it is lost. The rate for this additional coverage will be that for his or her attained age, not the age at which the policy was issued. The rider generally expires when the insured attains age 40.

The amount of insurance that can be purchased on the option dates is usually limited to the amount and type of the base policy. Thus, if the insured had a $10,000 whole life policy with the guaranteed insurability rider, she could purchase up to an additional $10,000 of whole life coverage on the option dates.

The biggest advantage offered by this rider is the opportunity to buy additional amounts of insurance as one's responsibilities and needs change, without proof of insurability.

10. 3. 6 Return of Premium

This rider was developed primarily as a sales tool to enable the agent to say, "In addition to the face amount payable at your death, we will return all premiums paid if you die within the first 20 years," for example. The rider is simply an increasing amount of term insurance that always equals the total of premiums paid at any point during the effective years. In reality, the rider does not return premium but pays an additional amount at death that equals the premiums paid up to that time—as long as death falls within the time specified in the rider. By purchasing this rider, the policyowner is buying term insurance and is, of course, charged for it accordingly.

10. 3. 7 Return of Cash Value

This rider, not often used, was designed to offset the invalid complaint, "When I die, the company confiscates the cash value." Such a complaint is based on lack of understanding of the mathematics involved in a level face value life insurance policy. However, if the agent can say, "We can attach a rider returning the cash value in addition to the face amount," the objection is more easily answered than if it is necessary to explain the mathematics involved. The return of cash value rider is similar to the return of premium rider in that it is merely an additional amount of term insurance that is equal to the cash value at any point while effective. Buying it, the policyowner is simply getting additional term insurance. In reality, this rider does not return the cash value; it pays an additional amount of insurance equal to the cash value.

The premium paid for either the return of premium or the return of cash value rider is actually equal to the cost of adding an increasing term insurance rider to the base policy. Accordingly, the term premium would take into account the age of the insured and the amount and duration of the term insurance.

10. 3. 8 Cost of Living

The high inflation years of the 1970s caused concern that the face amounts of policies would not be adequate to cover family expenses by the time the death benefit was paid.

With the **cost-of-living rider**, the policyowner has the option to increase the death benefit of his policy to match an increase in the cost-of-living index (usually the CPI-U, the Consumer Price Index-All-Urban). This is accomplished by either changing the face amount of an adjustable life policy (and increasing the premium accordingly) or attaching an increasing term rider to the base term or whole life policy and billing the policyholder for the additional coverage. (There is usually a cap on the increase—for example, 5%.)

An increase in the death benefit will mean an increase in premium. Subsequent decreases in the index will not result in a decrease in the policy's death benefit.

Suppose Louise has a whole life policy with a face value of $100,000 and a cost-of-living index rider. If the CPI-U has gone up by 2%, Louise may increase the face value of her policy by $2,000, up to $102,000.

Note that this increase will cause an increase in Louise's premium. Note also that when the CPI-U goes up, Louise is not required to increase the face value of her policy accordingly.

10. 3. 9 Additional Insureds

Riders are also commonly attached to life insurance policies to provide coverage on the lives of one or more additional insureds. Usually they are term insurance riders covering a spouse, one or more children, or all family members in addition to the insured policyholder. Many companies will issue additional insured riders on request. As discussed earlier in this unit, some companies actively market combination coverage policies for family members under the label *family protection policy*.

10. 3. 10 Substitute Insured Rider

Although it seems unusual to allow for the substitution of insureds in life insurance, the **substitute insured rider** actually does permit a change of insureds. This rider is also known as an **exchange privilege rider**.

The ability to substitute or exchange insureds is desirable, for instance, in business-owned life insurance, when a key employee or business executive is insured for the benefit of the corporation. If this employee terminates employment or retires, the insurance can be switched over to apply to the employee's replacement, subject to evidence of insurability. This way, the policy can continue (rather than be terminated and a new policy issued) with the same face amount, and premiums can be calculated on the basis of the new insured's age, sex, and other factors.

10. 3. 11 Accelerated Benefits

In the 1980s, many companies began offering an **accelerated benefits rider,** sometimes known as a **living benefits rider**. This rider allows policyowners who are terminally ill or who require long-term care or permanent confinement to a nursing home to collect all or part of their death benefit while they are still alive. This can help relieve some of the financial distress caused by an insured's inability to continue working and the rising costs of health care.

The purpose of this benefit is to provide the terminally ill person with necessary cash with which to take care of expenses related to the terminal illness—that is, medical expenses or nursing home expenses.

10. 3. 11. 1 *Effect on Death Benefit*

Death benefits payable under a policy are reduced by any amounts paid as accelerated benefits. For example, a $250,000 policy that provides for a 75% accelerated benefit would pay up to $187,500 to the terminally ill insured, with the remaining $62,500 payable as a death benefit to the beneficiary when the insured dies. Accelerated payment can be made in a lump sum or in monthly installments over a special period, such as one year.

This provision is given without an increase in premium. There are some companies that deduct an interest charge from the proceeds paid out to make up for what the company would have earned had the money not been withdrawn from the contract.

10. 3. 12 Living Benefits Provision

Long-term care (LTC) insurance, which reimburses health and social service expenses incurred in a convalescent or nursing home facility, can be marketed as a rider to life insurance policies.

LTC rider benefits are similar to those found in a LTC policy. The benefit structure includes the following.

- There are elimination periods of 10–100 days.
- Benefit periods are three to five years or longer.
- Prior hospitalization for at least three days may be required.
- Benefits may be triggered by impaired activities of daily living.
- Levels of care include skilled, intermediate, custodial, and home health care.

In addition, certain optional benefits also may be provided such as adult day care, cost-of-living protection, hospice care, and others.

There are two approaches to the LTC rider concept. The generalized or independent approach recognizes the LTC rider as independent from the life policy because the benefits paid to the insured will not affect the life policy's face amount or cash value. The integrated approach links the LTC benefits paid to the life policy's face amount and/or cash value.

The living benefit or living needs rider combines life insurance and LTC benefits, drawing on the life insurance benefits to generate LTC benefits. In a sense, it's like borrowing from the life insurance to pay LTC benefits. Under the LTC option, up to 70–80% of the policy's death benefit may be used to offset nursing home expenses. Under the terminal illness option, 90–95% of the death benefit may be used to offset medical expenses. Of course, payment of LTC benefits reduces the face amount of the life policy.

10. 4 SUMMARY

In this lesson, you learned about

- the use of riders in life insurance policies;
- how riders affect the provisions of a life insurance policy;
- various riders used in life insurance policies; and
- the effects of policy riders in enhancing, expanding, or reducing the benefits of a policy.

UNIT TEST

1. Garth has a $100,000 whole life insurance policy that has been in effect for 10 years. The policy includes a double indemnity rider. Garth jumps off a bridge and dies. How much will the policy pay?
   A. Nothing because all policies exclude death resulting from suicide
   B. $100,000 because the base policy excludes death resulting from suicide, but the multiple indemnity rider does not
   C. $100,000 because the multiple indemnity rider excludes death resulting from suicide, but the base policy's suicide exclusion has expired
   D. $200,000 dollars because death was accidental

2. Tammy has a total of $10,000 loan and interest outstanding against her $100,000 policy. The policy has a double indemnity rider. Tammy is killed in an automobile accident. How much will the policy pay?
   A. Nothing until the outstanding loan is repaid
   B. $180,000
   C. $190,000
   D. $200,000

3. Kumar has a life insurance policy with a rider that will pay him $1,000 per month if he is totally and permanently disabled. Which type of rider does he have?
   A. Waiver of premium rider
   B. Accidental death and disability rider
   C. Disability income rider
   D. Payor rider

4. Paul has a life insurance policy on his son for which he pays all the premiums. A rider to this policy states that if Paul becomes permanently and totally disabled, the premiums will be paid until his son reaches age 21, at which point his son will take over the premium payments. Which type of rider does he have?
   A. Waiver of premium rider
   B. Accidental death and disability rider
   C. Disability income rider
   D. Payor rider

5. Alberta is concerned that if she became totally and permanently disabled, she would not be able to pay her life insurance premiums and the policy will lapse. Which type of rider should she consider to protect against this possibility?
   A. Waiver of premium rider
   B. Accidental death and disability rider
   C. Disability income rider
   D. Payor rider

6. Which of the following riders is increasing term insurance that always equals the total premiums paid during the time the policy is in effect?
   A. Guaranteed insurability
   B. Return of premium
   C. Accidental death
   D. Waiver of premium

7. Double payment may be made because of which occurrence?
   A. Guaranteed insurability
   B. Return of premium
   C. Accidental death
   D. Waiver of premium

8. Which of the following is waiver of all future premiums in the event of total and permanent disability?
   A. Guaranteed insurability
   B. Return of premium
   C. Accidental death
   D. Waiver of premium

9. Which of the following is a guarantee that at specified ages, dates, or events, the insured may buy additional insurance without a medical exam?
   A. Guaranteed insurability
   B. Return of premium
   C. Accidental death
   D. Waiver of premium

10. The amount of money paid by an ADB rider if the insured dies in an accident is referred to as the
    A. principal sum
    B. principle sum
    C. capital sum
    D. capitol sum

11. The amount of money paid by an AD&D rider if the insured is disabled in an accident is referred to as the
    A. principal sum
    B. principle sum
    C. capital sum
    D. capitol sum

12. For the waiver of premium to apply under a waiver of premium rider, the disability must be
    A. total
    B. permanent
    C. total and permanent
    D. total, permanent, and disfiguring

13. Which of the following riders requires proof of insurability of the policyowner as well as of the insured?
    A. Payor rider
    B. Guaranteed insurability rider
    C. Waiver of premium rider
    D. Return of premium rider

ANSWERS AND RATIONALES TO UNIT TEST

1. **C.**
2. **C.** The policy will pay a death benefit of $200,000 minus the outstanding policy loan of $10,000.
3. **C.**
4. **D.** This is a payor rider because it provides for a waiver of premiums on the son's coverage if the payor (Paul) becomes disabled.
5. **A.** A waiver of premium rider will waive the premiums on Alberta's policy if she becomes disabled.
6. **B.** A return of premium rider is increasing term insurance that always equals the total premiums paid during the time the policy is in effect.
7. **C.** Double payment may be made in the case of accidental death.
8. **D.** Waiver of premium is waiver of all future premiums in the event of total and permanent disability.
9. **A.** Guaranteed insurability is a guarantee that at specified ages, dates, or events, the insured may buy additional insurance without a medical exam.
10. **A.** The amount of money paid by an ADB rider if the insured dies in an accident is referred to as the principal sum.
11. **C.** The amount of money paid by an AD&D; rider if the insured is disabled in an accident is referred to as the capital sum.
12. **C.** For the waiver of premium to apply under a waiver of premium rider, the disability must be total and permanent.
13. **A.** The payor rider requires proof of insurability of the policyowner as well as of the insured.

UNIT

11

Policy Options

11. 1 LEARNING OBJECTIVES

After completing this lesson, you will be able to:

- explain policy options, including settlement options, nonforfeiture options, and dividend options;
- explain what happens to money left with the insurer when the beneficiary dies; and
- know how quickly permanent policies are required to accumulate cash values.

11. 2 INTRODUCTION

The life insurance policy provides important policy options. These options give the life insurance contract flexibility to meet the needs of the insuring public. Of particular value are the settlement, nonforfeiture, and dividend options available under a life insurance contract.

11. 3 SETTLEMENT OPTIONS

At one time, life insurance policy proceeds were paid only in the form of a lump-sum cash payment. This often created as many problems for the beneficiary as it solved. For instance, the beneficiary, who is the sudden recipient of a large amount of cash, might have little or no idea of how to use or invest the money, or an immature beneficiary might launch into a great spending spree and be broke in a short time.

To avoid situations such as these, the life insurance industry developed methods by which the proceeds of a policy could be paid in forms other than a lump sum. These methods of receiving policy proceeds in other than a lump sum are known as settlement options or payment options. Although settlement options are not required by law, most policies today have them.

Most policy proceeds are still distributed in a lump sum. It is important that policyowners and beneficiaries understand that settlement options are available if conditions set forth in the policy are met and that such options may be tailored to meet individual needs.

When a settlement option is chosen, the proceeds of the policy are left with the company. The insurance company invests the proceeds and guarantees that the funds will earn interest. Now, think for a moment about money management. A beneficiary grieving from the recent loss of a spouse may be unprepared to handle money matters. The advantages of a settlement option are clear.

- The insurer invests the money, thus relieving the beneficiary from the care of managing and investing the funds.
- The money is safe with the insurance company.

- Interest earnings on the retained proceeds are guaranteed.

Finally, with a settlement option, the beneficiary can receive the proceeds in a manner that best suits his overall financial situation. Unless the policyowner specifies an irrevocable settlement option, the beneficiary may select any of the same options available to the policyowner when the proceeds become payable, even if that option differs from that originally selected by the policyowner. For example, a beneficiary can arrange to receive a monthly payment from the policy proceeds—a payment based on budgeted needs.

The settlement options we will be looking at provide benefits that take into account the following.

- Outstanding policy loans are always deducted from the chosen settlement option.
- All dividend accumulations, paid-up dividend additions, and term insurance riders serve to increase the benefits of the chosen settlement option.

There are four frequently used optional modes of settlement:

- Interest only
- Fixed-period installments
- Fixed-amount installments
- Life income

In addition, most companies will agree to distribute the proceeds under any reasonable and actuarially sound mode. The death proceeds include the death benefit plus any accumulated dividends, paid-up insurance additions, or one-year term insurance additions. The net death proceeds then will be used to determine the amount payable under any one of the following options.

11. 3. 1 Interest Only

The first settlement option to be described is the interest option, sometimes also called the interest-only option. Under the interest option, the life insurance company keeps the proceeds of the policy for a limited time and invests them for the beneficiary, paying the earned interest as income to the beneficiary.

Although the settlement option of a life insurance policy usually is selected by the policyowner, the beneficiary may change the option selected at the time the proceeds become payable or the policyowner may provide a means by which the beneficiary can withdraw all or part of the principal amount of the policy proceeds. Under the interest option, the right of withdrawal can take several forms. Consider this example.

The insurance company holds $100,000 of proceeds at interest. Interest is paid to the beneficiary at the rate of a certain number of dollars per month. In addition, the beneficiary may withdraw, at any time, any amount up to the full $100,000 principal. In this situation, the beneficiary can withdraw all or part of the principal if so desired.

The policy also can be arranged so that the beneficiary cannot withdraw any of the principal amount or cannot withdraw any of the principal until a specified number of years have elapsed or until a specified age is reached.

What happens to the remaining proceeds (principal) when the beneficiary is prevented from withdrawing it, or must wait a specified period before withdrawing it, and the beneficiary dies while the money is still on deposit with the company?

Money left with a company will go to either of two places when the beneficiary dies:

- To the deceased beneficiary's estate
- To a secondary beneficiary (or beneficiaries) named in the policy itself

As you know, the original beneficiary—the person named to receive the proceeds before any others—is called the primary beneficiary. Another named beneficiary or beneficiaries may be designated as secondary or contingent beneficiaries.

When the primary beneficiary has died and proceeds still on deposit are to be paid to the contingent beneficiary, the manner in which the amount remaining is to be distributed depends on what the insured originally stipulated in the policy. If the insured indicated that the contingent beneficiary should continue to receive income, the company pays the contingent beneficiary in the designated manner.

When the insured has not elected a settlement option for the contingent beneficiary, that beneficiary can select the manner in which the proceeds are to be paid.

11. 3. 2 Fixed Period Option

The fixed period option, along with the remaining two options that we'll look at, is actually a form of annuity. Under the fixed period option, the beneficiary receives a regular income for a specified period, comprising both principal and interest. So, under this option, the principal amount gradually decreases to zero.

Three factors that determine the amount the beneficiary or payee will receive each time a payment is made under the fixed period option are:

- the principal amount;
- the interest earned on the principal; and
- the length of time the payments are to be made.

Example

If the policy proceeds total $100,000, earn 6% annual interest, and are to be paid out over a 10-year period, the beneficiary can expect to receive approximately $1,100 each month for a total of $132,000. However, if the proceeds are paid out over a 15-year period, the beneficiary would receive approximately $845 per month for a total of $152,100. Note that in both examples the total amount paid exceeds the policy proceeds because of the interest earned.

As with other settlement options, if the primary beneficiary dies before receiving the full amount of the policy's proceeds, the money remaining is paid to the contingent beneficiary, if one is named in the policy, or into the estate of the primary beneficiary.

In addition, if the remaining proceeds are paid into the primary beneficiary's estate, they will eventually go to the heirs of that estate. If the policy names a contingent beneficiary (or beneficiaries), the money will be paid as the policyowner (or insured) has directed in the policy, or if there is no indication as to how the remaining money is to be paid, the contingent beneficiary has a choice as to how it will be received.

11. 3. 3 Fixed Amount Option

The third type of settlement option is the fixed amount option under which the payee receives payments, but the length of time for the payments is not specified. The amount of each periodic installment is established ahead of time, and payments continue until the combination of principal and interest has been exhausted.

The three factors that determine how long the payee will receive payments under the fixed amount option are:

- the specified amount of each payment;
- the principal amount, or the amount of the policy proceeds; and
- earnings on the principal, or the interest.

Suppose the beneficiary is to receive $10,000 per year from $100,000 in policy proceeds that are earning 6% interest annually from the insurer. Payments would extend over a 14-year period and total approximately $140,000. If the annual payment were increased to $15,000, the income would last for only 8 years and total $120,000. Just as with the fixed period option, the company guarantees that the total amount paid until the proceeds are exhausted will exceed the policy proceeds because of the interest earned.

In guaranteeing that the payee will receive more money in the long run by taking the proceeds in the form of an income stream, the company is encouraging the payee to leave the proceeds with the company. It also increases its total assets, thus increasing overall earnings for the company—and the payee.

11. 3. 4 Life Income Option

The fourth settlement option is the life income option. As its name implies, the life income option provides for payment of installments for the entire lifetime of the payee. Just as with an annuity, there are at least four distinct methods—many companies offer additional options—in which these installments can be paid:

- Straight life income (or life only), in which the payee receives a specified income for as long as she lives

- Refund annuity, in which an income is paid for the lifetime of the payee, and to a second payee if the first payee dies before having received an amount equal to the full proceeds of the policy
- Life income certain, in which the payee receives installments for life and a second payee receives the payments if the first payee dies before the end of the years specified in the certain period, for example, a period certain of 5, 10, or 20 years
- Joint and survivor life income, in which two payees are recipients of the income for the lifetime of the first payee and the surviving payee the recipient of income of a lesser amount (usually two-thirds or one-half) for the rest of her life

Using these four settlement options, custom tailoring may be done between the policyowner and the company. For instance, an insured policyowner might specify in her policy that if she dies, her husband is to receive only the interest on the proceeds until he reaches age 62; from that point on, he is to receive a life income certain for 20 years.

Additionally, because a beneficiary's needs change from time to time, most companies will allow the policyowner to change the settlement option as necessary during her lifetime.

11. 3. 5 Withdrawal Provisions

The withdrawal provision is used in connection with settlement options. Under this provision, the proceeds of a policy are held by the insurance company and earn interest. The insured has the right to withdraw the funds left on deposit with the insurer at any time. The beneficiary may withdraw only a limited amount each year. Quite often this withdrawal provision is used to pay for college.

11. 3. 6 Other Settlement Arrangements

Many policies are written with no provision for special arrangements in the settlement of proceeds. However, a large number of companies will permit other settlement arrangements. Special settlement arrangements are sometimes desirable to accomplish the estate planning objectives of some insureds, and insurance companies will cooperate with almost any arrangement that is reasonable. Whatever plan is selected, however, must be of such nature that it can be administered by the insurance company and with regard to proper actuarial principles. In other words, installments received under the special arrangement must be the actuarial equivalent of the other settlement options available under the contract.

Administration of the special arrangement must strictly follow the terms of the contract. An insurance company does not provide trustee services. If an insured, for example, requested a settlement arrangement whereby the insurance company would make payment of the proceeds to two beneficiaries according to their needs, the insurance company would probably reject the settlement arrangement because it would require that the insurance company make a judgment determination. The insurer will provide administrative services but will not provide judgment services. Insurance companies will handle settlement option elections by individually drafting such agreements and applying them to individual policies. The companies do, however, have rules to avoid arrangements that are uneconomical to administer. For example, a company may specify that a minimum of $1,000, or in some cases $2,000, may be placed under a settlement option. It may prescribe that minimum installments payable cannot be less than a certain amount per installment. It is not a good business practice and might not be legal to hold proceeds for an indefinite period. Consequently, a company may set a time limit for holding proceeds at interest, such as for the lifetime of the primary beneficiary or the lifetime of a contingent beneficiary.

11. 3. 7 Third-Party and Creditor's Rights

Although the life insurance contract is between the policyowner and the insurer, once the insured has died, a contractual arrangement exists between the insurer and the beneficiary. The beneficiary may sue the insurer if payment is not received upon proper proof of death.

Likewise, once the insured dies, the proceeds of a life insurance policy belong to the beneficiary and the insured's creditors have no right to them. The beneficiary's creditors, however, may have a right to the life insurance proceeds.

Even the cash value of life insurance is generally protected from creditors.

The only exception to these statements is if the premiums that paid for the insurance were from embezzled funds.

11. 3. 8 Advantages of Settlement Options

One of the principal advantages for the insured or beneficiary in selecting one of the various settlement options is freedom from investment concerns. If a beneficiary elects a lump-sum settlement of the death benefit, he must decide how to use or invest the money. In essence, by electing a settlement option other than a lump sum, the beneficiary is trusting in the expertise and knowledge of the insurance company to administer these proceeds and provide some form of income.

Another advantage of settlement options is the fact that any of the options will guarantee a greater return than by simply taking the face amount of the policy. A $100,000 policy will generate a greater death benefit than $100,000 if these proceeds, consisting of principal and interest, are paid to a beneficiary over time. For example, if a beneficiary elected an interest-only option, he would receive interest payments over a period and then possibly at some future date, the principal. This could result in a total sum of money many times greater than just the face amount of the policy.

11.4 NONFORFEITURE OPTIONS—GUARANTEED VALUES

Many years ago, life insurance policies were structured so that if a policyowner allowed the policy to lapse, he simply forfeited excess amounts paid in as premium. Now, almost all states operate under a law known as the **standard nonforfeiture law**. This law prescribes that any cash value accumulation or its equivalent must be made available to the policyowner if he stops paying the premiums for any reason.

The amount of cash value and the rate at which it accumulates depend on the type of policy purchased by the policyowner; the amount and rate vary from company to company and often from one type of policy to another. In many states, however, permanent policies are required to have at least a small cash value by the end of the policy's third year.

The following are common nonforfeiture options in cash value policies:

- Cash surrender value
- Extended term insurance
- Reduced paid-up insurance

11.4.1 Cash Surrender Value

The policyowner can receive the cash accumulation as cash or its equivalent.

The **cash surrender value** of a life insurance policy is the amount a policyowner is entitled to when the policy has been surrendered before maturity. The minimum cash value is determined by a formula established by law. A portion of each premium paid is allocated to the policy reserve, which is a fixed liability of the insurance company. The balance of the premium is used to cover certain expenses (e.g., acquisition costs, administrative expenses, and agents' commission). In the early years of the policy (the first two or three), all of the premium is used for the reserve requirement and other liabilities and expenses. The life insurance contract is a heavily loaded with expenses initially; thus, there is no cash value in the early years of the policy.

Usually about the third year of the policy, these initial expenses are covered and the policy's guaranteed cash value begins to grow. As the cash value grows, so do the values associated with the nonforfeiture options. If the policyowner elects to cash in the policy—that is, surrender it for its available cash—he may do so. This concept can easily be seen in the sample nonforfeiture table illustrated below. The longer the policy is in force, the higher is the cash surrender or loan value and the higher are the other nonforfeiture values.

$100,000 Whole Life Policy, Male, Age 35, Nonsmoker

End of Policy Year	Cash Surrender or Loan Value	Reduced Paid-Up Insurance	Extended Term Insurance	
			Years	Days
1	$ .00	$ 0	0	0
2	.00	0	0	0
3	641.00	3,658	2	169
4	1,632.00	8,927	5	312
5	2,659.00	13,944	8	246
6	3,727.00	18,741	11	4
7	4,832.00	23,304	12	316
8	5,978.00	27,656	14	116
9	7,165.00	31,803	15	174
10	8,395.00	35,759	16	146
11	9,657.00	39,483	17	40
12	10,965.00	43,042	17	236
13	12,320.00	46,442	18	18
14	13,727.00	49,705	18	123
15	15,183.00	52,822	18	197
16	16,691.00	55,807	18	244
17	18,251.00	58,666	18	268
18	19,860.00	61,397	18	271
19	21,519.00	64,010	18	256
20	23,225.00	66,506	18	222
25	31,461.00	75,080	17	29
27	34,993.00	77,940	16	124
30	40,464.00	81,688	15	59
35	49,800.00	86,687	13	42

With this option, policyowners need to realize that their life insurance protection ceases. Making such a choice is not to be taken lightly.

If the policyowner chooses the cash surrender value option, he is entitled to the full amount of the cash value, with this exception: if the policyowner has borrowed money on a policy loan, the amount yet to be repaid plus interest will be deducted from the cash surrender value.

So, if Sherry has a policy with a stated cash value of $1,500 and she still owes $350 (including interest) on a previous loan from this cash value, on the cash surrender value option the company would give her a total of $1,150 ($1,500 less $350). Besides this total policy surrender, universal life policies and some whole life policies allow for a partial surrender of cash value. In this case, the policy remains in force, although possibly with a reduced face amount.

11.4.2 Reduced Paid-Up Insurance Option

Another nonforfeiture option is called the reduced paid-up insurance option. Under this option, the policyowner essentially uses the cash value of a present policy to purchase a single premium insurance policy at attained age rates for a reduced face amount.

Here are some facts to remember about the reduced paid-up insurance option.

- Once the face amount of protection has been determined, it remains the same for the duration of the contract. The new policy will build cash values for the policyowner.
- No further premiums need be paid on the reduced policy—it's paid up because it's a single premium policy.
- The new protection is computed at the attained age of the insured (who also may be the policyowner).
- A full share of expense loading is usually not included in the premium on the reduced coverage because the costs of setting up the coverage are greatly reduced.

Note that reduced paid-up policies are of the same type of insurance as the original policy, except all riders, including those for disability and accidental death, are eliminated.

11.4.3 Extended Term Option

The third nonforfeiture option is called the *extended term option*.

With this option, the policyowner can use the policy's cash value accumulation as a single premium to purchase paid-up term insurance in an amount equal to the original policy face amount.

The length of the term depends on the net cash value that is applied as a net single premium at the insured's attained age.

Typically, the extended term nonforfeiture option goes into effect automatically if the policyowner isn't available to make a choice or simply fails to exercise an option (unless the paid-up insurance would provide more coverage). So, if a cash value policy is lapsed and the policyowner neither makes an effort to reinstate that policy nor requests a specific nonforfeiture option, the company automatically buys term coverage in the same amount as the original policy for whatever period the cash buys at the insured's attained age.

If a policy loan is outstanding at the time the extended term option is exercised, the company will first deduct the loan outstanding from the cash surrender value of the policy to cancel out the outstanding loan. The reduced cash value will provide term coverage for a shortened period and for a face amount that is likewise reduced by the amount of the outstanding loan.

Example

Suppose a policyowner has borrowed $10,000 from her cash value. She pays back $8,000 and then is unable to continue paying premiums and chooses the extended term option. If the cash value of the original policy was $30,000 and its face value was $75,000, then:

- the single premium available for the extended term policy is $28,000 ($30,000 minus the $2,000 remaining on the policy loan); and
- the face amount of the extended term insurance is $73,000 ($75,000 minus the $2,000 remaining on the policy loan).

Note: The reason the outstanding loan amount is deducted from both the cash value and the face amount is to prevent policyowners from borrowing heavily against their permanent policies if they learn they're soon going to die or if they may be contemplating suicide. Without this stipulation, policyowners could borrow up to the limit on their permanent policies, accept an extended term policy with the same face amount as their original policy, and take the insurance company for more money.

When the reduced paid-up option is selected, the policyowner receives a smaller amount of protection than existed with the original policy—usually quite a bit smaller, unless the policy has quite a sizable cash value. If the cash option is taken, the policyowner loses all life insurance protection in the policy. If you are asked which nonforfeiture option provides the most life insurance protection immediately, the answer usually is the extended term option.

11. 5 DIVIDENDS

Many of the life insurance policies sold in the United States today have a provision allowing the policyowner to participate in the favorable experience of the insurance company through dividends. Most, although not all, of these participating policies (sometimes referred to as par policies) are sold by mutual life insurance companies rather than by stock companies.

Policies that do not pay dividends are called nonparticipating (nonpar) policies.

Usually, the premium for a participating policy is calculated using very conservative assumptions, including an allowance for future dividend payments. The amount, or even the existence, of policy dividends is never guaranteed. By charging a slightly higher initial premium for participating policies, a company can be fairly sure that it will be able to return at least a small dividend.

As a matter of practice, many companies declare and pay dividends annually. The policyowner usually is offered several options for the settlement of these dividends. The following is a list of possible dividend payment options. Although these options are the most frequently used, the list is not inclusive:

- Cash dividend

- Accumulation at interest
- Paid-up additions
- Reduce premium
- Accelerated endowment
- Paid-up option
- One-year term option

11. 5. 1 Not Guaranteed, Not Taxable

When dividends are possible in participating policies, it is common for clients to believe that the dividends are earnings similar to those associated with stocks. Producers must explain that dividends are a return of premium, which is why they are not taxed. Most of all, producers must make sure they never give clients the impression that dividends are guaranteed. Producers should make this especially clear when giving cash value projections. Also, a company's past dividend performance must be presented as just that—a history of past performance, which in no way can be interpreted as a projection of future dividends.

11. 5. 2 Participating vs. Nonparticipating Company

Life insurance policies may be either participating or nonparticipating, and it is important to distinguish between the two to understand the source of policy dividends. At any given age, people who buy participating (par) policies normally pay premiums that are slightly higher than premiums paid by those who purchase nonparticipating (nonpar) policies. This is because an extra charge to cover unexpected contingencies is built into premiums for par policies.

At the end of each year, the insurance company analyzes its operations. If fewer insureds have died than was estimated, a "divisible surplus" results and the company can return to the policyowners a part of the premiums paid for participating policies. A company also can issue returns stemming from positive operating or investment income. These payments are called dividends but should not be confused with the dividends paid on stocks. Policy dividends are really a return of part of the premiums paid. As such, policy dividends are generally not taxable income, unlike corporate dividends, which are reportable for income tax purposes. However, policy dividends can be taxed when they exceed the cost of the policy.

11. 6 POLICY DIVIDEND SOURCES

The source of funds from which life insurance policy dividends are paid is the same (basically) as the three factors used in premium computations, which are as follows:

- Mortality—The mortality tables tell us that a certain number of persons (insureds) in each age group will probably die during the next year. If fewer people die than predicted, the life insurance company experiences a mortality savings.

- (Assumed) interest—A life insurance company estimates that invested money will earn a given rate over the long run, usually around 4%. If a company assumes its investments will earn 4% but the invested premiums actually earn 8%, the company has earned excess interest.
- Operating expenses or loading—Past experience tells a company that it will cost so many dollars per $1,000 coverage to keep the company going. Such costs as accounting, rent, office equipment, and so forth are relatively predictable. Let's say, however, that a given company installs a new accounting system that saves several thousand dollars. These savings help reduce operating expenses or loading.

In each of the cases outlined above, the company ends up with excess funds or surplus over those needed to pay claims and operating expenses and to make a respectable profit. Life insurance policy dividends are paid out of such funds.

11. 7 DIVIDEND OPTIONS

11. 7. 1 Cash Dividend Option

The policyowner has several dividend options available with respect to the receipt of dividends and when they are paid, and the policyowner notifies the insurer regarding which option she selects.

One dividend option is simply to have the company issue the policyowner a check for the dividend amount. This is known as the **cash dividend option**.

11. 7. 2 Accumulation at Interest Option

The policyowner can let dividends accumulate at interest with the company. The company will invest the policyowner's money and add interest earnings to the initial amount of the dividends as such earnings accrue. Of course, any interest is currently taxable. The interest on invested dividends builds up, or accumulates. For this reason, this dividend option is called the **accumulation at interest option**.

If an insured policyowner dies with a credit to the policy for accumulated dividends and interest, the dividends plus any accrued interest are paid to the beneficiary of the policy because this money belonged to the policyowner.

Dividends earned during the year of an insured's death, too, are paid along with any accrued dividends and interest accumulated on previous dividends. Dividends earned during the year of death and paid as a part of the death claim (in addition to the face amount of the policy) are called postmortem dividends. Both **postmortem dividends** and dividends from previous years that have accumulated interest are paid to the beneficiary of the policy when the insured dies.

Keep in mind, with respect to leaving dividends to accumulate at interest, that this money has nothing to do with the cash value accumulation of a permanent policy. This means that dividends left at interest can be used in a cash emergency—the policyowner can withdraw them—without in any way affecting the cash value of the policy.

11. 7. 3 Paid-Up Additions Option

If a policyowner decides to use dividends as a single premium to buy additional life insurance protection, the additional coverage is fully paid for, or paid-up, with that premium. For this reason, we call this option the **paid-up additions option**.

The amount of paid-up addition per $1 of dividend is based on the insured's age at the time the paid-up addition is purchased. The amount of the paid-up addition to a life insurance policy is therefore dependent on the amount of the dividend and the insured's attained age.

What the policyowner is saying to the company is this: "Take my dividend dollars this year and purchase single premium additional life insurance for me in whatever amount the money will buy at my attained age."

No new policies are issued. The base policy is simply amended to reflect the additional paid-up values. Each of these additions will also develop cash value. The face amount and the additions make up the total death benefit if the policy matures as a death claim. If the policyowner elects to surrender the policy for its cash value before that time, both the cash value of the policy and the addition would be paid.

When this arrangement is chosen, the insured need not prove that he is a standard risk. If the purchase of paid-up additions is the policyowner's dividend option, proof of insurability is not required each time a new dividend is credited.

If another dividend option is chosen originally and the policyowner later decides to change to the paid-up additions option, previous dividend amounts generally cannot be used to purchase these additions. However, the policyowner can use current and future dividends to purchase paid-up additions.

Now, let's summarize.

- When dividends are used to buy additional life insurance protection, the policyowner is using the paid-up additions dividend option.
- The single premium for the added coverage will be based on the insured's attained age.
- The policyowner can use current and future dividends to obtain this coverage.

The type of insurance purchased as a paid-up addition is usually restricted to the same type as provided in the original policy. If a policyowner is insured by a whole life policy and decides to use policy dividends to purchase paid-up additions, the paid-up additional insurance will be whole life insurance.

There is one more point concerning paid-up additions: the loading charges—the share of the company's operating expenses—borne by each policy. When current dividends are used to buy paid-up additions, no agent's commission is involved, nor is there any investigation of insurability. This means that the operating expenses of putting this coverage in force are lower than original policy expenses.

11. 7. 4 Reduce Premium Dividend Option

The policyowner can direct the insurer to apply the dividend toward the next premium due on the policy. In other words, the policyowner can use the dividend to pay all or part of the next premium due on the policy. Usually, if this option has been elected, the premium notice will show the gross premium minus the dividend and the policyowner simply pays the net amount. If the dividend equals or exceeds the premium amount, the premium payment may be suspended entirely.

Let's see how this works. Imagine that an insured has a policy with an annual premium of $480. The dividend due for one year is $150. If the insured chose the reduce premium dividend option, the net annual premium due would be $330 ($480 less $150).

11. 7. 5 Accelerated Endowment

As discussed earlier, endowment policies lost their tax advantages in 1985 and have been rare since that time. However, you still may encounter a policyowner with an endowment policy using dividends to accelerate the endowment.

At one time, dividends may have been applied to convert the policy into an endowment. This is unlikely today because of the adverse tax consequences. Dividends still may be used on an existing endowment policy to shorten the endowment term. The usual methods are described here.

- Dividends remain as accumulations until they, together with the cash value, equal the face amount of the policy, at which time the face amount will be paid as an endowment if so requested.
- The dividends are used each year to shorten the endowment period. The effect is to change the policy form each year by reducing its term. Under this option, a policy will mature more quickly because its cash value will reach the desired face amount of the insurance in a shorter time. The annual application of the dividend reduces the amount at risk. With less at risk, a smaller proportion of future premiums to be collected will be needed than originally anticipated to pay the cost of the insurance. This form of the endowment option endows the policy more quickly than the one in the first method described.

11. 7. 6 Paid-Up Option

This option actually allows the policyowner to pay up the policy early. For example, the insured has a 20-pay life policy. By using the dividends over the life of the policy, it may be paid up after 16 or 17 years instead of the full 20 years. If the insured owned a whole life contract, by using the dividends in this manner, he would not have to pay on the policy to age 100.

11. 7. 7 One-Year Term Dividend Option

If the policyowner chooses to do so, he can direct the company to use the dividends on the policy to purchase term insurance—term coverage that will be in force for a full year. We call this option the one-year term dividend option.

Under the one-year term dividend option, the dividend money is used to buy term coverage of one year's duration, based on the attained age of the insured. The amount usually is limited to the current cash value of the policy. If there is more than enough dividend money to buy that amount of one-year term coverage, any excess dividend money still belongs to the policyowner. These extra funds can be applied under other available dividend options.

In addition, the company usually will require a medical examination for the term coverage, only if the original policy has been in force and another dividend option has been in effect for several years. If this option has been in effect since the original policy went in force, the company usually requires no additional proof of insurability under the one-year term dividend option.

11. 8 CONCLUSION

A company's board of directors can declare a policy dividend annually if a surplus exists. This doesn't mean that the policyowner has to decide which dividend option to select every time the dividend is declared. The policyowner can set up any one of the options we've been discussing as a permanent option, to be handled automatically by the company every time dividends on the policy are made available.

11.9 SUMMARY

In this lesson, you learned about:

- policy options, including settlement options, nonforfeiture options, and dividend options;
- what happens to money left with the insurer when the beneficiary dies; and
- how quickly permanent policies are required to accumulate cash values.

UNIT TEST

1. Emily has chosen to receive the payout from her husband's life insurance policy so that she will receive an income for the next 15 years. At the end of that time, the entire proceeds from the policy will have been paid out. Emily has selected the
   A. interest-only option
   B. fixed-period option
   C. fixed-amount option
   D. life-income option

2. Heath has chosen to receive the payout from his wife's life insurance policy in such a way that he will have an income for the remainder of his life, regardless of how long he lives. Heath has selected the
   A. interest-only option
   B. fixed-period option
   C. fixed-amount option
   D. life-income option

3. Jim has selected to receive only the interest from his mother's life insurance policy. When Jim dies, his children will receive the lump-sum benefit in addition to the benefit from his life insurance policy. Jim has selected the
   A. interest-only option
   B. fixed-period option
   C. fixed-amount option
   D. life-income option

4. Carmen has selected to receive $10,000 per month until the principal and interest on her husband's life insurance policy have been paid out. Carmen has selected the
   A. interest-only option
   B. fixed-period option
   C. fixed-amount option
   D. life-income option

5. Tina has a whole life insurance policy on her life that has been in effect for 15 years. Tina and her husband review their insurance coverage and decide that this policy, which was purchased before their marriage, is no longer necessary for their financial future. If Tina decides to stop paying the premiums, what will happen?
   A. The policy will lapse when the grace period expires, and Tina will lose the cash values built up in the policy.
   B. The policy has not built up cash values because it is a whole life policy.
   C. The policy has not been in force long enough to have built up cash values, so when it lapses, Tina will receive nothing.
   D. The policy will lapse, and Tina will be able to select a nonforfeiture option to receive value for the cash value built up in the policy.

6. In most states, a whole life policy must have at least a small cash value by the end of the policy's
   A. first year
   B. second year
   C. third year
   D. fourth year

7. Ann quits paying premiums on her whole life policy that has been in effect for 17 years. She does not select a nonforfeiture option. What happens to the cash value in her policy?
   A. The insurer will issue a paid-up term insurance policy with the same face value as the policy with a term as long as the cash value will purchase.
   B. The insurer will issue Ann's beneficiary check for the eligible amount of cash value in the policy.
   C. The insurer will issue a check for the eligible amount of cash value in the policy.
   D. The insurer may keep the cash value if a nonforfeiture option is not selected.

8. Which of the following statements about reduced paid-up insurance option is NOT true?
   A. The new policy will build cash values for the policyowner.
   B. No further premiums need to be paid on the reduced policy—it is paid up.
   C. The new protection is for the same amount as the original policy.
   D. A full share of expense loading is usually not included in the premium on the reduced coverage, because the costs of setting up the coverage are greatly reduced.

9. Shawn takes out a $5,000 loan against his $100,000 whole life insurance policy. Shortly thereafter, he chooses to convert the policy using the extended term option. What will the face value of the term insurance be?
   A. $5,000
   B. $95,000
   C. $100,000
   D. $105,000

10. Why did insurance companies develop settlement options?
    A. A federal mandate required the development of settlement options in the 1970s
    B. To avoid problems for beneficiaries who might be unprepared or unable to wisely handle a lump-sum settlement
    C. To retain the bulk of death benefit payouts for as long as possible to improve insurers' investment experience
    D. A model law adopted by most states required the development of settlement options in the 1960s

11. Which of the following statements regarding settlement options is NOT true?
    A. Most insurers will agree to distribute the proceeds under any reasonable and actuarially sound settlement model.
    B. Interest earnings on the retained proceeds are guaranteed.
    C. The money is safe with the insurance company.
    D. The beneficiary invests the money at the suggestion of the insurer.

12. Ken is receiving interest-only payments on the settlement of his father's life insurance policy. If Ken dies before the lump sum is paid to him, what happens to the balance of the money?
    A. It is retained by the insurer.
    B. It is paid to any contingent beneficiary named in the original policy, or if there is no contingent beneficiary, it is paid to Ken's estate.
    C. It is paid to any primary beneficiary named in the original policy or into Ken's father's estate.
    D. It is paid directly into Ken's estate.

13. Which of the following is NOT a factor in determining the amount the beneficiary will receive each time a payment is made under the fixed period option?
    A. The age of the beneficiary
    B. The principal amount
    C. The interest earned on the principal
    D. The length of time payments are to be made

14. Which of the following is not a factor in determining the amount the beneficiary will receive each time a payment is made under the fixed amount option?
    A. The specified amount of each payment
    B. The principal amount
    C. The interest earned on the principal
    D. The capital amount

15. Thomas has chosen to receive the settlement from his wife's $100,000 life insurance policy according to the life income option. Under the option he chooses, he will receive an income for his life and his daughter will receive payments if he dies before receiving $100,000 in income. Thomas has selected a
    A. straight life income option
    B. refund annuity option
    C. life income certain option
    D. joint and survivor life income option

16. Walter is the beneficiary of his mother's life insurance policy. He wants to make sure the proceeds will last not only as long as he lives but also as long as his wife is alive. Walter should select the
    A. straight life income option
    B. refund annuity option
    C. life income certain option
    D. joint and survivor life income option

17. Which of the following factors does NOT affect the payment of dividends?
    A. Mortality
    B. Assumed Interest
    C. Morbidity
    D. Operating expenses or loading

18. Carl has not selected a dividend option for his nonparticipating policy. What happens to his dividends?
    A. No dividends are paid.
    B. They are used to purchase paid-up additions to the policy.
    C. They are used to purchase one-year term insurance.
    D. They are paid to Carl in cash.

19. Which of the following dividend options is least likely to be used on a policy issued today?
    A. Cash
    B. Accumulation at interest
    C. Accelerated endowment
    D. Paid-up additions

20. Which of the following statements about paid-up additions is TRUE?
    A. The dividends are used to purchase additional insurance protection.
    B. The additional protection is almost always restricted to term insurance.
    C. The single premium for the added coverage will be based on the insured's original age.
    D. The operating expenses of putting this coverage in force are higher than original policy expenses.

ANSWERS AND RATIONALES TO UNIT TEST

1. **B.**
2. **D.** This is an example of the life-income option because the proceeds will be paid over the beneficiary's life, regardless of how long that might be.
3. **A.** Because Jim has elected to receive only the interest, this example represents the interest-only option.
4. **C.** Carmen has elected to receive a fixed amount per month until all the proceeds have all been paid, so this is an example of the fixed-amount option.
5. **D.**
6. **C.** Most states require whole life policies to have a cash value by the end of the third year.
7. **A.** Usually, the extended term nonforfeiture option goes into effect automatically if the policyowner fails to make an election.
8. **C.** The reduced paid-up amount is simply the amount of paid-up insurance that can be purchased using the existing cash value.
9. **B.** Under the extended term option, the amount of term insurance is the same as the face amount of the whole life coverage, minus any outstanding policy loans.
10. **B.**
11. **D.** It is not true that the beneficiary invests the money at the suggestion of the insurer.
12. **B.** The balance of the money is paid to any contingent beneficiary named in the original policy. If there is no contingent beneficiary, it is paid to Ken's estate.
13. **A.** The age of the beneficiary is not a factor in determining the amount the beneficiary will receive each time a payment is made under the fixed period option.
14. **D.** The capital amount is not a factor in determining the amount the beneficiary will receive each time a payment is made under the fixed amount option.
15. **B.** Thomas has selected a refund annuity option.
16. **D.** Walter should select the joint and survivor life income option.
17. **C.** Morbidity does not affect the payment of dividends.
18. **A.** No dividends are paid.
19. **C.** The accelerated endowment option is least likely to be used on a policy issued today.
20. **A.** With paid-up additions, the dividends are used to purchase additional insurance protection.

UNIT

12

Annuities

12. 1 LEARNING OBJECTIVES

After completing this lesson, you will be able to:

- describe and explain the workings of the various types of annuities;
- list the three types of annuity premium payments;
- list the five factors used to determine annuity premiums;
- explain how variable annuities are regulated; and
- explain how accumulation units and annuity units are calculated.

12. 2 PURPOSES OF ANNUITIES

Life insurance is designed to protect the insured against premature death. An annuity is designed to protect the annuitant against the risk of living too long and possibly outliving her financial resources during retirement. Annuities offer a benefit unknown to other types of financial vehicles: a payout you cannot outlive. Other investments and savings can be depleted and leave an individual with no other resources in dire financial straits. Annuity payments, however, can be arranged to last for life.

Like all insurance, annuities are designed to transfer a risk from consumers to an insurance company. In the case of annuities, the risk being transferred is the risk of outliving your savings. Annuities technically are not life insurance, but because annuities are sold by life insurance companies, a basic understanding of the types of annuity policies available is necessary to qualify for a producer license.

12. 2. 1 Distribution of a Lifetime Income

Suppose you had a sum of money with which to support yourself for the rest of your life. If you spent too much each month, you would run out of money before you died. If you spent too little, you would not maximize the use of that money—you would die before it was all used up. An annuity eliminates this uncertainty by converting a sum of money into a series of period payments that can be guaranteed to last a lifetime, and sometimes longer as we'll see.

12. 2. 2 Lump Sum Settlements

If an annuitant dies before the annuity fund (the principal) is depleted, a lump-sum cash payment of the remainder is made to the annuitant's beneficiary. Thus, the beneficiary receives an amount equal to the beginning annuity fund less the amount of income already paid to the deceased annuitant.

12. 2. 3 Accumulation of a Retirement Fund

Suppose you don't have a sum of money that will serve as a fund for your retirement. An annuity can be structured to allow for the accumulation of such a fund over time so that when retirement finally arrives, income payments begin. These payments will continue as long as you live and even afterward to your spouse if he survives you.

12. 2. 4 Accumulation of Education Funds

While annuities are designed to create and accumulate income for retirement, they can be used for other purposes as well. For example, they can be used to create and accumulate funds for a college education. Annuities serve a variety of purposes for which a stream of income is needed for a few years or a lifetime.

12. 2. 5 Tax-Deferred Growth

Annuity benefit payments are a combination of principal and interest. Accordingly, they are taxed in a manner consistent with other types of income: the portion of the benefit payments that represents a return of principal (i.e., the contributions made by the annuitant) are not taxed; the portion representing interest earned on the declining principal is taxed. The result, over the benefit payment period, is a tax-free return of the annuitant's investment and the taxing of the balance.

Though a detailed discussion of how to compute the taxable portion of an annuity payment is beyond the scope of this text, the basics are not difficult to understand. An *exclusion ratio* is applied to each benefit payment the annuitant receives:

$$\frac{\text{Investment in the contract}}{\text{Expected return}} = \text{Exclusion ratio}$$

The investment in the contract is the amount of money paid into the annuity; the expected return is the annual guaranteed benefit the annuitant receives, multiplied by the number of years of her life expectancy. The resulting ratio is applied to the benefit payments, allowing the annuitant to exclude from income a like percentage.

Deferred annuities accumulate interest earnings on a tax-deferred basis. While no taxes are imposed on the annuity during the accumulation phase, taxes are imposed when the contract begins to pay its benefits (in accordance with the exclusion ratio just described). To discourage the use of deferred annuities as short-term investments, the Internal Revenue Code imposes a penalty as well as taxes on early withdrawals and loans from annuities. Partial withdrawals are treated first as earnings income (and are thus taxable as ordinary income); only after all earnings have been taxed are withdrawals considered a return of principal. Furthermore, a 10% penalty tax is imposed on withdrawals from a deferred annuity before age 59½. Withdrawals after age 59½ are not subject to the 10% penalty tax, but are still taxable as ordinary income.

12. 2. 6 Summation

Annuities exist to distribute a lifetime income or to accumulate a sum of money if necessary. This accumulation may be used for retirement, as has been described, or for any other purpose—perhaps an education fund to pay college expenses. Whatever the reason, the annuity can serve as a means of providing the money.

12. 3 HOW ANNUITIES WORK

Like an insurance policy, an annuity is a contract between a purchaser and an insurance company. The purchaser pays the premium and generally is the contract owner. The **contract owner** has certain rights under the contract.

Example

The contract owner names the annuitant. The annuitant is the insured, the person on whose life the annuity policy has been issued. In most cases, the annuitant is the intended recipient of the annuity payments. Many times, the contract owner and annuitant are the same person, but not always. The contract owner also names a beneficiary, who receives survivor benefits payable under the annuity upon the death of the annuitant.

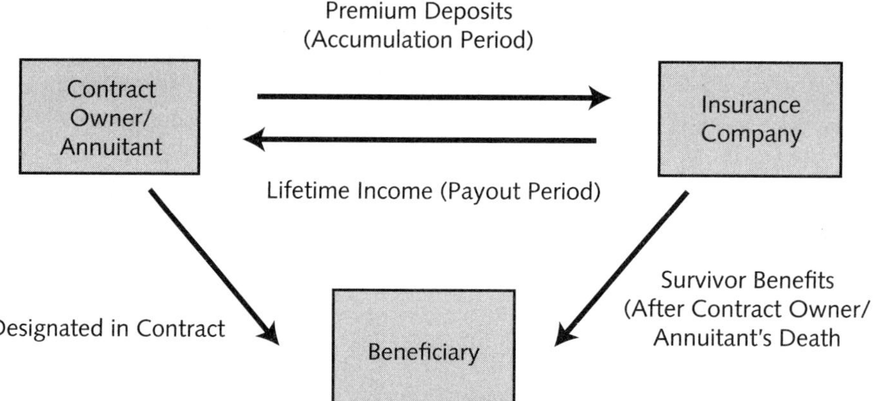

Annuities may be considered a true insurance product because there is an amount at risk. With an insurance policy, the insurer is counting on the insured living long enough so that the premiums paid and interest earned on them will equal or exceed the policy's death benefit. With an annuity, specifically a life annuity that provides benefits for as long as the annuitant lives, the insurer is counting on the annuitant not outliving the principal and interest used to provide payments.

From the standpoint of the consumer, it could be said that life insurance offers protection against dying too soon, whereas an annuity offers protection against living too long.

12. 3. 1 The Accumulation Period

The common purpose of all annuities is the distribution of an income. As we'll see, there are different ways an annuity can do this. Nonetheless, to accomplish this purpose, most annuities have an accumulation period. In fact, there will always be an accumulation period unless (1) the purchaser already has a lump sum with which to buy the annuity contract, and (2) the purchaser wants the payout to begin right away. The accumulation period may be initiated by the payment of a single lump sum or the first of a series of premium payments.

During this accumulation period, the principal earns interest and grows year by year. A so-called fixed annuity specifies a fixed, guaranteed minimum rate of interest that will be paid on the principal amount invested in the annuity. Under this arrangement, the contract owner knows exactly the minimum return that will be earned during the accumulation period. The insurer simply invests each premium in its general investment account and credits the current interest to the annuity's cash value, but never less than the minimum guaranteed.

A variable annuity, as we'll see, offers a variable, nonguaranteed rate of interest that offers the potential—but not a promise—to act as a hedge against inflation.

In all types of annuities, the principal earns interest. The first year's interest is added to the original principal, and the combined sum then earns more interest in the second year. In other words, we earn interest on interest, or compound interest, in the second and every subsequent year, as demonstrated by the following.

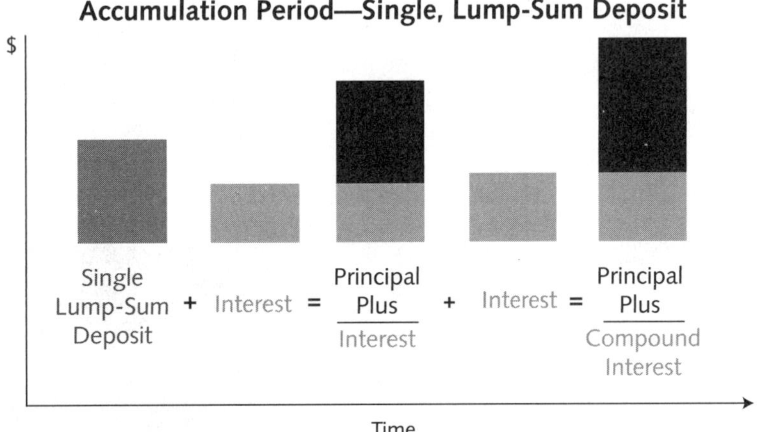

Compound interest also works when the accumulation is initiated with the first of several periodic deposits. The first deposit earns interest during year one, which is then added to the principal going into year two, along with the second deposit of principal. The entire sum then earns interest in year two, so again we have the compounding of interest, as shown.

Accumulation Period—Periodic Deposits

$

Deposit #2

Deposit #3

Deposit #1 + Interest

Deposit #1 Plus Interest

+ Interest

Deposit #1,2 Plus Compound Interest

+ Interest

Time

This brings us to an important point. The interest earned by the annuity contract is not currently taxed as it is with other savings investment vehicles. Instead, if an individual owns the annuity, the interest generally is not taxed until it is paid out of the contract. Meanwhile, during the accumulation period, this untaxed interest goes right on earning even more interest, which is also added to principal and not currently taxed. This tax advantage is an important reason why people buy annuities.

12. 3. 2 The Annuity Period

We reach the point in time at which we begin using the accumulated money—not all at once but just enough of it periodically so that we can live comfortably. Each periodic annuity payment can be considered a blend of our deposits and the interest those deposits have earned. In the illustration below, we see funds flowing out of both the principal deposits and the interest accumulation to make up each annuity payment. That is exactly how the federal income tax laws view annuity payments.

Payout Period

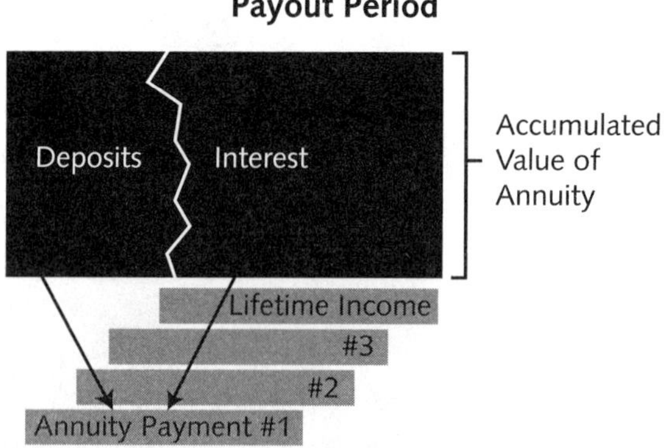

Of course, nobody knows exactly how long the annuitant is going to live. However, insurance companies have studied average life expectancies over many years, so that using the law of large numbers, the insurance company has a pretty good idea how long the average person will live. Some people will die before their life expectancy is up, leaving uncollected benefits for the people who live longer than their life expectancy.

So, an annuity is really a combination of three things:

- Deposits
- Interest
- A mortality factor

Even after the annuitant has exhausted all deposits and interest, he still can collect annuity payments for life because of the insurer's acceptance of longevity risk.

12. 3. 2. 1 *Fixed Payout*

For a fixed annuity, the cash value accumulation at the beginning of the annuity period is simply annuitized—that is, the accumulation is converted into a stream of periodic payments using actuarial principles that take into account the expected longevity of the annuitant, interest earned by the principal balance during the annuity (payout) period, and related factors. The result is a fixed dollar amount payout that remains the same for the rest of the contract.

12. 3. 2. 2 *Variable Payout*

A different payout measure is used for variable annuities, and we'll look at it in detail later in this unit. Suffice it to say, the payout can change, reflecting the investment experience of the principal.

12. 3. 3 Nonforfeiture Provisions

An annuity contract owner who stops making premium payments during the accumulation period does not lose the value accumulated in the annuity to that point. The contract holder may have several **nonforfeiture options**—the rights to the cash value accumulation up to the point the premiums stopped.

A common option is to permit the contract to become a paid-up contract under which the annuitant receives annuity payments based on that amount.

Another option is to surrender the contract for its cash value and take a lump-sum payment. Surrender is not permitted once annuity payments begin, but the contract owner may totally or partially surrender the annuity contract during the accumulation period. Most companies will level some kind of surrender charge, which often scales downward as time goes on.

12. 3. 4 Owner vs. Annuitant vs. Beneficiary

The **annuitant** is the insured person in an annuity contract, the person on whose life the annuity policy has been issued. As is the case with life insurance, the owner of the annuity may or may not be the annuitant. In most cases, the annuitant is the intended recipient of the annuity payments.

Depending on the type of annuity and the method of benefit payment selected, a beneficiary may also be named in an annuity contract. In such cases, annuity payments may continue after the death of the annuitant for the lifetime of the beneficiary or for a specified number of years.

12. 4 IMMEDIATE AND DEFERRED ANNUITIES

There are two categories of annuities based on when annuity payments are to begin—immediate and deferred annuities.

We call a contract an **immediate annuity** if income payments to the annuitant are to begin one payout interval (e.g., one month or one year) after purchase of the annuity.

We call a contract a **deferred annuity** if income payments are to begin at some further point in the future—perhaps as much as several years from the date of purchase.

Even with an immediate annuity, payments don't begin on the very next day after the contract is purchased. Instead, payments begin after one full payment period from the date of purchase has elapsed. If the contract calls for monthly installments, for example, payments will begin one month after the date of purchase. If the contract calls for annual payments, the annuitant will receive the first payment one year after the date of purchase.

Annuity benefit payments are made on either an annual, semiannual, quarterly, or monthly basis. The longest period between benefit payments is a year, so it follows that payments on an immediate annuity will begin no later than one year from the date of purchase.

With an immediate annuity, payments could begin as soon as one month from the date of purchase.

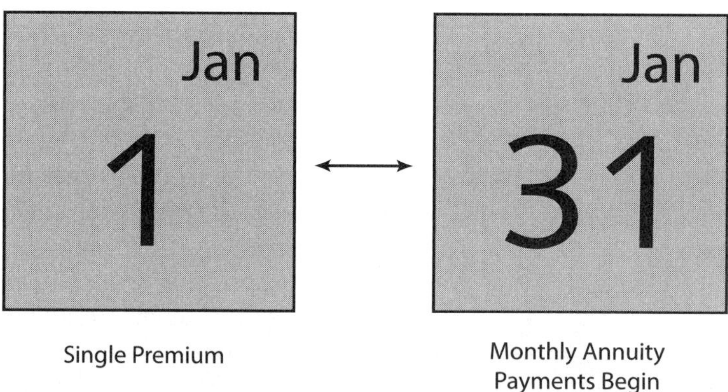

The point to remember is this: an immediate annuity is immediate only in relation to a deferred annuity, in which the first payment is deferred by as much as several years.

In addition, keep in mind that if the insurance company is to begin paying the annuitant shortly after the purchase of the contract, the purchaser must pay for the entire contract at once. An immediate annuity then must be paid for with a single premium and is known as a single premium immediate annuity (SPIA).

A deferred annuity also can be a single premium contract or single premium deferred annuity (SPDA). In fact, such persons as professional athletes frequently buy single premium deferred annuities while their incomes are quite high.

Sometimes the annuity payments do not begin until many years after the first (or only) premium is paid. This type of contract is a deferred annuity because the benefits are not immediate but are delayed until some specified future time. This deferral period allows a deferred annuity to be used as an accumulation vehicle during the annuitant's working years as well as a source of lifetime income after retirement, as illustrated by the following.

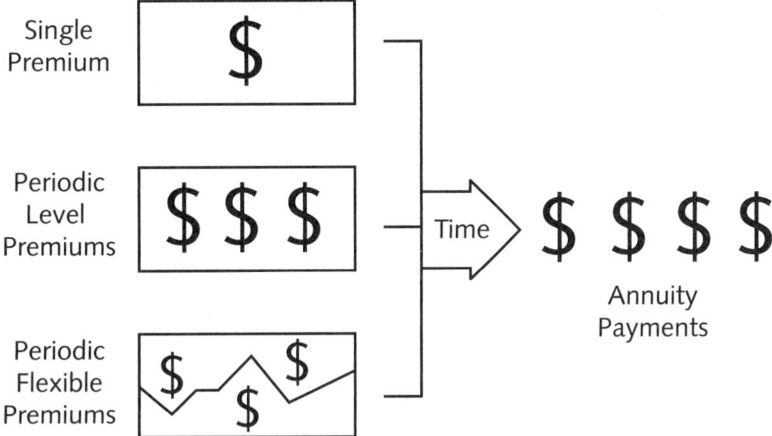

Example

Most of the time, deferred annuity premiums are paid in annual, semiannual, quarterly, or monthly installments over a period of years. With a deferred annuity, the start of income payments is delayed for a specified period—until age 55, 60, 65, or 70. Regardless of premium payment method, with a deferred annuity, income payments to the annuitant begin after the specified period has elapsed after the purchase date.

12. 5 DEFERRED ANNUITY DEATH BENEFITS

In the case of a deferred annuity contract, the annuitant could die before he received even one income payment under the contract—perhaps several years before the first income payment became due. Although company policy varies greatly as to what amount is paid to the annuitant's beneficiary or other heirs, most companies refund at least the amount the purchaser has paid for the contract at that point. Some may include interest on that amount.

When the annuitant dies before the start of annuity payments, some companies return both the aggregate, net premiums paid by the purchaser of a deferred annuity and a portion of the interest the money has earned. Still others deduct enough money from premiums paid to cover the expense incurred in setting up the contract. So, if you are asked what the death benefits of a deferred annuity are, the best answer you can give is that this is the amount returned when the annuitant dies before receiving payments under the annuity.

Not all companies return the premiums; fewer include interest. Still, this amount (the aggregate, net premiums paid for the annuity up to the point of the annuitant's death) is usually returned to the annuitant's beneficiary. Although these proceeds do not represent death protection like the benefits from a life insurance policy, we still may call the amount refunded from a deferred annuity a death benefit.

12. 6 ANNUITY PREMIUMS

12. 6. 1 Single Premium

As we'll see shortly, there are different types of annuities available. Let's first look, however, at the various ways to pay for an annuity. One of the most common is the single premium.

An annuity purchased by a single lump-sum payment is called a single premium annuity. For example, a life insurance policy could be cashed in at retirement and the cash value could be used to buy a single premium annuity. The annuity itself is a contract between the company and the annuitant. For the single premium, the company promises to pay the annuitant an amount each period (monthly, quarterly, semiannually, or annually).

12. 6. 2 Level Premium

A second method of buying an annuity is the level premium annuity.

Under this arrangement, the premiums are paid in periodic installments over the years before the date on which the annuity income begins. Level premiums have a forced savings aspect to them, much like making regular deposits into a passbook savings account. A common level premium arrangement is the annual premium annuity in which the premiums are paid in yearly installments up to the time the annuity benefits begin. Premiums also can be paid semiannually, quarterly, or monthly.

12. 6. 3 Flexible Premium

A flexible premium annuity is like the level premium annuity in that annuity premiums are made over time, usually years, until annuity benefits are scheduled to begin. The difference is that with a flexible premium annuity, the purchaser has the option to vary the amount of each premium payment, as long as it falls between a minimum and maximum amount—for example, between $200 and $10,000.

The flexible premium annuity can be advantageous to persons whose incomes may be subject to considerable fluctuation or who, for whatever reason, cannot pay for an annuity all at once or with periodic premiums that are the same amount each time.

If an annuity is used to fund an IRA, it must provide for flexible premiums.

There is, however, a disadvantage to a flexible premium annuity. The actual amount of the annuity benefit cannot be determined in advance because there's no way to determine in advance the amount of each premium that will be paid or how much will be paid in total for the annuity. The purchaser of a flexible premium annuity therefore must wait until the final premium payment has been made to determine the exact amount of the annuity benefit. Benefits can be projected on the basis of assumptions about premium payments.

12. 6. 4 Premium Determination

There are five factors used to determine annuity premiums:

- Annuitant's age
- Annuitant's sex
- Assumed interest rate
- Income amount and payment guarantee
- Loading for company expenses

The first factor used to determine annuity premiums is the age at which the annuitant will begin to receive a lifetime income. The annuitant's age is important, because the company must determine for how long it's likely to have to make income payments to the annuitant. If Mr. A were to receive $300 a month for life beginning at age 60 and Mr. B were to receive $300 a month for life beginning at age 65, the company will charge a higher premium for Mr. A than for Mr. B.

The annuitant's sex is also a factor used in most states to determine premiums. Statistics show that women live longer than men do. Therefore, if the annuitant is a woman, she'll pay higher premiums because she's likely to live longer—and will therefore receive more income payments—than would a man her age.

Some states have adopted unisex titles that disregard sex in determining annuity premiums. In such states, the premium for a female annuitant will be the same as that for a male annuitant.

As you know, life insurance companies invest premium dollars and earn a certain rate of interest on these investments. When determining premiums for annuities, the companies estimate, or assume, that invested premium dollars will earn a specified interest rate. This assumption is known as an assumed rate of interest, and it is the third factor in determining annuity premiums.

The fourth factor in annuity premium computation is made up of the amount of periodic income and any payment guarantees the company has made concerning the total amount (or total number of payments) to be paid. For example, the company may guarantee that no fewer than 120 monthly payments will be made even if the original annuitant dies before 120 months elapse.

With regard to annuity premiums, the higher the amount of periodic income and the longer it must be paid, the higher the annuity premium.

Finally, with annuity contracts, as with life insurance policies, the purchasers help pay the company's operating expenses. The premiums charged, therefore, must have an expense factor added to them. The premiums must be loaded for expenses. So, annuity premiums contain a fifth factor, which is an extra amount called loading, to pay the company's operating expenses.

12. 7 FIXED ANNUITIES

Annuities can be defined according to their investment configuration, which affects the income benefits they pay. The two classifications are *fixed annuities*, which provide a fixed, guaranteed accumulation or payout, and *variable annuities*, which attempt to offset inflation by providing a benefit linked to a variable underlying investment account. Equity indexed annuities, a form of fixed annuity, are fairly new but have become quite popular.

12. 7. 1 General Account Assets

As is the case with traditional whole life, insurance companies can keep annuity funds in the insurer's general accounts and invest them in conservative investments selected by the insurer to match its contractual guarantees and liabilities to the annuitant.

12. 7. 2 Interest Rate Guarantees

Fixed annuities provide a guaranteed rate of return. During the period in which the annuitant is making payments to fund the annuity (the *accumulation period*), the insurer invests these payments in conservative, long-term securities, typically bonds. This, in turn, allows the insurer to credit a steady interest rate to the annuity contract. The interest payable for any given year is declared in advance by the insurer and is guaranteed to be no less than a minimum specified in the contract. In this way, a fixed annuity has two interest rates: a minimum guaranteed rate and a current rate.

The *current rate* is what the insurer credits to the annuity on a regular schedule, typically each year. The current rate will never be lower than the minimum rate, which the insurer guarantees. In this way, the accumulation of funds in a fixed annuity is certain and the contract owner's principal is secure. The investment risk is borne by the insurer.

12. 7. 3 Level Benefit Payment

When converted to a payout mode, fixed annuities provide a guaranteed fixed benefit amount to the annuitant, typically stated in terms of dollars per $1,000 of accumulated value. This is possible because the interest rate payable on the annuity funds is fixed and guaranteed at the point of annuitization. The amount and duration of benefit payments are guaranteed. Because they provide a specified benefit payable for life (or any other period the annuitant desires), fixed annuities offer security and financial peace of mind. However, because the benefit amount is fixed, annuitants may see the purchasing power of their income payments decline over the years due to inflation. For many, a variable annuity is preferable.

12. 8 VARIABLE ANNUITIES

Except as otherwise indicated, the annuities we've been discussing up to this point have been fixed annuities—that is, annuities that grow at a fixed rate and pay fixed benefits when the annuitant reaches a certain age. Another type of annuity in which rate of growth of the annuity values varies according to the performance of the investment medium and from which benefits also vary is called a **variable annuity**.

Variable annuities provide annuitants the opportunity to experience large gains; they may, however, also produce a loss. Thus, variable annuities are characterized by a variable rate of growth and a variable benefit payable to the annuitant.

12. 8. 1 Regulation as Securities

Under traditional, fixed annuity contracts, the insurance company assumes the investment risk. If investment performance is more than what is required to fund the contract's guarantees, the difference is added to the company's surplus. If investment performance is unfavorable, the insurance company, not the contract owner, bears the loss.

With all variable contracts, including variable life insurance and variable annuities, the investment risk is borne by the contract owner. This allows investment gains to be passed through to the contract owner, but it means that investment losses will be passed through to the contract owner as well. Buyers usually can choose from a variety of investment accounts, including the company's (nonvariable) general account.

Because the contract owner bears the investment risk, the Securities and Exchange Commission (SEC)—as well as some individual states—considers variable annuities to be securities rather than simple life insurance products. As a result, variable annuities and those who sell them are subject to federal securities regulations as well as to state insurance regulations.

Variable contracts must be registered with the SEC under the Securities Act of 1933. This means that generally, the laws and rules that apply to securities also apply to variable annuities. People who sell variable annuities must be dually licensed. First, they must be licensed by a state to sell life insurance. Second, they must be licensed as registered representatives of a member of the Financial Industry Regulatory Authority (FINRA). FINRA registration requires passing an exam, either the series 6 limited registration exam or the series 7 general securities exam. Some states also require a separate state variable contracts or variable annuities license in addition to the life license and FINRA registration.

12. 8. 1. 1 Separate Account Assets

In a variable annuity, contributions made by the annuitant during the accumulation period, less a deduction for expenses, are converted to accumulation units and credited to the individual's account. This account is separate from the insurer's general account. The value of each accumulation unit varies, depending on the value of the underlying stock investment.

12. 8. 2 Accumulation Units

The money paid to an insurance company over the years by purchasers of variable annuities is accumulated in an account that is kept separate from all other fixed annuity and insurance sales. This separate account is used by the company to buy securities that hopefully will keep pace with the cost of living.

The variable annuity contract owner is actually buying accumulation units in the separate account. He is not buying shares of stock or other securities. The use of accumulation units is simply an accounting measure to determine a contract owner's interest in the separate account during the accumulation period, or purchase period, of a deferred variable annuity.

Not all purchase payments made by a contract owner go toward the purchase of accumulation units. Before units can be purchased, charges such as sales charges and taxes are deducted. Thus, the money used to buy accumulation units is the net purchase payment.

The number of units a net payment will buy depends on the value of an accumulation unit at that time. This value is determined periodically, usually daily. At the risk of oversimplification, the value of one accumulation unit is reached by dividing the value of the separate account by the number of accumulation units outstanding.

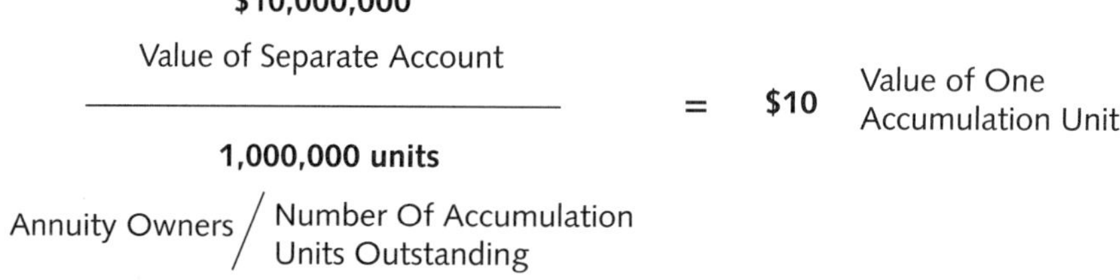

An annuitant can never end up with fewer accumulation units than he has purchased, although the value of each unit may become either greater or less.

Example

Assume that a net payment of $100 buys 100 accumulation units and the next day the value of the portfolio held by the separate account increases so that accumulation units are worth $1.05 each. The annuitant still has only 100 units, but each is now worth $1.05 instead of the $1.00 that was paid. If the value of the portfolio had decreased, the accumulation units each would be worth less.

As the contract owner continues to buy accumulation units, they are added to those already purchased. The dollar value of all the units owned by the contract holder equals the number of units the contract holder owns multiplied by the value of one accumulation unit. For example, if Frank owns 2,000 units and the value of one accumulation unit equals $5, Frank's dollar interest in the separate account equals $10,000.

12. 8. 3 Annuity Units

When the time arrives for the annuitant to start receiving payments, another accounting device replaces the accumulation unit. This is the annuity unit, which serves to determine the amount of each payment to the annuitant during the payout period.

Unlike the number of accumulation units, which increases with each payment into the separate account, the number of annuity units remains fixed. The first step in determining this fixed number is to find the dollar value of the accumulation account that is the contract holder's interest in the separate account. Recall that this is determined by multiplying the number of accumulation units by the value of each unit.

The second step in the process of finding the number of annuity units is to determine what the first monthly payment to the annuitant will be. Insurance company annuity tables, which take into account the annuitant's age and sex, the payout option chosen, and deductions for charges, show the monthly annuity payment per $1,000 applied.

Example

Suppose that the annuitant transfers $50,000 from the accumulation account and the table shows a value of $5 per $1,000. The first monthly payment to the annuitant would be 50 × $5, or $250.

If the annuity involved were fixed instead of variable, the annuitant would receive that first month's value for the remainder of the contract. With a variable annuity, this figure is converted into annuity units by dividing the first monthly payment by the value of an annuity unit at the time. If the first monthly payment is $250 and the value of an annuity unit is then $2.50, the annuitant will own 100 annuity units; once established, this number will never change.

This number of annuity units remains fixed throughout the remainder of the contract, but the annuity payment will vary according to the value of an annuity unit. If the value of an annuity unit is $2.55 the next month, the annuitant in the preceding frame would receive $255. If it is $2.45 the following month, the annuitant would receive $245.

12. 9 ANNUITY SETTLEMENT OPTIONS

12. 9. 1 Life Annuities

Life annuities is a general payout category in which the payout is guaranteed for life. Life annuities may be contrasted with temporary annuities, discussed later.

12. 9. 1. 1 Life Annuity—No Refund

Sometimes known as a **straight** life annuity, a **life annuity** pays a benefit for as long as the annuitant lives and then it ends. Whether the annuitant lives past age 100 or dies in one month, the annuity payments will continue only until the annuitant dies. In other words, there is no guarantee as to minimum benefits with a life annuity.

There is a risk to the annuitant that he might not live long enough once the annuity period begins to collect the full value of the annuity. If an annuitant dies shortly after benefits begin, the insurer keeps the balance of the unpaid benefits. This option will pay the highest amount of monthly income to the annuitant because it is based on life expectancy only, with no further payments after the death of the annuitant.

12. 9. 2 Guaranteed Minimum Payouts

Many people were not happy knowing that most or all of their investment would be lost if they were to die after receiving just a few payments. This caused insurance companies to start offering some alternatives that provided a minimum guaranteed payout.

12. 9. 2. 1 Refund Life Annuity

The length of time for which income payments will be made to the annuitant under a **refund life annuity** contract is the same as that for a straight life annuity. Thus, under a **refund life annuity**, the annuitant will receive payments for as long as he lives.

The main difference between the refund and the life annuity is that a refund annuity guarantees that an amount at least equal to the purchase price of the contract will be paid. If the annuitant lives for quite some time after the annuity income payments begin, he could receive more in benefits than the contract cost. If death occurs before an amount equal to the purchase price has been paid, the annuitant's beneficiary receives the rest of the money in cash or installment payments.

12. 9. 2. 2 Life Annuity Certain

Another type of annuity is the **life annuity with period certain**, which calls for payments for a guaranteed minimum number of years—often 10, 15, or 20. Most often, the period is 10 years because 10 years is approximately the average life expectancy of a male who retires at age 65. Obviously, the annuitant could outlive the minimum number of years specified in the contract, in which event the income payments continue until he dies.

Under a life annuity with period certain, income installments must be paid for the number of years guaranteed in the contract. Therefore, if the annuitant dies after payments have started but before the guaranteed number of years (the certain installments) have elapsed, the annuitant's beneficiary receives income payments until the remainder of the guaranteed (certain) period has elapsed. Thus, if Archie, the annuitant, retires at age 65 and selects life with 10 years certain and dies at age 70, his survivor will continue to receive the monthly annuity payments for the balance of the period certain, or five more years.

12. 9. 3 Joint Life and Survivorship and Joint Life Annuities

With a **joint life and survivorship (or last survivor) annuity**, there are more than one (usually two) annuitants, and both receive payments until one of them dies. A stated monthly amount is paid to the annuitant, and upon the annuitant's death, the same or a lesser amount is paid for the lifetime of the survivor. The joint and survivor option is usually classified as a joint and 100% survivor, joint and two-thirds survivor, or joint and 50% survivor option.

Example

If the annuitant was receiving $1,000 monthly under a joint and 50% survivor option, the survivor would receive $500 (50% of $1,000) monthly upon the death of the annuitant.

The joint and survivor annuity option should be distinguished from a **joint life annuity**, which covers two or more annuitants and provides monthly income to each annuitant until one of them dies. After the first annuitant's death, all income benefits cease. The joint life annuity can be viewed as a special case of the straight life annuity, with payments ending at the first death among the joint life annuitants.

12. 9. 4 Temporary Annuity Certain

As you know, under a life annuity with period certain, if the annuitant lives longer than the certain period stated in the contract, income payments continue for the lifetime of the annuitant. This is not the case with a **temporary annuity certain**, however. If the insured outlives the period of payments stipulated in the temporary annuity certain contract, payments stop at the end of the period.

Under a **temporary annuity certain**, the company guarantees that payments will be made for a specified number of years—often 10, 15, or 20 years. This income is guaranteed, so if the annuitant dies before receiving payments for the specified number of years, the annuitant's beneficiary receives the payments for the remaining number of years.

12. 10 TWO-TIERED ANNUITIES

An annuity may be taken in periodic payments as has been discussed. It may, however, also be taken as cash in a lump sum. If so, the amount will be different than if the annuity had been paid out under one or another of the usual annuity settlement options. A **two-tiered annuity** is one that has different values available for distribution at maturity depending on whether the value is taken in a lump sum before annuitization or left with the issuer for periodic payments.

These annuities offer relatively high rates, but only if the owner holds the contract for a certain number of years and then annuitizes it. If the annuity is surrendered at any point, interest credited to the contract is recalculated from the contract's inception using a lower tier of rates.

Although the higher tier of rates is designed to reward annuitization and to make the product more attractive than competing annuities, the lower tier of rates generally makes the contract very unattractive compared with other alternatives. And this interest penalty applies under some contracts even if the annuity is surrendered because of the death of the owner.

A few states do not permit sales of two-tiered annuities because of the potential for misunderstanding on the part of consumers or lack of disclosure on the part of agents regarding the conditions that must be met for the owner to earn the higher tier of rates. Agents who sell two-tiered annuities must make sure that clients know how the product works and are prepared to commit themselves and their beneficiaries to the annuity for a lifetime.

12. 11 TAX-SHELTERED ANNUITIES

To encourage public school systems and tax-exempt charitable, educational, and religious organizations to set aside funds for their employees' retirements, **tax-sheltered annuity plans (TSAs)** may be set up and the contributions may be excluded from the current taxable income of the employees. The plan must be established by the employer, and contributions must be used to purchase annuity contracts or mutual fund shares.

Payments received from TSAs at retirement are generally fully taxable to the recipient as ordinary income. However, payments may be spread over a long period, and taxable income at retirement is usually lower, perhaps making the tax bracket lower, too.

12. 12 RETIREMENT INCOME ANNUITIES

A **retirement income annuity** is an ordinary deferred annuity, but with an additional feature—a decreasing term life insurance rider that provides term life insurance with a face amount that decreases each year the policy is in force. The effect is that if the annuitant reaches retirement age, say 65, the decreasing term insurance death benefit expires and annuity payments begin providing retirement income. If, however, the annuitant dies before retirement, the decreasing term insurance death benefit is combined with the value of the annuity and then paid to the annuitant's beneficiary in any settlement option chosen.

12. 13 EQUITY-INDEXED ANNUITIES

Equity-indexed annuities are generally considered to be fixed annuities because they offer a guaranteed minimum interest rate and a guarantee against loss of principal if held to term. (As with other fixed annuities, surrender charges may reduce principal if the policy is surrendered early.) However, with an equity-indexed annuity, interest crediting in excess of the minimum guaranteed rate is linked to the upward movement of a designated equity index, such as the Standard and Poor's 500. If the index moves upward, the interest rate is based on some portion of the increase. If the index moves downward, the equity-indexed annuity credits the guaranteed minimum rate.

Let's see how this works. Suppose Frank has an equity-indexed annuity with a guaranteed minimum interest rate of 6% and is linked to the Standard and Poor's 500 Index. If that index goes up, Frank can expect his annuity interest rate to go up. If that index goes down, the lowest annuity interest rate Frank can expect to receive is 6%, the guaranteed minimum.

12. 14 MARKET VALUE-ADJUSTED ANNUITIES

Another fixed annuity product with a market-driven aspect is the **market value-adjusted (MVA) annuity**. Instead of having the annuity's interest rate linked to an index like an equity-indexed annuity, an MVA annuity's interest rate remains fixed. The market value adjustment feature applies only if the contract is surrendered before the contract period expires. These contracts must disclose on the first page that the nonforfeiture values may increase or decrease on the basis of the market value formula specified in the contract. Otherwise, the annuity functions the same way a fixed annuity does.

If an MVA annuity owner decides to surrender his contract early, a surrender charge and a market value adjustment applies. If interest rates decreased during the contract period, the market value adjustment will be positive and may add to the surrender value of the contract. However, if interest rates increased over that period, the market value adjustment will be negative, which would increase the contract's surrender charge.

Let's see how this would affect Martha. She owns a 10-year MVA annuity contract but decides to cash in the contract after the sixth year. By cashing it in early, Martha would be automatically subject to a surrender charge, and because interest rates increased by 2% since she purchased the contract, her market-value adjustment would be negative, forcing her to pay an even higher surrender charge.

Depending on whether the MVA annuity is registered, the market value adjustment may apply only to interest earned under the contract. However, if the MVA annuity is registered, both principal and interest will be susceptible to a market value adjustment. MVA annuities expose consumers to investment risk, so they are classified as securities, and people who sell them must be registered with FINRA.

12. 15 GROUP VS. INDIVIDUAL ANNUITIES

Annuities can benefit groups as well as individuals. Retired employees receiving a stream of income from their former employer are getting an annuity benefit. Small employers often purchase group annuities for employees during their working years. Larger employers often operate their own annuity pool, using a trust fund to hold investment assets and dispense benefits.

Increased longevity and early retirement may contribute to the rapid increase in the purchase of individual annuities. People retiring before age 65 should begin to fund their retirements earlier because mortality probability indicates they will have longer retirement periods than people retiring after age 65. A longer retirement period requires greater initial funding.

12. 16 COMPARISON OF ANNUITIES

Comparison of Annuities

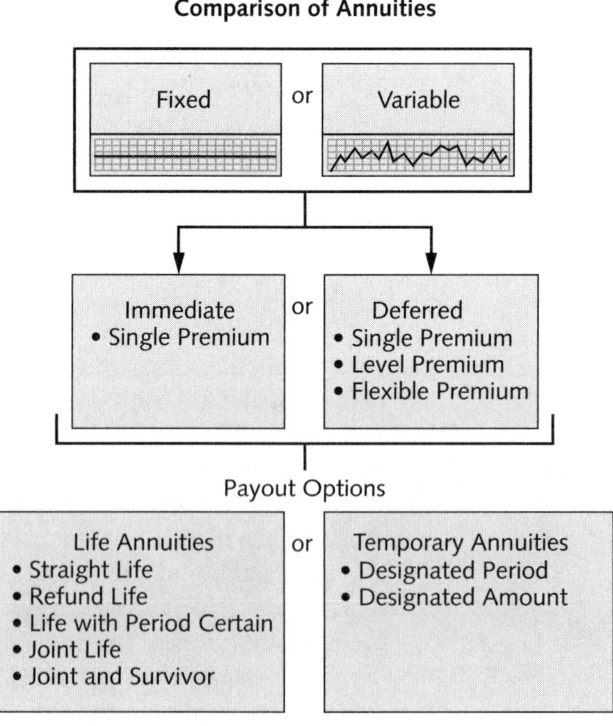

12.17 SUMMARY

In this lesson, you learned about:

- the workings of the various types of annuities;
- three types of annuity premium payments;
- five factors used to determine annuity premiums;
- how variable annuities are regulated; and
- how accumulation units and annuity units are calculated.

UNIT TEST

1. Annuities exist to
   A. accumulate a sum of money
   B. distribute a lifetime income
   C. both accumulate a sum of money and distribute a lifetime income
   D. neither accumulate a sum of money nor distribute a lifetime income

2. Tracey is paying money into an annuity she hopes will support her in her retirement years. Her contract currently is in which of the following periods?
   A. Accumulation period
   B. Nonforfeiture period
   C. Payout period
   D. Annuity period

3. Liz purchases an immediate annuity. The annuity contract must be a
   A. fixed annuity
   B. variable annuity
   C. deferred annuity
   D. single premium annuity

4. Which type of annuity is most likely to provide death benefits?
   A. Fixed annuity
   B. Variable annuity
   C. Deferred annuity
   D. Immediate annuity

5. Which of the following factors is NOT used to determine annuity premiums?
   A. Annuitant's retirement date
   B. Assumed interest rate
   C. Income amount and payment guarantee
   D. Applicant's sex

6. Which of the following types of annuities are regulated as securities?
   A. Fixed annuities
   B. Flexible annuities
   C. Variable annuities
   D. Structured annuities

7. Which of the following statements about variable annuities is TRUE?
   A. Variable annuities may be paid for with a single premium.
   B. Variable annuities can provide a lifelong income.
   C. Variable annuities may be paid for with level or flexible premiums.
   D. Variable annuities' growth varies according to investment performance.

8. Which of the following is a purpose of the annuity?
   A. The creation of a fund at the death of an individual
   B. The replacement of earnings upon the disability of an individual
   C. The distribution of a lifetime income
   D. The discounting of a principal sum back to its present value

9. An annuity might be called the flip side of
   A. compounding
   B. life insurance
   C. retirement planning
   D. Social Security

10. Annuities are a mechanism for transferring to an insurance company the risk of
    A. poor investment returns
    B. becoming uninsurable
    C. outliving financial resources
    D. outliving a spouse or child

11. An annuity that guarantees a minimum rate of return is a(n)
    A. immediate annuity
    B. deferred annuity
    C. variable annuity
    D. fixed annuity

12. Devon purchases an annuity that will pay a monthly income for the remainder of his life and then stop making payments. Devon has purchased a
    A. fixed annuity
    B. straight-life annuity
    C. variable annuity
    D. temporary annuity certain

13. Albert has purchased an annuity that will pay him a monthly income for the rest of his life. If Albert dies before the annuity has paid back as much as he put into it, the insurance company has agreed to pay the difference to Albert's daughter. Albert has purchased a
    A. straight-life annuity
    B. life annuity with period certain
    C. refund life annuity
    D. temporary annuity

14. Which type of annuity is most likely to be used to distribute lottery winnings?
    A. Flexible premium, temporary annuity with period certain
    B. Single premium, temporary annuity with amount certain
    C. Single premium life annuity
    D. Flexible premium, temporary annuity with amount certain

15. Marcus purchases an annuity that offers a guaranteed minimum interest rate and a guarantee against loss of principal if the contract is held to term. However, if the Nasdaq moves upward, Marcus's annuity might end up accruing more than the guaranteed minimum interest rate. Marcus has purchased a(n)
    A. equity-indexed annuity
    B. market value-adjusted annuity
    C. market value-indexed annuity
    D. equity-adjusted annuity

16. Eric purchased an annuity with favorable rates. However, because of unforeseen circumstances, he needs to surrender the annuity. If the market has gone up, Eric will need to pay a higher surrender charge than if the market has gone down. Eric owns a(n)
    A. equity-indexed annuity
    B. market value-adjusted annuity
    C. market value-indexed annuity
    D. equity-adjusted annuity

ANSWERS AND RATIONALES TO UNIT TEST

1. **C.** Annuities are useful for both accumulating a sum of money and for distributing a lifetime income.
2. **A.**
3. **D.** An immediate annuity is purchased with a single premium, and annuity payments begin one payout interval later.
4. **C.** A death benefit is paid if the annuitant dies before the annuity payments begin. This is more likely to occur with a deferred annuity.
5. **A.** All of these factors, except the annuitant's retirement date, are used to determine annuity premiums.
6. **C.** Variable annuities are regulated as securities because the contract owner bears the investment risk.
7. **D.** Fixed annuities provide a fixed, guaranteed growth rate. The growth of a variable annuity varies depending on the performance of the underlying subaccounts.
8. **C.**
9. **B.** An annuity might be called the flip side of life insurance.
10. **C.** A life annuity provides that payments will be made until the annuitant's death no matter how long he lives.
11. **D.** A fixed annuity guarantees a minimum rate of return.
12. **B.** A straight-life annuity will pay a monthly income for the remainder of Devon's life and then stop making payments.
13. **C.** Albert has purchased a refund life annuity.
14. **B.** Lottery winnings are most likely distributed through a single premium, temporary annuity with amount certain.
15. **A.** Marcus has purchased an equity-indexed annuity.
16. **B.** Eric owns a market value-adjusted annuity.

UNIT

13

Group Life Insurance

13. 1 LEARNING OBJECTIVES

After completing this lesson, you will be able to:

- list and explain the six basic characteristics of group insurance that are uniform throughout the majority of states;
- list and explain the required provisions of group policies;
- list the five main types of group life insurance marketed to eligible groups;
- describe the criteria to be listed as a dependent for life insurance coverage; and
- list and explain the four characteristics of conversion from group to permanent life insurance.

13. 2 INTRODUCTION

Social and economic changes resulting from the industrialization of our society, the growth of large cities, and the growth of the union movement in the United States have contributed to the development of group insurance. The influence and political strength of unionized workers have compelled employers to offer group insurance as an employee benefit. Group insurance is usually written as one-year term insurance.

13. 3 LEGAL REQUIREMENTS

In keeping with the NAIC Model Group Life Insurance bill, the legal requirements of group insurance are uniform throughout the majority of states and include six basic characteristics.

- All states define a **true group** as having at least 10 people covered under one master contract. Some states make allowance for even smaller groups.
- Coverage generally is available without individual medical examinations.
- The policy is issued to the employer, trust, union, or other association. Certificates of insurance are issued to the insured individual.
- The insurance cannot be obtained to benefit the employer, trust, union, or other association. It must be for the benefit of the covered employees or members and their dependents.
- Premiums are based on the experience of the group as a whole.

- Individuals covered under the plan are classified in such a way (usually by salary, position, or time on the job) that they do not choose the benefit levels.

13. 3. 1 Contributory vs. Noncontributory

The premium may be paid entirely by the policyowner, or it may be paid jointly by the policyowner and the insured. If premium is paid entirely by the policyowner (employer or association), it is a **noncontributory plan** and all eligible employees or members must be covered. If premium is paid by both policyowner and insured, the plan is a **contributory plan** and at least 75% of all eligible employees or members must be covered. **Eligible employees** refer to the eligible class of employees, such as full-time employees, salaried workers (as opposed to hourly workers), nonunion workers, and others. It is permissible to exclude certain groups of employees from the eligible class as long as these exclusions are based on some occupational criteria. The employer or association is always required to pay some portion of the premium. Insureds are, by law, not permitted to contribute more than a specified amount.

13. 4 STANDARD PROVISIONS

Group insurance policies have special provisions unique to group insurance. Some of these provisions are the same as those found in policies of individual insurance. Most states have enacted or adopted the standard provisions found in the NAIC Model Bill for Group Life Insurance. Group policies must contain provisions relating to the following:

- Grace period (usually 31 days)
- Incontestability (usually one or two years after the policy becomes effective; usually two years from the insured's effective date of coverage)
- Entire contract (application must be attached to and made part of the contract)
- Representations (statements regarding the individual's health are representations, not warranties)
- Evidence of insurability (individual insurability must be proven if the employee or member joins the plan after the enrollment period)
- Misstatement of age (premium is adjusted to the correct age; under individual insurance, benefits are adjusted)
- Facility of payment (allows payment of policy proceeds to a close relative or friend if no beneficiary is named or living)

- Conversion (the right to convert to an individual policy when the insured's coverage is terminated because of termination of employment or the elimination of a class of insureds)
- Termination of master policy (the right to convert to an individual policy because the master policy has been terminated)
- Individual certificates (issued as evidence of coverage under a master policy)

In addition to the rights of conversion listed, an insured who dies after coverage has terminated but before the end of the 31-day conversion period will receive the group policy benefit.

13. 5 CERTIFICATES OF INSURANCE

In group insurance, the policy is evidence of a contract between the insurer and the employer or association (the policyowner). The policy is purchased for the benefit of the individuals who are covered under the policy but is issued to the insured (the employer or sponsor). Because of this situation, it is obvious that the individual insureds would not receive a copy of the policy because there is no agreement between the insureds and the insurer. When an employee becomes covered by a group life plan, the employer, as the master policyowner, retains the life insurance policy itself. As proof of protection, the employee receives a form that certifies the coverage, the benefits under the plan, and the beneficiary's name.

Because it certifies or states all these things, we call this paper a certificate of insurance.

The certificate of insurance is evidence of the fact that a person has coverage under a group life insurance policy. The certificate shows two facts that are extremely important to the insured:

- The amount of the life insurance protection
- The name of the beneficiary

In addition, the insureds need to know something about the plan under which they are covered, and the certificate provides enough information so that they are aware of the benefits available to them and their rights and obligations.

The face page of the certificate has information on the coverage effective date, dependent coverage, and life insurance benefit amounts. The certificate covers such information as benefit amounts, benefit descriptions, age limits, notice of claim, proof of loss, and the insured's right to convert to individual coverage in the event of policy or employment termination.

13. 6 POLICY FORMS

Five main types of group life insurance are marketed to eligible groups: group term life, group permanent life, group creditor life, group paid-up life, and group survivor income benefit insurance. Group insurance is also written to include the dependents of the group members.

One disadvantage of group life insurance is that it is usually only temporary coverage, and an individual member of the group may lose that coverage when she leaves the group.

To lessen this disadvantage, group term policies must include provisions to provide for conversion to individual coverage. They also may include continuation of insurance provisions and waiver of premium provisions. Some employers continue group term insurance at reduced amounts for retired workers.

13. 7 DEPENDENT COVERAGE

In most cases, it's possible to include the dependents of employees who are insured under a group life plan. Dependents may be any of the following:

- The insured's spouse
- The insured's children
- The insured's dependent parents
- Any person for whom dependency can be proven

The insured's children can be stepchildren, foster children, or adopted children. Dependent children must be younger than a specified age, usually age 19, or age 21 if attending school full time. The law further requires that any other person dependent on the insured is eligible for coverage. Dependency is proven by the relationship to the insured, residency in the home, or the person being listed on the insured's income tax return as a dependent. A child may be a dependent beyond age 19 or 21 if that child is permanently disabled, either mentally or physically, before the specified age. Dependent coverage is not provided under credit life insurance.

13. 8 GROUP CONVERSION OPTION

By law in most states, any employee covered by a group life insurance plan must be allowed to convert to an individual permanent life policy upon termination of employment.

If an employee leaves the group, which normally happens when terminating employment, most states have laws that permit the departing employee to convert the coverage to an individual permanent life policy without evidence of insurability.

When converting a group life policy, however, the departing employee must select a form of insurance other than term. In other words, the employee must choose a whole life policy.

The departing employee will have to apply for conversion within a specified period after leaving the group, usually one month, or the conversion privilege is lost.

Finally, when converting from group life to a whole life policy, the premium charged for the new policy will be based on the insured's attained age and not the age when first covered by the group policy.

To summarize, here are the characteristics of conversion from group to permanent life insurance.

- No proof of insurability is required.
- Conversion must be to a whole life policy.
- Conversion must be applied for within one month of termination.
- Premiums for the new policy will be based on the insured's attained age.

This conversion privilege also may be used if, for any reason, an employer discontinues group coverage. The same rules apply, except that application must be made within one month of the policy's cancellation rather than one month following the employee's termination.

The conversion period is usually 30 or 31 days, and coverage is automatically in force during that period. Coverage is often limited to $5,000 or $10,000 or the amount of coverage under the group policy, whichever is less.

13. 9 SUMMARY

In this lesson, you learned about:

- the six basic characteristics of group insurance that are uniform throughout the majority of states;
- the required provisions of group policies;
- the five main types of group life insurance being marketed to eligible groups;
- the criteria to be listed as a dependent for life insurance coverage; and
- the four characteristics of conversion from group to permanent life insurance.

UNIT TEST

1. According to the NAIC Model Group Life Insurance bill, a true group has at least
   A. 2 people
   B. 5 people
   C. 10 people
   D. 25 people

2. A contributory life insurance plan must cover
   A. at least 50% of the eligible employees
   B. at least 75% of the eligible employees
   C. at least 85% of the eligible employees
   D. all of the eligible employees

3. Doris dies 15 days after her group coverage is terminated and before she has the chance to convert her policy to permanent coverage. Doris's beneficiary will receive
   A. the full benefit under the group policy
   B. the full death benefit under an individual policy
   C. the death benefit minus unpaid premium under the group policy
   D. the death benefit minus unpaid premium under the individual policy

4. Which of the following individuals would NOT qualify as a dependent for group insurance coverage?
   A. The insured's spouse
   B. The insured's parents, who live on their own and receive a small amount of financial support from the insured
   C. The insured's best friend, who lives with the insured and is listed as a dependent on the insured's tax return
   D. The insured's disabled 22-year-old daughter

5. Which of the following statements about conversion from group life insurance is TRUE?
   A. Coverage must be converted to a term policy
   B. Conversion must be applied for within 6 months of termination
   C. Proof of insurability will be required
   D. Premiums for the new policy will be based on the insured's attained age

ANSWERS AND RATIONALES TO UNIT TEST

1. **C.**
2. **B.** A contributory life insurance plan must cover at least 75% of the eligible employees.
3. **A.** Doris's beneficiary will receive the full benefit under the group policy.
4. **B.** The insured's parents, who live on their own and receive a small amount of financial support from the insured, would not qualify as a dependent for group insurance coverage.
5. **D.** In converting from group life insurance, the premiums for the new policy will be based on the insured's attained age.

UNIT

14

Social Security and Tax Considerations

14. 1 LEARNING OBJECTIVES

After completing this lesson, you will be able to:

- explain the Social Security system and how people become eligible for the various Social Security benefits;
- explain the taxation of insurance and annuity products; and
- explain Section 1035 policy exchanges and the tax benefits provided by them.

14. 2 SOCIAL SECURITY

Since the time of the Industrial Revolution, most individuals and families have not been self-sufficient economic entities. We no longer grow our own food, and many people live long distances from their families. Particularly since the Great Depression, society has wrestled with the problem of numbers of individuals being unable to care for themselves because of unemployment, disability, or death of the family wage earner. The Social Security System was a political response to this issue.

14. 2. 1 Covered Workers

Most US workers participate in Social Security, a benefit program run by the federal government. To some extent, Social Security competes with private insurance in that it provides a basic level of benefits for death, disability, and retirement.

The Social Security Act was originally passed in 1935 and took effect in 1937. Over the years, its coverage has been extended so that today nearly all private sector employees and self-employed persons are covered.

Social Security benefits have been liberalized considerably since the early days. Retirement benefits for workers are still the core of the program, but other assorted benefits have since been added. Furthermore, benefit amounts were periodically increased by Congress until the early 1970s when an automatic cost-of-living escalator was built into the program. This escalator currently operates to increase benefits each January to match the increase in inflation.

The Social Security Act covers a wide assortment of social insurance and public assistance (welfare) programs. What we refer to as Social Security is more properly called Old Age Survivors and Disability Insurance (OASDI).

14. 2. 2 Types of Benefits

Generally speaking, OASDI provides the following categories of benefits:

- Monthly retirement benefits for retired workers at least age 62
- Monthly benefits for spouses of retired workers
- Monthly survivor benefits for the spouse and certain other survivors of deceased workers
- Monthly disability benefits for disabled workers and their dependents
- A modest lump-sum death benefit payable at a worker's death

14. 2. 3 Eligibility for Social Security

Generally, most workers must be covered under Social Security, including common-law employers and employees, most self-employed persons, Armed Forces personnel, and employees of nonprofit organizations.

The main excluded worker groups are railroad workers and federal employees hired before 1984. Federal employees hired after 1984 are covered. Railroad workers contribute to their own railroad retirement system.

In addition, employees of state and local governments are not covered unless the government entity has entered into an agreement with the Social Security Administration or does not have a retirement program. Generally, most government workers are covered.

Finally, there are certain types of family employment situations in which a family member may not be covered under Social Security. These situations include employment of a minor child (under age 18) by his parent, employment of a parent as a domestic in the home of the parent's child, and employment of a parent to do work not in the course of a son's or daughter's business.

14. 2. 4 Insured Status

A covered worker becomes qualified for Social Security benefits by attaining either fully, currently, or disability insured status. Insured status depends on how many *quarters of coverage* a worker has earned. The term *quarters of coverage* comes from the middle part of the 20th century, when wages were reported to the government each quarter. Now, most employers report wages on an annual basis, but the terminology has stayed the same.

Since 1978, the amount of money needed to earn a quarter of coverage has increased automatically each year with increases in the national average wage index. In 2008, for example, a worker earns one quarter of coverage for every $1,050 in earnings.

A worker may not earn credit for more than four quarters of coverage during any given year. So, for example, if Bill earned $4,500 in 2008, and Bob earned $45,000 in 2008, both of them would be credited with four quarters of coverage. Since 1978, there is no requirement to work in different calendar quarters. For example, any worker who earned more than

$4,200 during January 2008 would have earned four quarters of coverage ($1,050 x 4) for the year even if no work was performed for the remainder of the year.

14. 2. 4. 1 Fully Insured

To achieve **fully insured** status, a worker must accumulate at least one quarter of coverage for each year after the person's 21st birthday and have a minimum of at least six quarters of coverage. This birthday rule allows young workers to achieve fully insured status within a relatively short time. The maximum requirement for fully insured status is 40 quarters of coverage, which gives the worker permanent status. Under the 40-quarter rule, once a worker accumulates credit for 40 quarters of coverage, that person is fully insured for life and the status cannot be lost even if the person drops out of the workforce.

14. 2. 4. 2 Currently Insured

A worker who is not fully insured still is **currently insured** if he has earned six credits within the last 13 calendar quarters. For example, a 35-year-old worker who did not have the 13 credits required to be fully insured is currently insured as long as he earned at least six credits within the last three years and three months.

14. 2. 4. 3 Disability Insured

A special insured status is required if a worker is eligible for disability benefits under Social Security. This status requires that the worker be fully insured and have earned at least 20 quarters of coverage in the 40 calendar quarter periods ending with the calendar quarter in which the disability begins. This requirement is modified slightly if a covered worker is disabled before age 31.

The individual's insured status determines eligibility for Social Security benefits. A fully insured person and eligible dependents are entitled to all Social Security benefits. A worker who is only currently insured has limited benefits available. If a worker is only currently insured at death, Social Security benefits would be payable only to a dependent child in addition to the lump-sum death benefit of $255.

The insured status required for some of the more important Social Security benefits is summarized in the table below.

Benefit	Insured Status
Retirement at 65	Fully
Disability	Fully or Disability
Lump-sum death benefit	Fully or Currently
Spouse's benefit (worker living)	Fully
Spouse's survivor benefit	Fully
Child's benefit (worker living)	Fully
Child's survivor benefit	Fully or Currently
Parent's survivor benefit	Fully

14. 3 PRIMARY INSURANCE AMOUNT

Social Security benefits are expressed as a percentage of the primary insurance amount (PIA). The PIA for a worker is based on her average level of earnings and is updated and published annually in tables by the federal government. Most types of Social Security benefits are some percentage of the PIA as set for the year for the worker's earnings level.

14. 4 NORMAL RETIREMENT AGE

To receive full Social Security retirement benefits, a person must wait until normal retirement age. If benefits are taken before this age, the monthly benefit amount is reduced.

The Social Security normal retirement age is currently 65. It will gradually increase to age 67 in accordance with the following table.

Year of Birth	Normal Retirement Age
1937 and before	65 years
1938	65 years, 2 months
1939	65 years, 4 months
1940	65 years, 6 months
1941	65 years, 8 months
1942	65 years, 10 months
1943-1954	66 years
1955	66 years, 2 months
1956	66 years, 4 months
1957	66 years, 6 months
1958	66 years, 8 months
1959	66 years, 10 months
1960 and after	67 years

14. 5 DUAL BENEFIT LIABILITY

Often a person is eligible to receive more than one Social Security benefit. For example, a spouse who has reached age 65 may be eligible to receive a retirement benefit based on her own earnings and also a benefit based on her late husband's earnings. In these cases, the person is entitled to receive only the larger of the two benefit amounts instead of both amounts.

14. 6 RETIREMENT BENEFITS

A worker receives 100% of his PIA as a retirement benefit if benefits are not taken until normal retirement age. For each month earlier the retirement benefit is taken, the monthly amount is reduced. At age 62—currently the earliest age at which retirement benefits may begin—the benefit is 80% of the PIA.

A worker's spouse is also eligible for a retirement benefit based on the worker's earnings. At age 65, this benefit is 50% of the PIA. The spouse can take a reduced benefit as early as age 62.

A retired worker's unmarried child is eligible for a benefit of 50% of the PIA if under age 18, if under age 19 and in high school, or at any age if disabled before age 22.

A retired worker's spouse is eligible for a benefit of 50% of PIA at any age if caring for an unmarried, dependent child of the worker who is under age 16 or was disabled before age 22.

14. 7 SURVIVOR BENEFITS

When a worker dies, several members of his family may be eligible for benefits. The surviving spouse is eligible for a benefit at any age if caring for an unmarried child under age 16 or a disabled child under age 22. This benefit is 75% of the deceased worker's PIA. When the youngest child reaches age 16, this benefit terminates.

However, the spouse's survivor will be eligible for a benefit again when he reaches age 60. At this point, the benefit is 71.5% of the deceased worker's PIA. The spouse could delay the benefit until he reaches age 65 and receive 100% of the PIA. Also, if the spouse is disabled, he can begin to receive the benefit as early as age 50.

The period during which the surviving spouse receives no Social Security benefits is sometimes referred to as the **blackout period.**

An unmarried child of a deceased worker is eligible for a benefit of 75% of the PIA if under age 18, under age 19 and in high school, or at any age if disabled before age 22.

A dependent parent age 62 or over who received at least half of his support from the deceased worker is eligible for a benefit of 82.5% of the PIA. If both parents receive benefits, each gets 75% of the PIA.

A lump-sum death benefit of $255 is paid to the deceased worker's spouse or a dependent child.

14. 8 DISABILITY BENEFITS

Social Security defines **total disability** as the inability to engage in any substantial gainful activity because of physical or mental disability, and the disability must be expected to last for at least 12 months or end in death.

Substantial work activity means significant mental and/or physical duties for which a person is compensated.

This definition does not refer to the individual's occupation before disability or to the level of predisability compensation. A surgeon earning $200,000 annually may be disabled to the degree that he could no longer perform surgery. However, if this person could perform other meaningful work duties (e.g., bank employee, school teacher, or salesperson), he probably would not be eligible for disability benefits because he could not meet the Social Security definition of total disability.

The amount of the disability benefit is equal to the worker's PIA, which in essence is the same as the individual's monthly retirement benefit. Disability benefits are only payable for total disabilities. Disability benefits begin with the sixth month of disability. No benefit is paid for a partial disability.

If the worker satisfies these conditions, there is still a five-month waiting period before benefits begin.

The worker is entitled to a disability benefit of 100% of her PIA. If the worker's spouse is caring for an unmarried child under age 16 or a disabled child under age 22, he gets a benefit of 50% of PIA. Finally, each unmarried child is entitled to a benefit of 50% of PIA if under age 18, under age 19 and still in high school, or disabled before age 22.

14. 9 MAXIMUM FAMILY BENEFIT

When several members of a worker's family are entitled to receive benefits, the family may run up against an overall limitation on benefit payments called the maximum family benefit. Like the PIA, a maximum family benefit is established for each level of average earnings and is updated annually.

14. 10 RETIREMENT EARNINGS LIMIT

Once a Social Security retiree reaches normal retirement age, there is no restriction on the amount he may earn from employment (or self-employment) without losing Social Security benefits. Retirees age 64 and under may earn only up to a certain amount without a reduction in benefits.

One earnings limit applies to retirees who have not yet reached their normal retirement age, and a modified limit applies in the year an individual reaches normal retirement age. The dollar amounts are indexed to inflation and change annually. For 2008, for example, a retiree who has not yet reached normal retirement age would face a reduction in retirement benefits of $1 for every $2 earned beyond $13,560.

In the year an individual reaches normal retirement age, $1 in benefits will be deducted for every $3 earned in excess of $36,120 (the limit for 2008).

14. 11 SOCIAL SECURITY TAXES

Social Security is a pay-as-you-go program—that is, the Social Security taxes collected from workers are not set aside in an account for each worker but are used to pay benefits to current beneficiaries of the program. Put another way, when someone begins receiving benefits, she is not drawing on a fund of some specific amount that consists of her previous tax deposits plus earnings. Those benefits are financed by the taxes currently collected from covered workers.

Social Security benefits are financed by a payroll tax on employers, employees, and the self-employed. There is no Social Security tax on investment income (e.g., interest or dividends) or any kind of income other than earnings from employment or self-employment.

The rate of tax is a flat amount set by Congress and adjusted upward from time to time. The tax rate for employers and employees is currently set at 6.2% (not counting the additional tax for Medicare). The self-employment tax rate is 12.4%—twice the employee rate—because self-employed individuals pay both the employee and the employer portion of the tax. The tax rate is multiplied by the relevant earnings figure to compute the Social Security tax.

So, if Clarice has $20,000 of earnings from her employer this year, she and her employer combined must pay in Social Security taxes on this income a total of $2,480: (.062 × $20,000) + (.062 × $20,000).

Not all of a worker's earnings are necessarily subject to the Social Security tax. The law puts a cap on the maximum amount that is taxed each year; 2008, the cap is $102,000.This is called the maximum taxable wage base. It is the same for employers, employees, and the self-employed. This wage base is indexed to inflation so that it rises each January.

The earnings of spouses are not combined for purposes of computing the Social Security tax as they usually are when computing the federal and state income taxes. Also, Social Security taxes may not be deducted in computing the federal income tax.

There is an additional payroll tax to help finance Medicare Part A (hospital insurance). The rate is 1.45% for both employers and employees and 2.9% for the self-employed. There is no cap on the amount of earned income subject to this Medicare tax.

14. 11. 1 Taxation of Social Security Benefits

A portion (up to 85%) of the Social Security benefit is includable in the worker's adjusted gross income for tax purposes. Various formulas apply depending on the level of adjusted gross income, whether the taxpayer is married or single, and if married, whether filing separate or joint returns.

14. 12 TAX CONSIDERATIONS

14. 12. 1 Individual Life Insurance

Life insurance policies have traditionally been given favorable tax treatment. There are two major tax advantages of life insurance.

- The annual earnings on the cash values generally accumulate on a tax-free basis (until they are distributed).
- The proceeds payable at the insured's death are generally income tax free to the beneficiary.

Because of these tax advantages and the competitive returns life insurance policies have paid in recent years, they sometimes have been purchased as accumulation vehicles in addition to their traditional uses.

To deter policyowners from quickly accumulating large sums of money in their life insurance contracts and thus using them primarily as an investment vehicle, Congress created a definition of life insurance that all life insurance policies must meet to qualify for these tax advantages. To qualify, a policy must meet one of the two following tests.

- Cash value accumulation test—the cash surrender value of the policy may never exceed the net single premium that would be required to fund future benefits. For example, a male age 35 owns a $100,000 policy with a cash value of $9,000. To meet the cash value accumulation test, the net single premium for the same size policy at his age must be $9,000 or more.
- Guideline premium and corridor test—the corridor test relates to the amount of pure insurance in the contract—the relationship between the cash value and the death benefit at any point in time. The cash value of a life insurance policy must not account for more than a certain percentage of the total death benefit. For example, at age 40 or younger, the total death benefit cannot be less than 250% of the cash value. If a policy had $100,000 of cash value at the insured's age 40, it would have to provide a total death benefit of $250,000. The additional $150,000 of coverage required to produce that total death benefit is the insurance corridor. After age 40, the cash value ratio begins to scale down. At age 95, the cash value may equal the total death benefit.

The guideline premium test is met if the total premiums paid do not exceed the greater of (1) the guideline single premium or (2) the total of the guideline level premiums.

The guideline single premium is the total premium payable at one time to fund the future benefits of the contract. The guideline level premium is the level annual amount payable over a period extending to at least the insured's 95th birthday to fund the future benefits of the contract.

If a contract fails to meet either the cash value or the guideline premium test, it will not qualify as life insurance. This has serious tax consequences for the contract owner.

- The inside buildup of earnings in the policy may be taxable each year as income to the policyowner to the extent these earnings, added to dividends received and the pure cost of insurance, exceed premiums paid.
- Only the pure insurance part of the death benefit proceeds (death benefit less the cash value) will be received income tax free by the beneficiary.

The taxation rules explained here all pertain to life insurance contracts that conform to the definition of life insurance in section 7702 of the Internal Revenue Code.

14. 12. 1. 1 *Modified Endowment Contract*

The tax consequences of a policy becoming a modified endowment contract (MEC) are serious, although not as serious as those for a policy failing to meet the definition of life insurance. Recall the discussion of MECs from an earlier unit. The penalties assessed against MECs primarily affect money taken out of the policy.

- Money distributed from a MEC is considered to come first from earnings (excess of cash value over cost basis) and is taxed as ordinary income.
- If the policyowner is younger than age 59½ and is not disabled, these taxable distributions are considered to be premature and are subject to a 10% penalty tax in addition to the regular income tax.

14. 12. 1. 2 *Premiums*

Now, let's look at life insurance premiums.

As a general rule, life insurance or annuity premiums paid by individuals are not deductible for federal income tax purposes. This is true regardless of the type of policy owned: term, whole life, variable life, universal life, variable universal life, or annuities.

Exceptions to this general rule include individual retirement accounts/annuities (IRAs). Under certain circumstances, as we'll discuss in the next unit, contributions to an IRA may be deducted from an individual's adjusted gross income up to an annual limit, or twice the annual limit if the individual also is contributing to a spousal IRA.

14. 12. 1. 3 *Policy Proceeds*

If the beneficiary of a life insurance policy receives the death proceeds in a lump sum, the entire amount of the payment is generally received income tax free. It makes no difference whether the death benefit is the face amount alone or whether it includes additional benefits such as double indemnity for accidental death.

Death benefits, however, may be paid out in ways other than a lump sum. These settlement options were covered earlier. Regardless of which option is chosen, only a portion of each individual payment is taxable to the beneficiary as income. That portion of each payment that is principal, derived from the lump-sum death benefit, is received income tax free.

In other words, the amount of the actual death benefit (equal to what would have been paid as a lump sum) is always paid to the beneficiary on an income tax free basis. However, if the proceeds are held by the insurance company and paid out to the beneficiary in the form of an income stream, the proceeds will earn additional income that will form a part of each payment to the beneficiary. It is only this income element that is subject to income tax.

14. 12. 1. 4 Accelerated Benefits

Accelerated, or living, benefits paid by a life insurance policy fall into the same category as a policy's death benefits—that is, accelerated benefits are received income tax free as long as they are qualified. **Qualified** means the insured has been certified by a physician as having an illness or physical condition that can reasonably be expected to result in death 24 months or less after the date of the certification. Other stipulations may be applied, but the end result is that those who require access to these benefits may receive the money without having to pay income taxes on it.

14. 12. 1. 5 Dividends and Surrender Values

Dividends paid to participating policyowners are generally not taxable as income. They are considered a return of premium. However, any interest earned on dividends is taxable, so the accumulation at interest dividend option explained earlier would incur income tax liability for the interest earned on the accumulated dividends.

Any dividend of a MEC that the insurer keeps to pay principal or interest on a policy loan is, just like the loan itself, considered to be money taken from the policy.

Generally speaking, when any proceeds are received from a surrendered or matured life insurance policy, the part of the proceeds, if any, that exceeds the cost of the policy is subject to ordinary federal income tax in the year received. Cost is equal to the total premiums paid (not including costs for qualified additional benefits) less the sum of any amounts previously received under the contract that were not includable in gross income.

Suppose Olaf surrenders his whole life policy, and it has a cash value of $25,000. During the time he held the policy, Olaf paid $22,000 in premiums. As a result, $3,000 ($25,000 less $22,000) of the cash surrender value will be subject to federal income tax.

14. 12. 1. 6 Annuity Payments

Like income payments made as a result of a settlement option in a life insurance policy, income payments made from an annuity are only partly subject to federal income taxation. Federal tax law holds that a fixed part of each annuity income payment is designated as a return of capital and as such is nontaxable. The remainder of each annuity income payment is considered to be income and is taxable.

Determining how much of each payment is a return of capital and how much is income is outside the scope of this course. However, once it is determined that the capital has been fully recovered during the course of annuity payments, all of the annuity payment becomes taxable.

14. 12. 1. 7 Cash Value Accumulation

As we've pointed out throughout this course, one of the most significant advantages of life insurance products is their ability to accumulate cash on a tax-deferred basis. Permanent life products, including variable and universal life products, may accumulate cash values that are not taxed unless and until withdrawn. The same is true of annuities, qualified retirement plans, and IRAs. All of a policyholder's current earnings are working for him, unreduced by a current tax liability.

Note, however, that annuities owned by corporations, for whatever purpose, do not accumulate cash on a tax-deferred basis.

On the other hand, bank accounts, stocks and bonds, and other kinds of noninsurance investments pay interest or dividends that are taxed currently.

14. 13 GROUP LIFE INSURANCE

Proceeds from a group life policy, like those from an individual life policy, are not subject to federal income tax when received by the beneficiary as a lump-sum payment.

Premiums for group life insurance policies, whether paid by the employer entirely or shared by employer and employee, are not deductible by the employee, but a company can deduct such premium payments as a business expense.

When all or part of the premiums for group life insurance are paid by the employer, these contributions are generally not considered as income to the employees covered by the group life policy. However, this rule applies only to the first $50,000 of employer-provided coverage. The cost of coverage in excess of $50,000 will be taxed to the employee.

14. 14 DOCTRINE OF ECONOMIC BENEFIT

This rule appears from time to time with respect to life insurance products, especially those paid for by employers but that are designed to benefit employees. Briefly, this doctrine holds that if an employee receives property or benefit in lieu of income and that property or benefit would have been taxable income if it were received in cash, an economic benefit has been received and will be taxed accordingly.

Nonqualified plans, such as deferred compensation, that are funded with life insurance and aimed at certain key and/or highly compensated employees, may be affected by this rule. Qualified plans containing insurance on the life of the plan participant also may be affected. Care must be taken if those employees are to escape current taxation on such plans.

14. 15 FEDERAL ESTATE TAX

Federal estate taxes are imposed on estates that exceed certain amounts. Life insurance proceeds are includable in a deceased insured's gross estate:

- if the proceeds are payable to the estate, either directly or indirectly;
- if the deceased possessed any incidents of ownership in the policy at death (such as the rights to change the beneficiary, to assign the policy, or to borrow against the policy); or
- if the policy was assigned by the insured, other than for full and adequate consideration, within three years of death.

14. 16 CHARITABLE USES OF LIFE INSURANCE

People give gifts to charities for a variety of reasons, and a common method of making such gifts is through life insurance. There are two basic ways to make charitable gifts of life insurance, the first of which is to make an outright gift of a policy on the life of the donor. The value of the policy at the time of the gift is generally deductible, with certain restrictions. The charity (the donee) is the beneficiary. The donor may give the charity enough cash each year to pay the premium on the policy; if so, the cash gifts are generally deductible.

When this method of giving is used, it is important that the donee, the charity, be given all the rights of ownership. If the donor retains any control over the policy, the tax advantages (deductions) are lost.

In the second common method of making charitable gifts of life insurance, the donor can retain ownership of the policy, make the charity the beneficiary, and continue to pay the premiums. In this case, the premium payments are not tax deductible. The amount of the proceeds will be included in the donor's estate but will wash out as a charitable deduction. One advantage of this method is that the donor retains the right to change beneficiaries if this becomes necessary or desirable. The principal disadvantage is that premium payments are not deductible on the donor's federal income tax return.

Life insurance also may be used to fund a number of charitable vehicles such as remainder trusts, pooled income funds, and so on. This, however, is a complex area and requires a working knowledge of charitable gift techniques and their tax consequences.

14. 17 GIFTS OF LIFE INSURANCE

Anyone who makes a gift of a large amount may have to pay a gift tax. Probably the most common method of making a gift of life insurance to someone other than a charity is literally to give a policy to the donee. If this gift involves the transfer of all the incidents of ownership from the donor to the donee, the gift will probably qualify for a present interest gift tax exclusion and the donor will not incur gift tax liability. This is true unless the replacement value of the policy, which is usually about equal to the cash value, is more than $12,000 in 2008 (more than $24,000 for a joint split gift by a donor and spouse in 2008). This threshold may increase in later years. The donor must consider all gifts of a present interest made to the donee during the year to determine whether the $12,000 threshold has been crossed.

The second most common method of making a gift of life insurance is to make a gift of the premiums on the insurance. An example of such a gift is when a new son-in-law takes out a life insurance policy and the father-in-law, the donor, gives the son-in-law the money to pay the premium. The policy belongs to the son-in-law, who is the donee of the amount of the premiums. As long as the amount of premium paid by the donor, plus all other gifts made during the same year to the same donee, is equal to or less than the annual gift tax exclusion—$12,000 annually for a single donor, $24,000 annually for a split gift by a donor and spouse—the donor should not incur federal gift tax liability.

A donor (or donors) may continue to make a tax-free gift of insurance premiums of up to $12,000 ($24,000 for donor and spouse) each year as long as desired. The recipient of the gift does not have to pay income tax on the gift.

14. 18 TRANSFER FOR VALUE RULES

Life insurance proceeds may not be exempt from income taxes if the benefit payment results from a transfer for value. If the benefits are transferred under a beneficiary designation to a person in exchange for valuable consideration (whether it be money, an exchange of policies, or a promise to perform services), the proceeds would be taxable as income. This section of the tax laws is designed to prevent a tax exemption for benefits that are purchased from another party because the intent of the transaction would be to exchange something of value for tax-free income.

Taxation under the transfer of value rules does not apply to an assignment of benefits as collateral security because a lender has every right to secure the interest in the unpaid balance of a loan. It also does not apply to transfers between a policyholder and an insured, transfers to a partner of an insured, transfers to a corporation in which the insured is an officer or stockholder, or transfers of interest made as a gift (where no exchange of value occurs).

14. 19 SECTION 1035 (POLICY EXCHANGES)

Insurance, endowment, and annuity policies are considered property so that gain or loss on an exchange of such policies ordinarily would be recognized for tax purposes. However, under Section 1035 of the Internal Revenue Code, no gain or loss is recognized on the exchange of the following:

- A life insurance contract for another life insurance contract or for an endowment or annuity contract
- An endowment contract for another endowment contract (provided the endowment contract that is received provides for regular payments beginning at a date not later than the date payments would have begun under the contract exchanged) or for an annuity contract
- An annuity contract for another annuity contract

Exchanges not coming within the above three categories are taxable exchanges.

14. 20 BUSINESS INSURANCE

The premiums paid by companies for life insurance policies used for business purposes are generally not deductible as business expenses, with the exception of group insurance. By the same token, the proceeds from life policies purchased for business purposes are received by the company income tax free. However, if the business is subject to the alternative minimum tax (AMT), that tax may apply to the death proceeds. Policy proceeds are usually not includable in the estate of an individual insured by a business unless the individual possessed some incident of ownership in the policy. This is true even if the insured was the owner or one of the owners of the business. If the insured is a controlling stockholder, the corporation's incidents of ownership may be attributed to the insured.

14. 21 SUMMARY

In this lesson, you learned about:

- the Social Security System and how people become eligible for the various Social Security benefits;
- the taxation of insurance and annuity products; and
- Section 1035 policy exchanges and the tax benefits provided by them.

UNIT TEST

1. Carla is age 32. How many quarters of coverage does she need to be fully insured?
   A. 6
   B. 8
   C. 10
   D. 12

2. Carol is eligible for a retirement benefit based on her own earnings and also a benefit based on her late husband's earnings. Carol will receive
   A. both benefits
   B. only the benefit based on her own earnings
   C. only the benefit based on her husband's earnings
   D. only the larger benefit

3. A person who begins receiving retirement benefits at normal retirement age receives what percentage of her PIA as a retirement benefit?
   A. 50%
   B. 75%
   C. 100%
   D. 150%

4. At what age can a surviving spouse who is disabled start receiving survivor benefits if the deceased was fully insured?
   A. 50
   B. 55
   C. 60
   D. 65

5. At what age can a surviving spouse who is not disabled start receiving survivor benefits if the deceased was fully insured?
   A. 60
   B. 62
   C. 65
   D. 67

6. Social Security taxes are often shared between the employer and employee. What do self-employed people pay?
   A. Just the employee's portion of the tax
   B. Just the employer's portion of the tax
   C. Both the employer's portion and the employee's portion of the tax
   D. Neither the employer's portion nor the employee's portion of the tax

7. Which of the following people would NOT be eligible for benefits under Social Security?
   A. Steve, 45, who loses his currently insured wife while still raising two young children
   B. Tina, 6, whose fully insured parent is killed in an auto accident
   C. Clarice, 60, whose fully insured son supported her
   D. Alice, 50, who is fully insured when she is disabled by cancer that is expected to kill her before she can return to work

8. At what age is an individual eligible to receive full Social Security retirement benefits?
   A. 65
   B. 67
   C. Nominal retirement age
   D. Normal retirement age

9. Social Security benefits are expressed as a percentage of the
   A. primary insurance amount
   B. presiding insurance amount
   C. potential insurance amount
   D. preferred insurance amount

10. Disability benefits under Social Security require at least a
    A. 3-month waiting period
    B. 5-month waiting period
    C. 7-month waiting period
    D. 12-month waiting period

11. Which of the following would NOT meet Congress's definition of life insurance?
    A. Tom, 35, owns a policy with a $100,000 death benefit and a $150,000 cash value.
    B. Alice, 27, owns a policy with no cash value and a $2,000 single premium.
    C. Calista owns a policy with a net single premium of $4,000 and a cash value of $2,500.
    D. Ken, 96, owns a $250,000 policy with $250,000 cash value.

12. What happens if the contract fails to qualify as life insurance?
    A. The entire death benefit will be taxed.
    B. Only the cost basis part of the death benefit proceeds will be taxed.
    C. The inside buildup earnings may be taxable each year as income to the policyowner if they exceed the cost basis of the policy.
    D. The cost basis of the earnings may be taxable each year as income to the policyowner if it exceeds the inside buildup of the policy.

13. The penalties assessed against MECs primarily affect
    A. the cost basis of the policy
    B. money put into the policy
    C. money taken out of the policy
    D. the death benefits of the policy

14. As a general rule, for federal tax purposes
    A. neither life insurance nor annuity premiums is tax deductible
    B. life insurance premiums are tax deductible but annuity premiums are not
    C. annuity premiums are tax deductible but life insurance premiums are not
    D. both life insurance and annuity premiums are tax deductible

15. Billy is receiving the proceeds of a life insurance policy as an income stream over a period of several years. What part of the money will be subject to tax?
    A. None of it; it is life insurance proceeds
    B. All of it; it is being paid out in an income stream
    C. Only the part that represents income earned on the original death benefit
    D. Only the part that represents the original death benefit and not the income earned on the original death benefit

ANSWERS AND RATIONALES TO UNIT TEST

1. **C.** To be fully insured, a person must accumulate at least one quarter of coverage for each year after the person's 21st birthday.
2. **D.** A person who is eligible to receive more than one Social Security benefit is entitled to receive only the larger of the two benefit amounts.
3. **C.** A person who retires at normal retirement age receives 100% of the person's PIA as a retirement benefit.
4. **A.**
5. **A.** A surviving spouse who is not disabled can begin receiving survivor benefits at age 60.
6. **C.** Self-employed people pay both the employer's portion and the employee's portion.
7. **C.**
8. **D.** An individual is eligible to receive full Social Security retirement benefits when that person reaches normal retirement age.
9. **A.** Social Security benefits are expressed as a percentage of the primary insurance amount.
10. **B.** Disability benefits under Social Security require at least a 5-month waiting period.
11. **A.** Tom's policy does not meet Congress's definition of life insurance.
12. **C.** If a contract fails to qualify as life insurance, the inside buildup earnings may be taxable each year as income to the policyowner if they exceed the cost basis of the policy.
13. **C.** The penalties assessed against MECs primarily affect money taken out of the policy.
14. **A.** As a general rule, for federal tax purposes, neither life insurance nor annuity premium is tax deductible.
15. **C.** Only the part that represents income earned on the original death benefit is subject to tax.

UNIT

15

Retirement Plans

15. 1 LEARNING OBJECTIVES

After completing this lesson, you will be able to:

- describe qualified and nonqualified retirement plans;
- list the benefits of qualified retirement plans;
- explain profit-sharing plans, pension plans, and 401(k) plans;
- explain IRAs, SIMPLE plans, and Keogh plans, including eligibility criteria;
- explain who is eligible to establish a tax-deferred annuity arrangement and how such a plan works;
- explain the rules governing plan distributions;
- explain when and how plan benefits are taxed;
- explain rollovers; and
- explain the purpose of ERISA and when it applies.

15. 2 QUALIFIED AND NONQUALIFIED RETIREMENT PLANS

People use many means to plan for retirement. Recognizing the necessity for working people to provide for their retirements, the government offers some significant tax benefits for certain kinds of retirement plans. They are called qualified retirement plans, and we'll be looking at them mostly as they apply to businesses and their employees.

To be qualified, a retirement plan must meet certain requirements of the Internal Revenue Code with respect to participation, funding, benefits, vesting, and so forth. Once qualified, a retirement plan offers significant tax advantages. If a plan qualifies, contributions made on behalf of participants to fund their retirement benefits are:

- tax deductible to the business;
- generally not currently taxable to the employee;
- allowed to accumulate in the plan on a tax-deferred basis; and
- axed at the time of distribution to retirees under special, advantageous rules.

This means that if a business is profitable, a qualified retirement plan can provide for employees' retirement security and lower the company's tax liability.

We've looked at certain nonqualified plans that can be used to provide retirement income. Deferred compensation is one of them. Because such plans do not have to meet the requirements of the Internal Revenue Code, they do not enjoy the tax advantages of qualified plans. Why would a business invest in a nonqualified plan if it does not have these tax advantages?

Participation in nonqualified plans can be limited to select employees, such as the businessowner and top executives. That isn't true of qualified plans.

Within the qualified category are two kinds of overall plans:

- Defined-benefit plans
- Defined-contribution plans

A **defined-benefit plan** offers benefits that are determined using a definite formula. Contributions to defined-benefit plans must be made in amounts that fund the benefits promised to plan participants.

A **defined-contribution plan** focuses on the contributions made to the plan and not the benefits the plan will pay out. By and large, defined contribution plans are tied to company profits, and the company generally is not obligated to provide a certain, specified retirement benefit to any employee. The general idea is that the better the company does, the more the company will be able to contribute to the plan (within legal limits) and thereby provide for retirement benefits. Those benefits may be determined at retirement, when the amount in the plan participant's account is totaled and a distribution is made.

A company has a number of defined-benefit and defined-contribution plans from which it can choose, depending on its objectives and circumstances. Study the following chart.

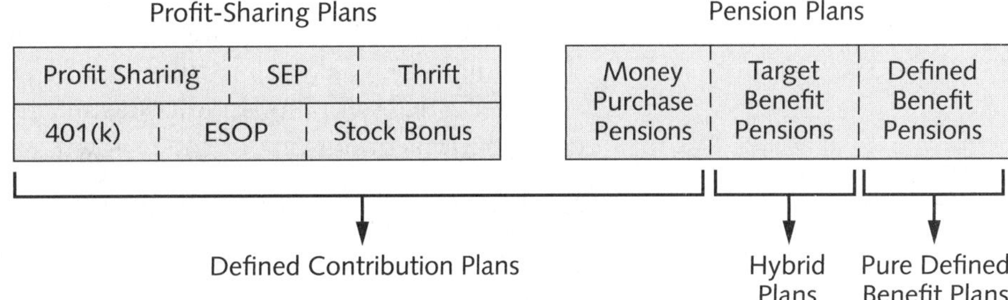

Explaining how each of these works and hoe to set up and administer qualified plans is outside the scope of this course. We'll take a brief look at the more common plans in a moment. For right now, the reason qualified retirement plans are included in this course is that:

- many of them are funded using life insurance products or are administered by life insurance companies; and
- the inclusion of insurance on the life of the plan participant in a qualified plan is permitted and can be used to pay estate costs or even to fund a buy-sell agreement.

Setting up and administering qualified plans is a complex, laborious task best left to those who specialize in it. There are numerous rules regarding eligibility, participation, and the amount of contribution that can be made or benefit that can be paid. However, a life insurance agent who understands the various qualified plans and how one or the other may meet the needs of a business client can do very well by selling qualified plans.

15.3 VESTING

To be tax qualified, a retirement plan, including multiemployer plans, must also satisfy the vesting rules included in the Internal Revenue Code. **Vesting** refers to the schedule an employer establishes that spells out the percentage ownership an employee has in the employer's contributions to the plan or the employee's accrued benefit. This percentage generally increases as the employee's length of service increases, until the employee owns 100% of the accrued benefit or the amount the employer has contributed to the account. At that time, the employee is considered to be 100% vested.

Note that any employee contributions to a plan, whether mandatory or voluntary, must vest 100% when made. In other words, employee contributions are always nonforfeitable.

The standard minimum vesting requirement follows one of these schedules:

- 100% vesting after five years of service
- A graduated vesting schedule providing 20% vesting after three years of service with an additional 20% vesting each year thereafter, resulting in 100% vesting after seven years of service

Special accelerated vesting requirements apply to employer matching contributions. These are employer contributions that must be made only if an employee makes contributions of an equal or greater amount, such as under a 401(k) plan. Employees must be vested in employer matching contributions under one of the following schedules:

- 100% vesting after three years of service
- 20% vesting after two years of service, with an additional 20% each year until 100% vesting is achieved after six years of service

15.4 DEFINED BENEFIT PLANS

15.4.1 Group Deferred Annuity

As mentioned previously, defined benefit plans are designed to provide a specific benefit to an employee upon retirement. The amount of the benefit usually depends on length of service, highest salary earned, or a combination of these. Be aware that most small- and medium-sized companies (which would be your most likely clients for a qualified plan) are no longer setting up defined-benefit plans. They are much more in favor of defined-contribution plans because they are leery of committing to specific pension amounts that must be paid regardless of how the company is doing. Nevertheless, there are many defined-benefit plans in place, and you should be aware of them in case you run into one or find a prospect that is interested in establishing one.

Funding for defined benefit plans can be provided through either a **group deferred annuity** or an individual deferred annuity, among other ways. With a **group deferred annuity**, the employer holds a master contract and certificates of participation are given to the persons covered by the plan. Specified amounts of deferred annuity are purchased each year in order to provide a specified retirement income to an employee.

Example

Beginning at age 65, $75 per month might be purchased every year for an employee, or perhaps an amount of deferred annuity equaling a certain percentage of an employee's monthly salary would be purchased. Whatever the amount, it would be multiplied by the number of years the employee worked before retirement and the result would be the monthly payment derived from the group deferred annuity when the employee retired.

Example

Suppose Calvin is an employee whose company funds its defined-benefit plan with a group annuity that bases its monthly payout to Calvin on $50 for each year of his employment. After 30 years, Calvin retires and can expect a monthly retirement income of $1,500 ($50 × 30).

15. 4. 2 Individual Deferred Annuity

Another means of funding a defined benefit plan is to take out individual deferred annuities on each plan participant. The premium rate is determined individually, on the basis of attained age and sex. Premiums are level to retirement unless an employee's compensation changes and an increase in retirement benefits is warranted. In that case, an additional annuity contract is purchased to fund the increase in the retirement benefit level.

15. 5 DEFINED CONTRIBUTION PLANS

15. 5. 1 Profit-Sharing Plans

A qualified **profit-sharing plan** is a plan established and maintained by an employer primarily to provide for the participation in its profits by its employees or their beneficiaries. The plan must provide a definite, predetermined formula for allocating among plan participants all contributions made to the plan. However, the amount of annual contributions, if any, is usually left to the discretion of the employer. Contributions are held in trust. When the employee retires or leaves under certain other circumstances, the contributions that have been allocated to that employee, plus all earnings on them, are distributed to the employee.

15. 5. 2 Pension Plans

Pension plans are established and maintained by employers interested in providing systematically for the payment of definitely determinable benefits to retired employees over a period of years—usually for life. Retirement benefits are generally measured by and based on such factors as years of service and compensation received. The amount of plan contributions or benefits is not determined by the employer's profits, nor is it left to the discretion of the employer.

A **money-purchase pension plan** requires the employer to make a fixed contribution to the plan each year, which is then allocated among the plan participants' accounts. At retirement, employees receive whatever benefit may be purchased with the money in his or her plan account.

A **target benefit pension plan** is a cross between a defined-contribution and defined-benefit plan that works much like a money-purchase plan except that a target benefit is specified. This target benefit looks like a defined-benefit plan, but it's only a target and may or may not be reached.

15. 5. 2. 1 401(k) Plans

When a profit-sharing or pension plan has been modified to provide a cash or deferred arrangement (CODA), the resulting plan is popularly called a **401(k) plan** after the section of the Internal Revenue Code that authorizes it.

The term *CODA* refers to two different methods by which an employee can defer a portion of his pay into a 401(k) plan. In the classic case, the employee will be offered a cash bonus, all or part of which may be placed in, or deferred into, the plan on a pretax basis. Alternately, the arrangement can take the form of a salary reduction agreement under which employee's elect to reduce their salary and place, or defer, the reduction portion into the plan, also on a before-tax basis. With either method, plan participants can avoid immediate taxation of the diverted bonus or salary deferral amount. Consequently, no income taxes are paid on these funds or their earnings until they are withdrawn. A 401(k) plan allows, within limits, plan participants, to augment the funds being contributed into their plan account on a tax-advantaged basis and thus provide for greater retirement income.

15. 6 INDIVIDUAL RETIREMENT ACCOUNTS AND ANNUITIES

The government offers individual retirement accounts (IRAs) and annuities as an incentive to individuals to plan for their own retirements. With an IRA, the amount an individual contributes to an IRA may be deductible, within limitations, from gross income before taxable income is determined. The contribution limit will increase in future years. The contribution limit for 2008 is $5,000.

In addition, individuals age 50 and up can make catch-up contributions of an additional $1,000 per year since 2006.

Whether an individual may make a fully deductible IRA contribution depends on the answer to this question: Is the individual, or the individual's spouse if filing jointly, covered by an employer-maintained retirement plan?

If the answer to this question is no, the IRA contribution is fully deductible up to the limit no matter what the adjusted gross income (AGI) of the individual or couple. If a married worker's spouse does not work, the married worker can contribute up to the limit to another IRA on behalf of the spouse in addition to the individual's own annual IRA contribution for a total tax-deductible contribution of double the contribution limit per year.

If the answer to this question is yes, the IRA contribution is fully deductible up to the limit (double the limit if also contributing to a spousal IRA) as long as one of the following holds true:

- the individual has an annual adjusted gross income of less than $53,000 (in 2008); or
- a married couple filing jointly has an annual adjusted gross income of less than $85,000 (in 2008).

Note: Married persons not covered by an employer-maintained retirement plan who file separate returns are considered covered if their spouses are covered by such a plan unless they have lived apart from their spouses for the entire year.

These income limitations will increase in future years. In addition, partial deductions are permitted if the limitations are exceeded, but only up to a certain dollar amount. The following table shows the income limitations for 2008.

15. 6. 1 Income Limits for IRA Deductibility

AGI Phase-Out Levels for Traditional IRA Deductions

Individuals who are actively participating in an employer-sponsored retirement plan will see the deductible portion of their traditional IRA contributions reduced or phased out once their adjusted gross incomes exceed certain threshold levels. Those with AGIs above these levels cannot take any IRA deduction. For 2008, these threshold levels are:

	Full Deduction Allowed	**Partial Deduction Allowed**	**No Deduction Allowed**
Filing Status	AGI level	AGI level	AGI level
Single	$0—$53,000	$53,001—$63,000	$63,001 and above
Married, filing jointly 2008	$0—$85,000	$85,001—$105,000	$105,001 and above

A separate limit of $158,999 applies to an individual who is married, filing jointly, and who is not an active participant in an employer-maintained retirement plan but whose spouse is. In that case, the limits in the preceding table apply to the participating spouse and the $158,999 limit applies to the nonparticipating spouse. If the couple's combined income is or exceeds $169,000, no deduction is permitted either spouse. (These limits are for 2008.)

Let's look at a couple of examples to see how this all works. Keep in mind that the income amounts given in the examples refer to adjusted gross incomes.

Example

Kelly is single and earned $100,000 in 2008 working for a company that has no employer-maintained retirement plan. Kelly made a 2008 contribution of $5,000 to an IRA and deducted the entire amount. In 2009, Kelly got married and earned $120,000 from the same company. Kelly's nonworking spouse had no income. Kelly made total IRA contributions of $10,000 ($5,000 to Kelly's IRA plus $5,000 to her spouse's IRA) and deducted the entire amount.

Example

In 2008, Mark earned $90,000 as an attorney and had no retirement plan. His spouse earned $30,000 and was a participant in his company's retirement plan. Mark made fully deductible 2008 IRA contributions of $10,000 ($5,000 to Mark's IRA plus $5,000 to his spouse's IRA) because their combined income was below $169,000.

All earnings that accumulate in an IRA do so tax deferred. That is, the interest earned on the contributions placed in an IRA is not taxed until withdrawn. This is also true for IRAs funded with nondeductible contributions.

Popular vehicles used to fund an IRA include:

- mutual funds;
- bank, savings and loan, or credit union accounts or CDs;
- bank trust accounts; and
- fixed or variable flexible-premium annuities.

This last category should be familiar to you from your study of annuities earlier in this course.

15. 7 ROTH IRAS

Since tax year 1998, taxpayers can make contributions to a Roth IRA (named after the Senator who proposed it), or IRA Plus. But the traditional, or regular, IRA that we just looked at still exists. To distinguish between these two types of IRAs, we will refer to them here as Roth IRAs and traditional IRAs, respectively.

The tax treatment of these two types of IRAs differs markedly. Traditional IRA contributions are deductible for some taxpayers. In addition, the earnings in traditional IRA accounts, which are tax deferred as long as they remain in the account, are taxable when they are withdrawn. In contrast, contributions to Roth IRAs are not deductible. In addition to not being taxed while they remain in the account, the earnings in Roth IRAs may generally be withdrawn tax free subject to certain restrictions.

To make tax-free withdrawals from a Roth IRA, the account owner must be at least age 59½ and must have held the account for at least five years. Tax-free Roth IRA distributions may also be taken after five years in the event of the account owner's death or disability or, with a limit of $10,000, for the purchase of a first home.

Roth IRA contributions are subject to the same contribution limits that affect other IRAs. Each spouse can contribute up to the limit to an IRA (Roth or traditional) in any combination. If both spouses take advantage of this rule, the combined contribution could be as much as double the limit. Availability of Roth IRAs is phased out between $159,000 and $169,000 of adjusted gross income (AGI) for married couples filing jointly and $101,000 and $116,000 of AGI for singles. Availability of the Roth IRA is not affected by participation in an employer-sponsored retirement plan.

Taxpayers with less than $100,000 of AGI, married or single, can convert existing traditional IRAs to Roth IRAs. This involves paying income tax on all deductible contributions and earnings.

15. 8 SIMPLE RETIREMENT PLANS

Since tax year 1998, certain small employers may establish a savings incentive match plan for employees (SIMPLE). To be eligible to establish a SIMPLE, a business must employ no more than 100 people who earned more than $5,000 the preceding year, and the business must have no other qualified plan.

A SIMPLE can take the form of either an employer-established IRA or a 401(k) plan. Under either format, employees may elect to make contributions of a percentage of their compensation up to $10,500 per year in 2008. In addition, individuals 50 and over can make catch-up contributions of $2,500 in 2008 and after.

These contributions are not included in the employees' taxable income, but they are subject to employment tax. Employers must contribute to the SIMPLE by either:

- matching each employee's contribution dollar-for-dollar up to 3% of the employee's income; or
- contributing 2% of compensation to the account of each eligible employee who has earned at least $5,000 that year.

Under the IRA format, employers who elect to match contributions dollar for dollar may in some years reduce the matching percentage to as low as 1% but may not reduce the matching percentage below 3% for more than two years in any five-year period. The option to reduce the matching percentage is not available under the 401(k) format.

Employer contributions are deductible from the employer's income, excludable from the employee's income, and not subject to employment tax. Employees must be immediately 100% vested in all contributions. Distributions from SIMPLE IRAs are generally taxed like distributions from regular IRAs. A 10% penalty tax generally applies to withdrawals made before age 59½ subject to the same exceptions as those for IRAs, but a 25% penalty tax applies to withdrawals made from a SIMPLE within its first two years.

15. 9 SIMPLIFIED EMPLOYEE PENSIONS (SEPS)

Simplified employee pensions are a cross between an IRA and a profit-sharing plan. Under a SEP, each eligible employee of an employer establishes an IRA. The employer then makes contributions to the employee's IRA according to a formula described in the SEP document. The maximum contribution that may be deducted by the employer is 25% of the total compensation paid to all participating employees.

Historically, contributions made by the employer were included in the employee's W-2 gross income, which was then offset by a tax deduction on the individual's tax return for the amount of the contribution. The net effect was that the employee had no tax liability for the contribution. However, the Tax Reform Act of 1986 changed this requirement and made SEP contributions excludible from the employee's gross income in the first place.

15. 10 KEOGH PLANS

Self-employed persons may set up their own retirement plans, known as Keogh plans. Self-employed persons may be sole proprietors, partners in a business, farmers, or professionals such as doctors or lawyers. Other individuals who are employed by a company and covered under the company retirement plan may establish a Keogh plan provided they also are self-employed in some other capacity.

There are two kinds of Keogh plans:

- Defined-contribution plan
- Defined-benefit plan

With a defined-contribution plan, the amount of each contribution is specified in the plan document. This can vary according to rules established by the IRS. Under a defined-contribution plan, the benefits the participant will receive are unknown, though they can be reasonably estimated.

With a defined-benefit plan, on the other hand, the participant's benefit is specified and contributions are calculated to produce the benefit specified in the plan document.

Contributions to a Keogh plan are not taxed as current income as long as they follow these guidelines.

- For a defined contribution Keogh plan, the contribution limit in 2008 for a common-law employee is the lesser of $46,000 or 25% of compensation. For self-employed persons, the Keogh contribution itself must be deducted in determining the individual's net earnings from self-employment. The limits are $46,000 or 20% of compensation, whichever is less.
- For a defined benefit Keogh plan, the contribution is limited to a sufficient amount, actuarially determined, to fund the maximum benefit allowable under the plan, but which cannot be more than $185,000 per year in 2008.

These dollar amounts are indexed to inflation and will increase in future years.

15. 11 TAX-DEFERRED ANNUITY ARRANGEMENTS (403(B) ARRANGEMENTS)

A 403(b) arrangement (sometimes referred to as a 403(b) plan) is an employee-sponsored qualified retirement arrangement available to employees of public school systems. Under this tax-deferred annuity arrangement, the employee agrees to let the employer withhold a part of the employee's salary, or perhaps the amount of a salary increase. The employer then uses this deferred salary to purchase an annuity. The employee's current taxable income does not include the amount withheld to purchase the annuity. Employees may only have a certain amount of their salary withheld for the arrangement. Net investment income and capital gains that accumulate in the annuity are not taxed until distributions begin, when they are taxed as current income.

15. 12 SECTION 529 PLANS

To encourage college attendance and facilitate payment for it, the federal government has made a number of plans available that allow individuals to save to meet college expenses as well as receive tax credits and deductions for certain higher education expenses. One of the most powerful vehicles for providing for higher education expenses is a Section 529 plan, named for the tax code that governs it. Although the formal name for such plans is Qualified Tuition Programs (QTPs), they are most often referred to as Section 529 Plans.

There are two types of Section 529 or Qualified Tuition Plans: prepaid tuition plans and college savings plans. *Prepaid tuition plans* allow contributors to prepay college tuition and other fees for a designated beneficiary for a set number of academic periods or course units while locking in current tuition costs. Contributors bear no investment or inflation risk because the accounts are generally guaranteed to grow at a rate equal to college tuition increases. *College savings plans* allow contributors to invest after-tax dollars in professionally managed accounts that contain a mix of stocks, bonds, and other investments selected to reflect a child's age or a family's investment preference. Contributors assume both inflation and investment risk.

Unlike certain other education incentives, such as Coverdell Education Savings Accounts (previously known as Education IRAs), Section 529 plans don't restrict eligibility or limit the amount of contribution based on the income of the contributor.

State residency also is not a restriction. A contributor can open a Section 529 plan in any state and the beneficiary can use the funds to attend college anywhere.

The designated beneficiary of a Section 529 plan does not need to report income when withdrawals are used for qualified college costs.

However, withdrawals from Section 529 plans are not limited to withdrawals to pay higher education expenses. A contributor may make a withdrawal from a Section 529 Plan for any purpose. For example, a contributor may take a withdrawal to pay taxes or to buy a new car. By doing so, however, the withdrawal is both taxable as ordinary income to the extent of the earnings that are withdrawn and subject to a penalty of 10% of the amount of the withdrawal that is includible in income.

15. 13 PLAN DISTRIBUTIONS

As a rule, funds from a qualified retirement plan or IRA may be distributed at any age when employment is terminated, the plan is terminated, or the employee retires. However, if the distribution is considered to be **premature** (i.e., made before age 59½), a 10% penalty tax is usually applied to it. This penalty is in addition to the regular income tax due on the distribution.

The law also places limits on when distributions from a qualified plan or an IRA (with the exception of a Roth IRA) must begin. Distributions to all qualified plan participants or IRA holders must begin no later than April 1 of the year following the calendar year in which the participant reaches age 70½. The minimum amount that must be distributed each year is set by regulation. The penalty for failure to comply with this distribution requirement is a nondeductible excise tax equal to 50% of the amount by which the minimum amount required to be distributed exceeds the amount actually distributed.

Early retirement, although an attractive idea to many, can be an expensive decision in the case of a participant in a defined benefit plan. This is because of the rules that reduce the maximum defined benefit for many who leave the workforce before normal retirement age. An actuarial reduction in benefits is made for those who retire before their normal Social Security retirement age. An additional penalty is imposed on those who retire and who have participated in a defined benefit plan for less than 10 years. The maximum benefit to which they are entitled must be further reduced by

10% for each year their number of years of plan participation at retirement is less than 10.

15. 14 INCIDENTAL LIMITATIONS

On a conditional basis, life insurance may be purchased with contributions to (or accumulations in) some types of qualified plans. There are, however, certain limits imposed by the IRS on the purchase of insurance as part of a qualified plan. These **incidental limitations** are designed to ensure that the death benefit of life insurance coverage purchased under a qualified plan are incidental to the other benefits provided by the plan. In a defined benefit plan, the face value cannot exceed 100 times the monthly pension benefit. With a defined contribution plan, when an ordinary life policy is used, 50% of the plan contribution is the limit. With universal life, the formula stipulates 25%.

15. 15 TAXATION OF PLAN BENEFITS

Now let's look at the tax treatment of funds paid to plan participants at retirement. The only funds that escape taxation at distribution are those that have already been taxed. For example, some plans allow participants to make voluntary, after-tax contributions to their plans. These funds would not be taxed at distribution.

Distributions may be made in the form of annuity installments or, in the case of a defined contribution plan, in a lump sum. Those made in the form of installments may be made partially income tax free. The portion of each payment that represents money that has already been taxed to the recipient, if any, is excluded from gross income. The remainder is taxed as ordinary income in the recipient's tax bracket.

Until the end of 1999, distributions taken in the form of a lump sum could use five-year income averaging to determine the tax liability. With this method, the entire distribution is considered ordinary income treated as if it were received in equal amounts over a five-year period. In addition, the amount is taxed separately from all other income, as if it were the only income the individual had received for the tax year in which it is distributed. It is then taxed as ordinary income using the tax schedule for unmarried taxpayers, regardless of the individual's marital status. Since 1999, income averaging has not been available.

Distributions from a qualified retirement plan may also be triggered by the plan participant's death. Lump-sum distributions of plan benefits upon a participant's death are considered *income in respect of a decedent* and are generally subject to income tax when received by the estate or other beneficiaries, less any amount the plan participant contributed using after-tax dollars. An itemized deduction may be available to the beneficiary for any federal estate taxes paid on income in respect of a decedent, even if the beneficiary is not the one who paid the estate tax.

Tax treatment of benefits received as annuity installments by beneficiaries after the plan participant's death are usually treated like those received by the participant—a portion of the payments may be income tax free if the participant made contributions to the plan with after-tax dollars.

15. 15. 1 Rollovers

A **rollover** occurs when the money in an IRA is transferred to a different IRA. This term can also refer to the transfer of funds from a qualified retirement plan to an IRA or to another qualified retirement plan.

Rollovers are accomplished for a number of reasons. Perhaps the investment experience in one IRA is disappointing and the owner wants to switch to another, or maybe someone is leaving a job before retirement age and needs to reinvest the money distributed from a qualified retirement plan. Whatever the reason, there are rules regarding taking money from a tax-sheltered account or transferring it to another tax-sheltered account. These rules are designed to discourage the use of retirement money for any purpose other than retirement income.

Rollovers between IRAs may be made only once within a 12-month period. Someone who maintains more than one IRA may roll over each IRA every 12 months. Transfers between funds within the same family of mutual funds are not considered rollovers. For example, suppose the Do-Well Mutual Fund has both a money market fund and a growth stock fund. Transfers made between these two funds are subject only to the limits placed by Do-Well.

The rollover need not be made directly to the new IRA. From the date funds are withdrawn from the old IRA, the IRA owner has 60 days to make the deposit to the new IRA. Any funds not rolled over within that 60-day period become taxable to the extent they consist of deductible contributions and earnings on any contributions. Premature distribution penalties will also apply. We'll examine those shortly.

For people changing jobs and receiving their vested interests in their former employer's qualified retirement plan, those funds will also become taxable unless rolled over into an IRA or another qualified plan within 60 days.

Other rules that apply to rollovers from one IRA to another or from a qualified retirement plan to an IRA include the following.

- Only full or qualifying partial lump-sum distributions qualify for a tax-free rollover. Amounts paid out in installments over more than one year do not qualify. The lump-sum distribution does not have to be made in one payment. As long as the entire balance of an account is paid out (even in several payments) within one tax year, the distribution is considered to be a lump-sum distribution.

- A partial lump-sum distribution may be rolled over, but any amount not rolled over will be subject to income tax to the extent of deductible contributions and earnings on any contributions.

- Qualified plan distributions following a participant's death subject a surviving spouse-beneficiary to the same rollover rules to which the original participant would have been subject.

Amounts received from a qualified plan may also be transferred to another qualified plan with the consent of the individual's new employer if the new employer's plan provides for acceptance of such amounts. So a person can receive a distribution from a qualified plan and either put it into a rollover IRA or reinvest it into the qualified plan of a new employer. But there is an important rule that applies only to transfers made from a qualified plan to an IRA or to another qualified plan.

Any such rollover must be made *directly* or it will be subject to a 20% withholding rate. This is true even if the rollover occurs within the 60-day limit. The key here is the word *directly*. To escape the withholding rate, the rollover must take place without the plan's funds being in the recipient's control for even an instant. If such control does occur and the 20% is withheld, the recipient must make up this amount out of other funds or the amount withheld will be subject to income taxation and, possibly, a penalty for premature distribution. The amount withheld is applied toward the tax liability, if any, of money distributed from the fund.

15. 16 THE EMPLOYEE RETIREMENT INCOME SECURITY ACT (ERISA)

ERISA was enacted to protect the interests of participants in employee benefit plans as well as the interests of the participants' beneficiaries. Much of the law deals with qualified pension plans, but some sections also apply to group insurance plans.

15. 16. 1 Fiduciary Responsibility

ERISA mandates very detailed standards for fiduciaries and other parties-in-interest of employee welfare benefit plans, including group insurance plans. This means that anyone with control over plan management or plan assets of any kind must discharge that fiduciary duty solely in the interests of the plan participants and their beneficiaries. Strict penalties are imposed on those who do not fulfill this responsibility.

15. 16. 2 Reporting and Disclosure

ERISA requires that certain information concerning any employee welfare benefit plan, including group insurance plans, be made available to plan participants, their beneficiaries, the Department of Labor, and the IRS. Examples of the types of information that must be distributed include:

- a summary plan description to each plan participant and the Department of Labor;

- a summary of material modifications that details changes in any plan description to each plan participant and the Department of Labor;
- an annual return or report (Form 5500 or one of its variations) submitted to the IRS;
- a summary annual report to each plan participant; and
- any terminal report to the IRS.

ERISA imposes severe monetary penalties for failure to comply with its reporting and disclosure requirements within prescribed time periods. In addition, civil and criminal action may be taken against any plan administrator who willfully violates any of these requirements or who knowingly falsifies or conceals ERISA disclosure information.

15. 17 SUMMARY

In this lesson, you learned about:

- qualified and nonqualified retirement plans;
- the benefits of qualified retirement plans;
- profit-sharing plans, pension plans, and 401(k) plans;
- IRAs, SIMPLE plans, and Keogh plans, including eligibility criteria;
- who is eligible to establish a tax-deferred annuity arrangement, and how such a plan works;
- Section 529 plans, formally known as Qualified Tuition Program, or QTPs;
- the rules governing plan distributions;
- when and how plan benefits are taxed;
- rollovers; and
- the purpose of ERISA and when it applies.

UNIT TEST

1. Allison's employer's contributions to her pension plan are 0% vested after 2 years of service. What percentage must be vested after 3 years of service, according to the standard minimum vesting schedules?
   A. 20%
   B. 40%
   C. 80%
   D. 100%

2. Curtis knows that when he retires, he will receive $100 a month for every year of service with his employer. This is an example of a
   A. defined-benefit plan
   B. defined-contribution plan
   C. profit-sharing plan
   D. money-purchase plan

3. All of the following statements about profit sharing plans are correct EXCEPT
   A. such plans are established by employer's so employees can participate in company profits
   B. the amount of annual contributions is set by law
   C. the plan must provide a formula for allocating contributions to the plan among plan participants
   D. plan contributions are held in trust

4. At what age can people begin making catch-up contributions to their retirement plans?
   A. 50
   B. 55
   C. 60
   D. 65

5. Which of the following types of retirement plans does NOT have a mechanism for making catch-up contributions past a certain age?
   A. IRA
   B. Roth IRA
   C. SIMPLE plan
   D. SEP

6. A qualified retirement plan does NOT offer which of the following tax advantages?

   A. The business sponsoring the plan may not deduct contributions to it.
   B. Qualified plan distributions may be taxed to recipients using favorable rules.
   C. Contributions to qualified plans are not currently taxable to plan participants.
   D. Contributions to qualified plans may accumulate on a tax-deferred basis.

7. Employer vesting schedules apply to
   A. all contributions made to qualified plans
   B. only employee contributions made to qualified plans
   C. only employer contributions made to qualified plans
   D. all contributions made to nonqualified plans

8. Who may contribute to an IRA?
   A. Anybody with earned income
   B. Only people who don't participate in company retirement plans
   C. Only people who earn less than certain specified amounts
   D. Only people who are self-employed

9. Who may NOT make fully deductible contributions to an IRA?
   A. Anybody with earned income above the specified income limits
   B. People who do not participate in company retirement plans
   C. People who participate in company retirement plans and who earn less than specified amounts
   D. People who are not eligible for company retirement plans

10. Under which of the following circumstances are qualified plan distributions likely to receive a tax penalty?
    A. Premature distributions only
    B. Late distributions only
    C. Both A and B
    D. Neither A nor B

11. Premature distribution from a qualified plan or an IRA can result in the amount being taxed as income plus a penalty tax of
   A. 5%
   B. 10%
   C. 15%
   D. 25%

12. A rollover from one IRA to another or from a qualified plan to an IRA must be accomplished within how many days if the owner is to avoid an income tax liability on the amount rolled over?
   A. 10
   B. 30
   C. 60
   D. 90

13. At what age is an individual no longer subject to early withdrawal penalties under an IRA?
   A. 55
   B. 55-1/2
   C. 59
   D. 59-1/2

14. Which of the following organizations would be eligible to offer a 403(b) arrangement?
   A. Fire department
   B. Public school system
   C. Any small business
   D. Any corporation

15. Carmen owns a business that provides a retirement plan to its employees whereby the business makes contributions of up to 25% of the total compensation paid to all participating employees to IRA plans owned by the individual employees. Carmen's plan is most likely a
   A. SIMPLE plan
   B. Keogh plan
   C. 403(b) plan
   D. SEP

16. Delbert is self-employed and sets up a retirement plan for himself. Delbert most likely sets up a
   A. SIMPLE plan
   B. Keogh plan
   C. 403(b) plan
   D. SEP

17. Kim is required to take a $2,000 minimum annual distribution from her IRA. She fails to comply and only takes a $1,000 distribution. Because of this failure, Kim will be subject to a
   A. deductible excise tax of $1,000
   B. nondeductible excise tax of $1,000
   C. deductible excise tax of $500
   D. nondeductible excise tax of $500

ANSWERS AND RATIONALES TO UNIT TEST

1. **A.**
2. **A.** This is a defined benefit plan because it is designed to provide a specific benefit amount at retirement.
3. **B.** Under a defined contribution plan, the amount of any annual contributions is usually left to the employer's discretion.
4. **A.** People age 50 and up can make additional catch-up contributions.
5. **D.** SEPs do not provide for catch-up contributions.
6. **A.**
7. **C.** Employer vesting schedules apply to only employer contributions made to qualified plans.
8. **A.** Anybody with earned income may contribute to an IRA.
9. **A.** Anybody with earned income above the specified income limits may not make fully deductible contributions to an IRA.
10. **C.** Tax penalties may apply to premature and late distributions.
11. **B.** Premature distribution from a qualified plan or an IRA can result in the amount being taxed as income plus a penalty tax of 10%.
12. **C.** A rollover from one IRA to another or from a qualified plan to an IRA must be accomplished within 60 days to avoid an income tax liability on the amount rolled over.
13. **D.** At age 59-1/2, an individual is no longer subject to early withdrawal penalties under an IRA.
14. **B.** A public school system is eligible to offer a 403(b) arrangement.
15. **D.** Carmen's plan is most likely a SEP.
16. **B.** A self-employed person will most likely set up a Keogh plan.
17. **D.** Kim is subject to a nondeductible excise tax of $500.

UNIT

16

Health Insurance Basics

16. 1 INTRODUCTION

Although it is not often recognized, the financial impact of total disability may be greater than the financial impact of death. A person may live for many years totally disabled and, therefore, unable to generate an income to pay for the higher medical and living expenses caused by the disability.

Health insurance provides payment of benefits for the loss of income and/or the medical expenses arising from illness or injury. Health insurance is often called accident and sickness insurance or accident and health insurance. Many different kinds of health insurance coverages are available. Health insurance varies according to the methods of underwriting, the injury or illness covered, the types of insurers, the types of benefits and services provided, the types of losses covered, and the amount of benefits available.

Health insurance originated in the United States in the mid-1800s. It was first provided by casualty insurance companies and then by riders to life insurance products. The earliest policies were designed to provide benefits for losses resulting from accidental injuries and to protect railroad travelers. Later coverage provided benefits for losses because of illness as well as accidents.

16. 2 LEARNING OBJECTIVES

After completing this lesson, you will be able to:

- explain the risk that health insurance is designed to protect against;
- list 12 types of loss that health insurance may be purchased to guard against;
- explain the difference between a limited policy and other health policies, and list six types of limited policies;
- list six environments where physicians might see patients;
- explain the difference between reimbursement, fee-for-service, and capitation payment;
- explain the role of Blue Cross/Blue Shield organizations, how they differ from commercial insurers, the corporate structure they usually employ, and the types of coverage and benefits they offer;
- explain how health maintenance organizations (HMOs) are different from traditional insurers, and the role government had in promoting the development of HMOs;
- list and describe four typical HMO structures;
- explain the difference between open- and closed-panel HMOs;

- explain the difference between basic and supplemental HMO services, and list what generally is included as basic and what may be included as supplemental;
- define the following HMO-related terms: co-payment, exclusion, limitation, gatekeeper, open enrollment, quality assurance, open-ended HMO, and open-access HMO;
- explain what an HMO's grievance system is designed to do, and how it must function;
- list practices that HMOs are commonly prohibited from engaging in;
- describe the basic characteristics of preferred provider organizations (PPOs), point-of service plans, exclusive provider organizations, and multiple option plans;
- explain how self-funding works, explain what a stop-loss contract is, and list the advantages and disadvantages of self-insurance;
- explain what a 501(c)(9) trust is, and when it is used;
- describe the basic characteristics of cafeteria plans, medical savings accounts, multiple employer trusts, multiple employer welfare arrangements, blanket policies, and franchise policies;
- list the major statutory health insurance programs offered by the federal government and state governments;
- list the types of benefits provided by Social Security;
- explain who is eligible for workers' compensation, and list the types of benefits provided under workers' compensation;
- explain the limits that apply to income benefits under workers' compensation;
- briefly explain who qualifies for Medicaid, the intent of the program, and how it functions; and
- briefly explain who qualifies for TRICARE, the intent of the program, and how it functions.

16. 3 TYPES OF LOSSES AND BENEFITS

16. 3. 1 Loss of Income from Disability

Disability income insurance, also referred to as loss-of-time insurance, pays a weekly or monthly benefit for disabilities resulting from accident or sickness. The primary purpose of disability income coverage is to replace loss of personal income due to a disability.

Disability income policies are issued on an individual basis or on a group basis through an employer-sponsored plan, labor union, or association. Benefits paid are in accordance with the policy's provisions and, to a degree, the insured's loss of income.

16. 3. 2 Accidental Death and Dismemberment

AD&D policies (or riders) pay the policy's **principal sum** for accidental death in accordance with the policy's provisions and definition of accidental death. The **principal sum** is similar in meaning to a policy's face amount. This same amount is paid if the insured suffers the actual severance of two arms, two legs, or the loss of vision in two eyes due to an accident. This amount is usually identified as the **capital sum** if the policy is paying an accidental dismemberment benefit.

AD&D benefits may be included as riders on life insurance policies, as part of disability income insurance, as part of health insurance, or as a separate policy (a type of limited coverage).

16. 3. 3 Medical Expense Benefits

Medical expense insurance, commonly referred to as hospitalization insurance, provides benefits for expenses incurred as a result of in-hospital medical treatment and surgery as well as certain outpatient expenses such as doctor's visits, lab oratory tests, and diagnostic services. Hospitalization insurance may be issued as an individual policy covering all family members or as a group insurance policy provided through an employer-sponsored program.

When medical expense coverage for proprietors and partners is paid for by the business, the premiums have traditionally been considered tax deductible to the business but includable as income to the individual. There is no limit to the amount of tax-free medical expense benefits the individual can receive.

16. 3. 4 Dental Expense Benefits

Dental expense benefits are generally sold as part of group health insurance coverage. Most insurers do not provide individual dental policies. Dental benefits are offered for preventive maintenance (cleanings and x-rays), repair (e.g., fillings or root canals) and replacement of teeth.

16. 3. 5 Long-Term Care Insurance

Long-term care (LTC) insurance pays for the care of persons with chronic diseases or disabilities and may include a wide range of health and social services provided under the supervision of medical professionals. LTC insurance often covers nursing home care, home-based care, and respite care.

16. 3. 6 Limited Health Exposures and Insurance Contracts

A variety of special health insurance policies are available that provide limited coverage. To ensure that the insured has sufficient notice that the coverage is limited, every policy that provides limited coverage must, by law, state plainly on the first page of the policy, "THIS IS A LIMITED POLICY."

Travel accident insurance provides coverage for death or injury resulting from accidents occurring while the insured is a fare-paying passenger on a common carrier.

Specified disease or **dread disease insurance** provides a variety of benefits for only certain diseases, usually cancer or heart disease.

Hospital income insurance pays a specified sum on a daily, weekly, or monthly basis while the insured is confined to a hospital. The amount of the benefit is not related to expenses incurred or to wages lost while the insured is hospitalized.

Accident only insurance provides coverage for injury from accident and excludes sickness. Benefits may be paid for all or any of the following: death, disability, dismemberment, and hospital and medical expenses.

Credit insurance is listed here because of the limited nature of its coverage. This policy is issued only to those who are in debt to a creditor. The coverage is limited to the total amount of the debtor's indebtedness.

Blanket insurance is a form of group insurance. Often the individual's name is not known because the individuals come and go. Such groups include students, campers, passengers of a common carrier, volunteer groups, and sports teams. Unlike other group insurance, the individuals are automatically covered under the blanket policy and do not receive certificates of insurance.

16. 3. 7 Prescription Coverage

Prescription medication coverage is normally provided as an optional benefit under a group medical expense policy. The insured and eligible dependents are provided with a stated cost for any prescription medication required. This specific cost is usually $2, $3, or $5 per prescription. Thus, regardless of the cost of the medication, the insured only pays the stated amount, and the balance of the prescription cost is paid by the insurance company.

16. 3. 8 Vision Care

Relatively new to the array of health care benefits offered to groups is coverage for vision care. In fact, vision care coverage is available only on a group basis.

Although basic, comprehensive, and major medical policies often cover disease and injury to eyes, there is generally no coverage for eye exams and corrections such as eyeglasses or contact lenses. To close this gap, insurers may offer vision care policies, which usually cover:

- eye examinations;
- cost of lenses and frames;
- cost of contact lenses; and
- other corrective items.

Typically, vision care policies operate with a network of eye doctors and providers of eyeglasses which the policyholder must use in order to receive benefits. Co-payments will vary according to the type of plan. The plan member simply presents the vision care card to the provider and is told the amount of the co-payment. Individual and family coverage is generally available.

Limitations normally apply. For example, the policy may pay for only one eye exam and one set of lenses per year. Common exclusions are:

- replacement frames or lenses required because of loss or breakage;
- sunglasses and safety glasses; and
- medical and surgical costs of the type covered by basic and major medical policies.

16. 4 DETERMINING INSURANCE NEEDS

Life insurance is designed to protect individuals and their families from the risk of premature death by providing specific amounts of money exactly when needed to cover necessary expenses. Health insurance is designed to protect the insured from the risk of medical and disability expenses.

Similar to life insurance, health insurance provides benefits exactly when needed. Disability income insurance can enable the insured to make mortgage payments and cover other necessary family expenses when total disability due to an accident or sickness cuts off the insured's income.

Medical expense insurance provides the insured with necessary funds to cover hospital and physician expenses associated with a serious illness, thus preserving the family's savings and other assets.

Basically, the process of determining health insurance needs is similar to identifying an individual's life insurance requirements. The principal difference is the risk being insured—premature death or health insurance expenses.

The individual's and family's health insurance needs must be identified. These needs are then prioritized in terms of their importance to the family. Other forms of health insurance should be reviewed with regard to this needs analysis. These benefits include:

- workers' compensation benefits for job-related disabilities;
- Social Security disability benefits;

- Medicare, if the individual is eligible;
- work-related benefits through employer-sponsored plans; and
- health coverage under any statutory plans.

Once the individual's total health insurance needs analysis has been completed, meaningful recommendations can be made as to the type and amounts of health insurance required.

16. 5 HEALTH CARE PROVIDER ORGANIZATIONS AND PLANS

Patients have traditionally been seen by physicians in office or hospital environments. Today, physicians also see patients in surgicenters and urgent care centers and at skilled nursing facilities. **Surgicenters** are health care facilities that are physically or geographically separate from hospitals and that provide surgical services to outpatients who do not require hospitalization. **Urgent care centers** provide primary and urgent care treatment on a less than 24-hour-per-day basis but are not equipped to treat true medical emergencies, such as heart attack or stroke victims, and do not provide continuity of care. **Skilled nursing facilities** are primarily engaged in providing skilled nursing care, which is nursing care for patients who do not require acute hospital nursing care but who need inpatient supervision by a registered nurse. **Home health care** involves the provision of services by staff of home health agencies in an individual's place of residence on a per-visit or per-hour basis to patients or clients who have or are at risk of an injury, illness, or disabling condition or who are terminally ill and require short- or long-term intervention by health professionals.

The traditional broad health coverage provided by insurance plans provides little incentive for efficient, cost-effective health care delivery. In the past decade, it has become clear that too much money is being spent on health care. One response from insurers and providers has been to reorganize the health care delivery system into a form of managed care. **Managed care** imposes controls on the use of health care services, the providers of health care services, and the amount charged for these services, usually through health maintenance organizations or preferred provider arrangements. Managed care organizations achieve efficiency by increasing beneficiary cost sharing, controlling inpatient admissions and lengths of stay, establishing cost-sharing incentives for outpatient surgery, selectively contracting with health care providers, directly managing high-cost health care cases, and so forth. Of all workers covered by employer-sponsored health plans in 1994, 63% were enrolled in managed care plans.

The traditional stock and mutual companies and Blue Cross and Blue Shield are not the only insurers of health care. The health maintenance organizations and preferred provider organizations formed by hospitals and physicians also to deliver health care directly to enrollees in their plans.

16. 5. 1 Commercial Insurers

Commercial insurers are stock and mutual life insurers and sometimes casualty companies. Commercial insurers have traditionally provided coverage on a reimbursement basis but have also begun to embrace alternative approaches. **Reimbursement** plans pay benefits directly to the insured, who is responsible for paying the providers of medical services.

Commercial insurers offer both individual and group health insurance products. These products include basic medical expense coverage, major medical plans, comprehensive medical plans, disability income policies, and other types of health products.

Recent developments from commercial insurers in response to the need for cost control include the preferred provider organizations (PPOs) and health maintenance organizations (HMOs).

16. 5. 2 Blue Cross and Blue Shield

The 65 Blue Cross and Blue Shield plans nationwide provide coverage to 64 million people. When considered in combination, they are the dominant health insurer of the United States. The nation's Blue Cross and Blue Shield plans are loosely affiliated through the national Blue Cross and Blue Shield Association but are independently managed.

16. 5. 2. 1 Differences from Commercial Insurers

Blue Cross and Blue Shield (the Blues) are different than traditional commercial insurers in the following important areas.

- The Blues provide the majority of their benefits on a service basis rather than on a reimbursement basis. This means that the insurer pays the provider directly for the medical treatment given the insured, instead of reimbursing the insured.
- The Blues have contractual relationships with the hospitals and doctors. As participating providers, the doctors and hospitals contractually agree to specific costs for the medical services provided to subscribers. Thus, there is no contractual arrangement between the Blues and the subscribers as there would be between the insurer and the insured.

16. 5. 2. 2 Corporate Structure

Blue Cross/Blue Shield organizations, which are often referred to as service organizations, are examples of producers' cooperatives. Physicians and hospitals that sponsor Blue Cross/Blue Shield plans provide the insurance, so they are considered to be the producers in the cooperative.

Traditionally, the Blues have operated as nonprofit organizations, which means any net gain realized from company operations is eventually returned to the subscribers in the form of reduced premiums or increased benefits. A few plans have been allowed to become for-profit companies, or form for-profit subsidiaries, to allow them to raise money for expansion and compete in the health care marketplace.

Blue Cross traditionally has been a hospital service plan and Blue Shield a physician service plan, but these distinctions are becoming blurred. In most states, Blue Cross and Blue Shield have merged, but each group still covers the expenses for which it was first developed: Blue Cross covers hospital expenses and Blue Shield covers medical and surgical expenses. In some states, both Blue Cross and Blue Shield serve as hospital and physician service plans. Under the hospital plan, the contract is between Blue Cross and the hospital providing the hospital care. Under the medical plan, the contract is between Blue Shield and the physicians providing the service. The contract is evidence of their joint cooperation in providing health care to the public. One purpose of these plans was to ensure that health care providers—hospitals and practitioners—received payment for their services. Thus, with occasional exceptions, reimbursements for incurred expenses are made directly to the providers, not to the subscribers.

The favorable tax environment for Blues organizations has eroded over the years, and some states have withdrawn the favored status Blue Cross/ Blue Shield previously enjoyed. In addition, the federal Tax Reform Act of 1986 made the Blues taxable as insurance companies.

16. 5. 2. 3 Enrollment and Premium Rates

Members of Blue Cross and Blue Shield are known as **subscribers**. Subscribers in either plan can transfer their membership from one Blues organization to another in other areas of town or to other cities or states. Subscribers may also change their coverage from individual to family, from family to group, or any combination of changes they need to make. When transfers or changes are made, the subscriber's coverage continues without interruption.

Blue Cross and Blue Shield plans are called **prepaid** plans because the plan subscribers pay a set fee, usually each month, for medical services covered under the plan.

16. 5. 2. 4 Types of Coverage and Benefits

Blue Cross offers broad coverages and pays claims on a service basis. The plan covers hospital daily room and board, outpatient services for minor surgery or accidental injury, medical emergencies, diagnostic testing, physical therapy, kidney dialysis, chemotherapy, and, in some cases, preadmission testing. Family plans may also include coverage for dependent handicapped children. Maternity benefits are also made available as for a disability.

Blue Cross also has a supplemental coverage for catastrophic loss, which is similar to commercial major medical plans. This supplement has a deductible and an 80 to 20% coinsurance feature.

Blue Shield offers prepaid medical coverage for physician services received by plan subscribers. Again, through the contractual arrangement with the providers, Blue Shield normally pays the participating physician a predetermined amount for the specific service provided. Usually, this amount is based on the usual, customary, and reasonable (UCR) fees charged by other physicians in the same geographical area for the same or similar medical procedures.

It is also possible to obtain dental coverage through Blue Cross/Blue Shield, which contracts with dental providers and pays fees on a service basis. An estimated 15% of people with dental insurance have their coverage through Blue Cross/Blue Shield plans.

16. 5. 2. 5 Blues and Managed Care

The Blues have also been strongly influenced by managed care. Many Blues subscribers are now covered by a Blues-affiliated HMO or PPO, or **point-of-service (POS) plan**, which is a type of health plan allowing the covered person to choose to receive a service from a participating or a non-participating provider, with different benefit levels associated with the use of in-plan and out-of-plan providers.

16. 5. 2. 6 Special Requirements for Consolidated Plans

Jointly operated (consolidated) Blue Cross/Blue Shield plans are often so comprehensive that supplementing them with major medical coverage is not necessary. Plan provisions applying to consolidated Blue Cross/Blue Shield plans are similar to plan provisions applying to comprehensive major medical plans.

16. 5. 3 Health Maintenance Organizations

16. 5. 3. 1 History and Development

The number of health maintenance organizations (HMOs) has grown rapidly in response to increasing health care costs. The purpose of HMOs is to manage health care and its costs through a program of prepaid care that emphasizes prevention and early treatment. This prepayment, which entitles the health care consumer to a wide range of services, is referred to as a **service-incurred** basis. In contrast, traditional health insurance coverage is handled on a reimbursement basis, with the insured or provider being reimbursed for all or part of medical expenses actually incurred.

The emphasis on prevention means HMOs cover preventive medicine, such as routine physical and well-child examinations and diagnostic screening paid for in advance. This is in sharp contrast to health insurance plans that traditionally did not cover preventive programs, paying only after the fact of disease or injury. Theoretically, the HMOs' focus on prevention ultimately leads to reduced health care costs. At the same time, HMOs provide for hospital, surgical, and medical treatment when such services are needed.

One way HMOs differ from traditional health insurance providers is that HMOs have a dual function not shared by insurance companies. The illustration that follows, which is oversimplified for clarity, shows that under traditional arrangements, consumers receive the health care itself from one group, the medical profession—physicians, hospitals, therapists, and so forth—while the financial coverage comes from a separate entity, the insurance company.

Traditional Health Insurance Arrangement

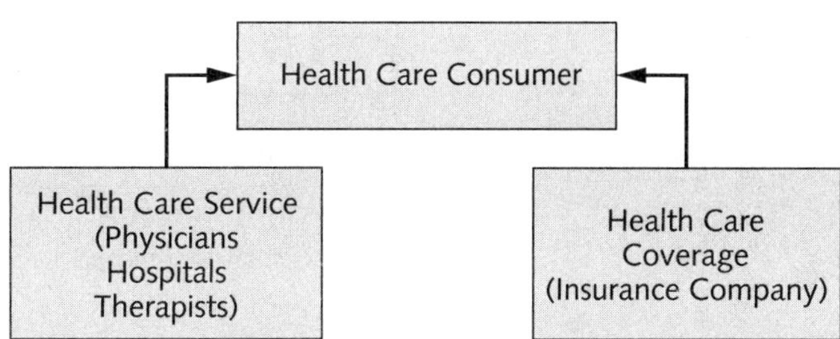

In contrast, as shown in the next illustration, an HMO provides both the health care services and the health care coverage.

Health Maintenance Organization Arrangement

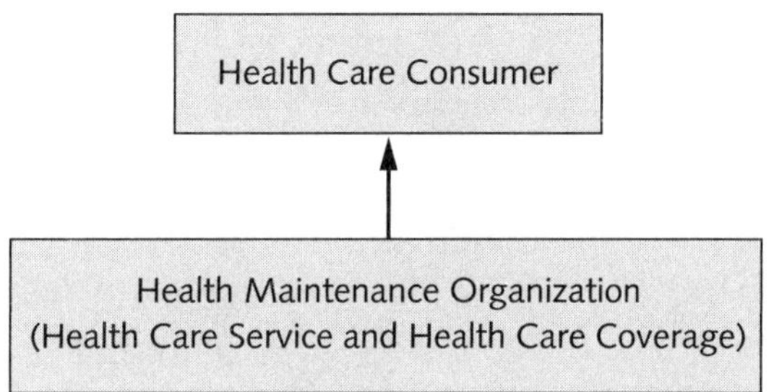

16. 5. 3. 2 Health Maintenance Organization Arrangement

These two functions are combined because the HMO comprises a group of medical practitioners who have contracted to provide specified services to HMO members at agreed-upon prices. In return, each consumer who is a member of the HMO agrees to pay the HMO a specified amount in advance to cover required hospital and medical services. Thus, the HMO both handles the financial arrangements and makes available the health care services.

16. 5. 3. 3 Federal Requirements

Although the emphasis on prevention and containing costs was a major factor in the development of HMOs, federal HMO laws further encouraged development by two primary means:

- Providing for government grants
- Requiring certain employers who provide health benefits to employees to offer enrollment in an HMO as an option

To receive government grants, HMOs must:

- maintain certain minimum financial requirements in terms of the net worth of the HMO or reserves to pay health claims;
- provide a defined package of health services that includes routine preventive care;
- require no more than nominal use charges or co-payments (in addition to the prepaid amounts) for services actually rendered to individuals; and
- establish premiums on a community rating basis without considering actual usage of services by individuals.

Once an HMO has met the minimum standards as well as other federal and state requirements, it is allowed to operate in a designated **service area**—often within a certain county or a specified distance surrounding the HMO facilities. Then, the federal law regarding employers comes into play.

The HMO Act of 1973 required employers with certain characteristics to offer HMO coverage by a federally qualified HMO as an alternative to an indemnity plan. Under this law, if the HMO operates in the service area of an employer that has 25 or more employees and that provides health care benefits, enrollment in the HMO must be offered as an alternative to traditional health insurance plans. This is often referred to as the dual choice option or dual choice law.

This requirement was repealed at the federal level in 1995, although some states still impose dual choice requirements. Federal law now simply requires that employers not financially discriminate in the amounts of employee contribution made toward HMO and indemnity plans. Employers are required to contribute equally to either type of health coverage for employees. However, the employer is never required to pay more for the HMO than it pays for any existing insurance plan already in place. If the HMO cost is greater, the employee choosing the HMO must make up the difference.

16. 5. 3. 4 HMO Organization

16. 5. 3. 4. 1 Profit Versus Nonprofit

There are a number of ways to analyze the organization of an HMO. The first concept we'll address is whether the HMO operates on a for-profit or a not-for-profit basis.

Usually, but not always, if the HMO is a producers' cooperative owned and operated by a group of physicians, the HMO is for-profit. If it is a consumers' cooperative in which the doctors are salaried employees of the HMO, it is usually not-for-profit.

16. 5. 3. 4. 2 Typical Structures: Group Model

The basic structure of an HMO involves contractual agreements with a variety of health care providers and facilities to provide services to HMO subscribers. Within that structure, four models are used, one of which is the **group model**.

More than two-thirds of HMOs existing in the late 1980s were based on the **group model**, sometimes called the medical group model or the group practice model. Under this arrangement, the HMO contracts with an independent medical group that specializes in a variety of medical services to provide those services to HMO subscribers. Under the agreement, the HMO pays the medical group entity, not the individual service providers. The medical group itself chooses how to pay its individual physicians, all of whom remain independent of the HMO rather than becoming salaried employees.

Often, the HMO pays the group a **capitation fee**, which is a fixed amount paid monthly for each HMO member. Thus, the medical group can make a profit on those members for whom a fee is paid but who use few or no services. On the other hand, the medical group can lose money on frequent users. The medical group model thus entails some financial risk on the part of the practitioners.

16. 5. 3. 4. 3 Typical Structures: Staff Model

A second type of arrangement is the **staff model**, so named because the contracting physicians are paid employees working on the staff of the HMO. They generally operate in a clinic setting at the HMO's physical facilities. When hospital services are required, the staff doctors and HMO administration arrange for those services. In some cases, the HMO may even own and operate a hospital. Unlike the group model, practitioners in the staff model are under no financial risk; they are simply employed by the HMO, and it is the HMO corporation that takes the risk.

16. 5. 3. 4. 4 Typical Structures: Network Model

The **network model** operates much like the group model, except the HMO contracts with at least two, and more likely several, medical groups rather than just one. In addition, the HMO may make similar contractual arrangements with independent doctors to provide services in their individual offices. The purpose of a network is to increase accessibility to providers as a convenience for HMO subscribers who might otherwise be required to visit a facility far from their homes or workplaces. Under the network model, medical groups are generally paid a capitation fee, and individual physicians may be paid either a capitation fee or a discounted fee.

16. 5. 3. 4. 5 Typical Structures: Individual Practice Association Model

The fourth and final model is one that gives HMO members the maximum freedom of choice of physicians and locations. The **individual practice association (IPA) model** allows the HMO to contract separately with any combination of individual physicians, medical groups, or physicians' associations. Some HMOs, in fact, have been started by such groups.

In the IPA model, there is no separate HMO facility. Physicians operate out of their own private offices, and their HMO patients may be individuals whom the physicians were already attending. Many people prefer this arrangement because it allows them to continue with their personal doctors. Payment is usually on a fee-for-service basis, whereby the fees have been negotiated in advance.

16. 5. 3. 4. 6 Open- and Closed-Panel Types

Open and closed panels are another way to characterize HMOs. Physicians, hospitals, and other health care providers who have contracts with an HMO are referred to as the HMO's panel. With an **open panel**, any and all providers who want to provide services for the HMO may do so as long as they agree to the HMO's requirements.

In contrast, a **closed panel** is a limited number of health care providers chosen by the HMO. HMO subscribers must receive their health care services from this closed panel of providers to have those services paid for on the prepaid plan. The theory is that, with a closed panel, the HMO is better able to manage costs with fewer providers.

16. 5. 3. 5 Sponsorship and Eligibility

Throughout this section, we've mentioned several types of groups that may sponsor HMOs. Other sponsoring groups include:

- medical schools or associations;
- physicians;
- hospitals;
- employers;
- service organizations (such as Blue Cross/Blue Shield);
- labor unions;
- consumer groups;
- insurance companies; and
- government entities.

Most HMOs, no matter who sponsors them, restrict membership to a specifically defined group. For example, an HMO organized by a labor union might limit enrollment to members of specific unions. An HMO sponsored by a Blue Cross/Blue Shield plan might accept only the employees of organizations within its service area that employ 500 or more individuals. Every rule has its exception, however, and some HMOs solicit individual enrollees from the entire population in the service area.

16. 5. 3. 6 Basic and Supplemental Services

The emphasis of HMOs is prevention, and the benefits offered are broader than those provided by commercial insurers or the Blues. HMO benefits are not limited to treatment resulting from illness or injury; they also include preventive health care measures such as routine physical examinations.

HMOs are required to provide for certain basic health care services.

- **Inpatient hospital and physician services** must be provided for a period of at least 90 days per calendar year for treatment of illness or injury. If inpatient treatment is for mental, emotional, or nervous disorders, including alcohol and drug rehabilitation and treatment, services may be limited to 30 days per calendar year. Treatment for alcohol and drug rehabilitation may be restricted to a 90-day lifetime limit. A partial list of the hospital services provided include room and board; maternity care; general nursing care; use of operating room and facilities; use of intensive care unit; x-rays, laboratory, and other diagnostic tests; drugs, medications, and anesthesia; and physical, radiation, and inhalation therapy.
- **Outpatient medical services** must be provided when prescribed or supervised by a physician and rendered in a non-hospital-based health care facility (e.g., physician's office, member's home). Outpatient medical services include diagnostic services, treatment services, short-term physical therapy and rehabilitation services, laboratory and x-ray services, and outpatient surgery.
- **Preventive health services** with the goal of protection against and early detection and minimization of the ill effects and causes of disease or disability must be provided. Specifically, this includes well-child care from birth, eye and ear examinations for children age 17 and under, periodic health evaluations, and immunizations.
- **In and out of area emergency services**, including medically necessary ambulance services, must be available on an inpatient or an outpatient basis 24 hours a day, seven days a week.

Many HMOs may but are not required to provide one or more of the following supplemental health care services:

- Prescription drugs
- Vision care
- Dental care
- Home health care
- Nursing services
- Long-term care
- Mental heath care
- Substance abuse services

Consumers who want supplemental services may purchase them from the HMO only as an adjunct to the basic health care services the HMO offers. For example, an employer could not ask an HMO to provide coverage only for prescription drugs without purchasing the basic package of services.

16. 5. 3. 6. 1 Co-Payments

Members of an HMO may be charged only nominal amounts—**co-payments**—for basic services in addition to the original monthly payment. In many cases, no additional payments are required for services. Any co-payments are described in the certificate of coverage or the evidence of coverage.

On the other hand, HMOs are permitted to require co-payments on supplemental services and to charge an amount that is added to the monthly fee. For example, suppose an HMO makes dental coverage available to members who want to pay for it. The basic package of services might cost $200 per month, and an additional $5 will buy the dental coverage. The HMO then might require the consumer to pay $3 for every routine dental checkup. (All figures are hypothetical.)

16. 5. 3. 6. 2 Exclusions and Limitations

Exclusions and limitations are used either to limit a benefit provided or specifically to exclude a type of coverage, benefit, medical procedure, and so forth. HMOs may not exclude and limit benefits as readily as commercial insurers. This is because the rationale of an HMO is to provide comprehensive health care coverage. Some of the benefits HMOs may (and often do) exclude from coverage include eye examinations and refractions for persons over age 17, eyeglasses or contact lenses resulting from an eye examination, dental services, prescription drugs (other than those administered in a hospital), long-term physical therapy (over 90 days), and out-of-area services (other than emergency services).

16. 5. 3. 7 Important Features of HMOs

16. 5. 3. 7. 1 Gatekeeper System

HMOs often have a gatekeeper system under which the member must select a primary care physician (PCP), who in turn provides or authorizes all care for the particular member. Any referrals, such as to specialists, must be made and authorized by the PCP. Think of this person as opening (or refusing to open) the gate between the member and the health care providers. In emergency situations, the member's needs are covered, but generally the individual must notify the PCP as soon as possible if it wasn't possible to do so when the emergency arose. Members are required to involve the PCP in all service decisions to ensure claims will be paid.

Suppose Ronald knows his PCP can't perform the open-heart surgery he needs. Ronald may not simply select a surgeon of his choice and assume the claim will be paid by his HMO. He must first consult with the gatekeeper, his personal PCP, who will make the referral and authorize treatment.

16. 5. 3. 7. 2 24-Hour Access

As a rule, members have 24-hour access to the HMO. Telephones are answered and referrals and authorizations are made 24 hours a day, seven days a week. Nursing and medical staff, including PCPs, must be willing to respond during nonbusiness hours as well. Therefore, an HMO member who needs to consult with a PCP late at night or on a weekend would likely be able to do so.

16. 5. 3. 7. 3 Open Enrollment

The term **open enrollment** can mean two different things:

In employer-sponsored group plans, a period each year when employees may choose to enroll or remain enrolled in the HMO or to change health plans

A period each year when an HMO must advertise availability to the general public on an individual basis

In the first case, open enrollment allows employees who have not yet joined the HMO to do so if they wish. Those who are already HMO subscribers may at this time also choose to continue in the HMO or to change plans if another health care plan is available.

In the second case, open enrollment may be required by state law, permitting all who apply to join. During this period, which usually lasts 30 days, the HMO generally may not reject any applicant for health reasons. However, some laws permit the HMO to refuse enrollment to people who are hospitalized during the enrollment period or who have chronic illnesses or permanent injuries. For the most part, the advantage of open enrollment lies completely with potential enrollees, who may have been rejected for traditional coverage because of their health but who will now be accepted by the HMO. The HMO, on the other hand, is placed at risk because it is more likely to lose money on such subscribers.

Example

Darren has been rejected for health insurance by several insurance companies because of a history of heart attacks. Darren's state requires HMOs to have a period of open enrollment. If Darren applies for HMO coverage during the open enrollment period, chances are he will be accepted even though he might not be able to obtain coverage elsewhere because of his medical history.

16. 5. 3. 7. 4 Nondiscrimination

When HMO coverage is offered to a group, the HMO may not refuse to cover an individual member of the group because of adverse preexisting health conditions, such as a history of heart trouble that predates enrollment in the HMO. This is different from traditional insurers, which generally have the option of refusing to cover certain group members and of excluding preexisting health conditions.

HMOs are permitted to refuse coverage for individuals with preexisting conditions, except during open enrollment as discussed previously.

16. 5. 3. 7. 5 Complaints

All HMOs are required to have a complaint system, often called a **grievance procedure**, to resolve written complaints by members. The HMO is required to provide forms for written complaints, including the address and telephone number to which complaints should be directed. In addition, upon providing the necessary forms for a complaint to a member, the HMO must notify the member of any time limits applying to a complaint. Complaints must be resolved within 180 days of being filed with the HMO (with a few exceptions). Complaints may be resolved through binding arbitration if so specified by the HMO and agreed to by the member.

HMOs must have mechanisms to handle complaints from subscribers for two categories:

- Coverage complaints
- Care complaints

The first category includes complaints about the coverage offered, payment or denial of health claims, and similar items. These complaints are reviewed internally and might eventually be referred to the state Insurance Department.

The second category refers to the quality of care received from an HMO provider. Medical personnel review this type of complaint. HMO subscribers must receive a document indicating how complaints can be registered. This information is usually included in the evidence or certificate of coverage.

16. 5. 3. 7. 6 Prohibited Practices

HMOs, like traditional commercial insurers, are not allowed to engage in certain types of business practices, policies, and so on. Specifically, HMOs are prohibited from excluding a member's preexisting conditions from coverage, and they are prohibited from unfairly discriminating against a member on the basis of age, sex, health status, race, color, creed, national origin, or marital status. HMOs are also prohibited from terminating a member's coverage for reasons other than nonpayment of premiums or co-payments, fraud or deception in the member's use of services, violation of the terms of the contract, failure to meet or continue to meet eligibility requirements prescribed by the HMO, or a termination of the group contract under which the member was covered.

16. 5. 3. 7. 7 Quality Assurance

Because HMOs provide service benefits rather than reimbursement benefits, they are required to follow guidelines prescribed by the state Insurance Department to ensure quality service to members. These guidelines specify the requirements for reasonable hours of operation, after-hours emergency health care, and standards to ensure that sufficient personnel will be available to attend to members' needs. The guidelines also require adequate arrangements to provide inpatient hospital services for basic health care and that the services of specialists are provided as a basic health care service.

16. 5. 3. 7. 8 Open-Ended Plans

An **open-ended HMO** (also known as a leaky HMO or a point-of-service HMO) is a hybrid arrangement whereby participants may use non-HMO providers at any time and receive indemnity benefits subject to higher deductible and coinsurance amounts. The out-of-pocket cost to the participant (and probably to the employer) is higher, but the arrangement allows participants to remain in control of choosing a health care provider.

16. 5. 3. 7. 9 Open-Access HMOs

Dissatisfaction with the gatekeeper mechanism, delays in receiving care, and problems in obtaining referrals have led many health plans to offer open access. An **open-access HMO** allows members to receive care from network specialists without first going through a primary care physician (gatekeeper) and receiving a referral. Alternatively, a point-of-service plan allows members to seek the care of a specialist outside of the HMO provider network. Because the plan does not control the outside provider, POS plans tend to be more expensive than open-access HMOs.

16. 6 PREFERRED PROVIDER ORGANIZATIONS

Other efforts to reduce medical costs have resulted in **preferred provider organizations (PPOs)**. A PPO is an arrangement under which a selected group of independent hospitals and medical practitioners in a certain area, such as a state, agrees to provide a range of services at a prearranged cost. The contracting agency or organizer of the PPO might be any one of a number of groups, including:

- traditional insurance companies;
- Blue Cross/Blue Shield;
- local groups of hospitals;
- local groups of physicians;
- an existing HMO;
- large employers; and
- trade unions.

The organizers and the providers agree on medical service charges that are generally lower than those the providers would charge patients not associated with the PPO. Unlike most prepaid HMO arrangements, the providers are paid on a fee-for-service basis rather than receiving a flat monthly amount for each user. Providers are willing to enter into this arrangement in return for guaranteed payment from the PPO and a potential increase in the number of patients.

People who receive services choose a preferred provider from a list the PPO distributes. As a general rule, the users have more choices among doctors and hospitals under a PPO than under an HMO arrangement. However, some recent HMO structures offer similar arrangements. PPOs fall somewhere between commercial insurers, wherein the user has unlimited choice of practitioners, and HMOs, wherein the user might be severely restricted. Even with the usually long list of PPO providers from which to choose, people may opt to go to another provider. However, the PPO agrees to pay its full benefits only when a preferred provider is used. If an individual uses a nonpreferred facility, the PPO usually pays a reduced amount and the individual must pay the balance.

Although a PPO generally pays less for services performed by a nonpreferred provider, this rule is mitigated for emergency services under most PPO plans. Recognizing that emergencies may require treatment in other than preferred facilities or by providers who have not agreed to the PPO arrangement, PPO plans generally pay in full for emergency treatment regardless of where and by whom it is performed.

Example

Dorian is a member of a PPO in his home town of Topeka, Kansas. While vacationing in Utah, he is injured in an auto accident and is rushed to the nearest hospital in Salt Lake City. Dorian's medical bills in Salt Lake City total $5,600 before he is returned to Topeka. The same treatment with his preferred providers in Topeka would have cost only $4,780. Under these circumstances, Dorian's PPO is likely to pay the full amount to the Salt Lake providers.

PPOs and HMOs are often lumped together and referred to as managed health care systems. Although they do share the concept of saving costs by proper health care management and are similar in many ways, they are distinguishable by the fact that PPOs have no separate physical facility and HMOs generally do. But even this distinction has become blurred somewhat by continuing refinements and variations in the way HMOs operate. Currently, an HMO may operate through a PPO arrangement rather than have its own facility.

A distinguishing characteristic that still exists concerns regulation. Although commercial insurance companies are regulated only by the states, HMOs have increasingly had to meet state requirements as well as the original standards established by the federal government. PPOs, on the other hand, are less stringently regulated, since any group that can agree upon the arrangements may call itself a PPO.

16. 7 POINT-OF-SERVICE PLANS

Point-of-service plans are another form of managed care. With POS plans, the insured is given a choice of receiving in-network care or out-of-network care. With in-network coverage, the insured receives care through a particular network of doctors and hospitals participating in the plan, and all care is coordinated by the insured's primary care physician. This includes referrals to specialists and arrangements for hospitalization, which must all be approved by the PCP. In-network coverage is the highest level of coverage within the plan, which means the plan will pay more for medical services and the insured won't have to submit claim forms. Out-of-network coverage applies when the insured receives care from a provider who does not participate in the plan's network, and the care is not coordinated by the PCP. An insured receiving out-of-network care usually pays more of the cost than if it had been in-network care (emergencies excepted). Out-of-network care also means that the insured must submit claim forms in order to receive benefits.

Example

Arnold is a member of a point-of-service plan. He develops a heart condition but decides not to follow his PCP's recommendation to see an in-network cardiologist. Instead, he becomes the patient of a famous cardiologist in another city who is out of network. Arnold can expect that his POS plan will pay less than it would pay if had he become the patient of the in-network cardiologist.

16. 7. 1 Exclusive Provider Organizations

Exclusive provider organizations (EPOs) are a type of PPO in which individual members use particular preferred providers instead of choosing among a variety of preferred providers. Providers are not paid a salary but are paid on a fee-for-service basis.

EPOs are characterized by a primary physician who monitors care and makes referrals to a network of providers (the gatekeeper concept), strong utilization management, experience rating, and simplified claims processing. EPOs can serve as an alternative to or companion with HMOs and PPOs.

16. 7. 2 Emerging Variations

Today there are many variations of managed health care providers, including physician hospital organizations (PHOs), practice management organizations (PMOs), and provider sponsored networks (PSNs).

The principal differences between these organizations are the parties to the contracts and their basic structure and organization. For example, with the physician hospital organization, the physicians and hospitals contract directly with employers to provide health care services. Most of these arrangements are funded through capitation fees much like HMOs.

16. 7. 3 Multiple Option Plans

A multiple option plan is an integrated health plan that may include services of an HMO, PPO, EPO, or indemnity plan, all of which are administered by a single vendor (usually an insurance company).

16. 8 EMPLOYER-ADMINISTERED PLANS

16. 8. 1 Self-Funding

If claim costs are fairly predictable, an employer may consider a self-funded health care plan. With a self-funded plan, an employer, not an insurance company, provides the funds to make claim payments for company employees and their dependents. In the event that claims are higher than predicted, a self-funded health insurance plan can be backed up by a **stop-loss contract**. A **stop-loss contract** is designed to limit the employer's liability for claims. There are two variations of this coverage. Specific stop-loss coverage begins to apply after an individual's medical expenses exceed a predetermined threshold such as $5,000. Aggregate stop-loss coverage applies when the employer's liability for group insurance claims exceeds a specified amount. The insurer pays all claims after the specified amount is reached.

An employer self-funded plan may be an indemnity program that reimburses covered employees for medical care they have received. **Or**, the employer may provide benefits through the service plan offered under an HMO or through an insurer's PPO network.

An insurer may also be used for a self-funded employer under an administrative services only contract. Under the **ASO contractual agreement**, the insurer provides claim forms, administers claims, and makes payments to health care providers, but the employer still provides the funds to make claims payments.

16. 8. 1. 1 Advantages of Self-Insurance

Self-insurance has four major advantages.

- The company can save money if actual losses are less than those predicted.
- The expense of carrying insurance may be reduced because of the elimination of administrative costs, agent commissions, brokerage fees, and premium tax.
- Because the company has assumed the entire risk, there may be a greater effort on its part to seek ways to reduce claims and encourage employees to actively participate in wellness programs and improved lifestyles.
- The company has use of the money that normally would be held by the insurance company.

16. 8. 1. 2 Disadvantages of Self-Insurance

The main disadvantages of self-insurance are as follows.

- Actual losses may be more than predicted, causing the unexpected loss of funds that were to be used for other purposes.
- Expenses could be higher than expected if additional personnel have to be hired to administer claims, manage risk, or offer employee information.
- Income taxes could be higher because the company will not be able to take premiums paid as a deduction; only the claims paid and operating expenses may be taken as tax deductions.
- Contracts usually are not regulated by the Insurance Department; therefore, the Department cannot assist consumers with problems.
- Contracts are not subject to mandated benefits laws.

16. 8. 2 501(c)(9) Trusts

Section 501(c)(9) of the Internal Revenue Code provides for the establishment of **voluntary employees' beneficiary associations, or 501(c)(9) trusts**, which are funding vehicles for the employee benefits offered to members. Liberalized tax treatment made 501(c)(9) trusts an attractive self-funding employee benefit plan alternative, but restrictive legislation in the Tax Reform Act of 1984 has caused their popularity to diminish.

Some employers may prefer to establish a 501(c)(9) trust for some of the tax advantages it provides. Under a regular self-funded plan, contributions to the plan cannot be deducted until benefits are distributed. But contributions to 501(c)(9) trusts are deducted immediately. Accumulated earnings on 501(c)(9) assets are also tax deductible, unlike earnings on funds in a regular self-insured plan.

Maintaining a 501(c)(9) trust can be quite costly, though, and administration of the plan must be exceptional to make it worthwhile to the employer. High losses under the plan may negate any tax advantages a 501(c)(9) trust offers.

16. 8. 3 Small Employers

Small employers (usually defined as those with fewer than 25 or 50 employees) have been hit especially hard by increases in health care insurance premiums. Because many group plans are experience rated, small employers see an immediate premium increase whenever claims are particularly high. If the average age of the participants is particularly high, if claims experience is high, or if there has been even one long or catastrophic illness in a small employer plan, it can have a devastating effect, making health insurance unaffordable for the whole group. Recent surveys by the Health Insurance Association of America (HIAA) indicate a substantial decline in the number of small firms that are able to offer health coverage to their employees.

Several states have acted to ensure that health insurance coverages are available at a reasonable cost and under reasonable conditions for small employers. The new requirements include the following:

- Standard benefit plans that must be offered to small employers
- Maximum waiting periods for preexisting conditions
- The insurer may not exclude particular individuals or medical conditions from coverage
- Carriers may cancel or nonrenew small employer plans only for nonpayment of premium, fraud, misrepresentation, or noncompliance with plan provisions

16. 8. 4 Cafeteria Plans

A **cafeteria plan** could be defined as a plan in which employees select health benefits from a variety of coverage options on the basis of their individual and family needs. Cafeteria plans tend to be more complex (and more expensive) than traditional plans, especially with regard to plan administration, and usually make the most sense for larger employers. Benefits are elected in advance of the year in which they will be used (for example, benefits to be used in 2009 would be elected at the end of 2008). Taxation of cafeteria plans is regulated by Section 125 of the Internal Revenue Code.

16. 8. 5 Medical Savings Accounts

Medical savings accounts (MSAs) were created to help employees of small employers, as well as self-employed individuals, pay for their medical care expenses. MSAs are tax-free accounts set up with financial institutions such as banks and insurance companies.

To qualify for an MSA, an individual must be one of the following:

- An employee (or spouse) who works for a small employer that maintains an individual or family high-deductible health plan for the employee
- A self-employed person (or spouse) who maintains an individual or family high-deductible health plan

A **small employer** is one that has averaged 50 or fewer employees during either of the last two calendar years. Using 2008 limits, a **high-deductible health plan** is one with an annual deductible between $1,950 and $2,900 for an individual policy, or between $3,850 and $5,800 for a family policy, with a maximum out-of-pocket of $7,050.

The self-employed individual or the employer funds an MSA with tax-deductible dollars. At the same time, the account holder is covered by a high-deductible health insurance policy. Qualified medical expenses are paid for with tax-free withdrawals from the MSA. The health insurance policy kicks in only when the high deductible is met. There may or may not be enough in the MSA to cover all medical expenses until the high deductible is met. If there isn't enough, the account holder must make up the difference out of pocket. Any funds left over at the end of the year in an MSA can be withdrawn (on a taxable basis) by the account holder or rolled over (on a nontaxable basis) into a new MSA the following year.

16. 8. 6 Flexible Spending Accounts

A variation of the traditional cafeteria plan is the **flexible spending account (FSA)**. The FSA is a cafeteria plan that is funded with employee money by means of a salary reduction. A salary reduction plan is a pretax plan; the employee agrees to a reduction in compensation, and this amount is used to cover certain medical expenses. This naturally results in a lower-cost plan from the employer's perspective, with an employer's expenses usually limited to administrative costs. FSAs typically are for moderate-sized to large employers.

The FSA plan provides the selectivity and flexibility of the regular cafeteria plan. Thus, desired benefits can be chosen by the employee, especially the employee whose spouse works and has a similar benefits package. Because of the coordination of benefits provision found in most group hospitalization policies, duplicate coverage will pay only once. If an employee is contributing toward the cost of the plan, it makes sense that payroll deduction dollars be used for selective benefits instead of duplicate benefits.

The salary reduction method results in the employees funding nontaxable benefits with nontaxed dollars. This also results in a reduced payroll and reduced payroll taxes for the employer.

16. 8. 7 High Deductible Health Plans

The Medicare Prescription Drug and Modernization Act of 2003 also established a new way for consumers to pay for medical expenses—health care savings accounts (HSAs). An HSA is a tax-favored vehicle for accumulating funds to cover medical expenses. Individuals under age 65 are eligible to establish and contribute to HSAs if they have a qualified high-deductible health plan. For an individual, a qualified high deductible health plan is one with a minimum deductible of $1,100 for 2008 ($1,150 for 2009) and a $5,600 for 2008 ($5,800 for 2009) cap on out-of-pocket expenses. (These limits are indexed annually). For a family, a qualified health plan is one with a minimum deductible of $2,200 for 2008 ($2,300 for 2009) and a $11,200 for 2008 ($11,600 for 2009) cap on out-of-pocket expenses. These limits are also indexed annually.

16. 8. 8 Health Savings Accounts

Since 2004, individuals under the age of 65 who are enrolled in certain high-deductible health plans have been able to establish **health care savings accounts (HSAs)**. For individual policies in 2009, a high-deductible health plan is one that has an annual deductible of at least $1,150 and an out-of-pocket limit of no more than $5,800. These amounts are doubled for family policies and will be indexed for inflation in future years.

The maximum HSA contribution in 2009 is the amount of the deductible under the taxpayer's high-deductible health plan (up to a limit of $3,000 for individual policies and $5,950 for family policies). People ages 55 to 64 can make an additional catch-up contribution of $900 in 2008 and $1,000 in 2009 and thereafter. Contributions by individuals are deductible from gross income.

Employers may set up HSAs for their eligible employees and contribute to them, subject to the dollar limits discussed previously. Employer contributions are excluded from employees' taxable income.

HSA distributions are tax free if used to pay qualified medical expenses, which generally include the same kinds of medical expenses that are deductible as itemized deductions. Distributions for any other purposes are subject to income tax; a 10% penalty tax also applies unless the account beneficiary has died, become disabled, or is age 65 or older.

16. 8. 9 Health Reimbursement Arrangements

Some employers provide employees with high-deductible medical expense plans and create a tax-favored savings account for each covered employee under which he can obtain reimbursement for certain medical expenses that are not covered under a high deductible plan. HRAs are the dominant form of consumer-directed health plans.

16. 8. 10 Consumer-Directed Health Plans

As described in the preceding sections, recent years have seen considerable interest in the concept of the consumer-directed health plan.

16. 8. 11 Multiple Employer Trusts

Multiple employer trusts (METs) provide health insurance benefits to small businesses through a series of trusts usually established on the basis of specific industries such as manufacturing, sales and service, real estate, and others.

Most states have group-size eligibility requirements for employer groups to qualify for group insurance. Generally, states may require a minimum of 5 to 10 participants for a group to be eligible for group benefits. METs typically have no such requirements, and, in reality, a group of one could be eligible for group benefits.

METs are formed by insurers or third-party administrators called sponsors. The sponsor develops the plan, sets the underwriting rules, and administers the plan. To prevent the possibility of adverse selection, the underwriter must make sure that the sponsor's underwriting rules are adequate and that the sponsor adheres to them. This is necessary because an employer with only two, three, or five employees could elect to join an MET because the employer knows of the poor health condition of one of the employees. The underwriting standards must be able to prevent this from happening.

If state law allows, METs may be **noninsured**. A **noninsured plan** is a self-funded plan—that is, a plan that operates without the services and funds of an insurance company. The trustee has charge of the funds and the policies, and all financial activities occur through the trust.

As with a traditional group insurance plan, a master policy is issued to a trustee operating under a trust agreement. The master contract has its own policy effective date and renewal dates, which the insurer may use for changing rates on the MET's entire block of business. Also, each individual employer under the MET has its own effective dates and anniversary dates. Rates are generally changed on the employer's anniversary date, but usually not more than once in 12 months.

16. 8. 12 Multiple Employer Welfare Arrangements

Multiple employer welfare arrangements (MEWAs) are created by small employers who join to provide health insurance benefits for their employees, often on a self-insured basis.

The federal Employee Retirement Income Security Act (ERISA), designed to protect group health insurance plan participants, restricts states' ability to regulate employee welfare benefit plans while preserving state insurance laws having to do with reserve requirements. A state may regulate insurance but may or may not consider an employee welfare benefit plan an insurance plan for the purpose of regulation.

Some self-funded MEWAs claim they are not subject to Insurance Department regulation and operate under a supposed preemption under ERISA. As a result, many have gone unregulated and have fraudulently collected premiums from small businesses, only to go out of business themselves and leave millions of dollars of unpaid claims.

State and federal regulators are attempting to resolve the question of jurisdiction. Meanwhile, in most states MEWAs need to obtain a certificate of authority to transact insurance business and must be fully insured by a licensed insurer. Usually, agents and brokers are prohibited from assisting MEWAs to transact insurance until and unless the agent or broker files a report with the Department of Insurance outlining the MEWA's organization, insurance contracts, benefit plan description, and the designated third-party administrator.

16. 9 OTHER FORMS OF GROUP INSURANCE

16. 9. 1 Blanket Policies

Many types of groups, such as the students of a single school or a group of campers, are indefinite in number and composition and are constantly changing. These characteristics prevent qualification for group insurance under the usual terms.

However, groups such as these can have health coverage at group rates under a **blanket policy**. Because no employer/employee relationship is involved, the members of such groups are not usually interested in covering themselves for loss of income resulting from their activities as a group. Instead, they usually want only hospital, medical, and surgical coverages.

Example

The dean of a college might make insurance available to all full-time students. The group members are constantly changing as students enroll, graduate, or drop out. By obtaining a blanket policy, the dean can secure student coverage at the same low premium rates as group coverage. However, the members of the group, the students, will not be identified by name. Instead, all who can prove they are enrolled full time will be covered by the insurance blanket.

Gina owns a small business and is the leader of a local Girl Scout troop. Through an insurance company, Gina has established insurance plans for both of these groups.

For her employees, Gina provides group health insurance. Under the group plan, Gina provides the insurance company with each group member's name.

For the scout troop, Gina provides a blanket policy, under which she does not give the insurance company a list of the group's members, because they change frequently.

The members of a group insured under a blanket policy may or may not help to pay the premiums for their coverage. In the case of the college students, the school might require that they pay at least part of the premiums. In the case of the scouts, perhaps Gina's scout council pays for the coverage, and the children are not required to pay anything. In any event, blanket policies may be either contributory or noncontributory.

16. 9. 2 Franchise Policies

Group policies require the number of insured persons to remain above a specified minimum. Many small businesses and other groups do not have enough members to qualify. An arrangement that allows very small groups to have some of the benefits of group insurance, especially the lower cost, is called **franchise insurance**.

Franchise insurance works much like group insurance, but it is established differently. There is no master policy. Instead, each member of the group receives an individual insurance policy. This allows group members to make some coverage choices, but they are required to provide health information on their applications, just as they would for individual policies.

Like true group coverage, franchise insurance offers hospital, surgical, medical, and disability income coverage. Plans may be contributory or noncontributory. One premium is paid for the whole group.

One example of franchise insurance is coverage sold by mail to groups, such as the members of a certain association or holders of certain credit cards. Purchasers receive individual policies at group rates, so this is a type of franchise insurance.

16. 10 GOVERNMENT HEALTH INSURANCE

Both the federal and state governments offer statutory health insurance programs. On the federal level, Social Security provides disability income benefits and administers the Medicare program. On the state level, all states have workers' compensation laws and Medicaid or some similar form of state-subsidized health care.

16. 11 SOCIAL SECURITY

Social Security pays four types of benefits:

- Disability income benefits to workers
- Medicare benefits
- Retirement benefits to workers and their dependents
- Survivors benefits to a worker's family

A special insured status is required if a worker is eligible for disability benefits under Social Security. This status requires that the worker be fully insured and have earned at least 20 quarters of coverage in the 40-calendar-quarter period ending with the calendar quarter in which the disability begins. This requirement is modified slightly if a covered worker is disabled before age 31.

A covered worker may be eligible for disability income benefits if the required insured status is achieved and the worker is under age 65 and can satisfy the Social Security definition of total disability.

Social Security defines **total disability** as the inability to engage in any substantial gainful activity because of physical or mental disability that is expected to last for at least 12 months or end in death. *Substantial work activity* means significant mental and/or physical duties for which a person is compensated.

This definition does not refer to the individual's occupation prior to disability or to the level of predisability compensation. A surgeon earning $200,000 annually may be disabled to the degree that the individual could no longer perform surgery. However, a surgeon who could perform other meaningful work duties (e.g., bank employee, school teacher, salesperson), would probably not be eligible for disability benefits because this person could not meet the Social Security definition of total disability.

The amount of the disability benefit is equal to the worker's primary insurance amount (PIA), which in essence is the same as the individual's monthly retirement benefit. Disability benefits are payable only for total disabilities. Disability benefits begin with the sixth full month of disability. This waiting period begins with the first full month of disability. No benefit is paid for a partial disability.

As a result of the disabled person's work record, family members such as the following may also receive disability benefits:

- An unmarried child under age 18, or under 19 if in high school full time
- An unmarried child disabled before age 22
- A spouse caring for a child under age 16 or disabled
- A spouse age 62 or older
- A disabled widow or widower age 50 or older
- A disabled surviving divorced spouse age 50 or older, if the marriage lasted at least 10 years

16. 12 WORKERS' COMPENSATION

Most states require employers to provide workers' compensation benefits for their employees. Workers' compensation is designed to help persons who suffer from loss of income due to injury or sickness that occurs as a result of their occupation.

16. 12. 1 Eligibility

To be eligible for workers' compensation benefits, the disabled worker must:

- work in an occupation that is covered by workers' compensation; and
- have had an accident or sickness that is work related.

16. 12. 2 Benefits

Workers' compensation laws provide for the payment of four types of benefits:

- Medical benefits
- Income benefits
- Death benefits
- Rehabilitation benefits

Medical benefits are provided without limit. An injured or diseased employee is entitled to receive all necessary medical and surgical treatment to cure or relieve the condition. Certain maximums or limits may apply to a type of care or a particular medical item, but overall benefits are unlimited.

Income benefits are paid to employees who suffer work-related disabilities. An elimination period applies before benefits for loss of wages begin. If the disability continues beyond a certain period, retroactive benefits are paid for the initial waiting period. A disability may be total (making employment impossible) or partial (resulting in a reduced ability to work). Either type of disability may be temporary or permanent. For permanent total disability or temporary total disability, the benefit is 66.66% of weekly wages, subject to minimum and maximum weekly limits. However, for permanent total disability, the dollar maximum and the benefit period are greater. (Benefits for permanent total disability often continue for life, while benefits for a temporary total disability are limited.) People with partial disabilities are able to perform some work, so the laws provide a benefit equal to a percentage of the wage loss (the difference between earnings before and after the accident). In addition to benefits for lost wages, the state provides scheduled benefits for specific permanent partial disabilities such as loss of limbs, sight, or hearing. Usually, these benefits are paid in addition to any other income benefits.

Death benefits provide two types of payments. Up to a certain dollar amount is provided as a burial allowance, and the state also provides weekly income payments for a surviving spouse and children. Weekly benefits are 66.66% of the deceased worker's wages, subject to minimum and maximum dollar amounts, a maximum time limit, and an aggregate payment limit. Surviving children generally receive benefits until a certain age.

Rehabilitation benefits are now recognized as a valuable tool for reducing workers' compensation costs and returning disabled employees to their jobs as soon as possible. Rehabilitation may include therapy; vocational training; devices such as wheelchairs; and the costs of travel, lodging, and living expenses while being rehabilitated.

16. 13 MEDICAID

Medicaid provides health care benefits for the financially needy. It is basically a state program with some federal financial support. Medicaid is designed to provide increased assistance to those who are unable to pay for their medical needs. For persons age 65 or over, Medicaid principally supplements Medicare for those who cannot pay the expenses not covered by Medicare. For not eligible for Medicare, it provides medical assistance for certain categories of people who are medically needy—the blind, the disabled, families with dependent children, or medically needy children under age 21.

Medicaid is a federal-state program. The federal government encourages states to increase medical assistance to the indigent, regardless of age, by paying one-half of the administration cost of state medical assistance programs and 50 to 80% of the fees to the providers of services to the needy. The actual federal matching proposition varies inversely with the state average per capita income; therefore, the poorer states receive the larger federal grants.

Generally, Medicaid helps to pay for medical services that the patient cannot pay for. Thus, Medicaid covers such services as hospitalizations, physician's services, diagnostic testing, pregnancies, and others.

In addition, Medicaid also serves as a supplement to Medicare in some situations. For example, Medicare currently offers extremely limited coverage for nursing home care. Often, Medicaid will supplement these limited benefits by paying for nursing home expenses. Other health care expenses not completely covered by Medicare may be paid for by Medicaid.

16. 14 SUMMARY

In this lesson, you learned about:

- the risk that health insurance is designed to protect against;
- the 12 types of loss that health insurance may be purchased to guard against;
- the difference between a limited policy and other health policies and six types of limited policies;
- the six environments where physicians might see patients;
- the difference between reimbursement, fee-for-service, and capitation payment;

- the role of Blue Cross/Blue Shield organizations, how they differ from commercial insurers, the corporate structure they usually employ, and the types of coverage and benefits they offer;
- how health maintenance organizations (HMOs) are different from traditional insurers and the role government had in promoting the development of HMOs;
- the four typical HMO structures;
- the difference between open- and closed-panel HMOs;
- the difference between basic and supplemental HMO services, and what generally is included as basic, and what may be included as supplemental;
- the following HMO-related terms: co-payment, exclusion, limitation, gatekeeper, open enrollment, quality assurance, open-ended HMO, and open-access HMO;
- what an HMO's grievance system is designed to do and how it must function;
- practices that HMOs are commonly prohibited from engaging in;
- the basic characteristics of preferred provider organizations (PPOs), point-of service plans, exclusive provider organizations, and multiple option plans;
- how self-funding works, what a stop-loss contract is, and the advantages and disadvantages of self-insurance;
- what a 501(c)(9) trust is and when it is used;
- the basic characteristics of cafeteria plans, medical savings accounts, multiple employer trusts, multiple employer welfare arrangements, blanket policies, and franchise policies;
- the major statutory health insurance programs offered by the federal government and state governments;
- the types of benefits provided by Social Security;
- who is eligible for workers' compensation and the types of benefits provided under workers' compensation;
- the limits that apply to income benefits under workers' compensation; and
- who qualifies for Medicaid, the intent of the program, and how it functions.

UNIT TEST

1. Julia has a policy that will pay any expenses she incurs as the result of in-hospital medical treatment, as well as some of the expenses she incurs on an outpatient basis. Julia probably has a
   A. disability income policy
   B. medical expense insurance policy
   C. long-term care policy
   D. hospital income insurance policy

2. George has a policy that will provide him an income if he is disabled from illness or injury and recuperating at home. George probably has a
   A. disability income policy
   B. medical expense insurance policy
   C. long-term care policy
   D. hospital income insurance policy

3. George's brother, Jerry, has a policy that will provide him an income if he is disabled from illness or injury, but only if he is confined to a hospital. George's brother probably has a
   A. disability income policy
   B. medical expense insurance policy
   C. long-term care policy
   D. hospital income insurance policy

4. Between George and his brother, Jerry, who has the more limited policy?
   A. George
   B. Jerry
   C. Neither; both policies probably have the same limitations
   D. It is not possible to tell from the information provided

5. The main difference between traditional health insurance arrangements and HMOs is that
   A. traditional health insurance companies provide both the health care service and the health care financing, but HMOs provide only the health care financing
   B. traditional health care insurance companies provide both the health care service and the health care financing, but HMOs provide only the health care service
   C. HMOs provide both the health care service and the health care financing, but traditional health care insurance companies provide only the financing
   D. HMOs provide both the health care service and the health care financing, but traditional health care insurance companies provide only the service

6. Which of the following types of health care insurers is an example of a producers' cooperative?
   A. Urgent care center
   B. Blue Cross/Blue Shield
   C. Commercial insurer
   D. Skilled nursing facility

7. The Hoosier HMO contracts with an independent medical group that specializes in a variety of medical services to provide those services to HMO subscribers. The Hoosier HMO is structured a(n)
   A. staff model HMO
   B. network model HMO
   C. group model HMO
   D. individual practice association model HMO

8. The Albuquerque HMO's contracting physicians are paid employees working on the staff of the HMO, operating in a clinic setting at the HMO's physical facilities. The Albuquerque HMO operates as a(n)
   A. staff model HMO
   B. network model HMO
   C. group model HMO
   D. individual practice association model HMO

9. Star HMO contracts with 14 medical groups to increase accessibility to providers as a convenience for subscribers. Each of the medical groups is paid on a capitation basis to provide services to Star's subscribers. The Star HMO operates as a(n)
   A. staff model HMO
   B. network model HMO
   C. group model HMO
   D. individual practice association model HMO

10. The Provider's Choice HMO was started by a group of individual physicians who each operate out of their own office. The physicians are paid on a fee-for-service basis with the fees negotiated in advance. Provider's Choice HMO operates as a(n)
    A. staff model HMO
    B. network model HMO
    C. group model HMO
    D. individual practice association model HMO

11. Gwyneth's HMO requires that she receive health care services from a specified, limited number of health care providers chosen by the HMO. Gwyneth's HMO is
    A. open panel
    B. closed panel
    C. choice panel
    D. guarded panel

12. All of the following are examples of managed care plans EXCEPT
    A. health maintenance organizations
    B. preferred provider organizations
    C. indemnity arrangements
    D. point-of-service plans

13. A method of payment in which a provider is paid a specific fee monthly for each subscriber is known as
    A. indemnity
    B. fee-for-service
    C. managed care
    D. capitation

14. Calvin is hit by a car while traveling out of state. When the bill for his emergency services arrives, Calvin's HMO will probably
    A. pay for the services, even though they were incurred out of network, because emergency coverage is a basic health care service
    B. deny the claim because the services were out of network
    C. pay the claim only if the HMO had an affiliation agreement with the facility where the services were provided
    D. pay the claim if the HMO had an affiliation agreement with the facility where the services were provided, or if there is no affiliated facility within 50 miles

15. Best Cleaners has a health plan that provides its employees with a high-deductible medical indemnity plan and an account funded by the business, which employees can use to pay for medical expenses throughout the year or withdraw at the end of the year as taxable income. The plan is probably a
    A. cafeteria plan
    B. medical savings account
    C. multiple employer trust
    D. third-party administrator

16. Bob's Balloons has a plan in which its employees can select benefits from a variety of coverage options based on individual and family needs. The plan is probably a
    A. cafeteria plan
    B. medical savings account
    C. multiple employer trust
    D. third-party administrator

17. The Gargantuan Garage company funds its own claims but uses another company to make sure the plan is run correctly, acting as a liaison between the insurer and the employer. This arrangement is probably a
    A. cafeteria plan
    B. medical savings account
    C. multiple employer trust
    D. third-party administrator

18. Which of the following individuals would probably qualify for Social Security disability benefits?
    A. George, a ski instructor who breaks his leg
    B. Carl, who becomes ill with a viral infection and is not expected to be able to work for the next 6 months
    C. Mike, a mechanic who loses his dominant hand in an accident
    D. John, who experiences serious early-onset Alzheimer's and is unable to remember how to get to work

19. Under workers' compensation, the permanent total disability benefit, while subject to minimum and maximum dollar amounts, is generally
    A. 50% of weekly wages
    B. 66.66% of weekly wages
    C. 70.5% of weekly wages
    D. 75% of weekly wages

20. Under workers' compensation, individuals with partial disabilities who are able to perform some work are eligible to receive
    A. no benefits
    B. 66.66% of weekly wages, subject to minimum and maximum dollar amounts
    C. the entire wage loss, subject to minimum and maximum dollar amounts
    D. a percentage of the wage loss, subject to minimum and maximum dollar amounts

ANSWERS AND RATIONALES TO UNIT TEST

1. **B**. A medical expense insurance policy pays for inpatient treatment and some outpatient expenses.
2. **A**. A disability income policy provides income to an individual disabled by illness or injury.
3. **D**. A hospital income insurance policy provides income to an indvidual who is disabled by illness or injury and confined to a hospital.
4. **B**. Jerry's policy pays only if he is confined to a hospital.
5. **C**.
6. **B**. Blue Cross/Blue Shield is an example of a producers' cooperative.
7. **C**. A group model HMO contracts with an independent medical group to provide services to its subscribers.
8. **A**.
9. **B**. A network model HMO contracts with medical groups, which it pays to provide services to its subscribers.
10. **D**. An individual practice association model HMO consists of individual physicians operating out of their own offices.
11. **B**. A closed-panel HMO specifies a limited number of health care providers from which its subscribers may receive services.
12. **C**. Indemnity arrangements are not managed care plans.
13. **D**. A method of payment in which a provider is paid a specific fee monthly for each subscriber is known as capitation.
14. **A**. Calvin's HMO will probably pay for the services, even though they were incurred out of network, because emergency coverage is a basic health care service.
15. **B**. A medical savings account is funded by an employer and can be used to pay for medical expenses or withdrawn at the end of the year.
16. **A**. A cafeteria plan provides a variety of coverage options based on an individual and family needs.
17. **D**. A third-party administrator funds its own claims but uses another company to make sure the plan is run correctly.
18. **D**. Social Security disability benefits are payable only to a totally disabled person who will not be able to return to work.
19. **B**. Under workers' compensation, the permanent total disability benefit, although subject to minimum and maximum dollar amounts, is generally 66.66% of weekly wages.
20. **D**. Under workers' compensation, individuals with partial disabilities who are able to perform some work are eligible to receive a percentage of the wage loss, subject to minimum and maximum dollar amounts.

UNIT

17

Policy Underwriting, Issuance, and Delivery

17. 1 UNDERWRITING OBJECTIVES

Health insurance underwriting is the process of selecting, classifying, and rating risks. Most companies offering health policies have a variety of policies available, and underwriting standards for each policy are usually established. Low-limit policies with limited coverages do not require the underwriting that broad coverage policies with high limits do; the greater the company's exposure, the more careful the underwriter must be. Generally, underwriting is more restrictive for individual than for group policies. The underwriter's principal functions are to review applications to eliminate those that do not meet underwriting standards, thus reducing adverse selection, and to classify risks to establish benefits and corresponding premium.

Certain underwriting factors for health insurance may be more or less important than for the underwriting of life insurance. For example, an individual with a serious back ailment presents a major risk for the health insurance underwriter because of the danger of such a chronic condition creating several expensive claim situations. However, for the life insurance underwriter, this same condition may be of little significance as a bad back is not likely to affect the individual's mortality.

17. 2 LEARNING OBJECTIVES

After completing this lesson, you will be able to:

- explain the underwriting objectives applicable to health insurance;
- define *earned* and *unearned* premium;
- list possible payment modes for health insurance, and explain which is used most frequently and which results in the highest overall cost to the insured;
- explain when health insurance policies go into effect;
- define the policy term for health insurance;
- list and explain three reasons for delivering a policy in person;
- define replacement and the advantages and disadvantages of replacing health insurance policies;
- define *fiduciary* and explain how it applies to health insurance producers; and
- summarize health insurance producers' responsibilities.

17. 3 PREMIUM PAYMENTS

17. 3. 1 Definition of Premium

The premium is a sum of money the insured pays the insurer in exchange for or in consideration of the benefits or indemnities provided in the policy.

Because a premium is paid in consideration of the benefits provided in the policy, it is frequently called just that, a consideration. So the premium is the consideration paid for the benefits provided by the policy.

17. 3. 2 Earned and Unearned Premium

Premium payment frequency varies, but regardless of frequency, the insured is always paying for the upcoming period. That is, insurance premiums are paid in advance.

Suppose Kathryn's health insurance premium is $500 per year, which she pays in full on January 1. Because the $500 covers an entire year, the insurer earns the premium as the time passes, having both earned and unearned premium on hand during the policy term. The illustration shows how it looks as the year passes.

Unearned and Earned Premium

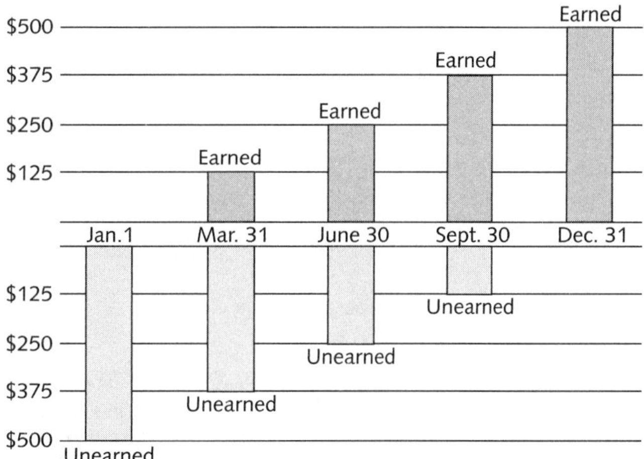

As shown in the illustration, as of March 31, the insurer has provided protection from January 1 through March 31. At this point, $125 represents the amount paid for the period for which protection has been provided, so $125 is the earned premium.

The remaining $375 of premium that Kathryn has paid is, as of March 31, the unearned premium.

17. 3. 3 Payment Modes

In the insurance industry, **mode** of premium payment refers to the frequency with which premiums are paid. Payments may be made in five ways:

- Annually—once a year
- Semiannually—twice a year
- Quarterly—once every three months
- Monthly—once a month
- Weekly—once a week

Of these five modes, the least-used frequency for individual policies is weekly. You probably know that in group health plans employers often deduct the employees' shares weekly, but it is likely that the employer actually sends the premium to the insurer less frequently.

Insurers generally calculate premiums on an annual basis. If the insured wants to pay by any of the other modes, the premium increases slightly as the frequency increases. The increases allow the insurer to recoup (1) the additional billing and handling costs and (2) the lost interest the insurer could have earned by having the full annual premium to invest all at once.

So, for example, a monthly premium mode results in a premium that is somewhat higher than a semiannual mode. An annual premium mode also results in a premium that is somewhat lower than a quarterly mode.

17. 3. 4 Initial Premium

The **initial premium**, as the name implies, is the first premium the applicant pays to place the policy into effect. A health insurance policy goes into force when:

- the initial premium has been paid; and
- the policy is delivered to the insured.

If the initial premium was paid with the application and the applicant satisfies all of the conditions of the conditional receipt, coverage takes effect just as if the policy had already been issued.

A producer should always try to obtain the initial premium with an application and submit the entire package for underwriting. This affords faster protection to applicants, and applicants are less likely to change their minds about purchasing policies once they have money invested in them.

The important thing to remember is that coverage never applies until the insured has paid for it. If the initial premium does not accompany the application, the premium must be collected at policy delivery along with a signed statement that the insured continues to be in good health. The policy is then effective as of the date stated in the policy.

When the policy is delivered, the producer should explain the provisions, point out any exclusions, and—very importantly—go over any significant rating that affects the insured's coverage and premium payments.

17. 3. 5 Policy Effective Date

Although it is generally true that a policy is effective when the initial premium has been paid and the policy delivered (or under the conditions of a conditional receipt), there is a better way for a producer to respond when asked when a particular policy takes effect.

The best approach is to state that the policy takes effect on the date specified in the policy as the effective date.

Remember that accident coverages usually take effect immediately when the policy is issued, whereas sickness coverages may require a probationary period. Therefore, different coverages under the same policy might have different effective dates.

17. 3. 6 Policy Term

Once a health insurance policy becomes effective, it will stay in force for the period for which the premium has been paid, unless the insurer or the insured cancels it. In other words, the policy will stay in force for a specified period or term.

The length of the term is governed by the length of time for which coverage is purchased by the premium payment. If a policy calls for annual premium payment, for example, one year is the term of the policy. If premiums are paid semiannually, the term extends for each six-month period for which the premium is paid.

17. 3. 7 Policy Fee

When a policy is issued, some companies charge a **policy fee**, which is generally a flat amount that helps defray such expenses as acquisition costs, producer commissions, administration, and maintenance of the policy. There are two ways a policy fee might be handled.

Usually, the policy fee is added to the premium and paid annually. For example, the company might charge an annual premium of $300 plus a $15 policy fee, for a total annual premium of $315, which the insured will pay every year.

Some companies, on the other hand, may charge a policy fee only once—at the time the policy is issued. For example, suppose the annual premium is $300 and the policy fee is $25. The insured will pay an initial premium of $325, which includes the one-time policy fee, but for succeeding years will pay only $300.

17. 4 DELIVERING THE POLICY

The surest way to be certain the policy is delivered is to do it personally. In addition to knowing the policy has been delivered, the producer has the following opportunities.

- The producer can explain the policy. It is important in health insurance for the policyowner to have basic understanding of what is and is not covered. With today's high health care costs, it is extremely important for the insured to know what the policy limitations are on the different types of medical expenses covered. Sometimes, policy premiums are higher than standard (rated up) because the insured does not meet certain basic health requirements or is involved in extra hazardous hobbies or avocations. These facts should be explained to avoid future misunderstandings and dissatisfaction. If the premium was not collected with the application, the company may require the producer to obtain a statement of good health from the insured at the time the policy is delivered and the premium is paid.

- The producer can reinforce the relationship and good will that have been established with the client.
- The producer can explain the possible need for additional health or other coverages.

Legally, the policy is considered delivered when it is mailed or turned over to the policyowner or someone acting on the policyowner's behalf. Some companies mail policies directly to policyowners; however, many prefer that the producer make a personal delivery. In some cases, a **constructive delivery** is deemed to occur when the insurer mails a policy to its producer for actual delivery to the policyowner, because the insurer has issued the policy and released it for delivery. However, a legal delivery has not yet occurred if the insurer requires personal delivery for verification of good health at the time of delivery, or if the policy is being provided to the applicant merely to review and inspect at that time and not necessarily to buy.

17. 5 SERVICING THE POLICY

In many industries, closing the sale means the end of the producer/consumer transaction. However, this is not so in insurance. Insurance policies require ongoing customer service throughout the policy period. Competition in the industry is another incentive to provide good customer service because it can make all the difference at renewal time. Good customer service makes insureds feel more comfortable doing business with you and makes them more likely to renew with your agency. Proper service of insurance policies also results in referrals, additional coverage, good public relations, and reduced errors and omissions exposure.

17. 6 REPLACEMENT

Producers attempting to replace the insured's current policy with a new policy need to take special care not to mislead the insured or provide coverage that is to the insured's detriment. Of particular concern is the fact that health conditions covered under an insured's existing policy may not be covered under a replacement policy because of the exclusion of preexisting conditions, or new waiting periods may be established.

A producer recommending replacement should give special attention to the exclusions and limitations in the proposed policy, compared with the existing policy. Not all policies cover the same things. If the contracts are different, the replacement policy might not provide the same coverages or the same level of benefits as the existing policy.

A producer should consider the underwriting requirements of the replacing insurer. Will the insurer cover the insured on a basis as favorable to the applicant as the present insurer? Will the underwriter accept the risk at a similar rate, or will differences in the insured's health or the underwriter's requirements result in a higher premium rate?

Some states have passed **no loss/no gain** legislation, which requires that when health insurance is replaced, ongoing claims under the former policy must continue to be paid under the new policy, thereby overriding any preexisting conditions exclusion. In replacing group health coverage, a transfer of benefits statement ensures that benefits provided under the old policy continue under the new policy.

One would assume there is no benefit to the insured (and great benefit to the producer) when an insurance policy undergoes **intracompany replacement**—that is, the policy is replaced by a similar policy with the same insurer. Therefore, most general agency and producer contracts specify that the producer's commission will be limited to a percentage of the increase in premium only when a policy is replaced within the same company. This discourages the producer from replacing existing policies with new policies from the same insurer unless the amounts of coverage (and thus the premium) are substantially increased.

Because the elderly are extremely vulnerable and often victimized insurance prospects, and are most susceptible to being penalized by preexisting conditions limitations, producers should be aware that there are often more-restrictive regulations for replacing Medicare supplement policies.

Certainly, there are legitimate circumstances when replacement of a policy makes sense and should be recommended—for example, when broader coverage or higher benefits can be obtained at a lower rate and preexisting conditions and waiting periods are not issues.

However, a producer needs to be very careful in recommending a change in policies or carriers when any potential factors could lead to an uninsured loss that might otherwise have been covered. Producers need to be aware of their own errors and omissions liability, particularly in the area of replacement. Replacement is not illegal, but it is heavily regulated.

17. 7 PROFESSIONALISM AND ETHICS

All business transactions are based to a certain extent on trust. When it comes to insurance, the trust factor is especially significant. When asked what factors matter most in a financial advisor, consumers choose ethical performance more than twice as often as financial performance. Ethics and professionalism are critical components of a successful career as an insurance producer.

Ethics means setting a standard of conduct or behavior based on established values. Insurance producers and other industry employees have long sought to distinguish themselves as professionals. A professional is defined as a person in an occupation requiring an advanced level of training, knowledge, or skill. *Professionals* enjoy privileges commensurate with their skills, but they also have higher responsibilities in caring for others because of the title of professional. *Professionals* relate to their clients in a way that reflects well on the entire industry. The highest standard of service is provided by preparing for new clients long before even meeting them.

17. 7. 1 Fiduciary Responsibility

Insurance producers have a **fiduciary** duty to just about any person or organization with whom they come into contact as a part of the day-to-day business of transacting insurance. By definition, a **fiduciary** is a person in a position of financial trust. Attorneys, accountants, trust officers, and insurance producers are all considered fiduciaries.

As a fiduciary, producers have an obligation to act in the best interest of the insured. The producer must be knowledgeable about the features and provisions of various insurance policies and know the use of these insurance contracts. The producer must be able to explain the important features of these policies to the insured. The producer must recognize the importance of dealing with the general public's financial needs and problems and offering solutions to these problems through the purchase of insurance products.

As a fiduciary, the producer must know and comply with the state's insurance laws. Many of these laws are for consumer protection. It is the producer's duty to comply with these laws and protect the interest of the insured at all times.

17. 7. 2 Summary of the Producer's Responsibilities

The insurance producer is a key person in the process of marketing, underwriting, and delivery of insurance policies. As a marketing representative of the insurer, the producer has a responsibility to represent and market the insurer's products in an ethical and professional manner. This requires knowledge of various insurance products, awareness of a prospect's insurance needs and problems, and the ability to solve these needs with the proper insurance products.

The producer also has a responsibility to be aware of insurance laws that pertain to marketing of insurance products, such as state-required standards for advertising and sales literature. In general, all advertising, sales presentations, and illustrations must be truthful and may not misrepresent or omit material information.

As part of the underwriting process, the producer is the primary source of underwriting information. It is the producer's duty to accurately and thoroughly complete all applications for insurance, collect initial premiums, and promptly submit them to the company. In addition, the producer is responsible for providing the insurance applicant with privacy notices and information such as the Notice of Insurance Information Practices and for providing the insurance applicant with necessary receipts for the initial premium collected.

Another objective of the producer as a field underwriter is to help protect the insurer from adverse risks. If an applicant is substandard, the producer is responsible for delivering the substandard policy and explaining its limitations or extra premium to the applicant.

17. 8 SUMMARY

In this lesson, you learned about:

- the underwriting objectives applicable to health insurance;
- earned and unearned premium;
- possible payment modes for health insurance and which is used most frequently and which results in the highest overall cost to the insured;
- when health insurance policies go into effect;
- the policy term for health insurance;
- three reasons for delivering a policy in person;
- replacement and the advantages and disadvantages of replacing health insurance policies;
- fiduciary and how that applies to health insurance producers; and
- health insurance producers' responsibilities.

UNIT TEST

1. The sum of money the insured pays the insurer in exchange for the benefits provided in the policy is the
   A. co-payment
   B. premium
   C. indemnity
   D. capitation

2. Ally pays for her health insurance monthly. Her identical twin, Georgia, has the same policy, but pays annually. Which of them probably pays more for her policy?
   A. Ally probably pays more.
   B. Georgia probably pays more.
   C. They probably pay the same.
   D. It is not possible to determine from the information provided.

3. Health insurance coverage never applies until
   A. the policy is delivered
   B. an underwriting decision is made
   C. the application is reviewed by underwriting
   D. the insured has paid for the policy

4. Once a health insurance policy becomes effective, unless it is canceled, it will stay in force for
   A. 1 year
   B. 6 months
   C. the length of the term
   D. indefinitely

5. Legally, the policy is considered delivered in all of the following situations EXCEPT
   A. when the policy is approved by the company
   B. when the policy is mailed to the policyowner
   C. when the policy is turned over to the policyowner
   D. when the policy is turned over to someone acting on behalf of the policyowner

6. An insurer might require personal delivery
   A. to ensure the policy goes to the right person
   B. for verification of the continued good health of the insured at the time of delivery
   C. to ensure the correct policy is delivered
   D. to verify information listed on the application

7. No loss/no gain legislation requires a replacing policy to
   A. have exactly the same premium as the policy it replaces
   B. have exactly the same limits of coverage as the policy it replaces
   C. continue to pay claims ongoing under the policy it replaces
   D. continue to use the same producer to manage the policy as the policy it replaces

8. A statement that ensures benefits provided under the old policy will continue under the new policy is
   A. a transfer of benefits statement
   B. a continuation of benefits statement
   C. a preexisting conditions coverage statement
   D. a replacement statement

9. Restrictions applying to the replacement of Medicare supplement policies are
   A. often less restrictive than regulations applying to the replacement of other policies
   B. generally the same as regulations applying to the replacement of other policies
   C. often more restrictive than regulations applying to the replacement of other policies
   D. prohibited entirely by federal law

ANSWERS AND RATIONALES TO UNIT TEST

1. **B.**
2. **A.** Ally probably pays more because premiums increase as frequency increases.
3. **D.** Health insurance coverage never applies until the insured has paid for the policy.
4. **C.**
5. **A.** The policy is not considered delivered when the policy is approved by the company.
6. **B.** An insurer might require personal delivery for verification of the continued good health of the insured at the time of delivery.
7. **C.** No loss/no gain legislation requires a replacing policy to continue to pay claims ongoing under the policy it replaces.
8. **A.** A statement ensuring that benefits provided under the old policy will continue under the new policy is a transfer of benefits statement.
9. **C.** Restrictions applying to the replacement of Medicare supplement policies are often more restrictive than regulations applying to the replacement of other policies.

UNIT

18

Policy Provisions

18. 1 INTRODUCTION

Because both state insurance laws and insurance policies vary greatly, an attempt has been made to make health insurance policies conform to certain standard regulations. To accomplish this, all states have adopted the Uniform Individual Accident and Sickness Policy Provisions Law. Nearly every state has modified the law to some extent, but all have adopted it in principle.

The law includes 12 mandatory provisions that must be included in individual health insurance policies and 11 optional provisions. Each of the mandatory provisions must be included in each policy, usually in a section of the policy titled "Mandatory or Required Provisions." Insurance companies need not use the exact wording of the provisions, but any variations must be at least as favorable to the insured as the original statutory wording. Each provision is presented as it appears in the law, followed by a short discussion of the content. Since the provision language is somewhat stilted legalese, don't be surprised if you have to read a provision more than once.

18. 2 LEARNING OBJECTIVES

After completing this lesson, you will be able to do the following:

- describe and explain the purpose of the following mandatory policy provisions;
- entire contract, changes;
- time limit of certain defenses;
- grace period;
- reinstatement;
- notice of claims;
- claim forms;
- proof of loss;
- time of payment of claims;
- payment of claims;
- physical examination and autopsy;
- legal actions;
- change of beneficiary;
- describe and explain the purpose of the following optional policy provisions:
  - — change of occupation,
  - — misstatement of age,

- other insurance with this insurer,
- other insurance with other insurers (1 and 2),
- relation of earnings to insurance,
- unpaid premium,
- cancellation,
- conformity with state statutes,
- illegal occupation, and
- intoxicants and narcotics; and

- describe and explain the purpose of the following other policy provisions:
  - the policy face,
  - free look,
  - insuring clause,
  - consideration clause,
  - renewability,
  - benefit payment clause,
  - exclusions and reductions,
  - preexisting conditions,
  - nonoccupational coverage, and
  - case management provisions.

18. 3 REQUIRED POLICY PROVISIONS

18. 3. 1 Required Provision 1: Entire Contract, Changes

Here is the exact wording of the provision.

This policy, including the endorsements and the attached papers, if any, constitutes the entire contract of insurance. No change in this policy shall be valid until approved by an executive officer of the insurer and unless such approval be endorsed hereon or attached hereto. No agent has authority to change this policy or to waive any of its provisions.

This provision defines an **entire contract** as:

- the insurance policy;
- endorsements, if any; and
- attachments, if any.

So, an entire contract means the policy itself, any endorsements, and any attached papers, such as the application and any riders. Nothing else is part of the contract.

An agent or producer may not change a policy or waive any of its provisions, but changes may be made if they are approved by an executive officer of the insurance company. The insured will be aware of any such changes because they will be endorsed on or attached to the policy.

18. 3. 2 Required Provision 2: Time Limit on Certain Defenses, Incontestability

A. *After two years from the date of issue of this policy, no misstatements, except fraudulent misstatements, made by the applicant in the application for such policy shall be used to void the policy or to deny a claim for loss incurred or disability (as defined in the policy) commencing after the expiration of such two-year period.*

B. *No claim for loss incurred or disability (as defined in the policy) commencing after two years from the date of issue of this policy shall be reduced or denied on the ground that a disease or physical condition, not excluded from coverage by name or specific description effective on the date of loss, had existed prior to the effective date of coverage of this policy.*

Unless an insured's misstatements are fraudulent, after two years from the date the policy is issued, the policy becomes incontestable. Part A says that no material misstatements in the application (except for fraud) can be used to void the policy or deny a claim after two years have passed (three years in some states). Fraud can void the health insurance contract whenever it is found and can be proven by the health insurer.

Part B states that after two years, the policy cannot be voided, a claim may not be denied, and benefits may not be reduced on the grounds that an illness or a condition was preexisting. This does not prevent an insurer from specifically excluding coverage for a certain condition, but to be excluded the condition must be named or specifically described in the policy when it is written.

18. 3. 3 Required Provision 3: Grace Period

A grace period of __ days (the period varies according to premium payment frequency: 7 days for weekly premium policies; 10 days for monthly premium policies; 31 days for all other policies) will be granted for the payment of each premium falling due after the first premium, during which grace period the policy shall continue in force.

A policy that contains a cancellation provision may add, at the end of the above provision, "*subject to the right of the insurer to cancel in accordance with the cancellation provision hereof.*"

A policy in which the insurer reserves the right to refuse any renewal shall state, at the beginning of the above provision, the following: "*unless not less than five days prior to the premium due date the insurer has delivered to the insured, or has mailed to the last address as shown by the records of the insurer, written notice of its intention not to renew this policy beyond the period for which the premium has been accepted.*"

The required grace period depends on how often the insured pays the policy premiums, as illustrated.

Required Grace Period, by Payment Frequency

Weekly Premium Policies Require a 7-day Grace Period							Monthly Premium Policies Require a 10-day Grace Period							All Other Policies Require a 31-day Grace Period						
JANUARY							JANUARY							JANUARY						
S	M	T	W	T	F	S	S	M	T	W	T	F	S	S	M	T	W	T	F	S
		1	2	3	4	5			1	2	3	4	5			1	2	3	4	5
6	7	8	9	10	11	12	6	7	8	9	10	11	12	6	7	8	9	10	11	12
13	14	15	16	17	18	19	13	14	15	16	17	18	19	13	14	15	16	17	18	19
20	21	22	23	24	25	26	20	21	22	23	24	25	26	20	21	22	23	24	25	26
27	28	29	30	31			27	28	29	30	31			27	28	29	30	31		

Insurers must allow the insured a period of grace for premium payment. This is a specified time following the premium due date during which coverage remains intact. During a grace period, the company continues coverage in full force and will accept the premium from the policyowner just as if it were not late.

If a policy is cancelable, the grace period is subject to the policy's cancellation provision. In an optionally renewable policy the company has decided not to renew, the company must follow certain steps to avoid having the grace period affect its right not to renew. The insurer is required to mail written notice of its intention not to renew to the insured's last known address at least five days before the premium due date. The insurer must keep a record of the mailing in order to protect its rights as well as the rights of the insured.

18. 3. 4 Required Provision 4: Reinstatement

Before you read this provision, let's cover some information not specifically mentioned in the provision itself. The insured, unlike the insurer, may cancel a policy at any time. In addition, the insured can simply refuse or fail to pay the premium when it is next due. When this occurs, we say that the policy has lapsed. Whether the policy is canceled by the insurer or the insured or it lapses, the end result is the same: the coverage terminates.

Because this provision is quite long, we'll cover it in two parts. Here is the first portion.

If any renewal premium is not paid within the time granted the insured for payment, a subsequent acceptance of premium by the insurer or by any agent duly authorized by the insurer to accept such premium, without requiring in connection therewith an application for reinstatement, shall reinstate the policy; provided, however, that if the insurer or such agent requires an application for reinstatement and issues a conditional receipt for the premium tendered, the policy will be reinstated upon approval of such application by the insurer or, lacking such approval, upon the 45th day following the date of such conditional receipt unless the insurer has previously notified the insured in writing of its disapproval of such application.

According to this part of the provision, with certain exceptions, a lapsed policy is reinstated when either the company or the company's authorized agent accepts subsequent premiums.

However, an application for reinstatement might be required, and a conditional receipt could be issued to the insured for any premium payment. The insurer will then generally notify the applicant whether or not the policy has been reinstated, but if the insurer does not so notify the applicant, the policy is automatically reinstated on the 45th day after the date of the receipt.

Here is the second portion of the reinstatement provision.

The reinstated policy shall cover only loss resulting from such accidental injury as may be sustained after the date of reinstatement and loss due to such sickness as may begin more than 10 days after such date. In all other respects, the insured and insurer shall have the same rights thereunder as they had under the policy immediately before the due date of the defaulted premium, subject to any provisions endorsed hereon or attached hereto in connection with the reinstatement. Any premium accepted in connection with the reinstatement shall be applied to a period for which premium has not been previously paid, but not to any period more than 60 days prior to the date of reinstatement.

The last sentence of that paragraph may be omitted from policies guaranteed renewable to age 50, or if issued after age 44, guaranteed renewable for at least five years.

Once the policy is reinstated, there is:

- a 10-day waiting period for sickness coverages; and
- no waiting period for accident coverages.

Otherwise, both the insurer and the insured have all the same rights each had the day before the policy lapsed, subject to any endorsements or riders attached at the time of reinstatement.

18. 3. 5 Required Provision 5: Notice of Claim

This lengthy provision is also presented in two parts. Here is the first portion.

Written notice of claim must be given to the insurer within 20 days after occurrence or commencement of any loss covered by the policy, or as soon thereafter as is reasonably possible. Notice given by or in behalf of the insured or the beneficiary to the insurer at ___________ (insert the location of such office as the insurer may designate for the purpose), or to any authorized agent of the insurer, with information sufficient to identify the insured, shall be deemed notice to the insurer.

When a claim arises, certain stipulations apply. If reasonably possible, the insured must give written notice of claim to the insurer within 20 days after the loss occurs. The insured may send the notice either to the address the insurer provides or to the agent.

Although the term *reasonably* is not defined, an example will illustrate one possibility. An insured is injured in an accident and remains in a coma for five weeks, thus failing to provide written notice of claim within the required 20 days. The company is still liable for the claim because it could not reasonably have required the claim to be filed during the time the insured was in a coma.

Here is the remainder of notice-of-claim provision.

Policies providing loss-of-time benefits payable for at least two years may insert the following between the first and second sentences of the above provision.

Subject to the qualifications set forth below, if the insured suffers loss of time on account of disability for which indemnity may be payable for at least two years, he shall, at least once in every six months after having given notice of claim, give to the insurer notice of continuance of said disability, except in the event of legal incapacity. The period of six months following any filing of proof by the insured or any payment by the insurer on account of such claim or any denial of liability in whole or in part by the insurer shall be excluded in applying this provision. Delay in the giving of such notice shall not impair the insured's right to any indemnity which would otherwise have accrued during the period of six months preceding the date on which such notice is actually given.

The essence of this provision is that if the policy provides disability income for an extended period, the insurer can require that the insured provide, every six months, written notice that the claim is continuing. This provision does not apply when the insured suffers a legal incapacity.

18. 3. 6 Required Provision 6: Claim Forms

The insurer, upon receipt of a notice of claim, will furnish to the claimant such forms as are usually furnished by it for filing proofs of loss. If such forms are not furnished within 15 days after the giving of such notice, the claimant shall be deemed to have complied with the requirements of this policy as to proof of loss upon submitting, within the time fixed in the policy for filing proofs of loss, written proof covering the occurrence, the character and the extent of the loss for which claim is made.

When an insurer receives a notice of claim, it should furnish the insured with forms to provide proof of loss within 15 days. If the insurer fails to do so, however, the insured is required to act to protect the claim by filing written proof of loss detailing the occurrence, the character, and the extent of the loss.

18. 3. 7 Required Provision 7: Proof of Loss

Written proof of loss must be furnished to the insurer at its said office in case of claim for loss for which this policy provides any periodic payment contingent upon continuing loss within 90 days after the termination of the period for which the insurer is liable, and in case of claims for any other loss within 90 days after the date of such loss. Failure to furnish such proof within the time required shall not invalidate nor reduce any claim if it was not reasonably possible to give such proof within such time, provided such proof is furnished as soon as reasonably possible and in no event, except in the absence of legal capacity, later than one year from the time proof is otherwise required.

The next illustration shows the difference between filing a proof of loss when benefits are paid periodically versus filing proof for a one-time, non-periodic loss as provided in the provision.

Filing Proof of Loss

Insured Xavier	Insured Yvonne
Receives periodic payments of disability income from May 1 through October 11.	Submits a claim for hospital expenses after an accident at home on April 25.
Must file proofs of loss within 90 days after October 11—the date the insurer's liability for payment has ended.	Must file proofs of loss within 90 days after April 25—the date of the loss since no periodic benefits are involved.
Both Insureds	
Have up to a year following the required filing dates to file proofs of loss if they cannot reasonably do so earlier. Legal incapacity excuses this limit.	

Normally, written proofs of loss must be furnished within 90 days after the date of loss. However, when the claim involves periodic payments because of a continuing loss, proofs must be furnished within 90 days after the end of the period for which the company is liable.

If it was not reasonably possible for the insured to provide proofs of loss within the time required, the claim is not invalidated. Nevertheless, unless the insured suffers legal incapacity, proofs of loss must be furnished no later than one year from the date they were otherwise due.

18. 3. 8 Required Provision 8: Time of Payment of Claims

Indemnities payable under this policy for any loss other than loss for which this policy provides any periodic payment will be paid immediately upon receipt of due written proof of such loss. Subject to due written proof of loss, all accrued indemnities for loss for which this policy provides periodic payment will be paid _______ (insert period for payment which must not be less frequently than monthly), and any balance remaining unpaid upon the termination of liability will be paid immediately upon receipt of due written proof.

According to this provision, except for claims involving periodic payments over a specified time span, the insurer must make the payment immediately after receiving proof of loss.

Payment of periodic indemnities (for disability, for instance) must be made at least monthly.

Let's look at an example of how this provision works.

Example

Serena has been receiving $700 a month for a total disability, but she is able to return to work two weeks after her most recent indemnity payment. She has two more weeks' benefits coming. She files a final proof of loss, including statements from her doctor (that she has been released) and her employer (that she has returned to work). Upon receipt of this final proof of loss, the insurer must pay the final two weeks' indemnity immediately.

Notice that in every case, the insured must provide written proof of loss to the insurer.

18. 3. 9 Required Provision 9: Payment of Claims

This long provision actually contains both a required portion and two optional paragraphs. Here is the required section.

Indemnity for loss of life will be payable in accordance with the beneficiary designation and the provisions respecting such payment which may be prescribed herein and effective at the time of payment. If no such designation or provision is then effective, such indemnity shall be payable to the estate of the insured. Any other accrued indemnities unpaid at the insured's death may, at the option of the insurer, be paid either to such beneficiary or to such estate. All other indemnities will be payable to the insured.

This required portion of the provision states that:

- death benefits will be paid to the named beneficiary;
- if there is no beneficiary designated, the company will pay the benefit to the insured's estate;
- if the insured was receiving monthly indemnities under the policy and some accrued benefits remain at the time of death, the company may pay these accruals to either the beneficiary or the insured's estate; and
- while the insured is alive, all other benefits are paid to the insured unless otherwise specifically designated in the policy.

Here is the first of the two optional paragraphs that are included in the payment-of-claims provision.

If any indemnity of this policy shall be payable to the estate of the insured, or to an insured or beneficiary who is a minor or otherwise not competent to give a valid release, the insurer may pay such indemnity, up to an amount not exceeding $_____ (insert an amount which shall not exceed $1,000), to any relative by blood or connection by marriage of the insured or beneficiary who is deemed by the insurer to be equitably entitled thereto. Any payment made by the insurer in good faith pursuant to this provision shall fully discharge the insurer to the extent of such payment.

This first optional paragraph is often called the **facility of payment** clause because it makes claim payment easier under the circumstances described. It stipulates two things.

- If the insured or the beneficiary cannot legally release the company from further liability, as when the insured or beneficiary is a minor or is legally incapacitated, the company may pay the benefits to any relative by blood or marriage who is deemed to be entitled to the money.
- The amount paid to this person cannot exceed $1,000.

If a claim is paid under this provision, the payment absolves the company of further liability.

Here is the second of the optional paragraphs that may be included with the payment-of-claims provision.

Subject to any written direction of the insured in the application or otherwise, all or a portion of any indemnities provided by this policy on account of hospital, nursing, medical, or surgical services may, at the insurer's option, and unless the insured requests otherwise in writing not later than the time of filing proofs of such loss, be paid directly to the hospital or person rendering such services, but it is not required that the service be rendered by a particular hospital or person.

According to this second optional paragraph, unless the insured specifically directs otherwise, the company may pay benefits to a hospital or person rendering medical or surgical services. However, the company may not require that the insured enter a specific hospital or see a particular doctor.

18. 3. 10 Required Provision 10: Physical Examination and Autopsy

The insurer at its own expense shall have the right and opportunity to examine the person of the insured when and as often as it may reasonably require during the pendency of a claim hereunder and to make an autopsy in case of death where it is not forbidden by law.

According to this provision, while the insured is alive and receiving benefits, the insurer may require that the insured submit to physical examinations.

If an insured has died, apparently accidentally, the insurer may have an autopsy performed to determine the exact cause of death. However, any applicable state laws that might prevent such an autopsy take precedence.

The insurer is required to pay for examinations or autopsies, and may require only reasonable examinations.

18. 3. 11 Required Provision 11: Legal Actions

No action at law or in equity shall be brought to recover on this policy prior to the expiration of 60 days after written proof of loss has been furnished in accordance with the requirements of this policy. No such action shall be brought after the expiration of three years after the time written proof of loss is required to be furnished.

When written proof of loss has been submitted, the company needs time to investigate the claim and make certain it is valid. To provide the insurer with this time, this provision prohibits the insured from suing the insurer for at least 60 days after filing a written proof of loss.

The maximum time during which suit can be filed is three years after written proof of loss is furnished.

18. 3. 12 Required Provision 12: Change of Beneficiary

Unless the insured makes an irrevocable designation of beneficiary, the right to change of beneficiary is reserved to the insured and the consent of the beneficiary or beneficiaries shall not be requisite to surrender or assignment of this policy or to any change of beneficiary or beneficiaries, or to any other changes in this policy.

The policyowner, who is usually the insured, may name a beneficiary either **revocably**, which means that the insured can change the beneficiary later, or **irrevocably**, which means the beneficiary designation may not be changed.

In other words, the right to change the beneficiary or dispose of the policy or its benefits in any manner one chooses is reserved to the insured unless the insured has named an irrevocable beneficiary.

Example

Ben has named his spouse the beneficiary of the accidental death benefit of his health insurance policy, and he has relinquished his right to change that designation. Now he wants to obtain a large loan, and the lender agrees to make the loan if Ben assigns any payments under his policy to the lender. Ben may assign the policy only with his spouse's permission because she is the irrevocable beneficiary. Ben would not need this permission if his spouse were a revocable beneficiary.

18. 4 OPTIONAL POLICY PROVISIONS

The optional provisions are not required to be included in the policy, but if the subject of any of them is contained in the policy, it must be worded in accordance with the wording of the appropriate optional provision. An insurer may reword any of the optional provisions so long as the new wording is not less favorable to the insured or the beneficiary.

18. 4. 1 Optional Provision 1: Change of Occupation

Here is the first optional provision.

If the insured be injured or contract sickness after having changed his or her occupation to one classified by the insurer as more hazardous than that stated in this policy, or while doing for compensation anything pertaining to an occupation so classified, the insurer will pay only such portion of the indemnities provided in this policy as the premium paid would have purchased at the rates and within limits fixed by the insurer for a more hazardous occupation. If the insured changes an occupation to one classified by the insurer as less hazardous than that stated in this policy, the insurer, upon receipt of proof of such change of occupation, will reduce the premium rate accordingly, and will return the excess pro rata unearned premium from the date of change of occupation or from the policy anniversary date immediately preceding receipt of such proof, whichever is the more recent. In applying this provision, the classification of occupational risk and the premium rates shall be such as have been last filed by the insurer prior to the occurrence of the loss for which the insurer is liable, or prior to date of proof of change in occupation with the state official having supervision of insurance in the state where the insured resided at the time this policy was issued; but if such filing was not required, then the classification of occupational risk and the premium rates shall be those last made effective by the insurer in such state prior to the occurrence of the loss or prior to the date of proof of change in occupation.

This provision relieves the insurer from paying benefits not anticipated when the premium was established. If an insured's occupation is more hazardous than the insurer knew, and resulted in injury or illness, the insurer might be required to pay a larger benefit than the premium warrants. Here's an example of how this provision works.

Example

If Max, the insured, had continued at the occupation he had when he purchased his disability income policy, disability from an accidental injury would have resulted in a benefit of $1,600 per month based on the premium Max paid. However, Max changed to a more hazardous occupation without notifying the insurer, and then suffered a disabling injury on the job. The insurer will pay only the amount of benefit that Max would have been able to purchase, with the premium already paid, for the more hazardous job, so Max's benefit is reduced.

Suppose Max had changed to a less hazardous occupation but paid premiums based on the more hazardous occupation. In this case, Max sends proof that he changed occupations to the insurer, the premium rate is reduced accordingly, and the insurer returns the excess premium to Max on a pro rata (proportionate) basis.

When calculating how much of the extra premium to return, the company uses the more recent of:

- the date the occupation changed; or
- the policy anniversary date immediately preceding receipt of the proof of change.

18. 4. 2 Optional Provision 2: Misstatement of Age

If the age of the insured has been misstated, all amounts payable under this policy shall be such as the premium paid would have purchased at the correct age.

When an insured is younger, a premium dollar buys a certain amount of insurance. As the insured ages, the same premium dollar buys less insurance. This provision is similar to the previous provision regarding a more hazardous occupation. If the insured has misstated his age on the application, the company may adjust benefits to the amount the premiums paid would have bought had the insured's correct age been known.

If an insured overstated his age—stated an older age than he actually was—when applying for the coverage, the insured has been paying a premium that is too high. Under this provision, the insurer could increase any benefits to the amount the premium paid for.

Or, if the insured had understated his age, the company would pay the insured (or a beneficiary, in the event of accidental death) a smaller benefit.

Whether the insured misstated his age intentionally or unintentionally, the company simply adjusts benefits accordingly.

18. 4. 3 Optional Provision 3: Other Insurance with This Insurer

If an accident or sickness policy or policies previously issued by the insurer to the insured be in force concurrently herewith, making the aggregate indemnity for ___________ (insert type of coverage or coverages) in excess of $______ (insert maximum limit of indemnity or indemnities), the excess insurance shall be void and all premiums paid for such excess shall be returned to the insured or to the estate.

Or,

Insurance effective at any one time on the insured under a like policy or policies in this insurer is limited to one such policy elected by the insured, his or her beneficiary or estate, as the case may be, and the insurer will return all premiums paid for all other such policies.

This provision deals with insurance of the same type with the same insurer.

If an individual has so much insurance that it is more profitable to see a doctor, enter a hospital, or stay home from work, there might be some temptation to do just that rather than to have a quick recovery. Such an individual is **overinsured**—a situation insurers try to avoid.

This optional provision allows an insurer to control overinsurance through its own policies. The company can establish maximum amounts payable to any one insured for certain coverages—disability income insurance being the most common—so no matter how many policies an insured has with this particular company, there is a limit on the amount of benefits that will be paid.

Either of the two provisions may be included in the policy. If the insurer chooses the first paragraph, it is the insurer's responsibility to decide on the maximum indemnity that will be paid and the type of coverage to which the provision applies. When these limitations are included in the policy, any amount of like insurance over the specified maximum is considered void, and the insurer will return premiums paid for these void benefits to the insured or to the insured's estate.

If the insurer uses the second paragraph, coverage is limited to one policy as selected by the insured, the beneficiary, or the administrator of the insured's estate. When the second optional provision is used, the premiums paid for the other policy or policies are refunded.

18. 4. 4 Optional Provisions 4 and 5: Insurance with Other Insurers

Although the previous optional provision concerned overinsurance with the same insurer, the next two deal with other insurers. Because they are closely related, they are presented together.

Provision 4

If there be other valid coverage, not with this insurer, providing benefits for the same loss on a provision-of-service basis or on a expense-incurred basis and of which this insurer has not been given written notice prior to the occurrence or commencement of loss, the only liability under any expense-incurred coverage of this policy shall be for such proportion of the loss as the amount which would otherwise have been payable hereunder plus the total of the like amounts under all such other valid coverages for the same loss, and for the return of such portion of the premiums paid as shall exceed the pro rata portion of the amount so determined. For the purpose of applying this provision when other coverage is on a provision of service basis, the like amount of such other coverage shall be taken as the amount which the services rendered would have cost in the absence of such coverage.

Provision 5

If there be other valid coverage, not with this insurer, providing benefits for the same loss on other than an expense-incurred basis and of which the insurer has not been given written notice prior to the occurrence or commencement of loss, the only liability for such benefits under this policy shall be for such proportion of the indemnities of which the insurer had notice (including the indemnities under this policy) bear to the total amount of all like indemnities for such loss, and for the return of such portion of the premium paid as shall exceed the pro rata portion for the indemnities thus determined.

The essence of the fourth and fifth optional provisions is this: if an insured has two or more policies from different companies that cover the same expenses, and if the insurers were not notified that the other coverage existed, each insurer will pay a proportionate share of any claim. This prevents the insured from receiving benefits greater than the loss. The concept is illustrated below.

Proportionate Benefit Payment

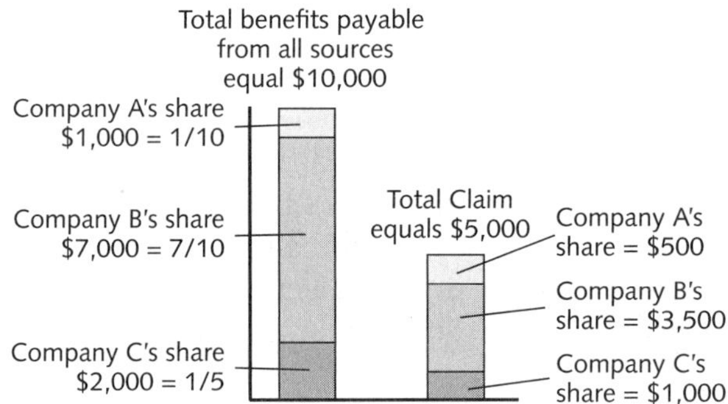

The insured would have paid for benefits that cannot be collected; each company also must refund a proportionate share of the excess premiums on a pro rata basis.

When both of these optional provisions appear in the same policy, **Provision 4** must be captioned *expense-incurred benefits* as it deals with losses to be reimbursed on that basis. Likewise, **Provision 5** must be captioned *other benefits* as it deals with overinsurance for losses reimbursed on any basis other than expense incurred.

The law also allows an insurer to include a definition of *other valid coverage* to cover more than just another insurer's individual health policy. This allows other benefit sources such as auto medical payments, union welfare plans, or Blue Cross/Blue Shield benefits to be taken into account.

18. 4. 5 Optional Provision 6: Relation of Earnings to Insurance—Average Earnings Clause

This provision specifically concerns loss of time, or disability income, coverage.

If the total monthly amount of loss of time benefits promised for the same loss under all valid loss of time coverage upon the insured, whether payable on a weekly or monthly basis, shall exceed the monthly earnings of the insured at the time disability commenced, or the average monthly earnings for the period of two years immediately preceding a disability for which claim is made, whichever is greater, the insurer will be liable only for such proportionate amount of such benefits under this policy as the amount of such monthly earnings or such average monthly earnings of the insured bears to the total amount of monthly benefits for the same loss under all such coverage upon the insured at the time such disability commences, and for the return of such part of the premiums paid during such two years as shall exceed the pro rata amount of the premiums for the benefits actually paid hereunder; but this shall not operate to reduce the total monthly amount of benefits payable under all such coverage upon the insured below the sum of $200 or the sum of the monthly benefits specified in such coverages, whichever is the lesser, nor shall it operate to reduce benefits other than those payable for loss of time.

This optional provision is also designed to prevent overinsurance malingering—remaining disabled in order to collect insurance. The provision specifically addresses the relationship between what the insured actually has been earning on the job and the amount of insurance available by failing to return to work. The illustration gives an example of how insurance might pay more than the insured earns.

Overinsurance

$2,500 benefits from **both** policies

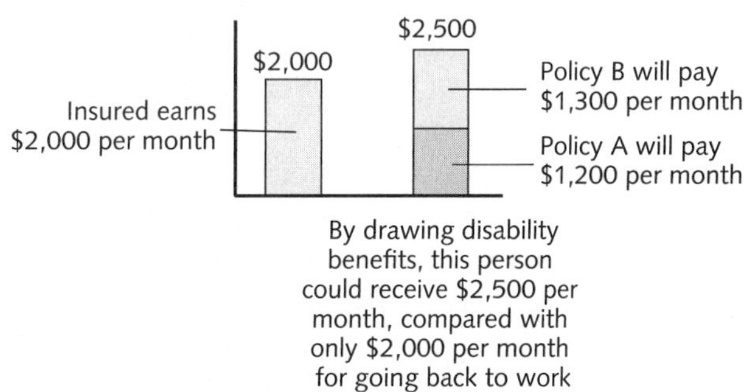

By drawing disability benefits, this person could receive $2,500 per month, compared with only $2,000 per month for going back to work

According to this provision, if the total monthly benefits from all policies are more than the insured's monthly income (and more than $200), each insurer will pay a proportionate share of the lost income. This will prevent the insured from receiving benefits greater than the loss. Because the insured paid for more coverage than can be collected, each company must refund a proportionate share of the excess premiums. Furthermore, benefits cannot be reduced below $200.

If the insurer that wrote Policy A in the previous illustration includes the sixth optional provision in the policy, here is how it might work.

Relation of Earnings to Insurance

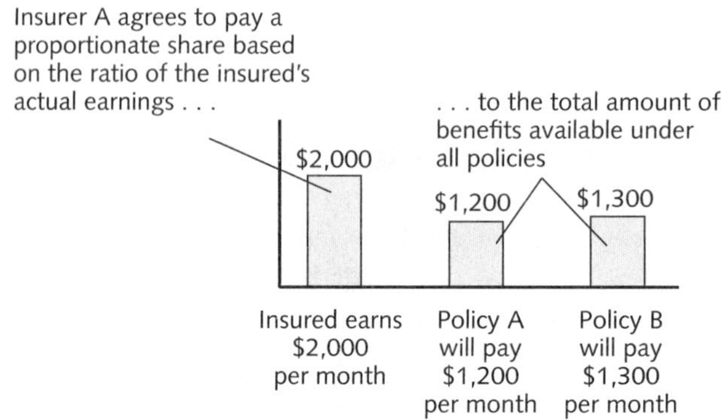

Relation of Earnings to Insurance

To determine the proper proportion, the insurer will divide the insured's earnings by the total benefits available from all policies

$\frac{\$2,000}{\$2,500} = \frac{4}{5}$ or 80%

Insured earns $2,000 per month

$2,000

$2,500

$1,200

Policy B will pay $1,300 per month

Policy A will pay $1,200 per month

Both policies will pay 80% of the benefit it would otherwise have paid

Policy A	Policy B
$1,200	$1,300
× .80	× .80
$ 960	$1,040

The insurer may define other valid loss of time coverage to take into account other benefit sources such as workers' compensation, union welfare plans, or employee benefit payments.

Because this provision allows for computation of the insured's average earnings over the course of two years, it is often called the **average earnings clause**. The following situation describes how it works.

Brian averages $3,000 a month income. He has two policies, each providing a $1,800 monthly disability income benefit. Total monthly benefits payable if neither policy contains an average earnings clause, nor any other provision limiting benefits in the event of overinsurance, are $3,600.

Average monthly earnings are 83% ($3,000 ÷ $3,600) of the total monthly benefits for which Brian is eligible. If the policy contains the provision we've been discussing, the insurer is liable to pay $1,494 each month because that is 83% of the $1,800 otherwise payable.

When an individual buys disability income coverage, the benefits are received tax free. So, if Brian is disabled and has a policy providing full monthly income, he will actually receive more than his take-home pay when he was working.

For this reason, many companies limit benefits to a percentage of monthly income, such as 60%. It's still possible to have two policies, each providing a high percentage of monthly income. Let's see what happens then.

Harold's average earnings are $4,000 a month. He has two policies, each providing 75% of monthly income in disability benefits—$3,000 each or a total of $6,000. Both policies contain the average earnings provision. To determine the proportion, divide average monthly earnings by total available benefits. Then multiply the resulting proportion (percentage or fraction) by the individual benefit for each policy—$3,000 each in this case.

Harold's average monthly earnings are 2/3, or 66%, of total monthly benefits for which Harold is eligible ($4,000 ÷ $6,000). Each insurer is liable to pay $1,980 (66% of $3,000) each month.

18. 4. 6 Optional Provision 7: Unpaid Premium

Upon the payment of a claim under this policy, any premium then due and unpaid or covered by any note or written order may be deducted therefrom.

This very simple optional provision allows an insurer to deduct premiums that are due or past due as part of settling a claim. Some companies will also accept a promissory note from an insured, indicating the insured will pay at a stipulated time in the future. In return, the company agrees to continue coverage in force as if the premium had already been paid. When a company holds such a note and a claim is made, this provision allows the insurer to deduct the amount of the premium before paying the indemnity. With or without a promissory note, here is how this provision would operate.

Example

Frederick sends his insurer a claim for $1,800 to cover hospital and medical expenses from an illness.

CLAIM $1,800

The insurer notes that Frederick owes a past-due premium of $300, which the insurer deducts from the claim...

UNPAID PREMIUM - $300

...then pays the $1,500 balance:

AMOUNT OF CLAIM PAID $1,500

18. 4. 7 Optional Provision 8: Cancellation

Let's break this optional provision into two parts. Here is the first part.

The insurer may cancel this policy at any time by written notice delivered to the insured or mailed to the last address as shown by the records of the insurer, stating when, not less than five days thereafter, such cancellation shall be effective; and after the policy has been continued beyond its original term, the insured may cancel this policy at any time by written notice delivered or mailed to the insurer, effective upon receipt or on such later date as may be specified in such notice.

Although this provision may not be used in noncancelable policies, in policies that may be canceled, the insurer may do so by delivering (usually by mail) written notice to the insured UNPAID PREMIUM - $300s last known address. Cancellation is effective no fewer than five days after the date of notice.

Here is the remainder of the optional provision regarding cancellation.

In the event of cancellation, the insurer will return promptly the unearned portion of any premium paid. If the insured cancels, the earned premium shall be computed by the use of the short rate table last filed with the state official having supervision of insurance in the state where the insured resided when the policy was issued. If the insurer cancels, the earned premium shall be computed pro rata. Cancellation shall be without prejudice to any claim originating prior to the effective date of cancellation.

When a policy is canceled before its expiration date, some of the prepaid premium is **unearned**—that is, the insurance company has not yet earned the premium, because the period of time it was intended to cover has not yet passed. The way in which unearned premium is returned to the insured depends on who canceled the policy—the insurance company or the insured. The explanations and illustrations that follow show what happens to a premium dollar.

When the insurance company cancels, the portion of the premium dollar the insurer has already earned is kept by the insurer and the entire unearned portion is returned to the insured. This is a **pro rata** return.

Pro Rata Return of Premium

Premium Dollar

Earned → Insurer

Unearned → Insured

When the insured cancels, the insurance company is allowed to retain a portion of premium over and above that which it has earned. So the insurer keeps earned premium and a portion of **unearned** premium, returning the balance of unearned premium to the insured. This is a **short-rate** return.

Short Rate Return of Premium

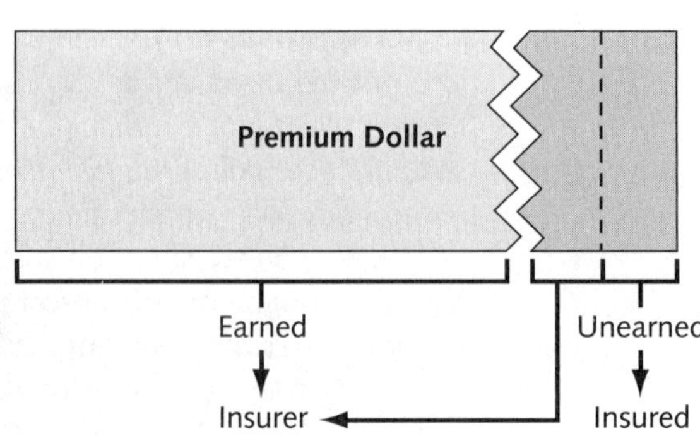

When a premium is paid, the insurer assumes the insured will keep the policy in force for the entire period for which that premium was paid. On the basis of this assumption, the company invests the money, or at least plans its investments. If the insured cancels before expiration of the term for which premium was paid, it costs the company money to return the premium—a cost initiated by the insured when requesting cancellation. To help pay for these costs, insurers are permitted to compute the amount of premium to be returned on a short-rate basis. Short-rate tables are established and filed in advance with the state Insurance Commissioner's office. Using short rates allows the insurer to retain more than a **pro rata** share of the premium.

Under the pro rata method, the insurer retains no more than the proportion of premium paid to the proportion earned during the period the policy was in force. Therefore, if an insurance company initiates the cancellation, it must bear the costs of cancellation as well.

A **flat cancellation** means that a policy is canceled as of its effective date. Usually this means that no premium is charged. For example, when an insured returns a policy during a free-look period, any premium payment will be fully refunded.

18. 4. 8 Optional Provision 9: Conformity with State Statutes

Any provision of this policy which, on its effective date, is in conflict with the statutes of the state in which the insured resides on such date is hereby amended to conform to minimum requirements of such statutes.

Although this provision is usually optional, some states insist that it be included in all policies; therefore, in some states, this provision is required.

Not only does the provision help insurers avoid issuing policies that conflict with existing state laws, it also can prevent reissuing policies that are in conflict with any ruling enacted during the time a policy is being or is about to be issued.

The provision applies to the laws of the insured's state of residence.

18. 4. 9 Optional Provision 10: Illegal Occupation

The insurer shall not be liable for any loss to which a contributing cause was the insured's commission of or attempt to commit a felony or to which a contributing cause was the insured's being engaged in an illegal occupation.

In our discussion of common exclusions, you learned that most companies exclude coverage for injuries or accidental death suffered while the insured is committing or attempting to commit a felony. Therefore, you can assume that most policies do include the illegal occupation provision.

Example

Dan's policy contains this provision. Dan's application stated that he is the proprietor of a small newsstand. After Dan was severely beaten one night by someone who apparently was trying to rob him, he applied for benefits under the hospital and medical provisions of his policy. Upon investigating the incident, police discover that Dan was using his newsstand simply as a front. His real employment is fencing stolen goods, and the beating he suffered was the result of a quarrel with other criminals. Since Dan was engaged in an illegal occupation that contributed to his injury, the insurer will not pay his claim.

If Dan's injury had resulted from an auto accident instead of a beating, a complete investigation might not have been made, nor his illegal occupation discovered. If this had been the case, the insurer probably would have paid the claim.

18. 4. 10 Optional Provision 11: Narcotics

The insurer shall not be liable for any loss sustained or contracted in consequence of the insured's being under the influence of any narcotic unless administered on the advice of a physician.

As with of the illegal occupation provision, many insurers include this optional provision. Injuries or death resulting while the insured is under the influence of either alcohol or narcotics is commonly excluded. Following are two examples of how this provision works.

Example

If Oliver wrecks his car and is injured while returning home from a party at which he used cocaine, even though this was his first experience with drugs, the insurance company will not pay any resulting claims.

Example

Because Amy was in great pain when she visited her doctor, the doctor prescribed a prescription containing morphine. Later, under the influence of the drug, Amy fell down the stairs in her home. In this case, because Amy was using a drug administered by her physician, the insurer will likely reimburse her for any resultant medical expenses.

18. 5 OTHER HEALTH INSURANCE PROVISIONS

18. 5. 1 The Policy Face

The face of the policy is a standard printed form containing the name of the insurance company and providing enough information to give the insured a capsule summary of what type of policy and what type of coverage are provided by the contract. The policy face identifies the insured and states the term of the policy (when it goes into effect and when coverage expires). The policy face also states how the policy can be renewed.

The policy face usually gives a brief statement of the type or types of benefits. However, it is essential to examine the benefit provisions within the body of the contract to obtain a complete understanding of the coverage provided.

18. 5. 2 Free Look

Many states require that health policies contain a **free-look** provision, allowing individuals to look over the policy for a specified period with the right to refuse it. Usually, this is a 10-day trial period, and in some states, may be a 15- or 20-day period, beginning on the day the individual receives the policy. If the individual decides to return the policy by the end of the trial period, that individual receives a full refund of the prepaid premium.

This free-look provision permits applicants to inspect the policy at their leisure and make a final decision about whether it meets their needs. If the individual cancels during the trial period, the insurance company is not liable for any claims originating during that period.

Example

Sheila receives a new health policy on March 11. On March 16, she is involved in an auto accident but suffers no apparent injury. On March 18, she exercises her 10-day free-look right and notifies the insurer, BBB Health Company, to cancel the policy. On March 20, she is hospitalized with a neck problem that her doctor says is the result of the March 16 auto accident. Sheila has not received a premium refund from BBB, so she files a claim for medical expenses related to the accident. Since she has returned the policy under the free-look provision, the insurer is not required to pay the claim but must fully refund the premium Sheila has already paid.

Under a free-look provision, the policy usually may be returned either to the insurer or to its agent within the time specified. Check your state laws and your health policies to see if a free-look provision is required. Your company may include such a provision even if it isn't required by state law.

18. 5. 3 Insuring Clause

The **insuring clause** is usually the initial policy clause. In general, it represents the insurer's promise to pay under the conditions stipulated in the policy. The insuring clause performs these functions:

- Describes the general scope of coverage
- Provides any definitions required
- Sets forth the conditions under which benefits will be paid

This clause is often viewed as the foundation of a health policy in terms of the insurer's general agreement to provide coverage. An example of such a case would be as follows:

"The insurer, ABC Mutual, agrees to pay disability income benefits to the insured upon receipt of proof of loss, and the timely payment of premiums by the insured. All benefits will be paid in accordance with the policy's provisions contained herein."

18. 5. 4 Consideration Clause

In legal terms, **consideration** is an exchange of something of value on which a contract is based. When both parties exchange consideration, the contract is validated.

In health insurance, the insurance company exchanges the promises in the policy for a two-part consideration from the insured. A health insurance contract is valid only if the insured provides consideration in the form of:

- the full minimum premium required; and
- the statements made in the application.

Example

If Joan completes an application but does not pay the first premium due, she does not have a valid contract even if the policy is issued. On the other hand, if she pays the first premium and the policy is issued as applied for, the contract is valid because she provided the correct consideration.

In health policies, the consideration clause not only defines consideration but also states:

- the date coverage begins; and
- the length of the initial coverage period.

This clause may be stated separately, or it may be part of a renewability clause in the policy.

18. 5. 5 Policy Continuation

18. 5. 5. 1 Optionally and Conditionally Renewable Policies

To remain in force, health policies must be renewed periodically, that is, the coverage remains in force only for the length of time for which premiums have been paid. When the premium is due again, the policy may be renewed or it may expire. Both the policyowner and the insurer have a role in the renewal process.

A policyowner has the option of canceling a policy at any time by notifying the insurer, or of allowing it to lapse at a premium due date by not paying the premium.

Health policies also include specific provisions that determine whether the insurance company may refuse to renew a policy. When the insurer has the option to refuse to renew, the policy may be one of two types:

- Optionally renewable, which means the insurer may elect not to renew for any reason or for no reason, but may exercise that right only on the premium due date
- Conditionally renewable, which means the insurer may elect not to renew only under conditions specified in the policy

To protect the insured when a valid claim is being paid or is eligible for payment at the time the premium is due, the insurer may not prejudice that claim. That is, the claim will be paid even if the insurer elects not to renew the policy.

18. 5. 5. 2 *Cancelable Policies*

With the optionally renewable policy, the company must wait until a premium is due before it can terminate the policy by refusing to renew. However, with a **cancelable policy**, the insurer may cancel coverage at any time, provided it returns any unearned premiums to the insured. As is true of optionally and conditionally renewable policies, cancellation does not relieve the insurer from paying valid existing claims.

Cancelable policies are not common and, obviously, are not advantageous to the insured. Unless the policy contains a clause that permits the company to cancel on other than a premium due date, it simply cannot be canceled. The company may refuse to renew the policy on a premium payment date, but, unless specifically stated in the policy, health insurance policies usually are not cancelable by the insurer.

When canceling a cancelable policy, the company must notify the insured in writing, mailing the notice and the unearned premium to the insured's last known address. In most states, cancellation is effective not less than five days from the date of the notice.

Example

An insurer decides to cancel Anthony's cancelable health policy. The company mails a notice of cancellation and a refund check for the amount of unearned premium to Anthony's last known address. A few months later, Anthony files suit to collect benefits for a claim that did not exist at the time the notice was mailed.

Anthony bases his suit upon the fact that he had moved and did not receive the notice of cancellation. Assuming the company has an accurate record of the transaction on file, including a copy of the cancellation notice and evidence that the unearned premium check was issued, the insurer is not liable for the claim because it followed proper cancellation procedures. However, if the claim had existed before the insurer canceled, the insurer would be liable.

18. 5. 5. 3 *Guaranteed Renewable Policies*

In some policies, the insurer relinquishes its rights to cancel at any time and to refuse renewal at a premium due date. This type of policy is called **guaranteed renewable**, and it includes several important features.

- Renewal is guaranteed as long as the insured pays the premium.
- The insurer may not cancel unless the insured fails to pay the premium.
- Premiums may not be increased on an individual basis.
- Premiums may be increased on the basis of an entire classification, such as occupation.
- The guarantee to renew ends at a specified age.

Nonpayment of premium is the only reason an insurer may cancel or refuse to renew a guaranteed renewable policy. Furthermore, the insurer is not permitted to increase the premiums on the basis of individual insured's experience. It may, however, increase the premiums on a class basis. One common classification, for example, is by occupational groups. On the basis of experience, insurers know that certain occupations are subject to a higher risk of accidental injury or death than are other occupations. For example, compare the different risks faced by a typist and by a construction worker.

With a guaranteed renewable policy, the company must renew. However, on the basis of new experience ratings within the insured's occupational class, the insurer may increase the premiums for all insureds in that class of risk. The guaranteed renewable feature is often limited. In some policies, the insurer regains the rights to cancel and to refuse to renew when the insured reaches a specified age. Commonly, the policy stipulates this right when the insured reaches a normally accepted retirement age, such as 60, 65, or 70. However, the company's right to do this is limited in many states if the insured is over age 54 when the policy is issued. In this case, the insurer may not cancel or refuse to renew until at least five years after the policy is issued.

Since insurers expose themselves to higher risks by relinquishing the rights to refuse renewal and to cancel a policy, guaranteed renewable policy premiums are higher than those for cancelable policies. Suppose a 56-year-old person buys a guaranteed renewable policy, paying the higher premiums required for that type of coverage. When the person reaches age 60, the company could conceivably cancel the policy if that age were stipulated in the policy. However, the insured has paid an extra premium to obtain the coverage. So, some states require that if an insured is over age 54 when the policy is issued, the company must keep the policy in force for a minimum of five years, even though it might otherwise have canceled or elected not to renew when the insured reached the specified age.

18. 5. 5. 4 Noncancelable Policies

The terms ***noncancelable*** and ***noncancelable and guaranteed renewable*** are often used interchangeably to describe a noncancelable policy. As the name implies, an insurer may not cancel or refuse to renew a noncancelable policy. Although this appears to be the same as a guaranteed renewable policy, there is one important difference. With a guaranteed renewable policy, the insurer may increase the premiums by classifications. With a noncancelable policy, however, the insurer may never increase the premiums. That is, the initial premium is the premium the insured will pay throughout the life of the policy.

Other features of noncancelable policies are the same as for guaranteed renewable policies.

- The only reason the insurer may cancel is for nonpayment of premium.
- The insurer regains the right to cancel or nonrenew at a stipulated age—usually 60, 65, or 70.
- If the insured is over age 54 when the policy is issued, the policy term must be at least five years.

You can see that the insurer assumes a higher risk by being unable to adjust future premiums. Therefore, premiums for noncancelable policies are somewhat higher than for other health policies. As a general rule, only disability income policies (not medical expense policies) are noncancelable.

To reiterate: Aside from the fact that premiums are somewhat higher for noncancelable policies, there is only one basic difference between these policies and guaranteed renewable policies. That is, the insurer may not increase the premiums on a noncancelable policy.

18. 5. 5. 5 Term Policies

In some situations, an individual may need health insurance for a fixed, limited time period. Coverage that extends only for a specified length of time is called **term insurance**. A term health policy cannot be renewed at all. When it expires, the insured must purchase another policy.

Flight insurance is a well-known example of term accident insurance. Coverage begins when the flight starts and terminates when the flight is over. Student accident policies are another example, beginning when the school term begins and ending when the term is over.

18. 5. 6 Benefit Payment Clause

Health insurance benefits are paid differently depending on the type of policy. How benefits will be paid is set out in the policy's **benefits provision**. Typically, benefits are paid in the form of:

- periodic income under disability policies;
- lump-sum reimbursements for expenses incurred under hospital, medical, surgical, and major medical policies; or
- lump-sum indemnity payments for death or dismemberment under accidental death and dismemberment policies.

Suppose the benefits provision of Mitchell's policy indicates that if he is unable to work under certain conditions, he will be paid a specified amount monthly. This is known as a **periodic income** payment under his disability income policy.

On the other hand, Tom's medical expenses resulting from hospitalization for surgery will be paid under his major medical policy in the form of a lump-sum reimbursement.

According to the benefits provision of Carla's policy, she will receive $10,000 if one of her limbs is accidentally amputated. This is an example of a lump-sum indemnity payment under an accidental death and dismemberment policy.

18. 5. 7 Exclusions and Reductions

These provisions limit the insurer's obligation to pay. An **exclusion or exception** is a provision that entirely eliminates coverage for a specified risk. A **reduction** is a decrease in benefits as a result of specified conditions.

Most health insurance policies exclude war and acts of war, self-inflicted injuries, aviation, military service, and overseas residence. Benefits will not be provided if the cause of a loss is due to military service, a war or civil disorder, a self-inflicted injury such as an attempted suicide, or if the loss is due to aviation as a pilot.

In general, coverage is temporarily suspended if an individual resides in a foreign country for a specified period of time or if the individual is serving in the military. Coverage is reinstated or reactivated when the insured returns to the United States or no longer is serving in the military.

18. 5. 8 Preexisting Conditions

Preexisting conditions can be excluded from coverage under a health insurance policy. This exclusion may be permanent or temporary. By definition, a preexisting condition is any condition for which the insured sought treatment or advice before the effective date of the policy.

Furthermore, a preexisting condition can also be defined as any symptom that would cause a reasonable and prudent person to seek diagnosis and medical treatment. This concept prevents an applicant who suspects that he may have a serious medical problem from buying health insurance and then going to a doctor for diagnosis and treatment.

Preexisting conditions may be covered by the insurer if they are indicated on the application. The insurer will then review the medical information and, depending on the condition, may elect to cover the problem or exclude it. Usually, only serious or chronic conditions will be excluded.

18. 5. 9 Nonoccupational Coverage

Some people work in occupations that are considered extremely hazardous, such as railroad switchers or steeplejacks. Many insurance companies won't assume the risk of covering such people for the hazards involved in their occupations. To provide these individuals with general accident and sickness or disability income coverage, some companies issue policies that contain a provision excluding job-related injuries.

Since policies with this provision do not cover occupational hazards, they are usually called **nonoccupational policies**. Without the exposure to everyday work hazards, the insurer takes a lesser risk, so the premiums are generally lower than for policies that cover occupational hazards. Remember, though, nonoccupational policies do not provide full coverage, either—for both on- and off-the-job injuries.

Occupational coverage is basically full coverage. If the health policy provides 24-hour coverage, occupational losses will be covered as well as any other type of loss.

18. 5. 10 Case Management Provisions

To control the costs associated with medical care, many insurers are instituting methods to reduce costs while giving the insured options for health care. As health care costs have risen, more and more policies provide for some type of administrative oversight in an attempt to contain costs. These provisions are variously called case management, managed care, claims control, cost containment or similar terms.

The **second surgical opinion** is a provision that can be included in policies that offer surgical expense benefits. This coverage allows the insured to consult a doctor, other than the attending physician, to determine alternative methods of treatment. Although the use of this provision is sometimes optional, it is more often mandatory for certain procedures, such as tonsillectomy, cataract surgery, coronary bypass, mastectomy, and varicose veins. Some insurance companies have medical examiners review claims, and the examiner's decision to approve or deny a claim is considered the required second opinion.

One cost control mechanism being used by insurers and employers is utilization review. **Utilization review** consists of an evaluation of the appropriateness, necessity, and quality of health care and may include preadmission certification and concurrent review.

Under the **precertification provision** (also known as precertification authorization or prospective review), the physician can submit claim information before providing treatment to know in advance whether the procedure is covered under the insured's plan and at what rate it will be paid. This way both the physician and the insured know in advance what the benefit will be and can plan accordingly. This provision allows the insurance company to evaluate the appropriateness of the procedure and the length of the hospital stay.

Under the **concurrent review** process, the insurer monitors the insured's hospital stay to make sure that everything is proceeding according to schedule and that the insured will be released from the hospital as planned.

Recent evidence has shown that many treatments can be satisfactorily provided without the need for a hospital stay. **Ambulatory outpatient care** is the alternative to the costly inpatient diagnostic testing and treatment. Today, ambulatory care is best known to operate in hospital outpatient departments. However, this care can be provided by special ambulatory care health centers, group medical services, hospital emergency rooms, multispecialty group medical practices, and health care corporations. These ambulatory facilities provide, in addition to diagnosis and treatment, preventive care, health education, family planning, and dental and vision care.

18. 5. 11 Waiver of Premium

Under this provision, the insurer waives premium payments after the insured has been totally disabled (as defined in the policy) for a specified period, usually three or six months. If the insured remains totally disabled, no further premium payments will be required from the insured. The insurer will pay the premiums until the insured attains age 65. If the insured recovers from the disability, the insured will resume paying the premiums.

18. 6 SUMMARY

In this lesson, you learned about:

- the purpose of the following mandatory policy provisions:
  - — entire contract, changes,
  - — time limit of certain defenses,
  - — grace period,
  - — reinstatement,
  - — notice of claims,
  - — claim forms,
  - — proof of loss,
  - — time of payment of claims,
  - — payment of claims,
  - — physical examination and autopsy,
  - — legal actions, and
  - — change of beneficiary;
- the purpose of the following optional policy provisions:
  - — change of occupation,
  - — misstatement of age,
  - — other insurance with this insurer,
  - — other insurance with other insurers (1 and 2),
  - — relation of earnings to insurance,
  - — unpaid premium,
  - — cancellation,
  - — conformity with state statutes,
  - — illegal occupation, and
  - — intoxicants and narcotics;

- the purpose of the following other policy provisions:
  - the policy face,
  - free look,
  - insuring clause,
  - consideration clause,
  - renewability,
  - benefit payment clause,
  - exclusions and reductions,
  - preexisting conditions,
  - nonoccupational coverage, and
  - case management provisions.

UNIT TEST

1. According to the entire contract provision, the entire contract includes all of the following EXCEPT
   A. the insurance policy
   B. the premium payment
   C. any endorsements
   D. any attachments

2. In most states, the policy becomes incontestable after
   A. 2 years
   B. 3 years
   C. 4 years
   D. 5 years

3. All insurance policies may be canceled at any time by
   A. the insurer only
   B. the insured only
   C. neither the insurer or the insured
   D. neither the insurer nor the insured

4. Normally, written proofs of loss must be furnished within how many days after the loss?
   A. 15
   B. 45
   C. 60
   D. 90

5. If there is no beneficiary listed on a policy, benefits will be paid to
   A. the state
   B. the insured's estate
   C. the insured's nearest blood relative
   D. the insured's nearest relative by marriage or blood

6. The insurer may generally require an autopsy at its own expense unless
   A. the deceased requests in writing that an autopsy not be performed
   B. the deceased's relatives request that an autopsy not be performed
   C. the deceased's relatives have proven religious objections to an autopsy being performed
   D. the state has an applicable law that forbids autopsy

7. When Betty purchased her insurance policy, her age was recorded as 32 when she was actually 34. Assuming her policy includes the misstatement of age provision and the insurance company discovers this 4 years later
   A. Betty's policy will be canceled for misrepresentation
   B. Betty's policy will be unchanged because the incontestable period has expired
   C. Betty's policy limits will be lowered
   D. Betty's policy limits will be raised

8. The optional provisions that deal with multiple insurance policies of the same type on a single insured deal with the problem of
   A. underinsurance
   B. overinsurance
   C. inappropriate insurance
   D. incorrect insurance

9. If a policyholder has two or more policies from different companies that cover the same expenses and the insurers were not notified that the other coverage existed, each insurer will
   A. have the option to cancel the policyholder's policy without notice
   B. have the option to cancel the policyholder's policy with appropriate notice
   C. pay the claim regardless, as long as the premiums have been paid
   D. pay a proportionate share of any claim

10. Laura stops to buy a newspaper at a newsstand without knowing that it's a front for illegal activity. She is injured in a drive-by shooting determined to be related to the illegal activity. Her insurer will probably
    A. not pay the claim because it is related to illegal activity
    B. not pay the claim because Laura cannot prove that she didn't know about the illegal activity
    C. pay the claim because Laura was not involved in any illegal activity that contributed to her injury
    D. appeal the necessity to pay the claim to the state Department of Insurance

11. If a policy includes the provision on conformity with state statutes, and the state changes the law to be in conflict with another provision of the policy
    A. the policy will automatically be void
    B. the provision will be automatically grandfathered and able to stay the same
    C. the insurer will be able to apply for a grandfather provision for those policies already in force
    D. the provision will automatically be amended to conform to the minimum requirement of the statutes

12. A pro rata return is one in which the insurer returns
    A. all of the unearned premium
    B. some of the unearned premium
    C. both earned and unearned premium
    D. neither earned nor unearned premium

13. The grace period varies according to
    A. premium payment frequency
    B. premium payment amount
    C. method of premium payment
    D. type of policy

14. Mike allows his policy to lapse, then applies for reinstatement using the company's required application. The company does not inform Mike either that the policy has been accepted or that the policy is being rejected. At what point can Mike consider the policy reinstated?
    A. Not until the insurer notifies him that it has been reinstated
    B. As soon as the application has been submitted
    C. After 45 days
    D. After 90 days

15. A reinstated policy will cover
    A. sickness immediately and accidents after 10 days
    B. both sickness and accidents after 10 days
    C. accidents after 10 days and sickness after 30 days
    D. accidents immediately and sickness after 10 days

16. If an insured is disabled for at least 2 years, the insurer may require proof of continuance of disability every
    A. month
    B. 2 months
    C. 6 months
    D. Year

17. Because the insurer needs time to respond to a claim, the law provides the insurer with a window during which the insured cannot sue to recover under a claim. This window lasts for
    A. 30 days
    B. 60 days
    C. 90 days
    D. 120 days

18. The maximum time during which suit can be filed is how many years after written proof of loss is furnished?
    A. 1
    B. 2
    C. 3
    D. 4

19. A revocable beneficiary
    A. has the right to refuse assignment of the policy
    B. may stop the policyowner from disposing of the policy
    C. may be changed without the beneficiary's consent
    D. is assigned for life

20. Which of the following is NOT a required provision under the Uniform Provisions Model Act?
    A. Grace period
    B. Change of occupation
    C. Time of payment of claims
    D. Proof of loss

21. Which of the following is an optional provision under the Uniform Provisions Model Act?
    A. Cancellation
    B. Physical examination and autopsy
    C. Legal actions
    D. Reinstatement

22. Julia worked as a race car driver until recently, when she took a job in the promotions office handling media inquiries. If she has the same health insurance, her premiums are likely to
   A. stay the same
   B. go up
   C. go down
   D. stop because the policy will be canceled

23. Joe took out a disability policy while working as a very successful stockbroker. A few years later, he decides to take a less stressful job at a not-for-profit organization, writing about financial issues. He loves his new job and doesn't mind the fact that he makes a lot less money. When he becomes disabled 3 years later, his disability benefit is more than he has made in salary in 3 years. If the policy contains an average earnings clause, Joe's benefit will
   A. be the same as listed in the policy
   B. be the lesser of Joe's monthly earnings at the time the disability started, or the average monthly earnings for the period of 2 years immediately preceding his disability
   C. be the greater of Joe's monthly earnings at the time the disability started, or the average monthly earnings for the period of 2 years immediately preceding his disability
   D. be the greater of Joe's monthly earnings at the time the disability started, or the average monthly earnings for the period of 2 years immediately preceding his disability. In addition, the insurer will return some of the excess premiums that paid for the benefit Joe is not eligible to receive.

24. Cindy has a claim for $2,000 and a past due premium of $200. The insurer will
   A. refuse to pay the claim until the past due premium is paid
   B. pay the claim minus the past due premium
   C. pay the claim and forgive the past due premium
   D. pay the claim and bill Cindy for the past due premium

25. If Lois cancels her health insurance policy, the insurer will
   A. issue a pro rata refund of all of the unearned premium
   B. issue a pro rata refund of most of the unearned premium
   C. issue a short-rate refund of all of the unearned premium
   D. issue a short-rate refund of most of the unearned premium

26. Joel is hit by a car while crossing the street against the light. If Joel's policy contains the illegal occupation provision
   A. the insurer is not liable for the claim because Joel was engaged in illegal activity at the time of the accident
   B. the insurer is not liable for the claim because Joel's illegal activity was the direct cause of the accident
   C. the insurer will pay the claim because crossing the street against the light is not a felony or a regular occupation
   D. the insurer may or may not pay the claim, depending on Joel's occupation

27. Carmen gets her health insurance policy on May 1, and on May 3 she decides she doesn't want it and returns it to the company. On May 6, she is hit by a car. The company
   A. will pay any resulting claim because she was injured within the 10-day free-look period
   B. will pay any resulting claim only if the premium has not yet been returned to Carmen
   C. will pay any resulting claim minus the amount of the returned premium
   D. will only return any premium Carmen has paid and not any resulting claim

28. The insuring clause does all of the following EXCEPT
   A. describe the insured
   B. describe the general scope of coverage
   C. provide any definitions required
   D. set forth the conditions under which benefits will be paid

29. Consideration for a health policy includes
    A. the premium only
    B. the statements made in the application only
    C. the statements made in the application and the insuring clause
    D. the statements made in the application and the premium

30. Jennifer takes out an optionally renewable health policy with an annual premium due on June 14. The insurer decides it no longer wants to insure people with first names longer than five letters. The insurer may
    A. not cancel the policy because it does not have a good reason
    B. not cancel the policy unless the number of letters in the first name is a condition specified in the policy
    C. cancel the policy, but only on June 14 of the next year
    D. cancel the policy whenever it wants to

31. CeeCee's policy is guaranteed renewable. Which of the following may the insurer NOT do?
    A. Refuse to renew the policy if CeeCee fails to pay the premium
    B. Increase the premiums on all members of CeeCee's class
    C. Increase the premiums on CeeCee's policy only
    D. Refuse to renew the policy when CeeCee reaches a specified age

32. George has a noncancelable policy. Which of the following may the insurer do?
    A. Cancel the policy if George fails to pay premiums
    B. Increase the premiums on all members of George's class
    C. Increase the premiums on George's policy only
    D. Cancel the policy if the insurer chooses no longer to do business in George's state

33. Which of the following statements is TRUE?
    A. An exclusion is a provision that eliminates coverage for a specified condition; a reduction is a provision that decreases benefits as a result of a specified condition.
    B. A reduction is a provision that eliminates coverage for a specified condition; an exclusion is a provision that decreases benefits as a result of a specified condition.
    C. A reduction is a provision that eliminates coverage for a specified condition; an exception is a provision that decreases benefits as a result of a specified condition.
    D. A reduction is another term for an exception.

ANSWERS AND RATIONALES TO UNIT TEST

1. **B.**
2. **A.** In most states, the policy becomes incontestable after 2 years.
3. **B.** All insurance policies may be canceled at any time by the insured only.
4. **D.**
5. **B.** If there is no beneficiary listed on a policy, benefits will be paid to the estate.
6. **D.** The insurer may generally require an autopsy at its own expense unless the state has an applicable law that forbids autopsy.
7. **C.**
8. **B.** The optional provisions that deal with multiple insurance policies of the same type on a single insured deal with the problem of overinsurance.
9. **D.** If a policyholder has two or more policies from different companies that cover the same expenses and if the insurers were not notified that the other coverage existed, each insurer will pay a proportionate share of any claim.
10. **B.**
11. **D.** If a policy includes the provision on conformity with state statutes, and if the state changes the law to be in conflict with another provision of the policy, the provision will automatically be amended to conform to the minimum requirement of the statutes.
12. **A.** A pro rata return is one in which the insurer returns all of the unearned premium.
13. **A.**
14. **C.** Mike can consider the policy reinstated after 45 days.
15. **D.** A reinstated policy will cover accidents immediately and sickness after 10 days.
16. **C.** If an insured is disabled for at least 2 years, the insurer may require proof of continuance of disability every 6 months.
17. **B.** The window lasts for 60 days.
18. **C.** The maximum time during which suit can be filed is 3 years after written proof of loss is furnished.
19. **C.** A revocable beneficiary may be changed without the beneficiary's consent.
20. **B.** Change of occupation is not a required provision under the Uniform Provisions Model Act.
21. **A.** Cancellation is an optional provision under the Uniform Provisions Model Act.
22. **C.** Her premiums are likely to go down because of a change of occupation provision.
23. **D.** If the policy contains an average earnings clause, Joe's benefit will be the greater of Joe's monthly earnings at the onset of disability, or the average monthly earnings for the period of 2 years immediately preceding the onset of disability. In addition, the insurer will return some of the excess premiums that were paid for the benefit Joe is not eligible to receive.
24. **B.** The insurer will pay the claim minus the past due premium.
25. **D.** The insurer will issue a short-rate refund of most of the unearned premium.
26. **C.** If Joel's policy contains the illegal occupation provision, the insurer will pay the claim, because crossing the street against the light is not a felony or a regular occupation.
27. **D.** The company will only return any premium Carmen has paid and not any resulting claim.
28. **A.** The insuring clause does not describe the insured.
29. **D.** Consideration for a health policy includes the statements made in the application and the premium.
30. **C.** The insurer may cancel the policy, but only on June 14 of the next year.
31. **C.** The insurer may not increase the premiums on CeeCee's policy only.
32. **A.** The insurer may cancel the policy if George fails to pay premiums.
33. **A.** An exclusion is a provision that eliminates coverage for a specified condition; a reduction is a provision that decreases benefits as a result of a specified condition.

UNIT

19

Disability Income Insurance

19. 1 INTRODUCTION

When people are disabled and unable to work, the chances are high their income will stop sooner or later. Unfortunately, even when income stops, the costs of day-to-day living continue. That's why disability is often called the "living death." Earning power, in a sense, dies while life goes on—expenses continue and may even increase.

Disability income insurance is available to continue a portion of earnings while an insured is disabled. Too few people consider the possibility that they will be unable to continue earning an income by working. However, it is a fact that a person who is 25 years old today has better than a 50% chance of being disabled for more than 90 days before reaching age 65, while the likelihood of dying before age 65 is much less. Yet people are likely to insure with life insurance and to buy health insurance to cover medical expenses, while ignoring the need for disability insurance.

Disability income insurance, sometimes referred to as **loss of time coverage**, is designed to protect an individual's most important asset—the ability to earn an income.

19. 1. 1 Financial Planning Considerations

The importance of disability income protection cannot be overestimated as it relates to the overall planning of family finances. No matter what other safeguards may have been taken, the family's future is at stake when the ability to work is in peril. The following are some practical considerations in determining disability income needs.

- Establish the minimum income that would be required if income stopped because of disability.
- Consider the need for retirement plan maintenance if the individual has such a plan that would be disrupted in the event of long-term disability.
- After establishing the insured's total needs, allow for any benefits that would be provided by Social Security and workers' compensation.
- Include enough long-term disability coverage for both occupational and nonoccupational sickness or injury as well as short-term disability coverage to provide income during the Social Security waiting period or to supplement workers' compensation.

19. 1. 2 Alternatives to Disability Income Insurance

When people consider purchasing disability income insurance, they may ask about other alternatives that would allow them to use money they would devote to premiums differently. Listed are some other options people might consider if they develop a disability, along with the consequences of each option:

- **Using savings**. According to one source, if an individual saved 5% of his income each year, 6 months of total disability could wipe out 10 years of savings—savings that may have been designated for another purpose such as retirement or children's education.

- **Borrowing**. The problem is, who will lend money to someone who can't work?
- **Depending on spouse's income**. Will it be enough? If two incomes were needed before, one income may be insufficient.
- **Liquidating assets**. Can the individual get a fair market price when forced to liquidate? By their very nature, disabilities are unexpected, and the market may be down for the stocks, real estate, or other asset to be liquidated.

19. 2 LEARNING OBJECTIVES

After completing this lesson, you will be able to:

- explain why disability insurance is an important part of an individual's insurance portfolio;
- list and describe four practical considerations to be taken into account when determining disability income needs;
- list four possible alternatives to disability income insurance and explain why they are less desirable than they may first seem;
- explain the importance of the elimination period and how it affects benefits;
- explain when the benefit period begins, and list some typical benefit periods;
- explain the factors that go into determining total disability and how it is defined in each policy;
- explain the difference between own occupation and any occupation when determining total disability;
- explain the difference between injury and sickness disability;
- explain the difference between occupational and nonoccupational disability;
- explain the concept of presumptive disability, and list three conditions generally considered to be presumptive disabilities;
- explain the criteria for partial disability;
- explain the concept of residual disability and how it is being used;
- explain the concept of recurrent disability and how it is used;
- explain the difference between permanent and temporary disability;
- explain the difference between confining and nonconfining disability;

- explain the difference between accidental bodily injury and injury by accidental means;
- explain the function of short-term disability coverage;
- explain the function of long-term disability coverage;
- list six common exclusions found in disability income policies; and
- explain the use and function of the following riders: rehabilitation benefit, future increase option, cost of living benefit, lifetime benefits, Social Security, social insurance supplements, additional monthly benefit, hospital confinement, nondisabling injury, waiver of premium, and accidental death and dismemberment.

19. 3 DEFINITIONS AND BENEFITS

Disability income insurance can be defined as a contract that normally pays a monthly benefit, following the elimination period, for total disability due to accident or sickness. Disability benefits may also be paid for partial or residual disability as well as total disability. An understanding of each of these terms is important because as a producer, you must be able to explain to insureds how this policy will work if they become disabled. Benefits will be paid in accordance with the policy's terms and conditions.

19. 3. 1 Probationary Period

A **probationary** or **qualification period** may be found in some disability income policies. It is a period that begins when a policy goes into effect. During this period, no benefits will be paid under the policy. The period is often 15 or 30 days, or even 60 days for long-term policies. This probationary period generally applies to sickness, but not to accidents. Its major purpose is to relieve the insurance company from paying benefits for **preexisting conditions**—health problems that existed before the policy's inception—but its effective result is that no benefits are paid for any otherwise covered events during the stipulated period.

19. 3. 2 Elimination Period

An elimination period is the period for which an insured person must be disabled before benefits begin. The elimination period may be thought of as a time deductible rather a dollar deductible, because benefits are not payable for the elimination period. Benefits begin only after this period of time is satisfied. For example, if an insured has an elimination period of 30 days and is totally disabled for 75 days, benefits would be payable only for the 45 days in excess of the elimination period.

The elimination period may be 30, 60, 90, or 180 days or longer, depending on the period elected by the insured. The longer the elimination period, the smaller the insurance premium, because the insured is willing to go without benefits for a longer period of time and the insurer will not have to pay for short-term claims.

19. 3. 3 Benefit Period

After the elimination period has been satisfied and monthly disability benefits begin, they will be paid for a specific period, provided the insured remains totally disabled. This period is the **benefit period**. Typical benefit periods are one year, two years, five years, and to age 65.

Thus, if an insured has a disability income policy with a monthly benefit of $1,000 payable after a 30-day elimination period with a benefit period of five years, the insured would be entitled to five full years of benefits following the elimination period for each total disability (assuming that the insured continues to be totally disabled throughout the benefit period).

The longer the benefit period, the higher will be the policy's premium.

Important Disability Policy Periods

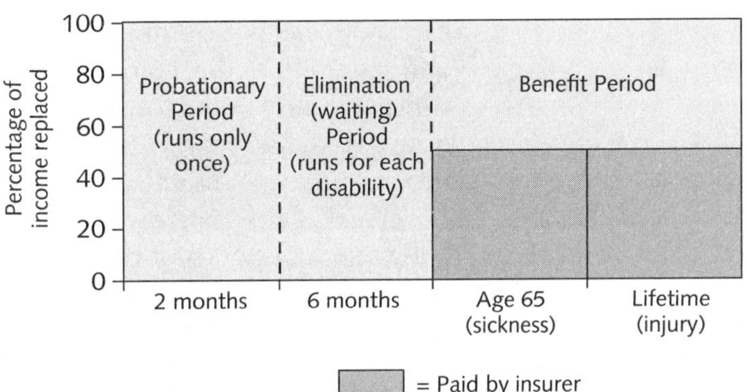

19. 3. 4 Defining Total Disability

Because the major purpose of disability income policies is to provide income when the insured is totally disabled and unable to work, the meaning of total disability is important. **Total disability** is always defined in the policy, and different companies may use different definitions. These definitions are based on work activity, and insurers look at work activity in terms of two dimensions: the insured's own occupation and any occupation the insured may be qualified to perform.

19. 3. 4. 1 Own Occupation

The first way total disability might be defined concerns the occupation in which the particular individual is normally engaged. In this case, total disability is defined as an insured's inability to perform any or all of the duties of the insured's own occupation.

This refers to the insured's own occupation at the time disability begins. Suppose Lee, who is a word-processing typist, is involved in an accident in which three fingers on one hand and four on the other are severed. Using the definition given, Lee has a total disability because he is unable to use the keyboard—a primary duty of his occupation.

19. 3. 4. 2 Any Occupation

An alternative and more restrictive definition of total disability is an insured's inability to perform the duties of any occupation for which the insured is reasonably qualified by education, training, or experience.

Again, consider Lee, the word-processing typist whose fingers were severed. Under the first definition, he was totally disabled because he was unable to perform the duties of his own occupation. Suppose, however, that Lee is qualified to teach word processing. Under this second definition, Lee is not totally disabled because he can work as an instructor, an occupation for which he is qualified by training and experience.

The own-occupation definition, which is less restrictive and therefore more favorable to the insured, is used more commonly than the any-occupation definition.

Later in this unit, we'll talk about both short- and long-term disability income policies. Long-term policies generally use both definitions to cover different periods during the insured's disability. The own-occupation definition generally is used for the initial period of disability, which might extend from two to five years as stated in the policy. Then the any-occupation definition applies to disability continuing beyond the initial period.

Once again, remember Lee, the word-processing typist. Suppose Lee's policy includes both of these provisions, and it identifies the initial period as two years. If Lee performed no work at all during the two years following the loss of his fingers, he could collect total disability benefits under the own-occupation definition.

Suppose Lee wants neither to be a word-processing instructor nor to do any other kind of work except his previous occupation, which he is now unable to do. After two years, he could no longer claim total disability and continue receiving benefits, because the any-occupation definition becomes effective. Because he is qualified and able to perform other work, he is no longer classified as totally disabled.

19. 3. 4. 3 Loss of Earnings

Between these two definitions of **total disability**, there are several variations. In fact, some policies use a two-tier definition that refers to the insured's own occupation during an initial period of disability and then shifts to any occupation. These policies usually define **total disability** as the inability to perform the duties of the insured's own occupation for a period of two to five years, and thereafter the inability to perform the duties of any occupation for which the insured is suited by reason of education, training, experience, or prior economic status. This is known as the **loss of earnings** test for disability.

19. 3. 4. 4 Injury Versus Sickness

Total disability is occasionally further defined in terms of its cause. For example, some policies may cover only, or cover differently, disability caused by accidental injury, and some may cover only disability caused by sickness. In these cases, the terms *total accident (or injury) disability* and *total sickness disability* might be used.

If you see these terms, you know that total accident disability is disability caused by an accident, and total sickness disability is caused by sickness.

19. 3. 4. 5 Occupational Versus Nonoccupational

Although short-term policies often cover only nonoccupational disability, most long-term plans cover both occupational and nonoccupational sickness and accidents. When occupational benefits are provided, they are often reduced by benefits received from workers' compensation and Social Security.

19. 3. 4. 6 Medically Defined

Some older policies also require that in addition to meeting the definition of total disability, the insured must also be confined to the house and under the treatment of a doctor. This is called **medically defined** disability.

19. 3. 5 Presumptive Disability

Aside from the occupational considerations, many disability income policies have another criterion by which total disability may be classified. This is called **presumptive disability**, which is a condition that automatically qualifies insureds for total disability classification, whether or not they can work. Conditions generally considered to be presumptive disabilities include:

- loss of use of any two limbs;
- total and permanent blindness; and
- loss of speech and hearing.

Under these criteria, if Bruce's right arm and leg are severed in an accident, he is presumptively disabled. However, if Allen's left leg is amputated, he is not because only one limb is involved.

Presumptive disability may also be determined using a loss of earnings test. The insured's level of earnings before disability is compared to the level of earnings after disability. If postdisability earnings fall below predisability earnings by a given percentage, the insured is considered totally disabled and eligible for a full benefit even if some level of earnings remains.

19. 3. 6 Partial Disability

Although total disability is the insured's inability to perform any duties of the insured's own occupation, not every disability is total. Some people may suffer a partial disability. This means the person cannot perform every duty of the occupation but can perform one of more important duties of the occupation.

Example

Bob works in a warehouse where his duties involve moving materials both with a mechanical lift-truck and by hand. Bob injures his back and is unable to perform the part of his job that involves moving heavy materials by hand, but he can use the lift-truck. Because Bob is able to perform some of the duties of his occupation, but not all of them, he is partially disabled.

Partial disability is generally not a factor in sickness disability. The insured usually either is or is not sick enough to stay off the job. Partial disability applies largely to accident disability, although some policies apply the concept to certain illnesses, such as heart attacks or ulcers.

Therefore, to receive sickness benefits from a disability income policy, the insured usually must be totally disabled. However, certain accident benefits may be payable when the insured is either totally or partially disabled.

The usual partial disability indemnity is 50% of the monthly or weekly indemnity for total disability. If a policy pays, for example, $3,000 per month for total disability, it will probably pay $1,500 for partial disability. These benefits are usually paid for a relatively short period—commonly three or six months.

An insured might receive both total and partial disability benefits as the result of a single accident. For example, a person might be totally disabled for three months, then be able to return to work but able to perform only a few of the usual duties for some time—let's say two months. If the policy so stipulates, the individual described would be eligible to receive total disability benefits during the first three months and partial disability benefits for the next two months.

19. 3. 7 Residual Disability

Many recent policies have replaced the partial disability provision with a **residual disability** provision. A **residual disability** benefit is usually a percentage of the total disability benefit for periods of partial disability as defined in the policy.

Earnings come into play in the residual benefit provision. Earnings during partial disability must be at least a stated percentage less than earnings before disability—20% less, for example. For instance, if earnings before disability were $2,000 per month and the policy required earnings during partial disability to be reduced at least 20% to receive residual benefits, a partially disabled person could earn no more than $1,600 per month.

The percentage of reduction in earnings is multiplied by the normal benefit to determine the residual benefit. So, if in the previous example, the normal benefits were $1,000 per month, the residual benefit would be $200: 20% (reduction in earnings) × $1,000 (normal benefit). If the reduction in earnings is not at least the minimum stated percentage, no benefits are payable under this option.

19. 3. 8 Recurrent Disability

Occasionally, after a period of disability appears to be over, the disability will recur as a result of the same illness or accident. A second period of disability from the same or a related cause of a prior disability is a **recurrent disability**.

Most disability income policies stipulate that if the insured returns to work for a specified period of time after the original disability, a recurrence must be handled as a new claim for a new period of disability, requiring a new elimination period, rather than as a continuation of a prior claim. Usually, the specified period is 90 days, although some insurers permit six months.

Assume a policy specifies that no new elimination period is required if the disability recurs within 90 days. The insured suffers a disability as the result of an accident, returns to work for six months, and then suffers the same type of disability. In this situation, the disability claim would be treated as a new event rather than a recurrent disability because more than 90 days have passed. Had the insured returned to work for only two months before the disability recurred, no new elimination period would have been required.

19. 3. 9 Permanent Disability

Disability is usually defined as permanent or temporary, in addition to total or partial. A permanent disability is one that reduces or eliminates the insured's ability to work for the rest of the insured's life. Permanent disability results from any injury from which the insured is not expected to recover, such as loss of sight or one or more limbs.

19. 3. 10 Temporary Disability

A temporary disability occurs when an insured is unable to work while recovering from an illness or injury but is expected to fully recover from that illness or injury. Examples would be a broken leg or a sprained back.

19. 3. 11 Confining Versus Nonconfining Disability

Some policies may include a provision that differentiates between disabilities in still another way: whether the disability is confining or nonconfining.

A total, **confining disability** is a condition that requires the individual to stay indoors, perhaps in the hospital or at home except for visits to the doctor.

Example

Lana is at home recuperating from tuberculosis. If she may not leave her home until she is completely recovered, she has a total, confining disability.

A total, **nonconfining disability** refers to a condition that disables but does not require the individual to remain confined indoors.

Example

While Warren was recovering at home from a serious illness, his doctor encouraged him to take a short walk each day. Warren's is a total, nonconfining disability.

You should be aware of this terminology, but unless a policy specifically includes this provision, the absence or presence of confinement does not affect the total disability classification.

19. 3. 12 Accidental Means

Of the terms used to define accident, the two that will be discussed here are **accidental bodily injury** and **accidental means**.

A policy that includes the "accidental means" wording is more restrictive than one that refers simply to accidental bodily injury. To help you understand the restrictive nature of accidental means, let's look at an example.

Example

Mary is carrying a heavy bag of groceries and strains her back. This accident would be defined as accidental bodily injury, because Mary did not intentionally strain her back. However, while the injury was caused by accident, it could not be defined as accidental means because the cause of the accident was foreseeable. That is, using reasonable judgment, Mary could foresee that carrying too heavy a load could produce problems, such as the bag breaking and the contents spilling out and injuring her foot, or, as in this example, the heavy load creating a strain on her back. If the policy under which Mary was covered defined accident in terms of accidental means, she would not receive benefits.

Example

On the other hand, if while carrying this same heavy bag of groceries, a dog runs in Mary's path, causing her to fall and break her arm, she would be covered under the definition of accidental means. This is because the injury was caused by circumstances that could not reasonably be foreseen. Mary could not possibly foresee that a dog would run in her path; that in running in front of her, the dog would cause her to fall; and that in falling, she would break her arm. There are too many contingencies to be planned for. Also, the cause of the fall was not based on any action taken by Mary or by any activity in which Mary was engaged.

The term *accidental bodily injury* encompasses almost all but self-inflicted injuries, subject to any other events the policy excludes. On the other hand, *accidental means* involves a more literal interpretation of accident—an event that is completely unforeseen and unintended.

There is a line of distinction between accidental bodily injury and injury by accidental means—so fine, in fact, that the courts have often been required to determine whether an insurer is liable. Most courts have interpreted policies in favor of the insureds or their beneficiaries. As a result, though at one time many policies contained the "accidental means" stipulation, today most—but not all—policies use only the "accidental bodily injury" wording.

Because some policies being issued today do contain this wording, you should be aware of the implications. If your company's policies do not use accidental means as a criterion for receiving accidental injury or death benefits, you may be able to use this as a sales point. For example, a prospective client might be considering the purchase of either your policy or a competitor's. If your competitor's policy contains the "accidental means" wording, you could point out that your policy's wording is more favorable.

19. 3. 13 Definition of Sickness

Sickness or **illness** may not be defined in any manner that is more restrictive than "sickness or disease that first manifests itself after the effective date of the policy." If a policy provides nonoccupational coverage only, the definition of sickness may exclude work-related disabilities.

Example

Susan applies for and is issued a disability income policy with an effective date of May 1, 2008. Approximately one month later, she begins to have a digestive problem, which is diagnosed on August 15, 2008, as a gall bladder problem requiring surgery. Medically, her symptoms first appeared after the effective date of the policy and, thus, this sickness claim would be honored by the insurer.

Example

On the other hand, let's assume that Susan begins to have the digestive problem on May 1, 2008. She contacts her doctor, and he suggests that she take some antacid medication, which she purchases from her local drug store. By June 1, the problem appears to be no better, but Susan does nothing about it. Susan purchases some disability income insurance with an effective coverage date of July 1, 2008. One month later, she consults with her doctor who, after conducting some tests, diagnoses her gall bladder problem. Even though the diagnosis occurred after the effective date of the disability income policy, the symptoms appeared before the effective date of the policy. Should a claim arise and all the facts become known, the insurer could determine that the gall bladder problem preexisted the effective date of the insurance and deny the claim.

The definition of sickness is very important because it could be used to permanently exclude benefits for conditions that existed prior to the effective date of coverage.

19. 4 BENEFIT CALCULATIONS

Following are some sample benefit calculations that use the concepts discussed thus far.

Beth has a disability income policy with a 30-day elimination period, a $2,000 monthly income benefit for total disability, and a benefit period to age 65. Beth becomes totally disabled on January 1 and is unable to work for three months. She returns to work on a part-time basis on April 1 and is able to earn 40% of her predisability compensation during April. In May, she earns 60% of her predisability income. By June 1, she is working full time, earning 100% of her predisability income. Let's consider how Beth's benefits would differ under a policy that provides total and residual disability benefits and a policy that provides total disability benefits only.

It can be seen in the benefit calculation that a policy that pays residual disability benefits provides an incentive for the insured to return to work because it pays proportional benefits. A more traditional "total disability only" policy implies that an insured cannot return to work for any length of time without losing all benefits. While it appears that the insurance company in the example would pay less (by terminating benefits as soon as Beth returned to work part time in April), it might actually end up paying as much or more than the policy providing residual benefits (because without partial benefits, Beth might not return to work until she is fully recovered in June, and she might claim total disability benefits for two additional months).

Benefit Calculation

Month	Income Loss	Total And Residual Benefit Policy	Total Disability Only Policy
January	100%	None—satisfying the elimination period	None—satisfying the elimination period
February	100%	$2,000—100% of the total disability benefit	$2,000—total disability benefit
March	100%	$2,000—100% of the total disability benefit	$2,000—total disability benefit
April	60%	$1,200—60% of the total disability benefit	None—performing occupational duties
May	40%	$800—40% of the total disability benefit	None—performing occupational duties
June	0	None—no loss of income	None—performing occupational duties

19. 5 TYPES OF DISABILITY BENEFITS AND EXCLUSIONS

19. 5. 1 Short-Term Disability

Most group short-term policies provide for short elimination periods (usually 30 days or less) and short benefit periods. The benefit period is normally for six months but not longer than one year. The benefit amount is limited to a percentage of compensation, such as 60 or 70%.

One of the rationales for short-term disability has been that the worker presumably is eligible for Social Security disability benefits after the five-month Social Security waiting period. In reality, this may or may not be true, depending on whether the worker can qualify for Social Security disability benefits. In addition, if the person does qualify for benefits, the first benefit check will likely not be received before one year from the onset of disability. In any event, short-term disability benefits were designed to fill the gap until Social Security began paying benefits to the claimant.

19. 5. 2 Long-Term Disability (LTD)

LTD policies provide for longer elimination and benefit periods than do short-term policies. Typically, the elimination period is 90 days or six months, with benefits provided for two or five years or to age 65. Most often, LTD policies provide benefits to age 65.

The amount of the long-term benefit is limited to a percentage of the worker's compensation, such as 60 or 70%. As with short-term policies, LTD coverage may be occupational or nonoccupational.

Additionally, LTD policies usually provide for integration of plan benefits with other disability income benefits payable to the insured. The LTD benefit may be offset by any of the following:

- Any benefits provided by another formal employer plan
- Benefits payable under workers' compensation or any similar statutory program
- Any benefits payable under Social Security

The purpose for having integration with these other sources of disability income is to prevent overinsurance on the part of the insured.

19. 5. 3 Lump-Sum Benefits

Lump-sum payments under disability policies were once paid more often than they are today. Modern safety measures and enforcement, coupled with advancements in medical technology, have made total and permanent disabilities less common. Although lump-sum benefits may be paid for presumptive disability, or under special disability policies covering business buy-sell agreements, it is more common for disability income benefits to be received in the form of installment payments.

19. 6 EXCLUSIONS

Common exclusions found in disability income policies are losses arising from war, military service, attempted suicide, overseas residence, aviation under certain circumstances (pilot or crew of aircraft), and losses that result when an insured is injured while committing a felony.

19. 7 OPTIONAL BENEFITS AND RIDERS

19. 7. 1 Rehabilitation Benefit

Because of disability, insureds may not be able to return to their normal occupation but still be able to work at some kind of job. The rehabilitation benefit facilitates vocational training to prepare insureds for a new occupation.

The rehabilitation benefit applies when the insured is totally disabled and receiving benefits. If that is the case and the insured chooses to participate in a vocational rehabilitation program approved by the insurer, then total disability benefits will continue as long as the insured actively participates in the training program and remains totally disabled.

Some insurers may provide a lump-sum benefit for vocational training. Whether a lump-sum or a monthly disability benefit, this benefit enables the insured to take positive steps toward returning to work, even though it may be in another occupation. Thus, this option benefits both insureds and the insurer.

19. 7. 2 Future Increase Option

This option also may be referred to as the **guaranteed insurability option** or **guaranteed purchase option** because it enables the insured to purchase additional disability income protection, regardless of insurability, at specified future dates. However, the rate for this additional coverage will be at the insured's attained age at the time of purchase, not the age when the policy was originally issued.

This benefit has some limitations. The insured will be able to purchase only a specified, predetermined amount of disability income insurance at each option date. To guard against overinsurance, the insurer will usually limit the amount of additional coverage to possibly $500 or less on each option date. Also, the insured's earned income must warrant additional coverage. That is, it is assumed that every few years, the insured's earned income will increase substantially, thus leaving room for additional disability insurance.

Another limitation is the number of option dates on which the insured may purchase additional coverage. Usually, these option dates will be every two or three years from ages 25 to 40, or possibly even to age 50. These dates may be arbitrarily selected by the insurer, or they may coincide with the insured's birthdays, marriage, and the birth of children.

19. 7. 3 Cost-of-Living Benefit

The purchasing power of fixed disability benefits may be eroded because of inflation and increases in the cost of living. To protect against these trends, most insurers will offer an optional cost-of-living benefit.

Under the provisions of this option, the insured's monthly disability benefit (total or residual) will be increased automatically once the insured is on claim (receiving disability income benefits). Typically, this increase will occur after the insured is on claim for 12 months and each 12-month period thereafter as long as the insured remains on claim.

19. 7. 4 Lifetime Benefits

This option extends the benefit period from age 65 to lifetime. This extension may apply to accident-only benefits or to accident and sickness benefits. Normally, if the total disability is due to an accident and it occurs before age 65, benefits will be paid for the lifetime of the insured, provided the insured remains totally disabled.

Most companies will place some time limitations for the lifetime sickness benefit. That is, the disabling sickness must begin before a specified age such as 50, 55, or 60. A policy providing lifetime sickness benefits may stipulate that if the sickness begins at age 55 or earlier, then 100% of the total disability benefit will be provided for the lifetime of the insured. However, if the disability begins after age 55 but before age 65, a reduced benefit will be paid for life.

Example

A policy might state the following.

If total disability due to sickness begins at age 55 or earlier, total disability benefits will be paid for the lifetime of the insured. If total disability benefits begin at age:

- 56, total benefits are paid to age 65, then 90% of the benefit for the lifetime of the insured;
- 57, total benefits are paid to age 65, then 80% of the benefit for the lifetime of the insured;
- 58, total benefits are paid to age 65, then 70% of the benefit for the lifetime of the insured;
- 59, total benefits are paid to age 65, then 60% of the benefit for the lifetime of the insured; and
- 60, total benefits are paid to age 65, then 50% of the benefit for the lifetime of the insured.

This progression of benefits would continue in this manner until age 65. If the total disability began at age 65 (normally the policy is not renewed past age 65), the payment of total disability benefits would be limited to one or two years.

19. 7. 5 Social Security Rider

The Social Security Administration defines **total disability** as the "inability to perform any substantial gainful work which may exist in the national economy." In addition, the disability must be expected to last at least 12 months or end in death. This is a very rigid and ultraconservative definition of total disability. As a result, many disabled people do not qualify for Social Security disability benefits. In fact, the Social Security Administration denies about two-thirds of all disability claims.

Even when Social Security benefits are payable, there is a five-month waiting period, and benefits do not begin until the sixth month of disability. When a Social Security rider is added to an individual's disability income policy, an additional monthly benefit is payable during the waiting period.

The rider may or may not continue to pay benefits after Social Security benefits begin. There are two different methods by which this type of rider may provide benefits.

- **All or nothing rider**. Under this approach, the insured will be paid a benefit only if Social Security pays nothing. Conversely, if Social Security provides any benefit, then the rider pays nothing.
- **Offset rider**. Under this approach, the benefit provided by the rider will be reduced, or offset, by the amount of any benefit provided by Social Security.

19. 7. 6 Social Insurance Supplements

Some insurers offer social insurance supplements designed to fill gaps left by various government benefit programs. The concept is similar to the Social Security rider, except that this coverage also may mesh with workers' compensation benefits and benefits provided by state disability funds. These supplemental benefits may be included as part of the disability income policy or may be added to the policy by rider. The benefits are usually payable during any waiting periods for social insurance benefits or if the social insurance benefits are denied. Benefits will be paid monthly until government benefits begin. If, for any reason, the government benefits stop, the insurer will step in and begin the monthly payments again. However, the benefits are only payable during the benefit period specified in the contract and only while the insured remains disabled.

19. 7. 7 Additional Monthly Benefit (AMB) Riders

Most insurers offer short-term riders to provide additional benefits during the first 6 or 12 months of a claim. Some companies may call these Social Security riders because the benefit is payable during the Social Security waiting period, although the rider itself may not even refer to Social Security benefits. More commonly, the term *additional monthly benefit rider* is used. The additional benefits during the early months of disability may be used to supplement government benefits or short-term disability benefits provided by an employer, or they may be used to help pay extra transitional expenses that might be incurred when an insured is first disabled.

19. 7. 8 Hospital Confinement Rider

This optional benefit results in the elimination period being waived when the insured is hospitalized as an inpatient. The payment of any disability benefits usually requires satisfying the elimination period. The hospital confinement benefit pays the regular total disability benefit during the elimination period when the insured is hospitalized.

The factor that triggers the payment of the benefit is any period of hospitalization during the elimination period. Benefits will be paid only as long as the insured is hospitalized.

Example

An insured has a disability income policy with a 30-day elimination period and a $1,000 per month benefit for total disability, payable to age 65. The insured also has the hospital confinement option and is hospitalized for minor surgery for two days. Following the hospitalization, the insured returns to work within three days. Total disability benefits will be paid for the two days. The amount paid will be 2/30 (1/15) of $1,000, or $67.

19. 7. 9 Impairment Rider

When an applicant for insurance has an existing medical problem or chronic condition, an insurer might attach an **impairment rider** to the standard policy. This rider excludes coverage for a specific ailment or condition that otherwise would be covered. Because the condition currently exists, the insurance company will be unlikely to take the risk, so will normally refuse coverage. Using the impairment rider to exclude this specific condition, however, benefits both the applicant and the insurer in the following ways.

- The applicant is able to obtain coverage that might not otherwise be available for other health care needs.
- The insurance company is able to protect itself from undue risk from this particular condition and is still able to provide health coverage.

Impairment riders are written on an individual basis for a specific person's medical condition, such as heart disease, cancer, or diabetes. The exclusion in the rider applies only to the person with the impairment and not to any other insureds, such as family members covered by the same policy.

19. 7. 10 Nondisabling Injury Rider

This benefit does not pay a disability benefit but rather provides for the payment of medical expenses incurred as the result of injury that does not result in total disability.

19. 7. 11 Waiver of Premium (with Disability Income)

This rider specifies that in the event of disability, premiums will be waived retroactively to the beginning of the disability. The definition is usually permanent and total disability. Again, however, a few companies have gone to a definition in terms of occupation, as previously discussed.

19. 7. 12 Accidental Death and Dismemberment (AD&D)

Accidental death policies or riders include a death benefit that is payable in the event of death resulting from accidental bodily injury. A companion coverage is provided for loss of limbs or sight, often called dismemberment coverage.

A schedule is made a part of the policy that lists various dismemberments and losses of sight for which a specified sum will be paid to the insured. In policies with weekly disability income benefits, the sum payable is usually expressed as a multiple of the weekly indemnity. In policies without weekly disability income benefits, the sums payable are usually expressed as percentages of the death benefit limit or sometimes as percentages of a limit in the policy known as the **capital sum**. The capital sum might be $20,000 and the death benefit is usually the same amount ($20,000).

Sample Schedule

Loss Of	Sum Equal To Weekly Indemnity For
Both hands, or feet, or sight of both eyes	200 weeks
One hand and one foot	200 weeks
Either hand or foot and sight of one eye	200 weeks
Either hand or foot	100 weeks
Sight of one eye	65 weeks
Thumb and index finger of either hand	50 weeks

The intent of the dismemberment feature is to provide insureds with a lump sum that will help them over the period when they go through rehabilitation and, probably, training for work other than that for which they previously were qualified. If the policy has a disability income feature, once a dismemberment sum is paid, the disability income payments stop. In some cases, the insured might be disabled for a while and, during the disability, suffer one of the losses listed above. In that event, the insured would be paid disability income up to the time of the loss of limb or sight only.

Most company policies provide that, even if the insured is not disabled after an accident, if a loss of limb or sight occurs within 90 days of the date of the accident, the sums in the schedule will be paid.

Accidental death and dismemberment coverage provides both a life insurance and a health insurance benefit. However, the life insurance benefit applies only to accidental death and is not paid for death by natural causes.

19. 7. 13 Other Provisions

Although disability income policies do not typically accumulate cash value or have a life insurance component, it is possible to purchase riders to the policy that provide benefits similar to those of life insurance policies. Thus, an **annual renewable term** life insurance feature may be attached to a disability income policy, providing a death benefit as well as disability income coverage.

Similarly, a **return of premium rider** may be attached to a disability income policy. This rider provides for the return of a percentage of premiums paid (usually 80%) during a specific term period (usually every 10 years) minus the claims paid during the term period. The refund is made every 10 years and at age 65 or as of the date of death. Essentially, for an additional premium, the policyholder gets 80% of the money back either in claims, premium refunds, or a combination of both. Various settlement options are offered for receiving the premium refund. Amounts left on deposit with the insurance company earn interest and constitute cash value or may be applied toward future premium payments.

19. 8 BUSINESS USES

Disability income insurance is designed to protect an individual's most important asset—the ability to earn an income. By protecting against the loss of income during periods of disability, this type of coverage enables the disabled insured to continue to provide for the basic necessities of life. The application and use of disability income coverage is not confined to individuals but also is very relevant in business situations.

The life insurance section of this book identifies business uses of life insurance—that is, to fund buy-sell agreements, key person insurance, and so on. Life insurance benefits are paid to the business upon the death of a key person or the businessowner so that the business may continue. A similar concept applies for the business with regard to the disability of a key person or the businessowner. The living death of disability can have a serious impact on the continued existence and profitability of a business.

19. 8. 1 Business Overhead Expense (BOE)

The BOE policy is designed for the small businessowner. Its purpose is to cover certain overhead expenses that continue when the businessowner is disabled. Most insurers will limit the BOE policy to relatively small businesses.

Example

General Motors would not be eligible for a BOE policy, but a small firm consisting of the owner and three to four employees could purchase a BOE policy.

The policy will indemnify the business (not the owner) for such business expenses as rent, taxes, insurance premiums, utility bills, employees' compensation (not the owner's salary), and so forth. By covering these expenses when the owner is disabled, the business is able to keep its doors open and continue to operate.

Naturally, the overall concept is that the small businessowner is so important to the profitability of the business that when the bussinessowner becomes totally disabled, the business will suffer economically and may even be forced to close. An example of such a situation would be a dentist. Typically, if the dentist cannot practice, business income will eventually be impaired and the few employees working in the dentist's office may lose their jobs. As the business income slows, the bills still have to be paid, as do the employees. The BOE policy will solve this problem.

Generally, BOE policies have elimination periods of 15 or 30 days and benefit periods of one or two years. The benefit amount will be determined by the average eligible overhead expenses of the business. If the businessowner becomes disabled, after the elimination period is satisfied, the business will receive benefits equal to the actual overhead expenses incurred during the owner's disability.

BOE premiums are tax deductible to the business. The disability benefits received are thus taxable to the business. However, these taxable benefits are then used to pay tax-deductible business expenses.

19. 8. 2 Key Person Disability Insurance

Just as key person life insurance indemnifies the business for the lost services of a key person, so does a key person disability income policy. This type of coverage pays a monthly benefit to a business to cover expenses for additional help or outside services when an essential person is disabled. The key person could be a partner or working stockholder of the business. The key person could also be a management person who is personally responsible for some very important functions, such as a sales manager.

The key person's economic value to the business is determined in terms of the potential loss of business income that could occur, as well as the expense of hiring and training a replacement for the key person. The key person's value then becomes the disability benefit that will be paid to the business. The benefit amount may be paid in a lump sum or in monthly installments. Generally, the policy's elimination period will be 30 to 90 days, and the benefit period will be one or two years.

The business is the owner and premium payor of the policy. Benefits are received by the business tax free, because the premium paid is not tax deductible.

19. 8. 3 Disability Buy-Sell Insurance

When there is a buy-sell agreement funded with life insurance to buy out the interest of a deceased owner or partner, there should also be a provision in the agreement for the buyout of the owner's business interest in the event of disability. Naturally, this disability provision should be funded with buy-sell disability income insurance.

One of the critical considerations with reference to the disability buy-sell policy is the elimination period. Once the elimination period is satisfied, benefits will begin to be made to the business for the purpose of buying out the interest of the disabled owner or partner. Generally, once the buyout begins, it cannot be stopped. Thus, for example, a disabled partner does not want to be bought too soon and then possibly recover from the disability and find that he has no job and no business interest.

For this reason, the elimination period for disability buy-sell insurance will normally be one or two years. The buy-sell agreement will specify the value or a method of determining the value of the owner's business interest. This value will be paid to the business following the elimination period. The benefits may be paid in a lump sum or in monthly installments. If the policy provides a monthly benefit, usually the benefit period will not exceed five years. The business, of course, uses the policy proceeds to buy out the interest of the disabled person.

Usually, the business is the owner and premium payor for the policy or policies. The premiums are not deductible, but the benefits are received by the business tax free.

19. 9 SUMMARY

In this lesson, you learned about:

- why disability insurance is an important part of an individual's insurance portfolio;
- four practical considerations to be taken into account when determining disability income needs;
- four possible alternatives to disability income insurance and why they are less desirable than they may first seem;
- the importance of the elimination period and how it affects benefits;
- when the benefit period begins and some typical benefit periods;
- the factors that go into determining total disability and how it is defined in each policy;
- the difference between own occupation and any occupation when determining total disability;
- the difference between injury and sickness disability;
- the difference between occupational and nonoccupational disability;
- the concept of presumptive disability and three conditions generally considered to be presumptive disabilities;
- the criteria for partial disability;
- the concept of residual disability and how it is used;
- the concept of recurrent disability and how it is used;
- the difference between permanent and temporary disability;
- the difference between confining and nonconfining disability;
- the difference between accidental bodily injury and injury by accidental means;
- the function of short-term disability coverage;
- the function of long-term disability coverage;
- six common exclusions found in disability income policies; and

- the use and function of the following riders: rehabilitation benefit, future increase option, cost-of-living benefit, lifetime benefits, Social Security, social insurance supplements, additional monthly benefit, hospital confinement, nondisabling injury, waiver of premium, and accidental death and dismemberment.

UNIT TEST

1. To receive benefits from a disability income policy for disability due to sickness, the insured must be
   A. totally disabled
   B. partially disabled
   C. either totally or partially disabled
   D. deceased

2. Social insurance supplements provide disability income
   A. before workers' compensation and Social Security begin payments
   B. after workers' compensation and Social Security end payments
   C. both A and B
   D. neither A nor B

3. The benefit that enables a disabled insured to learn to work in another occupation is known as the
   A. cost-of-living benefit
   B. rehabilitation benefit
   C. guaranteed insurability option
   D. lifetime benefit option

4. The benefit that protects against the erosion of purchasing power for fixed disability benefits is known as the
   A. cost-of-living benefit
   B. rehabilitation benefit
   C. offset rider
   D. lifetime benefit

5. The rider that provides more benefits during the first 6 months or year of a claim is known as the
   A. cost-of-living rider
   B. rehabilitation rider
   C. additional monthly benefit rider
   D. lifetime benefit rider

6. The benefit that pays the regular total disability benefit during the elimination period when the insured is hospitalized is known as the
   A. hospital confinement rider
   B. rehabilitation benefit
   C. nondisabling injury rider
   D. offset rider

7. The option that allows an insured to purchase additional amounts of disability income protection is known as the
   A. lifetime benefit option
   B. additional monthly benefit option
   C. all or nothing option
   D. future increase option

8. Social insurance supplements provide disability income
   A. before workers' compensation and Social Security begin payments
   B. after workers' compensation and Social Security end payments
   C. both A and B
   D. neither A nor B

9. The elimination period may be thought of as
   A. a dollar amount deductible
   B. a time deductible
   C. a dollar amount co-payment
   D. a time co-payment

10. The longer the benefit period
    A. the higher the policy's premium
    B. the lower the policy's premium
    C. the higher the policy's benefits
    D. the lower the policy's benefits

11. Which definition of total disability is more favorable to the insured?
    A. Own occupation
    B. Any occupation
    C. They are the same in terms of benefits to the insured
    D. There is no way to determine from the information provided

12. Occupational disability benefits are often reduced by benefits received
    A. from Social Security only
    B. from workers' compensation only
    C. from either Social Security or workers' compensation
    D. before the end of the elimination period only

13. Which of the following generally is NOT considered to be a presumptive disability?
    A. Loss of the dominant hand
    B. Loss of use of any two limbs
    C. Total and permanent blindness
    D. Loss of speech and hearing

14. Which of the following statements about partial disability is NOT true?
    A. The person is not able to perform every duty of the prior occupation.
    B. The person is able to perform one or more important duties of the occupation.
    C. Sickness disability is more likely to be partial than accident disability.
    D. An insured might receive both total and partial disability benefits as the result of a single accident.

15. Some policies have replaced the partial disability provision with a
    A. reduced disability provision
    B. redundant disability provision
    C. recurrent disability provision
    D. residual disability provision

16. Brandon injures his back working at a warehouse. Six months later, he is well enough to go back to work lifting boxes. Two weeks into working, however, he strains his back again and has to go back on bed rest. This is an example of a
    A. redundant disability
    B. residual disability
    C. recurrent disability
    D. reduced disability

17. Lee is helping a friend move his pool table when he strains his back, causing a disability. The insurer declines coverage, saying the injury was not accidental under the terms of Lee's policy. Lee's policy must include
    A. an accidental bodily injury definition of accidental
    B. an accidental means definition of accidental
    C. a confining definition of accidental
    D. a nonconfining definition of accidental

18. Most often, LTD policies provide benefits
    A. for 2 years
    B. for 5 years
    C. to age 60
    D. to age 65

19. Common exclusions under disability policies include all of the following EXCEPT
    A. disability caused by flying as a passenger on a commercial aircraft
    B. disability resulting when an insured is injured while committing a felony
    C. disability caused by self-inflicted injury
    D. disability caused by an act of war

20. Which of the following statements regarding the future increase option rider is NOT true?
    A. The rate for additional coverage will be at the insured's attained age at the time of purchase.
    B. The rider guarantees the ability to increase coverage to a predetermined limit regardless of change in the insured's income.
    C. The rider generally limits the number of option dates on which the insured may purchase additional coverage.
    D. The rider usually limits the amount of additional coverage available at each option date.

21. Disability benefits will generally be paid for the lifetime of the insured if total disability due to sickness begins at age
    A. 45 or earlier
    B. 50 or earlier
    C. 55 or earlier
    D. 65 or earlier

22. Which of the following statements regarding Social Security disability benefits is TRUE?
    A. For benefits to be paid, the disability must be permanent and expected to end in death.
    B. For benefits to be paid, the disability must prevent the individual from being able to perform any substantial gainful work existing in the national economy.
    C. Most of the people who apply for disability under Social Security are able to get benefits.
    D. Social Security provides a fairly liberal definition of total disability in order to keep individuals able to spend and support the national economy.

23. Which of the following statements about accidental death and dismemberment coverage is NOT true?
    A. A schedule listing various dismemberments and the sums that will be paid for them will be listed in the policy.
    B. The sums payable are generally expressed as percentages of the death benefit limit or the capital sum.
    C. If the policy has a disability income feature, the disability income payments continue even after the dismemberment sum is paid.
    D. Even if the insured is not disabled after an accident, if a loss of limb or sight occurs within 90 days of the date of the accident, the sums in the schedule will be paid.

24. Which of the following organizations would be most likely to be eligible for business overhead expense insurance?
    A. A law firm with 15 partners
    B. A doctor's office
    C. A major multinational corporation
    D. A public library

25. To protect the businessowner, the elimination period for disability buy-sell insurance normally is
    A. 1 to 2 weeks
    B. 3 to 6 months
    C. 6 months to 1 year
    D. 1 to 2 years

ANSWERS AND RATIONALES TO UNIT TEST

1. **A.** To receive benefits from a disability income policy for disability due to sickness, the insured must be totally disabled.
2. **C.** Social insurance supplements provide disability income before workers' compensation and Social Security begin payments and after workers' compensation and Social Security end payments.
3. **B.**
4. **A.** The benefit that protects against the erosion of purchasing power for fixed disability benefits is known as the cost-of-living benefit.
5. **C.** The rider that provides more benefits during the first 6 months or year of a claim is known as the additional monthly benefit rider.
6. **A.** The benefit that pays the regular total disability benefit during the elimination period when the insured is hospitalized is known as the hospital confinement rider.
7. **D.** The option that allows an insured to purchase additional amounts of disability income protection is known as the future increase option.
8. **C.** Social insurance supplements provide disability income before workers' compensation and Social Security begin payments and after workers' compensation and Social Security end payments.
9. **B.**
10. **A.** The longer the benefit period the higher the policy's premium.
11. **A.** The own occupation definition of total disability is more favorable to the insured.
12. **C.** Occupational disability benefits are often reduced by benefits received from either Social Security or workers' compensation.
13. **A.** Loss of the dominant hand is not considered to be a presumptive disability.
14. **C.** Sickness disability is less likely to be partial than accident disability.
15. **D.** Some policies have replaced the partial disability provision with a residual disability provision.
16. **C.** A recurrent disability is when a second period of disability arises from the same or a related cause of a prior disability.
17. **B.** An accidental means definition of accidental means that the accident is completely unforeseen and unintended.
18. **D.** Most often, LTD policies provide benefits to age 65.
19. **A.** Disability caused by flying as a passenger on a commercial aircraft is not a common exclusion under disability policies.
20. **B.** The rider does not guarantee the ability to increase coverage to a predetermined limit regardless of change in the insured's income.
21. **C.** Disability benefits will generally be paid for the lifetime of the insured if total disability due to sickness begins at age 55 or earlier.
22. **B.** For benefits to be paid, the disability must prevent the individual from being able to perform any substantial gainful work existing in the national economy.
23. **C.** If the policy has a disability income feature, the disability income payments do not continue even after the dismemberment sum is paid.
24. **B.** A doctor's office would be most likely to be eligible for business overhead expense insurance.
25. **D.** To protect the businessowner, the elimination period for disability buy-sell insurance normally is 1 to 2 years.

UNIT

20

Medical Expense Insurance

20. 1 INTRODUCTION

Medical expense insurance provides benefits for medical care. Contracts may provide for payment of medical expenses incurred on a reimbursement basis (by paying benefits to the policyowner), payment on a service basis (by paying those who provide the services directly), or payment of an indemnity (by paying a set amount regardless of the amount charged for medical expenses). Medical expense or hospitalization insurance may be written on an individual or group basis. Benefits provided cover the individual and eligible dependents.

Although there are many types of benefits available, medical expense insurance can generally be categorized as basic medical expense insurance, major medical insurance, comprehensive medical insurance, and special policies. Note that these products have largely been replaced by managed care alternatives and are no longer sold as stand-alone coverages. These types of plans have been modified and replaced in response to changes in the health care field relative to cost containment and market competition. However, an understanding of basic medical, hospital, and surgical plans can serve as a foundation for understanding the hybrid plans currently being marketed.

20. 2 LEARNING OBJECTIVES

After completing this lesson, you will be able to:

- explain the purpose of medical expense insurance;
- describe the types of coverage generally offered under basic medical expense policies;
- explain the difference between a scheduled and a nonscheduled plan;
- list and describe 18 exclusions common to medical expense policies but not disability income policies;
- explain the difference between basic and major medical expense policies;
- list and describe the two main groups of major medical expense policies;
- explain the function of deductibles, coinsurance, stop-loss limits, and maximum benefits;
- describe how supplemental major medical benefits work;
- list and describe 19 things covered in most major medical plans;
- list and describe 15 items generally subject to limitations on benefits under medical expense plans;
- explain when alternative providers may be able to receive payment under medical expense policies; and

- list and describe five types of benefits sometimes added to medical expense policies.

20. 3 BASIC MEDICAL EXPENSE

Basic coverages provided by an individual medical expense policy include hospital expense, surgical expense and medical expense. These three basic coverages may be sold together or separately. Frequently this is written as "first dollar" coverage, which means it does not have a deductible.

20. 3. 1 Hospital Expense Benefits

As the name implies, **hospital expense** coverage provides benefits for expenses incurred during hospitalization. Hospital indemnities are usually classified into two broad groups:

- Room and board, including nursing care and special diets
- Miscellaneous medical expenses, including x-rays, laboratory fees, medications, medical supplies, and operating and treatment rooms

In some cases, surgical benefits may be included for certain types of surgery and associated costs.

20. 3. 1. 1 Room and Board Benefit

Hospital expense coverage provides benefits for daily hospital room and board and miscellaneous hospital expenses (not including telephone and television) while the insured person is confined to the hospital. The policy may provide for a certain dollar amount for the daily hospital room and board benefit, although the trend is toward coverage of not more than the semiprivate room rate unless a private room is medically necessary.

The room and board benefit may be paid on either an indemnity basis or a reimbursement basis, depending on the particular policy.

When room and board are covered on an indemnity basis, the insurer pays a specified, preestablished amount per day, as shown in a schedule in the policy, for a stated maximum number of days. For example, the policy might pay $125 per day for up to 90 days. Thus, if the hospital's room and board charge is $135 per day and an insured is hospitalized for 10 days, the total charge will be $1,350 ($135 × 10), and the policy will pay $1,250 ($125 × 10). If the insured were hospitalized for more than 90 days, no additional room and board would be covered.

Indemnity policies are sometimes called dollar amount plans. Room and board rates vary by geographic location, but it is not unusual to find room and board rates ranging from $300 to $500 per day or more. Typically, the maximum number of days is from 90 to 365.

More commonly, room and board expenses are paid on a **reimbursement** basis. This is also referred to as an expenses-incurred basis. Under this arrangement, the policy will pay in one of two ways.

- The actual charges for a semiprivate room are covered.
- A percentage of the actual charges is paid, with no specific dollar limit.

Under the first reimbursement option—actual charges —the insurer will pay the full actual semiprivate room rate, regardless of what it is, as indicated in the illustration that follows.

Actual Charges/Option A

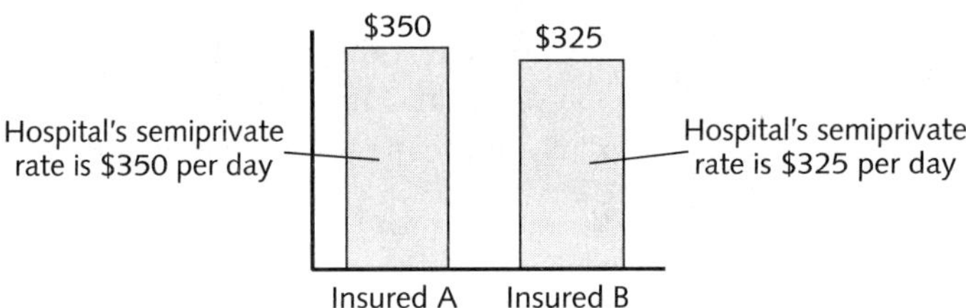

Under this same arrangement, however, the insurer still pays only the semiprivate room rate if the insured must be in a private room, as indicated in the following chart.

Option B

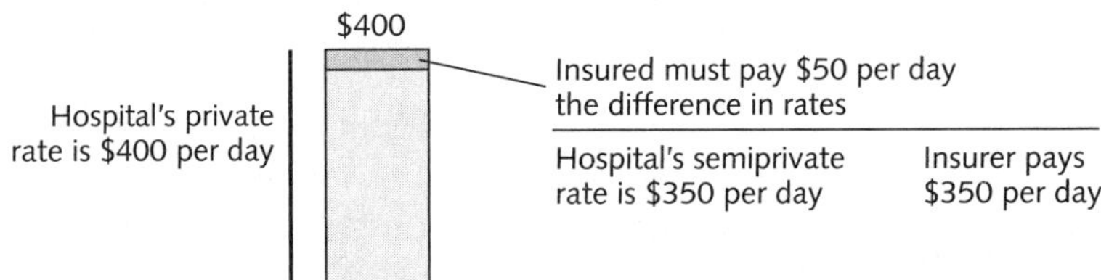

Under the second reimbursement option—payment of a percentage of the actual charges —the insurance company pays a specified percentage, regardless of what the actual charges are. A common percentage is 80%. Here is how it would apply to Insureds A and B from the previous illustration.

Pecentage of Actual Charges

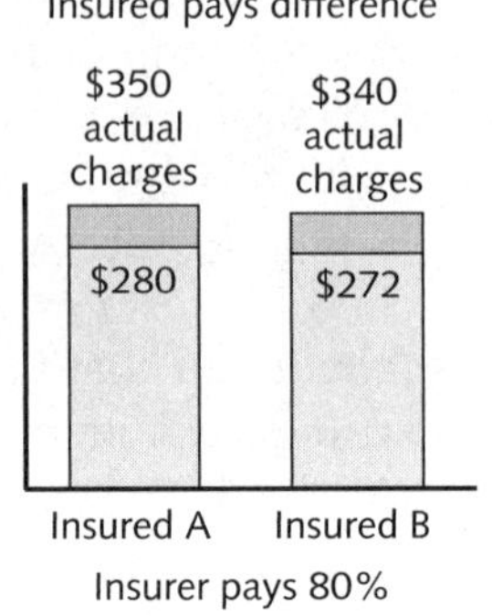

To summarize, under the actual charges type of reimbursement plan, the policy will pay the actual amount charged for a semiprivate room without regard to a specific dollar limit. Under the percentage type of reimbursement plan, the policy will pay a specified percentage of the actual charges.

Some room and board benefits include intensive care, which may be paid in full or in part. Hospital plans with this provision generally provide for a maximum intensive care benefit of some multiple of the room and board maximum—usually two or three times. For example, if the room and board maximum is $400 per day, the plan might pay twice that amount, or $800 per day, for intensive care. A limit might also be placed on the number of days for which this benefit will be paid.

20. 3. 1. 2 Miscellaneous Medical Expenses Benefit

Benefits for miscellaneous medical expenses are generally stated as a limit separate from the room and board benefits. Usually, the limit is expressed as some multiple of the per-day limit for room and board—such as 10 or 20 times—for each period of hospital confinement. For example, a policy might state that it will pay 10 times the semiprivate room rate. If the semiprivate rate is $500 per day, a total of $5,000 (10 × $500) is available for miscellaneous expenses during this single stay in the hospital. If, a year later, the rate has increased to $550 per day, $5,500 will be available.

20. 3. 2 Surgical Expense Benefits

20. 3. 2. 1 Scheduled Plan

Surgical expense policies pay surgeons' fees and related costs incurred when the insured has an operation. Related costs might include fees for an assistant surgeon, an anesthesiologist, and even the operating room, when it is not covered as a miscellaneous medical item.

Basic surgical coverage is often included in the same policy as basic hospital and medical expense. Benefit amounts are included in a schedule that lists major commonly performed operations and benefits payable for each. The fact that a particular type of surgery is not listed in the schedule does not mean that no benefit is available to cover it. Instead, insurers indemnify on the basis of the absolute value and the relative value of each surgical procedure.

For example, suppose the insurer has determined that the prevailing value, or cost, of a certain type of surgery is $4,000 as indicated in the schedule that accompanies the policy. This is the **absolute value** of that procedure. Another procedure, not listed in the schedule, might be relatively less complicated. Let's say the company has determined that it is only 50% as complex as the $4,000 procedure. Therefore, its **relative value** is $2,000, and that is the benefit that will be paid for the unscheduled, less complicated procedure.

In some cases, the schedule itself may be referred to in terms of the maximum benefit paid for the most costly procedure, with all other surgical benefits paid as a percentage of that maximum. For example, under a $10,000 schedule, that amount might be paid for open-heart surgery. A less complex procedure, such as a tonsillectomy, might trigger a benefit equal to 10% of that, or $1,000.

20. 3. 2. 2 *Nonscheduled Plan*

When surgical benefits (and sometimes other benefits) are not listed by a specific dollar amount in a schedule, a policy will pay on the basis of what is considered **usual, customary, and reasonable (UCR)** in a certain geographic area. This type of indemnity is found more often in the major medical and comprehensive policies discussed later in this unit.

Under this type of arrangement, the definition of UCR is based on the amount physicians in the area usually charge for the same or similar procedures. These nonscheduled plans allow policies to stay apace of inflation and to avoid policy restructuring every time medical costs increase. The insurer still reserves the right to agree or disagree that a particular charge is usual, customary, and reasonable.

20. 3. 3 Regular Medical Expense Benefits

Another category, regular medical expense benefits, is sometimes called physicians' nonsurgical expense. Remember that some states refer to this particular category as basic medical expense. Coverage is for nonsurgical services a physician provides. Sometimes, it is narrowly applied to physician visits to patients confined in the hospital. If so, the benefit will usually pay for:

- a specified maximum number of visits per day;
- a specified maximum dollar amount per visit; and
- a specified maximum number of days that coverage applies.

For example, this type of limited benefit might pay for up to three visits per day at $10 per visit for no more than 30 days.

In other policies, the benefit might be for nonsurgical services a physician performs whether or not the patient is in the hospital. Again there are limits, such as $25 per visit for up to 50 visits a year.

20. 3. 4 Other Medical Expense Benefits

In addition to the hospital, surgical, and medical benefits just discussed, there are other benefits that might be included, that may be added at the insured's option, or for which separate policies might be written. Different insurers may include different options as part of their standard policies, so each policy must be considered individually. Some coverage options are:

- maternity;
- convalescent/nursing home;

- emergency first aid;
- home health care;
- mental infirmity;
- hospice care;
- prescription drugs;
- dread disease;
- outpatient treatment;
- dental;
- private-duty nursing; and
- vision.

We will discuss the most common options here, and in another lesson you'll learn about those that are more typically written as separate policies.

20. 3. 4. 1 In-Hospital Physician Visits

Frequently, a basic medical expense policy will include a daily benefit for expenses incurred when the insured's physician visits him in the hospital. This benefit is limited to a dollar amount such as $25 or $30 per day. This amount would be paid for any charges made by the doctor for visiting the patient.

20. 3. 4. 2 Maternity Benefits

Some policies provide maternity benefits subject to certain conditions and limitations—the most usual of which is a 10-month waiting period designed to prevent purchase of health insurance solely to cover pregnancy and childbirth expenses. You should be aware, however, that group policies for employee groups of 15 or more are required by law to provide maternity benefits on the same basis as nonmaternity benefits. Thus, under a group plan with 15 or more employees, a 10-month waiting period would not apply unless nonmaternity benefits also required a 10-month waiting period.

Note: Since June 1, 1997, pregnancy may not be subject to a waiting period if the worker has already met the waiting period required by the group coverage of a previous employer.

Aside from group plans as described, many policies exclude maternity benefits but make them available at extra cost. Often, a maternity benefit is a lump sum paid for normal childbirth. The actual amount might be:

- usual, customary, and reasonable charges;
- a specified amount; or
- a multiple of the daily hospital benefit.

The benefit generally includes routine newborn care while the mother is hospitalized.

Other benefits that might be available under the same maternity coverage but scheduled at amounts different from the benefit for normal childbirth include:

- cesarean deliveries;
- natural abortions; and
- elective abortions.

20. 3. 4. 3 *Emergency First Aid Coverage*

An accident may require immediate first aid on the scene. When a medical professional who happens upon an accident provides first aid service, that person might bill the insured. Sometimes, such treatment must be performed without the insured's knowledge or assent. Some policies offer coverage for such contingencies by including emergency first aid coverage for treatment expenses incurred within a very short time after an accident. This length of time is specified in the policy.

20. 3. 4. 4 *Emergency Accident Benefits*

A basic plan may include a specific benefit for expenses incurred as the result of an accident when the insured is taken to the emergency room of a hospital as an outpatient. Typically, this benefit is stated as $300 or possibly $500. The benefit is to cover the cost of treatment in the emergency room including physician expenses, x-rays, stitches, and other services.

20. 3. 4. 5 *Mental Infirmity*

Although some policies exclude coverage for mental infirmities, more now include this coverage than before. Typically, the benefits will be lower than for physical infirmities, usually a stated percentage of the benefit paid for other types of medical care. For example, the physical infirmity benefit might be $100,000 and the mental infirmity benefit 70% of that amount.

Alternatively, a policy might specify a particular dollar amount for mental infirmity that is different from the amount for physical infirmity, such as $50,000 for physical infirmity and $25,000 for mental infirmity.

Suppose Brad's policy will pay a maximum benefit of $100,000 for any one hospitalization but only 60% of the maximum benefit if the impairment is mental. The most Brad could receive under his particular policy if he is hospitalized for mental infirmity is $60,000, which is 60% of $100,000.

20. 3. 4. 6 *Hospice Care*

Most states require that any hospitalization policy (individual or group) include benefits for hospice expenses. The hospice is a facility designed to control pain and suffering of terminally ill patients until their death. It does not treat diseases, nor does it attempt to cure. In addition, the hospice also provides counseling for the patient and the family of the terminally ill. Expenses covered include room and board, medication, and outpatient services and expenses.

20. 3. 4. 7 Home Health Care

This is usually an optional benefit that provides for reimbursement of expenses incurred by the insured for the services of a visiting nurse, a therapist, or some other support-type person who, because of a medical necessity, visits the insured in the home and provides necessary medical services.

20. 3. 4. 8 Outpatient Care

Outpatient care refers to expenses incurred by the insured for doctor's office visits and out-of-the-hospital diagnostic services, such as laboratory work and x-rays. Often a basic medical expense policy only covers in-hospital expenses (inpatient) whereby treatment is provided to the patient who has been assigned a room and a bed and is staying in the hospital for some period of time. Basic plans may add coverage for certain medical services provided to the insured as an outpatient.

20. 3. 5 Common Exclusions and Limitations

Both disability income and medical expense policies exclude or limit coverage for certain types of injuries and illnesses. One example of a limitation is the smaller benefit for mental infirmity just discussed. Exclusions, on the other hand, are conditions that are completely omitted from coverage.

The exclusions and limitations in the list that follows are representative of items a policy might include. Many policies will, in fact, include benefits for all or part of some in the list. It is important for you to be aware of your own state laws and your company's policies regarding each of the following items:

Preexisting conditions, as defined in the policy and according to state law (however, some states have no loss/no gain laws that require a replacing health insurance policy to cover any conditions for which there are ongoing claims under existing coverage, thus overriding the preexisting conditions exclusion in the replacing policy)

- Hernia, although the trend is to cover this condition
- Self-inflicted injuries
- Suicide
- War or acts of war resulting in death or injury, whether or not war is officially declared
- Military duty, usually a suspension of the policy that ends when the insured is released from such duty

- Noncommercial air travel, which is any air travel other than as a scheduled airline passenger
- Injury while committing a felony
- Injury, illness, or death while under the influence of intoxicants or narcotics
- Cosmetic surgery, except for surgery required as the result of an accidental injury or a congenital defect
- Dental expense, although some policies cover such expenses resulting from accidental injury
- Vision correction, such as eye exams and eyeglasses
- Care provided in a government facility, normally paid by the Veterans Administration or by workers' compensation
- Sexually transmitted diseases
- Experimental procedures
- Organ transplants
- Infertility services
- Alcohol or drug abuse treatment

Here are some examples of situations that would be excluded by most policies:

- The insured is severely cut while breaking the plate glass window of a jewelry store from which he intends to steal gems (injury while committing a felony).
- When the insured is injured in an auto accident, the police administer an alcohol test and discover he is legally intoxicated (injury while under the influence of intoxicants).
- The insured is injured by shellfire while touring another country torn by guerrilla fighting (injury caused by an act of war).

In summary, it is quite evident that basic medical expense plans definitely have time and/or benefit amount limitations. Thus, the insured may well expect to have to pay a considerable amount out of pocket for medical expenses. The solution to this problem is another type of hospitalization coverage referred to as major medical insurance.

20. 4 MAJOR MEDICAL INSURANCE

We have discussed basic benefits designed to cover even some hospital, medical, and surgical costs that are considered relatively minor. When these basic benefits are purchased piecemeal, the total benefits provided can be substantially less than the actual expenses incurred. Providing more complete coverage with fewer gaps, **major medical insurance** covers a much broader range of medical expenses with generally higher individual benefits and policy maximums.

These more extensive health policies are divided roughly into two groups:

- **Comprehensive** major medical expense, in which the more traditional basic coverages and essentially any other type of medical expense are combined into a single comprehensive policy
- **Supplemental** major medical expense, in which coverage begins with a traditional basic policy, which pays first, and the major medical coverage is added to pick up expenses not covered by the basic policy

20. 4. 1 Comprehensive Major Medical Benefits

20. 4. 1. 1 Deductibles

Most major medical benefits begin to be paid after the deductible is satisfied. The policy's deductible is considered satisfied as long as the insured can show evidence of having incurred the necessary expense.

There are essentially two types of comprehensive major medical plans: one with first dollar coverage and one without.

First dollar coverage means that as soon as covered medical expenses are incurred, the policy begins to pay. Policies with first dollar coverage effectively have a deductible of zero. Without first dollar coverage, the insured must pay a specified deductible amount first, and when that amount of expenses incurred has been paid by the insured, the policy starts reimbursing. Deductibles are generally an important feature of major medical policies.

For example, before Jim's major medical policy will pay benefits, Jim must pay the first $400 of medical expenses each year. He does not have first dollar coverage; that is, he must pay a deductible. On the other hand, as soon as Rona was hospitalized, her major medical policy began reimbursing her for expenses. She has first dollar coverage.

20. 4. 1. 2 Coinsurance

Another important feature of major medical coverage is coinsurance. **Coinsurance** means that the insurer and the insured share any expenses above the deductible amount. The insurer always carries the bulk of the expense, usually paying 80% of covered expenses compared with 20% for the insured. Other proportions, such as 75/25%, may be used, so it is important to read the policy. In some areas, coinsurance is referred to as percentage participation.

Here's an example of how coinsurance works. An insured's major medical policy includes a $200 deductible and 80/20% coinsurance. The insured incurs medical expenses totaling $1,200. The insured will pay $400 of this amount—the initial $200 deductible—leaving $1,000 to be shared 80/20, of which the insured pays 20%, or an additional $200. The insurance company will pay $800 of the $1,200 total. This is 80% of the $1,000 remaining after the insured has paid the deductible.

In some policies, certain types of medical expenses are not subject to the deductible whereas others are. It is not uncommon, for example, for no deductible to apply to initial hospital or surgical expenses up to a specified amount, say the first $5,000 of such expenses. In this case, the insured would pay no deductible—in essence would get first dollar coverage on the first $5,000 of hospital and surgical expenses—but would be required to pay the deductible before major medical covered any additional expenses. Then, the insurer and the insured would share the remaining expenses at 80/20% or whatever percentage applies.

The illustration that follows shows how a comprehensive major medical plan works both with and without first dollar coverage on specified hospital/surgical benefits.

Comprehensive Major Medical Expense

Without First Dollar Coverage

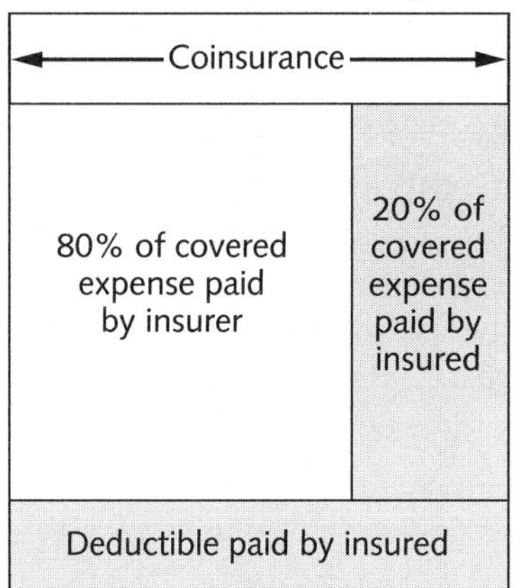

With First Dollar Coverage

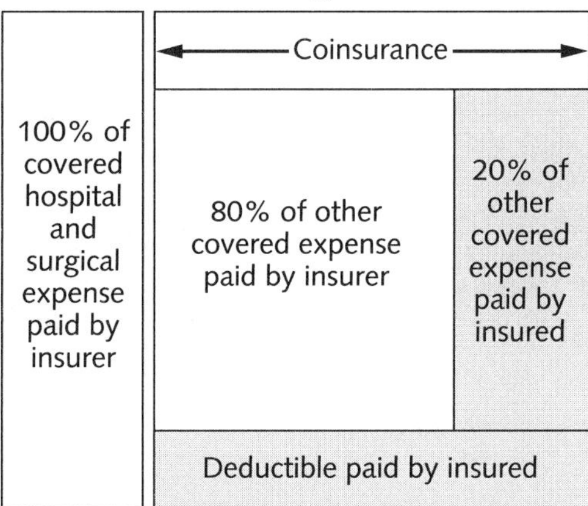

20. 4. 1. 3 Stop-Loss Limit and Maximum Benefits

More and more major medical policies include a **stop-loss limit**, which is a dollar amount beyond which the insured no longer participates in payment of the expenses. The stop-loss limit is sometimes known as the out-of-pocket limit. After the insured's total coinsurance and deductible payments reach that amount, the insurer picks up the entire cost of remaining expenses, up to a stated **maximum benefit**. Currently, the lifetime maximum limits on health policies might range from $100,000 to $1,000,000, and some policies even have unlimited benefits.

Just as the maximum benefit varies considerably, so does the amount of the stop loss limit, depending on the insurer. The next illustration shows how the stop-loss limit and the maximum benefits limit work, assuming a $5,000 stop loss and $1,000,000 lifetime maximum.

Stop-Loss Limit and Maximum Benefits

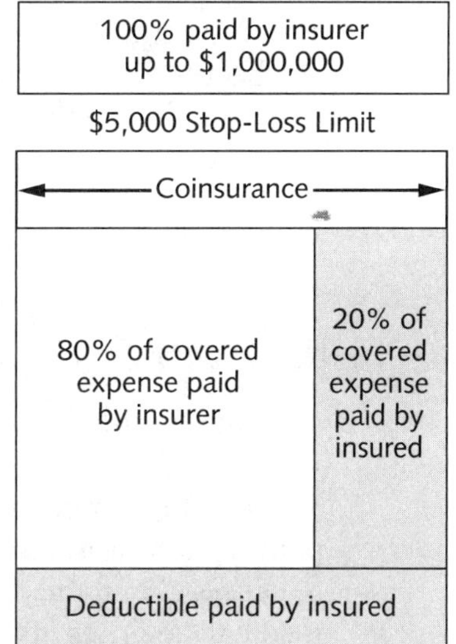

Assume an insured has the comprehensive plan illustrated, with a $300 deductible. Following a severe injury, the insured incurs covered medical expenses totaling $28,000. The insured will pay a total of $5,000, which is the stop-loss limit. The insurance company will pay $23,000, the balance remaining after the insured has paid up to the stop-loss limit.

20. 4. 2 Supplemental Major Medical Benefits

Supplemental Major Medical

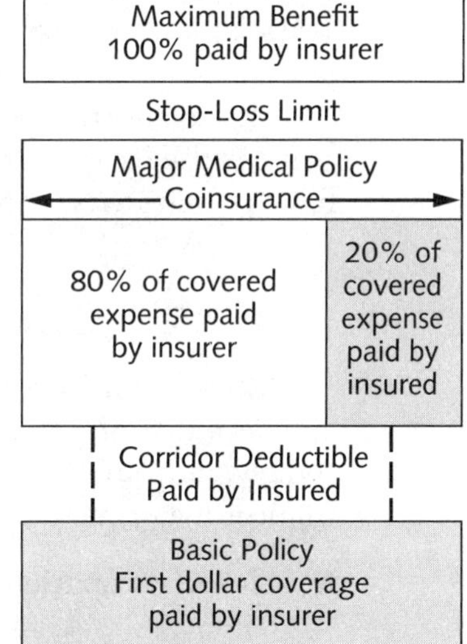

When major medical benefits are provided through a **supplemental policy**, the major medical portion supplements a basic policy that includes hospital, surgical, and medical coverage with an additional policy covering the broader range of medical expenses.

Generally, the basic plan will pay covered medical expenses with no deductible, up to the policy limit. Above that limit, the supplemental policy operates identically to a comprehensive policy that provides no other first dollar coverage. That is, after the basic policy limits are exhausted, the insured must pay a deductible, after which the major medical coverage begins. Because the deductible comes between the basic policy and the major medical policy, it is often called a **corridor** deductible.

Like the comprehensive major medical policy, a supplemental plan is likely to include a stop-loss limit and a maximum benefit limit. Here is how a supplemental major medical plan looks.

20. 4. 2. 1 Supplemental Major Medical

Suppose Jill has a supplemental major medical policy. The basic policy will pay $500 for her scheduled surgery. The corridor deductible is $250, and the plan includes an 80/20% coinsurance provision above the base plan, up to a stop-loss level of $5,000. The policy will pay 100% of covered expenses above the $5,000 limit, up to a limit of $1 million. Jill has covered medical expenses of $4,750 following an illness. Here is how these expenses are paid:

	Insurance Pays	**Jill Pays**
First $500 of expenses	$500	$0
Deductible	$0	$250
Remaining expenses = $4,000 at 80/20%	$3,200	$800
Total insurance payment	$3,700	$1,050

Let's change the scenario slightly. If Jill's expenses had totaled over $5,000, she would pay nothing over that amount because the insurer pays 100% of covered expenses over the stop-loss limit, which is $5,000 in Jill's policy.

Here's another possibility. If Jill's expenses had totaled only $400 for benefits the basic policy provides, she would have paid nothing because her basic policy provides first dollar coverage.

20. 4. 2. 2 Covered Expenses

Major medical policies, whether supplemental or comprehensive, cover a wide range of medical expenses. The precise services covered may vary somewhat from policy to policy, but many of the following will be included in most major medical plans:

- Hospital inpatient room and board, including intensive and cardiac care
- Hospital medical and surgical services and supplies
- Physicians' diagnostic, medical, and surgical services
- Other medical practitioners' services
- Nursing services, including private-duty service outside a hospital

- Anesthesia and anesthetist services
- Outpatient services
- Ambulance service to and from a hospital
- X-rays and other diagnostic and laboratory tests
- Radiological and other types of therapy
- Prescription drugs
- Blood and blood plasma
- Oxygen and its administration
- Dental services resulting from injury to natural teeth
- Convalescent nursing home care
- Home health care services
- Prosthetic devices when initially purchased
- Casts, splints, trusses, braces, and crutches
- Rental of durable equipment such as hospital-type beds and wheelchairs

Expenses that are excluded from major medical policies generally parallel the exclusions listed previously in this unit.

20. 4. 3 Other Major Medical Concepts

20. 4. 3. 1 Deductible Features

There are a number of ways deductibles might be handled in major medical policies. Some policies include a **per-cause**—injury or sickness—deductible, whereas others may have an **all-cause** deductible, which is also referred to as a cumulative, or calendar year, deductible.

With a **per-cause** deductible, the insured pays one deductible for all expenses incurred for the same injury or illness. The benefit period for each cause begins when the deductible for that particular injury or illness has been satisfied and may run for one or two years. It works like this: Yu-Long suffered a major illness early in the year that required his incurring continuing medical expenses through mid-year. Then, in September, he was injured in an auto accident that hospitalized him for two weeks. Yu-Long had to pay a separate deductible for each of these incidents because his policy has a per-cause deductible.

On the other hand, with an **all-cause** deductible, expenses for any number of different or the same type of illness or accidents are accumulated to meet the deductible during a single calendar year. Once enough expenses have been paid by the insured to meet the stated deductible, all other covered charges are paid during the remainder of the calendar year.

Under the all-cause deductible arrangement, there is also usually a **carryover provision** that permits expenses incurred during the last three months of the calendar year to be carried over into the new year if needed to satisfy the deductible for the next year. For example, suppose Laura had no medical expenses until November and December. Her illness continued into January. Laura will be able to count the expenses in November and December toward her deductible in the new year.

Policies that cover entire families usually have a **family deductible** rather than individual deductibles. For example, although a policy's individual deductible might be $200, the family deductible amount might be $400. Thus, even a family with six members would pay no more than a $400 deductible as opposed to the $1,200 that would be required if each member had to meet the $200 deductible.

Another deductible provision that can be advantageous to families is the **common injury or illness provision**. Under this provision, only one deductible must be paid when two or more members of the same family are injured in a common accident or become ill concurrently from the same sickness. Suppose Myra and Rick, wife and husband, are riding in Rick's car when they are both injured in an accident on the freeway. The deductible for each person under their health policy is $200, but their policy requires them to pay only $200 in this case.

20. 4. 3. 2 Benefit Periods and Inside Limits

The time during which benefits are paid, known as **benefit periods**, are generally tied to the deductible and to any inside or internal limits included in the major medical policy.

When a deductible must be paid, the benefit period might begin either on the first day of the accident or illness or on the date the insured has satisfied the deductible (if later than the date of the event) and may extend for up to two years. In other cases, the benefit period ceases at the end of the calendar year and begins anew with the new deductible.

Inside or **internal limits** are benefit limitations placed on specified coverages in a major medical policy. For example, the policy might limit both the room and board benefit and the number of days benefits will be paid. In this case, the benefit period for hospital room and board would be the number of days specified. Other examples of internal limits might be restrictions placed on convalescent care days, mental health care, x-rays per claim, and similar items.

20. 4. 3. 3 Restoration of Benefits

Since lifetime maximums on major medical policies have increased dramatically to $1 million and more, the restoration or reinstatement of plan benefits is not as important as in the past when maximums were much lower. However, some policies in force today carry fairly low maximums, and most major medical policies still include a provision that allows restoration of the maximum to the original level.

For example, a lifetime level might be $100,000. An insured with a severe injury or illness could easily use half or more of that in a single year, leaving only $50,000 for the rest of the insured's life. Generally, a policy allows the maximum to be restored after a certain amount of benefits are used, though sometimes the insured must prove insurability again. Many policies have an automatic reinstatement provision that restores a specified number of dollars each January 1, or after a given period elapses, without requiring the insured to prove insurability.

20. 4. 4 Medical Expense Limitations

Reimbursement-type medical expense policies frequently provide limited coverage or benefits for certain medical conditions. Many plans will include limitations on the benefits to be provided for the following:

- Rehabilitation and skilled nursing/extended care facilities care
- Home health care
- Hospice care
- Ambulance services
- Outpatient treatment
- Medical equipment and supplies
- Reconstructive cosmetic surgery
- Treatment of AIDS
- Infertility and sterilization
- Maternity/complications of pregnancy/well-baby care
- Psychiatric conditions
- Substance abuse
- Organ transplants
- Preexisting conditions
- Reimbursement for nonphysician services

20. 4. 4. 1 Mental or Emotional Disorders

Lifetime benefit amounts are limited for outpatient treatment of these disorders. For example, a major medical policy may have a lifetime maximum of $1 million, but the policy may limit coverage for outpatient treatment of mental or emotional disorders to a lifetime benefit of $25,000. In addition, frequently there may be a limitation with regard to the number of outpatient psychiatric visits per calendar year (such as a maximum of 26 visits per year) or the benefit amount paid per visit (such as a maximum benefit of $50 per visit or coverage for no more than 50% of the actual charges). These limits would not apply to inpatient treatment of mental or emotional disorders.

Note: New federal laws effective in 1997 removed these limitations for group coverage.

20. 4. 4. 2 Maternity

As previously discussed, maternity benefits are often optional. When elected, the amount of the maternity benefit is often limited. This limitation is frequently the result of the high cost of a maternity claim and the corresponding high premium charged for the benefit.

For example, a maternity benefit may be limited to a total benefit of $1,000 regardless of the actual expenses incurred. Usually, the only time additional benefits are paid is when there are certain complications during the pregnancy or at the time of delivery. A very liberal maternity benefit (and a costly one) would be that maternity is treated as an illness and thus a full range of benefits are payable.

20. 4. 4. 3 Substance Abuse

Outpatient treatment for drug or alcohol problems is usually limited in much the same way that coverage for nervous or emotional disorders is limited. Usually, if the insured is hospitalized as an inpatient for treatment of the substance abuse problem, then regular medical expense benefits are payable.

20. 4. 4. 4 Chiropractic Services

The treatment rendered by a chiropractor is normally a covered expense subject to a limitation with regard to total benefits (e.g., $10,000 lifetime) or a limitation with regard to the number of visits that will be covered in a given year and/or the amount that may be paid per visit.

20. 4. 4. 5 Preexisting Conditions

Generally, a preexisting condition is any condition for which the insured sought treatment or advice before the effective date of coverage. Many policies contain a preexisting conditions limitation that excludes coverage for unspecified conditions for a certain period (usually six months). If an insurer wants to permanently exclude a preexisting condition, it usually has to specify the condition by name in the issued policy. Depending on the severity of the condition, it may be permanently excluded or temporarily excluded (i.e., the first 12 months following the effective date of coverage). Seldom is a preexisting condition covered by means of limited benefit amounts. Generally, it is either excluded or covered in full as any other condition.

20. 5 BENEFITS FOR OTHER PRACTITIONERS

In past years, many health insurance contracts placed limitations on the kind of provider who could perform covered treatments and services. In many cases, coverage was limited to treatment rendered by a physician. In effect, this eliminated coverage for treatments rendered by chiropractors, midwives, and other nontraditional healers.

In recent years, it has become recognized that many alternative providers who are subject to state licensing and/or standards of conduct imposed by professional organizations are qualified health care providers. Use of alternative providers can help to minimize health care costs and reduce the demand on hospitals and doctors. Under current laws in many states, policies must provide benefits for services given by various providers if benefits would be payable for the same services when given by a physician, as long as the providers are properly qualified and are acting within the scope of their profession. As a result, benefits for various services are often provided and may not be excluded when performed by the following types of health care professionals, if they are practicing within the scope of their license when rendering treatment:

- Chiropractors
- Optometrists
- Opticians
- Psychologists
- Podiatrists
- Clinical social workers
- Dentists
- Physical therapists
- Professional counselors

20. 6 MEDICAL EXPENSE EXCLUSIONS

Medical expense policies contain many exclusions that are found in all health and disability policies: preexisting conditions, war, intentionally self-inflicted injuries, and active military duty. Medical expense policies also commonly exclude the following:

- Workers' compensation
- Government plans (care in government facilities)
- Well-baby care
- Cosmetic surgery
- Dental care
- Eyeglasses
- Hearing aids
- Custodial care
- Routine physicals and medical care

Workers' compensation and other government plans are excluded to prevent overpayment of claims or overinsurance. If an injured employee will have his claim taken care of by workers' compensation because the injury was work related, individual or group medical expense plans will not pay the same claim. The same concept applies if, for example, an individual's medical care is to be provided by a veterans' administration facility.

Some plans exclude well-baby care because the purpose of medical expense coverage is to indemnify an individual who sustains a loss due to an accident or an illness. If a newborn baby is normal and healthy (a well baby) following delivery, then no benefits will be paid for any hospital claim while the child is in the hospital's nursery pending discharge of the mother. If the newborn has a medical problem following birth, normal benefits will be paid.

Cosmetic surgery is usually excluded unless the reason for the surgery is a medical necessity, such as an accident or a disease that disfigures a person. Cosmetic surgery is viewed as voluntary and thus not covered.

Routine dental care is usually excluded with individual medical expense policies but is frequently offered as an optional benefit under a group contract. Again, if a person is injured, such as in an automobile accident, and needs dental surgery for repair of damaged teeth, this type of care is normally covered.

Eyeglasses and hearing aids are normally excluded unless there is a medical reason for acquiring these devices such as injury that causes loss of hearing or vision. Reduced hearing or vision due to age and similar factors are not covered.

Custodial care is care provided to assist the individual in the activities of daily living that does not contribute to the improvement of a medical condition and that can be performed by a person who does not have medical training. Coverage for these types of services may be excluded by a medical expense policy.

Routine physicals are normally also excluded from coverage. Routine physicals include a person's annual check-up when the reason for the physical is simply that it has been a year since the individual had a physical. Also excluded would be preemployment physicals or a child's school physical. There must be a medical reason for the physical before it is considered a covered expense.

Routine medical care such as immunizations is usually excluded. On the other hand, if an insured is injured and requires a tetanus shot as a result of an accident, the immunization is covered. If a doctor simply told a patient that he or she should have a tetanus shot because it has been 10 years since the last shot, it would not be covered.

It should be noted that some insurers offer coverage for routine physicals and medical care because it is generally recognized that these preventive health care measures benefit the insured and the insurer. A routine physical exam could result in the diagnosis of a potential major medical problem before it develops into a large claim for the insurer.

20. 7 OPTIONAL FEATURES AND BENEFITS

20. 7. 1 Prescription Drugs

The prescription drug benefit is most often found in group health insurance policies. Some individual health insurance policies offer this benefit as a rider. Different policies offer different prescription card benefits. For example, some policies will cover birth control pills as part of the benefit, and in other policies they are specifically excluded. Usually prescription drug coverage requires a small deductible, typically $2, $3, or $5.

A prescription drug benefit generally works one of two ways. Either insureds can be reimbursed for their prescription drug expenses using standard claim forms, or a prescription drug card can be issued. A prescription drug card allows prescriptions to be received by paying only the deductible with each prescription purchase. The pharmacy bills the insurer issuing the card directly for the prescription.

For example, Sally has a prescription drug card as part of her group medical plan, which has a $5 deductible per prescription. Her doctor prescribes two medications for a serious cold. Each of these medications would cost Sally $5. The balance of the prescription cost will be billed to the insurer by the pharmacy.

20. 7. 2 Vision Care

Vision care includes eye examinations (refractions) and eyeglasses. It is usually offered as an optional benefit under group health insurance. Generally, this option will pay a specific amount or the entire cost of an annual eye examination. It normally also covers all or part of the cost of prescribed eyeglasses once in every two-year period.

20. 7. 3 Hospital Indemnity Rider

A hospital indemnity benefit provides for the payment of a daily benefit for each day that the insured is hospitalized as an inpatient. Available amounts are usually $50 to $100 per day or possibly slightly higher. In addition to any other medical benefits paid to the insured, the hospital indemnity benefit will pay the daily amount as long as the insured is hospitalized, usually for a benefit period of one or two years.

20. 7. 4 Nursing or Convalescent Home

Under this benefit, a daily maximum amount is paid for each day the insured is confined to a nursing or convalescent home after a hospital stay. Benefits are paid generally for as short as one month or up to one year.

20. 7. 5 Organ Transplants

More insurers are offering this coverage as it becomes less experimental and more commonplace. To provide coverage, many insurers require that a transplant be performed only in life-threatening situations. Some of the more commonly covered transplants include bone marrow and kidney.

20. 8 SUMMARY

In this lesson, you learned about:

- the purpose of medical expense insurance;
- the types of coverage generally offered under basic medical expense policies;
- the difference between a scheduled and a nonscheduled plan;
- 18 exclusions common to medical expense policies but not disability income policies;
- the difference between basic and major medical expense policies;
- the two main groups of major medical expense policies;
- the function of deductibles, coinsurance, stop-loss limits, and maximum benefits;
- how supplemental major medical benefits work;
- 19 things covered in most major medical plans;
- 15 items generally subject to limitations on benefits under medical expense plans;
- when alternative providers may be able to receive payment under medical expense policies; and
- five types of benefits sometimes added to medical expense policies.

UNIT TEST

1. Lauren's policy covers hospital expenses by paying a specified, predetermined amount per day, as shown in a schedule in the policy. Lauren's policy pays on a
   A. reimbursement choice
   B. expenses-incurred basis
   C. indemnity basis
   D. capitation basis

2. Intensive care benefits under hospital plans are
   A. never included
   B. generally provided at the same level as the room and board maximum
   C. generally provided at some multiple of the room and board maximum
   D. generally provided without limit based on the need of the insured

3. When benefits are not listed by a specific dollar amount in a schedule, a policy will generally pay
   A. the usual, customary, and reasonable charge for the procedure
   B. the universal, customary, and reasonable charge for the procedure
   C. the usual, capitated, and reasonable charge for the procedure
   D. the usually charged rate for the procedure

4. The out-of-pocket limit is also known as the
   A. deductible
   B. co-payment
   C. stop-loss limit
   D. maximum benefit

5. Which of the following is least likely to be covered by a major medical policy?
   A. Outpatient services
   B. Vision correction
   C. Prescription drugs
   D. Blood and blood plasma

6. Which of the following is least likely to be covered by a major medical policy?
   A. Surgery performed on an outpatient basis
   B. Replacement of an artificial limb
   C. Nursing home care for a month following release from a hospital
   D. Purchase of blood for transfusion during an operation

7. Carmen falls and breaks her leg, incurring $2,000 in medical expenses. Her policy pays the entire amount. Carmen has a
   A. hospital expense policy
   B. surgical expense policy
   C. medical expense policy
   D. policy with first dollar coverage

8. A hospital room and board benefit may be paid
   A. on an indemnity basis
   B. on a reimbursement basis
   C. on either an indemnity basis or a reimbursement basis
   D. on neither an indemnity basis nor a reimbursement basis

9. The type of health insurance providing high maximum coverage for medical care is
   A. a basic medical expense policy
   B. a major medical expense policy
   C. a comprehensive medical expense policy
   D. a supplemental medical expense policy

10. The type of policy that has a major medical portion that provides benefits once the basic policy limits are exhausted and a deductible has been paid is
    A. a basic medical expense policy
    B. a major medical expense policy
    C. a comprehensive medical expense policy
    D. a supplemental medical expense policy

11. A combination of basic medical expense coverage and major medical expense coverage is
    A. a basic medical expense policy
    B. a major medical expense policy
    C. a comprehensive medical expense policy
    D. a supplemental medical expense policy

12. The type of policy covering doctor visits while the insured is in the hospital is
    A. a basic medical expense policy
    B. a major medical expense policy
    C. a comprehensive medical expense policy
    D. a supplemental medical expense policy

13. Maternity benefits must be provided on the same basis as nonmaternity benefits
    A. in all cases
    B. only if the insurer chooses to do so
    C. if the policy covers an employee group of 15 or more people
    D. if the policy provides disability income coverage

14. Among individual policies that include coverage for mental infirmities, the benefit will generally be
    A. lower than the benefit for physical infirmities
    B. higher than the benefit for physical infirmities
    C. unlimited
    D. the same as the benefit for physical infirmities

15. A hospice works
    A. to treat diseases only, not accident-related medical issues
    B. to control pain and suffering as well as to treat illness
    C. alleviate pain and suffering for terminally ill patients until death, but does not attempt to cure
    D. with medical professionals when they become ill, to provide treatment in a private setting away from lay patients

16. No loss/no gain laws require
    A. replacing health insurance policies to cover any conditions for which there are ongoing claims under existing coverage
    B. replacing health insurance to remove preexisting condition exclusions from all policies replaced
    C. existing insurers to continue to cover ongoing claims after a policy has been replaced
    D. existing insurers to remove preexisting condition exclusions from all policies being replaced

17. Purchasing basic benefits on an individual basis usually
    A. provides a broader range of coverage than a single major medical policy
    B. provides less-complete coverage with more gaps than a major medical policy
    C. provides exactly the same coverage as a major medical policy
    D. is prohibited by state law

18. The dollar limit beyond which the insured no longer participates in payment of expenses is the
    A. deductible
    B. coinsurance
    C. stop-loss limit
    D. maximum benefit

19. The dollar limit beyond which the insurer no longer participates in payment of expenses is the
    A. deductible
    B. coinsurance
    C. stop-loss limit
    D. maximum benefit

20. The expense that must be incurred before major medical benefits begin to be paid is the
    A. deductible
    B. coinsurance
    C. stop-loss limit
    D. maximum benefit

21. The sharing of expenses between the insured and the insurer is an example of
    A. deductible
    B. coinsurance
    C. stop-loss limit
    D. maximum benefit

22. A deductible that runs between the first dollar coverage of a basic policy and the comprehensive coverage of a supplemental policy is known as a
    A. stop-loss deductible
    B. capitated deductible
    C. corridor deductible
    D. limited deductible

23. Which of the following would most likely be covered under a medical expense policy?
    A. Gertrude steps on a rusty nail and requires a tetanus shot.
    B. Carmelita decides to get a flu shot this year.
    C. Gary goes to the doctor each year for an annual check-up.
    D. Earl requires some help getting dressed in the morning.

ANSWERS AND RATIONALES TO UNIT TEST

1. **C.**
2. **C.** Intensive care benefits under hospital plans are generally provided at some multiple of the room and board maximum.
3. **A.** When benefits are not listed by a specific dollar amount in a schedule, a policy will generally pay the usual, customary, and reasonable charge for the procedure.
4. **C.** The out-of-pocket limit is also known as the stop-loss limit.
5. **B.**
6. **B.** Replacement of an artificial limb is least likely to be covered by a major medical policy.
7. **D.**
8. **C.** A hospital room and board benefit may be paid on either an indemnity basis or a reimbursement basis.
9. **B.** A major medical expense policy provides high maximum coverage for medical care.
10. **D.** A supplemental medical expense policy has a major medical portion that provides benefits once the basic policy limits are exhausted and a deductible has been paid.
11. **C.** A comprehensive medical expense policy is a combination of basic medical expense coverage and major medical expense coverage.
12. **A.** A basic medical expense policy covers doctor visits while the insured is in the hospital.
13. **C.** Maternity benefits must be provided on the same basis as nonmaternity benefits if the policy covers an employee group of 15 or more people.
14. **A.** Among individual policies that include coverage for mental infirmities, the benefit will generally be lower than the benefit for physical infirmities.
15. **C.** A hospice works to alleviate pain and suffering for terminally ill patients until death, but does not attempt to cure.
16. **A.** No loss/no gain laws require replacing health insurance policies to cover any conditions for which there are ongoing claims under existing coverage.
17. **B.** Purchasing basic benefits on an individual basis usually provides less-complete coverage with more gaps than a major medical policy.
18. **C.** The stop-loss limit is the dollar limit beyond which the insured no longer participates in payment of expenses.
19. **D.** The maximum benefit is the dollar limit beyond which the insurer no longer participates in payment of expenses.
20. **A.** The deductible must be incurred before major medical benefits begin to be paid.
21. **B.** The sharing of expenses between the insured and the insurer is an example of coinsurance.
22. **C.** A corridor deductible runs between the first dollar coverage of a basic policy and the comprehensive coverage of a supplemental policy.
23. **A.** Gertrude would most likely be covered under a medical expense policy.

UNIT

21

Special Types of Medical Expense Policies

21. 1 INTRODUCTION

In this lesson, we will discuss several special types of health insurance plans that are designed for very specific and limited insurance needs, including the following:

- dental care policies;
- limited policies, including dread disease, travel accident, hospital income, vision care, and long-term care; and
- credit insurance policies.

In each case, a special type of policy is one that covers a limited number of situations as described in the policy itself.

21. 2 LEARNING OBJECTIVES

After completing this lesson, you will be able to:

- describe how special policies differ from other types of policies;
- list the two types of traditional dental coverage and describe which is more commonly issued and how they differ;
- list eight types of dental care generally considered to be nonroutine and explain how they are generally covered under comprehensive policies;
- list six common exclusion or limitations;
- explain what a closed list is and why it is used;
- list and describe seven methods insurers use to minimize adverse selection;
- explain how prepaid dental plans differ from traditional plans;
- explain the difference between an open-panel and closed-panel system;
- describe the function of limited policies;
- explain what is covered by the following types of policies: dread disease, travel accident, hospital income, vision care, and prescription drug;
- explain the purpose of credit insurance; and
- describe how credit health insurance differs from credit life insurance.

21. 3 DENTAL CARE INSURANCE

21. 3. 1 Traditional Dental Coverages

The number of companies offering dental care insurance is increasing rapidly, as coverage for dental care is being offered more frequently as part of group health plans. Occasionally, dental insurance is part of a health benefits package with a single deductible called an integrated deductible, applying to both medical and dental coverages. More often, dental coverage and dental claims are handled separately (though they may be part of a larger package) with a separate deductible for health insurance coverage and for dental insurance coverage. There also may be a probationary period in group dental insurance to help hold down coverage for preexisting conditions.

Some dental policies are scheduled; that is, benefits are limited to specified maximums per procedure, with first dollar coverage. Most, however, are comprehensive policies that work in much the same way as comprehensive medical expense coverage.

In addition to deductibles, coinsurance and maximums may also affect the level of benefits payable under a dental plan. Coinsurance percentages may apply to reimbursements that are either the reasonable and customary (R&C) type or the scheduled type. A plan based on R&C will apply coinsurance percentages to the dentist's usual and customary fee, provided it is reasonable. This type of plan is also known as usual, customary, and reasonable (UCR) or usual and prevailing (U&P). A plan that is scheduled will apply coinsurance percentages to a schedule or list of fixed-dollar amounts for each covered benefit. Scheduled benefits are generally lower than R&C allowances.

Comprehensive dental plans usually provide routine dental care services without deductibles or coinsurance to encourage preventive dental care. Generally, there is a specified maximum dollar amount payable per year and, sometimes, per family member covered. There also may be a lifetime maximum per individual.

Nonroutine dental care includes the following:

- Restorative—repairing or restoring dental work that has been damaged in some way
- Oral surgery—surgery performed in the oral cavity, for example, the removal of wisdom teeth
- Endodontics—treatment of the pulp (the soft tissue substance located in the center of each tooth)
- Periodontics—treatment of the supporting structures of the teeth
- Prosthodontics—artificial replacements
- Pediatric dentistry—patient management and preventive and restorative techniques particularly suited to children and adolescents

- Oral pathology—microscopic analysis of tissue biopsy material for diagnosis of oral diseases including oral cancer
- Orthodontics—correction of irregularities of the teeth; most commonly, braces

For nonroutine treatments, a comprehensive policy pays a percentage, such as 80%, of the reasonable and customary charges. The patient pays an annual deductible and whatever expense remains. Typically, the deductible is per person or per family, and most policies limit benefits to stated maximums per year.

Policies that provide for orthodontic care generally have separate limits and deductibles for orthodontia. The coinsurance percentage is likely to be 50% rather than the higher 75% or 80% that applies to other types of nonroutine dental care.

Many plans offer a selection of providers from which plan participants must choose. In some plans, if a course of treatment is expected to exceed a certain amount, say $200, a report must be submitted to the insurer by the dentist. The report describes the proposed treatment and itemizes the expected charges. The insurer reviews and evaluates this report and sends the dentist an estimate of benefits to be paid.

Benefits may be on a fixed prepaid basis rather than a fee-for-service plan in which the plan participant is reimbursed. Such plans often provide 100% coverage for:

- routine visits to the dentist;
- protective fluoride treatments;
- diagnostic x-rays;
- dental exams and diagnosis;
- local anesthetics;
- teeth cleanings (usually once every six months); and
- preventive care.

21. 3. 2 Exclusions and Limitations

An insurer will often reduce its liability for payment of dental expenses by contractual provisions that state what a plan does and does not cover. A closed list is a method of defining which procedures are covered. If an unlisted procedure is performed, coverage is either denied or paid on the basis of the most similar procedure included on the list. The following are examples of common exclusions and limitations.

- The cosmetic exclusion stipulates that benefits are not payable for dental work that is not necessary for sound dental health.
- The missing tooth provision excludes coverage for teeth that are missing at the time coverage becomes effective.

- The five-year replacement exclusion does not allow replacement of prosthetic appliances (such as retainers or spacers) for five years after a benefit is paid.
- The vertical dimension, splinting, and restoring occlusion exclusion limits liability for exotic and highly optional procedures.
- Expenses for oral hygiene instructions and plaque control programs are often limited or excluded.
- Some plans may offer members coverage up to a certain amount for emergency dental treatment required when outside the service area.

21. 3. 3 Minimizing Adverse Selection

Because the nature of dental coverage is quite different from that of medical coverage, the underwriting of dental coverage requires a few special considerations. There are three circumstances that make dental coverage unique.

- Patients have wider choices in treatment options. For instance, a patient can choose bridgework that is fixed or removable and inlays that are gold or nongold. These choices represent a wide range in treatment costs.
- A person who needs dental work can often postpone treatment until an insurance plan becomes effective, causing the insurer to be liable for larger benefits than it would otherwise expect to pay. (For this reason, few individual dental plans exist; most plans are sold on a group basis to further offset this type of adverse selection.)
- Many dental expenses are cosmetic; therefore, underwriting must often limit benefits for cosmetic procedures in order to avoid paying excessive claims.

To offset these additional (and often costly) factors, a new program of dental insurance will often include provisions to minimize adverse selection. The following are examples of such provisions:

- A reduced maximum annual benefit to encourage an insured to choose less costly courses of treatment whenever possible
- A lower coinsurance percentage for optional expenses
- A graduated coinsurance factor that begins at 60% and increases each plan year
- An advance approval requirement for treatment plans that exceed a certain minimum, usually $200
- A provision that bases the benefit on the least costly treatment option
- A longer eligibility period before an employee's coverage is effective
- A limited benefit for late entrants

21. 3. 4 Prepaid Dental Plans

Another increasingly popular way to offer dental insurance is a through a prepaid dental plan. A **prepaid dental plan** is a corporation, partnership, or other entity that, in return for a prepayment, provides or arranges for the provision of dental care services to enrollees or subscribers. The plan may be owned by a corporation, partnership, association trust, or other entity and operated by a board of directors or trustees, executive committee, or principal officers.

Prepaid dental plans operate in much the same way as health maintenance organizations. They offer services based on capitation, or fixed per-member per-month payments whereby the provider assumes the full risk for the cost of contracted services without regard to the type, value, or frequency of the services provided.

21. 3. 5 Dentist Access to Membership

A prepaid dental plan must provide that any licensed dentist may participate as a provider in the prepaid dental plan.

21. 3. 6 Benefits

Individual group contracts, evidence of coverage, and solicitation materials must provide a statement of the services and benefits each member may receive. Reasonable exclusions, limitations, co-payments, and deductibles may be included, provided they are clearly disclosed in contracts, evidence of coverage, and solicitation documents.

21. 3. 7 Member Choice of Provider

Subscribers must have the right to select any participating dentist as a provider. If a prepaid dental plan would restrict an enrollee's ability to receive services from a class of providers, the limitations must be described in the evidence of coverage and in all solicitation documents.

21. 3. 8 Provider Contracts

The prepaid plan may contract with licensed dentists to provide dental care to subscribers in a specific service area or geographic location.

The dentists are paid (other than the co-payment or deductible) by the prepaid dental plan. Provider contracts are subject to state laws designed to protect enrollees from becoming liable for services the prepaid dental plan fails to pay because of insolvency.

In an open-panel system, dentists render services to both prepaid dental plan subscribers and to nonmembers. In a closed-panel system, services are provided only to subscribers of the prepaid dental plan. The plan must publish a list of participating providers, and enrollees are asked to choose a primary provider.

Under the precertification or prior authorization requirement, when the enrollee's dentist prescribes any course of treatment expected to exceed a specific amount (such as $200), the treatment must be outlined on a precertification form and submitted to the insurer for review and approval before it may be undertaken.

21. 3. 9 Evidence of Coverage

All enrollees must be issued an evidence of coverage describing the dental services covered, limitations on those services (including deductibles and co-payments), how to obtain services and information, and methods for resolving complaints.

21. 3. 10 Complaint Procedure

The complaint system must establish reasonable procedures for resolving written complaints from both enrollees and providers. The organization must respond promptly to written complaints. Responses to written complaints regarding quality or appropriateness of care must include a statement that the complainant may have the complaint reviewed by a consulting dentist and may submit the complaint to a professional peer review organization. Copies of complaints and responses must be maintained for three years.

21. 3. 11 Service Area—Geographic Location

Subscribers must have reliable access to qualified providers in the geographic area served by the prepaid dental plan. They also must have access to short-term emergency dental care services within the areas served, and the plan must pay for services when a dental emergency occurs outside the service area.

21. 3. 12 Quality Assurance Program

Each prepaid dental plan must provide appropriate, necessary, cost-effective, and professional services. Prepaid dental plans must have a quality assurance program to evaluate the quality of care given to enrollees and provide for ways to correct deficiencies in provider or organizational performance. Provider contracts must give disincentives (including termination) for providers rendering inappropriate, unnecessary, excessively costly, or low quality care.

21. 3. 13 Underwriting

The underwriting procedures for group dental insurance are similar to those that apply to other types of group health insurance. Generally, when a group dental plan is initially effective, all employees or members must be covered or eligible for coverage. Under a contributory plan in which the employee pays all or part of the premium, each eligible employee must elect to be covered. To minimize adverse selection, a probationary period usually applies to new employees who join the group after the effective date. Limitations on benefits may also be imposed on any employees who do not choose to be covered when first eligible, to avoid premium payments, but who elect coverage at a later date when they know they need dental treatment.

Because dental coverage is usually available only on a group basis, most plans do not include a conversion privilege. Members cannot convert to individual insurance when their membership in the group ends or the group plan is terminated.

21. 3. 14 Integrated Deductible vs. Stand-Alone Plan

As noted before, dental insurance may be part of a health benefits package with a single deductible, called an integrated deductible, which applies to both medical and dental coverages. In most cases, however, dental coverage and dental claims are treated separately with a separate deductible for health insurance coverage and for dental insurance coverage.

21. 4 LIMITED POLICIES

21. 4. 1 Dread Disease

In this section, we will look at a series of policies, each of which covers only a limited, specified risk. Collectively, they are called limited policies, and the first of these is often referred to as a dread disease policy.

Dread disease policies can be purchased to cover specific diseases as named in the policy, such as heart disease or cancer. Generally, these policies cover illnesses that do not occur frequently but incur significant costs when they do occur. Because of the low frequency of the disease covered, these policies are often fairly inexpensive in comparison to full health coverage.

Insurance regulatory bodies do not always look favorably upon these policies because less sophisticated insurance buyers have sometimes purchased them believing the coverage was much broader, when major medical coverage was actually needed instead.

21. 4. 2 Travel Accident Insurance

Special policies can be purchased to cover loss from travel accidents. Travel accident insurance may be offered as a benefit of either an individual or a group accidental death and dismemberment policy. Benefits are limited to losses caused by accidents while traveling, usually by common carriers such as airlines or bus lines.

A frequent use of such coverage under a group policy limits benefits to losses suffered while traveling on business for one's employer. Air travel insurance purchased at airports for individual, one-time coverage is probably the best known type of travel accident policy.

21. 4. 3 Hospital Income (Indemnity) Insurance

A policy that pays a specific amount of insurance for each day an individual is hospitalized is called hospital income or hospital indemnity coverage. These policies pay an indemnity directly to the insured, not to the hospital. They are not intended to cover expenses for hospitalization but to provide a flow of income that begins when the insured is confined to the hospital and ends on the final day of hospitalization. Some individuals use this kind of policy to meet the deductible and coinsurance requirements of their medical expense policies.

Limitations may apply. Some hospital indemnity policies include an elimination period, in which case coverage does not begin on the first day of confinement. Limits also may be placed on benefits paid for preexisting conditions.

Usually, the amount of insurance available is indicated as a monthly amount for a specified number of months. For example, Sin Lan has a policy that pays $3,000 per month for up to 12 months. However, Sin Lan will be indemnified only for actual continuous days in the hospital, and the monthly amount is the aggregate of a daily amount times 30 days. Sin Lan's $3,000 policy, then, pays $100 for each day the insured is hospitalized.

Because these policies provide a fixed number of dollars, they should be updated periodically to stay apace of inflation.

21. 4. 4 Vision Care Insurance

Although basic, comprehensive, and major medical policies often cover disease and injury to eyes, there is generally no coverage for eye exams and corrections such as eyeglasses or contact lenses. To close this gap, insurers may offer vision care policies, which usually cover:

- eye examinations;
- cost of lenses and frames;
- cost of contact lenses; and
- other corrective items.

Typically, vision care policies operate with a network of eye doctors and providers of eyeglasses, which the policyholder must use to receive benefits. Co-payments will vary according to the type of plan. The plan member simply presents the vision care card to the provider and is told the amount of the co-payment. Individual and family coverage is generally available.

Limitations normally apply. For example, the policy may pay for only one eye exam and one set of lenses per year. Common exclusions are:

- replacement frames or lenses required because of loss or breakage;
- sunglasses and safety glasses; and
- medical and surgical costs of the type covered by basic and major medical policies.

- Suppose Avtar has a vision care policy with the features described above. The policy also covers Avtar's spouse and children. Avtar's family incurs costs for the following:
- A pair of glasses to replace a pair Avtar lost
- Eye surgery for Avtar's spouse
- One eye exam each year for each member of the family
- Contact lenses just prescribed for Avtar's son
- A new lens prescription for Avtar to correct a further deficiency since his last exam 18 months ago

Only the last three items will be covered under the policy described.

21. 4. 5 Prescription Drug Policies

Prescription drug policies can be described as discount plans for members. Very often, an individual health policy does not cover prescription drugs. For an annual fee or premium, an individual can join a plan that provides discounts of one degree or another for doctor-prescribed drugs. Prescription drug plans operate with a network of pharmacies that members must use in order to receive benefits. Sometimes a mail order service may be provided for drugs used on a regular basis. Plan members receive cards that must be presented to the pharmacy when a prescription is filled. There is a co-payment. Usually generic drugs are dispensed. Some drugs may be excluded, such as fertility drugs, vitamins, experimental drugs, or drugs covered by other programs. There is a dispensing limit such as 34 days' worth or 100 units, whichever is larger. Premiums are guaranteed for one year. Individual and family coverage is generally available.

21. 5 CREDIT INSURANCE

Credit health insurance covers a debtor, with the creditor receiving the benefits to pay off the debt if the debtor is disabled or dies accidentally. Credit insurance may be written as an individual policy covering a single debtor, or it can be sold to a master policyowner on a group basis to cover more than one debtor.

Individual credit health insurance is handled in essentially the same way as any other individual health insurance policy. The applicant applies for the policy and receives it on the basis of individual selection. In this case, the policyowner is the debtor and he names the creditor as the recipient of the policy's benefits.

The most common type of credit health insurance is group coverage sold as a master policy to a creditor that acquires many new debtors each year. For example, an auto dealership that provides financing for the vehicles it sells might have a group credit policy to cover all clients who finance their cars through the dealership.

Group credit health insurance is somewhat more complicated than individual coverage. In most states, a creditor must have a minimum number of debtors per year, often 100, before it qualifies for group credit insurance. Check your own state laws to determine minimum group size requirements.

Group credit health insurance has many of the same features as any other group coverage. No individual selection occurs, so no evidence of insurability is required. Group credit coverage is nearly always contributory, and a high percentage, usually 75%, of those to whom it is offered must want the coverage.

21. 5. 1 Limits on Coverage Amounts

The objective of credit insurance is to ensure that the outstanding indebtedness will be paid if the insured is disabled or dies accidentally before the loan is repaid. Therefore, the accidental death benefit may not exceed the total amount of indebtedness at any given point, nor may the monthly disability benefit exceed the amount of the monthly payment on the loan. Consider this situation.

Raoul has a loan for which he makes payments of $340 a month. His creditor provides group credit health insurance. The monthly disability indemnities covering Raoul under this policy must be no more than $340, the amount of the monthly loan payment.

Now suppose the policy that covers Raoul contains accidental death benefits. Raoul's original loan was for $13,500. Raoul is accidentally killed when the balance due is $7,180. The benefit payable to the creditor is $7,180 because at any given time the death benefit may be no more than the total outstanding loan at the time of death.

Debtors usually pay for group credit health insurance as a portion of the monthly loan payment. Some lending institutions have their own or affiliated insurance companies through which they would like to write all of their credit insurance. However, a debtor is not required to carry insurance through the company suggested by the creditor.

In some states, and under certain conditions, a creditor can insist that the debtor have some type of insurance to help secure the loan. Even so, the debtor, not the creditor, has the option of selecting the insurer.

Suppose Joan finances her car through the Friendly Loan Company. Friendly Loan has its own wholly owned subsidiary insurance company. In Joan's state, a lender may require the debtor to purchase credit insurance, and Friendly Loan would like Joan to purchase coverage from its subsidiary. As a prerequisite to financing the car, Friendly Loan may insist that Joan buy the coverage, but it may not require that she buy coverage from Friendly's subsidiary.

21. 5. 2 Notice of Proposed Insurance

When the loan is closed, the creditor must inform the debtor that he may be covered by the group plan if desired. Even if the creditor pays the full cost of the coverage, the debtor must be notified. Creditors are not permitted to place insurance on debtors without telling them about it.

The notification to a debtor that he will be covered under a credit health policy is called a notice of proposed insurance. This notice takes the place of the certificate of insurance until the certificate can be prepared by the insurer and forwarded to the debtor.

In some states, a modified application, rather than a notice of proposed insurance, can be furnished in lieu of the certificate of insurance when the loan is closed.

In still other states, a creditor is permitted to incorporate the notice of proposed insurance in the loan or sales contract. This means that the debtor receives the notice when signing for the loan. If the debtor doesn't read the contract carefully, he may not be aware of the insurance because no verbal notification is required. In states where this practice is allowed, including the notice in the contract fulfills the creditor's obligation to provide notice of proposed insurance.

Once a debtor has received a notice of proposed insurance, the certificate of insurance must be delivered within 30 days of the date the indebtedness is incurred.

Sometimes, coverage might be terminated because the debtor pays off the loan early or because of refinancing. Any such termination requires the insurance company to refund unearned premiums.

Sid obtains a loan from a local finance company, and at the same time agrees to have credit health insurance placed on the amount of indebtedness. Sid receives a notice of proposed insurance at the time he signs for the loan. Because this is group coverage, Sid will receive a certificate of insurance rather than an insurance policy, and he must receive it within 30 days.

After the loan is four months old, Sid decides he needs more money. He asks the loan company to refinance his loan, giving him an additional $1,000. This causes termination of the credit insurance, and the insurer must return the unearned premium to Sid.

21. 5. 3 Credit Life: A Corollary Coverage

Let's talk briefly about credit life insurance. In the previous section, you learned that credit health insurance covers death only when it is accidental. Therefore, if a debtor were to die a natural death, the credit health insurance policy would not apply.

Credit life, on the other hand, will pay death benefits whether death occurs accidentally or by natural causes. If you are required to take an examination for your health insurance license, you may encounter a test question concerning credit life insurance. Keep in mind that it is not considered health insurance, because it provides for natural death benefits; health insurance covers only accidental death.

Credit life insurance, which may be either individual or group coverage, names the creditor as the beneficiary of the policy. The proceeds or face amount of the policy may not exceed the indebtedness at the time of death. A credit life policy intended to cancel a given indebtedness is usually decreasing term life insurance. This means that the policy is in force for the period of indebtedness, and the face amount of the policy equals the amount owed at any given time, as shown in the illustration.

Decreasing Term Life Insurance

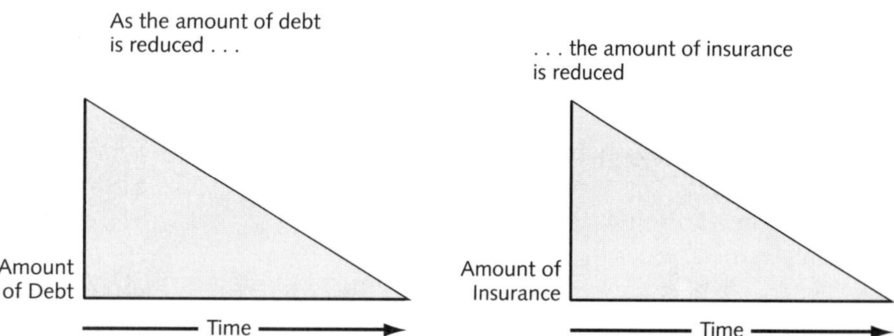

21. 6 SUMMARY

In this lesson, you learned about:

- how special policies differ from other types of policies;
- the two types of traditional dental coverage, which is more commonly issued, and how they differ;
- eight types of dental care generally considered to be nonroutine and how they are generally covered under comprehensive policies;
- six common exclusion or limitations;
- what a closed list is and why it is used;
- seven methods insurers use to minimize adverse selection;
- how prepaid dental plans differ from traditional plans;
- the difference between an open-panel and closed-panel system;
- the function of limited policies;
- what is covered by the following types of policies: dread disease, travel accident, hospital income, vision care, and prescription drug;
- the purpose of credit insurance; and
- how credit health insurance differs from credit life insurance.

UNIT TEST

1. Scheduled benefits are generally
   A. lower than reasonable and customary allowances
   B. higher than reasonable and customary allowances
   C. the same as reasonable and customary allowances
   D. paid in addition to reasonable and customary allowances

2. Which of the following is NOT a common exclusion or limitation of dental policies?
   A. Benefits are generally not payable for dental work that is not necessary for sound dental health.
   B. Teeth that are knocked out in an accident will generally not be replaced under a dental policy.
   C. Oral hygiene instructions and plaque control programs are often limited or excluded.
   D. Prosthetic appliances generally may not be replaced for 5 years after a benefit is paid.

3. The ability of an individual to wait until covered by dental insurance before seeking treatment for dental issues is an example of
   A. improper insurance
   B. improper selection
   C. adverse selection
   D. adverse insurance

4. Prepaid dental plans offer services based on
   A. capitulation
   B. captive member selection
   C. concentration
   D. capitation

5. Sin Lan has a hospital income policy that will pay $1,500 per month for up to 12 months. There is no elimination period. If Sin Lan is hospitalized, to whom will the insurer make payments?
   A. The hospital
   B. Sin Lan

6. Sin Lan has a hospital income policy that will pay $1,500 per month for up to 12 months. There is no elimination period. If Sin Lan is hospitalized for 10 days, how much will the policy pay?
   A. $50
   B. $500
   C. $1,000
   D. $1,500

7. Which of the following drugs may be excluded from a prescription drug policy?
   A. Ginseng
   B. Fertility drugs
   C. Rogaine
   D. All of these

8. A special type of policy tends to cover
   A. more areas than basic medical expense
   B. a broad number of situations as described in the policy itself
   C. a limited number of situations as described in the policy itself
   D. whatever the insured wants to be covered

9. Comprehensive dental policies
   A. limit benefits to specified maximums per procedure
   B. work in much the same way as comprehensive medical expense coverage
   C. never require deductibles
   D. seldom require coinsurance

10. Which of the following is NOT likely to be considered nonroutine dental care?
    A. Treatment of the soft tissue substance located in the center of each tooth
    B. Microscopic analysis of tissue biopsy material for diagnosis of oral diseases including oral cancer
    C. Annual checkups and cleaning of teeth, including x-rays to check the health of the teeth
    D. Repairing or restoring dental work that has been damaged in some way

11. For nonroutine treatments, a comprehensive policy generally pays
    A. the full amount
    B. a percentage of the reasonable and customary charges from the first dollar
    C. a percentage of the reasonable and customary charges after a deductible
    D. nothing

12. Which of the following is NOT a common way dental insurance programs work to minimize adverse selection?
    A. Increasing the maximum annual benefit to encourage the insured to maintain dental health for the long term
    B. Lowering the coinsurance percentage for optional expenses
    C. Basing the benefit on the least costly treatment option
    D. Graduating the coinsurance percentage to increase each plan year

13. What is the main difference between a prepaid dental plan and a comprehensive dental plan?
    A. Comprehensive dental plans pay on the basis of reasonable and customary charges, whereas prepaid dental plans pay on a capitation basis.
    B. Comprehensive dental plans pay on a capitation basis, whereas prepaid dental plans pay based on reasonable and customary charges.
    C. Comprehensive dental plans cover routine services, whereas prepaid dental plans do not.
    D. Comprehensive dental plans do not cover routine services that are covered by prepaid dental plans.

14. A prepaid dental plan that wants to restrict an enrollee's ability to receive services from a class of providers
    A. is out of luck because such limitations are prohibited by law
    B. must request permission from the Insurance Commissioner for the limitations
    C. must request permission from the federal Department of Insurance for the limitations
    D. must describe the limitations in the evidence of coverage and in all solicitation documents

15. Dread disease policies
    A. are purchased to cover a variety of conditions that fall under the category of dread diseases
    B. cover any disease defined by the ADA as a dread disease
    C. cover specific diseases as named in the policy, such as heart disease or cancer
    D. are a good replacement for general health insurance

16. Benefits of travel accident insurance are limited to
    A. losses caused by accidents while traveling, usually by common carriers such as airlines or bus lines
    B. losses caused while in transit, generally in personal vehicles such as cars or vans
    C. accident losses caused while outside of the state of residence
    D. accident or illness losses caused while outside of the state of residence

17. Hospital indemnity insurance pays
    A. medical costs only while the insured is confined to the hospital
    B. supplemental costs, such as television or phone charges, while the insured is confined to the hospital
    C. an income for each day the insured is confined to the hospital
    D. an income for each month the insured spends partially confined to the hospital

18. Vision care insurance is generally needed to cover all of the following EXCEPT
    A. injury to the eye
    B. eye examinations
    C. costs of contact lenses
    D. costs of prescription lenses

19. Prescription drug policies generally exclude
    A. any narcotic substance
    B. any drugs not covered by other programs
    C. experimental drugs
    D. drugs for ongoing medical conditions

20. Credit health insurance covers
    A. a creditor
    B. a debtor
    C. either a creditor or a debtor
    D. neither a creditor nor a debtor

21. The amount of coverage available under a credit insurance policy is generally limited to
    A. the total amount of indebtedness at any given point
    B. the total amount of the loan covered
    C. the amount the policy is written for
    D. there is no limit

22. The creditor must notify the debtor that he may be covered by the group insurance plan
    A. only if the debtor is to be charged the full premium for the insurance
    B. if the debtor is to be charged more than half the premium amount
    C. even if the creditor pays the full cost of the coverage
    D. only if the creditor chooses to make the disclosure

ANSWERS AND RATIONALES TO UNIT TEST

1. **A.**
2. **B.** The fact that teeth knocked out in an accident will generally not be replaced under a dental policy is not a common exclusion or limitation of dental policies.
3. **C.** The ability of an individual to wait until covered by dental insurance before seeking treatment for dental issues is an example of adverse selection.
4. **D.** Prepaid dental plans offer services based on capitation.
5. **B.**
6. **B.** The daily amount is $50, or $1,500 ÷ 30 days. The total payment will equal $50 per day for 10 days, or $500.
7. **D.** All of the listed drugs may be excluded from a prescription drug policy.
8. **C.**
9. **B.** Comprehensive dental policies work in much the same way as comprehensive medical expense coverage.
10. **C.** Annual checkups and cleaning of teeth, including x-rays to check the health of the teeth, are not likely to be considered nonroutine dental care.
11. **C.** For nonroutine treatments, a comprehensive policy generally pays a percentage of the reasonable and customary charges after a deductible.
12. **A.** Dental insurance programs do not increase the maximum annual benefit to encourage the insured to maintain dental health for the long term.
13. **A.** The main difference between prepaid dental plans and comprehensive dental plans is that comprehensive dental plans pay on the basis of reasonable and customary charges, whereas prepaid dental plans pay on a capitation basis.
14. **D.** A prepaid dental plan that wants to restrict an enrollee's ability to receive services from a class of providers must describe the limitations in the evidence of coverage and in all solicitation documents.
15. **C.** Dread disease policies cover specific diseases, such as heart disease or cancer, as named in the policy.
16. **A.** Benefits of travel accident insurance are limited to losses caused by accidents while traveling, usually by common carriers such as airlines or bus lines.
17. **C.** Hospital indemnity insurance pays an income for each day the insured is confined to the hospital.
18. **A.** Vision care insurance generally does not cover injury to the eye.
19. **C.** Prescription drug policies generally exclude experimental drugs.
20. **B.** Credit health insurance covers a debtor.
21. **A.** The amount of coverage available under a credit insurance policy is generally limited to the total amount of indebtedness at any given point.
22. **C.** The creditor must notify the debtor that he may be covered by the group insurance plan even if the creditor pays the full cost of the coverage.

UNIT

22

Group Health Insurance

22. 1 INTRODUCTION

Most people have at least a superficial acquaintance with group insurance because the most common type of group coverage is provided through employment. Many employers make health insurance available to their employees—either by paying the premiums for the employees, sharing in premium payment, or deducting the premiums from employees' paychecks.

22. 2 LEARNING OBJECTIVES

After completing this lesson, you will be able to:

- list and describe five common types of group health insurance plans;
- list and describe five coverage provisions that apply solely or primarily to group policies;
- list the events that generally trigger an employee's conversion privilege;
- explain who qualifies as a dependent under group coverage and how dependency is legally determined;
- explain how the coordination of benefits rule determines which insurer is primary and what each insurer pays;
- explain how the coordination of benefits rule determines which parent's insurance plan is primary for covered children;
- describe what happens if a clerical error prevents information from getting to an insurer;
- explain the scope and impact of the following federal regulations: HIPAA, COBRA, OBRA, TEFRA, ERISA, the Age Discrimination in Employment Act, and the Americans with Disabilities Act;
- explain how pregnancy is treated under the Civil Rights Act; and
- describe some of the types of regulation commonly adopted by states in regard to group insurance.

22. 3 POLICY TYPES

Group health plans may include any of the several types of insurance discussed earlier, so this section will serve as a review of those individual coverages. Group plans need not include all coverages, but most will include at least two or more. In addition, disability income coverage may be offered under a group arrangement, but it is usually offered separately from hospital, medical, and surgical coverage.

The first possible group coverage, then, pays benefits for lost earnings resulting from accident or sickness disability, and it is commonly called disability income insurance.

Another common type of group coverage deals with accidental loss of life and accidental loss of one or more limbs or of eyesight. You'll recall that accidental loss of life is referred to as accidental death, and accidental loss of one or more limbs or of eyesight is known as dismemberment.

Still another type of group coverage is hospital expense. These policies can pay for hospital expenses whether treatment is on an inpatient or resident basis, whereby the insured is admitted to the hospital, or on an outpatient basis, whereby the insured is not admitted for an overnight stay but is treated and released the same day. The fees of an attending physician during hospital treatment may also be covered.

Example

Eloise's employer provides a group insurance plan covering expenses incurred for hospital care of any type. Eloise is involved in an auto accident on her way home from work, and she is rushed to the hospital for emergency treatment. She is not admitted to the hospital but does receive emergency room treatment. In this particular case, Eloise is an outpatient.

If Eloise's group insurance covers only situations such as the one described and does not provide disability income or any other benefits, the coverage is strictly a hospital expense policy.

If Eloise's group coverage provides a separate benefit in the event Eloise loses her sight in an accident, this type of benefit is called accidental dismemberment.

Some group policies might cover only surgical expenses. Suppose Paul is hospitalized to have his appendix removed. His group policy specifies that the surgeon who performs an appendectomy will receive $450. The hospital charges are not paid. Although this would be fairly unusual today, such policies do exist, and in this situation, Paul's group policy covers only reimbursement for surgical expenses.

Group health policies frequently provide coverage for medical expenses involving physician or nursing services, but no surgical expense. If Mihail becomes ill and must see his physician regularly as well as remain under the care of a private nurse for several weeks, any health care reimbursement for these expenses is considered medical expense coverage.

We've now mentioned five forms of group health coverage, all of which have counterparts in individual policies. They are:

- disability income;
- accidental death and dismemberment;
- hospital expense;
- surgical expense; and
- medical expense.

22. 4 GROUP COVERAGE PROVISIONS

Several provisions apply solely or primarily to group policies. They are provisions that:

- describe who is eligible for the group plan;
- describe when individuals become eligible for the plan;
- specify the minimum number of individuals and the minimum participation by eligible people required to sustain the plan;
- specify the amounts of insurance to which individual group members are entitled; and
- describe the responsibilities of the master policyowner.

As was mentioned, not all members of a group are necessarily eligible for coverage under a group plan. An employer may establish certain eligibility requirements, such as limiting coverage to people who have been employed for a specified period.

Often, an employee becomes eligible for coverage after working with a company for a given period, commonly 90 days. The employee is then eligible to apply for coverage during another period, usually 31 days, within which no medical examination will be required. This is the eligibility period discussed previously.

Any such qualifications or limitations must be indicated in the policy.

22. 4. 1 Conversion Privilege

The conversion privilege allows the insured to convert his group coverage to individual coverage without evidence of insurability. This privilege goes into effect only when the insured is no longer eligible for group coverage because of the following circumstances.

- The insured's employment is terminated.
- The insured becomes ineligible for coverage because the class he was insured under is no longer eligible for coverage. (For example, to save expenses, a company that formerly provided coverage for all employees working not less than 20 hours per week may now only provide coverage to the class of employees who do not work less than 40 hours per week.)
- The insured's dependent child reaches the age specified in the policy as the age of terminating dependent coverage.

The insured has 31 days from the time of ineligibility to convert to the new plan of insurance. The new plan of insurance is an individual plan, normally a hospitalization policy, which will not provide the same benefits that the group plan did. Usually, the group medical expense benefits are more liberal than the converted policy's benefits. Often, those who elect to exercise this conversion privilege do so because frequently they may have insurability problems. To limit adverse selection against the company, the insurer typically offers this conversion plan with reduced or limited benefits.

22. 4. 2 Dependent Coverage

Life or health insurance benefits may be extended to the primary insured's dependents. Dependents may be any of the following individuals:

- The insured's spouse
- The insured's children
- The insured's dependent parents
- Any other person who is dependent on the insured

The insured's children can be stepchildren, foster children, or adopted children. Dependent children must be younger than a specified age (usually age 19, or 21 if attending school full time). The law further requires that any other person dependent on the insured is eligible for coverage. Such dependency is proved by the relationship to the insured, residency in the home, or being listed on the insured's income tax return as a dependent.

A child may be a dependent beyond the ages of 19 or 21 if that child is permanently mentally or physically disabled before the specified age.

Also, a dependent child may be offered coverage beyond the limiting age of 19 if that child is a full-time college student in an accredited college. Usually, dependent coverage for a student will be extended until age 21 or even to age 25.

22. 4. 3 Coordination of Benefits Provision

Many working couples are doubly covered by group health insurance. Both husband and wife often have employer-provided group coverage, and each is covered as a dependent by the other's plan. This type of double coverage can result in individuals being **overinsured**, creating the temptation to realize a profit from being ill.

To avoid this situation, a special provision is required by law in most states. The **coordination of benefits provision** is designed to give insureds as much coverage as possible while eliminating overinsurance. Here is an example of how it works.

In double coverage situations, the insurer covering the employee who has the claim is called the **primary** insurance company. The primary company must pay as much of the claim as the policy limits permit.

Basil and Kendra, a married couple, work at different companies. Both are covered by group plans that extend to dependents, so they have double coverage. Let's assume that Basil has $2,200 in medical bills resulting from an illness. Basil's policy is primary. Basil has major medical coverage and a $200 deductible, so the primary insurer (Basil's insurance company) first deducts that amount from the $2,200 bill, leaving $2,000.

The primary insurer then pays 80% of $2,000, which is $1,600, leaving $600 unpaid—the $200 deductible plus $400, which is Basil's share of the other $2,000.

Kendra's company also covers Basil. For Basil's claim (because he is covered as a dependent of Kendra's), her company is called the **secondary** or **excess** insurer. The secondary company will pay whatever the primary company will not pay, up to its own limits.

Therefore, assuming the remaining $600 is within the limits, Kendra's company pays the full additional $600, which is Basil's percentage participation (20% of $2,000, or $400) plus his deductible ($200). Because double coverage existed, Basil's expenses were fully covered. However, he did not receive more than his actual expenses.

To restate the coordination of benefits rule: the primary company pays the claim as if there were no double coverage, and the secondary company pays whatever the primary company will not pay, within its policy limits.

When a working couple is doubly covered by group insurance, any children they support will also be doubly covered. Before June of 1985, the usual way to coordinate benefits for children was to make the father's group plan primary and the mother's plan secondary.

This procedure is being phased out. Instead, the birth months and days of the parents are often used to decide which plan is primary. The plan of the parent whose birthday comes first during the year is primary. The other parent's plan is secondary. That is, if Sue's birthday is March 4 and her spouse's is March 8, Sue's plan is primary.

Or, if Juan's birthday is April 25 and his spouse's is July 22, Juan's plan is primary because his birthday falls first in the year.

If parents are separated or divorced, the plan of the parent with custody is primary, barring any other legal arrangements.

22. 4. 4 Records and Recordkeeping

This provision contains information as to whether the insurer or the policyholder will maintain records on the insureds. It provides for the policyholder to furnish the insurance company with necessary information to determine premiums and administer coverage.

22. 4. 4. 1 Clerical Error

A clerical error provision provides that if there is an error or omission in the administration of a group policy, the person's insurance is considered to be what it would be if there had been no error or omission.

For example, an employer has the responsibility to send group enrollment forms for newly hired employees to the insurer. Sean is a new employee, and through an administrative error, his enrollment form is never forwarded to the insurance company. A few months later, he submits a medical expense claim to the insurer and is told that they have no record of his coverage.

This recordkeeping and clerical error provision protects the new employee in this type of situation. Usually, the insurer would accept an enrollment form and all of the past due premium and proceed to pay the medical claim.

22. 5 FEDERAL AND STATE REGULATIONS AFFECTING GROUP POLICIES

A number of federal regulations enacted over the past 20 years affect group life and health insurance policies. These are known by the acronyms COBRA, OBRA, TEFRA, and ERISA. Also, the health reform package, HIPAA, passed in 1996, has major implications for group health insurance policies.

22. 5. 1 Health Insurance Portability and Accountability Act (HIPAA)

The **Health Insurance Portability and Accountability Act (HIPAA)**, which took effect July 1, 1997, ensures portability of group insurance coverage and includes various mandated benefits that affect small employers, the self-employed, pregnant women, and the mentally ill.

22. 5. 1. 1 Portability

The new law makes it easier for individuals to change jobs and still maintain continuous health coverage. If an employer offers health benefits to its employees, the employer now must make full health care coverage available immediately to newly hired employees who were previously covered at another job (the individual must have had coverage for at least 18 months). Before this change, coverage for preexisting conditions could be delayed for six months to one year, and new hires were subject to a waiting period before being eligible for health insurance. If the worker goes without health insurance for more than 63 days between jobs, the waiting period can be reinstated.

Also, an individual with group health insurance who leaves to become self-employed cannot be denied coverage (although the premium charged may be higher).

Group plans cannot impose more than a 12-month preexisting conditions exclusion for a person who sought medical advice, diagnosis, or treatment within the previous 6 months. However, this exclusion cannot be applied in the case of newborns, adopted children, or pregnancies existing on the effective date of coverage.

22. 5. 1. 2 Mandated Benefits

The law guarantees coverage for a 48-hour hospital stay for new mothers and their babies after a regular delivery (96 hours for a cesarean section birth). Also, it expands coverage for mental illness by requiring similar coverage for treatment of mental and physical conditions. The law eliminates the special limitations included in many policies, such as lifetime spending limits and annual limits applied only to mental health coverage.

Small employers (those with 2–50 employees) now cannot be denied group health insurance coverage because one or more employees are in poor health.

22. 5. 2 Continuation of Benefits

The **Consolidated Omnibus Budget Reconciliation Act (COBRA)** is a federal law that requires employers with 20 or more employees to provide former employees and their families a continuation of benefits under the employer's group health insurance plan. Coverage may be continued for 18 to 36 months. Employees and other qualified family members who would otherwise lose their coverage because of a qualifying event are allowed by COBRA to continue their coverage at their own expense at specified group rates. COBRA specifies the rates, coverage, qualifying events, qualifying beneficiaries, notification of eligibility procedures, and time of payment requirements for the continuation of insurance. Here are the terms and concepts most important to the understanding of COBRA and its limitations.

22. 5. 2. 1 Qualifying Event

A **qualifying event** is an occurrence that triggers an insured's protection under COBRA. Qualifying events include the death of a covered employee, termination or reduction of work hours of the covered employee, Medicare eligibility for the covered employee, divorce or legal separation of the covered employee from the covered employee's spouse, the termination of a child's dependent status under the terms of the group insurance plan, and the bankruptcy of the employer. Termination of employment is not a qualifying event if it is the result of gross misconduct by the covered employee. In short, a qualifying event occurs when the employee, spouse, or dependent child becomes ineligible for coverage under the group insurance contract.

22. 5. 2. 2 Qualified Beneficiary

A **qualified beneficiary** is any individual covered under an employer-maintained group health plan on the day before a qualifying event. Usually this includes the covered employee, the spouse of the covered employee, and dependent children of the employee. Changes made in 1996 amend the definition of *qualified beneficiary* to include children born or adopted during the 18-month coverage period.

22. 5. 2. 3 Notification Statements

Employers are obligated to provide notification statements to individuals eligible for COBRA continuation. This notification must be provided under the following circumstances:

- When a plan becomes subject to COBRA
- When an employee is covered by a plan subject to COBRA
- When a qualifying event occurs

In addition to notifying current employees, the company must also notify new employees when they are informed of other employee benefits. Initial notification made to the spouse of an employee or to the employee's dependents must be made in writing and sent to the last known address of the spouse or dependent.

Following the notification of eligibility for continuation of benefits, an individual has 60 days in which to elect continuation. If continued coverage is not elected within 60 days, the option to do so is forfeited.

22. 5. 2. 4 Duration of Coverage

An employer is not required to make continuation coverage available indefinitely. The rationale behind COBRA is to provide transitional health care coverage until the employee or family member can obtain coverage or employment elsewhere. The maximum period of coverage continuation for termination of employment or a reduction in hours of employment is 18 months. For all other qualifying events the maximum period of coverage continuation is 36 months. There are also certain disqualifying events that can result in a termination of coverage before the specified time periods. The dates of these events are as follows:

- The first day for which timely payment is not made
- The date the employer ceases to maintain any group health plan
- The first date on which the individual is covered by another group plan (even if coverage is less)
- The date the individual becomes eligible for Medicare

It should be remembered that COBRA deals with continuation of the exact same group coverage that the employee had as a covered employee. This distinction is important so as not to confuse this provision with the conversion of group coverage to a lesser amount of insurance as part of an individual plan.

Not only is the type of coverage the same the insured had while employed, the premium is also the same, except now the terminated employee pays the entire premium to the employer for the privilege of continuing the group benefits. To cover any administrative expense that the employer may incur, the terminated individual may also pay an additional amount each month not to exceed 2% of the premium. Only the health benefits can be continued under COBRA. Any group life insurance under the plan may not be continued. It can, of course, be converted.

Recent amendments to COBRA require the continuation of coverage if a preexisting condition limitation is included in the new group health coverage. However, the new group health coverage is primary, and the continuation coverage is secondary.

22. 5. 2. 5 *Plan Termination*

In most states, if an employer discontinues its group insurance plan, employees must have the opportunity to convert to individual insurance without a medical exam or other evidence of insurability.

Suppose Giovanni has been employed by the same company for 15 years. He is now 53 years of age and has battled a number of skin cancers during the last four years. Giovanni's employer terminates its group health plan but offers employees the opportunity to convert to individual coverage. To get this coverage, it is likely that Giovanni will not be required to have a physical examination or otherwise show that he is insurable. Giovanni is fortunate; he otherwise might not be able to get health insurance at standard rates.

22. 5. 3 Omnibus Budget Reconciliation Act (OBRA)

The **Omnibus Budget Reconciliation Act of 1989 (OBRA)** extended the minimum COBRA continuation of coverage period from 18 to 29 months for qualified beneficiaries disabled at the time of termination or reduction in hours. The disability must meet the Social Security definition of disability, and the covered employee's termination must not have been for gross misconduct. Changes to COBRA in 1996 permit individuals who become disabled during the first 60 days of the 18-month coverage period to extend their coverage to 29 months, so as to extend coverage until the person would become eligible for Medicare (the 5 month waiting period plus 24 months of eligibility for Social Security disability benefits).

Under OBRA 1989, an employer may terminate COBRA coverage because of coverage under another health plan, provided the other plan does not limit or exclude benefits for a beneficiary's preexisting conditions.

OBRA 1989 also clarifies that COBRA coverage may be terminated only because of Medicare entitlement, not merely eligibility. Before terminating COBRA coverage for beneficiaries at age 65, an employer must first be certain that the individual has actually enrolled under Medicare. Also, 36 months of COBRA coverage must be provided for the spouse and dependent children of a covered employee whose group insurance terminates because of entitlement to Medicare.

22. 5. 4 Tax Equity and Fiscal Responsibility Act (TEFRA)

The **Tax Equity and Fiscal Responsibility Act of 1982 (TEFRA)** is intended to prevent group term life insurance plans (usually part of group health insurance programs) from discriminating in favor of **key employees**. Key employees include officers, the top 10 interest-holders in the employer, individuals owning 5% or more of the employer, or individuals owning more than 1% who are compensated annually at $150,000 or more.

TEFRA amends the Social Security Act to make Medicare secondary to group health plans. TEFRA applies to employers of 20 or more employees and to active employees and their spouses between ages 65 and 69. TEFRA also amends the Age Discrimination in Employment Act (ADEA) to require employers to offer these employees and their dependents the same coverage available to younger employees.

22. 5. 5 Employee Retirement and Income Security Act (ERISA)

The **Employee Retirement Income Security Act of 1974** was intended to accomplish pension equality, but it also protects group insurance plan participants. ERISA includes stringent reporting and disclosure requirements for establishing and maintaining group health insurance and other qualified plans. Summary plan descriptions must be filed with the Department of Labor, and an annual financial report must be filed with the IRS. For other qualified plans, legal documentation of the trust agreement, plan instrument, plan description, plan amendments, claim and benefit denials, enrollment forms, certificates of participation, annual statements, plan funding, and administrative records must all be maintained.

22. 5. 6 Age Discrimination in Employment Act (ADEA)

This act applies to employers with 20 or more employees and is directed toward employees age 40 or older. In general, this act prohibits compulsory retirement, except for those in executive or high policymaking positions. Employee benefits, which in the past usually ceased or were severely limited when an employee turned 65, must be continued for older workers, although some reductions in benefits may be allowed. Some states have even stricter laws with regard to retirement and benefits.

22. 5. 7 Americans with Disabilities Act (ADA)

This act has a widespread impact on almost all facets of American life. With respect to group insurance, it makes it unlawful for employers with 15 or more employees to discriminate on the basis of disability against a qualified individual with respect to any term, condition, or privilege of employment. Employees with disabilities must be given equal access to whatever health insurance coverage the employer provides to other employees, although certain coverage limitations may be acceptable for mental and nervous conditions as opposed to physical conditions, as long as such limitations apply to employees without disabilities as well those with disabilities.

Among other things, the law forbids exclusion or limitation of benefits for:

- specific disabilities such as deafness or AIDS;
- individually distinct groups of afflictions, such as cancer, muscular dystrophy, or kidney disease; and
- disability in general.

22. 5. 8 Pregnancy Discrimination

In the past, pregnancy was treated differently from other medical conditions under both individual and group health policies. However, an amendment to the Civil Rights Act requires that women affected by pregnancy, childbirth, or related medical conditions be treated the same for employment-related purposes as other persons who are not affected in the same way but are in similar positions. This includes receiving benefits under an employee benefit plan, such as group health insurance. Although the federal law applies only to employers who have 15 or more employees, various state laws may affect employers with fewer than 15 employees.

22. 5. 9 Experience Rating vs. Community Rating

In general, premiums for group insurance are based on experience rating. This is a method of establishing the premium for a group based on the group's previous claims experience. The larger and more homogenous the group, the closer it comes to reflecting standard mortality and morbidity rates.

In contrast, the practice of community rating sets premiums by using the same rate structure for all subscribers to a medical expense plan, regardless of their past or potential loss experience, and regardless of whether coverage is written on an individual or a group basis.

22. 5. 10 State Regulation

Many states have some form of mandated group health benefits. These commonly include required coverage for adopted or newborn children, continued coverage for handicapped dependents, coverage for treatment of alcoholism or drug abuse, and coverage for mammograms and pap smears.

Some state statutes mandate continuation of coverage for individuals whose group insurance has terminated. Most often, COBRA satisfies the state continuation of coverage requirements. In instances where the state requirements are more generous than COBRA, the employer must follow the more generous plan.

Extension of benefits is similar to continuation of coverage. In this case, benefits that began to be paid while a health insurance policy was in force continue, or are extended, after the insurance contract is terminated. Some states require group policies to provide for extension of benefits for a covered member who is totally disabled at the time of policy discontinuance.

States often regulate the marketing and advertising of accident and health insurance policies to ensure truthful and full disclosure of pertinent information when selling these policies. As a rule, the insurer is held responsible for the content of advertisements of its policies. Advertisements cannot be misleading or obscure, or use deceptive illustrations, and must clearly outline all policy coverages as well as exclusions or limitations on coverage (such as preexisting condition limitations).

22. 6 INDIVIDUAL VERSUS GROUP INSURANCE

The chart that follows summarizes how individual and group plans differ.

Comparison of Individual and Group Plans

Individual	Group
Anyone can apply for coverage.	Only group members are covered. Group must meet size and purpose definitions.
Each person has a policy.	There is one master contract.
Individual selects coverage options.	Benefits are essentially the same for all group members.
Individual's health is evaluated.	Group as a whole is evaluated; no individual underwriting.
Coverage renewable at option of the insured, sometimes insurer.	Coverage stops when insured leaves the group.
All accidents are covered.	Only off-the-job accidents are generally covered.

22. 7 SUMMARY

In this lesson, you learned about:

- five common types of group health insurance plans;
- five coverage provisions that apply solely or primarily to group policies;
- the events that generally trigger an employee's conversion privilege;
- who qualifies as a dependent under group coverage and how dependency is legally determined;
- how the coordination of benefits rule determines which insurer is primary and what each insurer pays;
- how the coordination of benefits rule determines which parent's insurance plan is primary for covered children;
- what happens if a clerical error prevents information from getting to an insurer;
- the scope and impact of the following federal regulations: HIPAA, COBRA, OBRA, TEFRA, ERISA, ADEA, and ADA;
- how pregnancy is treated under the Civil Rights Act; and
- some of the types of regulation commonly adopted by states in regard to group insurance.

UNIT TEST

1. The conversion privilege allows the insured to continue group coverage without
   A. paying individual premiums
   B. filling out an application
   C. providing proof of termination of employment
   D. providing evidence of insurability

2. All of the following could be considered dependents except the insured's
   A. adopted children
   B. parents
   C. 25-year-old child who became physically disabled at 24
   D. 21-year-old child who is attending college full time

3. The coordination of benefits provision provides that when a person is covered under more than one plan, the total benefits cannot exceed
   A. the greater of the benefits provided
   B. the lesser of the benefits provided
   C. both of the benefits combined
   D. the total medical expenses or loss of wages

4. An individual is NOT eligible for the conversion privilege if
   A. the insured's employment is terminated
   B. the insured becomes ineligible for coverage because the insured's class is no longer eligible for coverage
   C. the insured fails to make the conversion within 31 days
   D. the insured's dependent child reaches the age specified in the policy as the age of terminating dependent coverage

5. Which of the following is NOT part of the qualification process for legal dependency?
   A. Relationship to the insured
   B. Residency in the home
   C. Eligibility for insurance
   D. Listing on the insured's tax return as a dependent

6. When both parents have employer-provided group coverage, the children are covered under
   A. the father's plan
   B. the mother's plan
   C. the plan of the parent whose birthday falls closest to the child's birthday
   D. the plan of the parent whose birthday falls closest to the start of the calendar year

7. Under the coordination of benefits rule, the primary company pays
   A. if there is no other coverage
   B. as if there were no other coverage
   C. whatever the other coverage does not pay, up to the policy limits
   D. only if the other coverage refuses the claim

8. Under the coordination of benefits rule, the secondary company pays
   A. if there is no other coverage
   B. as if there were no other coverage
   C. whatever the other coverage does not pay, up to the policy limits
   D. only if the other coverage refuses the claim

9. Carla enrolls in group insurance when she is eligible under her employer's plan. Because of an administrative error, her enrollment form is never sent to the company. When she later has a claim, the insurer will
   A. deny the claim because it has no record of her policy
   B. force the employer to pay the claim because it was the employer's error
   C. pay the claim only if the insurer is proven to have made an error
   D. accept the enrollment form and all of the past due premium and pay the medical claim

10. Which federal law requires employers with more than 20 employees to include in their group insurance plan a continuation of benefits provision for all eligible employees?
    A. COBRA
    B. OBRA
    C. ERISA
    D. TEFRA

11. Which federal law is intended to prevent group term life plans from discriminating in favor of key employees?
    A. COBRA
    B. OBRA
    C. ERISA
    D. TEFRA

12. Which federal law extends the minimum continuation of coverage period from 18 to 29 months for qualified beneficiaries disabled at the time of termination or reduction in hours?
    A. COBRA
    B. OBRA
    C. ERISA
    D. TEFRA

13. Which federal law is intended to accomplish pension equity but also protects group insurance plan participants?
    A. COBRA
    B. OBRA
    C. ERISA
    D. TEFRA

14. Which of the following provisions is NOT a part of HIPAA?
    A. Employers must make full health care coverage available immediately to newly hired employees who were previously covered for at least 18 months.
    B. New mothers and their babies must be allowed to stay in the hospital for at least 48 hours after a regular delivery.
    C. Small employers may not be denied group health insurance coverage because one or more employees is in poor health.
    D. Annual limits and lifetime spending limits may be applied to mental health coverage.

15. Which of the following is considered a disqualifying event under COBRA?
    A. The employer ceases to maintain any group health plan.
    B. The employee is no longer eligible for the group health plan because of a change in the covered classes.
    C. The employee voluntarily leaves employment with the employer.
    D. The employee's employment is terminated by the employer.

16. Under OBRA, an employer may terminate COBRA coverage because of coverage under another health plan
    A. as soon as the coverage is in force
    B. as long as the other health plan does not limit benefits for the insured's preexisting conditions
    C. as long as the other health plan limits benefits for the insured's preexisting conditions
    D. only if the premiums for the new plan are paid entirely by the insured's new employer

17. The Age Discrimination in Employment Act applies to employees age
    A. 40 or older
    B. 45 or older
    C. 50 or older
    D. 55 or older

18. The Americans with Disabilities Act
    A. does not apply to acquired diseases such as AIDS
    B. permits exclusion of benefits for individual distinct groups of afflictions, such as cancer, muscular dystrophy, or kidney disease
    C. applies to all employers with 25 or more employees
    D. requires that employees with disabilities be given equal access to whatever health insurance is provided to other employees

ANSWERS AND RATIONALES TO UNIT TEST

1. **D.** The conversion privilege allows the insured to continue group coverage without providing evidence of insurability.
2. **C.** The insured's 25-year-old child who becomes physically disabled at age 24 cannot be considered a dependent.
3. **D.** The coordination of benefits provision provides that when a person is covered under more than one plan, the total benefits cannot exceed the total medical expenses or loss of wages.
4. **C.**
5. **C.** Eligibility for insurance is not part of the qualification process for legal dependency.
6. **D.** When both parents have employer-provided group coverage, the children are covered under the plan of the parent whose birthday falls closest to the start of the calendar year.
7. **B.** Under the coordination of benefits rule, the primary company pays as if there were no other coverage.
8. **C.** Under the coordination of benefits rule, the secondary company pays whatever the other coverage does not pay, up to the policy limits.
9. **D.** In case of an administrative error, the insurer will accept the enrollment form and all of the past due premium and pay the medical claim.
10. **A.** COBRA requires employers with more than 20 employees to include in their group insurance plan a continuation of benefits provision for all eligible employees.
11. **D.** TEFRA is intended to prevent group term life plans from discriminating in favor of key employees.
12. **B.** OBRA extends the minimum continuation of coverage period from 18 to 29 months for qualified beneficiaries disabled at the time of termination or reduction in hours.
13. **C.** ERISA is intended to accomplish pension equity but also protects group insurance plan participants.
14. **D.** Applying annual limits and lifetime spending limits to mental health coverage is not a part of HIPAA.
15. **A.** Ceasing to maintain any group health plan is considered a disqualifying event for an employer under COBRA.
16. **B.** Under OBRA, an employer may terminate COBRA coverage because of coverage under another health plan as long as the other health plan does not limit benefits for the insured's preexisting conditions.
17. **A.** The Age Discrimination in Employment Act applies to employees age 40 or older.
18. **D.** The Americans with Disabilities Act requires that employees with disabilities be given equal access to whatever health insurance is provided to other employees.

UNIT

23

Social Health Insurance

23. 1 INTRODUCTION

The term *social health insurance* refers to health coverages subsidized and implemented through government administration of tax money and social programs. We will look at four types of social health insurance:

- Medicare and associated private coverages
- Medicaid
- Social Security
- Workers' compensation

23. 2 LEARNING OBJECTIVES

After completing this lesson, you will be able to:

- list the four main types of social health insurance provided in the United States;
- describe the Medicare system, its purpose, and its administration;
- explain who is eligible for Medicare and how individuals can enroll;
- list and explain the benefits provided under the Original Medicare Plan: Medicare Parts A and B;
- explain the purpose of Medicare supplement insurance;
- list and describe the core and optional benefits available in Medicare supplement policies;
- describe Medicare Select and explain how it differs from other Medicare supplement plans;
- describe Medicare Plans C and D;
- explain how Medicare benefits coordinate with employer-provided benefits;
- describe the Medicaid program, its purpose, and its administration;
- explain who is eligible for Medicaid and how individuals can enroll;
- explain the spousal impoverishment rule;
- list and describe the costs Medicaid is required to pay;
- describe the Social Security program, its purpose, and its administration;
- explain the purpose of TRICARE and who is eligible;
- describe workers' compensation, its purpose, and its administration;
- list the four categories of benefits incorporate by all states;

- explain which injuries and illnesses are compensable under workers' compensation;
- list and explain the four types of disability defined under workers' compensation law; and
- describe an extraterritorial provision under workers' compensation.

23. 3 MEDICARE PARTS A AND B

23. 3. 1 Medicare

Medicare is the US version of national health insurance, at least as far as the elderly and disabled are concerned. It was originally enacted by Congress in 1965 and has been modified many times since. Medicare is a federal program. It is administered by the Centers for Medicare and Medicaid Services (CMS), a division within the US cabinet-level Department of Health and Human Services. At the local level, district offices of the Social Security Administration accept Medicare enrollment applications, process claims, and provide general information to the public about the Medicare program. However, Social Security does not make Medicare policy; it simply handles the paperwork.

To make Medicare benefit payments, the US government enters into contracts with selected private insurance companies. The insurance companies that make coverage and payment decisions with respect to services provided by hospitals, skilled nursing facilities, home health agencies, and hospices are called **intermediaries**. The insurance companies that handle claims with respect to services provided by physicians and other providers are called **carriers**.

23. 3. 2 Eligibility

Eligibility for Medicare benefits is not determined by financial need. Practically everyone age 65 or older, as well as many people classified as disabled, are eligible for Medicare Part A and Medicare Part B. A person is eligible for Medicare benefits who:

- is age 65 or over and has qualified for Social Security or Railroad Retirement monthly cash benefits;
- is entitled to benefits under the Social Security program for 24 months as a disabled worker, disabled widow(er), or as a child age 18 or over who was disabled before age 22;
- is diagnosed as having permanent kidney failure and requiring dialysis or a kidney transplant; or
- was born before 1929 and has few or no quarters of coverage under the Social Security system.

Medicare Eligibility

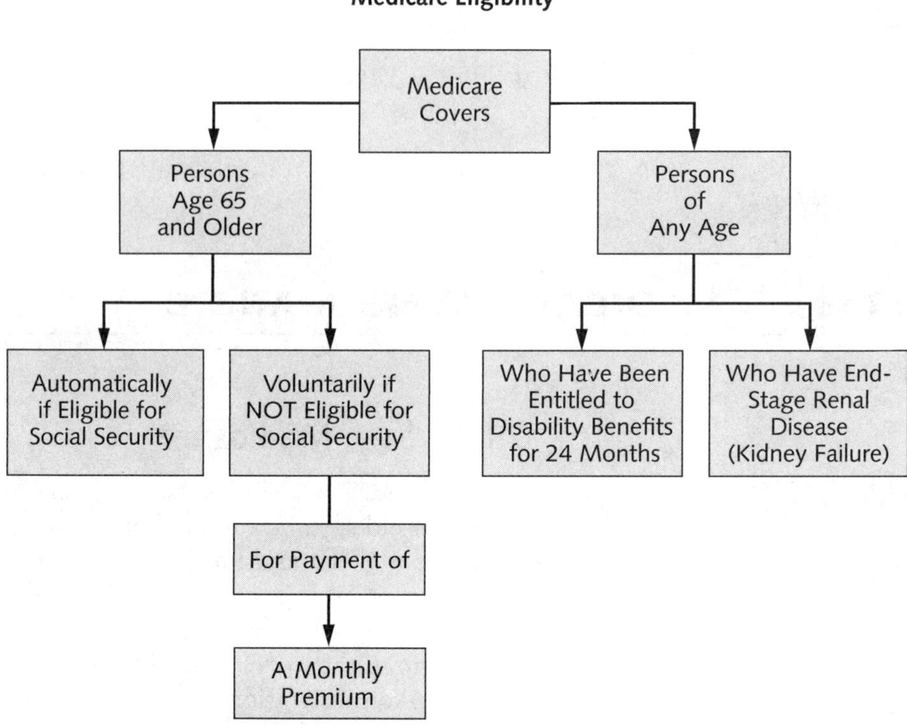

Survivors and dependents of these individuals may also qualify for Medicare coverage under certain circumstances. A common example is the surviving spouse of an individual who qualified for Social Security before the individual's death. A survivor who is at least age 65 can qualify for Medicare after the spouse's death. Other restrictions apply in other situations.

Here are just a few examples of people who would be eligible for Medicare:

- Chris, age 65, the surviving spouse of Stacy, who was age 68 and eligible for Social Security at the time of death
- Orlando, age 49, who is suffering from kidney failure
- Harry, age 85, who was born in 1921 and has few quarters of coverage under Social Security

23. 3. 3 Overview

Medicare covers inpatient care in hospitals (Part A), doctors' services, outpatient care, and some other medical services (Part B), as well as prescription drug coverage (Part D). Medicare also offers what are called Medicare Advantage plans (Part C). Medicare Advantage plans include Medicare managed care plans, such as HMOs, Medicare preferred provider organization plans (PPOs), Medicare private fee-for-service (PFFS) plans, and Medicare special needs plans.

What the Original Medicare Plan Covers

Part A	Part B
Inpatient hospital services, including semiprivate room and board and nursing services	Physicians' and surgeons' services, whether in a hospital, clinic, or elsewhere
Posthospital skilled nursing care, in an accredited care facility	Medical and health services, such as x-rays, diagnostic lab tests, ambulance services, medical supplies, medical equipment rental, and physical and occupational therapy.
Posthospital home health services, including nursing care, therapy, and part-time home health aides	
Hospice benefits for the care of terminally ill patients (to the exclusion of all other Medicare benefits, except for physician services)	
Inpatient psychiatric care, on a limited basis	

Medicare provides basic health insurance protection to approximately 42 million Americans. Contrary to popular belief, Medicare does not cover all medical expenses. To control costs, Medicare limits the scope of its coverage and its benefit amounts, thus making the consumer and the service provider more cost conscious and less likely to overuse or overcharge the program. For example, Medicare does not pay for most routine physicals, eye and hearing exams, dental care, and many other medical products and services. In addition, many long-term health problems requiring custodial or private nursing care (such as Alzheimer's disease) are not covered. Medicare coverage is also subject to deductibles, co-payments, and limitations.

23. 4 THE ORIGINAL MEDICARE PLAN

The Original Medicare Plan (sometimes called the original fee-for-service plan) has two parts: Hospital Insurance (Part A) and Medical Insurance (Part B). Part A covers inpatient care in hospitals and skilled nursing facilities, and it covers care provided in a hospice and some care provided at home. Part B provides medical insurance for required doctors' services, outpatient services and medical supplies, and many services not covered by Part A hospitalization coverage.

23. 4. 1 Enrollment

Enrollment in Part A is free and automatic for individuals entitled to Social Security benefits. These persons are eligible for Part A benefits as of the first day of the month in which they reach age 65. It should be noted that individuals who are not eligible for premium-free Part A may be able to purchase it under certain circumstances.

Enrollment in Part B, on the other hand, is voluntary and requires payment of a monthly premium. When individuals become eligible for the hospital insurance coverage under Part A, they are enrolled and their premium payment is established for Part B coverage also, unless they sign a form indicating they do not want the Part B coverage.

If individuals enroll before the month in which they reach age 65, Part B coverage begins as of the first day of the month when they are 65, just as it does for Part A. If enrollment takes place later, coverage also begins later.

Part B Initial Enrollment Period

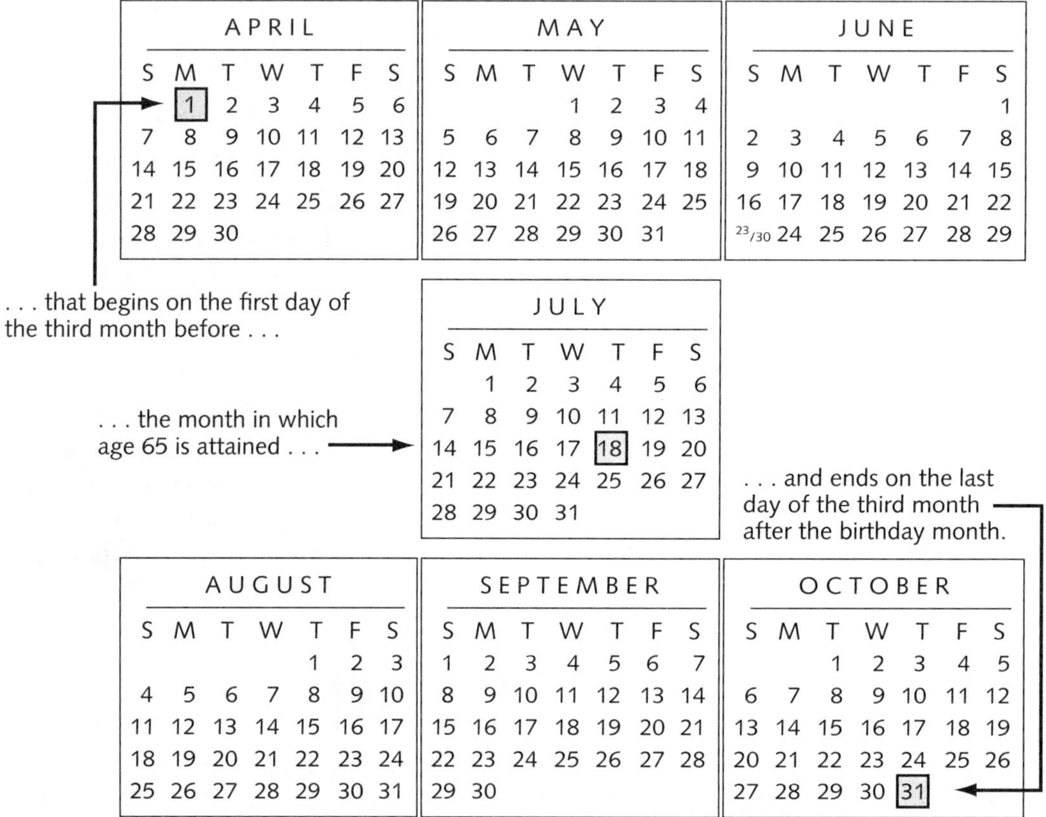

Since 2007, high-income beneficiaries pay higher premiums for Medicare Part B coverage. Premiums are tied to income levels. Previously, everyone paid an amount equal to 25% of the total cost of coverage, and the government picked up the rest of the cost. In 2008, beneficiaries who make more than $82,000 ($164,000 if filing jointly) pay a greater percentage of the premium costs. Individuals with incomes between $82,000 and $102,000 pay 35%, and those with incomes from $102,000 to $153,000 pay 50%. Individuals who make more than $153,000 are responsible for 65% to 85% of costs. These amounts are adjusted annually for inflation.

People who choose not to enroll in Part B during their initial enrollment period may do so later. A **general enrollment period** occurs each year from January 1 through March 31. When enrollment occurs during this period, coverage begins on the following July 1.

23. 4. 2 Benefits Under the Original Medicare Plan: Medicare Part A

Part A provides coverage for four different kinds of care:

- Inpatient hospital care
- Skilled nursing facility care
- Home health care
- Hospice care

The services covered under each of these arrangements are subject to certain limitations that we will discuss later.

Examples of the four types of care follow.

- An individual who is hospitalized with pneumonia is receiving **inpatient hospital care.**
- An individual receives skilled nursing services in a facility designed for that purpose. **Skilled nursing care** is for patients whose professional nursing needs do not require acute hospital nursing care but who need inpatient supervision by a registered nurse.
- An individual receives assistance several days a week at home following major surgery. This is **home health care**.
- An individual with a terminal illness who will spend the remainder of his life in a hospice receives **hospice care**.

23. 4. 2. 1 Inpatient Hospital Care

Medicare's inpatient hospital care benefit helps pay the reasonable charges that result from hospitalization in a semiprivate room for medically necessary care. This includes meals, regular nursing services, special care units, drugs taken in the hospital, tests, medical supplies, operating room, and many other supplies and services.

For each benefit period, Medicare will pay the full cost of up to 60 days' of inpatient hospital care, after the patient pays a deductible, which changes annually. From the 61st through 90th days of hospitalization, Medicare pays all but a specified coinsurance amount per day. This figure also changes annually. For a stay over 90 days, the patient may draw upon 60 lifetime reserve days, which may be used only once in a lifetime. The patient's daily co-payment amount increases substantially when these reserve days are used.

A benefit period begins upon admission and ends 60 days after hospital discharge. A readmission during these 60 days is considered part of the same benefit period; a readmission after the 60 days run out is the beginning of a new benefit period.

23. 4. 2. 2 Skilled Nursing Facility Care

Medicare will share the cost of skilled nursing facility (SNF) care for up to 100 days in each benefit period.

The patient must pay a specified dollar amount (coinsurance) for the 21st through 100th days of confinement. This amount changes annually. Medicare pays all reasonable charges for the first 20 days.

Medicare defines the skilled nursing facility benefit quite narrowly. The patient must be receiving medically necessary services provided by a highly skilled staff in a Medicare-approved facility, following a prior hospital stay of at least three days. The care must be of a type that can be performed only by or under the supervision of licensed nursing personnel, and only as the result of a doctor's orders.

Any type of intermediate or custodial, as opposed to skilled, nursing care is not covered. Custodial care includes board, room, and nonmedical personal assistance services, such as help performing activities of daily living, for example, dressing, eating, and bathing.

23. 4. 2. 3 Home Health Care

If a patient is confined at home, the home health care benefit provides for certain services performed by a participating home health agency. This is a public or private agency that provides skilled nursing or therapeutic services in the home. Eligible expenses include:

- intermittent part-time nursing care;
- physical, occupational, or speech therapy;
- home health aides;
- medical social services;
- medical supplies; and
- 80% of certain durable medical equipment, such as wheelchairs or hospital beds.

No benefits will be paid for housekeeping services, meal preparation or delivery, shopping, full-time nursing care, blood transfusions, drugs, or biologicals.

The home health care benefit pays for an unlimited number of home visits as medically necessary, provided they are intermittent rather than constant or full time. Note that this is not the same benefit that is found in long-term care policies.

23. 4. 2. 4 Hospice Care

A hospice is organized primarily for the purpose of providing support services to terminally ill patients and their families. For terminally ill patients, the hospice care benefit provides inpatient and outpatient hospice care. Payments are made for pain relief and symptom management but not for curative or other types of treatment.

It is possible for Medicare to cover hospice care for an unlimited period, as long as a physician certifies need.

Medicare pays virtually all costs for hospice treatment, with no deductible. Only two services require co-payments:

- Prescription drugs, for which patients must pay 5% or $5 per prescription, whichever is less
- Respite care, for which patients must pay 5% of the Medicare-approved rate up to a specified dollar amount, which changes annually

The **respite care** benefit covers temporary care in a hospice for a patient who is normally cared for in the home. The respite is for the usual caregivers and may last no more than five consecutive days.

Example

Ellis is admitted to a hospice in March. Medicare begins paying covered charges immediately, with no deductible required from Ellis.

In July and again in October, Ellis is recertified as being terminally ill. Medicare continues to pay hospice benefits for Ellis.

During this time, Ellis receives experimental medical treatments that could conceivably halt the progress of his illness. Medicare will not cover these treatments, so Ellis must find other funding to pay for them.

Now let's suppose that Ellis is instead being cared for at home by his brother, Bradley, who needs some time off from the responsibility of caring for Ellis. If Bradley wants to take Ellis to a hospice for several days, Medicare will pay for five consecutive days of respite care.

23. 4. 3 What Part A Does Not Cover

Hospital insurance under Medicare does not cover:

- private-duty nursing;
- charges for a private room, unless medically necessary;
- conveniences, such as a telephone or television in an insured's room; and
- the first three pints of blood received during a calendar year (unless replaced by a blood plan).

23. 4. 4 Benefits Under the Original Medicare Plan: Medicare Part B

Medicare Part B provides coverage for three general kinds of medical services:

- Doctors' services
- Home health care (if not covered by Part A)
- Outpatient medical services and supplies

Part B is an optional program of medical insurance designed to supplement Part A. Persons who enroll in Part A are automatically enrolled in Part B unless they request otherwise. Part B requires payment of a monthly premium, which many people simply have deducted from their Social Security or Railroad Retirement checks.

23. 4. 4. 1 Common Deductible and Co-Payment

Medicare Part B requires cost-sharing by the patient. There is an annual deductible and a coinsurance percentage that applies to all Part B covered services across the board. This contrasts with Part A, in which each benefit provided has its own unique co-payment requirements for the patient.

Under Part B, a patient is always responsible for these co-payments:

- An annual deductible amount
- 20% of all reasonable charges for covered, medically necessary services
- The first three pints of blood

The deductible can be met by any combination of expenses covered under Part B. The patient does not have to meet a separate deductible for each type of covered service.

Medicare determines what is a reasonable charge for a particular service. If the actual charge is more than that, the patient must pay the difference, unless the doctor or supplier agrees to accept assignment. **Assignment** means that the doctor or supplier will accept Medicare's approved amounts as full payment and cannot legally bill the patient for anything above that amount. Doctors and suppliers are not required to accept assignment, but many will.

If Medicare decides that an expense is medically unnecessary, the patient must pay the entire cost. Neither Medicare nor most private insurance policies will provide benefits.

23. 4. 4. 2 Doctors' Services

Part B covers most physicians', surgeons', and osteopaths' services and supplies furnished as part of such services. It does not matter where such services are provided—in a hospital, in a skilled nursing facility, in a clinic, at the doctor's office, at the patient's home, or anywhere else in the United States.

Some of the specific services covered are:

- medical and surgical services, including anesthesia;
- office visits, house calls, and hospital calls;
- radiological and pathological services provided by a physician;
- medical supplies furnished as part of a physician's professional services;

- second opinions before surgery;
- diagnostic tests that are part of the patient's treatment;
- x-rays;
- services of the doctor's office nurse;
- physical, occupational, and speech therapy services;
- blood transfusions; and
- drugs and biologicals that cannot be self-administered.

Specifically excluded from Part B coverage are physicians' services for:

- routine physical exams (note: Part B does cover one physical examination within the first six months of enrollment);
- routine foot care, treatment of flat feet, and treatment for subluxations of the foot;
- eye exams and fitting of eyeglasses or contact lenses;
- hearing exams and fitting of hearing aids;
- most types of dental care;
- most immunizations; and
- cosmetic surgery (unless needed to repair an accidental injury or to correct a malformed body part).

23. 4. 4. 3 Preventive Care

Medicare Part B covers the following preventive services:

- Bone mass measurements for qualified individuals
- Screening blood tests, including cholesterol, lipid, and triglyceride levels, for early detection of cardiovascular disease (since 2005)
- Colorectal cancer screenings
- Diabetes screening tests for enrollees who are at risk for diabetes (since 2005)
- Glaucoma testing once every 12 months
- Pap tests, pelvic examinations, and clinical breast exams for women
- Annual prostate cancer screenings for men age 50 and over
- Annual screening mammograms for women age 40 and over

Note that these preventive services are covered by other types of Medicare plans. However, the amount a person pays for these services varies depending on the type of plan.

23. 4. 4. 4 *Home Health Care Services*

Recall that Medicare Part A covers home health care services. For persons who participate in Part B but not Part A, Part B pays the full cost of medically necessary home health visits for patients requiring home nursing care. The patient pays no deductible or coinsurance, except for 20% of the cost of durable medical equipment, provided under the home health care benefit (e.g., wheelchairs and hospital beds).

The home health care expenses of persons with Part A are paid under Part A.

23. 4. 4. 5 *Outpatient Medical Services and Supplies*

Medicare Part B will help pay for certain services received as an outpatient from a Medicare-certified hospital for the diagnosis or treatment of an illness or injury.

The following is a relatively comprehensive list of some of the outpatient medical services and supplies covered under Medicare Part B:

- Outpatient clinic services
- Emergency room services
- X-rays, whether for therapy or diagnosis billed by the hospital
- Medically necessary ambulance services
- Purchase or rental of durable medical equipment used in the patient's home
- Artificial limbs and eyes
- Artificial replacements for internal organs (e.g., colostomy bags and supplies)
- Braces for neck, back, or limbs
- Casts, splints, and surgical dressings
- Blood transfusions (after the first three pints) furnished to an outpatient
- Outpatient physical, occupational, and speech therapy provided in a therapist's office, as an outpatient, or in the patient's home
- Drugs and biologicals that cannot be self-administered
- Mammograms, Pap smears, and colorectal screenings
- Diabetes glucose monitoring and education
- Flu shots

Outpatient services not covered by Part B are:

- routine physical exams (other than the one-time exam mentioned earlier);

- eye exams, fitting of eyeglasses or contact lenses;
- hearing exams and fitting of hearing aids;
- most immunizations; and
- routine foot care.

23. 4. 5 What Part B Does Not Cover

Medical insurance under Medicare Part B does not cover:

- private-duty nursing;
- skilled nursing home care costs over 100 days per benefit period;
- intermediate nursing home care;
- physician charges above Medicare's approved amount;
- most outpatient prescription drugs;
- care received outside the United States (limited coverage for Canada and Mexico);
- custodial care received in the home;
- dental care, routine physicals and immunizations, cosmetic surgery, eyeglasses, hearing aids, orthopedic shoes, and acupuncture expenses; and
- expenses incurred as a result of war or act of war.

23. 4. 6 Claims and Appeals

If a doctor has not accepted a Medicare assignment, the doctor sends the bill directly to the patient. The patient fills out a Medicare claim form and attaches itemized bills from the doctor including date of treatment, place of treatment, description of treatment, doctor's name, and charge for service. The form and accompanying documents are sent to the Medicare carrier (also known as a fiscal intermediary—a private insurance company) in the patient's area. Upon receiving the claim, the carrier sends a form called **Explanation of Medicare Benefits**. This form shows which services are covered and the amounts approved for each service.

If Medicare claims are denied, a patient can go through an appeal process. Within six months of the receipt of the Explanation of Medicare Benefits notice, the patient must file a written request for review. The carrier will check for miscalculations or other clerical errors. If the carrier, after review, declines to make a change, an appeal can be made (if the amount disputed is $100 or more) to the Social Security office. The patient must appear in person to attend a hearing and present evidence, such as a doctor's letter, to support the patient's point. A written notice of the decision is sent after the hearing.

23. 5 MEDICARE SUPPLEMENT INSURANCE

As we have seen, the Original Medicare Plan provides substantial hospital and other medical benefits for beneficiaries of the program. However, even after Medicare pays its share, the patient may still owe large amounts because of:

- deductibles;
- coinsurance;
- noncovered services; and
- actual charges by service providers in excess of the approved amount that Medicare will pay.

Several methods are available to supplement Medicare and cover most of the remaining expenses.

- Medicaid, discussed later in this unit, covers expenses not paid by Medicare for eligible low-income people. In other words, these people do not need supplemental insurance.
- Many employers offer their retiring employees an opportunity to continue their group insurance coverage or to convert it to Medicare supplement coverage. For those who continue to work after age 65, Medicare may become the secondary payer to an employer group health care plan. This means that the employer plan will pay first on hospital and medical bills. If the employer plan does not pay all expenses, Medicare may pay secondary benefits for Medicare-covered services to supplement the amount paid by the employer group health care plan. Medicare is also the secondary payer to employer plans for beneficiaries who have Medicare because of or permanent kidney failure.
- Associations and groups may offer supplemental Medicare coverage to their members who are age 65 and over.
- Members of certain HMOs can sign up for a Medicare Replacement Plan, which eliminates Medicare's deductibles and co-payments and provides additional benefits.
- More often, a Medicare supplement policy is purchased from an insurer to help cover the costs not paid by Medicare. This may also be referred to as a Medigap policy.

This section concentrates on the last option: Medicare supplement policies purchased from private insurers.

Some kind of supplement to Medicare is needed by almost everyone covered by Medicare except those whose income is low enough to qualify for help from Medicaid.

23. 5. 1 Medicare Supplement Plans

A **Medigap** policy is a Medicare supplement insurance policy sold by private insurance companies to fill "gaps" in Medicare Parts A and B. Medigap policies do not pay costs for Medicare Parts C and D. A person who has a Medicare Advantage plan does not need a Medigap policy because these plans generally cover many of the same benefits that a Medigap policy would cover. In fact, it is illegal for anyone to sell a Medigap policy to a person who is in a Medicare Advantage plan.

There are 12 standardized Medigap plans. Each of the 12 plans has a letter designation ranging from A to L. These policies were standardized by the National Association of Insurance Commissioners (NAIC) to help consumers understand and compare them and thus make informed buying decisions. These standards can be found in NAIC's Medicare Supplement Insurance Minimum Standards Model Act. The benefits in each plan may not be altered by insurers, nor may the letter designation be changed (although insurers may add names or titles to the letter designations).

Medigap Plan A covers basic benefits. Medigap Plans B through J include the Plan A basic benefits and some extra benefits. Plans K and L offer different benefits than Medigap Plans A through J and lower premiums than those plans. However, Plans K and L require higher out-of-pocket costs from beneficiaries because these plans were designed to give beneficiaries an incentive to control costs. Although Plans K and L are similar, they differ in the percentage of coverage for claims and in the maximum amount of out-of-pocket costs. Note that insurance companies that sell Medigap policies don't have to offer every Medigap plan. Each insurance company decides which Medigap policies it wants to sell. The front of each Medigap policy must state that it is Medicare supplement insurance.

Three states—Massachusetts, Minnesota, and Wisconsin—are referred to as waiver states because they are permitted by statute to have different standardized Medigap plans.

23. 5. 2 Basic Benefits

Each standardized Medigap policy must cover basic benefits. Plans A through J have one set of basic benefits, and Plans K and L have different benefits than Medigap Plans A through J. Medicare Plan A covers only the basic benefits. Medigap Plans B through J include the basic benefits and some extra benefits.

12 Standard Medigap Plans

A	B	C	D	E	F**	G	H	I	J**	K	L
Basic Benefits*	Basic Benefits*	Basic Benefits*	Basic Benefits*	Basic Benefits*	Basic Benefits*	Basic Benefits*	Basic Benefits*	Basic Benefits*	Basic Benefits*	Basic Benefits***	Basic Benefits***
	Part A Deductible	Part A Deductible	Part A Deductible	Part A Deductible	Part A Deductible	Part A Deductible	Part A Deductible	Part A Deductible	Part A Deductible	50% Part A Deductible	50% Part A Deductible
		Skilled Nursing Coinsurance	Skilled Nursing Coinsurance	Skilled Nursing Coinsurance	Skilled Nursing Coinsurance	Skilled Nursing Coinsurance	Skilled Nursing Coinsurance	Skilled Nursing Coinsurance	Skilled Nursing Coinsurance	50% Skilled Nursing Coinsurance	50% Skilled Nursing Coinsurance
		Part B Deductible			Part B Deductible				Part B Deductible		
					Part B Excess (100%)	Part B Excess (80%)		Part B Excess (100%)	Part B Excess (100%)		
		Foreign Travel Emergency	Foreign Travel Emergency	Foreign Travel Emergency	Foreign Travel Emergency	Foreign Travel Emergency	Foreign Travel Emergency	Foreign Travel Emergency	Foreign Travel Emergency		
			At-Home Recovery			At-Home Recovery		At-Home Recovery	At-Home Recovery		
							Basic Drugs ($1,250 Limit) ***	Basic Drugs ($1,250 Limit) ***			
				Preventive Care Not Covered by Medicare					Preventive Care Not Covered by Medicare		
					Annual Deductible **				Annual Deductible **	Annual Deductible ****	Annual Deductible ****

*The Basic Benefits policy covers 100% of the Part A hospital coinsurance amount for each day used from the 61st through the 90th day in any Medicare benefit period and 100% of the Part A hospital coinsurance amount for each Medicare lifetime inpatient reserve day used from the 91st through the 150th day in any Medicare benefit period; 100% of the Part A-eligible hospital expenses for 365 additional days after all hospital benefits are exhausted; Part B coinsurance amount (generally 20% of Medicare-approved expenses) after the annual deductible is met, and the cost of the first three pints of blood each year.

**Plans F and J have a high deductible plan option that pays the same benefits as Plans F and J after one has paid a calendar year deductible. Benefits from high deductible Plans F and J will not begin until out-of-pocket expenses exceed the deductible. Out-of-pocket expenses for this deductible are expenses that would ordinarily be paid by the policy. These expenses include the Medicare deductible for Part A and Part B, but do not include the plan's separate foreign travel emergency deductible.

***The basic benefits under Plans K and L provide for different costsharing for items and services than Plans A through J. Plan K pays 100% of Part A hospitalization coinsurance plus coverage for 365 days after Medicare benefits end, 50% of hospice cost-sharing, 50% of Medicare-eligible expenses for the first three pints of blood, and 50% of Part B coinsurance, except 100% coinsurance for Part B preventive services. Plan L pays 100% of Part A hospitalization coinsurance plus coverage for 365 days after Medicare benefits end, 75% of hospice costsharing, 75% of Medicare-eligible expenses for the first three pints of blood, and 75% of Part B coinsurance, except 100% coinsurance for Part B preventive services.

Once a person reaches the annual limit, the plan pays 100% of the Medicare copayments, coinsurance, and deductibles for the rest of the calendar years. The out-of-pocket annual limit does not include charges from a provider and that exceed Medicare-approved amounts. Such charges are called "excess charges," and the policyowner is responsible for paying them.

****These out-of-pocket annual limits increase each year for inflation.

23. 5. 3 Extra Benefits

The table shows extra Medigap benefits for Medigap Plans B through J.

Extra Benefits of Medigap Plans B Through J

Benefit	Medigap Beneficiary Pays
Skilled Nursing Facility Care Coinsurance	With Medigap Plan C, D, E, F, G, H, I, or J, beneficiary pays: – nothing for the first 20 days; – nothing for days 21-100; and – all costs after day 100.
Medicare Part A Deductible	With Medigap Plan B, C, D, E, F, G, H, I, or J, beneficiary pays nothing for days 1-60 of a hospital stay.
Medicare Part B Deductible	With Medigap Plan C, F, or J, beneficiary pays nothing of the annual deductible for Part B-covered services and supplies.
Medicare Part B Excess Charges	With Medigap Plans F, I, or J, beneficiary pays none of the excess charges. With Plan G, beneficiary pays 20% of the excess charges.
Foreign Travel Emergency	With Medigap Plan C, D, E, F, G, H, I, or J, beneficiary pays the first $250 and then 20% of the remaining costs of emergency health care during the first 60 days of each trip. There is a $50,000 lifetime maximum.
At-Home Recovery	With Medigap Plan D, G, I, or J: – beneficiary pays nothing for Medicare-approved home health services; – beneficiary pays nothing for up to eight additional weeks of at-home help after skilled care is no longer needed; and – Medigap policies will pay up to $40 each visit and $1,600 each year.
Prescription Drugs Starting January 1, 2006 (The Medicare Prescription Drug Modernization Act of 2003 and its effect of those benefits will be discussed later)	With Medigap Plan H, I, or J, beneficiary pays for the first $250 of outpatient prescription drugs each year. Then beneficiary pays 50% for all prescription drugs not covered by Medicare. Plans H and I have a $1,250 per year limit. For Plans H and I to be of full value, beneficiary should have at least $2,750 in drug costs per year (beneficiary pays $1,250 plus $250; plan pays $1,250). Plan J has a $3,000 per year limit. For Plan J to be of full value, beneficiary should have at least $6,250 in drug costs per year (beneficiary pays $3,000 plus $250; plan pays $3,000).
Medicare-Covered Preventive Services	With Medigap Plan E or J, beneficiary pays: – a yearly deductible for Part B; and – nothing for Medicare-covered preventive services.
Non-Medicare Covered Preventive Services	Beneficiary may pay nothing for routine yearly check-ups and any non-Medicare covered preventive services recommended by a doctor. This benefit has a $120 per year limit. Beneficiary pays 100% after meeting the yearly limit. Note that Medicare Part B covers a one-time Welcome to Medicare physical exam within the first 6 months of having Part B.

The table shows extra Medigap benefits for Medigap Plan K and Plan L. Beneficiaries will pay part of the cost-sharing of some covered services until they meet the annual out-of-pocket limit of $4,440 for Plan K or $2,220 for Plan L. (These limits are for 2008 and are subject to increase due to inflation.)

Extra Benefits of Medigap Plan K and Plan L

Basic Benefit	Plan K	Plan L
Skilled Nursing Facility Care Coinsurance	Beneficiary pays: – nothing for the first 20 days; – up to 50% of coinsurance amount per day for days 21-100*; and – all costs after day 100	Beneficiary pays: – nothing for the first 20 days; – up to 75% of coinsurance amount per day for days 21-100*; and – all costs after day 100
Medicare Part A Deductible	Beneficiary pays 50% of deductible for days 1-60 of a hospital stay.	Beneficiary pays 75% of deductible for days 1-60 of a hospital stay.
Annual Cap on Out-of-Pocket Expenditures for Medicare Parts A and B	Full coverage of all Medicare Parts A and B deductibles, co-payments, and coinsurance amounts after beneficiary pays out-of-pocket limit.	Full coverage of all Medicare Parts A and B deductibles, co-payments, and coinsurance amounts after beneficiary pays out-of-pocket limit.

*These amounts count toward the annual limit.

As long as a person pays the premium, a Medigap policy is automatically renewed each year. No provision of any Medicare supplement plan duplicates benefits provided under Medicare—instead, each plan provides supplemental coverage.

23. 5. 4 Medicare Part D and Medicare Supplement Plans

The **Medicare Prescription Drug and Modernization Act of 2003** contains provisions that affect Medicare supplement plans. The prescription drug coverages that Medicare began offering on January 1, 2006, affect Medigap policies that offered prescription drug coverage, specifically Plans H, I, and J. The law prohibits the sale of these Medigap policies with prescription drug coverage since 2006. Although these policies are still sold, they can no longer include prescription drug coverage.

Individuals who have such policies are given several options by their insurance company so they can decide which drug option best meets their needs. If a beneficiary chooses to enroll in a Part D prescription drug plan, that person can keep his current Medigap policy, but without the drug coverage and with the premium reduced accordingly. These beneficiaries also have the option to switch to another Medigap policy offered by the same insurer, but only if they elect Part D during the initial enrollment period. A beneficiary also can keep a Medigap policy with prescription drug coverage if the beneficiary does not enroll in a Medicare Part D plan. However, in this case, the beneficiary's drug coverage would be more expensive than and not as extensive as the benefits offered by a standard Part D plan, because the Medigap Plan H, I, or J prescription drug benefit is capped and does not have the catastrophic benefit that Part D plans must offer to their enrollees.

23. 5. 4. 1 Medicare SELECT

Medicare SELECT is another version of the standard Medigap policies we have been discussing. It offers the same 12 plans with the same coverages. The only difference between Medicare SELECT and standard Medigap insurance is that Medicare SELECT is operated on a **preferred provider** basis. Each insurer has a list of doctors and hospitals from which the insured must make a choice for treatment to receive benefits. As a result of this requirement, Medicare SELECT policies generally have lower premiums than standard Medigap policies.

23. 6 MEDICARE PART C: MEDICARE ADVANTAGE PLANS

The Original Medicare Plan as adopted in the 1960s allows beneficiaries to receive health care from any physician who accepts Medicare patients. No referrals are necessary. Under this plan, Medicare pays for medically necessary, Medicare-approved services, and the patient is responsible for the remaining expenses. This plan is known as the **original fee-for-service plan**.

The Balanced Budget Act of 1997 (BBA) authorized the use of alternative health care plans, including some types of managed care plans, to provide Medicare benefits. The goals were twofold: to give Medicare beneficiaries more options in choosing a health care plan and to help control Medicare costs, which were beginning to increase at an alarming pace. The alternative health care program authorized by the BBA was known as **Medicare+Choice**, or **Medicare Part C**.

23. 6. 1 Medicare Part C: Medicare Advantage Plans

The Medicare Prescription Drug, Improvement, and Modernization Act of 2003 made additional refinements to the Medicare+Choice program and renamed it **Medicare Advantage**. Plans available under the Medicare Advantage program include the following:

- Medicare private fee-for-service plans
- Medicare managed care plans
- Medicare preferred provider organization plans
- Medicare specialty plans

The original fee-for-service plan is still available to all Medicare beneficiaries nationwide. Beneficiaries who are happy with the original plan are not required to change to a Medicare Advantage plan. They will remain enrolled under the original plan unless they choose to enroll in a Medicare Advantage plan.

To enroll in a Medicare Advantage plan, a person must be enrolled in Medicare Part A and Part B. The enrollee must still pay the monthly Part B premium and also may have to pay an additional premium to the Medicare Advantage plan. People who are enrolled in a Medicare Advantage plan don't need a Medicare supplement policy because Medicare Advantage plans usually provide most of the same benefits provided by Medicare supplements.

23. 6. 2 Medicare Private Fee-for-Service Plans

Medicare private fee-for-service (PFFS) plans are similar to the Medicare original fee-for-service plan, except that they are offered by private companies. They allow beneficiaries to receive care from any Medicare-approved provider who is willing to accept the terms of the plan's payment schedule. But the private company, rather than Medicare, negotiates with providers to determine how much the plan will pay and what enrollees must pay for the services they receive.

Enrollees may have to pay a premium to join the plan and may have to pay other costs, such as co-payments, for some services. These costs may be different from the costs under the Original Medicare Plan. In exchange, however, enrollees often get extra benefits that are not provided under the Original Medicare Plan, such as extra days in the hospital.

23. 6. 3 Medicare Managed Care Plans

Medicare managed care plans share many of the same features found in managed care plans provided under employer-sponsored health plans. They often take the form of **Medicare health maintenance organizations (HMOs).** In these HMOs, enrollees are usually limited to using network providers except for emergencies and may be required to choose a primary care physician. Enrollees who want to see a specialist typically must obtain a referral from their primary care physician.

In most Medicare managed care HMOs, enrollees who go outside the plan for nonemergency services must pay the entire bill out of their own pockets. Some Medicare managed care plans offer a **point-of-service (POS)** option, which allows enrollees to use out-of-network providers but requires them to pay a greater portion of the provider's charges if they do.

Medicare HMOs generally charge enrollees a monthly premium, which must be paid in addition to the usual Medicare Part B premium. They often charge a small co-payment each time an enrollee uses a service, such as $5 for a doctor's visit, but there are usually no additional charges. Enrollees do not have to pay the Medicare deductibles and coinsurance amounts, and they often receive coverage for services the original Medicare fee-for-service plan doesn't cover, such as routine physical exams and dental care.

23. 6. 4 Medicare Preferred Provider Organization Plans

Medicare preferred provider organization (PPO) plans are similar to Medicare managed health care plans but have the following differences.

- Enrollees generally aren't required to name a primary care physician and can see any doctor or provider that accepts Medicare, but they may pay more if they use providers who aren't part of the plan's network
- Enrollees don't need referrals to see a specialist, although they may need plan approval for certain services.

Since 2006, the Medicare Advantage program includes regional PPOs designed to bring the benefits of Medicare Advantage to rural areas. Medicare beneficiaries in many rural areas did not have access to the Medicare+Choice plans authorized by the Balanced Budget Act of 1997 and were limited to the original Medicare fee-for-service plan. The Medicare Prescription Drug, Improvement, and Modernization Act of 2003 provides additional financial incentives for providers who establish regional PPOs that serve those areas.

23. 6. 5 Medicare Specialty Plans

Medicare specialty plans provide more focused health care for people with specific conditions. A person who joins one of these plans gets health care services as well as more-focused care to manage a specific disease or condition. The goal is to provide quality health care as efficiently and effectively as possible.

23. 7 MEDICARE PART D: MEDICARE PRESCRIPTION DRUG PLANS

The Medicare Prescription Drug and Modernization Act of 2003 established a new Medicare Part D prescription drug benefit. Since January 2006, Medicare offers insurance coverage for prescription drugs to anyone who has Medicare Part A or Part B. Prescription drug coverage is needed because medical practice today relies on drug therapies to treat chronic conditions. As a result, most Medicare beneficiaries sooner or later will need prescription drugs to stay healthy.

Under the standard benefit for 2008, Medicare beneficiaries pay a monthly premium of $27.93 and a $275 annual deductible. Beneficiaries then pay 25% of the first $2,510 of prescription drug costs, and Medicare pays the other 75%. (In 2009, beneficiaries will pay an estimated monthly premium of $29 to $31 and an annual deductible of $295. They will then pay 25% of the first $2,700 of prescription drug costs, and Medicare will pay the other 75%.) Coverage then stops completely. However, if a beneficiary's total drug costs are more than $5,726.25 ($6,153.75 in 2009) after the beneficiary has spent another $4,050 ($4,350 in 2009), then catastrophic coverage starts and beneficiaries pay co-payments of $2.25 ($2.40 in 2009) for generic drugs and $5.60 ($6.00 in 2009) for brand name drugs or 5% of total costs, whichever is higher. (These dollar thresholds are scheduled to increase each year.) In 2008, a person would have had to spend $5,726.25 ($6,153.75 in 2009) in out-of-pocket costs before receiving catastrophic coverage. Although companies have considerable flexibility in designing their own plans, the overall value of the drug coverage offered must be the same or greater than the basic plan. Of course, companies that offer more benefits can charge higher premiums.

Coverage is available only through private plans that are either stand-alone prescription drug plans (PDPs) or Medicare private plans such as HMOs, PPOs, or PFFSs. A stand-alone plan only offers prescription drug benefits. People in these plans get other medical services through the Original Medicare Plan. Most Medicare private plans provide all Medicare-covered services, including prescription drug coverage. Individuals in private fee-for-service plans that don't offer drug coverage can enroll in a stand-alone prescription drug plan. However, individuals in HMOs or PPOs must receive all of their medical and drug coverage through these plans.

The law provides federal subsidy payments to employers and unions that sponsor qualified retiree prescription drug plans.

Three Medigap benefit plans (H, I, and J) include coverage for prescription drugs. The new law prohibits the sale of these Medigap policies with prescription drug coverage since 2006.

23. 8 MEDICARE AND EMPLOYER COVERAGE

Many individuals continue working beyond the age of 65 or have spouses who are working. In such cases, Medicare beneficiaries may be covered by their own or their spouse's employer group health plan. When this occurs, Medicare may be the secondary payer to any group health plan provided by an employer with 20 or more employees. This means that the group health plan pays first on hospital and medical bills. If the plan does not pay all of the expenses incurred, Medicare may pay secondary benefits for Medicare-covered services to supplement the amount paid by the group health plan.

Note that employers with 20 or more employees must offer the same health benefits to employees age 65 or older, as well as to their spouses who are age 65 or older, as they offer to younger employees and spouses. The older employee has the option of rejecting such group health coverage, in which case Medicare becomes the primary payer for Medicare-covered health services.

Medicare may also be a secondary payer to employer-provided group health coverage for certain individuals under age 65 who are entitled to Medicare on the basis of their . To be the primary payer, the group health plan must generally be that of an employer or employee organization that covers the employees of at least one employer with 100 or more employees. Such plans are known as large group health plans (LGHPs). An LGHP may not treat disabled employees differently from other employees because of their disability.

23. 9 MEDICAID

Medicaid is a welfare health care program for indigent persons. It was established by the federal government but is administered by the states. The eligibility requirements for Medicaid vary somewhat from state to state. Generally, to be eligible for Medicaid, a person must qualify for either (1) Aid for Families with Dependent Children (also known as public assistance or welfare) or (2) Supplemental Security Income, an assistance program under Social Security for indigent persons who are age 65 or over, blind, or disabled. For those who do qualify, Medicaid covers most health care costs, including hospital and doctor bills and nursing home care.

23. 9. 1 Financial Tests

Each state establishes its own limit on the income and financial resources that a Medicaid recipient may have and still qualify for Medicaid. The recipient must spend down or exhaust income and resources to a minimum amount before Medicaid becomes available.

The recipient—an individual, couple, or family—is permitted to retain a small amount of monthly income plus certain assets (or what the law refers to as resources). The recipient is allowed to keep his home. Within important limits, the recipient may also be able to keep some personal property.

23. 9. 2 Spousal Impoverishment Rule

In the case of a married couple, suppose that only one spouse requires nursing home care. Without some relief in the law, the institutionalized spouse would have to impoverish the other spouse to qualify for Medicaid. The law now provides that the spouse who is not institutionalized is permitted to keep a portion of the couple's resources, as determined by state and federal guidelines.

The law also allows the noninstitutionalized spouse to retain some of the couple's assets or to receive a transfer of assets from the institutionalized spouse to bring assets up to a specified minimum level that is adjusted annually.

If the institutionalized spouse has any resources remaining after making a transfer to the spouse, they are applied toward the nursing home bill. Medicaid then pays only the difference between the actual bill from the nursing home and the institutionalized spouse's contribution toward that bill out of his income and resources.

23. 9. 3 Medicare Cost Assistance

Medicaid is required by law to pay certain Medicare costs of indigent Medicare patients:

- Medicare deductibles
- Part B premium
- Medicare co-payments
- Part A premiums (when required)

The Medicare Secondary Payer Statute (MSP) reduces Medicare costs by making parties responsible for a Medicare beneficiary's injury or illness pay the costs of the injury or illness. Medicare does not cover an injury or illness if the costs were, or can be, paid under workers' compensation, an automobile or liability insurance policy, or under no fault insurance. If the responsible party cannot pay, Medicare will cover the cost. However, these conditional payments are subject to reimbursement from the responsible party. The Centers for Medicare and Medicaid Services (CMS) pursue recovery from the responsible party through subrogation.

23. 9. 4 Medicare-Aid

Medicare-Aid is a Medicare program for persons who have limited income and financial resources. It helps pay Medicare premiums, co-payments, and deductibles. Three levels of Medicare-Aid are based on a person's income.

- Comprehensive Medicare-Aid (MQB-Q) covers the Medicare Part B premium, Medicare Part A premiums, Medicare hospital deductible, Medicare annual deductible, 20% of the Medicare copayment, and the first 20 days of a nursing home stay.
- Limited Medicare-Aid (MQB-B) covers the Medicare Part B premium.
- Limited Medicare-Aid Capped Enrollment (MQB-E) covers the Medicare Part B premium, subject to fund limits.

Medicare-Aid for Working Individuals with a Disability is also available for employed individuals who are disabled. It continues coverage under Medicare Part A even after they have returned to work and earn income following a disability. Persons are eligible if they are under 65, disabled, and eligible for Medicare Part A.

23. 10 SOCIAL SECURITY DISABILITY

The Social Security program in the United States provides death benefits, survivor benefits, retirement benefits, and disability benefits, the last of which is a type of social health insurance. Social Security disability benefits are available to people who meet these requirements:

- Total and permanent disability for at least five months
- Disability expected to last for at least 12 months or end in death
- **Fully insured** and **disability insured** as defined under Social Security regulations

Fully insured means the individual has been credited with the appropriate number of quarters of coverage required by Social Security laws.

Disability insured means the individual is fully insured, has the required quarters of coverage, and meets the first two qualifications in the list above.

On the basis of these definitions, here are examples of two people who could qualify for Social Security benefits. Bill, who was totally and permanently disabled in an auto accident, is fully and disability insured. Mary has been totally and permanently disabled for six months and is not expected to live.

On the other hand, here are examples of two people who do not qualify for Social Security benefits. Lionel is 50% disabled from a military wound. Iona is fully and disability insured and disabled, but she expects to return to work after a nine-month recuperation period.

Benefits available are equal to 100% of the individual's **primary insurance amount (PIA)**, which is the amount the person would normally receive as a retirement benefit. After being entitled to disability benefits for two years, an individual may also receive Medicare benefits.

Social Security disability benefits are based on the level of a worker's earnings up to the time of disability. However, they are not designed to replace the entire amount of a worker's earnings. A worker's average earnings are reduced by a formula to calculate primary insurance amount. Benefit amounts are based on the PIA as follows.

- A disabled worker receives a benefit equal to 100% of PIA.
- A spouse caring for the worker's unmarried child who is under age 16 or was disabled before age 22 also receives a benefit, equal to 50% of the worker's PIA.
- Each unmarried child under age 18 (19 if in high school) or disabled before age 22 receives a benefit equal to 50% of the worker's PIA.

The total dollar amount a family may receive is capped by a maximum family benefit amount that is also based on the worker's average earnings. If the total amount a family is eligible for would exceed the maximum family benefit, the disabled worker receives the full amount for which the worker is eligible, but dependents' benefits are scaled back proportionately until the total amount equals the maximum family benefit. Social Security disability payments generally continue as long as the recipient cannot engage in any substantial gainful activity. This is essentially the same as the any-occupation definition discussed in a previous lesson.

Suppose that Lavonia, formerly a professional dance instructor, was disabled for 34 months. At the end of that period, she was well enough to work at a telephone answering service to pay her bills and fixed expenses. However, she will never again be able to teach dance. Even if Lavonia had qualified for Social Security disability payments previously, it is unlikely she will continue to qualify because she is able to engage in a substantial gainful activity. Whether she can resume her former occupation is not an issue in making this determination.

23. 11 TRICARE

TRICARE is a regionally managed health care program for active duty and retired members of the military uniformed services and their families as well as survivors who are not eligible for Medicare. Participants choose among three health care options: TRICARE Standard, a fee-for-service plan; TRICARE Extra, a preferred provider plan; and TRICARE Prime, for those who seek care at military treatment facilities (MTFs).

23. 12 WORKERS' COMPENSATION

23. 12. 1 Types of Benefits

All state workers' compensation laws incorporate four categories of benefits:

- Disability (loss of income) benefits
- Medical benefits
- Survivor (death) benefits
- Rehabilitation benefits

Disability benefits compensate for loss of income or earning capacity suffered by individuals injured in their occupation. How and in what amounts benefits are paid depend on the severity and permanency of the injury.

Payments may be made on a weekly basis, a lump-sum basis, or some combination. For example, an employee temporarily off work with a broken leg will probably receive a weekly payment based on a percentage of regular wages, subject to an upper limit.

On the other hand, an employee who suffers a permanent loss, such as amputation of a limb, will probably receive a flat lump-sum payment based on a predetermined schedule in the state's workers' compensation law.

Some state laws prescribe both methods of payment for permanent injuries. It is important to be aware of your own state's workers' compensation provisions.

Medical benefits compensate for the cost of medical treatment resulting from job-related injury. In most cases, workers' compensation will pay for the full cost of this treatment.

Suppose an employee of Spaulding Mattress Manufacturers breaks a leg while on the job and is taken to a hospital to have it casted. The resulting hospital bills will be payable under workers' compensation medical benefits because the employee was injured on the job.

If this same employee had broken a leg in an accident while driving home from work, workers' compensation medical benefits would not apply because the injury was not job-related.

Survivor benefits attempt to compensate the widowed spouse or other survivor of an employee whose death results from a job-related injury. The amount of the benefit depends on:

- the deceased's earnings, subject to fixed minimums and maximums; and
- the number of surviving dependents.

A fixed amount is also available for burial expenses. Benefits normally extend until the spouse remarries or until the children become adults.

Rehabilitation benefits are not specifically named in some state workers' compensation acts. However, rehabilitation is provided in every state because all states accept the provisions of the Federal Vocational Rehabilitation Act, which provides federal aid toward the costs incurred.

Diligent rehabilitation and determination on the part of the disabled employee can make the difference between a partial disability and a total one. Rehabilitation for gainful employment serves to reduce insurance losses while restoring the injured worker's dignity. Therefore, rehabilitation is considered worthy of federal help.

23. 12. 2 Compensable Injuries

To be considered compensable, as interpreted in workers' compensation law, an injury must meet three basic criteria.

- It must be accidental.
- It must arise out of the individual's employment.
- It must arise in the course of the individual's employment.

Accidental means that the injury was not intended to happen as far as the injured person is concerned. For example, injury resulting from falling from a loading dock would meet the criteria, whereas injury resulting from deliberately jumping from the loading dock would not.

The second requirement for a compensable injury is that it must arise out of employment. This means the employment must be the source of the accident. If Bud is a welder and is injured while welding on the job, the injury is compensable—provided the third criterion is also met.

The third criterion is that the injury must arise in the course of employment. The time, place, and circumstances of the accident are important in determining whether it results from the employment. If Bud from the previous paragraph were injured while welding at his place of employment but the injury occurred after hours while Bud was welding for his personal use, the injury would not be compensable.

23. 12. 3 Occupational Diseases

To be classified as an occupational disease under a workers' compensation law, the disease must meet these requirements:

- Arise out of employment
- Be due to causes or conditions characteristic of, and peculiar to, the particular trade, occupation, process, or employment

The requirement of peculiarity to a particular employment means that workers' compensation coverage does not apply for any ordinary diseases to which the general public is exposed.

It is possible that an employee might contract a disease that arises out of, and in the course of, employment but is not an occupational disease. Consider a heart attack, ulcers, or even alcoholism. These are not deemed occupational diseases, yet employment could have played a part in inducing any of them. Different states treat this type of situation differently; some states may award compensation, and others may not.

If a chemical engineer develops a throat disease caused by working with toxic materials in his employer's laboratory, this would likely qualify as an occupational disease. However, if a school teacher develops bronchitis in the classroom, this probably is not an occupational disease, even if the teacher was exposed to students with bronchitis. Bronchitis is a condition to which the general public is exposed.

All states mandate coverage for most occupational diseases as part of the workers' compensation system. In most states, occupational diseases are eligible for the same compensation that applies to occupational injuries.

23. 12. 4 Types of Disability

Four types of disability are defined under workers' compensation law:

- Permanent total
- Permanent partial
- Temporary total
- Temporary partial

The difference between permanent and temporary is as simple as it appears: it will last forever, or it will not last forever.

The difference between total and partial depends on the disabled person's ability to work. If a worker is disabled to the extent that the worker cannot perform any job, this is considered a total disability.

On the other hand, if a worker is disabled but able to perform some job (even if it is not the same as the previous employment), then this is considered a partial disability. You'll recognize the parallels between these definitions and those of *own occupation* and *any occupation* discussed in the lesson covering income insurance.

Now let's look individually at each of the four types of disability.

A **permanent total disability** usually results in a complete and permanent loss of earning power, with no ability to perform gainful employment. Many state compensation laws specify that certain injuries, such as total loss of sight or loss of both hands or both feet, constitute permanent total regardless of the insured's ability to do some type of work.

Tanika, a research physicist, permanently loses her eyesight when a batch of chemicals in the laboratory explodes in her face. She suffers a permanent total disability.

A **permanent partial disability** usually refers to a permanent physical impairment that leaves the individual incapable of performing the previous regular job, yet results in only partial loss of earning power because other jobs may be performed. In other words, the employee may be able to perform some other type of work.

Simon, a machinist, severs his leg when it is caught in a machine. Simon can no longer perform his former job, but he has had experience as a dispatcher and has been transferred to that position within his company. This is a permanent partial disability.

A **temporary total disability** usually refers to a total disability that lasts for a short period, after which the employee is fully able to return to work. For example, Andre strains his back while lifting heavy boxes at work. He is in traction and off work for five months before he is able to resume his former job.

A **temporary partial disability** usually refers to a temporary disablement that allows the employee to continue the same job, but with a diminished capability. Francesca, who is a photographer and a graphic designer, twists her ankle and is unable to shoot on location. However, she can complete a graphic illustration for her client, so she is only partially disabled and will be temporarily disabled only until her ankle heals.

23. 12. 5 Compulsory and Elective Compensation Laws

State workers' compensation laws are either compulsory or elective, with the majority being compulsory. This means the employer must accept and comply with all the provisions of the law.

If the state law is elective, however, the employer and employee both have the option of accepting or rejecting the law.

Some state workers' compensation laws are deemed compulsory for specific types of work and elective for other types. However, if an employer chooses not to be subject to a state's elective workers' compensation law, the employer is denied any rights provided under its law and loses use of most pro-employer law defenses as well.

In compulsory states, employers with fewer employees than a minimum established by law do not have to purchase compensation coverage. Most states do allow the employer to voluntarily provide protection by electing to be subject to the law. Once an employer volunteers the state workers' compensation law applies as if it were mandatory.

In states where the workers' compensation law is elective, the option is usually available only to private employers, since public (governmental) employers are required to provide compensation benefits to their employees.

Both compulsory and elective states often exclude two classifications of employees from required coverage:

- Farm workers
- Domestic servants

The direction of changes to workers' compensation law is to require coverage for farm workers. Currently, slightly more than 70% of the jurisdictions cover agricultural workers to greater or lesser extent. Fewer jurisdictions require domestic employees to be covered. In both cases, where coverage is required, the details of the law vary widely by jurisdiction.

23. 12. 6 Extraterritorial Provisions

Most state workers' compensation laws contain an **extraterritorial provision**. This means that a worker who is employed in a particular state is covered under that state's workers' compensation law, even while temporarily working in another state.

Example

Earl is employed by Stockhausen Sporting Goods Manufacturing Company in a state where the workers' compensation law includes an extraterritorial provision. If Earl travels to Texas for a Sporting Goods Distributors convention and injures his back while working at the convention, he is entitled to workers' compensation benefits under the laws of his own state.

While most states have extraterritorial provisions, there is a distinct lack of uniformity among them. This results from the fact that each state law is different and is written broadly in order to protect all types of workers within the state.

23. 12. 7 Second Injury Funds

Second injury funds have been established in almost every state to promote the hiring of previously injured or physically handicapped workers. These funds provide that if a handicapped employee is injured a second time, the employer will be charged only for the loss accrued by that specific second injury, not for the total disability. The employee will collect total benefits as the law provides, the difference being paid out of the second injury fund.

The financing of second injury funds differs among the states. Some states directly assess all of the insurance companies writing workers' compensation insurance in the state. Others insist that the insurance companies make a special contribution to the second injury fund whenever certain claims are processed. These funds serve to spread the cost of benefits among the insurers, encouraging the employment of handicapped persons.

23. 13 SUMMARY

In this lesson, you learned about:

- the four main types of social health insurance provided in the United States;
- the Medicare system, its purpose, and its administration;
- who is eligible for Medicare and how individuals can enroll;
- the benefits provided under the Original Medicare Plan: Medicare Parts A and B;
- the purpose of Medicare supplement insurance;
- the core and optional benefits available in Medicare supplement policies;
- Medicare Select and how it differs from other Medicare supplement plans;
- Medicare Plans C and D;
- how Medicare benefits coordinate with employer-provided benefits;
- the Medicaid program, its purpose, and its administration;
- who is eligible for Medicaid and how individuals can enroll;
- the spousal impoverishment rule;
- the costs Medicaid is required to pay;
- the Social Security program, its purpose, and its administration;
- the purpose of TRICARE and who is eligible;
- workers' compensation, its purpose, and its administration;
- the four categories of benefits incorporated by all states;
- which injuries and illnesses are compensable under workers' compensation;
- the four types of disability defined under workers' compensation law; and
- an extraterritorial provision under workers' compensation.

UNIT TEST

1. Which of the following individuals is least likely to be eligible for Medicare?
   A. Mannie, who is 65 and just registered for his Social Security benefits
   B. Margaret, who is not eligible for Social Security, but is willing to pay a fee for her insurance
   C. Karl, who has been diagnosed with end-stage liver disease
   D. Genevieve, who has been receiving benefits from Social Security for 3 years

2. Under Medicare Part B, individuals pay a deductible each
   A. benefit period
   B. week
   C. month
   D. year

3. After the deductible is satisfied, Part B pays what percentage of all approved charges?
   A. 10%
   B. 20%
   C. 80%
   D. 100%

4. Doctors and suppliers who agree to accept the amount Medicare will pay are said to have agreed to
   A. payment
   B. assignment
   C. assessment
   D. capitation

5. All of the following outpatient services are covered under Part B EXCEPT
   A. artificial limbs
   B. emergency room services
   C. most immunizations
   D. physical therapy

6. Which of the following outpatient services is excluded from Part B coverage?
   A. Casts and splints
   B. Laboratory tests billed by hospitals
   C. Medically necessary ambulance services
   D. Hearing exams

7. The Original Medicare Plan consists of
   A. Medicare Part A
   B. Medicare Part B
   C. Medicare Parts A and B
   D. Medicare Parts C and D

8. Michelle is 65 and starting to receive Social Security benefits. To receive Medicare Part A, she needs to
   A. fill out an enrollment form at her local Social Security office
   B. pay a monthly premium
   C. prove eligibility
   D. do nothing

9. The annual general enrollment period for Medicare Part B begins on
   A. January 1
   B. March 1
   C. March 31
   D. July 1

10. Does Medicare pay all medical costs for its beneficiaries?
    A. Yes
    B. No

11. Some kind of supplement to Medicare is needed by almost everyone covered by Medicare. Which of the following individuals would NOT need Medicare supplement insurance?
    A. George, whose medical conditions are currently under control
    B. Ken, whose income is low enough to qualify him for help from Medicaid
    C. Carl, whose net worth is high enough to cover any medical bills that might incur

12. Medicare SELECT policies offer ________________ coverage, compared with standard Medigap policies.
    A. the same
    B. more extensive
    C. less extensive

13. Which type of policy requires use of approved doctors and hospitals to receive benefits?
    A. Medicare SELECT
    B. Standard Medigap policies
    C. Both A and B
    D. Neither A nor B

14. Medicare supplement policies are also known as
    A. Medicare policies
    B. Medigap policies
    C. Medicaid policies
    D. Medichoice policies

15. All of the following statements about Medigap insurance are correct EXCEPT
    A. Medigap policies are available through Medicare
    B. Medigap policies are sold by private insurance companies
    C. Medigap policies were standardized by the NAIC
    D. Medigap Plan A covers basic benefits

16. Which of the following benefits are NOT required in any Medicare supplement policy?
    A. Skilled nursing care benefit that covers the Part A co-payments for the 21st through the 100th day of skilled nursing facility care
    B. Part A co-payments for the 61st through the 90th day of hospitalization
    C. Part B co-payments on Medicare-approved charges for physician's and medical services
    D. All charges for 365 days of hospitalization after all Part A inpatient hospital and lifetime reserve days are used up

17. Which of the following individuals is NOT likely to be eligible for Medicaid?
    A. Pam, a single mom who relies on Aid to Families with Dependent Children to help feed her family
    B. Darrell, who has been unable to work since becoming blind 2 years ago
    C. Carmen, who has not been able to work since losing both legs in an accident
    D. Ginny, who is over 65 and working as a manager of a retail outlet

18. Fully insured and disability insured are defined by
    A. state legislatures
    B. Social Security regulations
    C. individual insurers
    D. state departments of insurance

19. Under Social Security benefits, disabled workers receive a benefit equal to
    A. their earnings at the time of the
    B. 66% of their earnings at the time of the
    C. their preferred insurance amount
    D. their primary insurance amount

20. Carla is 67 and eligible for Social Security and Medicare. When she comes out of retirement to work at a large corporation that provides health benefits
    A. her private benefits become secondary to Medicare benefits
    B. her Medicare benefits become secondary to her private benefits
    C. the employer is not required to offer her private benefits
    D. she will cease to be eligible for Medicare benefits

21. Medicare is administered by the
    A. Social Security Administration
    B. individual state governments
    C. Health Care Financing Administration
    D. Health Care Focus Association

22. Medicare Part A covers all of the following EXCEPT
    A. charges for a private room
    B. skilled nursing facility care
    C. home health care
    D. hospice care

23. For each benefit period, Medicare will pay the full cost of up to how many days of hospital care?
    A. 30
    B. 60
    C. 90
    D. 365

24. Medicare will pay the entire cost for skilled nursing facility care for the first
   A. 0 days
   B. 20 days
   C. 80 days
   D. 100 days

25. Individuals who are eligible for Social Security benefits become eligible for Medicare Part A benefits as of
   A. the day they become eligible for Social Security benefits
   B. the first day of the month in which they become eligible for Social Security benefits
   C. the day they turn 65
   D. the first day of the month in which they turn 65

26. Medicare Part A provides coverage for all of the following kinds of care EXCEPT
   A. private-duty nursing
   B. skilled nursing facility care
   C. home health care
   D. hospice care

27. Medicare Part B provides coverage for all of the following kinds of care EXCEPT
   A. skilled nursing facility care not covered by Part A
   B. doctors' services
   C. home health care not covered by Part A
   D. outpatient medical services and supplies

28. Which of the following Medicare supplement plans covers the Part A and Part B deductible?
   A. Plan B
   B. Plan C
   C. Plan D
   D. Plan E

29. Which of the following Medicare supplement plans covers the Part B excess at 80%?
   A. Plan E
   B. Plan F
   C. Plan G
   D. Plan H

30. Which of the following statements about Medicare supplement plans is NOT true?
   A. Benefits must automatically change to coincide with changes in Medicare deductibles and co-payments.
   B. Losses resulting from sickness may not be treated differently than losses resulting from accidents.
   C. The definition of accident may employ an accidental means test.
   D. Policies must be at least guaranteed renewable.

31. To be compensable as interpreted in workers' compensation law, an injury must meet all of the following criteria EXCEPT
   A. it must be accidental
   B. it must arise out of the individual's employment
   C. it must arise in the course of the individual's employment
   D. it must be unforeseeable

32. Juanita is employed in California. She takes a business trip to Colorado to demonstrate some techniques to workers in another facility and is injured in the process. Her workers' compensation benefits will be paid according to the laws of
   A. California
   B. Colorado
   C. whichever state would provide the greater benefit
   D. whichever state would provide the lesser benefit

ANSWERS AND RATIONALES TO UNIT TEST

1. **C.** An individual diagnosed with permanent kidney failure (not end-stage liver disease) would be eligible for Medicare.
2. **D.**
3. **C.** After the deductible is satisfied, Part B pays 80% of all approved charges.
4. **B.** Doctors and suppliers who agree to accept the amount Medicare will pay are said to have agreed to assignment.
5. **C.**
6. **D.** Hearing exams are excluded from Part B coverage.
7. **C.**
8. **D.** To receive Medicare Part A, she needs to do nothing.
9. **A.** The annual general enrollment period for Medicare Part B begins on January 1.
10. **B.**
11. **B.** Low-income people eligible for Medicaid do not need Medicare supplement insurance.
12. **A.**
13. **A.** Medicare SELECT policies require the use of approved doctors and hospitals to receive benefits.
14. **B.**
15. **A.** Medigap policies are not available through Medicare.
16. **A.** A skilled nursing care benefit covering the Part A co-payments for the 21st through the 100th day of skilled nursing facility care is not required in any Medicare supplement policy.
17. **D.**
18. **B.** Fully insured and disability insured are defined by Social Security regulations.
19. **D.** Under Social Security benefits, a disabled worker receives a benefit equal to the worker's primary insurance amount.
20. **B.**
21. **C.** Medicare is administered by the Health Care Financing Administration.
22. **A.** Medicare Part A does not cover charges for a private room.
23. **B.** For each benefit period, Medicare will pay the full cost of up to 60 days of hospital care.
24. **B.** Medicare will pay the entire cost for skilled nursing facility care for the first 20 days.
25. **D.** Individuals who are eligible for Social Security benefits become eligible for Medicare Part A benefits as of the first day of the month when they turn 65.
26. **A.** Medicare Part A does not cover private-duty nursing.
27. **A.** Medicare Part B does not cover skilled nursing facility care not covered by Part A.
28. **B.** Medicare supplement plan C covers the Part A and Part B deductible.
29. **C.** Medicare supplement plan G covers the Part B excess at 80%.
30. **C.** The definition of accident may not employ an accidental means test.
31. **D.** The injury need not be unforeseeable.
32. **A.** Her workers' compensation benefits will be paid according to the laws of California.

UNIT

24

Long-Term Care

24. 1 INTRODUCTION

Better and better medical care means many individuals are living into their 80s, 90s, and beyond. Unfortunately, although life expectancy has increased, many older individuals have serious health problems that keep them from living on their own or completely caring for themselves. Long-term care pays for the kind of care needed by individuals who have chronic illnesses or disabilities. It often covers the cost of nursing home care and provides coverage for home-based care—visiting nurses, chore services, and respite care for daily caregivers who need time away from these difficult duties. Such coverage becomes important when one considers that the annual cost for nursing home confinement can reach $67,000 or more.

Many people believe Medicare or Medicare supplement policies will pay for this care if they need it. Medicare will cover nursing home care if it is part of the treatment for a covered injury or illness, but care needed because of aging is not covered by Medicare or Medicare supplements. Medicare and supplementary insurance pay for skilled nursing care, but the coverage is extremely limited (the care must immediately follow a period of hospital confinement, and no benefits are provided after the 100th day). Medicaid does pay for nursing home care but provides coverage only for needy families. Sadly, many people must pay for their own nursing home care and eventually turn to Medicaid when their life savings are gone.

24. 2 LEARNING OBJECTIVES

After completing this lesson, you will be able to:

- explain the purpose of long-term care (LTC) insurance;
- describe candidates for whom LTC insurance would be a suitable purchase;
- explain the likelihood of an individual needing long-term care;
- list and describe options other than LTC insurance for taking care of long-term care costs, and explain the drawbacks to each;
- explain who is eligible for LTC insurance;
- explain how premiums for LTC insurance are set and the rating factors that affect them;
- list and describe the different care levels covered under LTC policies;
- explain how benefit amounts are generally defined in an LTC policy;
- explain other provisions that affect LTC policies, including waiver or premium, benefit periods, preexisting conditions, and elimination periods;
- define activities of daily living, and explain how they affect LTC policies; and

- describe the standards required of qualified LTC plans.

24. 3 HISTORY OF LTC COVERAGE

The earliest long-term care policies were relatively more restrictive than the current generation of plans, often requiring prior hospitalization and a level of service greater than mere custodial care. Many covered care in a nursing facility only, rather than also providing coverage for services in the home of the individual or in an adult day care center. Most excluded Alzheimer's and dementia—two common illnesses of the elderly and the reason many older persons require such care.

Some long-term care policies were so closely tied to Medicare's restrictions that they paid little that Medicare did not already pay. During the early development period, policies often had so many restrictions that few insureds qualified for payment of benefits.

LTC policies are still evolving. However, with attention to the problem of long-term care firmly focused, legislators and the insurance industry have begun to come to grips with the far-reaching ramifications of health services for an older population. With the federal government responding to consumer interests in long-term care coverages, the National Association of Insurance Commissioners (NAIC) developed a model to help state legislatures in an effort to keep regulation on a state level. More than half of the states currently use the NAIC or a similar model. Key issues include the following:

- A benefit period of at least one year
- Strict restrictions on cancellation, specifically prohibiting cancellation because of the insured's aging; most policies now guarantee renewability
- Standards for covering preexisting conditions
- A free-look period
- Prohibition of exclusions for Alzheimer's disease

Another factor in the evolution and increasing availability of LTC policies is that consumers, too, are more aware that:

- Medicare does not cover long-term care (much to the surprise of most of the population, who at one time believed Medicare did cover most nursing home care);
- one in four people are likely to spend at least some time in a nursing home after age 65, increasing to about one in three if they live to age 85; and
- the average cost for nursing home confinement is currently about $3,300 per month and can be as high as $5,000 per month, depending on location and level of care. These costs are likely to continue growing.

The increased knowledge of insurance buyers has played a part in the development and refinement of LTC policies. In addition, law changes have clarified the tax status of long-term care policies, which now are treated like accident and health policies. Proceeds of qualified long-term care policies are generally received income tax free, and premiums may be deductible as a medical expense, within certain limitations. Federal law now determines what constitutes a qualified long-term care policy eligible for these tax advantages. The law spells out when benefits must be paid and what options must be offered to prospects for long-term care insurance.

Note, however, that insurers are not required to offer and consumers are not required to purchase qualified long-term care policies. Nonqualified policies may offer benefits that are more attractive or easier to obtain than qualified policies and may be more desirable to certain consumers even if the nonqualified policies do not offer the tax advantages of qualified policies.

24. 4 WHO NEEDS LTC INSURANCE?

LTC insurance enables senior citizens to maintain their independence. With adequate coverage, the individual does not have to rely on friends or family to provide custodial needs or necessary funds to help defray the costs of a nursing home stay.

Protection of personal assets may be the most important reason for purchasing LTC insurance. Possibly, the question isn't, "Can I afford to buy LTC insurance?" but rather, "Can I afford not to purchase LTC insurance?"

When an individual has substantial financial assets (and retirement income), the possibility that LTC expenses could mean a significant reduction in the person's assets and standard of living is a real threat. Thus, the purchase of LTC insurance to protect one's personal financial resources may be a wise financial decision.

Paying periodic premiums is a more efficient and manageable way to provide for future LTC costs than having to rely on personal savings. LTC insurance provides that a person's financial resources need not be liquidated either to pay for nursing home expenses or to spend down to satisfy Medicaid eligibility.

For example, an individual with no dependents and few financial responsibilities may not have a very big need for life insurance. Likewise, a person without substantial assets at risk may have little need to purchase LTC insurance.

If a senior citizen's sole source of income is a relatively small pension and the individual's financial assets are very minimal, this person may already be eligible for Medicaid reimbursement of LTC expenses. Also, because of the individual's low income and limited financial resources, LTC insurance premiums may be unaffordable.

Joe and Irene Brown are both 67 years old. Their only source of income is Social Security and a small pension ($200 monthly). They rent an apartment in a senior citizen complex, have a very small amount of life insurance (enough for burial), and usually maintain a savings account balance of no more than $1,000. They have no assets other than personal possessions and an automobile. Are Mr. and Mrs. Brown prospects for LTC insurance? Probably not. First, it's doubtful that they could afford the premiums on the basis of their relatively small retirement income. Second, they have no assets of any consequence to protect. They do not own a home, maintain a large savings account, or have other investments. In essence, they probably are already eligible for Medicaid benefits in case they are forced into a nursing home.

24. 5 PROBABILITY OF NEEDING CARE

In 2004, there were 36.3 million Americans 65 and older, and it is estimated that by the year 2030, there will be more than 64 million Americans age 65 and over.

In addition, life expectancy is increasing in the United States. People reaching 65 today can expect to live 10 or even 20 years in retirement. These retirees will face a greater potential need for long-term medical care simply because of longer life expectancy.

The likelihood of a nursing home confinement increases as age increases. In 2005, there were approximately 7 million Americans 65 or older who needed long-term care. This figure is expected to exceed 20 million by 2050.

24. 6 OPTIONS OTHER THAN INSURANCE

What are the available options for the senior citizen facing a stay in a nursing home? Following are some of the alternatives:

- Using personal assets
- Depending on relatives
- Depending on government programs

Depending on friends and relatives for custodial care may not be practical because of changing socioeconomic trends. Today's family is no longer a cohesive unit but a fragmented group; family members live great distances from each other.

The Medicare program is not designed to provide custodial care. It will cover a limited amount of rehabilitative care in a skilled nursing facility approved by Medicare. Because Medicare will pay only for rehabilitative services, it requires prior hospitalization before admission to the skilled nursing facility. Another avenue is Medicaid, which requires the individual to prove financial need. This normally requires that the individual get rid of financial resources and spend down to a poverty level to obtain Medicaid eligibility. The Health Care Financing Administration reports that about one-half of all Medicaid spending goes to people who had financial resources when they entered a nursing home but reached the poverty level while in the nursing home.

24. 7 RATING FACTORS

One way in which LTC policies differ from other health plans concerns how risks are rated. Although people afflicted with heart disease or diabetes, for example, would be rated as substandard risks under most health insurance plans, LTC policies, because of their focus on aging people, use a different means of classification. The key for LTC policies is whether an individual can perform the activities of daily living (ADLs) and, if so, with what degree of proficiency. ADLs include such things as dressing, bathing, eating, walking, and similar activities to care for oneself. Thus, an individual who has a heart disease but is still able to perform ADLs is a standard risk under LTC policies.

Example

Corey, age 60, has had several strokes during the past five years but is completely capable of performing the activities of daily living. Under a major medical policy, it is likely that Corey would be classed as a substandard risk. Under an LTC policy, Corey would be classified as a standard risk.

24. 8 TYPES OF BENEFITS

Three terms regarding the type of long-term care an individual requires are important to understand in order to determine what an LTC policy covers.

- **Skilled nursing care** is nursing and rehabilitative care that is required daily and can be performed only by skilled medical practitioners on a doctor's orders.
- **Intermediate care** is nursing and rehabilitative care that is required occasionally and can be performed only by skilled medical practitioners on a doctor's orders.
- **Custodial or residential care** is help in performing ADLs and can be performed by someone without medical skills or training, but still must be based on a doctor's orders.

Of these, custodial, or residential, care is the type most elderly people will require at some time in their later years, and it is also the type that is not covered by Medicare.

Other important terms are as follows:

- **Home health care** refers to services performed from time to time in the individual's home. It may include skilled nursing, various types of therapy, help with ADLs, and help with housework.
- **Adult day care** provides company, supervision, and social and recreational support during the day for people who live at home and need assistance. This service is especially useful for those who are cared for by relatives who work during the day.

24. 9 COMMON PROVISIONS

Now that you understand some of the terms and concepts involved in long-term care policies, let's look at provisions that are commonly included in these coverages. You might also want to glance back at the NAIC model requirements for comparison purposes.

Currently, most LTC policies include provisions or options to include those described in the following paragraphs.

24. 9. 1 Eligibility

What are the youngest and oldest ages at which LTC policies may be purchased? Most minimum ages range between 50 and 60 years, but more recent policies may include a much lower minimum age, including some as low as age 18. Upper age limits at which policies may be purchased range from age 69 to 89.

24. 9. 2 Renewability

Virtually all of the current generation of LTC policies are guaranteed renewable and cannot be canceled except for nonpayment of premium. The insurer cannot cancel the policy but does reserve the right to increase premiums in accordance with the policy provisions. If the premiums are to be increased, they will be changed on the policy anniversary, and the increased premium will be for an entire class of insureds, not just a single individual.

Some LTC policies are noncancelable, which means the insured has the right to continue the coverage by timely payment of premiums, and the insurer has no right to make any change in policy provisions, cannot decline to renew, and cannot change the premium rate at renewal for any reason.

24. 9. 3 Premiums

Similar to life insurance, premiums are generally based on when an individual purchases this insurance. The younger the individual is at the time of purchase, the lower the premium. In addition, premiums will fluctuate according to the elimination and benefit periods selected—the longer the elimination period, the lower the premium; the longer the benefit period, the higher the premium. Finally, premium variations may result from underwriting considerations. Underwriters consider risk factors, including an applicant's current ability to perform activities of daily living. The premium will be higher if an applicant needs assistance with an ADL at the time of application than it would if the applicant did not need such assistance.

24. 9. 4 Waiver of Premium

Nearly all LTC policies include a waiver of premium provision that takes effect after the insured has been confined for a specified period of time. The usual period is 90 days, but it is as long as 180 days in some policies. A few policies have no such provision, which means the insured will be required to continue premium payments no matter how long care continues. When waiver of premium applies, premium payment generally resumes when the care ceases.

24. 9. 5 Prior Hospitalization

Formerly, most nursing home policies required a hospital stay before confinement to a nursing home in order for benefits to be paid. This is no longer the case.

24. 9. 6 Care Level

This refers to whether the policy pays only if skilled nursing, intermediate, or custodial care, as specified in the policy, is required at the time the individual enters the nursing home. This is extremely important, since some policies pay only if intermediate or skilled care is involved, whereas custodial care, which is the most common type required by elders, may not be included. The best policies are those that will pay regardless of the level of care.

24. 9. 7 Hospice Care

Hospice care is often offered as an optional benefit under LTC policies. The primary focus of hospice care is pain control, comfort, and counseling for the terminally ill patient and the patient's family. A hospice is simply a facility whose purpose is to help terminally ill patients die with dignity and with as little suffering as possible. Typically, the expenses incurred in a hospice will be room and board and medication for pain.

24. 9. 8 Respite Care

Respite care is normally associated with hospice care. With this benefit, the patient is admitted to a nursing home for needed care for a short period, or the LTC policy will cover the cost of replacing for a short period (a day or weekend perhaps) the primary care giver, usually a family member, who is looking after an elderly person in the home.

24. 9. 9 Home Health Care

Most LTC policies now cover home health care as an alternative to nursing home care. Home health care is provided in the individual's home and must begin within a prescribed period following a nursing home stay. Usually, the home health care benefit under the policy will be 60% of the regular daily nursing home benefit. Home health care is an extension of intermediate custodial care. The patient is in need of some health care but is able to generally function without the need to be confined to a nursing home. Home health care might include physical therapy and some custodial care, such as meal preparation.

24. 9. 10 Adult Day Care

LTC policies also increasingly make provision for adult day care to allow primary caregivers who work the opportunity to tend to their employment responsibilities. The day care may be provided in the home or in an adult day care facility. Adult day care is basically social and health care services for functionally impaired adults. This benefit provides reimbursement for expenses pertaining to an adult day care center such as a neighborhood recreational center, a community center, and others. Typically, adult day care includes transportation to and from a day care center and a variety of health, social, and related activities. This care usually also includes meals and certain medical services. Specialized care for patients with Alzheimer's is usually included in adult day care benefits.

24. 9. 11 Professional Care Advisor

Coverage may be provided for the services of a care coordinator to help design the most appropriate plan of treatment.

24. 9. 12 Benefit Amount

The prospective insured may be offered a choice of the maximum daily benefit amount for a nursing home stay or covered home health care. Naturally, higher daily benefits mean higher annual premiums.

Most LTC policies provide a daily benefit during confinement. Traditionally, this benefit has been provided as a maximum daily amount (reimbursement for charges up to the stated limit, but not more than the daily limit). Benefit amounts range from $50 per day to $150 or $200 per day. However, some insurers provide coverage on an expense-incurred basis (full reimbursement for the actual charges incurred). The maximum policy benefit may be calculated by multiplying the daily benefit by the number of days in the benefit period.

To illustrate these points, let's use the example of Kim, who has an LTC policy with a 30-day elimination period, a daily benefit of $75 per day, and a two-year benefit period. Her maximum policy benefit is $54,750 ($75 a day times 730 days). If Kim is confined to a nursing home for a total of seven months, her benefit calculation will be as follows:

- First 30 days: no benefit paid (elimination period)

- Next six months: $75 per day (assumes 30-day month)
- $75 × 180 = $13,500

If Kim's actual charges were more than $75 per day, she would have to pay the additional amount.

Most policies specify the dollar amount per day that will be paid for skilled nursing care. Some policies may include sublimits for special types of care or services (e.g., home health care or adult day care). The benefit for home health care or adult day care is usually a fixed percentage of the specified daily benefit, usually 50%. In addition, there may be a deductible amount that must be satisfied before the policy begins to pay.

24. 9. 13 Benefit Periods

LTC policies vary as to the maximum period for which benefits will be paid, usually from three to five years. Some policies offer unlimited benefit periods. Some policies may contain both a benefit period per stay plus a lifetime maximum benefit period. The benefit period may also end when a maximum amount has been paid out.

24. 9. 14 Exclusions

Each policy should be read carefully to determine what is excluded. A major stride in current policies is that most now cover Alzheimer's disease and organic-based mental illness, both of which formerly were often excluded. However, some exclusions remain. Among these are war and acts of war, alcohol or drug dependency, self-inflicted injuries, mental illness and nervous disorders without a demonstrable organic cause, and treatment provided without cost to the insured (such as that received in a veteran's hospital).

24. 9. 15 Preexisting Conditions

Most—but not all—LTC policies do not cover conditions that existed during the six months before the policy effective date. A few policies have no such exclusion.

24. 9. 16 Elimination Period

Similar to a disability income policy, no LTC benefits will be paid until the elimination period is satisfied. Most long-term care policies provide for a period, usually expressed in days or months, at the beginning of a confinement in a long-term care facility, during which no benefits are payable. The elimination period could be defined as a "time deductible." The elimination period could be 30 days or longer. Thus, after the insured is confined to a nursing home for a period of 30 days, LTC benefits begin.

The longer the waiting period, the lower the premium, all other facts being equal. The waiting period can be viewed as the deductible in an LTC policy.

24. 10 BENEFIT TRIGGERS

24. 10. 1 Activities of Daily Living

ADLs are functions or activities that are performed by individuals without assistance, thus allowing personal independence in everyday living. These functions are used as measurement standards to determine the level of personal functioning capacity. Examples of ADLs would include:

- mobility (or transferring)—the ability to walk;
- dressing—being able to adequately clothe one's self;
- personal hygiene—being able to go to and from the toilet and remain continent;
- eating—being able to take in food; and
- bathing.

An individual who cannot accommodate these needs will need some type of care.

Some LTC policies base eligibility for nursing home benefits on the inability to perform some of the activities of daily living in lieu of sickness or injury. These contracts do not require prior hospitalization or that the insured be admitted to a nursing facility as a result of sickness or injury. Federal standards that determine whether an LTC policy is tax qualified also base eligibility on ADLs.

24. 10. 2 Cognitive Impairment

This means a deficiency in the ability to think, perceive, reason, or remember, which results in the inability of individuals to take care of themselves without the assistance or supervision of another person. LTC policies may base eligibility for nursing home benefits on cognitive impairment.

24. 10. 3 Medical Necessity

An LTC policy by definition provides coverage only for medically necessary diagnostic, therapeutic, rehabilitative, maintenance, or personal care services.

24. 11 QUALIFIED PLANS

A qualified long-term care policy must stipulate that the insured be incapable of performing at least two of the ADLs without assistance for at least 90 days to qualify for benefits. The cognitively impaired must require substantial supervision. A physician must certify that the insured is chronically ill and provide a plan of care. A long-term care policy will not be qualified if it does not conform to these standards.

Remember, however, that nonqualified long-term care policies do not have to conform to these federal standards. A nonqualified policy, for example, might require that the insured need assistance with only one ADL with no stipulated time period in order to be eligible for policy benefits. The prospective insured's concern over qualification for benefits must be weighed against tax consequences when considering qualified versus nonqualified long-term care policies.

24. 12 REGULATION

Just as with Medicare supplement insurance, long-term care policies are heavily regulated by the state Insurance Departments. States frequently regulate minimum standards, renewability, the insured's right to return the policy, replacement, marketing standards, and the appropriateness of recommending the purchase of LTC insurance. As with Medicare supplement insurance, frequently the delivery of a buyers guide and outline of coverage is mandatory.

Federal law allows the sale of long-term care coverage that "substantially" duplicates that provided under Medicare or Medicaid (but not multiple policies) to Medicare beneficiaries, provided the company discloses the duplication and the policy pays without regard to other benefits.

24. 13 EMERGING LTC ISSUES

Long-term care insurance is still in an evolutionary state. There are literally hundreds of individual contracts, which have not been standardized like Medicare supplement policies. Some emerging issues in the LTC field include inflation protection and nonforfeiture provisions. New federal standards that determine whether an LTC policy is tax qualified require consumer protections, such as the offer of inflation protection and nonforfeiture provisions, as well as imposing additional disclosure requirements.

24. 13. 1 Inflation Protection

Many states require that insurers offer optional inflation protection at the time of policy purchase. The feature must either increase benefit levels annually or cover a specific percentage of actual or reasonable charges, or allow the insured to periodically increase benefit levels without needing to provide evidence of continued insurability.

24. 13. 2 Nonforfeiture Provisions

These protect the policyholder from forfeiting all policy values or benefits when the policyowner stops paying premiums and lapses the policy for any reason. Standard nonforfeiture options may include cash surrender value (a lump sum payable upon policy surrender), reduced paid-up insurance (a reduced daily benefit payable for the policy's benefit period with no further premium payments required), or extended term insurance (a limited extension of coverage for the full amount of policy benefits, without further premium payments required). Nonforfeiture provisions are not commonly included in LTC policies but are beginning to appear in some contracts.

24. 14 MARKETING LTC COVERAGE

In addition to individual LTC policies, a growing number of insurers offer group LTC plans with provisions similar to those mentioned previously. Still, a third marketing device involves attaching an LTC rider to a life insurance policy called an accelerated benefits rider or a living benefits rider.

Accelerated benefits may be available to insureds who are chronically ill and need money for long-term care. Such riders are subject to the same rules as individual long-term care policies, especially with respect to benefit triggers. They also may be designed to cover home health care and nursing home care. Adding an accelerated benefits rider to a life policy costs money in the form of additional premium.

How much may be paid by such a rider varies from policy to policy. Some limit benefits to 50 or 75% of the policy's face value. Others place an absolute ceiling on the amount paid out, for example, $250,000. All, however, take into consideration any outstanding loans against the policy. Payments are ordinarily made to the insured on some kind of periodic basis. Naturally, any accelerated benefits paid out are subtracted from the death benefit paid to the beneficiary when the insured dies.

24. 15 SUMMARY

In this lesson, you learned about:

- the purpose of LTC insurance;
- candidates for whom LTC insurance would be a suitable purchase;
- the likelihood of an individual needing long-term care;
- options other than LTC insurance for taking care of long-term care costs, and the drawbacks to each;
- who is eligible for LTC insurance;
- how premiums for LTC insurance are set and the rating factors that affect them;
- the different care levels covered under LTC policies;

- how benefit amounts are generally defined in an LTC policy;
- other provisions that affect LTC policies, including waiver or premium, benefit periods, preexisting conditions, and elimination periods;
- activities of daily living and how they affect LTC policies; and
- the standards required of qualified LTC plans.

UNIT TEST

1. Nursing home care is generally covered by
   A. Medicare
   B. Medicare supplements
   C. long-term care policies
   D. all of the above

2. Which of the following would be least likely to be a good candidate for an LTC policy?
   A. George, whose law practice has allowed him to fund a generous retirement fund for himself and his wife
   B. Nina, a single mother whose financial struggles raising her children have left her with few assets and no independent retirement savings
   C. Carla, whose 25 years of civil service have provided a generous retirement, but who worries about the legacy she will leave her children
   D. Darrell, whose inherited estate has provided him with over $6 million in net worth

3. An individual age 75 or older has what chance of being confined to a nursing home?
   A. 25%
   B. 50%
   C. 75%
   D. 90%

4. Early long-term care policies were
   A. more restrictive than current policies
   B. less restrictive than current policies
   C. the same as current policies
   D. prohibited by law

5. Which of the following individuals is most likely to be rated a substandard risk under an LTC policy?
   A. Gerald, who lives alone and has no trouble taking care of himself, but who has been diagnosed with an inoperable brain aneurysm that, if it bursts, would almost certainly kill him immediately
   B. Ken, who is on medication to bring down his blood pressure, but who gets around and takes care of himself easily
   C. Brenda, whose diabetes is under control
   D. Garrison, who has been diagnosed with early-stage Alzheimer's disease

6. Which of the following is the type of care most people will require at some time during their later years?
   A. Inpatient hospital care
   B. Skilled nursing care
   C. Custodial or residential care
   D. Intermediate care

7. Virtually all of the current LTC policies are guaranteed renewable. This means the insurer cannot cancel the policy
   A. but does reserve the right to increase policy premiums on specified classes of policies
   B. but does reserve the right to increase policy premiums on individual policies
   C. or increase policy premiums on specified classes of policies
   D. or increase policy premiums on individual policies

8. When waiver of premium applies
   A. the premium is waived immediately upon disability
   B. the premium payment is suspended permanently once it is invoked
   C. the premium payment generally resumes when care ceases
   D. the premium payment is waived only if disability is considered permanent and total

9. Typically, the expenses incurred in a hospice will be
   A. surgical and room and board
   B. room and board and physical therapy
   C. surgical and physical therapy
   D. room and board and medication for pain

10. The elimination period may be thought of as
   A. a dollar amount deductible
   B. a time deductible
   C. a dollar amount co-payment
   D. a time co-payment

11. Which of the following is NOT considered an activity of daily living?
   A. Transferring
   B. Dressing
   C. Bathing
   D. Working

ANSWERS AND RATIONALES TO UNIT TEST

1. **C.** Nursing home care is generally covered by long-term care policies.
2. **B.** A good candidate for an LTC policy has substantial financial assets to protect.
3. **B.** An individual age 75 or older has a 50% chance of being confined to a nursing home.
4. **A.**
5. **D.** LTC policies rate risks according to how well the individual can perform ADLs.
6. **C.** Most people will require custodial or residential care at some time during their later years.
7. **A.** Guaranteed renewable means the insurer cannot cancel the policy but does reserve the right to increase policy premiums on specified classes of policies.
8. **C.** When waiver of premium applies, the premium payment generally resumes when care ceases.
9. **D.** Typically, the expenses incurred in a hospice will be room and board and medication for pain.
10. **B.** The elimination period may be thought of as a time deductible.
11. **D.** Working is not an activity of daily living.

UNIT

25

Health Insurance and Taxation

25. 1 INTRODUCTION

To understand how health insurance is taxed, we need to organize coverage into the following groups:

- Individually owned
- Group
- Sole proprietors and partners
- Business

Then we'll discuss the taxation of disability insurance, Medicare Supplement insurance, and long-term care insurance. We'll conclude by addressing the taxation of government health programs.

25. 2 LEARNING OBJECTIVES

After completing this lesson, you will be able to:

- explain how Social Security health benefits are funded;
- explain how the various types of health insurance are taxed, when premiums are deductible, and when the benefits are taxed;
- explain when and how disability insurance premiums and benefits are taxed; and
- explain when and how Medicare supplement and long-term care insurance premiums and benefits are taxed.

25. 3 TAXATION OF HEALTH INSURANCE POLICIES

25. 3. 1 Individual Policies

The premiums for individually owned accident, health, disability, or long-term care policies generally are not deductible to the individual taxpayer. However, if the taxpayer's medical expenses exceed 7.5% of adjusted gross income during a taxable year, any medical expenses, including premiums for accident and health insurance (but not disability insurance), incurred above the 7.5% threshold can be deducted. For long-term care insurance, there is an annual dollar limit for deductions. This limit is based on the taxpayer's age. Benefits paid by individually owned accident, health, disability, or long-term care policies generally are received income-tax free by the taxpayer, provided the benefits do not exceed actual expenses.

Congress has determined that individual long-term care insurance policies must be treated the same as accident and health policies tax wise, as long as such policies are qualified according to federal law. Individual premiums may be deductible if the 7.5% of adjusted gross income threshold is exceeded. All qualified long-term care policy benefits are received income-tax free, so long as they do not exceed actual expenses. As for nonqualified long-term care policy premiums and benefits, it's not clear what their precise status is. Until Congress or the IRS clarifies that status, however, it would be wise to treat nonqualified policies as if they did not have the tax advantages of qualified policies.

25. 3. 2 Group Policies

The premiums paid by a company for group accident, health, and dental coverage for its employees are generally deductible by the company as a business expense. The premiums are not taxed to the employees. The benefits are received by the employees income-tax free to the extent the benefits do not exceed actual expenses.

The premiums paid by a company for group disability insurance for its employees are generally deductible by the company as a business expense. The premiums are not taxed to the employees, but the benefits are taxable. However, if an employee pays all or part of the premiums for group disability coverage, he may not deduct these premiums, but the benefits will be received income-tax free to the extent that the employee paid the premiums. Let's look at an example to see how this works.

Wanda's company pays the entire premium for her group disability coverage. If Wanda became disabled, all of her benefits from this coverage would be subject to tax. However, if Wanda paid 50% of the premiums, then 50% of her benefits would be tax free. And if she paid 100% of the premiums, all of her benefits would be tax free.

Note, however, that disability benefits are subject to Social Security tax (FICA) and federal unemployment tax (FUTA) for the first six calendar months following the last month the employee was on the job.

Group accidental death and dismemberment coverage premiums may be deducted as a business expense by companies. The premiums are not taxable to the employees, and the benefits are received income-tax free.

Qualified group long-term care insurance, like individually owned long-term care, is treated the same as other group health policies. Companies offering this coverage may deduct any premiums paid as a business expense. The employee is not taxed on these premiums, and the benefits are tax exempt.

Companies offering group long-term care coverage can deduct any premiums paid as a business expense. The employee is not taxed on these premiums, and the benefits are tax exempt. However, these tax advantages do not apply to group long-term care coverage provided through a Section 125 cafeteria plan, and expenses for long-term care services cannot be reimbursed under flexible spending arrangements.

25. 3. 3 Sole Proprietors and Partnerships

Self-employed persons are allowed to deduct from their gross incomes 70% of the amount they pay for health insurance (including qualified long-term care insurance). This percentage was raised to 100% in 2003 and remains so. To claim this deduction, however, self-employed persons (1) must show a net profit for the year and (2) cannot claim the deduction for any month in which they were eligible to participate in a health plan subsidized by their employer or by the employer of their spouse.

Payments of premiums by a partnership for a partner's health and accident insurance is generally deductible by the partnership. The amount of the premiums is included in the partner's gross income, but it is deductible on the same basis as that for self-employed persons—70% in 2002 and 100% in 2003 and thereafter.

25. 3. 4 Business Policies

The premiums paid for business overhead expense insurance are deductible as a business expense whether the business is a sole proprietorship, partnership, or corporation. The proceeds of business overhead expense insurance, however, are taxable.

The premiums paid for a disability policy used to fund a buy-sell agreement are not deductible, nor are the proceeds taxable.

Similarly, the premiums paid for a key employee disability policy are not deductible, nor are the proceeds taxable.

25. 4 DISABILITY INCOME INSURANCE

Premiums paid by the insured for individually owned disability income insurance are not tax deductible. However, benefits paid in this type of situation are tax free to the insured.

In situations in which the business is providing disability income coverage for its employees, the premium paid by the business is tax deductible as a business expense. This is true whether the coverage is provided by a group policy or individual contracts. Naturally, the benefits received by the employees would then be taxable as income.

In situations where the business is providing disability income coverage to protect itself (e.g., key person or disability buy-sell insurance), premiums paid by the business are not tax deductible as a business expense. The basic premise is that either the premium or the benefit will be taxed. If the premium is not deductible to the business, the benefits will be received tax free. If the premium is deductible, then the benefits are taxable as with the BOE policy.

25. 5 MEDICARE SUPPLEMENT AND LONG-TERM CARE INSURANCE

Individual Medicare supplement insurance premiums are considered deductible medical expenses to the extent that the combination of premiums paid plus other unreimbursed medical expenses exceeds 7.5% of adjusted gross income. Benefits are considered reimbursements for medical expenses already incurred and are therefore received tax free. Premiums paid by an employer for group Medicare supplement insurance are tax deductible to the employer, and benefits are received tax free.

The Health Insurance Portability and Accountability Act of 1996 provided that premiums paid for individually owned long-term care insurance are tax deductible to the extent that combined premiums and unreimbursed medical expenses exceed 7.5% of adjusted gross income. This tax deductibility is subject to age-related limits ranging from $310 per year for taxpayers under age 40 to $3,850 per year for taxpayers age 71 and older. (These limits are for 2008 and are subject to annual indexing for inflation.)

Premiums for group LTC insurance paid by employers are deductible as a business expense, but the coverage cannot be part of a cafeteria plan or flexible spending account. Benefits are received tax free up to specified limits, which are indexed annually for inflation.

LTC policies issued on or after January 1, 1997, must meet federal standards for tax-qualified status. LTC policies issued before that date are grandfathered and are automatically tax qualified.

The federal standards establish new eligibility requirements. The individual must be certified by a licensed health care professional to be chronically ill with a condition that is expected to last at least 90 days and must have a plan of care. **Chronically ill** means that the individual:

- is unable without substantial help from another person to perform at least two of five (or six) activities of daily living for at least 90 days (ADLs include bathing, dressing, toileting, transferring, eating, and continence; state legislatures determine whether to include five or all six of the ADLs); and
- needs substantial supervision because of a cognitive impairment (i.e., Alzheimer's disease).

The individual must be recertified as chronically ill on an annual basis.

The new federal standards also establish consumer protection standards such as guaranteed renewability and the option to add inflation protection and nonforfeiture benefits (but not in the form of cash surrender values) and impose new disclosure requirements.

25. 6 TAXATION OF GOVERNMENT HEALTH PROGRAMS

25. 6. 1 Medicare

As a government social program, Medicare is largely paid for by federal taxes.

Medicare Funding

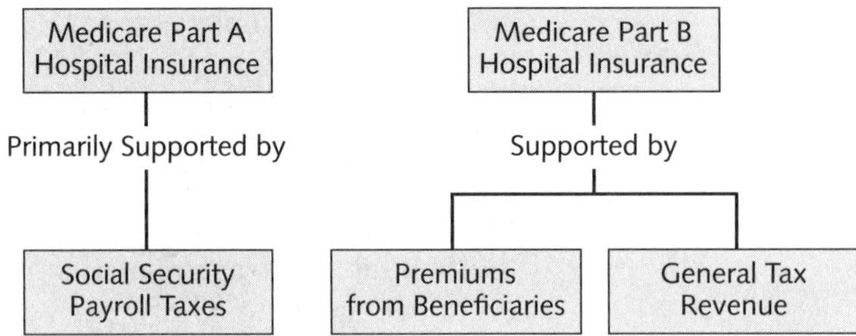

25. 6. 2 Social Security Disability Benefits

Social Security disability benefits are financed through a payroll tax. The tax rate is applied to an employee's gross wages (up to the current wage base), and an appropriate amount is deducted from the employee's wages each pay period. A like amount is contributed by the employer. Self-employeds must pay 100% of the combined employee/employer tax rate.

Although employers may take a tax deduction for contributions on behalf of their employees as a routine and necessary cost of doing business, employees are not entitled to a deduction for their share of the Social Security tax. In other words, employee Social Security taxes are paid with after-tax dollars.

25. 6. 2. 1 Taxation of Social Security Benefits

Social Security benefits are generally received free of income tax. However, federal income taxes are imposed on some benefits if the taxpayer has a substantial amount of additional income.

The specifics of the calculations are not important at this stage of your training. However, it is important to understand that Social Security benefits may not be entirely free from federal income taxes.

25. 7 SUMMARY

In this lesson, you learned about:

- how Social Security health benefits are funded;
- how the various types of health insurance are taxed, when premiums are deductible, and when the benefits are taxed;
- when and how disability insurance premiums and benefits are taxed; and
- when and how Medicare supplement and long-term care insurance premiums and benefits are taxed.

UNIT TEST

1. Wanda's company pays the entire premium for her group disability coverage. If Wanda became disabled, how much of her benefits from this coverage would be subject to tax?
   A. All
   B. None
   C. Half

2. If Wanda paid 50% of premiums, what percentage of her benefits would be tax free?
   A. 0%
   B. 50%
   C. 100%

3. If Wanda paid 100% of her premiums, what percentage of her benefits would be taxed?
   A. 0%
   B. 50%
   C. 100%

4. The Delectable Doughnut Company may deduct its premiums for business overhead expense insurance
   A. only if it is a corporation
   B. only if it is a partnership or a corporation
   C. whether it is a corporation, partnership, or sole proprietorship

5. The premiums are deductible for which of the following?
   A. Disability policy to fund a buy-sell agreement
   B. Key employee disability policy
   C. Both A and B
   D. Neither A nor B

6. Social Security disability income and medical benefits are financed through
   A. voluntary contributions
   B. Mandatory payroll taxes

7. The taxes to finance Social Security benefits are paid
   A. solely by employees
   B. solely by employers
   C. equally by employees and employers

8. Medicare Part A hospital insurance is primarily funded by
   A. general tax revenue
   B. premiums from beneficiaries
   C. state government taxes
   D. Social Security payroll taxes

9. Social Security taxes are paid by employees with
   A. pretax dollars
   B. tax-deductible dollars
   C. after-tax dollars
   D. tax-deferred dollars

10. Premiums for individually owned health policies may be deductible if the taxpayer's medical expenses exceed
    A. 5% of their adjusted gross income during the taxable year
    B. 5% of their adjusted net income during the taxable year
    C. 7.5% of their adjusted gross income during the taxable year
    D. 7.5% of their adjusted net income during the taxable year

11. The premiums paid by a company for group health for its employees are
    A. not tax deductible to either the company or the business
    B. tax deductible by the company and not considered taxable income to the employees
    C. tax deductible by the company and considered taxable income to the employees
    D. tax deductible to the employees and the company

12. Benefits paid by individually owned accident, health, disability, or long-term care policies generally are
    A. received income-tax free by the taxpayer, provided benefits do not exceed actual expenses
    B. received income-tax free by the taxpayer even if benefits exceed actual expenses
    C. received partially tax free by the taxpayer, provided benefits do not exceed actual expenses
    D. taxed upon receipt by the taxpayer

13. Qualified group long-term care coverage is
    A. deductible by both the company and the employee
    B. not deductible by either the company or the employee
    C. deductible by the company but not the employee
    D. deductible by the employee but not the company

14. Individual disability insurance premiums are
    A. deductible to the insured, and the benefits are received tax free
    B. not deductible to the insured, but the benefits are received tax free
    C. deductible to the insured, but the benefits are taxed
    D. not deductible to the insured, and the benefits are taxed

15. An individual who is considered chronically ill must be recertified as such
    A. every month
    B. every 6 months
    C. annually
    D. every 2 years

ANSWERS AND RATIONALES TO UNIT TEST

1. **A.**
2. **B.** 50% of her benefits would be tax free.
3. **C.** 100% of her benefits would be tax free.
4. **C.**
5. **D.** The premiums are not deductible for either a disability policy to fund a buy-sell agreement or a key employee disability policy.
6. **B.**
7. **C.** The taxes to finance Social Security benefits are paid equally by employees and employers.
8. **D.** Medicare Part A hospital insurance is primarily funded by Social Security payroll taxes.
9. **C.** Social Security taxes are paid by employees with after-tax dollars.
10. **C.** Premiums for individually owned health policies may be deductible if the taxpayer's medical expenses exceed 7.5% of their adjusted gross income during the taxable year.
11. **B.** The premiums paid by a company for group health for its employees are tax deductible by the company and not considered taxable income to the employees.
12. **A.** Benefits paid by individually owned accident, health, disability, or long-term care policies generally are received income-tax free by the taxpayer, provided benefits do not exceed actual expenses.
13. **C.** Qualified group long-term care coverage is deductible by the company but not the employee.
14. **B.** Individual disability insurance premiums are not deductible to the insured, but the benefits are received tax free.
15. **C.** An individual who is considered chronically ill must be recertified as such annually.

Glossary

A

absolute assignment Policy assignment under which the assignee (person to whom the policy is assigned) receives full control over the policy and also full rights to its benefits. Generally, when a policy is assigned to secure a debt, the owner retains all rights in the policy in excess of the debt, even though the assignment is absolute in form. (*See* **assignment**)

accelerated benefits rider A life insurance rider that allows for the early payment of some portion of the policy's face amount should the insured suffer from a terminal illness or injury.

acceptance (*See* **offer and acceptance**)

accident and health insurance Insurance under which benefits are payable in case of disease, accidental injury or accidental death. Also called health insurance, personal health insurance and sickness and accident insurance.

accidental bodily injury provision Disability income or accident policy provision that requires that the injury be accidental in order for benefits to be payable.

accidental death and dismemberment (AD&D) Insurance providing payment if the insured's death results from an accident or if the insured accidentally severs a limb above the wrist or ankle joints or totally and irreversibly loses his or her eyesight.

accidental death benefit rider A life insurance policy rider providing for payment of an additional benefit when death occurs by accidental means.

accidental dismemberment Often defined as "the severance of limbs at or above the wrists or ankle joints, or the entire irrevocable loss of sight." Loss of use in itself may or not be considered dismemberment.

accidental means provision Unforeseen, unexpected, unintended cause of an accident. Requirement of an accident-based policy that the cause of the mishap must be accidental for any claim to be payable.

accumulation unit Premiums an annuitant pays into a variable annuity are credited as accumulation units. At the end of the accumulation period, accumulation units are converted to annuity units.

acquired immune deficiency syndrome (AIDS) A life-threatening condition brought on by the human immunodeficiency virus; insurers must adhere to strict underwriting and claims guidelines in regard to AIDS risks and AIDS-related conditions.

acute illness A serious condition, such as pneumonia, from which the body can fully recover with proper medical attention.

adhesion A life insurance policy is a "contract of adhesion" because buyers must "adhere" to the terms of the contract already in existence. They have no opportunity to negotiate terms, rates, values, and so on.

adjustable life insurance Combines features of both term and whole life coverage with the length of coverage and amount of accumulated cash value as the adjustable factors. Premiums may be increased or decreased to fit the specific needs. Such adjustments are not retroactive and apply only to the future.

administrative-services-only (ASO) plan Arrangement under which an insurance company or an independent organization, for a fee, handles the administration of claims, benefits and other administrative functions for a self-insured group.

admitted insurer An insurance company that has met the legal and financial requirements for operation within a given state.

adult day care Type of care (usually custodial) designed for individuals who require assistance with various activities of daily living, while their primary caregivers are absent. Offered in care centers.

adverse selection Selection "against the company." Tendency of less favorable insurance risks to seek or continue insurance to a greater extent than others. Also, tendency of policyowners to take advantage of favorable options in insurance contracts.

Advertising Code Rules established by the National Association of Insurance Commissioners (NAIC) to regulate insurance advertising.)

agency Situation wherein one party (an agent) has the power to act for another (the principal) in dealing with third parties.

agent Anyone not a duly licensed broker, who solicits insurance or aids in placing risks, delivering policies or collecting premiums on behalf of an insurance company.

agent's report The section of an insurance application where the agent reports his or her personal observation about the applicant.

aleatory Feature of insurance contracts in that there is an element of chance for both parties and that the dollar given by the policyholder (premiums) and the insurer (benefits) may not be equal.

alien insurer Company incorporated or organized under the laws of any foreign nation, providence or territory.

ambulatory surgery Surgery performed on an outpatient basis.

amount at risk Difference between the face amount of the policy and the reserve or policy value at a given time. In other words, the dollar amount over what the policyowner has contributed of cash value toward payment of his or her own claim. Because the cash value increases every year, the net amount at risk naturally decreases until it finally reaches zero when the cash value or reserve become the face amount.

annually renewable term (ART) A form of renewable term insurance that provides coverage for one year and allows the policyowner to renew his or her coverage each year, without evidence of insurability. Also called **yearly renewable term** (YRT).

annuitant One to whom an annuity is payable, or a person upon the continuance of whose life further payment depends.

annuity A contract that provides a stipulated sum payable at certain regular intervals during the lifetime of one or more persons, or payable for a specified period only.

annuity unit The number of annuity units denotes the share of the funds an annuitant will receive from a variable annuity account after the accumulation period ends and benefits begin. A formula is used to convert accumulation units to annuity units.

any occupation A definition of total disability that requires that for disability income benefits to be payable, the insured must be unable to perform any job for which he or she is "reasonably suited by reason of education, training or experience."

apparent authority The authority an agent appears to have, based on the principal's (the insurer's) actions, words, deeds or because of circumstances the principal (the insurer) created.

application Form supplied by the insurance company, usually filled in by the agent and medical examiner (if applicable) on the basis of information received from the applicant. It is signed by the applicant and is part of the insurance policy if it is issued. It gives information to the home office underwriting department so it may consider whether an insurance policy will be issued and, if so, in what classification and at what premium rate.

appointment The authorization or certification of an agent to act for or represent an insurance company.

approval receipt Rarely used today, a type of conditional receipt that provides that coverage is effective as of the date the application is approved (before the policy is delivered).

Armstrong Investigation Investigation of a large number of insurance companies in the United States in 1905 that led to the enactment of stricter state supervision and insurance requirements.

assessment insurance Plan by which either the amount of insurance is variable or the number and amount of the assessments are variable. It is offered by assessment associations, either pure or advance.

assessment mutual insurer An insurance company characterized by member-insureds who are assessed an individual portion of each loss that occurs. No premium payment is payable in advance.

assignee Person (including corporation, partnership or other organization) to whom a right or rights under a policy are transferred by means of an assignment.

assignment Signed transfer of benefits of a policy by an insured to another party. The company does not guarantee the validity of an assignment.

assignment provision (health contracts) Commercial health policy provision that allows the policyowner to assign benefit payments from the insurer directly to the health care provider.

assignor Person (including corporation, partnership or other organization or entity) who transfers a right or rights under an insurance policy to another by means of an assignment.

attained age With reference to an insured, the current insurance age.

authority The actions and deeds an agent is authorized to conduct on behalf of an insurance company, as specified in the agent's contract.

authorized company Company duly authorized by the insurance department to operate in the state.

automatic premium loan provision Authorizes insurer to automatically pay any premium in default at the end of the grace period and charge the amount so paid against the life insurance policy as a policy loan.

average indexed monthly earnings (AIME) The basis used for calculating the primary insurance amount (PIA) for Social Security benefits.

average monthly wage (AMW) The average wage base for computing virtually all Social Security benefits prior to 1979.

aviation exclusion Either attached by rider or included in standard policy language excepting from coverage certain deaths or disabilities due to aviation, such as "other than a fare-paying passenger."

B

back dating The practice of making a policy effective at an earlier date than the present.

basic medical expense policy Health insurance policy that provides "first dollar" benefits for specified (and limited) health care, such as hospitalization, surgery or physician services. Characterized by limited benefit periods and relatively low coverage limits.

beneficiary Person to whom the proceeds of a life or accident policy are payable when the insured dies. The various types of beneficiaries are: primary beneficiaries (those first entitled to proceeds); secondary beneficiaries (those entitled to proceeds if no primary beneficiary is living when the insured dies); and tertiary beneficiaries (those entitled to proceeds if no primary or secondary beneficiaries are alive when the insured dies).

benefit May be either money or a right to the policyowner upon the happening of the conditions set out in the policy.

benefit period Maximum length of time that insurance benefits will be paid for any one accident, illness or hospital stay.

Best's Insurance Report A guide, published by A.M. Best, Inc., that rates insurers' financial integrity and managerial and operational strengths.

binding receipt Given by a company upon an applicant's first premium payment. The policy, if approved, becomes effective from the date of the receipt.

blackout period Period following the death of a family breadwinner during which no Social Security benefits are available to the surviving spouse.

blanket policy Covers a number of individuals who are exposed to the same hazards, such as members of an athletic team, company officials who are passengers in the same company plane, and so on.

broker Licensed insurance representative who does not represent a specific company, but places business among various companies. Legally, the broker is usually regarded as a representative of the insured rather than the company.

business continuation plan Arrangements between the business owners that provide that the shares owned by any one of them who dies or becomes disabled shall be sold to and purchased by the other co-owners or by the business.

business health insurance Issued primarily to indemnify a business for the loss of services of a key employee, partner or active close corporation stockholder.

business overhead expense insurance A form of disability income coverage designed to pay necessary business overhead expenses, such as rent, should the insured business owner become disabled.

buyer's guides Informational consumer guide books that explain insurance policies and insurance concepts; in many states, they are required to be given to applicants when certain types of coverages are being considered.

buy-sell agreement Agreement that a deceased business owner's interest will be sold and purchased at a predetermined price or at a price according to a predetermined formula.

C

cafeteria plan Employee benefit arrangements in which employees can select from a range of benefits.

cancellable contract Health insurance contract that may be terminated by the company or that is renewable at its option.

capital sum Amount provided for accidental dismemberment or loss of eyesight. Indemnities for loss of one member or sight of one eye are percentages of the capital sum.

career agency system A method of marketing, selling and distributing insurance, it is represented by agencies or branch offices committed to the ongoing recruitment and development of career agents.

case management The professional arrangement and coordination of health services through assessment, service plan development and monitoring.

cash or deferred arrangements A qualified employer retirement plan under which employees can defer amounts of their salaries into a retirement plan. These amounts are not included in the employee's gross income and so are tax deferred. Also called 401(k) plans.

cash refund annuity Provides that, upon the death of an annuitant before payments totaling the purchase price have been made, the excess of the amount paid by the purchaser over the total annuity payments received will be paid in one sum to designated beneficiaries.

cash surrender option A nonforfeiture option that allows whole life insurance policyowners to receive a payout of their policy's cash values.

cash surrender value Amount available to the owner when a life insurance policy is surrendered to the company. During the early policy years, the cash value is the reserve less a "surrender charge"; in later policy years, it usually equals or closely approximates the reserve value at time of surrender.

cash value The equity amount or "savings" accumulation in a whole life policy.

churning The practice by which policy values in an existing life insurance policy or annuity contract are used to purchase another policy or contract with that same insurer for the purpose of earning additional premiums or commissions without an objectively reasonable basis for believing that the new policy will result in an actual and demonstrable benefit.

class designation A beneficiary designation. Rather than specifying one or more beneficiaries by name, the policyowner designates a class or group of beneficiaries. For example, "my children."

classification Occupational category of a risk.

cleft lip A congenital furrow or groove in the upper lip that results from incomplete embryonic development. This condition may be associated with a cleft palate. Also called a hare lip.

cleft palate A congenital furrow or groove in the roof of the mouth that results from incomplete embryonic development. This condition may be associated with a cleft lip.

close corporation A corporation owned by a small group of stockholders, each of whom usually has a voice in operating the business.

COBRA "Consolidated Omnibus Budget Reconciliation Act of 1985," extending group health coverage to terminated employees and their families for up to 18 or 36 months.

coinsurance (percentage participation) Principle under which the company insures only part of the potential loss, the policyowners paying the other part. For instance, in a major medical policy, the company may agree to pay 75 percent of the insured expenses, with the insured to pay the other 25 percent.

collateral assignment Assignment of a policy to a creditor as security for a debt. The creditor is entitled to be reimbursed out of policy proceeds for the amount owed. The beneficiary is entitled to any excess of policy proceeds over the amount due the creditor in the event of the insured's death.

combination company Company whose agents sell both weekly premium life and health insurance and ordinary life insurance. Also called a multi-line company.

commercial health insurers Insurance companies that function on the reimbursement approach, which allows policyowners to seek medical treatment then submit the charges to the insurer for reimbursement.

commissioner Head of a state insurance department; public officer charged with supervising the insurance business in a state and administrating insurance laws. Called "superintendent" in some states, "director" in others.

Commissioner's Standard Ordinary (CSO) Table Table of mortality based on intercompany experience over a period of time, which is legally recognized as the mortality basis for computing maximum reserves on policies issued within past years. The 1980 CSO Table replaced the 1958 CSO Table.

common disaster provision Sometimes added to a policy and designed to provide an alternative beneficiary in the event that the insured as well as the original beneficiary dies as the result of a common accident.

competent parties To be enforceable, a contract must be entered into by competent parties. A competent party is one who is capable of understanding the contract being agreed to.

comprehensive major medical insurance Designed to give the protection offered by both a basic medical expense and major medical policy. It is characterized by a low deductible amount, coinsurance clause and high maximum benefits.

concealment Failure of the insured to disclose to the company a fact material to the acceptance of the risk at the time application is made.

conditional contract Characteristic of an insurance contract in that the payment of benefits is dependent on or a condition of the occurrence of the risk insured against.

conditionally renewable contract Health insurance policy providing that the insured may renew the contract from period to period, or continue it to a stated date or an advanced age, subject to the right of the insurer to decline renewal only under conditions defined in the contract.

conditional receipt Given to the policyowners when they pay a premium at time of application. Such receipts bind the insurance company if the risk is approved as applied for, subject to any other conditions stated on the receipt.

consideration Element of a binding contract; acceptance by the company of payment of the premium and statements made by the prospective insured in the application.

consideration clause The part of an insurance contract setting forth the amount of initial and renewal premiums and frequency of future payments.

contestable period Period during which the company may contest a claim on a policy because of misleading or incomplete information in the application.

contingent beneficiary Person(s) named to receive proceeds in case the original beneficiary is not alive. Also referred to as secondary or tertiary beneficiary.

continuing care Type of health or medical care designed to provide a benefit for elderly individuals who live in a retirement community; addresses full-time needs, both social and medical. Also known as residential care.

contract An agreement enforceable by law whereby one party binds itself to certain promises or deeds.

contract of agency A legal document containing the terms of the contract between the agent and company, signed by both parties. Also called agency agreement.

contributory plan Group insurance plan issued to an employer under which both the employer and employees contribute to the cost of the plan. Generally, 75 percent of the eligible employees must be insured. (*See* **noncontributory plan**)

conversion factor A stated dollar-per-point amount used to determine benefit amounts paid for the cost of a procedure under a health insurance plan. For example, a plan with a $5-per-point conversion factor would pay $1,000 for a 200-point-procedure.

conversion privilege Allows the policyowner, before an original insurance policy expires, to elect to have a new policy issued that will continue the insurance coverage. Conversion may be effected at attained age (premiums based on the age attained at time of conversion) or at original age (premiums based on age at time of original issue).

convertible term Contract that may be converted to a permanent form of insurance without medical examination.

coordination of benefits (COB) provision Designed to prevent duplication of group insurance benefits. Limits benefits from multiple group health insurance policies in a particular case to 100 percent of the expenses covered and designates the order in which the multiple carriers are to pay benefits.

corridor deductible In superimposed major medical plans, a deductible amount between the benefits paid by the basic plan and the beginning of the major medical benefits.

cost of living (COL) rider A rider available with some policies that provides for an automatic increase in benefits (typically tied to the Consumer Price Index), offsetting the effects of inflation.

coverage requirements Standards of coverage that prevent retirement plans from discriminating in favor of highly compensated employees. A plan must pass an IRS coverage test to be considered qualified.

credit accident and health insurance If the insured debtor becomes totally disabled due to an accident or sickness, the policy premiums are paid during the period of disability or the loan is paid off. May be individual or group policy.

credit life insurance Usually written as decreasing term on a relatively small decreasing balance installment loan that may reflect direct borrowing or a balance due for merchandise purchased. If borrower dies, benefits pay balance due. May be individual or group policy.

credit report A summary of an insurance applicant's credit history, made by an independent organization that has investigated the applicant's credit standing.

cross-purchase plan An agreement that provides that upon a business owner's death, surviving owners will purchase the deceased's interest, often with funds from life insurance policies owned by each principal on the lives of all other principals.

currently insured Under Social Security, a status of limited eligibility that provides only death benefits.

custodial care Level of health or medical care given to meet daily personal needs, such as dressing, bathing, getting out of bed, and so on. Though it does not require medical training, it must be administered under a physician's order.

D

death rate Proportion of persons in each age group who die within a year; usually expressed as so many deaths per thousand persons. (*See* **expected mortality**)

debit insurer (*See* **home service insurer**)

decreasing term insurance Term life insurance on which the face value slowly decreases in scheduled steps from the date the policy comes into force to the date the policy expires, while the premium remains level. The intervals between decreases are usually monthly or annually.

deductible Amount of expense or loss to be paid by the insured before a health insurance policy starts paying benefits.

deferred annuity Provides for postponement of the commencement of an annuity until after a specified period or until the annuitant attains a specified age. May be purchased either on single-premium or flexible premium basis.

deferred compensation plan The deferral of an employee's compensation to some future age or date. These plans are frequently used to provide fringe benefits, such as retirement income, to selected personnel.

defined benefit plan A pension plan under which benefits are determined by a specific benefit formula.

defined contribution plan A tax-qualified retirement plan in which annual contributions are determined by a formula set forth in the plan. Benefits paid to a participant vary with the amount of contributions made on his or her behalf and the length of service under the plan.

delayed disability provision A disability income policy provision that allows a certain amount of time after an accident for a disability to result, and the insured remains eligible for benefits.

dental insurance A relatively new form of health insurance coverage typically offered on a group basis, it covers the costs of normal dental maintenance as well as oral surgery and root canal therapy.

dependency period Period following the death of the breadwinner up until the youngest child reaches maturity.

deposit term Has modest endowment feature. Normally is sold for ten-year terms with a higher first-year premium than for subsequent years. If policy lapses, insured forfeits his or her "deposit" and receives no refund.

disability Physical or mental impairment making a person incapable of performing one or more duties of his or her occupation.

disability buy-sell agreement An agreement between business co-owners that provides that shares owned by any one of them who becomes disabled shall be sold to and purchased by the other co-owners or by the business using funds from disability income insurance.

disability income insurance A type of health insurance coverage, it provides for the payment of regular, periodic income should the insured become disabled from illness or injury.

disability income rider Typically a rider to a life insurance policy, it provides benefits in the form of income in the event the insured becomes totally disabled.

discrimination In insurance, the act of treating certain groups of people unfairly in the sale and/or pricing of policies; treating any of a given class of risk differently from other like risks. Discrimination is expressly prohibited in most state insurance codes.

dividend Policyowner's share in the divisible surplus of a company issuing insurance on the participating plan.

dividend options The different ways in which the insured under a participating life insurance policy may elect to receive surplus earnings: in cash; as a reduction of premium; as additional paid-up insurance; left on deposit at interest; or as additional term insurance.

domestic insurer Company within the state in which it is chartered and in which its home office is located.

dread disease policy (*See* **limited risk policy**)

E

elimination period Duration of time between the beginning of an insured's disability and the commencement of the period for which benefits are payable.

employee benefit plans Plans through which employers offer employees benefits such as coverage for medical expenses, disability, retirement and death.

employee stock ownership plan (ESOP) A form of defined contribution profit-sharing plan, an ESOP invests primarily in the securities or stock of the employer.

endowment Contract providing for payment of the face amount at the end of a fixed period, at a specified age of the insured, or at the insured's death before the end of the stated period.

endowment period Period specified in an endowment policy during which, if the insured dies, the beneficiary receives a death benefit. If the insured is still living at the end of the endowment period, he or she receives the endowment as a living benefit.

enhanced whole life A whole life insurance policy issued by a mutual insurer, in which policy dividends are used to provide extra death benefits or to reduce future premiums.

enrollment period Period during which new employees can sign up for coverage under a group insurance plan.

entire contract provision An insurance policy provision stating that the application and policy contain all provisions and constitute the entire contract.

entity plan An agreement in which a business assumes the obligation of purchasing a deceased owner's interest in the business, thereby proportionately increasing the interests of surviving owners.

equity indexed annuity A fixed deferred annuity that offers the traditional guaranteed minimum interest rate and an excess interest feature that is based on the performance of an external equities market index.

errors and omissions insurance Professional liability insurance that protects an insurance producer against claims arising from service he or she rendered or failed to render.

estate Most commonly, the quantity of wealth or property at an individual's death.

estate tax Federal tax imposed on the value of property transferred by an individual at his or her death.

estoppel Legal impediment to denying the consequences of one's actions or deeds if they lead to detrimental actions by another.

evidence of insurability Any statement or proof regarding a person's physical condition, occupation, and so forth, affecting acceptance of the applicant for insurance.

examiner Physician authorized by the medical director of an insurance company to make medical examinations. Also, person assigned by a state insurance company to audit the affairs of an insurance company.

excess interest Difference between the rate of interest the company guarantees to pay on proceeds left under settlement options and the interest actually paid on such funds by the company.

exclusion ratio A fraction used to determine the amount of annual annuity income exempt from federal income tax. The exclusion ratio is the total contribution or investment in the annuity divided by the expected ratio.

exclusion rider Health insurance policy rider that waives insurer's liability for all future claims on a preexisting condition.

exclusions Specified hazards listed in a policy for which benefits will not be paid.

exclusive provider organization (EPO) A variation of the PPO concept, an EPO contracts with an extremely limited number of physicians and typically only one hospital to provide services to members; members who elect to get health care from outside the EPO receive no benefits. (*See also* **preferred provider organization**)

expected mortality Number of deaths that theoretically should occur among a group of insured persons during a given period, according to the mortality table in use. Normally, a lower mortality rate is anticipated and generally experienced.

experience rating Review of the previous year's claims experience for a group insurance contract in order to establish premiums for the next period.

express authority The specific authority given in writing to the agent in the contract of agency.

extended term insurance Nonforfeiture option providing for the cash surrender value of a policy to be used as a net single premium at the insured's attained age to purchase term insurance for the face amount of the policy, less indebtedness, for as long a period as possible, but no longer than the term of the original policy.

extra percentage tables Mortality or morbidity tables indicating the percentage amount increase of premium for certain impaired health conditions.

F

face amount Commonly used to refer to the principal sum involved in the contract. The actual amount payable may be decreased by loans or increased by additional benefits payable under specified conditions or stated in a rider. (141)

facility-of-payment provision Clause permitted under a uniform health insurance policy provision allowing the company to pay up to $1,000 of benefits or proceeds to any relative appearing entitled to it if there is no beneficiary or if the insured or beneficiary is a minor or legally incompetent.

Fair Credit Reporting Act Federal law requiring an individual to be informed if he or she is being investigated by an inspection company.

family plan policy All-family plan of protection, usually with permanent insurance on the primary wage earner's life and with spouse and children automatically covered for lesser amounts of protection, usually term, all included for one premium.

FICA Contributions made by employees and employers to fund Social Security benefits (OASDI).

fiduciary Person in a position of special trust and confidence, e.g., in handling or supervising affairs or funds of another.

final expense fund Basic use for life insurance; reserve to cover costs of last illness, burial, legal and administrative expenses, miscellaneous outstanding bills, and so on. Also called cleanup fund.

fixed-amount settlement option A life insurance settlement option whereby the beneficiary instructs that proceeds be paid in regular installments of a fixed dollar amount. The number of payment periods is determined by the policy's face amount, the amount of each payment and the interest earned.

fixed annuity A type of annuity that provides a guaranteed fixed benefit amount, payable for the life of the annuitant.

fixed-period settlement option A life insurance settlement option in which the number of payments is fixed by the payee, with the amount of each payment determined by the amount of proceeds.

flat deductible Amount of covered expenses payable by the insured before medical benefits are payable.

foreign insurer Company operating in a state in which it is not chartered and in which its home office is not located.

franchise insurance Life or health insurance plan for covering groups of persons with individual policies uniform in provisions, although perhaps different in benefits. Solicitation usually takes place in an employer's business with the employer's consent. Generally written for groups too small to qualify for regular group coverage. May be called wholesale insurance when the policy is life insurance.

fraternal benefit insurer Nonprofit benevolent organization that provides insurance to its members.

fraud An act of deceit; misrepresentation of a material fact made knowingly, with the intention of having another person rely on that fact and consequently suffer a financial hardship.

free look Provision required in most states whereby policyholders have either 10 or 20 days to examine their new policies at no obligation.

fully insured A status of complete eligibility for the full range of Social Security benefits: death benefits, retirement benefits, disability benefits and Medicare benefits.

funding In a retirement plan, the setting aside of funds for the payment of benefits.

G

general agent Independent agent with authority, under contract with the company, to appoint soliciting agents within a designated territory and fix their compensation.

government insurer An organization that, as an extension of the federal or state government, provides a program of social insurance.

grace period Period of time after the due date of a premium during which the policy remains in force without penalty.

graded premium whole life Variation of a traditional whole life contract providing for lower than normal premium rates during the first few policy years, with premiums increasing gradually each year. After the preliminary period, premiums level off and remain constant.

gross premium The total premium paid by the policyowner, it generally consists of the net premium plus the expense of operation minus interest.

group credit insurance A form of group insurance issued by insurance companies to creditors to cover the lives of debtors for the amounts of their loans.

group insurance Insurance that provides coverage for a group of persons, usually employees of a company, under one master contract.

guaranteed insurability (guaranteed issue) Arrangement, usually provided by rider, whereby additional insurance may be purchased at various times without evidence of insurability.

guaranteed renewable contract Health insurance contract that the insured has the right to continue in force by payment of premiums for a substantial period of time during which the insurer has no right to make unilaterally any change in any provision, other than a change in premium rate for classes of insureds.

guaranty association Established by each state to support insurers and protect consumers in the case of insurer insolvency, guaranty associations are funded by insurers through assessments.

H

hazard Any factor that gives rise to a peril.

Health Care and Insurance Reform Act This 1993 act establishes a new model for health care delivery in Florida called "managed competition."

health insurance Insurance against loss through sickness or accidental bodily injury. Also called accident and health, accident and sickness, sickness and accident or disability insurance.

health maintenance organization (HMO) Health care management stressing preventive health care, early diagnosis and treatment on an outpatient basis. Persons generally enroll voluntarily by paying a fixed fee periodically.

Holocaust Victims Insurance Act Requires insurers that receive claims from Holocaust victims or beneficiaries, descendents or heirs, to allow, investigate and pay their rightful claims under the policy regardless of any statute of limitations. Claimants must have submitted their claims within 10 years of the effective date of the law or by July 1, 1998.

home health care Skilled or unskilled care provided in an individual's home, usually on a part-time basis.

home service insurer Insurer that offers relatively small policies with premiums payable on a weekly basis, collected by agents at the policyowner's home.

hospital benefits Payable for charges incurred while the insured is confined to, or treated in, a hospital, as defined in a health insurance policy.

hospital expense insurance Health insurance benefits subject to a specified daily maximum for a specified period of time while the injured is confined to a hospital, plus a limited allowance up to a specified amount for miscellaneous hospital expenses, such as operating room, anesthesia, laboratory fees, and so on. Also called hospitalization insurance. (*See* **medical expense insurance**)

hospital indemnity Form of health insurance providing a stipulated daily, weekly or monthly indemnity during hospital confinement; payable on an unallocated basis without regard to actual hospital expense.

human life value An individual's economic worth, measured by the sum of his or her future earnings that is devoted to his or her family.

I

immediate annuity Provides for payment of annuity benefit at one payment interval from date of purchase. Can only be purchased with a single payment.

implied authority Authority not specifically granted to the agent in the contract of agency, but which common sense dictates the agent has. It enables the agent to carry out routine responsibilities.

incontestable clause Provides that, for certain reasons such as misstatements on the application, the company may void a life insurance policy after it has been in force during the insured's lifetime, usually one or two years after issue.

increasing term insurance Term life insurance in which the death benefit increases periodically over the policy's term. Usually purchased as a cost of living rider to a whole life policy. (*See* **cost of living rider**)

indemnity approach A method of paying health policy benefits to insureds based on a predetermined, fixed rate set for the medical services provided, regardless of the actual expenses incurred.

independent agency system A system for marketing, selling and distributing insurance in which independent brokers are not affiliated with any one insurer but represent any number of insurers.

indexed whole life A whole life insurance policy whose death benefit increases according to the rate of inflation. Such policies are usually tied to the Consumer Price Index (CPI).

individual insurance Policies providing protection to the policyowner, as distinct from group and blanket insurance. Also called personal insurance.

individual retirement account (IRA) A personal qualified retirement account through which eligible individuals accumulate tax-deferred income up to a certain amount each year, depending on the person's tax bracket.

industrial insurance Life insurance policy providing modest benefits and a relatively short benefit period. Premiums are collected on a weekly or monthly basis by an agent calling at insured's homes. (*See* **home service insurer**)

inspection receipt A receipt obtained from an insurance applicant when a policy (upon which the first premium has not been paid) is left with him or her for further inspection. It states that the insurance is not in effect and that the policy has been delivered for inspection only.

inspection report Report of an investigator providing facts required for a proper underwriting decision on applications for new insurance and reinstatements.

installment refund annuity An annuity income option that provides for the funds remaining at the annuitant's death to be paid to the beneficiary in the form of continued annuity payments.

insurability All conditions pertaining to individuals that affect their health, susceptibility to injury, or life expectancy; an individual's risk profile.

insurability receipt A type of conditional receipt that makes coverage effective on the date the application was signed or the date of the medical exam (whichever is later), provided the applicant proves to be insurable.

insurable interest Requirement of insurance contracts that loss must be sustained by the applicant upon the death or disability of another and loss must be sufficient to warrant compensation.

insurance Social device for minimizing risk of uncertainty regarding loss by spreading the risk over a large enough number of similar exposures to predict the individual chance of loss.

insurance code The laws that govern the business of insurance in a given state.

insurer Party that provides insurance coverage, typically through a contract of insurance.

insuring clause Defines and describes the scope of the coverage provided and limits of indemnification.

integrated deductible In superimposed major medical plans, a deductible amount between the benefits paid by the basic plan and those benefits paid by the major medical. All or part of the integrated deductible may be absorbed by the basic plan.

interest adjusted net cost method A method of comparing costs of similar policies by using an index that takes into account the time value of money.

interest-only option (interest option) Mode of settlement under which all or part of the proceeds of a policy are left with the company for a definite period at a guaranteed minimum interest rate. Interest may either be added to the proceeds or paid annually, semiannually, quarterly or monthly.

interest-sensitive whole life Whole life policy whose premiums vary depending upon the insurer's underlying death, investment and expense assumptions.

interim term insurance Term insurance for a period of 12 months or less by special agreement of the company; it permits a permanent policy to become effective at a selected future date.

intermediate nursing care Level of health or medical care that is occasional or rehabilitative, ordered by a physician, and performed by skilled medical personnel.

irrevocable beneficiary Beneficiary whose interest cannot be revoked without his or her written consent, usually because the policyowner has made the beneficiary designation without retaining the right to revoke or change it.

J

joint and last survivor policy A variation of the joint life policy that covers two lives but pays the benefit upon the death of the second insured.

joint and survivor annuity Covers two or more lives and continues in force so long as any one of them survives.

joint life policy Covers two or more lives and provides for the payment of the proceeds at the death of the first among those insured, at which time the policy automatically terminates.

juvenile insurance Written on the lives of children who are within specified age limits and generally under parental control.

K

Keogh plans Designed to fund retirement of self-employed individuals; name derived from the author of the Keogh Act (HR-10), under which contributions to such plans are given favorable tax treatment.

key-person insurance Protection of a business against financial loss caused by the death or disablement of a vital number of the company, usually individuals possessing special managerial or technical skill or expertise.

L

lapse Termination of a policy upon the policyowner's failure to pay the premium within the grace period.

law of large numbers Basic principle of insurance that the larger the number of individual risks combined into a group, the more certainty there is in predicting the degree or amount of loss that will be incurred in any given period.

legal purpose In contract law, the requirement that the object of, or reason for, the contract must be legal.

legal reserve Policy reserves are maintained according to the standard levels established through the insurance laws of the various states.

level premium funding method The insurance plan (used by all regular life insurance companies) under which, instead of an annually increasing premium that reflects the increasing chance of death, an equivalent level premium is paid. Reserves that accumulate from more than adequate premiums paid in the early years supplement inadequate premiums in later years.

level term insurance Term coverage on which the face value remains unchanged from the date the policy comes into force to the date the policy expires.

license Certification issued by a state insurance department that an individual is qualified to solicit insurance applications for the period covered; usually issued for one year, renewable on application without need to repeat the original qualifying requirements.

licensed insurer (*See* **admitted insurer**)

lien system Plan for issuing coverage for substandard risks. A standard premium is paid, but there is a lien against the policy to reduce the amount of insurance if the insured dies from a cause that resulted in the substandard rating.

life annuity Payable during the continued life of the annuitant. No provision is made for the guaranteed return of the unused portion of the premium.

life expectancy Average duration of the life remaining to a number of persons of a given age, according to a given mortality table. Not to be confused with "probable lifetime," which refers to the difference between a person's present age and the age at which death is most probable, i.e., the age at which most deaths occur.

life income settlement option A settlement option providing for life insurance or annuity proceeds to be used to buy an annuity payable to the beneficiary for life-often with a specified number of payments certain or a refund if payments don't equal or exceed premiums paid.

life insurance Insurance against loss due to the death of a particular person (the insured) upon whose death the insurance company agrees to pay a stated sum or income to the beneficiary.

limited pay life insurance A form of whole life insurance characterized by premium payments only being made for a specified or limited number of years.

limited policies Restrict benefits to specified accidents or diseases, such as travel policies, dread disease policies, ticket policies, and so forth.

limited risk policy Provides coverage for specific kinds of accidents or illnesses, such as injuries received as a result of travel accidents or medical expenses stemming from a specified disease. (*See* **special risk policy**)

Lloyd's of London An association of individuals and companies that underwrite insurance on their own accounts and provide specialized coverages.

loading Amount added to net premiums to cover the company's operating expenses and contingencies; includes the cost of securing new business, collection expenses and general management expenses; excess of gross premiums over net premiums.

loan value Determinable amount that can be borrowed from the issuing company by the policyowner using the value of the life insurance policy as collateral.

long-term care Refers to the broad range of medical and personal services for individuals (often the elderly) who need assistance with daily activities for an extended period of time.

long-term care policy Health insurance policies that provide daily indemnity benefits for extended care confinement.

loss sharing (*See* **risk pooling**)

lump sum Payment of entire proceeds of an insurance policy in one sum. The method of settlement provided by most policies unless an alternate settlement is elected by the policyowner or beneficiary.

M

major medical expense policy Health insurance policy that provides broad coverage and high benefits for hospitalization, surgery and physician services. Characterized by deductibles and coinsurance cost-sharing.

managed care A system of delivering health care and health care services, characterized by arrangements with selected providers, programs of ongoing quality control and utilization review and financial incentives for members to use providers and procedures covered by the plan.

mandatory second opinion To control costs, many health policies provide that, in order to be eligible for benefits, insureds must get a second opinion before receiving non-life-threatening surgery.

master contract Issued to the employer under a group plan; contains all the insuring clauses defining employee benefits. Individual employees participating in the group plan receive individual certificates that outline highlights of the coverage. Also called master policy.

maturity value Proceeds payable on an endowment contract at the end of the specified endowment period, or payable on an ordinary life contract at the last age of the mortality table if the insured is still living at that age. Maturity value of a policy is the same as the face amount of the policy and is equal to the reserve value of the contract on this maturity date. Actual amount payable by the company may be increased by dividend additions or accumulated dividend deposits, or decreased by outstanding loans.

McCarran-Ferguson Act Also know as Public Law 15, the 1945 act exempting insurance from federal antitrust laws to the extent insurance is regulated by states.

Medicaid Provides medical care for the needy under joint federal-state participation (Kerr-Mills Act).

medical cost management The process of controlling how policyholders utilize their policies. (*See* **mandatory second opinion**, **precertification**, **ambulatory surgery** and **case management**)

medical examination Usually conducted by a licensed physician; the medical report is part of the application, becomes part of the policy contract, and is attached to the policy. A "nonmedical" is a short-form medical report filled out by the agent. Various company rules, such as amount of insurance applied for or already in force, or applicant's age, sex, past physical history and data revealed by inspection report, and so on, determine whether the examination will be "medical" or "nonmedical."

medical expense insurance Pays benefits for nonsurgical doctors' fees commonly rendered in a hospital; sometimes pays for home and office calls.

Medical Information Bureau (MIB) A service organization that collects medical data on life and health insurance applicants for member insurance companies.

medical report A document completed by a physician or other approved examiner and submitted to an insurer to supply medical evidence of insurability (or lack of insurability) or in relation to a claim.

Medicare Federally sponsored health insurance and medical program for persons age 65 or older; administered under provisions of the Social Security Act.

Medicare Part A Compulsory hospitalization insurance that provides specified inhospital and related benefits. All workers covered by Social Security finance its operation through a portion of their FICA tax.

Medicare Part B Voluntary program designed to provide supplementary medical insurance to cover physician services, medical services and supplies not covered under Medicare Part A.

Medicare Part C Medicare Part C is called Medicare Advantage. The program offers a variety of managed care plans, a private fee-for-service plan, and Medicare specialty plans. These specialty plans provide services that focus care on the management of a specific disease or condition.

Medicare Part D A program that offers a prescription drug benefit to help Medicare beneficiaries pay for the drugs they need. The drug benefit is optional and is available to anyone who is entitled to Medicare Part A or enrolled in Part B. This benefit is available through private prescription drug plans (PDPs) or Medicare Advantage (PPO) plans.

Medicare supplement policy Health insurance that provides coverage to fill the gaps in Medicare coverage.

minimum deposit insurance A cash value life insurance policy having a first-year loan value that is available for borrowing immediately upon payment of the first-year premium.

minimum premium plan (MPP) Designed to support a self-insured plan, a minimum premium plan helps insure against large, unpredictable losses that exceed the self-insured level.

miscellaneous expenses Hospital charges, other than for room and board, e.g., X rays, drugs, laboratory fees, etc., in connection with health insurance.

misrepresentation Act of making, issuing, circulating or causing to be issued or circulated, an estimate, illustration, circular or statement of any kind that does not represent the correct policy terms, dividends or share of the surplus or the name or title for any policy or class of policies that does not in fact reflect its true nature.

misstatement of age or sex provision If the insured's age or sex is misstated in an application for insurance, the benefit payable usually is adjusted to what the premiums paid should have purchased.

misuse of premium Improper use of premiums collected by an insurance producer.

modified endowment contract (MEC) A life insurance policy under which the amount a policyowner pays in during the first years exceeds the sum of net level premiums that would have been payable to provide paid-up future benefits in seven years.

modified whole life Whole life insurance with premium payable during the first few years, usually five years, only slightly larger than the rate for term insurance. Afterwards, the premium is higher for the remainder of life than the premium for ordinary life at the original age of issue, but lower than the rate at the attained age at the time of charge.

money-purchase plan A type of qualified plan under which contributions are fixed amounts or fixed percentages of the employee's salary. An employee's benefits are provided in whatever amount the accumulated or current contributions will produce for him or her.

moral hazard Effect of personal reputation, character, associates, personal living habits, financial responsibility and environment, as distinguished from physical health, upon an individual's general insurability.

morale hazard Hazard arising from indifference to loss because of the existence of insurance.

morbidity The relative incidence of disability due to sickness or accident within a given group.

morbidity rate Shows the incidence and extent of disability that may be expected from a given large group of persons; used in computing health insurance rates.

mortality The relative incidence of death within a group.

mortality table Listing of the mortality experience of individuals by age; permits an actuary to calculate, on the average, how long a male or female of a given age group may be expected to live.

mortgage insurance A basic use of life insurance, so-called because many family heads leave insurance for specifically paying off any mortgage balance outstanding at their death. The insurance generally is made payable to a family beneficiary instead of to the mortgage holder.

multiple employer trust (MET) Several small groups of individuals that need life and health insurance but do not qualify for true group insurance band together under state trust laws to purchase insurance at a more favorable rate.

multiple employer welfare arrangement (MEWA) Similar to a multiple employer trust (MET) with the exception that in a MEWA, a number of employers pool their risks and self-insure.

multiple protection policy A combination of term and whole life coverage that pays some multiple of the face amount of the basic whole life portion (such as $10 per month per $1,000) throughout the multiple protection period (such as to age 65).

mutual insurer An insurance company characterized by having no capital stock, it is owned by its policyowners and usually issues participating insurance.

N

National Association of Health Underwriters (NAHU) NAHU is an organization of health insurance agents that is dedicated to supporting the health insurance industry and to advancing the quality of service provided by insurance professionals.

National Association of Insurance and Financial Advisors (NAIFA) NAIFA is an organization of life insurance agents that is dedicated to supporting the life insurance industry and to advancing the quality of service provided by insurance professionals.

National Association of Insurance Commissioners (NAIC) Association of state insurance commissioners active in insurance regulatory problems and in forming and recommending model legislation and requirements.

natural group A group formed for a reason other than to obtain insurance.

needs approach A method for determining how much insurance protection a person should have by analyzing a family's or business's needs and objectives should the insured die, become disabled or retire.

net premium Calculated on the basis of a given mortality table and a given interest rate, without any allowance for loading.

nonadmitted insurer An insurance company that has not been licensed to operate within a given state.

noncancellable and guaranteed renewable contract Health insurance contract that the insured has the right to continue in force by payment of premiums set forth in the contract for a substantial period of time, during which the insurer has no right to make unilaterally any change in any contract provision.

noncontributory plan Employee benefit plan under which the employer bears the full cost of the employees' benefits; must insure 100 percent of eligible employees.

nondisabling injury Requires medical care, but does not result in loss of time from work.

nonduplication provision Stipulates that insureds shall be ineligible to collect for charges under a group health plan if the charges are reimbursed under their own or spouse's group plan.

nonforfeiture options Privileges allowed under terms of a life insurance contract after cash values have been created.

nonforfeiture values Those benefits in a life insurance policy that by law, the policyowner does not forfeit even if he or she discontinues premium payments; usually cash value, loan value, paid-up insurance value and extended term insurance value.

nonmedical insurance Issued on a regular basis without requiring a regular medical examination. In passing on the risk, the company relies on the applicant's answers to questions regarding his or her physical condition and on personal references or inspection reports.

nonparticipating Insurance under which the insured is not entitled to share in the divisible surplus of the company.

nonqualified plan A retirement plan that does not meet federal government requirements and is not eligible for favorable tax treatment.

notice of claims provision Policy provision that describes the policyowner's obligation to provide notification of loss to the insurer within a reasonable period of time.

O

offer and acceptance The offer may be made by the applicant by signing the application, paying the first premium and, if necessary, submitting to a physical examination. Policy issuance, as applied for, constitutes acceptance by the company. Or, the offer may be made by the company when no premium payment is submitted with application. Premium payment on the offered policy then constitutes acceptance by the applicant.

Old-Age, Survivors, Disability and Hospital Insurance (OASDI) Retirement, death, disability income and hospital insurance benefits provided under the Social Security system.

open-panel HMO A network of physicians who work out of their own offices and participate in the HMO on a part-time basis.

optionally renewable contract Health insurance policy in which the insurer reserves the right to terminate the coverage at any anniversary or, in some cases, at any premium due date, but does not have the right to terminate coverage between such dates.

ordinary insurance Life insurance of commercial companies not issued on the weekly premium basis; amount of protection usually is $1,000 or more.

other insureds rider A term rider, covering a family member other than the insured, that is attached to the base policy covering the insured.

outline of coverage Informational material about a specific plan or policy of insurance that describes the policy's features and benefits; in many states, an outline of coverage is required to be given to consumers when certain types of coverages are being considered.

overhead insurance Type of short-term disability insurance reimbursing the insured for specified, fixed, monthly expenses, normal and customary in operating the insured's business.

overinsurance An excessive amount of insurance; an amount of insurance that would result in payment of more than the actual loss or more than incurred expenses.

own occupation A definition of total disability that requires that in order to receive disability income benefits the insured must be unable to work at his or her own occupation.

P

paid-up additions Additional life insurance purchased by policy dividends on a net single premium basis at the insured's attained insurance age at the time additions are purchased.

paid-up policy No further premiums are to be paid and the company is held liable for the benefits provided by the contract.

parol evidence rule Rule of contract law that brings all verbal statements into the written contract and disallows any changes or modifications to the contract by oral evidence.

partial disability Illness or injury preventing insured from performing at least one or more, but not all, of their occupational duties.

participating Plan of insurance under which the policyowner receives shares (commonly called dividends) of the divisible surplus of the company.

participating physician A doctor or physician who accepts Medicare's allowable or recognized charges and will not charge more than this amount.

participation standards Rules that must be followed for determining employee eligibility for a qualified retirement plan.

partnership A business entity that allows two or more people to strengthen their effectiveness by working together as co-owners.

payor rider Available under certain juvenile life insurance policies, upon payment of an extra premium. Provides for the waiver of future premiums if the person responsible for paying them dies or is disabled before the policy becomes fully paid or matures as a death claim, or as an endowment, or the child reaches a specific age.

per capita rule Death proceeds from an insurance policy are divided equally among the living primary beneficiaries.

peril The immediate specific event causing loss and giving rise to risk.

period certain annuity An annuity income option that guarantees a definite minimum period of payments.

permanent flat extra premium A fixed charge added per $1,000 of insurance for substandard risks.

personal producing general agency system (PPGA) A method of marketing, selling and distributing insurance in which personal producing general agents (PPGAs) are compensated for business they personally sell and business sold by agents with whom they subcontract. Subcontracted agents are considered employees of the PPGA, not the insurer.

per stirpes rule Death proceeds from an insurance policy are divided equally among the named beneficiaries. If a named beneficiary is deceased, his or her share then goes to the living descendants of that individual.

policy In insurance, the written instrument in which a contract of insurance is set forth.

policy loan In life insurance, a loan made by the insurance company to the policyowner, with the policy's cash value assigned as security. One of the standard nonforfeiture options.

policy provisions The term or conditions of an insurance policy as contained in the policy clauses.

portability Provision under the Florida Health Care Access Act in which a worker or dependent will have to meet the waiting period for an existing condition.

precertification The insurer's approval of an insured's entering a hospital. Many health policies require precertification as part of an effort to control costs.

preexisting condition An illness or medical condition that existed before a policy's effective date; usually excluded from coverage, through the policy's standard provisions or by waiver.

preferred provider organization (PPO) Association of health care providers, such as doctors and hospitals, that agree to provide health care to members of a particular group at fees negotiated in advance.

preferred risk A risk whose physical condition, occupation, mode of living and other characteristics indicate a prospect for longevity for unimpaired lives of the same age.

preliminary term insurance Term insurance attached to a newly issued permanent life insurance policy extending term coverage of a preliminary period of 1 to 11 months, until the permanent insurance becomes effective. The purpose is to provide full life insurance premium and the anniversary to a later date.

premium The periodic payment required to keep an insurance policy in force.

premium factors The three primary factors considered when computing the basic premium for insurance: mortality, expense and interest.

prescription drug coverage Usually offered as an optional benefit to group medical expense plans, this coverage covers some or all of the cost of prescription drugs.

presumptive disability benefit A disability income policy benefit that provides that if an insured experiences a specified disability, such as blindness, he or she is presumed to be totally disabled and entitled to the full amount payable under the policy, whether or not he or she is able to work.

primary beneficiary In life insurance, the beneficiary designated by the insured as the first to receive policy benefits.

primary insurance amount (PIA) Amount equal to a covered worker's full Social Security retirement benefit at age 65 or disability benefit.

principal An insurance company that, having appointed someone as its agent, is bound to the contracts the agent completes in its behalf.

principal sum The amount under an AD&D policy that is payable as a death benefit if death is due to an accident.

private insurer An insurer that is not associated with federal or state government.

probationary period Specified number of days after an insurance policy's issue date during which coverage is not afforded for sickness. Standard practice for group coverages.

proceeds Net amount of money payable by the company at the insured's death or at policy maturity.

producer A general term applied to an agent, broker, personal producing general agent, solicitor or other person who sells insurance.

professional liability insurance (*See* **errors and omissions insurance**)

profit-sharing plan Any plan whereby a portion of a company's profits is set aside for distribution to employees who qualify under the plan.

proof of loss A mandatory health insurance provision stating that the insured must provide a completed claim form to the insurer within 90 days of the date of loss.

proper solicitation High professional standards that require an agent to identify himself or herself properly, that is, as an agent soliciting insurance on behalf of an insurance company.

pure endowment Contract providing for payment only upon survival of a certain person to a certain date and not in the event of that person's prior death. This type of contract is just the opposite of a term contract, which provides for payment only in the event the injured person dies within the term period specified.

pure risk Type of risk that involves the chance of loss only; there is no opportunity for gain; insurable.

Q

qualified plan A retirement or employee compensation plan established and maintained by an employer that meets specific guidelines spelled out by the IRS and consequently receives favorable tax treatment.

R

rate-up in age System of rating substandard risks that assumes the insured to be older than he or she really is and charging a correspondingly higher premium.

rating The making of insurance also creates the premium classification given an applicant for life or health insurance.

reasonable and customary charge Charge for health care service consistent with the going rate of charge in a given geographical area for identical or similar services.

rebating Returning part of the commission or giving anything else of value to the insured as an inducement to buy the policy. It is illegal and cause for license revocation in most states. In some states, it is an offense by both the agent and the person receiving the rebate.

reciprocal insurer Insurance company characterized by the fact its policyholders insure the risks of other policyholders.

recurrent disability provision A disability income policy provision that specifies the period of time during which the reoccurrence of a disability is considered a continuation of a prior disability.

reduced paid-up insurance A nonforfeiture option contained in most life insurance policies providing for the insured to elect to have the cash surrender value of the policy used to purchase a paid-up policy for a reduced amount of insurance.

re-entry option An option in a renewable term life policy under which the policyowner is guaranteed, at the end of the term, to be able to renew his or her coverage without evidence of insurability, at a premium rate specified in the policy.

refund annuity Provides for the continuance of the annuity during the annuitant's lifetime and, in any event, until total payment equal to the purchase price has been made by the company.

reimbursement approach Payment of health policy benefits to insured based on actual medical expenses incurred.

reinstatement Putting a lapsed policy back in force by producing satisfactory evidence of insurability and paying any past-due premiums required.

reinsurance Acceptance by one or more insurers, called reinsurers, of a portion of the risk underwritten by another insurer who has contracted for the entire coverage.

relative value scale Method for determining benefits payable under a basic surgical expense policy. Points are assigned to each surgical procedure and a dollar per point amount, or conversion factor, is used to determine the benefit.

renewable option An option that allows the policyowner to renew a term policy before its termination date without having to provide evidence of insurability.

renewable term Some term policies prove that they may be renewed on the same plan for one or more years without medical examination, but with rates based on the insured's advanced age.

replacement Act of replacing one life insurance policy with another; may be done legally under certain conditions. (*See* **twisting**)

representation Statements made by applicants on their applications for insurance that they represent as being substantially true to the best of their knowledge and belief, but that are not warranted as exact in every detail. (*See* **warranties**)

reserve Fund held by the company to help fulfill future claims.

reserve basis Refers to mortality table and assumed interest rate used in computing rates.

residual disability benefit A disability income payment based on the proportion of income the insured has actually lost, taking into account the fact that he or she is able to earn some income.

respite care Type of health or medical care designed to provide a short rest period for a caregiver. Characterized by its temporary status.

results provision (*See* **accidental bodily injury provision**)

revocable beneficiary Beneficiary whose rights in a policy are subject to the policyowner's reserved right to revoke or change the beneficiary designation and the right to surrender or make a loan on the policy without the beneficiary's consent.

rider Strictly speaking, a rider adds something to a policy. However, the term is used loosely to refer to any supplemental agreement attached to and made a part of the policy, whether the policy's conditions are expanded and additional coverages added, or a coverage of conditions is waived.

risk Uncertainty regarding loss; the probability of loss occurring for an insured or prospect.

risk pooling A basic principle of insurance whereby a large number contribute to cover the losses of a few. (*See* **loss sharing**)

risk selection The method of a home office underwriter used to choose applicants that the insurance company will accept. The underwriter must determine whether risks are standard, substandard or preferred and adjust the premium rates accordingly.

rollover IRA An individual retirement account established with funds transferred from another IRA or qualified retirement plan that the owner had terminated.

S

salary continuation plan An arrangement whereby an income, usually related to an employee's salary, is continued upon employee's retirement, death or disability.

salary reduction SEP A qualified retirement plan limited to companies with 25 or fewer employees. It allows employees to defer part of their pretax income to the plan, lowering their taxable income. (*See* **simplified employee pension plan**)

savings incentive match plan for employees (SIMPLE) A qualified employer retirement plan that allows small employers to set up tax-favored retirement savings plans for their employees.

schedule List of specified amounts payable, usually for surgical operations, dismemberment, fractures, etc.

secondary beneficiary An alternative beneficiary designated to receive payment, usually in the event the original beneficiary predeceases the insured.

Section 457 plans Deferred compensation plans for employees of state and local governments in which amounts deferred will not be included in gross income until they are actually received or made available.

Self-Employed Individuals Retirement Act Passed by Congress in 1962, this Act enables self-employed persons to establish qualified retirement plans similar to those available to corporations.

self-insurance Program for providing insurance financed entirely through the means of the policyowner, in place of purchasing coverage from commercial carriers.

self-insured plan A health insurance plan characterized by an employer (usually a large one), labor union, fraternal organization or other group retaining the risk of covering its employees' medical expenses.

service insurers Companies that offer prepayment plans for medical or hospital services, such as health maintenance organizations.

service provider An organization that provides health coverage by contracting with service providers, to provide medical services to subscribers, who pay in advance through premiums. Examples of such coverages are HMOs and PPOs.

settlement options Optional modes of settlement provided by most life insurance policies in lieu of lump-sum payment. Usual options are: lump-sum cash; interest-only; fixed-period; fixed-amount; and life income.

simplified employee pension plan (SEP) A type of qualified retirement plan under which the employer contributes to an individual retirement account set up and maintained by the employee.

single dismemberment Loss of one hand or one foot, or the sight of one eye.

single-premium whole life insurance Whole life insurance for which the entire premium is paid in one sum at the beginning of the contract period.

skilled nursing care Daily nursing care ordered by a doctor; often medically necessary. It can only be performed by or under the supervision of skilled medical professionals and is available 24 hours a day.

sliding The act of telling an insurance applicant that the law requires him to buy a specific ancillary coverage or product with the purchase of insurance when that coverage or product is not required. It is also the act of telling an applicant that a policy includes a specific ancillary coverage or product with- out additional charge when such a charge is required. Sliding also occurs when an insurer charges for a specific ancillary coverage or product, in addition to the cost of the coverage applied for, without the applicant's informed consent.

small employer An employer who employs not more than 50 employees, the majority of whom are employed in Florida.

Social Security Programs first created by Congress in 1935 and now composed of Old-Age, Survivors and Disability Insurance (OASDI), Medicare, Medicaid and various grants-in-aid, which provide economic security to nearly all employed people.

sole proprietorship The simplest form of business organization whereby one individual owns and controls the entire company.

special agent An agent representing an insurance company in a given territory.

special class Applicants who cannot qualify for standard insurance, but may secure policies with riders waiving payment for losses involving certain existing health impairments.

special questionnaires Forms used when, for underwriting purposes, the insurer needs more detailed information from an applicant regarding aviation or avocation, foreign residence, finances, military service or occupation.

special risk policy Provides coverage for unusual hazards normally not covered under accident and health insurance, such as a concert pianist insuring his or her hands for a million dollars. (*See* **limited risk policy**)

specified disease insurance (*See* **limited risk policy**)

speculative risk A type of risk that involves the chance of both loss and gain; not insurable.

spendthrift provision Stipulates that, to the extent permitted by law, policy proceeds shall not be subject to the claims of creditors of the beneficiary or policyowner.

split-dollar life insurance An arrangement between two parties where life insurance is written on the life of one, who names the beneficiary of the net death benefits (death benefits less cash value), and the other is assigned the cash value, with both sharing premium payments.

spousal IRA An individual retirement account that persons eligible to set up IRAs for themselves may set up jointly with a nonworking spouse.

standard provisions Forerunners of the Uniform Policy Provisions in health insurance policies today.

standard risk Person who, according to a company's underwriting standards, is entitled to insurance protection without extra rating or special restrictions.

stock bonus plan A plan under which bonuses are paid to employees in shares of stock.

stock insurer An insurance company owned and controlled by a group of stockholders whose investment in the company provides the safety margin necessary in issuance of guaranteed, fixed premium, nonparticipating policies.

stock redemption plan An agreement under which a close corporation purchases a deceased stockholder's interest.

stop-loss provision Designed to stop the company's loss at a given point, as an aggregate payable under a policy, a maximum payable for any one disability or the like; also applies to individuals, placing a limit on the maximum out-of-pocket expenses an insured must pay for health care, after which the health policy covers all expenses.

straight life income annuity (straight life annuity, life annuity) An annuity income option that pays a guaranteed income for the annuitant's lifetime, after which time payments stop.

straight whole life insurance (*See* **whole life insurance**)

subscriber Policyowner of a health care plan underwritten by a service insurer.

substandard risk Person who is considered an underaverage or impaired insurance risk because of physical condition, family or personal history of disease, occupation, residence in unhealthy climate or dangerous habits. (*See* **special class**)

successor beneficiary (*See* **secondary beneficiary**)

suicide provision Most life insurance policies provide that if the insured commits suicide within a specified period, usually two years after the issue date, the company's liability will be limited to a return of premiums paid.

supplemental accident coverage Often included as part of a group basic or major medical plan, this type of coverage is designed to cover expenses associated with accidents to the extent they are not provided under other coverages.

supplementary major medical policy A medical expense health plan that covers expenses not included under a basic policy and expenses that exceed the limits of a basic policy.

surgical expense insurance Provides benefits to pay for the cost of surgical operations.

surgical schedule List of cash allowances payable for various types of surgery, with the respective maximum amounts payable based upon severity of the operations; stipulated maximum usually covers all professional fees involved, e.g., surgeon, anesthesiologist.

surrender value (*See* **cash surrender value**)

T

taxable wage base The maximum amount of earnings upon which FICA taxes must be paid.

tax-sheltered annuity An annuity plan reserved for nonprofit organizations and their employees. Funds contributed to the annuity are excluded from current taxable income and are only taxed later, when benefits begin to be paid. Also called tax-deferred annuity and 403(b) plan.

temporary flat extra premium A fixed charge per $1,000 of insurance added to substandard risks for a specified period of years.

temporary insurance agreement (*See* **binding receipt**)

term insurance Protection during limited number of years; expiring without value if the insured survives the stated period, which may be one or more years, but usually is 5 to 20 years, because such periods generally cover the needs for temporary protection.

term of policy Period for which the policy runs. In life insurance, this is to the end of the term period for term insurance, to the maturity date for endowments and to the insured's death (or age 100) for permanent insurance. In most other kinds of insurance, it is usually the period for which a premium has been paid in advance; however, it may be for a year or more, even though the premium is paid on a semiannual or other basis.

tertiary beneficiary In life insurance, a beneficiary designated as third in line to receive the proceeds or benefits if the primary and secondary beneficiaries do not survive the insured.

third-party administrator (TPA) An organization outside the members of a self- insurance group which, for a fee, processes claims, completes benefits paperwork and often analyzes claims information.

third-party applicant A policy applicant who is not the prospective insured.

time limit on certain defenses A provision stating that an insurance policy is incontestable after it has been in force a certain period of time. It also limits the period during which an insurer can deny a claim on the basis of a preexisting condition.

total disability Disability preventing insureds from performing any duty of their usual occupations or any occupation for remuneration; actual definition depends on policy wording.

traditional net cost method A method of comparing costs of similar policies that does not take into account the time value of money.

transacting insurance The transaction of any of the following, in addition to other acts included under applicable provisions of the state code: solicitation or inducement; preliminary negotiations; effecting a contract of insurance; transacting matters subsequent to effecting a contract of insurance and arising out of it.

travel-accident policies Limited to indemnities for accidents while traveling, usually by common carrier.

trust Arrangement in which property is held by a person or corporation (trustee) for the benefit of others (beneficiaries). The grantor (person transferring the property to the trustee) gives legal title to the trustee, subject to terms set forth in a trust agreement. Beneficiaries have equitable title to the trust property.

trustee One holding legal title to property for the benefit of another; may be either an individual or a company, such as a bank and trust company.

twisting Practice of inducing a policyowner with one company to lapse, forfeit or surrender a life insurance policy for the purpose of taking out a policy in another company. Generally classified as a misdemeanor, subject to fine, revocation of license and sometimes imprisonment. (*See* **misrepresentation**)

U

unallocated benefit Reimbursement provision, usually for miscellaneous hospital and medical expenses, that does not specify how much will be paid for each type of treatment, examination, dressing, etc., but only sets a maximum that will be paid for all such treatments.

underwriter Company receiving premiums and accepting responsibility for fulfilling the policy contract. Company employee who decides whether or not the company should assume a particular risk. The agent who sells the policy.

underwriting Process through which an insurer determines whether, and on what basis, an insurance application will be accepted.

Unfair Trade Practices Act A model act written by the National Association of Insurance Commissioners (NAIC) and adopted by most states empowering state insurance commissioners to investigate and issue cease and desist orders and penalties to insurers for engaging in unfair or deceptive practices, such as misrepresentation or coercion.

Uniform Individual Accident and Sickness Policy Provisions Law NAIC model law that established uniform terms, provisions and standards for health insurance policies covering loss "resulting from sickness or from bodily injury or death by accident or both."

Uniform Simultaneous Death Act Model law that states when an insured and beneficiary die at the same time, it is presumed that the insured survived the beneficiary.

unilateral Distinguishing characteristic of an insurance contract in that it is only the insurance company that pledges anything.

uninsurable risk One not acceptable for insurance due to excessive risk.

universal life Flexible premium, two-part contract containing renewable term insurance and a cash value account that generally earns interest at a higher rate than a traditional policy. The interest rate varies. Premiums are deposited in the cash value account after the company deducts its fee and a monthly cost for the term coverage.

utilization review A technique used by health care providers to determine after the fact if health care was appropriate and effective.

V

valued contract A contract of insurance that pays a stated amount in the event of a loss.

variable annuity Similar to a traditional, fixed annuity in that retirement payments will be made periodically to the annuitants, usually over the remaining years of their lives. Under the variable annuity, there is no guarantee of the dollar amount of the payments; they fluctuate according to the value of an account invested primarily in common stocks.

variable life insurance Provides a guaranteed minimum death benefit. Actual benefits paid may be more, however, depending on the fluctuating market value of investments behind the contract at the insured's death. The cash surrender value also generally fluctuates with the market value of the investment portfolio.

variable universal life insurance A life insurance policy combining characteristics of universal and variable life policies. A VUL policy contains unscheduled premium payments and death benefits and a cash value that varies according to the underlying funds whose investment portfolio is managed by the policyowner.

vesting Right of employees under a retirement plan to retain part or all of the annuities purchased by the employer's contributions on their behalf or, in some plans, to receive cash payments or equivalent value, on termination of their employment, after certain qualifying conditions have been met.

viatical broker An insurance producer licensed to solicit viatical settlement agreements between providers and policyowners of life insurance contracts.

viatical provider A company that buys a life insurance policy from a policyowner who is suffering from a terminal illness or a severe chronic illness.

viatical settlement contract An agreement under which the owner of a life insurance policy sells the policy to another person in exchange for a bargained-for payment, which is generally less than the expected death benefit under the policy.

viator An individual suffering from a terminal illness or severe chronic illness who sells his or her life insurance policy to a viatical company. The company becomes the policyowner and assumes responsibility for paying premiums. When the insured dies, the company receives the death benefits.

vision insurance Optional coverage available with group health insurance plans, vision insurance typically pays for charges incurred during eye exams; eyeglasses and contact lenses are usually excluded.

void contract An agreement without legal effect; an invalid contract.

voidable contract A contract that can be made void at the option of one or more parties to the agreement.

voluntary group AD&D A group accidental death and dismemberment policy paid for entirely by employees, rather than an employer.

W

waiting period (*See* **elimination period**)

waiver Agreement waiving the company's liability for a certain type or types of risk ordinarily covered in the policy; a voluntary giving up of a legal, given right.

waiver of premium Rider or provision included in most life insurance policies and some health insurance policies exempting the insured from paying premiums after he or she has been disabled for a specified period of time, usually six months in life policies and 90 days or six months in health policies.

war clause Relieves the insurer of liability, or reduces its liability, for specified loss caused by war.

warranties Statements made on an application for insurance that are warranted to be true; that is, they are exact in every detail as opposed to representations. Statements on applications for insurance are rarely warranties, unless fraud is involved. (*See* **representation**)

whole life insurance Permanent level insurance protection for the "whole of life," from policy issue to the death of the insured. Characterized by level premiums, level benefits and cash values.

wholesale insurance (*See* **franchise insurance**)

workers' compensation Benefits paid workers for injury, disability or disease contracted in the course of their employment. Benefits and conditions are set by law, although in most states the insurance to provide the benefits may be purchased from regular insurance companies. A few states have monopolistic state compensation funds.

Y

yearly renewable term insurance (YRT) (*See* **annually renewable term**)

Index

Symbols

A

B

C

D

E

N

O

P

T

U

V

W